3

Economic and Social Security
Social Insurance
and Other Approaches

Economic and Social Security
Social Insurance
and Other Approaches

C. Arthur Williams, Jr.
University of Minnesota

John G. Turnbull
University of Minnesota

Earl F. Cheit
University of California, Berkeley

FIFTH EDITION

A RONALD PRESS PUBLICATION
JOHN WILEY & SONS
New York · Chichester · Brisbane · Toronto · Singapore

Library of Congress Cataloging in Publication Data

Williams, C. Arthur (Chester Arthur), Jr. 1924–
    Economic and social security.

    "A Ronald Press publication."
    Rev. ed. of: Economic and social security / John
G. Turnbull, C. Arthur Williams, Jr., Earl F. Cheit.
4th ed. [1973]
    Includes bibliographies and index.
    1. Economic security—United States. 2. Social
security—United States. I. Turnbull, John Gudert,
1913–   . II. Cheit, Earl Frank. III. Title.
HD7125.W49   1981   368.4′3′00973   81-16271
ISBN 0-471-08409-3   AACR2

Printed in the United States of America

10 9 8 7 6 5 4 3 2 1

Preface

Like its predecessors, this fifth edition of *Economic and Social Security* deals with the nature of economic insecurity and the system our society has developed to deal with these insecurities. This system includes social security programs plus legislation designed to correct substandard working conditions, wage rates, hours of employment, and child labor. Social security programs are defined broadly so as to include all public and private programs dealing with (1) the financial losses caused by death, old age, poor health, and unemployment and (2) poverty. Social security programs may, through loss control, attempt to reduce (1) the likelihood of loss or (2) the seriousness of the loss, should it occur. Other programs, through alleviation, help finance the losses that do occur.

Also like its predecessors, this fifth edition emphasizes public alleviative programs, which include (1) social insurance and related public programs and (2) the welfare system. This book, however, again includes two chapters on private employee-benefit plans and individual life and health insurance. Indeed the thesis of this book is that only by studying both public and private programs can one understand and intelligently evaluate the performance of plans in either sector.

Since the first edition of this book in 1957, the United States has dramatically expanded its economic security system. New programs have been added, old programs have been modified in significant ways. Most programs cover a much larger share of the population. For most individuals the system's benefits and costs play a far more important role in their economic lives. The system deserves closer study and evaluation than ever before.

How does this fifth edition differ from its predecessor? First, the material has been updated to include the many important changes that have occurred in the system in recent years. These changes by themselves justified a new edition. The publication date is also fortunate in that it has permitted us to discuss the thought-provoking 1981 reports of several national commissions plus the views of the Reagan Administration. Second, because of the increasing significance and complexity of Old-Age, Survivors, Disability, and Health Insurance (OASDHI), popularly called "Social Security," two chapters are now devoted to the Old Age and Survivors Insurance component of that program: the first deals with coverage

v

and benefits, the second with financing and administration. Third, this edition has fewer chapters. The chapters in the fourth edition that have been omitted here are those formerly entitled "The Problems of Occupational Illness," "Private Approaches to Unemployment," "Fair Labor Standards Act," and "Conclusions and New Directions." Instead of two separate chapters on the problems of occupational and nonoccupational illness, this material has, in our opinion, been more effectively and efficiently presented in one chapter entitled "The Problems of Poor Health." Because private approaches to handling unemployment problems are neither as important nor complex as private approaches to handling the problems associated with death, old age, or poor health, the discussion of these approaches has been condensed into a separate section in the chapter entitled "The Problems of Unemployment." The separate chapter on the Fair Employment Standards Act has become part of an abbreviated, but still comprehensive, one-chapter discussion of "The Problems and Treatment of Substandard Conditions." Most of the concluding observations in the final chapter have been incorporated in other parts of the book. In our opinion, the result of these chapter changes is a more compact, better organized presentation. Fourth, in the previous edition the problems of death and old age, unemployment, and poor health were discussed in that order. Poor health is now discussed prior to unemployment for two reasons: poor health is more closely related to death and old age than is unemployment, and OASDHI, the nation's major social insurance program, covers death, old age, and poor health. Finally, a major portion of the book has been rewritten to make it a more readable and effective learning aid.

Professor Williams assumed primary responsibility for this edition. Professor Turnbull, who was primarily responsible for earlier editions, prepared Chapters 11, 14, and 16. Because of other demanding responsibilities, Dean Cheit did not participate in this revision, but many parts of the book still reflect his contributions to past editions.

As in the past, many persons have responded to our requests for information concerning the present economic security system. We are deeply indebted to them for their help, without which this edition would not have been possible. We also thank those individuals who contributed to earlier editions. David Beech, a graduate student at the University of Minnesota, read the entire manuscript and made several valuable suggestions. Finally, for typing the manuscript from what at times was an almost illegible handwritten copy we thank Pam Jonckowski, Allison Rice, and Lu Anne Moe.

C. ARTHUR WILLIAMS, JR.
JOHN G. TURNBULL
EARL F. CHEIT

Minneapolis, Minnesota
Berkeley, California
January 1982

Contents

Chapter One

Economic Security in Our Society

CHARACTERISTICS AND CAUSES OF ECONOMIC INSECURITY

What is economic insecurity?

A primary breadwinner dies at age 35, leaving a spouse and four children, with food and clothing still to be bought, mortgage payments to be made, medical expenses to be paid.

Compulsory retirement or poor health causes a worker to stop working for pay at age 70.

A worker is laid off because of a downturn in the level of economic activity.

An employee is injured on the job and is out of work for two months; not only is there a loss of earnings, but the worker incurs medical expenses.

Two members of a family become seriously ill and have to be hospitalized for a long period of time.

An individual finds it difficult to get a job because of employer discrimination or finds it possible to secure employment only at substandard wages.

A father deserts a family with three small children; the mother cannot look for work because of the family responsibility.

These examples highlight the two basic characteristics of economic insecurity: (1) a loss of income, in whole or in part; and (2) additional expenses such as high medical bills. In essence, income is insufficient to meet some minimal budget or to cover extra costs.

What "causes" these insecurities? At the proximate level, rather than in some ultimate philosophical sphere, the answers can be specified as follows:

1 A loss of income that results from job separation, which may occur from premature death, old age, economic layoff, an accident, or sickness.

2 Extra—and sometimes costly—expenses incurred when members of a family become ill.

3 The inability or incapability of an individual to get a job that provides more than substandard wages—a mother with small children, or a member of a minority group.

Behind these "causes" are other "causes," and yet other "causes," and so on. For example, when a person is laid off because of a downturn in economic activity, what "causes" the downturn? An individual is injured on the job. What "caused" the accident? Behind the proximate "cause," can it be shown that the injured employee was accident prone? If so, what is the "cause" of this?

In our discussion we shall focus upon proximate causes, going behind the scene only when the analysis calls for it. To seek ultimate causes is beyond not only the scope of this book but the competence of the authors.

THE PLURALISTIC APPROACH TO ECONOMIC INSECURITY

If a society is not to sit by idly in cases of economic insecurity, what choices are open to it? In the United States, as well as in many other Western countries, a pluralistic approach has evolved—pluralistic not only as to what is done, but as to who does it and how it is done.

Let us first make an important distinction, since the structure and presentation in this volume are contingent upon it:

1 One broad and comprehensive set of programs designed to combat economic insecurity is labor-market oriented. Protection is provided at the workplace for those normally employed. Social insurance and employee-benefit plans are examples.

2 But what of the mother with small children when the father has left the family? Workplace-oriented economic security programs would not be applicable in such a case. How could the mother collect unemployment insurance benefits if she has never been employed or has not worked in years? Programs designed to aid these persons must be of a quite different nature than those with a labor-market focus. Public assistance illustrates this approach.

Economic security programs can also be classified according to whether they use (1) the loss control approach or (2) the alleviative approach.

The Loss Control Approach

One way of combating economic insecurity is through loss control, that is, attempting to reduce the likelihood of loss or to minimize the severity of the losses that do occur. Whether loss control can ever be completely effective is a matter of the nature and dimensions of each risk is followed by analyses of public-sector programs and, to a lesser extent, private-sector plans. Alleviation will receive more attention than loss control.

Chapters 14 through 17 focus on a quite different set of problems and treat a quite different "population." These chapters address mainly the issues of poverty and the poor: their nature and numbers and the programs designed to cope with their problems. These programs are quite different from those analyzed in the earlier chapters. They tend to be non-labor-market oriented (or, if labor-market oriented, they are "regulatory" in nature, concerning such things as wage and hour laws). They are generally noninsurance in nature and focus on long-run rather than transitory economic insecurity.

ECONOMIC SECURITY APPROACHES: SOME IMPORTANT DISTINCTIONS

Let us examine in some detail three important distinctions in society's approaches to economic insecurity, namely, (1) service versus income payments, (2) social insurance versus public assistance, and (3) social insurance versus private insurance.

Service Versus Income Payments

Under a service program the recipient receives payments in kind instead of in cash, while under an unrestricted income program the recipient receives cash that may be used to purchase services needed or desired. Both service and income programs exist in the United States, although, as will be seen, the latter tend to predominate.

The recipient of service benefits must accept the program services, but the recipient of unrestricted income benefits can purchase those services that he or she deems most important. The recipient loses freedom of economic choice when a loss of income is replaced with specific services. For example, there is a loss of freedom if an individual is provided with free room and board instead of, say, an unrestricted cash payment of $400 a month. The loss of freedom is less, however, when the program provides specific services instead of reimbursing the individual in cash for expenses incurred in purchasing these same types of services. In fact, the loss of freedom may be very slight if the services under the service program may be obtained from all or most of the available providers of that service. For example, a medical expense program may provide service benefits or cash reimbursements for expenses incurred. In either case, the program is limited to medical services. The loss of freedom under the service program depends on the ability of the insured to choose his or her own doctors, hospitals, nurses, and other suppliers of medical service. If the service program makes available all or most of the medical facilities of the nation on equal terms, the relative loss of freedom of choice under the service program as compared with a cash reimbursement program is slight.

Various other considerations, some administrative and some economic, are relevant to the issue of service versus income payments. Among them are the following:

1   Service benefits make it possible for the sponsoring body to exercise more control over the quality and cost of the services.
2   An insured person may use unrestricted cash payments for purposes that are not socially or economically desirable; hence service programs provide more rigorous controls, not only in quality and cost, but also in use.
3   Service benefits may, however, be more costly to administer, for there may be many more administrative and other details to be considered.
4   Public service benefits may make it necessary for the government to enter an area that had been reserved for private enterprise in the past.
5   Promises to provide service benefits become more valuable to the promisee and more costly to the promisor when the cost of that service increases. A promise to provide a stated dollar income that can be used to purchase that same service becomes less valuable to the promisee. The cost to the promisor is not affected. For example, a promise to provide hospital care in a semiprivate room for 90 days is made more valuable to the promisee and more costly to the promisor by an increase in the cost of providing this service. A specific per-day allowance may be sufficient to pay all the cost when the promise is made, but only part of the cost later.
6   Service benefits replacing lost income may be less "popular" than income benefits because of some loss of freedom of economic choice. Therefore, some who are eligible may not apply for the benefits. This means that the program may not service some of the people for whom it was intended. As stated earlier, however, the relative loss of freedom under some service programs is slight.

Most of the alleviative payments under the U.S. economic security system are cash payments.[2] Certain service programs do, however, play a major role in the current economic security scene. Public housing is one example of a public system utilizing the service approach. A currently important private illustration is provided by medical expense associations known as Health Maintenance Organizations, in which alleviation is in the form of direct provision of the service rather than via cash payment.

[2]Eveline M. Burns, *Social Security and Public Policy* (New York: McGraw-Hill, 1956), pp. 5–9. This excellent book discusses in detail the major questions arising in connection with public social security programs. Although published some years back, this source, and the one given in footnote 4, still provide as good an analysis of the possible options as is currently available.

Public Assistance Versus Social Insurance[3]

Public assistance benefits customarily are paid only to those individuals who can demonstrate need, and the amount of the benefit is based on the extent of the demonstrated need. Final decisions on both eligibility and benefit amounts are made on a discretionary basis by the officials administering the public assistance programs.

Social insurance and related benefits are paid regardless of need to all persons who satisfy certain eligibility requirements. The benefit amounts are also determined on some basis other than actual need, although under many social insurance programs one of the factors affecting general benefit schedules is the presumed average need of the beneficiaries. The actual need may be more or less than the social insurance benefits. The officials administering the social insurance programs exercise little or no discretion in the determination of eligibility or benefit amounts.

Other differences between public assistance and social insurance programs may be summarized as follows:

1 The only direct participants under a public assistance program are recipients. The direct participants under a social insurance plan are the insureds, only a small fraction of whom are beneficiaries at any given time. Thus many more persons are directly concerned with social insurance programs.

2 Many persons who would otherwise be eligible for public assistance benefits do not apply because of the test of need. Participation in most social insurance programs is compulsory, but the participants need not claim their benefits. Of course, very few persons eligible for social insurance benefits refuse to make a claim, for there is no stigma attached to the receipt of the benefits.

3 Because of the character of public assistance programs, they are financed out of general revenues, which are usually derived from a highly progressive tax system, rather than earmarked revenues. Social insurance programs, on the other hand, are generally financed out of earmarked taxes, and there is usually some relationship between an individual's benefit and the contributions made by or in behalf of the individual. Generally it is held desirable to maintain some relationship between contributions and benefits because of the presumably favorable effect on economic incentives. This relationship, it is claimed, also encourages participants and their elected representatives to pay more attention to the cost of the program.

4 Public assistance programs are generally administered by state or local government units who are closer to the recipients. The amount of discretion involved in these programs is the principal reason advanced for the lack of

[3]For an extensive discussion see Eveline M. Burns, *The American Social Security System* (Boston, Mass.: Houghton Mifflin, 1951), pp. 28–39. As noted in Mrs. Burns' volume, some programs are "hybrids," such as "income-conditioned" systems.

direct federal administration. An exception is Supplemental Security Income, which is federally financed and administered.[4] Eligibility and benefits under SSI, however, are generally determined on the basis of criteria more objective than public assistance. Because the amount of discretion involved in social insurance programs is slight and because uniformity among the states is highly desirable, many of these programs are administered solely or in large part by the federal government.

5 Because most American families do not expect to be needy, they do not consider public assistance benefits to be part of their economic security plans (except as emergency measures). Social insurance benefits, on the other hand, do not depend on need. Furthermore, these benefits can be reasonably forecast. Therefore, social insurance benefits are and should be included in a family's economic security plans.

Social insurance programs are much more "popular" than public assistance programs because definite benefits payable as a matter of right are preferred to indefinite benefits payable on the basis of need. Therefore, as interest in more adequate public economic security schemes has increased, social insurance programs have gradually replaced public assistance programs as the basic approach to these financial problems. Public assistance programs today protect only those persons who are both needy and ineligible for adequate social insurance benefits. Public assistance programs also cover some economic insecurities such as desertion of a family by the husband that are not covered at all by social insurance.

Social Insurance Versus Private Insurance

Insurance may be defined as a social device that enables many persons to combine their exposure to loss through actual or promised contributions to a fund out of which those persons who suffer a loss receive benefits as a matter of right.[5] As the number of persons or objects independently exposed to the loss increases it becomes more likely, according to the law of large numbers, that the losses incurred by a group of insureds will be closer, in the short run, to their expected losses, defined as the losses those insureds would experience on the average in the long run. In other words, the group's insured losses become more predictable the larger the number of exposure units. Thus, by insuring a large group of persons,

[4]The Supplementary Security Income program is sometimes classified as a third approach—a universal benefit or demogrant system. Generally these programs cover the entire population, not just the employed population, and benefits are conditioned on such demographic characteristics as age, sex, residence, and family status. There may be an income test, but it can be mathematically administered. See Robert J. Myers, *Social Security* 2nd ed. (Homewood, Ill.: Richard D. Irwin, 1981), pp. 7–8.

[5]We define private insurance so as to include all types of definite benefit plans, because all such benefit plans of which we are aware can and usually do involve some pooling of the risks of many persons. Furthermore, under our definition, a "self-insured" employee-benefit plan is not insurance from the viewpoint of the employer, but it is insurance from the viewpoint of the employee.

an insurer can reduce its risk, which is defined as the relative variation in the short-run losses around their expected value.[6]

Insurance is beneficial *to insureds* because (1) they will be indemnified if a loss occurs and (2) even if no loss occurs, they can conduct their lives with less uncertainty because the insurer promises to bear any covered loss that might occur. The insurer assumes the risks of the individual insureds but, through the operation of the law of large numbers, the insurer converts these individual risks into a much smaller one. *Society* benefits from the existence of insurance because (1) the unfortunate insureds who suffer losses are indemnified, (2) the risk and uncertainty in society is reduced, and (3) insurance substitutes many small losses in the form of premiums for a few large losses, thus reducing the *real* economic burden on society. The economic burden is less because, according to the law of diminishing utility, the loss in utility is much less if $100 is taken from each of 1,000 families than if $10,000 is taken from each of 10 families.[7]

Not all potential losses are insurable. Ideally, an insurable exposure should possess the following characteristics. First, the number of insureds with such an exposure should be large and they should be independently exposed to the potential loss, otherwise the risk is not reduced sufficiently to permit the insurer to operate safely. Second, to facilitate loss adjustments the losses covered should be definite as to cause, time, place, and amount. Third, the expected losses for all insureds combined should be calculable, otherwise the insurer will be unable to determine an accurate premium for the coverage. Fourth, the loss should be accidental from the viewpoint of the insured; it is unwise to insure against losses that the insured can bring about or that are bound to happen. (Death is "bound to happen," but the date is uncertain.) In practice, exposures judged insurable by private or public insurers seldom, if ever, possess all these characteristics. In most cases the departures are small; in other cases they are significant, but there are compelling economic or social reasons to offer the protection.

For example, the exposures covered by life insurance come close to being ideally insurable. The number of insured exposures is extremely large; for practical purposes these exposures can be assumed to be independent. As Chapter 2 will indicate, estimating accurately enough for insurance payments the financial losses caused by death is impossible. Insurers avoid this problem by promising to make certain dollar payments if death occurs. On this basis the insurer can estimate quite accurately the expected losses for a large group of insureds. State laws

[6]Life is not as certain for insurers as this sentence implies. The Law of Large Numbers reduces the effects of chance fluctuations but not changes in the underlying environment that affect the expected losses as well as the actual losses. For example, in the short run there may be a significant increase in the frequency and severity of disability claims, which is tied to the liberality of the benefits or conditions in the workplace, and not to chance.

[7]See Paul Samuelson, *Economics,* 10th ed. (New York: McGraw-Hill Book, 1976), pp. 433–436; Allan H. Willett, *The Economic Theory of Risk and Insurance* (New York: Columbia University Press, 1901; reprinted, Philadelphia, Pa.: University of Pennsylvania Press, 1951); and Irving Pfeffer, *Insurance and Economic Theory* (Homewood, Ill.: Richard D. Irwin, 1956).

require private insurers to cover suicides one or two years after the contract is in force, but such an event is unlikely. On the other hand, many insurers refuse to write sickness insurance because, as Chapter 6 will suggest, it is difficult to determine whether a person is sick and, if so, how sick. Others write sickness insurance with various degrees of reluctance for various reasons. For example, they may believe that they are obligated to insure such an important exposure, that sickness insurance enables the insurer to sell more life insurance, or that private insurers should not surrender any field of insurance to the government. Some insurers, it should be noted, consider sickness insurance much less troublesome than this analysis would suggest.

Private insurance generally possesses the following characteristics, although from the viewpoint of the insured worker there are some important exceptions associated with employee-benefit plans:

1   The protection is voluntary. Insureds must be "sold" on the need for protection. As a result, some persons buy either no protection or inadequate protection. On the other hand, they do retain their freedom of economic choice.

2   The insurance contract is a legal instrument that cannot be changed without the consent of the insured except in unusual cases, and that can be enforced in court.

3   The cost of each individual's protection is determined on an actuarial basis. The benefit amount and loss and expense-producing potential are considered in determining the price, for the price of the protection should equal the expected cost. It is true that most insureds are not rated individually, for there is a desire to base rates on past experience, and the experience of a single insured is not usually credible. (This is obvious in the case of death.) Moreover, rating each person individually is a complicated procedure. Therefore, usually all insureds with *approximately* the same loss and expense characteristics are grouped together in a class and charged the same rate. For example, life insurance premiums vary with the amount and type of life insurance purchased, but for a given benefit the rates depend only on two factors—age and sex. There are undoubtedly differences among standard lives in the same age and sex groups, but these differences are assumed to be slight.[8] Insofar as practical considerations will permit, price equals expected cost for the group.

Private insurers may become bankrupt if their premiums (plus assessments, if any) are consistently insufficient to pay their actual expenses and losses, which may differ considerably from their expected losses and expenses. Private insurer experience in this respect has, however, been excellent.

4   The protection is provided by many insurers of various types who compete with one another for insureds. There are stock insurers, mutual insurers,

[8]Substandard lives may pay a higher premium, but there are relatively few substandard lives. The use of sex as a rating variable in pricing life insurance and other types of insurance has been seriously questioned recently and prohibited in some cases.

self-insurers, medical service associations, and many others. Competition forces these insurers to reassess their contracts and prices periodically.

Social insurance includes a variety of insurance arrangements. Under one definition, social insurance includes all insurance arrangements in which the government acts as the insurer, subsidizes the operation, or requires insureds to purchase the protection. At one extreme this definition includes the type of private insurance required by law, such as workers' compensation insurance, and voluntary public insurance, such as government life insurance for veterans, which operate on essentially the same basis as private insurance. At the other extreme social insurance includes programs that differ from private insurance in many respects and which some persons believe should not be considered as insurance. However, these programs do satisfy the definition of insurance used in this book, in that they provide a mechanism for pooling exposures to accidental losses.

The most important social insurance program—Old-Age, Survivors, Disability, and Health Insurance—is the best example of this latter "extreme." This program carries out a social and economic public policy decision: it provides a floor of protection for all participants against financial losses caused by premature death, poor health, or old age.[9] It differs from the most common forms of private insurance in four important respects:

1 Participation is compulsory (with a few exceptions) for all eligible persons. Otherwise some individuals would elect not to be covered and the policy objective of a floor of protection for all members of a defined group would be thwarted.

2 The benefits are prescribed by law. There are no contracts, and it is possible (but highly improbable) that Congress will rescind the benefits in the future. Periodic changes in the benefit structure are very likely through changes in the law.

3 The system redistributes income in addition to providing protection through a pooling arrangement. Lower-income groups, insureds with many dependents, and participants who were elderly when the system was inaugurated receive more benefits for their contributions than most other participants. If this were not true, it would be impossible to achieve the public policy objective of a floor of protection for all participants, since some insureds would be unable to afford adequate protection. Old-age benefits during the early years of the system would also be limited. The benefits are not equitable in the private insurance sense, but they are not meant to be. Other standards of performance have been deemed more important. In short, the system stresses

[9]For a concise description of the principles underlying this program, see J. Douglas Brown, "Concepts in Old-Age and Survivors Insurance," *Proceedings of the First Annual Meeting of the Industrial Relations Research Association,* 1948, pp. 100–106. (We use the "complete" title here—OASDHI—even though different parts of the program are applicable to different parts of our discussion.)

"social adequacy" rather than "individual equity."[10] The contribution rates are scheduled, but Congress may and has revised the schedule periodically. Consequently, bankruptcy is impossible as long as the government has an effective taxing power, although it is conceivable that the taxes may become unbearable.

4 The government system is monopolistic. However, public pressure forces a continual reassessment of benefits and contribution rates.

In 1964 the Committee on Social Insurance Terminology,[11] one of the operating committees of the Commission on Insurance Terminology of the American Risk and Insurance Association, recommended a more restrictive definition of social insurance. If an insurance program is to be labeled "social insurance," it must possess the following characteristics:

1 Persons eligible for coverage must be covered except in unusual cases.

2 Eligibility for benefits is derived, in fact or in effect, from contributions having been made to the program by or in respect to (a) the claimant or (b) the person as to whom the claimant is a dependent; there cannot be any requirement that the individual demonstrate inadequate financial resources, although a dependency status may have to be established.

3 The method for determining the benefits is specifically prescribed by law.

4 The benefits for any individual can be directly related to contributions made by or in respect to him, but this should not usually be the case; instead, most "social insurance" programs would be expected to redistribute income in such a way as to favor certain groups such as those with low former wages or a large number of dependents. In other words, the usual program stresses social adequacy.

5 There is a definite plan for financing the benefits and it is designed (even though the design may be unsuccessful in view of the many long-range imponderables) to be adequate in terms of long-range considerations. The adequacy of the financing arrangements may involve reliance on some financial support from taxes or from contributions made with respect to *new entrants*.

---

[10]For the original statement of this feature of OASDHI in these terms by an actuary for the Metropolitan Life Insurance Company, see R. A. Hohaus, "Equity, Adequacy, and Related Factors," in W. Haber and W. Cohen, *Social Security: Programs, Problems, and Policies* (Homewood, Ill.: Richard D. Irwin, 1960), pp. 61–63. This article appeared originally in the June 1938 issue of *The Record*, a publication of the Institute of Actuaries. For a recent thoughtful critique of the distinction between social adequacy and private equity, see Gary W. Eldred, "Social Security: A Conceptual Alternative," *The Journal of Risk and Insurance*, XLVIII, No. 2 (June 1981), pp. 220–234.

[11]This committee included private insurance representatives, a risk manager for a large business, social insurance personnel, a union spokesman, and several academicians. For explanatory comments on the definition, see *Bulletin of the Commission on Insurance Terminology*, I, No. 2 (May 1965), 2–4. For a discussion of the alternative definitions considered, see C. A. Williams, Jr., " 'Social Insurance' —Proper Terminology?," *Journal of Insurance*, XXX, No. 1 (March 1963), 112–128.

6 The cost of the program is borne primarily by contributions that are usually made by covered persons, their employers, or both. Although some contributions may be made from general governmental funds, these contributions should not be the major source of financial support.

7 The plan is administered or at least supervised by the federal, state, or local government. Direct supervision, however, may be limited to settling contested cases or checking compliance with insurance requirements, with most of the daily operations being conducted by private insurance.

8 The plan was not established by the government solely for its present or former employees. Social insurance programs must cover some persons other than government employees.

Under this definition the following programs (to be described later in this text) *are* social insurance programs because they meet all the prescribed conditions:

Old-Age, Survivors, Disability, and Health Insurance (but not the Supplementary Medical Insurance part, which is voluntary).

Unemployment compensation or insurance.

Workers' compensation.

Temporary disability insurance.

Railroad Retirement System.

Railroad unemployment and temporary disability insurance.

The following programs are *not* social insurance programs because they fail to meet at least one of the prescribed tests:

Civil Service Retirement System, because this plan was established by the government solely for its employees.

National Service Life Insurance, because it is not compulsory and because it was established by the government solely for its present or former employees.

Public assistance, because the individual must demonstrate that he or she has inadequate financial resources, the method of determining the benefits is not prescribed by statute, and the cost is not borne primarily by employers and their employees.

Veterans' benefits, because the program is wholly financed out of general revenues, it was established by the government solely for its former employees, and some of the benefits require the individual to demonstrate that income falls below a specified level.

On the other hand, all of these programs, except public assistance and veterans' benefits that involve an income test, can be included under the label "social insurance and related programs."

The definition does not limit social insurance programs to the risks associated with death, accidental injury, sickness, family breakups, unemployment, and the like, but this book does. The only major subjects not discussed because of this restriction are automobile compensation ("no-fault" automobile insurance), which, at least in some modified form, applies the principles of workers' compensation to automobile accidents, plans designed to make property insurance available in urban core areas, government-subsidized flood insurance, and government crime insurance.[12]

Notice that under this definition social insurance programs still include different types of insurance arrangements, but these differences are much less marked than under the broader definition. Variety is still possible, however, with respect to the following: (1) the relative roles of social adequacy and private equity, but the program that stresses private equity is an unusual one; (2) whether the government contributes to program costs from general funds, but in any event their role should be minor; and (3) whether the government functions as a monopoly insurer or exercises various degrees of supervision over private insurers. Notice also that social insurance programs such as workers' compensation are not as different from private insurance as is OASDHI, an "extreme" case. We shall not consider these less extreme programs here, but as each is discussed in detail in later chapters the reader should compare and contrast that program with private insurance in order to increase his or her appreciation and understanding of the important differences between private and social insurance. Since the purposes of the two devices differ, we should not be surprised to find differences in their nature and application.

One final comment should be made here concerning the differences between private insurance and social insurance. Because social insurance benefits and contribution rates can be made noncontractual and flexible, and because the government can make participation compulsory, some risks that are noninsurable by sound private insurance standards are insurable under social insurance programs. To illustrate, assume that it is extremely difficult to estimate the expected losses for a particular kind of insurance. A private insurer might be reluctant to write this coverage because it would not be able to determine with much confidence the price to be charged. If the insurer did write the coverage and the price proved to be too low, the insurer might be able to charge more in the future, but only to cover future losses and expenses, not to make up the deficit incurred in the past. If the coverage were written for a long term at a price fixed in the contract, the insurer could not even change the price for the future until the term of the contract expired. Under either short- or long-term contracts, if the private insurer raised the price at the end of the contract term, it would face the possibility that some insureds would not insure or purchase their insurance from a lower-price competitor. On the other hand, if a social insurance program does not guarantee the benefits or price and the program is compulsory, the benefits or the

---

[12]For a discussion of these programs see, for example, C. A. Williams, Jr., and R. M. Heins, *Risk Management and Insurance,* 4th ed. (New York: McGraw-Hill, 1981), pp. 146–152, 668–673.

prices can be changed to make up past deficits without losing any insureds. For example, Old-Age, Survivors, Disability, and Health Insurance, as it presently exists, could not be underwritten by a private insurer because there are too many unpredictable variables in the program. Another case in point is unemployment insurance, which is not underwritten by private commercial insurers because they consider the expected losses to be unpredictable and the exposure units to be interdependent. However, some employers have developed self-insured unemployment "insurance" plans, to be discussed subsequently.

RECENT GROWTH

The U.S. insurance system, as a component of the economic security system, has expanded tremendously in the past 50 years. In 1929, the year the Great Depression started, but before its greatest impact and several years before the passage of the Social Security Act of 1935, the "typical" U.S. worker's only insurance consisted of a small amount of private life insurance plus a workers' compensation insurance program that would cover part of the worker's medical expenses and loss of income occasioned by an industrial injury.

Currently the typical worker has some public or private protection against all four perils: death (OASDHI, a private employee-benefit plan, and private individual life insurance), old age (OASDHI and private individual life insurance and annuities, plus a private pension plan for almost half the workers), unemployment (state unemployment compensation), occupational injuries and diseases (workers' compensation), and nonoccupational injuries and sicknesses (OASDHI—Medicare, a private employee-benefit plan, and private individual health insurance).

Table 1.1 presents a bird's-eye view of the social insurance, public assistance, and related programs that will be the major focus of this book. In addition to emphasizing the substantial impact and growth of these programs Table 1.1 allows a comparison of the relative importance and growth of each program. Tables in Chapters 5 and 10 contain data on private employee-benefit plans and individual life insurance, annuities, and health insurance. Later in the book we will present more detailed statistics for each of the public programs listed.

Tables 1.2 and 1.3 show how social insurance, public aid, and veterans benefits have grown since 1950 as a percentage of the gross national product and as a dollar amount per capita. In Tables 1.2 and 1.3 social insurance and related programs includes

Old-Age, Survivors, Disability and Health Insurance.

Workers' compensation.

Temporary disability insurance.

Unemployment compensation.

Railroad Retirement System.

Public employee retirement systems.

Public aid includes

Public assistance.

Food stamps.

Other aid programs such as emergency aid.

Table 1.1 Benefits Paid Under U.S. Social Insurance, Public Assistance, and Related Programs, 1940, 1950, 1960, 1970, and 1980 (In Millions of Dollars)

	1940	1950	1960	1970	1980
Cash benefits					
Monthly payments					
Old-Age, Survivors and Disability					
Insurance	24	928	11,080	31,570	120,262
Workers' compensation	161	415	860	1,981	11,000[a]
Temporary disability insurance					
State laws	—	89	311	665	1,200[a]
Railroad system	—	28	57	56	101
Unemployment Compensation					
State laws	519	1,407	2,867	4,184	15,013
Railroad system	16	60	158	39	179
Railroad Retirement System	116	298	942	1,756	4,867
Civil Service Retirement System	62	184	804	2,797	15,042
Public employee retirement programs other than the Civil Service Retirement System	183	600	1,793	6,369	25,000[a]
Veterans pensions and compensation	423	2,224	3,437	5,480	11,358
Supplemental Security Income	—	—	—	—	7,858
Public assistance other than Supplemental Security Income	1,020	2,354	3,277	8,864	14,000[a]
Lump-sum payments					
Old-Age, Survivors, and Disability					
Insurance	12	33	164	294	250
Other	25	54	135	289	214
Total	4,191	8,676	25,873	64,470	226,344[a]
Medical care benefits					
Medicare					
Hospital Insurance	—	—	—	5,124	23,073
Supplementary Medical Insurance	—	—	—	1,975	10,635
Workers' compensation	95	200	435	1,050	4,000[a]
Temporary disability insurance	—	7	41	66	50
Veterans benefits	70	573	848	1,793	6,122
Medicaid	—	—	—	5,507	22,000[a]
Public assistance other than Medicaid	—	52	522	99	1,000[a]
Total	165	832	1,846	15,614	66,880[a]

Source: Social Security Bulletins.

[a]Estimated by author.

Table 1.2 Social Insurance and Public Aid Expenditures as a Percentage of the Gross National Product, Selected Fiscal Years, 1950–1978

Fiscal Year	Social Insurance and Related Programs	Public Aid
1950	1.9	0.9
1955	2.6	0.8
1960	3.9	0.8
1965	4.3	1.0
1970	5.7	1.7
1975	8.5	2.8
1978	7.5	2.9

Source: "Social Welfare Expenditures, Fiscal Year 1978," *Social Security Bulletin,* XLIII, No. 5 (May 1980), Table 3.

Social insurance expenditures in 1978 were 7.5% of the gross national product, compared with 1.9% in 1950. This 7.5%, however, is less than the 1976 peak of 9.0%. Similarly, 1978 public aid expenditures were 2.9% of the gross national product. The peak percentage was 3.0 in 1976.

Social insurance per capita expenditures in 1978 were almost 25 times 1950 per capita expenditures. Even in constant dollars they were nine times as great. Public aid expenditures in 1978 were over 17 times 1950 per capita expenditures. In constant dollars they were over six times the 1950 amount. Social insurance expenditures were about three times public aid expenditures in 1978, compared with twice the public aid amount in 1950.

Most of these public programs were initiated under the Social Security Act of 1935 or its many important amendments. Other countries had adopted extensive public social insurance programs at a much earlier date. Germany had a fairly complete national insurance system in operation by the close of the nineteenth

Table 1.3 Social Insurance and Public Aid per Capita Expenditures in Actual and 1978 Prices, Selected Fiscal Years, 1950–1978 (In Dollars)

Fiscal Year	Social Insurance and Related Programs		Public Aid	
	Actual Prices	1978 Prices	Actual Prices	1978 Prices
1950	32	85	16	43
1955	59	134	18	42
1960	105	219	22	47
1965	142	275	32	62
1970	262	427	79	129
1975	565	682	188	227
1978	787	787	269	269

Source: See Table 1.2.

century. Great Britain introduced a series of public programs during the first two decades of this century. Other foreign countries were also active about the same time. Why did the United States lag behind?

This lag has been explained by the superior economic status and individualistic nature of our population, our federal form of government, the retention by the states of powers not expressly delegated to the federal government, social and economic variations among the states, and competition among the states for business interests. The Great Depression and changes in our social mores lessened the retarding effect of these factors and an extensive social insurance program was born. However, the program characteristics reflect the continuing importance of these factors.

Private insurance, on the other hand, was important in the nineteenth century, but it was much less developed and much less popular than it is today. In fact, private insurance in the United States dates back to the colonial period, but the industry was a very small one until the middle of the nineteenth century, when it began a period of steady growth. The Depression marked the beginning of a period of extremely rapid growth. The factors favoring the tremendous increase in the benefits and proportion of the insured population are the Depression experiences, the excellent solvency record of private commercial insurers during this period, increased public interest in economic security, the introduction of public programs, the increasing importance of employee-benefit plans, the government insurance program for service personnel and veterans, the changes in income distribution, an improved insurance industry sales force, the introduction of new coverages, and a higher average level of education among our population.

Forecasting is a hazardous occupation, but we can be almost certain that the protection afforded the typical employee will continue to improve. Existing benefits should cover a larger proportion of the loss and new benefits will be added. The improvements, however, will be much less dramatic than in the past because (1) the need for further improvements is less critical and (2) the cost of existing benefits is high and increasing.

BASIC DECISIONS IN DESIGNING ECONOMIC SECURITY PROGRAMS

This bird's-eye view omits, of necessity, detailed information about each part of the U.S. economic security system; this information will be presented in later chapters of this book. However, to be systematic in our presentation of the details, let us note the basic decisions that must be made in designing any economic security program.

Once a society decides to handle a given peril such as old age or poor health through its economic security system, it must decide whether to use loss control, alleviation, or both. If alleviation is selected, a choice must be made between insurance or assistance, or both. More decisions must then be made concerning

(1) who is covered, (2) what covered persons must do to collect benefits, (3) what benefits will be paid, (4) who should finance the system and when, and (5) who should administer the program. To simplify the discussion it is assumed below that either a social insurance plan or an employee-benefit plan is being designed, but most of the concepts are relevant to other approaches.

The choices that are made depend on many factors including, but by no means limited to, the following: the level of protection considered to be adequate, the importance assigned to personal choice, the effect on incentives and motivation, the role considered appropriate for private insurance, states' rights, and administrative problems. Private plans may be forced to operate within legal constraints such as the Employee Retirement Income Security Act (ERISA).

Coverage of the Program

The program may cover all persons, all workers, all workers except those in certain occupations, only workers with a minimum period of service, or some other group. In public programs administrative, constitutional, economic, political, and other pressures are intertwined, along with "need," in determining coverage. The Old-Age, Survivors, Disability, and Health Insurance program will serve as an example. In the early years following its passage certain classes of employees such as agricultural laborers and domestic servants were excluded, partly because of the administrative difficulties involved in handling their records. As record-keeping experience was gained by the OASDHI administration, this became less of a problem, and such employees were given coverage. There is little doubt that economic considerations were important in originally excluding farm groups, for example, from coverage. Again, the political representation of medical practitioners was probably instrumental in enabling them to remain out of the OASDHI program until the amendments of 1965.

In unemployment insurance differences in early coverage were based in part on the number of employees the employer had and, additionally, in some states, upon the size of the community in which the company was located. As of January 1, 1972, the federal law extended coverage to employers of one or more employees. Hence this kind of differentiation is no longer possible.

Similar considerations enter into private programs, such as employer-sponsored or collectively bargained pension programs or "guaranteed-wage" programs. A wage guarantee may be extended only to employees with two years' service with the company, this restriction arising in part out of the belief that the company does not have such an obligation to employees who do not intend to remain with it, that is, to "floaters"; or, if such a plan is collectively bargained, it may extend only to "seniority" workers. In part this may be based on cost factors, in part upon ethical considerations noted above. Other reasons may also be involved, varying to some extent with the specific program concerned. ERISA, for example, limits the choices available under private pension plans.

In general, there is a tendency for the coverage of both public and private economic security programs to become more extensive. The increase in OASDHI coverage illustrates this for public programs, and the extension of company and union medical expense programs to the employee's family provides an example for private programs.

Qualifications for Collection of Benefits

To receive benefits a "covered" individual must also meet certain other requirements. These are usually of three types. First are requirements relating to coverage itself, which must be satisfied before benefits begin. The individual frequently must have been in the program for a certain minimum period of time and in some cases also have had certain minimum wages or earnings. The specific requirements vary with program types and are again a result of a combination of administrative, economic, political, and other considerations. The reasoning behind such requirements is that benefits should only be payable to one who has a "genuine" attachment to the labor force or to a given company and there should be some sort of "ethical" minimum to this attachment. For example, it is not held to be economically or ethically desirable to pay unemployment benefits to a housewife who works as a retail clerk during the Christmas season but who retires from the labor force after the season is over. This is not universally true: a covered employee is protected by workers' compensation the moment the job begins. As will be described later, the worker gives up the right to sue a negligent employer under this program.

A second requirement relates to the specific factor "causing" the economic insecurity. In the most general sense programs typically cover one or more specified perils such as death, poor health, unemployment, or old age. Workers' compensation requires that the injury, sickness, or death be job related. Under unemployment compensation where discharge is for cause, or where an individual quits for certain reasons, benefits may be denied or a longer waiting period required. Subsequent to job separation other qualifications relating to the cause of the insecurity may also be found. Disability insurance requires the person to remain totally or partially unable to work. In unemployment compensation a person must be able to work and be willing to work.

Third, some public programs involve other continuing requirements, once benefits have started. Under unemployment compensation a beneficiary may lose part or all of the benefits if he or she earns above a certain maximum amount in part-time, casual, or other employment while technically unemployed. OASDHI beneficiaries under age 70 will lose some or all of their benefits if their earnings exceed a certain amount. Remarriage may cause a widow or widower to lose some workers' compensation or OASDHI death benefits.

The net effect of all these restrictions is to set up a series of rules under which benefits can or cannot be claimed or continued. Ethical and economic reasons underlie such requirements, with political pressures evident in a variety of instances. Public assistance programs illustrate, in a different way, all of the above characteristics.

Benefits

Benefits may differ according to their general level, how they vary among individuals, and whether they are service or income benefits.

The objective of the OASDI cash benefit program is ostensibly to provide a floor of protection. To some this objective means a subsistence level of protection; to others it means enough protection to meet the needs of most of the population, making it unnecessary for them to depend on private protection. In workers' compensation the basic promise is two-thirds of the lost wage, but in unemployment insurance the replacement objective is one-half. Presumably this difference reflects the different obligations society feels to these two groups of unemployed workers and the incentives they should have to return to work. Cost is, of course, an important factor in determining this general level. Private pension plans commonly set as their target a retirement income, including OASDHI benefits, that will replace a certain percentage of the worker's income before retirement.

Once the general level of benefits has been established, one must decide how the benefits are to be distributed among the participants. Here public and private programs differ markedly. In private insurance there is usually a close correspondence with actuarial principles. A person collects what is related actuarially to the specific contributions made to the program in his or her behalf. In public insurance programs such as OASDHI or unemployment compensation actuarial relations are less important. These social insurance systems emphasize the social aspect more than they do the actuarial aspect. Thus, under OASDHI, per given dollar of in-payment, a low-wage worker receives a proportionately greater benefit than does the high-wage earner because the benefit computation formula is structured to pay a higher percentage benefit for the lower-wage increments.

Finally, a choice must be made between cash benefits and service costs. As noted earlier, usually, but not always, cash benefits are the choice.

Who Pays the Costs

Who pays the costs depends on the persons asked to contribute (employers, employees, the "government"), and their respective shares. Here again diverse pressures are evident. In public programs political and constitutional considerations are relevant. In the OASDHI program both employer and employee contribute. In the unemployment compensation program only the employer contributes. Why this difference? One reason was a belief that the unemployment compensation program would have a greater chance of meeting the test of constitutionality if the given approach were used. Another was that old age is inevitable and hence both parties should "help," whereas unemployment might not fall on everyone. In private programs both ethics and economics are involved. Some persons hold that the employee as well as the employer should contribute to security programs as a matter of "right." Against this is the fact that employer contributions are usually not considered taxable income for the employee. Employee contributions, on the other hand, are not tax deductible. Also, it has been held that it is much more economical to administer a program where only the employer contributes. Compromise, not necessarily in the worst sense of the term, usually produces the final result.

A final comment relates to public programs only. Some early critics took the point of view that it would be cheaper to finance, say, an economic security program such as OASDHI by direct government revenue sources, without any intermediate in-payment plan. With a few exceptions, however, the system continues to be financed by earmarked payroll taxes. However, general revenues do support some of the costs of the medical expense programs under OASDHI and there is a strong movement to support more OASDHI costs in this way.

In addition to determining who pays the costs, the program must state the share of the cost to be paid by each contributer. As will be apparent from the discussion of specific programs, the cost can be shared in a variety of ways.

When the Costs Are Paid

Should the program be put completely on a pay-as-you-go basis or should there be some advance funding to cover some future costs as well as current costs?

In general, the type of insecurity involved, and hence the program utilized, has an important bearing on the answer to this question. For example, medical expense insurance programs tend to operate on a pay-as-you-go basis because they are usually short-term contracts.[13] They cover medical expenses arising out of injuries or sicknesses commencing during, say, the next year. The premiums collected should therefore be sufficient to cover those expenses. No advance funding is necessary to prepare for the future when, as the insured ages, these expenses will probably rise. Public unemployment insurance programs stand in an intermediate position: in part the employer (given varying state laws) pays in yearly on a pay-as-you-go basis, but if the firm pays in additional amounts to build up its own account and has little unemployment, rates in subsequent years may be lowered. At the other extreme are situations, primarily involving retirement, where both approaches can be found. Under ERISA private pension plans must accumulate some monies in advance of an employee's retirement. In the OASDHI program the approach has veered from some advance funding to pay-as-you-go, with political and other pressures being as important as economic ones. Currently, OASDHI operates essentially on a pay-as-you-go basis. In passing, it ought to be noted that the same type of financial logic need not necessarily

---

[13]Strictly speaking, a pay-as-you-go plan collects enough money each year to finance the benefits paid that year. The medical expense insurance programs discussed here collect enough to finance the expense payments made that year or to be made in future years because of injuries or sickness that start that year. It does not finance payments that year because of injuries or sicknesses that started in prior years.

hold for both public and private programs. "Pay-as-you-go" may have different implications for private in contrast to public programs.

Administration of the Program

The program may be administered by a public or private agency or some mix of these two groups. The level of government may be federal, state, or local. Administrative organizations and procedures may also vary greatly under either public or private agencies. In public programs administrative procedure is basically a matter of law. The administrative agency is conventionally set up by statute, as is the broad framework within which it operates. Within this framework the agency exercises, of necessity, some degree of discretion in its day-by-day operations. Thus, within limits, the agency makes rulings on eligibility, disqualifications, and the myriad phases of administration encountered daily. Commonly, there are procedures for appeal, so a person or group aggrieved by the ruling of an administrator has the opportunity to petition for review. The exact nature of the administrative organization and process is in part a result of the specific administrators named or elected and their policies.

The administrative organization and procedure in private programs are largely a matter of what the party or parties wish, with some external regulation imposed. A given pension plan may be self-administered or it may be turned over to a third party, such as an insurance company. The Labor Management Relations Act of 1947, as amended, contains restrictions for those plans arrived at through collective bargaining. These restrictions relate mainly to the fact that "joint" administration must be exercised and that out-payments must meet certain stipulations. ERISA also affects the administration of private pension plans.

YARDSTICKS FOR EVALUATING ECONOMIC SECURITY PROGRAMS

In addition to describing economic security programs, this book will discuss the major issues surrounding the most important programs. Three yardsticks that can be used to assess these programs are the following:

1   Did the economic security program accomplish its purpose? Or was it self-defeating? For example, in a narrower sense, was a minimum wage law self-defeating in that it reduced the total wage bill? In a broader sense, do economic security programs "reduce" incentives to the point where the economy is worse off than if the program had not been introduced?

2   Is the specific economic security program soundly structured and administered? Subsidiary standards are involved here: what is meant by soundly structured? By soundly administered? The second question is easier to answer

than the first; we would suggest that sound administration involves, first, execution of the program in terms of its intent and, second, that such execution be honest. Structural soundness implies not only an economical plan, but one whose features make sense organizationally.

3   Does the program produce undesirable economic consequences? Does it artificially distort resource allocation? Pricing? What is its impact on the functioning of the economy? For example, do different state unemployment insurance laws artificially influence the location of industry? Does experience rating in unemployment compensation add to cyclical movement rather than act as a countercyclical force? Do private pension programs unduly restrict labor mobility?

The criteria problem not only involves the choice of yardsticks but also requires the collection of information so as to apply the yardsticks. Information is becoming increasingly available in many areas of economic security, and this is perhaps a less difficult problem than is the specification of standards.

VALUE JUDGMENTS

Value judgments are important in a field such as economic security. To make our position clear on several important points that will come up from time to time, let us briefly indicate our beliefs:

1   Some causes of insecurity, such as industrial deaths, have decreased over time; others, such as nonoccupational highway accidents, have increased. On balance it is not easy to say which trend is uppermost; but insecurity is *not* a problem that has been solved at present, hence continuing attention is necessary.

2   What happens to incentive as security increases? What happens to progress? These are not easy questions to answer, and empirical evidence is mostly lacking.[14]

   We would tentatively conclude that (a) the present economic security system in the United States has not damaged our well-being, but (b) abuses and dangers exist and should be guarded against.

3   The government has a legitimate role to play in economic security programming. In some cases, as in the regulatory field, it may be the only body capable of doing the job. We further hold that it plays a useful role in providing a "floor of protection."

---

[14]Literary allusions are not lacking, however. If one broadens one's notion of security, one is deluged by mankind's conclusions. To cite but one example, listen to Macbeth:

"As you all know, security
Is mortals' chiefest enemy."

But, beyond regulation, government action and activity may be necessary, based on the principle of "subsidiarity."[15] This principle suggests that "higher" levels should not undertake to meet responsibilities if "lower" levels can. Thus private action is to be preferred over public action, and state action over federal action. But, where lower levels cannot meet the responsibility, the higher ones must. In the case of unemployment the loss control approach (maintaining high levels of economic activity) has become a basic responsibility of the public (federal level) sector. The alleviative approach is, however, largely at state, local, and private levels. It has become increasingly accepted for the government to play a useful role in providing a "floor of protection." Our judgment is, however, that given these constraints, the area in which private enterprise can operate should be maximized.

TERMINOLOGY

We have noted in this chapter many terms used in the field of economic security. Here we should like to present a more detailed picture and, in so doing, provide an overall view of the pattern of terminology. Then, in later sections of this book, the meaning of and relationship among terms should be clear.

Our presentation is in diagrammatic form. It should be noted that loss control, alleviation, and regulatory methods are intertwined in a complicated fashion. Our subject is economic security. We will concentrate on social security (as more narrowly defined), especially public and private alleviation. Public alleviative programs will be investigated in more detail than will be private programs.

A SUPPLEMENTARY COMMENT

The American approach to economic security seems unnecessarily complicated when reviewed on a strictly logical basis. We may wonder how such a complex system came into being. The major reason is that the system was developed piecemeal in response to what seemed to be the most important need at the time. This statement applies to both public and private programs.

Political factors as well as social and economic needs have been important. Thus our public system is a compromise between the desire to provide the optimum economic security at the minimum cost, make the system self-supporting, maintain individual responsibility, respect states' rights, produce the correct economic by-products (improve the allocation of resources, make labor more mobile, and counteraffect business cycles), and please the voting public. Few, if

---

[15]We are indebted to A. Edward Hunter for provocative discussions on this topic. The principle has had a long standing among political scientists and public administration specialists.

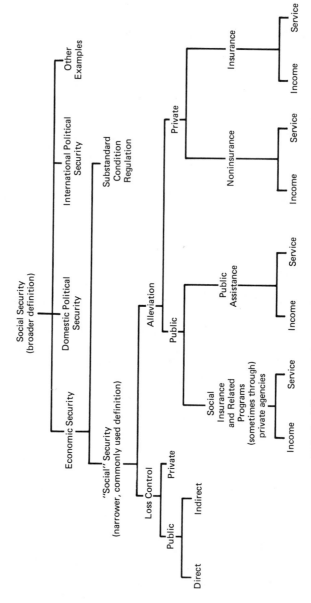

Principal Economic Security Terms and Their Relationships

any, persons are completely satisfied with the present system, but the critics, with feelings ranging from mild to intense, are not united in their objections. Some argue for a completely logical system, however that be defined. Others believe that some, but not all, of the other considerations should be ignored, while still others believe that it is possible to establish a superior compromise system. Each of these three groups may be divided into many subgroups on other bases, such as the method of implementing proposals. As this text is being written, a new set of value judgments seems to be replacing those that prevailed in recent decades, with resulting changes in program objectives and structures. The Omnibus Budget Reconciliation Act of 1981 tightened the eligibility requirements for several programs, lowered the benefits, and increased the penalties for fraud and other abuses. Some responsibility for economic security was passed from the federal government to state and local governments and to the private sector.

SUMMARY

Economic insecurity usually involves a loss of income or additional expenses such as medical expenses. The United States has adopted a pluralistic approach to dealing with economic and social security. One broad set of programs focuses primarily on labor-market-oriented "transitory" risks such as death, old age, poor health, or unemployment. The other programs deal with the problems of the poor and with substandard conditions of employment. These programs include two basic tools: (1) loss control, which attempts to reduce loss frequency or severity; and (2) alleviation, which promises to provide a substitute or supplemental income if a loss occurs. The responsibility for these programs may be entrusted to the government, business enterprises and unions, or individuals.

Alleviative programs may provide cash or service benefits. Public alleviative programs are usually public assistance or social insurance. Public assistance programs pay benefits only in case of need; social insurance programs pay benefits to persons who meet certain conditions, but need is not one of those conditions. Other differences involve the manner in which a program is financed and the party administering the system.

Not all public insurance is social insurance. Social insurance, even though more narrowly defined, includes programs with widely varying characteristics. Social insurance is considered to be insurance in this book because it shares with private insurances the essential characteristic of insurance—pooling risks. Most social insurance programs differ from private insurance ones in that they are compulsory, redistribute income in order to achieve some social objective, make no contractual promises, and are underwritten by a government insurer. Both social insurance and private insurance have increased dramatically in the past few decades.

In designing an economic security program against a peril such as death or poor health, decisions must be made regarding (1) who is covered, (2) what requirements covered persons must meet to collect benefits, (3) the benefits to be provided, (4) who pays the cost and when, and (5) who administers the program.

SUGGESTIONS FOR ADDITIONAL READING

Ball, Robert M. *Social Security, Today and Tomorrow.* New York: Columbia University Press.
A comprehensive, clear description and analysis of OASDHI plus recommendations for change by the Commissioner of Social Security under Presidents Kennedy, Johnson, and Nixon. This book also contains observations relevant to social insurance in general.

Chen, Yung-Ping. *Social Security in a Changing Society.* Bryn Mawr, Pa.: McCahan Foundation, 1980.
Chapter 1 of this highly readable short book presents an overview of social security, including the conceptual framework of social insurance.

Bowen, William G., Frederick H. Harbison, Richard A. Lester, and Herman M. Somers (Eds.). *The American System of Social Insurance.* New York: McGraw-Hill, 1968.
A useful series of essays on the philosophy, impact, and future development of social insurance concepts and programs.

Burns, Eveline M. *Social Security and Public Policy.* New York: McGraw-Hill, 1956.
A highly respected student of social security presents a brief and stimulating discussion of the historical development of social security measures and the important decisions to be made before establishing a program.

Carlson, Valdemar. *Economic Security in the United States.* New York: McGraw-Hill, 1962.
A historical and analytical treatment of economic security in this country. It is useful not only for its treatment of the development of problems and programs, but also for the ways in which economic security approaches are analyzed in terms of the market mechanism.

Chambers, Clarke A. *Seedtime of Reform: American Social Service and Social Action, 1918–1933.* Minneapolis, MN: University of Minnesota Press, 1963.
A detailed history of the social welfare movement in the United States from World War I to the year of Franklin Delano Roosevelt. Written by a historian, the volume covers topics such as unemployment, but also treats many broader issues and developments.

Myers, Robert J. *Social Security,* 2nd ed., Homewood, Ill.: Robert D. Irwin, 1981.
Chapter 1 of this comprehensive book discusses social security concepts. The author was Chief Actuary of the Social Security Administration from 1947 to 1970 and is currently Deputy Commissioner for Policy.

Rejda, George E. *Social Insurance and Economic Security.* Englewood Cliffs, N.J.: Prentice-Hall, 1976.
Chapters 1 and 2 of this comprehensive book present some fundamental concepts on economic security and its treatment.

Turnbull, John G. *The Changing Faces of Economic Insecurity.* Minneapolis, Minn.: University of Minnesota Press, 1966.
A qualitative and quantitative comparison of economic insecurity from 1910 to 1960 and of social adjustments thereto. The volume analyzes trends of the past half-century.

The reader can also peruse with profit the *Monthly Labor Review,* the *Social Security Bulletin,* the *Health Care Financing Review* and the annual *Economic Report of the President,* all of which contain useful articles and items of information.

Chapter Two

The Problems of Death
and Old Age

All workers face the possibility of premature death cutting short their earning period or of living to such an advanced age that their earning power will have stopped and they will have consumed all of their accumulated assets. Both situations pose serious financial problems that most persons are anxious to solve in advance through private or public means. We start our discussion of security programs with the topics of death and old age, since these are the most "final" forms of job severance. Injuries, sickness, and unemployment are usually of limited duration.

In this chapter we shall explore the nature and importance of the financial problems associated with premature death and old age. We shall also consider the probability of a person dying prematurely and that of a person surviving to retirement age and beyond and how these probabilities are related to economic insecurity.

The general loss control and alleviative approaches to these problems will then be discussed. Social insurance and private insurance—the two most important approaches—are discussed in detail in the next three chapters.

Finally, note will be made of the current economic resources of survivors and the aged, from all private and public sources, in order to evaluate the adequacy of present approaches to the problems of death and old age.

THE ECONOMIC PROBLEMS OF PREMATURE DEATH

Nature and Importance

Premature death of a worker causes two types of financial loss to dependents. First, the deceased's earning power stops. If the worker rendered services such as household care instead of contributing earnings, the imputed value of these services stops. Death of a spouse may also adversely alter the tax status of the survivor. Second, extra expenses are incurred in the form of burial expenses, probate costs, estate and inheritance taxes, forced liquidation losses, and others.

The earning power loss is the more important for most families, but few persons appreciate its possible magnitude. An example will illustrate this point. Assume that an individual, age 35, is earning $20,000 a year after income taxes. To simplify the explanation, further assume that this salary is not expected to change until age 65, at which time the worker expects to retire. Under these assumptions the future income will total 30 × $20,000 = $600,000. If the worker should die at age 35, this income will never be earned. However, it is not fair to state that dependents will suffer a loss of $600,000, because, first, the worker would have consumed some of this income if he or she had lived and, second, this income would have been spread over a 30-year period.

If it is assumed that $5,000 would have been required each year to maintain the deceased and prepare for his or her retirement, the annual income loss to the dependents is $15,000, making a total income loss of $450,000. The proportion of the lost income that would have been spent on the deceased worker depends on several factors, such as the deceased's personal tastes and habits, the size of the family, and the number of wage earners in the family. The fact that this income would have been spread over a 30-year period means that some allowance must be made for the interest earnings on a lump sum available at the present time. In more technical terms, it is necessary to discount the future incomes to determine their present value. If it is assumed that this lump sum can earn 5% interest after taxes, compounded annually, and that the incomes would have been available at the end of the year in which they were earned, the lump sum (or the present value of the future incomes) is computed as follows:

$$\$15,000 \ (1 + 0.05)^{-1} = \$ \ 15,000 \ (0.9524),$$
$$15,000 \ (1 + 0.05)^{-2} = \ 15,000 \ (0.9070),$$
$$15,000 \ (1 + 0.05)^{-3} = \ 15,000 \ (0.8638),$$

$$\vdots \qquad\qquad\qquad \vdots$$

$$15,000 \ (1 + 0.05)^{-28} = \ 15,000 \ (0.2551),$$
$$15,000 \ (1 + 0.05)^{-29} = \ 15,000 \ (0.2429),$$
$$15,000 \ (1 + 0.05)^{-30} = \ \underline{15,000 \ (0.2314)},$$
$$\$230,600 \ (\text{approximately}).$$

In other words, if $230,600 is invested at 5% interest compounded annually, periodic withdrawals of $15,000 at the end of each year for 30 years would exhaust the fund. Therefore $230,600 is a good *estimate* of the earning power loss to the dependents in this case. Even if it were in error by as much as $20,000 or $40,000, it is still a useful figure because it reveals the magnitude of the loss.[1]

Because salaries generally increase over most of a person's working career, assuming a constant salary understates the magnitude of the loss. For example, if this individual's salary increased by 5% a year, the same rate as the discount percentage, the loss would be $450,000.

The earning power loss varies inversely with age. To illustrate, when the individual used in our example reaches age 50, the possible earning power loss will have dropped to approximately $155,600. At retirement age it will be $0. Because annual income typically increases instead of remaining level, the drop in earning power loss with age is not usually this rapid.[2] However, it is still generally true that, other things being equal, the family suffers the greatest earning power loss when the breadwinner dies at an early age.

The earning power loss also varies inversely with the assumed interest rate. For example, in the case cited the loss would be about $294,000, $186,100, and $141,000 under 3%, 7%, and 10% assumptions respectively.

The Probability of Premature Death

Because of medical advances and improved social and economic conditions premature death is much less probable today than it was in the earlier part of the 20th century. However, a large number of people still die early in life and the probability of this occurring is greater than most people choose to believe. Table 2.1 shows the mortality rates at various ages for the first eight decades of this century. Notice that most of the improvement has occurred at the younger ages. This improvement is expected to continue, but at a less rapid pace, in the future.

On the average, on the basis of current mortality rates, about one out of five 20-year-olds will have his or her earning period shortened by death prior to age 65. By age 60 the odds drop to 1 out of 10.

---

[1]Unless the earnings figure includes some allowance for the non-wage income that this individual would have earned (for example, employer-paid insurance that would have paid the medical expenses incurred by his or her spouse or children), the loss is even greater than this analysis suggests. Some allowance should also be made for the fact that the individual performs certain services in his or her household to which a money value can be imputed.

[2]If the difference between the starting and final incomes is great, it is possible that decreasing interest discounts on the future larger salaries may result in an increasing earning power loss during the first few years. For a more detailed and sophisticated discussion of the human life concept, and tables expressing the human life value as a multiple of present gross earnings for selected occupations and ages, see Alfred E. Hofflander, Jr., "Human Life Value Concepts," unpublished doctoral dissertation, University of Pennsylvania, Pa., 1964. For example, the multiple for an engineer, age 25, is 36.

Table 2.1 Deaths Per 1,000 Total Population Living at Specified Ages, 1910–1978[a]

Age	1909–1911	1919–1921[b]	1929–1931[b]	1939–1941	1949–1951	1959–1961	1969–1971	1978
0	114.6	80.2	62.3	47.1	29.8	25.9	20.0	13.8
10	2.3	2.1	1.5	0.9	0.5	0.4	0.3	0.2
20	4.7	4.3	3.2	2.2	1.4	1.2	1.4	1.3
30	6.5	5.7	4.1	3.1	1.8	1.4	1.6	1.3
40	9.4	7.5	6.8	5.2	3.7	3.0	3.1	2.4
50	14.4	11.7	12.8	10.8	8.8	7.7	7.4	6.2
60	28.6	24.6	26.4	22.5	19.8	17.6	17.0	14.9
70	59.5	54.6	58.0	48.7	42.5	38.7	36.6	31.1
80	130.3	119.7	130.0	114.9	98.4	92.1	83.9	75.1
90	249.6	283.2	245.5	230.8	212.5	227.1	185.0	n.a.
100	401.9	442.4	470.4	360.0	389.0	392.4	307.0	n.a.

Sources: U.S. Department of Commerce, Bureau of the Census, *United States Life Tables: 1910, 1930, 1940, and 1950* (Washington, D.C.: Government Printing Office, 1916, 1936, 1946, and 1954). Data for 1959–1961 and 1969–71 are from the U.S. Department of Health, Education, and Welfare, Public Health Service, *United States Life Tables: 1959–1961* (Washington, D.C.: Government Printing Office, 1964) and *United States Life Tables: 1969–1971* (Washington D.C.: Government Printing Office, 1975). Data for 1978 were derived from abridged life tables in U.S. Department of Health and Human Services, *Vital Statistics of the United States, 1978,* Vol. II, Sec. 5 Life Tables (Washington, D.C.: U.S. Government Printing Office, 1980). These data are not as accurate as the *United States Life Tables,* which are based on decennial census data.

[a]Death registrations were not available for all states until 1933.

[b]Data for 1919–1921 and 1929–1931 apply to white males only.

THE ECONOMIC PROBLEMS OF OLD AGE

Nature and Importance

Old age also presents serious economic security problems. Earnings may stop or be considerably reduced, but expenses continue. The economic security problem involved is how to meet expenses not covered by current earnings. Again it is fair to say that the average person does not appreciate the magnitude of this problem. For example, assume that a retired person, age 65, has expenses totaling $10,000 a year. If these expenses are to be paid at the end of each year solely out of interest payments on accumulated investments, the principal would have to be $200,000 if the interest return after taxes were 5%, $333,333 if that return were 3%, and $142,857 if the return were 7%.

If it is assumed that expenses are to be paid out of periodic withdrawals of the principal plus interest on the unpaid balance, one would have to know how many years the person will live in order to determine the amount he or she must have accumulated by the date of retirement. If he or she will live 10 more years, the required principal is about $77,200 at 5% interest, $85,400 at 3%, and $70,200 at 7%. If he or she will live 20 more years, the required principal is $124,600 at

5% interest. If he or she will live to age 100, the amount required is $163,800 at 5% interest. The amount varies directly with the living expenses and number of years, and inversely with the interest rate.

Even a short period of retirement, therefore, requires the accumulation of a large sum of money. One never knows, however, whether one will live to retirement age and, if so, how long after retiring. Consequently the problem is compounded because the amount that needs to be accumulated is unknown.

The Probability of Survival to Retirement Age and Beyond

A person either dies or lives. Consequently, the chance of a person living to reach a certain age is equal to unity minus the probability of dying before reaching that age. Table 2.2 shows the probability of a person, age 20, 30, 40, 50, or 60, reaching age 65.

Table 2.2 also indicates the average life expectancy for each age, or the average number of years that persons in each age group will live beyond their present age. For ages 20 and 40 the median number of remaining life years is slightly higher than the average; for age 60 the median is less. The final column in Table 2.2 shows the number of years by which the average life expectancy will carry the person beyond age 65. Notice that these figures increase as the person grows older, because the person has moved closer to age 65 and the chance of surviving to that age has improved.

As mortality rates decrease over a period of time, the probability of surviving to retirement age and beyond increases. Table 2.3 shows how average life expectancies at birth and at ages 20, 40, 60, and 80 have increased over time. Improvements at the older ages have been slight, but those at the younger ages have been great.

Factors Other Than Age Causing Variation in Mortality Rates

Mortality rates also vary according to factors other than age. The effects of sex and race, the two other most important variables, are illustrated in Table 2.4. As

Table 2.2 Probability of Survival to Age 65 and Average Life Expectancy at Specified Ages, 1978

Present Age	Probability	Average Life Expectancy	Average Life Expectancy Beyond Age 65
20	.78	55.0	10.0
30	.79	45.7	10.7
40	.80	36.4	11.4
50	.83	27.6	12.6
60	.91	19.7	14.7

Sources: See Table 2.1 for 1978 data.

Table 2.3   Average Life Expectancies at Specified Ages, 1910–1978[a]

Age	1909–1911	1919–1921[b]	1929–1931[b]	1939–1941	1949–1951	1959–1961	1969–1971	1978
0	51.5	56.3	59.1	63.6	68.1	69.9	70.8	73.3
20	43.5	45.6	46.0	48.5	51.2	52.6	53.0	55.0
40	28.2	29.9	29.2	31.0	32.8	33.9	34.5	36.4
60	14.4	15.2	14.7	15.9	17.0	17.7	18.3	19.7
80	5.2	5.5	5.3	5.7	6.3	6.4	7.1	8.1

Sources: See Table 2.1.

[a]Death registrations were not available for all states until 1933.

[b]Data for 1919–1921 and 1929–1931 apply to white males only.

Table 2.4 indicates, females experience lower mortality rates than do males at all ages. At all except possibly the most advanced ages, the nonwhite population has higher mortality rates than does the white population.

Causes of Death

In 1980 the five leading causes of death and the proportion of the deaths for which they were responsible were as follows[3]

Cardiovascular–renal diseases	48%
Cancer	23%
Accidents	6%
Bronchitis and other respiratory diseases	3%
Pneumonia and influenza	3%

In 1900 the five leading causes, in order of importance, were pneumonia and influenza, tuberculosis, diarrhea and enteritis, cardiovascular–renal diseases, and accidents.

Table 2.4   Average Life Expectancies Classified by Age, Sex, and Race, 1978

Age	White		Nonwhites		All Races	
	Male	Female	Male	Female	Male	Female
0	70.2	77.8	65.0	73.6	69.5	77.2
20	52.0	59.1	47.4	55.6	51.4	58.7
40	33.6	39.9	30.4	37.0	33.2	39.5
60	17.2	22.3	16.5	21.2	17.1	22.1
80	6.7	8.8	8.8	11.5	6.9	8.9

Sources: See Table 2.1 for 1978 data.

[3]*1981 Life Insurance Fact Book* (Washington, D.C.: American Council of Life Insurance, 1981), p. 96.

Age Composition of the Total Population

As Table 2.5 indicates, the proportion of the population that is 65 and over has almost tripled since the turn of the century. The increase in the *number* of aged persons during that time has been even more dramatic.

Increased life expectancy, low birth rates during the 1930s, and reduced immigration rates have combined to produce this result, which has caused society to pay increasing attention to the social and economic problems of the aged.

Table 2.5 also shows that the proportion of the population that is 65 and over is expected to continue to increase, especially during the first half of the next century. The major reason for this changing composition is the steep decline in birth rates in the 1960s (from 3.61 per woman in 1960 to 2.43 in 1970) and the continuing decline through the 1970s until 1977, when there was a slight increase to 1.79 from 1.72 in 1976. The proportion of the population that is aged is expected to increase even under "high" fertility assumptions, which are less plausible in view of trends in life styles and the strong support for zero population growth.

Table 2.5 Age Composition of the U.S. Total Population, 1900–2040

Year	Percentage of Population in Each Age Group[a]		
	Under 20	20–64	65 and over
1900	44	52	4
1920	40	54	5
1940	34	59	7
1960	38	53	9
1980	31–31	58–58	11–11
2000	26–30	61–58	13–12
2020	23–29	60–56	17–15
2040	21–29	57–55	22–16

Sources: 1900–1960 data from Jacob Siegel, Meyer Zitter, and Donald S. Akers, *Current Population Reports, Population Estimates,* Series P-25, No. 286, July, 1964. 1980–2020 projections calculated from the Social Security Administration, Office of the Actuary, *United States Population Projections for OASDHI Cost Estimates,* Actuarial Study No. 77, June 1978.

[a]The first figure for each age group in the projections for 1980, 200, 2020, and 2040 is the "low" population estimate, which is based on the assumption that the ultimate fertility rate will be 1.7 children per women. The second figure is the "high" population estimate, based on an assumption that women will ultimately bear 2.3 children on the average. Under the low estimate the population will be 241 million in the year 2040. The high estimate is 377 million.

GENERAL APPROACHES TO THE ECONOMIC PROBLEMS OF PREMATURE DEATH

Society has attacked the problems of premature death in many ways. Private and public bodies have applied both loss control and alleviative methods to these problems.

Loss Control Methods

Loss control methods have reduced mortality rates, as is evident from the data presented in Tables 2.1 and 2.3. Advances in medical knowledge and their widespread application have been the most important factors, but higher average standards of living have also contributed to the increasing life spans.

Private Loss Control Measures

Private loss control measures have taken many forms and involve many different groups. The following five measures illustrate their nature and importance. The first is *health education,* which may consist of personal conversations between a physician and a patient or may instead be a program affecting many persons. Health education may be sought and paid for by an individual or it may be sponsored by an employer, a union, a nonprofit foundation, a commercial insurer, or some other private institution. The major objective of health education is to teach persons how to conserve their health, how to recognize danger signals, and the reasons for seeking early treatment. *Medical care* itself is a second loss control technique whose importance is obvious. A third example is a *safety program* aimed at preventing or reducing the effects of accidents on the job, on the highway, in the home, and elsewhere. At least some parts of most safety programs can be viewed as a kind of health education, but the program usually includes some measures that fall outside the scope of education, such as the removal of unsafe machinery. Employers, unions, nonprofit foundations such as the National Safety Council, and commercial insurers are especially active in this area. A fourth example is *individual health examinations,* which, it is hoped, will reveal at an early date conditions that might result in death if not treated in time. This examination might be a condition or privilege of employment, part of an application for an insurance contract, a service sponsored by a nonprofit foundation, or part of an individual's program of preventive medicine. The fifth example is *medical research,* which seeks to push back the frontiers of medical knowledge. Conducted by individuals, universities, hospitals, drug firms, and other groups, this research is sponsored by the four groups named as well as by nonprofit foundations, commercial insurers, and others.

Public Loss Control Measures

Our society first recognized the need for public loss control methods on an effective scale over a century ago.[4] Government action was requested because (1) only the government had the authority to *require* the public to supply information, meet certain standards, or stop practices considered to be undesirable, and (2) certain services such as sewage disposal were obviously more economically and efficiently provided by the government. At first state and local governments were almost entirely responsible for public health activities. A National Board of Health functioned from 1879 to 1883,[5] but it was not until the second decade of the present century, when the Public Health Service, Children's Bureau, and other federal agencies were established, that the national government became an important factor. At present the federal government is responsible for international and interstate quarantines, assembles and disseminates vital statistics, conducts research itself and encourages research by others, inspects and establishes standards for food and drugs, and stimulates through several grants-in-aid programs varied activities of state and local governments. Specialized services that cannot be obtained at the local level are also provided by the federal government.[6] The activities of the federal government were considerably increased by the Social Security Act of 1935, which provided for the allocation of considerably more funds among the states to establish and maintain adequate public health services and to promote the health of mothers and children.

Examples of activities of state and local governments are quarantine regulations, water sanitation and sewage disposal, immunization requirements and services for school children, inspection of food handlers, fluoridation of community water supplies, industrial and highway safety campaigns, school lunch and milk programs, public housing, physical examinations for school children, provision of hospital and medical facilities, health education, and medical research. Some of these programs are directed primarily toward the poor or low-income families.

Loss control methods are seldom completely successful, however, and there is tremendous variation in the extent to which they are used by each person. For these reasons alleviative measures are also necessary.

Private Alleviative Methods

Private methods of alleviating the financial loss caused by premature death have changed materially since the beginning of the Industrial Revolution. As long as

[4]The enactment of the New York Metropolitan Health Bill of 1866 is considered to be a turning point in the history of public health in the United States. See George Rosen, *A History of Public Health* (New York: M. D. Publications, Incorporated 1958), p. 247.

[5]George Rosen, *ibid.,* p. 249.

[6]George Rosen, *ibid.,* p. 470. The federal government also provides medical services for certain groups such as the Coast Guard, the American Indians, and the Alaskan Eskimos.

families were largely self-sufficient—a common occurrence in a predominantly agricultural economy—the dependents of a deceased person were welcome in some relative's home because they were able to make valuable contributions to the household's consumption needs. Today these dependents can usually make a positive contribution only if they have some source of money income, such as wages or savings.

Furthermore, even if the dependents have sufficient money income, it has become less "convenient" for relatives to care for them because of smaller living quarters, longer and more expensive dependency periods for children, different interests, a desire for a higher standard of living, and increased mobility. More-over, the size of the average family has decreased and hence there are fewer relatives to turn to for support. Finally, these relatives may not have maintained close family ties.

Dependents still move in with relatives (for example, a widowed daughter and her children still may live with her parents), but in general, social and economic forces have reduced the frequency and effectiveness of this approach to the problem.

Dependents may seek work to replace the earnings of the deceased, but jobs may not be available, the jobs available may not be desirable, or working may force some dramatic shifts in living styles or future plans. For example, a widow with young children may find it difficult to leave home to go to work. A teen-age son or daughter may have to defer or abandon plans to attend college.

Private charities help in alleviation, but this aid is necessarily very limited. United Way agencies exemplify this approach. Churches, labor unions, fraternal societies, and charitable institutions of various types have also been active in providing assistance. However, if private aid of this sort is the only support available, a drastic reduction in the family's standard of living is almost certain to result. Furthermore, most families do not consider charity to be an acceptable solution to their financial problems.

Accumulated capital in the form of real estate, savings accounts, securities, and the like may be an important source of income for middle-age survivors, but, as explained later in this chapter, there are many reasons why it may be difficult to accumulate substantial assets, even by the age of retirement. Younger persons are, of course, much less likely to have substantial ac-cumulated capital.

Private life insurance is an excellent way to accumulate capital in case of premature death. This device is particularly useful for young survivors because through a life insurance contract an insured can leave dependents a large sum of money even if death should occur at an early age.

Private life insurance, however, is by no means a complete solution to the problem. Some applicants do not qualify for insurance issued on an individual basis[7] because of poor health or other reasons, while other persons consider the

---

[7]The differences between individual insurance and group insurance are explained more fully in Chapter 5.

cost too high for them. Many individuals with dependents mistakenly feel that they need little or no insurance.

Group insurance, which is usually associated with the individual's place of employment and which originated in this century, has been a very important development because insurance is made available to every member of an eligible group and the wholesale merchandising of the coverage cuts the cost. However, many persons are not members of an eligible group and the amount of protection available under a group plan is usually limited.

Still another private approach to the financial problems created by premature death is to cut expenses by becoming more self-sufficient. More than very limited use of this approach, however, is not easy, nor, in some cases, even possible.

Public Alleviative Methods

Because the financial loss caused by premature death is so great, and because most families, for various reasons, have not voluntarily adequately protected themselves against this loss, the government has often been forced to aid the deceased's dependents. Poorhouses and orphanages represent the major approach used prior to the 20th century. Limited state cash assistance programs made their appearance at the beginning of this century, but they varied greatly among states and were, in general, inadequate.

The Social Security Act of 1935 was responsible for the first large-scale use of public alleviative methods. This act provided, among other things, for federal grants-in-aid to state public assistance programs dealing with the problems caused by premature death. All states have such programs, but they help only the needy. The most important public death protection was added in 1939, when the social insurance provisions of the Social Security Act were amended to include what Congress considered to be basic minimum death benefits. Today these benefits are a major source of protection for most of the population.

Death benefits are also available under the federal government's Railroad Retirement System, Civil Service Retirement System, veterans' programs, and uniformed services' programs, a selective discussion of which is found in Chapter 13. The special occupational death benefits payable under workers' compensation statutes are discussed in Chapter 7.

Financial Resources of Families With Children

How well has this system worked? One measure is the adequacy of the financial resources of families with children who have lost one parent and who are receiving survivorship benefits under Old-Age, Survivors, Disability, and Health Insurance. Periodically the Social Security Administration surveys such beneficiaries. The most recent Survey of Survivor Families with Children shows their situation in 1978.[8]

[8]Robert I. K. Hastings and Philip B. Springer, "Preliminary Findings from the 1978 Survey of Survivor Families with Children," *Research and Statistics Note No. 12* (Washington, D.C.: Office of

During that year about 2.3 million children under 18 and 692,000 parents received OASDI benefits for at least one month. During the spring of 1978 about 5,752 survivor families were interviewed for the survey. Two-thirds of the survivor families were headed by persons who were currently widows. About 20% were headed by a remarried widow, and 13% by a widower.

Some facts about each of these three types of survivor families are presented in Table 2.6. Because the families headed by current widows are the most numerous and have the most vulnerable economic status, the remainder of this discussion will concentrate on these families.

The median size of these households was 3.2 persons. About 22% contained one child; 26% had four or more children. The median age of the surviving widows was 46. About 7% were age 29 or younger, about 11% 55 or older. Almost half were working, most as clerical workers (27%), service workers (23%) or operatives (15%). About 35% reported a physical condition that prohibited or limited work. About 19% said they were not working because of family care responsibilities. About 5% could not find a job, 3% did not want to work, and 2% lacked the necessary training. About 6% gave other reasons.

Their median total family income in 1977 was $10,770. No frequency distribution of total family income is available at this writing, but the following data shed some light on this distribution:

	Total Earnings	Total Income Other Than Earnings
None (%)	27	—
$1–$2,999 (%)	24	8
$3,000–$5,999 (%)	16	30
$6,000–$8,999 (%)	11	33
$9,000 or more (%)	22	29

These families depend heavily upon sources of income other than earnings, such as OASDHI, public assistance, private pensions, income from insurance and trust funds, dividends and interest, and rents. Of such sources the most important were the public sources, which alone produced a median income of $6,570.

Median earnings increased with the age of the youngest child, but median total family income was not related to this age except at the extremes. The median income was $11,600 when the child was 17, $9,400 when the child was under 6.

Research and Statistics, Social Security Administration, November 7, 1980). See also Tim Sass, "Demographic and Economic Characteristics of Nonbeneficiary Widows: An Overview," *Social Security Bulletin*, LXII, No. 11 (November 1979), 3–14. This study reports the economic study of widows under age 60 with no dependents and thus no OASDI benefits after one year of widowhood. A related report is Lucy B. Mallan, "Young Widows and Their Children: A Comparative Report," *Social Security Bulletin*, XXXVIII, No. 5 (May 1975), 3–21. Unlike the Hastings–Springer report, the Mallan article described the status in 1971 of all widows under age 60 with or without children.

Table 2.6   Selected Characteristics of OASDHI Survivor Families, 1978

Characteristic	Current Widow	Remarried Widow	Widower	Total
Median number in household	3.2	4.3	3.7	3.5
Median age of surviving spouse	46	39	47	44
Race (%)				
White	72	89	84	77
Black	24	8	12	19
Other	4	3	4	4
Homeownership (%)				
Own	63	83	81	70
Rent	33	16	17	27
Other	4	1	2	3
Current labor force status (%)				
Working	49	47	90	55
Not working owing to				
Physical incapacity	16	8	4	13
Family care	19	27	1	18
Inability to find job	5	1	1	4
Unwillingness to work	3	11	1	4
Other reasons	8	6	3	6
Median total family income, 1977 ($)	10,770	20,100	21,140	13,280
Median total income excluding earnings ($)	7,050	5,940	3,230	6,310
Median total public income maintenance including OASDHI ($)	6,570	5,410	2,750	5,820
Financially "satisfied" (%)				
Pretty well	22	44	37	29
More or less	48	43	42	46
Not at all	30	13	22	25

Source: Robert I. K. Hastings and Philip B. Springer, "Preliminary Findings from the 1978 Survey of Survivor Families with Children," *Research and Statistics Note No. 12* (Washington, D.C.: Office of Research and Statistics, Social Security Administration, November 7, 1980).

About 63% of these families had received some private life insurance payments, usually in a lump sum, when the husband had died. The median face value was $12,160. About 26% indicated that they currently had no insurance to cover their medical expenses; 13% reported some public program coverage such as Medicaid.

What standards can be used to judge the economic status of these families? First, in the opinion of the families themselves, about 23% said they were "pretty well" satisfied with their financial condition, 47% were "more or less" satisfied, and 30% "not at all" satisfied. Second, a substantial proportion were poor according to the poverty line developed by the Social Security Administration.[9] Third,

[9]In 1978 the poverty threshold for a family of three was $5,201. See Chapter 14 for more details.

the U.S. Department of Labor periodically publishes the *City Worker's Family Budget,* which, in a modified form, can serve as a comparison point. This budget was developed for an urban family of four persons: an employed husband, age 38, a wife not employed outside the home, and two children, ages 8 and 13. In autumn of 1978 the total "intermediate" budget cost was about $18,600.[10] If it is assumed that the absence of the father would have cut expenses by 25% to about $14,000, the median income of survivor families headed by a current widow would still be less. The incomes of many such families were substantially less. These disturbing findings are partially mitigated by the fact that many of these families received important noncash assistance such as food stamps and public housing. Also the Bureau of Labor Statistics' budgets assume taxable earnings, whereas OASDHI, public assistance, and other similar payments to these survivors are nontaxable income.

By all three standards many survivor families have inadequate incomes. If it were not for the payments from OASDI and public assistance, they would be substantially worse off. During the past two decades, fortunately, the economic status of these families has improved. Nevertheless, much remains to be done to (1) increase public and private life insurance protection and (2) expand widows' earning opportunities through more and better day-care centers, training programs, job placement assistance, and reduction of some disincentives in public assistance programs.

GENERAL APPROACHES TO THE ECONOMIC PROBLEMS OF OLD AGE

Methods of attacking the economic problems of old age are largely alleviative, but the loss control programs discussed in connection with premature death diminish old-age problems if a larger proportion of the persons attaining advanced ages are capable of earning a limited income and a place can be found to apply their talents. Otherwise, increasing average life expectancies intensify the financial problems of old age.

Loss Control Methods

Loss control efforts, then, include all measures designed to facilitate continued employment of the aged, but the prospects for this approach are not bright. As Table 2.7 indicates, the proportion of the labor force that is 65 or over was less in 1980 than in 1945, despite that fact that the aged were a much larger percentage of the total population in 1980 than in 1945. The principal reason for this decrease is that the proportion of men 65 and over in the labor force dropped from almost

---

[10]The "lower" budget was $11,546, the higher budget $27,420. See "Family Budget Increases in 1978 Were the Largest in 4 Years," *Monthly Labor Review,* CIII, No. 1 (January, 1980), 44–47.

Table 2.7   Aged Persons in the Labor Force, 1945–1980

Year[a]	Proportion of Labor Force 65 Years and Over			Proportions of Persons 65 Years and Over in the Labor Force	
	Total	Men	Women	Men	Women
1945	4.4	3.7	0.7	48.7	9.0
1950	4.7	3.8	0.9	45.7	9.7
1955	4.8	3.7	1.1	39.6	10.6
1960	4.5	3.2	1.3	33.1	10.8
1965	4.1	2.8	1.3	27.9	10.0
1970	3.7	2.5	1.2	26.8	9.7
1975	3.0	1.9	1.1	21.7	8.3
1980	2.8	1.8	1.0	19.1	8.1

Sources: Data for 1945 to 1970 from *Historical Statistics of the United States, Colonial Times to 1970,* Part 1 (Washington, D.C.: U.S. Bureau of the Census, 1975), pp. 131–132. Data for 1975 from *Employment and Earnings,* XXII, No. 7 (January 1976), 134, 135. Data for 1980 from *Employment and Earnings,* XVIII, No. 1 (January 1981), 164, 165.
[a]Averages of monthly figures for 1945–1970, December figures for 1975 and 1980.

one-half to about one-fifth. The proportion of women was about the same in both years, but less than in 1960.

For males the same dominant trend in labor force participation exists among the 55 to 64 age group.[11] Their participation rate dropped from 87% in 1960 to 74% in 1977. Women, on the other hand, increased their participation rate from 37% to 41%.

One reason why more aged do not belong to the labor force may be that the demand for their services is not strong enough to absorb all the qualified aged persons. Other possible explanations are that (1) the aged prefer not to work, (2) many of the aged are in poor health or do not possess the talents in demand, or (3) institutional pressures cause forced retirements. The major institutional pressures are those imposed by public and private pension plans.

Social Security Administration Reports on the Work Experience of the Aged

According to the first of a biennial series of reports scheduled for publication in the *Social Security Bulletin,* about 39% of the aged couples in 1976 (defined as a couple in which the husband is at least 65) had worked.[12] A couple was considered to have worked if at least one member had been employed at least part of the year. About 19% of the nonmarried women had been so employed.

[11]Carl Rosenfeld and Scott Campbell Brown, "The Labor Force Status of Older Workers," *Monthly Labor Review,* CII, No. 11 (November 1979), 12–18.
[12]Susan Grad and Karen Foster, "Income of the Population Aged 55 and Older, 1976," *Social Security Bulletin,* XLII, No. 7 (July 1979), 17.

However, only 16% of the couples had full-time, year-round employment. For nonmarried men the corresponding proportion was 7%, for nonmarried women 3%.

From an earlier Survey of Newly Entitled Beneficiaries the Social Security Administration found that among the nonemployed men (wage and salary workers plus the self-employed) awarded OASI retirement benefits in late 1968 the most important reasons for retiring were as follows:[13]

Poor health	23%
Compulsory retirement age	36%
General retirement age	14%
Wanted to retire	16%
Other	11%

Some men who reported "general retirement age" may have been affected by a compulsory retirement age, but most implied that they initiated their own retirement because "it was time." The fact that age 65 is the normal retirement age under OASDI may have contributed to this decision.

Because the self-employed are not affected by compulsory retirement ages, it is not surprising to find that a much larger percentage of the beneficiaries who had been wage and salary workers cited compulsory retirement as the reason for having stopped working. This reason was given by 52%, 21% cited poor health, 5% had lost their jobs, and 22% quit their job for non-health-related reasons. About three-fifths of the beneficiaries who stopped working because of a compulsory retirement age did not want to retire. Among all the beneficiaries who had stopped working for any reason, about half would have preferred to continue working.

Poor health and compulsory retirement, therefore, have kept many of the aged out of the labor force. As indicated later, compulsory retirement should be a less important reason in the future because, starting in 1979, federal legislation has prohibited employers from forcing workers under age 70 to retire because of age. Compulsory retirement at age 70, however, will remain an important reason for retirement.

The arguments against retaining workers beyond some advanced age can be summarized as follows. Elderly employees are often in poor health, they are relatively inflexible at a time when our economy demands flexibility, they raise insurance and pension costs, they resent being supervised by younger people, and they block the promotion lanes for younger persons. Furthermore, because of minimum wage laws and collective bargaining, the production of the aged is often

[13]Virginia Reno, "Why Men Stop Working Before Age 65," Chapter 4 in *Reaching Retirement Age: Findings from a Survey of Newly Entitled Workers 1968–1970,* Research Report No. 47 (Washington, D.C.: U.S. Department of Health Education, and Welfare, Social Security Administration, Office of Research and Statistics, 1976), pp. 43–51.

exceeded by the wages they must be paid. A discretionary policy would permit a firm to select the more able among the aged, but many businessmen believe that a discretionary retirement policy is unworkable, breeds discontent, and hinders programs preparing older workers for retirement.

Other researchers argue that poor health and compulsory retirement ages are only two of many variables affecting a worker's decision to leave the labor force. In their opinion both the healthy and unhealthy consider the total advantages and disadvantages of retiring.[14] Among the strong economic disincentives to continue working are the actuarial penalties for later retirement that are built into most present public and private pension plans. For example, by delaying retirement from age 65 to age 70, a worker may receive at most a small increase in his or her pension.

The Social Security Administration has also reported the work experience of persons age 62–64: in 1976 only 80% of the couples and 49% of the nonmarried persons in this age group worked; only 55% of the couples and 26% of the nonmarried persons worked full-time year round.[15] The major reason most units in this age group were not working was poor health. Other reasons were loss of job due to automation, other technological and structural changes, age discrimination in employment, more liberal unemployment benefits, and early retirement provisions in public and private pension plans.[16]

If the present trends prevail, employment of the aged will become less and less frequent. Because there is a strong relationship between work and income adequacy in old age, this is disturbing. Some close observers claim, however, that the trends can and should be reversed. They argue that many of the aged who do not consider themselves well enough to work might change their attitude if they had something challenging to which they could look forward. Furthermore, many of the aged might have retained their health had they continued their normal work.

These authorities remind us that employers are placing increasing emphasis on training and decreasing emphasis on physical strength, which should improve employment opportunities for the aged. They point to the fact that the educational levels of the aged and the nonaged will be more similar in the future. In addition, aged workers, in their opinion, are more responsible, loyal, and stable. They believe, therefore, that modern industry should take another look at retirement plan provisions, because many able persons have been forced or encouraged to retire too early in life, thus wasting human resources and destroying for the

[14]See, for example, R. V. Burkhauser and G. S. Tolley, "Older Americans and Market Work," *The Gerontologist,* XVIII, No. 5 (1978), 449–453.

[15]Grad and Foster, "Income of the Population Aged 55 and Older, 1976," *Social Security Bulletin,* XLII, No. 7 (July 1979), 17.

[16]Virginia Reno, "Why Men Stop Working Before Age 65," Chapter 4 in *Reaching Retirement Age: Findings From a Survey of Newly Entitled Workers 1968–1970,* Research Report No. 47 (Washington, D.C.: U.S. Department of Health, Education, and Welfare, Social Security Administration, Office of Research and Statistics, 1976), p. 43.

individual the noneconomic attractions of work.[17] They also seek stronger protection against age discrimination in employment practices.

An alternative to continued full-time employment for the aged is part-time employment, which would be less physically taxing and interfere less with the desire for leisure. One version would gradually reduce the hours of work or transfer the worker to duties more consistent with his or her abilities or interest. Aged persons can also be made more employable by redesigning jobs to match their capacities and by providing more job information and continued training. In a strong brief for employing more aged persons Harold Sheppard and Sara Rix have recently argued that because the aged will constitute such a large proportion of the population in the future, if we are genuinely concerned about the welfare of the very old, we should continue to employ the "young-old."[18] Otherwise the working population may find the burden of supporting the aged unacceptable. They also expressed deep concern over the trends to early retirement.

The Older Americans Act of 1965

The Older Americans Act of 1965, which created an Administration of Aging within the Department of Health and Human Services (then the Department of Health, Education, and Welfare), established as one of its many objectives programs to help older persons obtain employment. The general purpose of the Act, however, is much broader: to help older people enjoy "wholesome and meaningful" living, which includes noneconomic values (such as income, housing, and employment). To accomplish its objectives the Administration of Aging conducts research and demonstration projects, provides technical assistance to state and local programs, gathers statistics on the aged, makes research grants, and engages in other related activities.

The Age Discrimination in Employment Act of 1967 as Amended in 1977

In 1967 Congress passed an Age Discrimination in Employment Act that created a protected class of persons age 40–65. It prohibited discrimination based on age with respect to hiring, compensation, or conditions of employment. Employers, however, were permitted to forcibly retire an employee within the protected class if that retirement was consistent with a bona fide employee retirement plan. In 1977 Public Law 95-256 amended the Age Discrimination in Employment Act to prohibit for most employers any mandatory retirement age prior to age 70. As a result workers now have the option of continuing their employment until age 70, assuming that they are not discharged for reasons other than age. As a result

---

[17]For example, work may be attractive because it enhances a person's self-respect and provides associations with others, opportunities for service to mankind, and a check on anxieties. See Otto Pollak, *The Social Aspects of Retirement,* Pension Research Council Monograph Series (Homewood, Ill.: Richard D. Irwin, 1956).

[18]Harold L. Sheppard and Sara E. Rix, *The Graying of Working America* (New York: The Free Press, 1977), pp. 142–143, 161.

employers have had to revise employee-benefit plans, work arrangements, and other human resource management programs.[19] The number of workers who will take advantage of this option is not known. For most workers early retirement is a more pressing question, but inflation, attractive continuation opportunities for the aged, and an increase in the OASDI retirement age could change this situation. There are some pressures toward removing the age limit completely.

Private Methods of Alleviation

The importance of private and public alleviative measures increases as the percentage of the employed aged decreases. Attention will be first centered on private methods.

In preparation for retirement, individuals may participate in private pension plans, purchase from life insurers individual annuity contracts that will pay them a lifetime income after they retire, or accumulate other assets that will either (1) pay them interest, dividends, or rent during their retirement years, (2) reduce their living expenses, or (3) permit them to supplement their incomes through withdrawals or sales. However, only about half of the currently employed workers are covered under pension plans.

Because even fewer of the current aged were covered under pension plans during their working years, pension benefits are not currently a major source of income for the aged. Individual annuity benefits are even less common. The current aged's accumulation of other assets was hindered by such factors as the relatively low income status of a large part of the population, an upward trend in prices, high income taxes, the American emphasis on "keeping up with the Joneses," the bank and business failures of the 1930s, personal misfortunes, the weakening of family ties, and a human tendency to postpone preparation for retirement. Most of these forces, which continue to affect preparations for retirement, are beyond the control of the individual, but the last is not.

Although the situation is improving, largely because of the growth and liberalization of private pension plans, present private sources of support are inadequate for most families. Of course it must be recognized that these private sources might have been greater if it had not been for the existence of public sources that meet part of the need and perhaps siphon off some funds which would have otherwise become private sources of support.

Public Methods of Alleviation

Before the 20th century government assistance to the aged consisted almost entirely of poorhouses. A few states made cash grants to the needy aged during the first 30 years of this century, but, until the federal government made grants-in-aid through the Social Security Act to the states the vast majority of the states made no cash grants, and those that did paid very small amounts to very few

[19]For a discussion of the impact of this change on employee-benefit plans see Chapters 5 and 10.

people. In 1974 a federal program of Supplemental Security Income began gua-
ranteeing a minimum income nationally for the aged. Federal and state income
and property tax relief programs reduce expenses, but these programs do little
or nothing for many aged persons.

Social insurance plans for the aged originally took the form of retirement plans
for persons rendering service to the government. State and local government
employees, federal government civil service employees, and members of the
armed services have been covered for the greater part of this century. Railroad
workers became the first nongovernmental employees to be covered under a social
insurance plan, when the Railroad Retirement System began to operate in 1937
as a substitute for private employer plans. The most important social insurance
program—Old-Age, Survivors, Disability, and Health Insurance—began to operate in the same year and has expanded its coverage and benefits since that time.

Money Income of the Aged

One measure of the adequacy of the combined public and private layers of
protection against old age is the present money incomes of the aged, including
their earnings. Two sources of information on these incomes are (1) the biennial
series of reports in the *Social Security Bulletin* already cited in this chapter and
(2) data from a Social Security Administration longitudinal *Retirement History
Study.*

Social Security Bulletin Biennial Reports

The focus of the biennial reports to be published in the *Social Security Bulletin*
is the income of the population age 55 and older.[20] We shall concentrate our
attention on the money incomes of the population age 65 and older.

Table 2.8 shows the 1976 *median incomes* for all aged units and for each of
the three kinds of aged units. Table 2.8 also shows the proportion in each group
with incomes under selected amounts and below the poverty line. The median
income of all aged units was $4,700; 30% had incomes of $3,000 or less; and 25%
had incomes below the poverty line.

One *measure of the adequacy of these incomes* is to compare them with the
budgets the Bureau of Labor Statistics believed a retired couple required in 1976
to maintain different standards of living in urban areas. The budgets included a
lower budget, an intermediate budget, and a higher budget. According to the
Bureau of Labor Statistics, the budgets were developed for an urban family—a
husband, age 65 or over, and his wife—that is self-supporting, living independently, in reasonably good health, and able to take care of itself. All three budgets
provide for the maintenance of health and allow normal participation in commu-

---

[20]The first of these reports was published in 1979. See Grad and Foster, "Income of the Population
Aged 55 and Older, 1976, "*Social Security Bulletin,* XLII, No. 7 (July 1979), 17.

Table 2.8 Total Money Income of Aged Units by Marital Status and Sex, 1976

	Units	Couples	Nonmarried Men	Nonmarried Women
Median income	$4,700	$7,890	$3,870	$3,230
Percentage with income less than				
$1,000	2	1	2	3
$3,000	28	5	34	45
$5,000	53	22	65	75
$10,000	82	63	91	92
$20,000	96	90	98	99
Percent below poverty line	25	9	27	38

Source: Susan Grad and Karen Foster, "Income of the Population Aged 55 and Older, 1976," *Social Security Bulletin,* XLII, No. 7 (July 1979), pp. 22–24.

nity life. Within this framework the three budgets differ because of variations in the assumptions concerning the manner of living and provisions of different quantities and qualities of goods and services.

The average annual total costs under these three budgets are presented in Table 2.9. Also shown are the amounts provided for the major categories of consumer goods and services. Equivalent consumption costs for single retired persons living alone were estimated to be 55% of the consumption total for the retired couple at each level. The intermediate budget for couples living in metropolitan areas was estimated to be about 18% higher than the nonmetropolitan area budget. The budget also varied among cities. For example, the Anchorage budget was 139% of the national average budget, the New York City budget 118%, and the Baton Rouge budget 88%. In 1976 about 40% of the aged couples had incomes less than the intermediate budget. Over half of the aged persons living alone had incomes less than the equivalent budget for the single aged.

Table 2.9 Annual Costs Under the Lower, Intermediate, and Higher Budgets for Retired Couples, by Major Components,[a] 1976 (In Dollars)

Item	Lower	Intermediate	Higher
Total	4,695	6,738	10,048
Allowances			
Food	1,443	1,914	2,402
Housing	1,613	2,334	3,653
Transportation	332	629	1,161
Clothing and personal care	534	549	831
Medical care	571	574	579
Other consumption items	200	332	657
Other items such as gifts, insurance, and taxes	202	405	767

Source: M. Louise McGraw, "Budgets for Retired Couples Rose Moderately in 1976," *Monthly Labor Review,* C, No. 10 (October 1977), 53.

[a]Weighted average costs of renter (35%) and homeowner (65%) families.

Table 2.10 Sources of Money Income for the Aged, by Marital Status and Sex, 1976

Source	Percentage Having Income From Specified Sources				Percentage With Income From Each of Five of Specified Sources Having at Least Half of Their Total Income From the Specified Sources			
	All Units	Married Couples	Nonmarried Men	Nonmarried Women	All Units	Married Couples	Nonmarried Men	Nonmarried Women
Earnings	25	41	21	14	43	46	41	38
Retirement benefits	92	93	92	92				
OASDI	89	90	87	88	79	72	83	83
Other public pensions	13	16	12	11	66	56	70	74
Private pensions	20	28	21	12	9	6	15	13
Interest, dividends, rents, and other income from assets	56	66	44	51				
Veterans benefits	6	6	7	6				
Unemployment insurance	2	3	1	1				
Workers' compensation	1	1	1	1				
Public assistance	11	6	15	15	32	25	29	35
Contributions by relatives or friends not in household	1	1	[a]	1				

Source: Same as for Table 2.8, pp. 18–20, 29, 30.

[a]Less than 0.5%.

The *sources from which the aged derived their money income* in 1976 are indicated in Table 2.10. OASDI was clearly the most frequent source of income and the source from which the aged with income from this source most frequently derived at least half their income. About 89% of the aged units reported income from OASDI; 79% of the recipients received more than half their income from this source. The second most frequent source (56%) was interest, dividends, rents, and other income from assets, but few units derived much of their income from this source. For three-fifths of the units this asset income amounted to less than one-fifth of their total income. Earnings were the third most frequent source, the percentages slightly exceeding the proportions who reported working in 1976. For 43% of the aged units with earnings, these earnings were at least half of their total income. Units with earnings had median incomes of $8,560, compared with $3,860 for those without earnings, thus demonstrating the importance of earnings in determining economic status. About 20% of the aged units reported income from private pensions, but only 9% of the units with pensions received at least half their income from this source. About 11% were receiving some form of public assistance. For 32% of these welfare recipients the public assistance payments made up at least half of their income.

Since 1962 two income sources have become much more frequent. The proportion of aged units with OASDI benefits increased from 69% to 89%, the proportion with private pensions from 9% to 20%.

Social Security Longitudinal Retirement History Study

In 1969 the Social Security Administration interviewed a national sample of about 11,000 persons age 58–63 for the first time in what was designed to be a 10-year study of the retirement process. Information was collected on their work lives, health, living arrangements, financial resources and assets, expenditures, and retirement plans.[21]

Of the men 17% were not in the labor force at the time of the interview. Poor health was the most frequently cited reason for not working.

By December 1974 the persons in the Retirement History Study (RHS) sample were age 63–69.[22] Of the married men 61% were receiving an OASDI retired workers' benefit. Of this 61% almost one-fourth were less than 65 years of age. About one-fourth of their wives were receiving OASDI benefits as retired workers on the basis of their own earnings; about one-third received a benefit as the dependent of the male worker, and 9% as a disabled person or widow. About 30% of the wives received no OASDI benefit. About 47% of the wives were at

---

[21]*Almost 65: Baseline Data from the Retirement History Study,* Research Report No. 49 (Washington, D.C.: U.S. Department of Health, Education, and Welfare, Social Security Administration, Office of Research and Statistics, 1976), p. 1.

[22]The section is based largely on Alan Fox, "Earnings Replacement Rates of Retired Couples: Findings From the Retirement History Study," *Social Security Bulletin,* XLII, No. 1 (January 1979), 17–39.

least four years younger than the husband, 9% three years younger, and 11% two years younger. In only 22% of the couples were the spouses born within one year of each other.

How did the income of these couples compare with their income prior to retirement? Table 2.11 shows the median earnings replacement rates of retired couples at the time of retirement assuming that (1) the couple's combined OASDI benefit was their only income and that (2) the couple's combined OASDI benefit and a second pension, if any, was their total income. OASDI provided a median earnings replacement rate of 41%, which is less than the 60–75% target com-

Table 2.11 Initial Earnings Replacement Rates of Retired Couples by Second-Pension Receipt and Year Husband's Benefit First Paid

Year Husband's Benefit First Paid	Median Pre-Retirement Earnings ($)	Median OASDI Replacement Rate (%)[a]	Median Total Replacement Rate (%)[b]
All Couples			
Total	8,670	41	52
1968–1970	6,970	35	45
1971–1972	8,750	42	55
1973–1974	9,690	45	55
Couples With No Second Pension[c]			
Total	6,315	46	46
1968–1970	4,640	41	41
1971–1972	6,275	48	48
1973–1974	7,905	49	49
Couples With a Second Pension			
Total	10,810	36	59
1968–1970	10,210	28	50
1971–1972	10,815	37	61
1973–1974	11,315	41	62

Source: Alan Fox, "Earnings Replacement Rates of Retired Couples: Findings from the Retirement History Study," *Social Security Bulletin,* XLII, No. 1 (January 1979), Table 22.

[a]Couple's combined OASDI benefit as a percentage of the couple's estimated combined total earnings in their three consecutive years of highest earnings.

[b]Couples combined OASDI benefit and second pension, if any, as a percentage of the couple's estimated combined total earnings in their three consecutive years of highest earnings.

[c]Private employer and union pensions as well as public employee pensions that are combined with OASDI benefits. Public pension systems whose employees are not simultaneously covered under OASDI are excluded.

monly quoted as the percentage required if the couple is to maintain its pre-retirement standard of living.[23] The target percentage varies inversely with the worker's income level. If prices rise following retirement, the pension should be adjusted upward to preserve its purchasing power. Furthermore, the target was designed for persons with reasonable incomes prior to retirement. For many poorer families the target would be 100%. (To the extent that even 100% replacement would not produce what society considers to be a minimum standard of living, the problem is one of poverty, not old age). On the other hand, many of these couples had other sources of income that would increase their replacement rates.[24] The earnings replacement rates were higher for those retiring in 1973–1974 than in 1968–1970.

About 45% of the couples had second pensions (35% had private employee pensions and 10% had public employee pensions). These couples had higher median pre-retirement incomes than the other couples. As will be described in Chapter 3, the OASDI benefit replacement rate tends to vary inversely with pre-retirement earnings. Consequently the median OASDI replacement rate for the couples with a second pension drops to 36%. On the other hand, the OASDI replacement rate for the couples with no pension rises to 46%, which is still much less than the amount required to maintain the pre-retirement standard of living. The median pension first payable in 1973–1974, 49% of $6,315, or $3,873, is also much less than the Bureau of Labor Statistics 1974 intermediate budget total for a retired couple. This intermediate budget total was $6,041; the lower budget was $4,228; and the higher budget $8,969.

For couples with a second pension OASDI and the second pension combined replaced about 59% of the pre-retirement income. Other income sources may have pushed the median earnings into the target retirement range. The median pension (62% of $11,315) payable in 1973–1974 was slightly more than the Bureau of Labor Statistics 1974 intermediate budget total. However, although OASDI benefits are adjusted automatically for price increases following retirement, second pensions are seldom fully adjusted for inflation.[25] Furthermore, for half these families the replacement rate was less than 59%.

On balance it is reasonable to conclude that a substantial proportion of the aged must reduce their standard of living following retirement.

[23]Dan M. McGill, *Fundamentals of Private Pensions* 4th ed., (Homewood, Ill.: Richard D. Irwin, 1979), pp. 92–95.

[24]In 1976 about 72% of the married couples age 65 or older with pensions reported that at least 50% of their income came from these pensions. About one-third said that at least 90% of their income came from this source. Grad and Foster, "Income of the Population Aged 55 and Older, 1976," *Social Security Bulletin,* XLII, No. 7 (July 1979), p. 29.

[25]For the experience of the pensioners included in the Retirement History Study see Gayle B. Thompson, "Impact of Inflation on Private Pensions of Retirees, 1970–1974: Findings From the Retirement History Study," *Social Security Bulletin,* XLI, No. 11 (November 1978), 16–25.

PUBLIC VERSUS PRIVATE ACTION

The need for some level of public action is obvious. However, since increased public benefits may occur at the expense of increased or present private benefits, it is not clear at present whether the two types of action have been combined in the optimum proportions. An answer to this question would, of course, contain important policy implications for the future. However, to discuss the question it is necessary to understand the major characteristics of present social and private insurance plans. We shall consider the public plans in Chapters 3, 4, and 13, and the private plans in Chapter 5.

SUMMARY

Premature death causes a loss of earning power and unexpected expenses such as funeral costs and estate taxes. For the majority of families the most important loss is that of the present value of future incomes. About one out of five 20-year-olds will die prior to age 65.

When a person reaches an advanced age, earnings may stop or be reduced, but expenses continue, even if at a lower level. He or she must save during his or her earning career to prepare for retirement but does not know how much to save because the date of death is unknown. On the average, about four out of five 20-year-olds will reach age 65. Decreasing mortality rates, low birth rates during the Depression, and reduced immigration have greatly increased the proportion of our population faced with the problems of old age.

Loss control methods such as medical research and safety programs have reduced the probability of premature death, but alleviative methods are still essential. Prior to the Industrial Revolution, the dependents of deceased persons moved in with relatives, but social and economic forces have reduced the importance of this solution. Insurance is the most acceptable and effective private alleviative approach, but relatively few persons are adequately protected through this medium for various reasons.

The Social Security Act initiated the first extensive public programs dealing with premature death. State public assistance programs became eligible for federal grants-in-aid in 1935 and the social insurance system was amended in 1939 to include death benefits.

The current incomes of many survivors, however, are still low. In 1978, for example, the median total income of OASDI survivor families headed by a widow was only $10,770.

The most important loss control approach to the problems of old age is continued employment of the aged. However, in 1980 only about 18% of the aged males and 8% of the aged females were in the labor force, and this participation is declining. Compulsory retirement ages are only one reason for this decline. It will become less important in the future. In 1977 the Age Discrimination in

Employment Act was amended to prohibit compulsory retirement prior to age 70. Poor health and, increasingly, a preference for leisure are other important reasons. Private pension plans, though growing in importance, still provide income for relatively few aged persons. The accumulation of other assets has been hindered by such factors as the low income status of part of the population, high taxes, and personal failures to prepare for retirement.

The Social Security Act also initiated the public programs dealing with old age. State old-age assistance programs were made eligible for federal grants-in-aid and a social insurance pension system was established. A new federal Supplemental Security Income program, which guarantees a minimum income for the aged, started operations in 1974.

Despite the public and private layers of protection and the continued employment of some aged persons, the current economic resources of the aged are inadequate. In 1976, for example, aged units had a median money income of only $4,700. About 25% of these units had incomes below the poverty level.

SUGGESTIONS FOR ADDITIONAL READING

Huebner, Solomon S. *The Economics of Life Insurance,* rev. ed. New York: Appleton-Century-Crofts, 1944.
A pioneering discussion of human life values and their relationship to property values.

Rejda, George E. *Social Insurance and Economic Security.* Englewood Cliffs, N.J.: Prentice-Hall, 1976.
Chapters 3 and 4 discuss in detail the economic, social, and psychological problems of premature death and old age.

Sheppard, Harold L., and Sara E. Rix. *The Graying of Working America.* New York: The Free Press, 1977.
A comprehensive study of the employment and employability of the aged.

U.S. Department of Health, Education, and Welfare, Office of Research and Statistics, Social Security Administration. *Almost 65: Baseline Data from the Retirement History Study,* Research Report No. 49. Washington, D.C.: U.S. Government Printing Office, 1976.
A summary of the Retirement History Study procedures and initial findings.

U.S. Department of Health, Education, and Welfare, Public Health Service. *United States Life Tables: 1969–1971.* Washington, D.C.: Government Printing Office, 1975.
Detailed mortality tables applicable to the total population.

The Widows Study, Vols. 1 and 2. Hartford, Conn.: Life Underwriter Training Council and Life Insurance Agency Management Association, 1971 and 1972.
A detailed study of the economic status of widows before and after widowhood.

Chapter Three

Old-Age and Survivors Insurance: Coverage and Benefits

The major social insurance program created under the Social Security Act is known as Old-Age, Survivors, Disability, and Health Insurance, or, in abbreviated form, OASDHI. This program is divided into (1) Old-Age and Survivors Insurance (OASI), (2) Disability Insurance, (3) Hospital Insurance, and (4) Supplementary Medical Insurance. OASI, which provides old-age and death benefits, is the subject of this chapter and Chapter 4. Disability Insurance will be discussed in Chapter 8, and the two medical expense programs in Chapter 9.

A brief discussion of the events leading to the Social Security Act of 1935 will be followed by an analysis and evaluation of the present OASI program. In order to emphasize the major features of the system and the important issues involved, no attempt has been made to cover all of the situations that can arise under the program. On the other hand, the treatment is detailed enough to provide a working knowledge of the system.[1]

This chapter deals with coverage and benefits, Chapter 4 with financing and administration.

HISTORICAL BACKGROUND

Until the mid-1930s the only major social insurance program in the United States was workers' compensation, which provided cash benefits and medical care for workers injured or killed on the job. (Workers' compensation is discussed in Chapter 7.) Public assistance plans at the state and local level provided benefits for some needy aged persons and widowed mothers, but many poor persons were ineligible for these programs because of severe eligibility requirements. The eligible poor generally received inadequate benefits. The Depression increased the number of persons in need of assistance and posed serious financial problems for

---

[1]The reader who is interested in a detailed explanation of the laws and regulations affecting OASDHI is referred to *Social Security Explained* (Chicago, Ill.: Commerce Clearing House, latest edition).

these plans. (Chapter 15 provides more details on the welfare system and its development.)

Pressure for some federal action increased as the Depression situation worsened. By 1931 President Hoover was convinced that the federal government should intervene in some direct fashion. Later that year, at his suggestion, Congress established the Reconstruction Finance Corporation, which made loans to businesses and banks in danger of failing. Under the Emergency Relief and Construction Act of 1932 this agency also made loans to states to be used in connection with public works projects and, later, for relief payments. Franklin Delano Roosevelt advocated more extensive federal action during the 1932 presidential campaign and his election was considered to be a mandate for more such programs.

In 1933 the Federal Emergency Relief Administration was established to make grants to states for direct relief and for work relief. Some closely related programs established under the "New Deal" included the following: (1) the Civilian Conservation Corps (1933), which employed young men on conservation projects; (2) the Public Works Administration (PWA) (1933), a Hoover-conceived project, which made loans and grants to states for large public building projects; (3) the Civil Works Administration (CWA) (1933), which made funds available to those local governments that could arrange work relief projects on short notice; (4) the Federal Surplus Relief Corporation (1933), which distributed surplus foods to the needy; and (5) the Works Progress Administration (1935), which replaced the PWA and CWA.

In June 1934 President Roosevelt appointed a Committee on Economic Security to study the general problem of economic security. This action was prompted by the obvious need for some action, the growing interest in and acceptance of social legislation, and the fear that some unwise proposal might be adopted without careful study. The Committee was composed of several cabinet members and the head of the Federal Emergency Relief Administration. Professor Edwin Witte of the University of Wisconsin was appointed Executive Director.[2] General advisory committees, a technical board of specialists from within and outside the government, and a special committee of four private actuaries aided the Committee in its work. After extensive deliberations concerning the perils to be included, the approaches to be used, the employments to be covered, the benefits to be provided, and the method of financing, the Committee reported its findings in January 1935. In response to this report[3] Congress passed, just seven months later, the Social Security Act—the most extensive piece of social legislation in our history.

---

[2]For the Executive Director's own account of this period, see Edwin E. Witte, *The Development of the Social Security Act* (Madison, Wisc.: University of Wisconsin Press, 1962).

[3]Although Congress accepted in principle most of the Committee's recommendations, it did not accept all of them. For example, a proposal to set up a government insurer to sell annuities in competition with private insurers was rejected.

The original Act provided for the following:

1 Grants to the states for assistance to the needy aged, blind, and, under certain conditions, families with dependent children.[4]
2 Grants to the states for the administration of state unemployment compensation systems.
3 Increased grants to the states for public health services and rehabilitation facilities and increased appropriations for the Public Health Service and the Federal Vocational Rehabilitation Service.
4 Grants to the states for maternal and child health services, services for crippled children, and child welfare services, and an increased appropriation for the Children's Bureau.
5 Federal old-age insurance benefits.
6 Taxes on employers and employees to support the old-age insurance benefits.
7 Taxes on employers designed to encourage the establishment of state unemployment compensation systems.

Important amendments to the Act were passed starting in 1939. The most significant changes are the following:

1 Grants are still made to the states for cash assistance to families with dependent children, but there is now a federal Supplemental Security Income program providing cash aid to the needy aged, blind, and long-term totally disabled. Federal grants also help finance state Medicaid programs, which provide medical assistance for the medically needy as well as needy aged, blind, and long-term totally disabled, and, under certain conditions, families with dependent children.
2 The Public Health Service and the Federal Vocational Rehabilitation Service provisions have been expanded and transferred to the Public Health Service Act and Vocational Rehabilitation Act, respectively.
3 The federal old-age insurance benefits have become old-age, survivorship, and disability insurance benefits.
4 A hospital insurance system and a supplementary medical expense insurance program have been established for the aged and the long-term disabled.
5 The OASDHI tax provisions have been transferred to the Internal Revenue Code. The part of the Code dealing with contributions is called the Federal Insurance Contributions Act. These tax provisions were originally assigned

[4]Professor Carlson argues that categorical programs were established only for the aged, the blind, and dependent children because Congress was made more aware of the needs of these groups and because its preference for outdoor relief caused it to concentrate on those groups for whom institutional care seemed to be the least adequate. Valdemar Carlson, *Economic Security in the United States* (New York: McGraw-Hill, 1962), p. 90.

to separate titles in the Social Security Act and deliberately not related to the other titles to prevent any attack on their constitutionality from destroying the other provisions. Their constitutionality, however, was upheld by the U.S. Supreme Court in 1937.[5] The change to the Internal Revenue Code was made in 1939 at the same time that Congress appropriated all tax collections from this source to the OASI system. At that time the Disability Insurance and medical expense parts of OASDHI did not exist.

The grants under the public assistance programs were designed to solve an immediate problem by strengthening and extending state special public assistance programs. The OASDI system and the medical expense insurance programs represent a long-range approach to the problems of death, old age, and poor health. The other grants deal with loss control approaches, which have already been discussed, or unemployment compensation, which will be discussed in Chapter 12. The discussion now turns to the OASI part of the OASDHI program.

COVERAGE

Classes of Coverage

For workers and their dependents and survivors to receive OASI benefits the worker must be either "fully insured" or "currently insured." The "fully insured" status entitles a worker to all the types of survivorship and retirement benefits provided by the system; "currently insured" workers are eligible only for some types of survivorship benefits.

A decreasing number of elderly people currently receive some OASI payments even though they never worked in covered employment. These special payments, which are the same for all recipients (currently $117 for single persons and $175.60 for couples), were authorized in 1966 on the grounds that people who were already retired when OASI started or who were working when many jobs were not covered should not be left out of the program for those reasons. These special payments, which started at age 72, were payable only to persons who reached age 72 before 1968. Those who became age 72 in 1968 or later were also made eligible for these special payments if they had at least three quarters of coverage plus three more quarters per year for each year after 1968 that they turned 72. As will be apparent from the next section, men who reached age 72 after 1971 and women who reached this age after 1969 found it just as easy to meet the requirements for fully insured status and receive regular benefits. Relatively few such special payments were ever paid and they will eventually disappear. Persons who receive these special payments must not be receiving public

[5]*Carmichael versus Southern Coal and Coke Co.,* 301 U.S. 495, *Steward Machine Co. versus Davis,* 301 U.S. 548, and *Commissioner versus Davis,* 301 U.S. 619.

assistance. Furthermore, this benefit is reduced by any pension from a state or local government, a veteran's pension, or any other pension from the federal government. Each June this special benefit is adjusted upward, as explained later in this chapter, to reflect increases in the Consumer Price Index.

Quarters of Coverage and Covered Employment

To understand how one may become fully or currently insured it is necessary to define "a quarter of coverage." A quarter of coverage was until recently a calendar quarter during which a worker earned at least a specified amount in "covered" employment. In 1977 this amount was $50. For work performed in 1978 a worker received credit for one quarter of coverage for each $250 of *annual* earnings. Since 1978 the 1978 rule has applied, except that the $250 amount has been increased each year to reflect changes in average national earnings. The 1982 amount is $340.[6]

Most employments are covered employments on a compulsory or elective basis. The easiest way to define covered employment is to consider the employments that are excluded from coverage or included only under special conditions. The excluded occupations are the following:

1 Family employment except when the service is performed in a trade or business by a child 21 years of age or over or by a parent in the employ of his or her child.
2 Local newsboys under 18 years of age.
3 Student nurses.
4 Student workers in institutions of learning.
5 Students performing domestic services for college clubs, fraternities, and sororities.
6 Long-service (over 10 years) railroad workers.
7 Police and fire fighters covered under an existing retirement system (except in some states where the situation is similar to that explained below for state and local government employees).
8 Federal government civilian employees covered by a retirement system established by a law of the United States.
9 Some special types of federal and state civilian employees.[7]

[6]Until 1978 a worker received credit for four quarters of coverage for each year in which his or her income exceeded the maximum earnings subject to tax. Self-employed persons received four quarters of coverage for each year in which their self-employment annual income was $400 or more. A farm laborer was credited with one quarter of coverage for each $100 of annual wages, the maximum annual credits being four quarters of coverage. Self-employed persons must still earn $400, and farm laborers $150, a year to be covered, but they earn only one quarter of coverage for each $250, as adjusted, of annual earnings.

[7]For example, the President of the United States.

The occupations included under special conditions are the following:

1 Self-employment is covered employment if the net earnings are $400 or more.
2 Agricultural labor is considered covered employment if the laborer earns $150 or more from any one employer in a calendar year or if he or she works for one employer on 20 or more days for cash pay figured on a time basis rather than a piece-rate basis.
3 Nonfarm domestic workers and casual laborers must earn $50 or more from one employer in a calendar quarter for that quarter to be a quarter of coverage.
4 Clergymen and members of religious orders (except those who have taken a vow of poverty) are covered unless they apply for exemption on or before the due date of their tax returns for the second taxable year in which they have net earnings of $400 or more, any part of which was derived from their duties in the ministry. The application must assert conscientious or religious opposition to participation in the program. Coverage may be extended to those who have taken a vow of poverty if the order makes an irrevocable election to cover these members as employees of the order.
5 Members of recognized religious sects such as the Amish, who, in adhering to the teaching of their sect, are conscientiously opposed to receiving any private or public insurance benefits in case of death, old age, or poor health, may elect not to be covered as to their self-employment income.
6 In order for employees of nonprofit organizations to be covered, the employer must consent. All new employees are automatically covered, but current employees have a choice.
7 State and local government employees not already under a retirement system may be covered if the state agrees. The employees under a retirement system may be covered if the state consents and at least half the employees under each separate system agree.

The exclusions have been justified on the following grounds. Railroad workers are covered under a separate public retirement system as are the federal employees excluded under the Act. As indicated in Chapter 13, however, the Railroad Retirement System is closely coordinated with OASI. Because nonprofit organizations have a tax-exempt status, they cannot be taxed without their consent. States also cannot be taxed without their consent. Some state and local government employees fear that they will lose some of their benefits under their present public retirement systems if they are covered under OASI. The exclusion of certain religious sects such as the Amish is considered necessary to assure these people religious liberty. In order to be exempt, however, the sect must have been in existence since 1950 and its members must have a reputation for making reasonable provision for dependent members. Most of the other occupations are excluded for administrative reasons. Either the administrative problems seem insoluble at the present time or the efforts necessary to solve the problems are not considered to be justified by the benefits to be gained.

Determination of Insured Status

To determine whether an individual is fully insured at retirement age or death the first step is to count the number of years elapsing between the end of the year in which the person became 21 (or December 31, 1950, if later) and the beginning of the year in which he or she became 62 years of age, or died, if earlier.

If the quarters of coverage credited to this person since January 1, 1937, are equal to at least this number, he or she is fully insured.[8] However, the person must have at least six quarters of coverage. Furthermore, years included wholly or partly in a "period of disability" are not counted as elapsed years.[9] The maximum requirement is 40 quarters of coverage.

Illustrations

The following illustrations are designed to clarify the above definition:

1   Assume that a worker will be 65 in March 1982. If she earned, say, $10,000 a year in covered employment during 1964–1971 inclusive, she has been credited with 32 quarters of coverage. She would be fully insured because the number of quarters of coverage would exceed the number of years (28) that have elapsed between December 31, 1950, and January 1, 1979, the year in which she became 62.

2   Another worker will reach age 65 in July 1982. If he earned at least $50 per quarter in covered employment during 1968–1977 inclusive, he has 40 quarters of coverage. It is not necessary to apply the elapsed-years rule in this case to determine whether he is fully insured, because he has satisfied the maximum requirement. Under the elapsed-years rule he needs 28 quarters.

3   Assume that a worker dies shortly after reaching age 30 in February 1982. If she earned $20,000 a year in covered employment during 1976–1981 inclusive, she would be fully insured because she would have 24 quarters of coverage, 16 more than the 8 required for this status in her age 30 birthday year.

4   A student will be 21 years of age in December 1982. He expects to work in covered employment for five years beginning January 1, 1983, after which time he expects to go into some noncovered employment. He will not be fully insured when he reaches age 65 for he will have only 20 quarters of coverage. This case is not typical. Most students will qualify by working 10 years in

[8]Some men attaining age 72 before 1964, plus some women who attained this age before 1967, qualified under certain conditions as transitional insureds even though they had less than 6 quarters of coverage.

[9]For more details on the effect of disability on this determination, see Chapter 8.

covered employment. Some will be well on their way to a permanent fully insured status by the time they graduate (because of part-time work in college).

It is possible to achieve currently insured status at an early date, for the only requirement is that the person have 6 quarters of coverage out of the last 13 quarters, including the quarter in which he or she dies or becomes entitled to old-age or disability benefits. However, the quarter in which the person becomes disabled is not counted in the 13-quarter period unless it is a quarter of coverage. It is, of course, possible to be currently insured without being fully insured and vice versa.

BENEFITS

The benefits under the OASI system may be divided into retirement and survivorship benefits. Unless otherwise stated, the worker must be fully insured to qualify for these benefits. The exceptions are some survivorship benefits for which currently insured status is sufficient.

Retirement Benefits

Life Income to the Worker

When an insured worker reaches age 65, he or she is entitled to a monthly income for life.

Calculating the amount of this income, called the "primary insurance amount" (PIA), is a complicated process. For persons who reached age 62 prior to 1979 the benefit is determined using a formula based on average (nonindexed) wages that is being phased out. For persons who reached age 62 or will reach 62 in 1979–1983 a Transitional Guarantee Method applies. Under this method the benefit is the higher of two calculations, one using a modified version of the old formula, and one a new method called the "Decoupled Formula Method." As will be explained later, the old formula contained a technical error that would have produced benefits that would have been far too high in the future. The Transitional Guarantee Method moves the benefit determination gradually from the old formula to the new Decoupled Formula Method. For many persons who reached or will reach age 62 prior to 1984 the modified old formula will produce higher benefits than will the Decoupled Formula Method. For persons who will reach 62 in 1984 or later only the Decoupled Formula Method will be used. *To simplify the discussion, only the Decoupled Formula Method, which will ultimately be the only method, will be discussed and illustrated in this text.*

Average Indexed Monthly Earnings. [10]

Under the Decoupled Formula Method the PIA is a function of the average monthly earnings on which the worker paid an OASI tax during his or her working career, adjusted or indexed to reflect the changes in the average earnings of all persons covered and not covered under OASI over that period. More specifically, the time span over which the average indexed monthly earnings is calculated extends from the end of the year in which the person became 26 years of age (or 1955 if later) to the beginning of the year in which he or she attained age 62. As will soon become apparent, the effect of this time span is to permit the worker to drop the five years of lowest earnings between the end of the year in which he or she was 21 (or 1950 if later) and the beginning of the 62nd birthday year. Starting in 1991, all persons reaching age 62 will have been 26 in 1955 or later. For these persons the time span will be 35 years; for persons reaching age 62 before 1991 the averaging period will be less than 35 years.

If the worker had earnings during years before or after this computation period, the earnings during any of these years can be substituted for earnings during years within this period if this substitution would increase the worker's average indexed monthly earnings. For example, a worker who retires at age 65 may substitute earnings during the years when he or she became age 62, 63, or 64 for earlier years when the average indexed monthly earnings were lower.

The earnings used to calculate the worker's average indexed monthly earnings over his or her working career are not the actual earnings. First, earnings in excess of the maximum taxable amount in any year are ignored in calculating the average. This taxable earnings base was $3,000 from 1937–1954, $4,200 from 1955–1958, $4,800 from 1959–1965, $6,600 from 1966–1967, $7,800 from 1968–1971, $9,000 in 1972, $10,800 in 1973, $13,200 in 1974, $14,100 in 1975, $15,300 in 1976, $16,500 in 1977, $17,700 in 1978, $22,900 in 1979, $25,900 in 1980, and $29,700 in 1981. The 1982 base is $32,400. Each year from now on, the base will be adjusted automatically to match increases in average national earnings. The concept of automatic adjustments first became effective in 1975, but in 1977 Congress decided to increase the taxable portion of covered payrolls through larger ad hoc adjustments in 1979, 1980, and 1981.

Second, each year's actual taxed earnings, except for the earnings during the last year of the period, are adjusted to reflect changes in average national earnings from that year to the second last year of the period. For retirement PIA calculations this base year for indexing is the year when the worker turned 60. The second last year in the computation period is used as the base year because the average earnings of all workers in the last year will not be known at the time the worker's average indexed monthly earnings are calculated if the worker elects, as described below, to retire as early as age 62. For example, assume that in an

[10] For a discussion of the various formulas used during the transition see Steven F. McKay, "Computing a Social Security Benefit after the 1977 Amendments," *Actuarial Note No. 100* (Washington, D.C.: Office of the Actuary, Social Security Administration, February 1980).

earlier year the worker paid taxes on $10,000. If average earnings increased by 50% from that year to the second last year of the period, the amount used in the calculation would be $15,000. Through this indexing procedure the worker's earnings are adjusted for increases in the cost of living and for productivity gains or losses that may have occurred over this period.

To determine the adjustments to be used in this indexing procedure the Social Security Administration has determined the average earnings for each year since 1950 to be the amounts shown in Table 3.1. The average earnings for 1981 are supposed to be announced no later than November 1, 1982, in the *Federal Register.*

For a worker retiring in 1982 at age 65 earnings are indexed to 1977, the second last year of the computation period and the year in which that worker turned 60. For example, if this worker earned the maximum taxable amount in 1960, these 1960 earnings would be indexed as follows:

$$\frac{\text{Earnings in}}{1960} \times \frac{\text{Average earnings in } 1977}{\text{Average earnings in } 1960} = \$4,800 \times \frac{\$9,779.44}{\$4,007.12} = \$11,714.48.$$

For a worker who elected to retire early at age 62 in February 1981, the earnings were indexed to 1979. If this person earned $4,800 in 1960, the indexed 1960 earnings were $4,800 ($11,479.46/$4,007.12) = $13,750.88. For a worker retiring at age 62 in 1982 the index base year will be 1980.

To illustrate how the average indexed monthly earnings (AIME) are calculated assume that a male worker retires in October 1982 at age 65. Because this person was 26 in 1943, the period over which his average indexed monthly earnings will be calculated will include 23 years, starting with 1956 and ending with 1978, his 61st birthday year. His actual earnings, limited to the maximum amount taxable each year over this period, will be adjusted to account for changes in average national earnings up to 1977, when the average earnings were $9,779.44. If the *indexed* taxable earnings are $6,000 each year from 1956 to 1965, $7,500 from 1966 to 1969, and $10,000 from 1970 to 1977, the average indexed monthly earnings will be

$$\frac{10(\$6,000) + 4(\$7,500) + 8(\$10,000)}{23 \times 12} = \frac{\$170,000}{276} = \$616.$$

If the worker had no earnings from 1956 to 1965, the AIME would be only

$$\frac{4(\$7,500) + 8(\$10,000)}{23 \times 12} = \$399.$$

Table 3.1 presents a worksheet that systemizes this calculation.

Table 3.1 Worksheet for Calculating Average Indexed Monthly Earnings (General Wage Increases After 1980 Not Shown)[a,b] (In Dollars)

Calendar Year	Actual Covered Wages (1)	Maximum Taxable Wage Base (2)	Smaller of (1) or (2) (3)	Average Earnings for All Workers (4)	Indexed Earnings (3) × (4) for Base Year ÷ (4) (5)
1951	————	3,600	————	2,799.16	————
1952	————	3,600	————	2,973.32	————
1953	————	3,600	————	3,139.44	————
1954	————	3,600	————	3,155.64	————
1955	————	4,200	————	3,301.44	————
1956	————	4,200	————	3,532.36	————
1957	————	4,200	————	3,641.72	————
1958	————	4,200	————	3,673.80	————
1959	————	4,800	————	3,855.80	————
1960	————	4,800	————	4,007.12	————
1961	————	4,800	————	4,086.76	————
1962	————	4,800	————	4,291.40	————
1963	————	4,800	————	4,396.64	————
1964	————	4,800	————	4,576.32	————
1965	————	4,800	————	4,658.72	————
1966	————	6,600	————	4,938.36	————
1967	————	6,600	————	5,213.44	————
1968	————	7,800	————	5,571.76	————
1969	————	7,800	————	5,893.76	————
1970	————	7,800	————	6,186.24	————
1971	————	7,800	————	6,497.08	————
1972	————	9,000	————	7,133.80	————
1973	————	10,800	————	7,580.16	————
1974	————	13,200	————	8,030.76	————
1975	————	14,100	————	8,630.92	————
1976	————	15,300	————	9,226.48	————
1977	————	16,500	————	9,779.44	————
1978	————	17,700	————	10,556.03	————
1979	————	22,900	————	11,479.46	————
1980	————	25,900	————	12,513.46	————
1981	————	29,700	————	12,513.46	————
1982	————	32,400	————	12,513.46	————

[a]AIME for retirement benefits:

1 Complete the above table using as the base year for column (5) the year in which the person retiring was age 60.
2 Determine the number of years to be included in the period, that is, the number of years after attaining age 26 (or 1955 if later) and before attaining age 62 (cannot be less than 5).
3 Total highest entries in column (5) for number of years determined in Step 2.
4 Divide total determined in Step 3 by 12 times the number of years determined in Step 2.

[b]AIME for death benefits:

1 Complete the above table using as the base year for column (5) the second year before the year of death.
2 Determine the number of years in the averaging period, that is, the number of years after attaining age 26 (or 1955 if later) and before the year of death (cannot be less than 2).
3 Total highest entries in column (5) for number of years determined in Step 2.
4 Divide total determined in Step 3 by 12 times the number of years determined in Step 2.

The Primary Insurance Amount

For persons retiring at age 65 in January through May 1982 the PIA will be determined by the following formula:

$$\text{PIA} = 90\% \text{ of the first \$180 of the AIME}$$
$$+ 32\% \text{ of the next \$905 of the AIME}$$
$$+ 15\% \text{ of the AIME in excess of \$1,085,}$$

increased by 39.7% to reflect the cumulative effect of the automatic cost of living adjustments in benefits described below in 1979, 1980, and 1981.

As will be explained later in this chapter, if the cumulative cost of living adjustment is omitted, this formula was the one used to determine the PIA for persons retiring at age 62 in 1979, the year when persons age 65 in 1982 were age 62. For this reason this formula, except for the Consumer Price Index (CPI) adjustments, will be called the 1979 PIA formula.

For the $616 AIME calculated above the PIA is [0.90($180) + 0.32($436)] (1.397) = $421. For the $399 AIME the PIA would be $324.

In addition to a special minimum benefit that benefits only long-service workers, there was until 1981 amendments a regular minimum PIA equal to the regular minimum amount payable in December 1978, which was $122. Workers now receive the PIA formula amount unless the special minimum benefit is higher. The special minimum benefit is currently $16.07 times the number of years of service in covered employment (years generally in which the worker had covered earnings equal to at least one quarter of the maximum taxable earnings base[11]) minus 10. Only the first 30 years of service are counted in determining this benefit. Thus the special minimum PIA for a worker with 30 or more years of service is $321.

The PIA formula reflects a compromise between (1) a desire to provide the same floor of protection for all families—a complete social adequacy objective—and (2) a desire to maintain an actuarial relationship between contributions and benefits—a private equity objective. The PIA increases as the AIME increases, but the ratio of the PIA to the AIME decreases. The formula thus redistributes income from persons with higher AIMEs to those with lower AIMEs.

Each June after the worker retires the PIAs are adjusted to reflect changes in the CPI. For example, if prices increase by 10% from the first quarter of 1981 to the first quarter of 1982, in June 1982 the PIA being paid to retired workers will be increased by 10%. Thus through the AIME computation the worker is protected against increases in *average earnings* before age 62. Starting at age 62, the worker is protected by the automatic CPI adjustments against *price increases.*

For workers retiring at age 65 in June through December 1982, the PIA will be determined using the formula presented above for workers retiring in January

[11]The maximum taxable earnings base for this purpose is the 1978 base adjusted only for changes in average earnings, not the higher ad hoc adjustments Congress made for 1979–81.

through May with one exception: instead of increasing the basic formula amount by 39.7% to reflect the automatic cost of living adjustments for 1979, 1980, and 1981, this amount will be increased by a larger percentage to reflect the automatic adjustment for 1982, as yet unknown, in addition to the 1979, 1980, and 1981 adjustments. If that adjustment is 10%, as assumed in the preceding paragraph, the increase will be close to 54%. The effect of this change is to give workers retiring in June or later the same benefit they would have received had they retired earlier in the year and received a cost of living adjustment in June.

The special minimum benefit is increased each June to reflect CPI increases. For example, in June 1981 the dollar value in the formula was raised from $14.45 to $16.07 because the 1981 CPI adjustment called for an 11.2% increase. In June 1982 this dollar value will be increased by the 1982 CPI adjustment.

Workers retiring at age 65 in January through May of 1983 will have their PIAs calculated in the same manner as those retiring at age 65 in January through May 1982 except for two changes. First, because these workers turned 62 in 1980, the starting point will be the 1980 PIA formula. The $180 and $905 "bend points" will be changed to $194 and $1,171, respectively, to reflect the almost 8% increase in national average earnings from 1977 to 1978. Second, the CPI adjustment will reflect the cumulative effect of the automatic CPI adjustments for 1980, 1981, and 1982. Workers retiring at age 65 later in 1983 will also receive a CPI adjustment based on the increase in prices from the first quarter of 1982 to the first quarter of 1983. Similar adjustments will be made in the PIA formula for those retiring at age 65 in 1984 or later. Table 3.2 summarizes the PIA formulas that have been used in the recent past or will be used in the near future under different conditions.

For workers who prefer to retire before or after age 65 OASI permits early or delayed retirement under certain conditions. A worker can retire as early as age 62, but the monthly benefit is reduced to $\frac{5}{9}$ of 1% below what it would otherwise be for each month the worker retires before age 65. For example, if the worker elects to retire at age 62, the benefit will be reduced by $36 \times \frac{5}{9}$, or 20%. If the worker delays retirement beyond age 65, the benefit is increased by $\frac{1}{4}$ of 1% for each month the retirement is delayed. For example, if retirement is deferred to age 67, the monthly benefit is increased by $24 \times \frac{1}{4}$, or 6%. The PIA formula used to determine the benefit that is to be reduced or increased by the above percentages depends on the year in which the worker is age 62. For example, for workers retiring at age 62 in early 1979 the PIA formula was the same as the PIA formula for workers retiring at age 65 in early 1982, except that, of course, there were no CPI adjustments. In other words, the 1979 PIA formula was used. For workers retiring at age 62 in early 1982 the PIA formula is the same, except for the CPI adjustment, as for those retiring at age 65 in early 1985. Table 3.2 demonstrates this relationship. The general rule is that, except for the CPI adjustment, the year in which the worker turns 62 determines the PIA formula to be used for retirements at age 62 or later.

Table 3.2 Primary Insurance Amount Formulas Under the Decoupled Formula Method for January through May of Selected Years

For workers retiring[a] at age 62, dying at age 62 or earlier, or becoming disabled in

	1979	1980	1981	1982	1983
90% of the first	$180 of AIME	$194	$211	$230	1979 dollar values adjusted for increase in average national earnings from 1977 to 1981
+32% of the next	$905 of AIME	$977	$1,063	$1,158	
+15% of the	AIME in excess of $1,085	$1,171	$1,274	$1,388	

For workers retiring[b] or dying at age 65 in

	1982	1983	1984	1985	1986
90% of the first	$180 of AIME	$194	$211	$230	1982 dollar values adjusted for increase in average national earnings from 1977 to 1981,
+32% of the next	$905	$977	$1,063	$1,158	
+15% of the	AIME in excess of $1,085	$1,171	$1,274	$1,388	to be determined
Sum multiplied by 1.397					
to match cumulative CPI benefit adjustment in	1979, 1980, and 1981	1980, 1981, and 1982	1981, 1982, and 1983	1982, 1983, and 1984	1983, 1984, and 1985

[a]The worker who retires at age 62 receives a benefit equal to 80% of this PIA because of the reduction for early retirement. See also footnote b.

[b]Many workers reaching age 62 prior to 1984 will receive higher PIAs under the Transitional Guarantee Method. Note that under the Decoupled Formula Method the basic PIA formula before CPI adjustments is the one in effect when the worker was age 62. Persons who retire at age 70 in 1987 will use the 1979 basic formula plus CPI adjustments for 1979 through 1986.

Dependents' benefits

The benefits for dependents of a retired worker are the following:

1 *Life Income to Spouse of Retired Worker* The spouse of a worker who retires at age 65 will receive 50% of the worker's monthly pension if the spouse is 65 or older and has been married to the retired worker for at least one year. If the worker retires earlier or later than age 65, thus reducing or increasing the monthly pension, the spouse's benefit is based on the amount the worker would have received had the retirement age been 65. This same rule applies to all dependents' benefits.

If the spouse wishes, he or she may take reduced benefits beginning as soon as age 62, but the worker must be retired. The reduction in benefits is $\frac{25}{36}$ of 1% times the number of months prior to age 65 that the benefits begin. Thus if benefits begin on the spouse's 63rd birthday, he or she will receive $83\frac{1}{3}$% of the amount payable at age 65.

A divorced spouse is eligible for benefits if he or she had been married to the worker for at least 10 years. The divorced spouse loses benefit rights upon remarriage, but regains those rights if the subsequent marriage ends.

2 *Income Till Age 18 for Unmarried Children of a Retired Worker or Till the End of the Semester or Quarter in Which the Child Reaches Age 22 if He or She is a Full-Time Student at an Accredited School* Each child of a retired worker will receive 50% of the worker's PIA until he or she reaches 18 (22 if a full-time student) or marries. (For the effect of a child's disability upon this benefit see Chapter 8.) At the time the child applies for this benefit, the worker must be supporting the child or have some legal obligation to do so. The child may be a stepchild, a legally adopted child, or even an illegitimate child. Grandchildren not adopted by their grandparents are not eligible if their parents have died or are totally disabled and some other conditions are met. Because of a 1981 amendment, effective August 1982, no child's benefits will be paid beyond age 18 unless the child is attending elementary or secondary school, in which case benefits stop at age 19. Post-secondary students already receiving benefits by that date will receive gradually reducing dollar amounts.

3 *Income to a Mother or Father Until the Youngest Child Eligible for a Child's Benefit is 16 Years of Age.* The wife or husband of a person receiving a PIA will receive 50% of that amount as long as she or he has an eligible child of the worker under 16 (18 until 1981 amendments). Divorced spouses are eligible for these benefits under the conditions discussed above.

The maximum family benefit is a function of the PIA. For workers retiring at age 65 in early 1982 the maximum family benefit is

150% of the first $230 of the PIA before the 1.397 CPI adjustment

+ 272% of the next $102

+ 134% of the next $101

+ 175% of the PIA in excess of $433,

this sum being adjusted to reflect the 39.7% cumulative effect of the CPI adjustment in benefits in 1979, 1980, and 1981. For workers retiring in late 1982 this maximum will be further increased for price increases from early 1981 to early 1982.

The dollar components of this formula are adjusted each year by the same earnings adjustment used to change the dollar amounts in the PIA formula. For example, when the 1981 PIA formula is used, the dollar figures in the corresponding maximum family benefit formula are $270, $120, $118, and $508. As a final point, a benefit paid to a divorced spouse is ignored in applying this maximum benefit.

Illustrations

The following cases show the application of these rules. All examples have been rounded to the nearest dollar to simplify the illustrations. Table 3.3 summarizes the benefits for various average monthly earnings and dependency statuses but does not show the special minimum benefits for long-term workers.

1. A male worker, age 65, retires in early 1982 with an AIME of $800. His PIA is $503. If his wife is also 65, the family benefit will be (1.00 + 0.50) $503, or $755. The maximum rule does not affect this benefit.

If his wife is 62 and elects to receive a reduced benefit, the family benefit will be [1.00 + (0.75) 0.50] $503, or $692.

If the worker has a wife, age 45, with a child, age 10, in her care, the computed family benefit will be (1.00 + 0.50 + 0.50) $503, or $1,007. However, the maximum family benefit rule applies here. The family will receive instead only $923 a month for eight years until the child reaches age 16. If the child is then a full-time student, the family will receive (1.00 + 0.50) $503 or $755 until the child reaches age 22. Unless the wife elects to receive a reduced wife's benefit between the ages of 62 and 65, the worker will receive $503 a month for the next eight years until his wife is 65. The benefit will then be increased to $755.

2. A female worker, age 65, retires in early 1982 with an AIME of $200. Because she has over 30 years of OASDI coverage, she is entitled to the minimum long-service benefit—(30 − 10) $16.07, or $321.

In both of these examples, starting in June 1982, the benefits will be adjusted each June to reflect increases in the CPI. The benefit amounts may also be reduced because the worker or dependents have earnings exceeding the limit described later in this chapter. Furthermore, if a dependent spouse also qualifies for a worker's benefit, then he or she cannot receive both the dependent's benefit and the worker's benefit. Only the higher amount is paid.

Survivorship Benefits

OASI provides some important survivorship benefits, which are expressed as a percentage of the deceased worker's PIA calculated in the same way as the retired worker's PIA except for two major differences. First, the period used to calculate

Table 3.3 Decoupled Formula Method, Illustrative January through May 1982 Monthly Cash Benefits Under Old-Age, Survivors, and Disability Insurance[a]

Family Situation	Average Indexed Monthly Earnings					
	$200	$400	$800	$1,200	$1,600	$2,000
PIA (1982 Formula)	$180	$261	$389	$517	$609	$669
Retirement						
Worker, age 62	144	208	311	414	487	535
Worker and spouse, both age 62	212	306	457	608	715	786
Worker and spouse, both age 62, and one child	212	306	573	754	868	954
Survivorship						
Widow or widower, age 65	180	261	389	517	609	669
Widow or widower, age 60, no child	129	187	278	370	435	478
Widow or widower, under 60, and 1 child	270	392	584	776	914	1,004
Widow or widower, under 60, and 2 children	270	392	700	922	1,067	1,172
Lump-sum death benefit	255	255	255	255	255	255
Disability						
Worker	180	261	389	517	609	669
Worker and spouse with child	180	340	584	776	914	1,004
Maximum family benefit[b]	270	392	700	922	1,067	1,172

[a]Rounded to nearest dollar.

[b]The maximum family benefit for the 1982 PIA formula is 150% of the first $294 of the PIA, 272% of the next $129, and $175 of the PIA in excess of $554.

A special maximum family benefit applies to disability benefits—the lesser of (1) 85% of the average indexed monthly earnings or, if greater, the PIA or (2) 150% of the PIA. In late 1981 the Senate passed a bill that would have applied this formula to all OASDI benefits.

The maximum family benefit is calculated first under the assumption that workers retire at age 65 and that spouses, widows, and widowers do not elect reduced benefits at earlier ages than they would be eligible to receive unreduced benefits. If workers do retire before or after 65 or if spouses, widows, and widowers do elect earlier reduced benefits, the amounts available for other beneficiaries are calculated on the assumption that this did not happen. To illustrate, assume a worker's AIME is $1,200. The maximum family benefit is $922. If the worker retires at age 62, the worker receives only $414 monthly, but the amount available for other beneficiaries is only $922 − $517 or $405. If the worker retires at age 62 with a spouse aged 65, the spouse would receive .50($517) or $259 leaving $922 − $776 or $146 for other beneficiaries. If the worker retires at age 62 with a spouse aged 62, the spouse would receive only .75($259) or $194, but the maximum amount available for other beneficiaries would remain $146. This explains why a child would increase the total benefit only to $414 + $194 + $146 or $754 the AIME may be much shorter and more recent. If the worker dies before age 62, the period ends with the year preceding the year of death. For example, if a worker dies at age 35, the period includes eight years, starting with the year in which the worker attained age 27 and ending with the year in which the worker reached age 34. On the other hand, if the worker dies at age 62 or later, the period is the same as that used to calculate the PIA for retirement benefits.

Second, if the worker dies before age 62, the PIA decoupled formula used is the one that becomes effective the year the worker dies. For example, if the worker died in the period January through May 1979, the formula was the 1979 PIA formula, 90% of the first $180 of AIME + 32% of the next $905 + 15% of the AIME in excess of $1,085. For workers who die in the period January through May 1982, the 1982 formula, for which the three dollar figures are $230, $1,158, and $1,388, respectively, will be used. Table 3.3 shows PIA formulas for early 1979 through early 1983. For workers dying later in those years the amounts were or will be increased by the CPI adjustments for those years (9.9% in 1979 and an amount still to be determined for 1982). If the worker dies at age 62 or later but is not receiving retirement benefits, the PIA is calculated as if the worker had elected to retire as of the date of death. If the worker dies at age 62 or later and is receiving retirement benefits, the benefit the worker is receiving (minus any reduction that had been made for early retirement) is the PIA used as a base to determine survivorship benefits.

The survivorship benefits are as follows:

1 *Life Income to Widow or Widower* The widow or widower of a *fully insured* person will receive 100% of the deceased's PIA if she or he is 65 years of age and has not remarried. Remarriage after attaining age 60, however, does not reduce benefits. Moreover, if the surviving spouse does remarry earlier and that marriage ends, the benefit is payable.

The widow or widower may elect to take reduced benefits as early as age 60. The percentage reduction in benefits is $\frac{19}{40}$ of 1% for each month before age 65 that the benefits begin.

A divorced spouse of a deceased worker is eligible for a widow's or widower's benefit under the same conditions as the divorced spouse of a retired worker.

If the deceased worker had been receiving an old-age benefit that was reduced or increased because of early or delayed retirement, this widow's or widower's benefit is set equal to that adjusted benefit. The other survivorship benefits listed below are not affected by this adjustment.

2 *Income Till Age 18 for Children of a Fully or Currently Insured Deceased Worker or Till the End of the Semester or Quarter in Which the Child Reaches age 22 if He or She is a Full-Time Student at an Accredited School* Until reaching age 18 (22 if a full-time student) or getting married each child of a deceased worker will receive 75% of the deceased's PIA. (For the effect of disability on the continuance of the benefit and the mother's benefit described below see Chapter 8). The child may have been a stepchild, an adopted child, or an illegitimate child, but it must have been dependent on the deceased at the date of death. Grandchildren not adopted by their grandparents qualify for these benefits under the conditions noted above for dependent retirement benefits. As indicated earlier in the discussion of retirement benefits, effective August 1982 this benefit will stop at age 18 (19 if the child is in elementary or secondary school).

3 *Income to the Surviving Spouse of a Fully or Currently Insured Worker With Surviving Children Until the Youngest Eligible Child Reaches 16 Years of Age* The surviving mother or father will receive 75% of the deceased worker's PIA as long as there is an eligible child of the deceased under 16 years of age (18 until 1981 amendments). The benefit stops if the parent remarries, but the children's benefits continue even if they are adopted by their stepparent.

4 *Life Income to Parents* Each parent of a *fully* insured deceased worker will receive 75% of the PIA if the parent is 62 years of age, depended on the deceased for at least one-half of his or her support, and has not remarried since the death of the deceased. The benefit is 82.5% if only one parent is receiving this benefit.

5 *Lump-Sum Death Benefit* If the deceased was *either fully or currently* insured, a lump-sum death benefit of $255, is paid to a surviving spouse who was living with the deceased worker or is eligible to receive a monthly cash survivor benefit. If there is no eligible spouse, this lump sum is paid to any child of the deceased eligible to receive monthly cash benefits. No lump sum benefit is payable if there is no eligible surviving spouse or children.

The maximum family benefit payable to survivors is determined in the same way as the maximum family retirement benefit.

Illustrations

A few examples, will illustrate the application of these benefits. Table 3.2 summarizes the survivorship benefits payable under various conditions. In all cases the worker is assumed to have died in early 1982. CPI adjustments in 1982 and later years are ignored. Because the student's benefit will soon be eliminated, it is also ignored in these examples.

1 A currently insured worker dies, leaving a wife, age 35, and one child, age 8. If his AIME is $1,200, his PIA is $517. The lump-sum benefit is $255, and the wife and child will receive (0.75 + 0.75) $517, or $776 monthly for 8 years. The child will continue to receive $388, monthly for 2 more years to age 18. If the worker had been fully insured, the widow would also begin to receive $517 after she reaches age 65. If she wished, she could start receiving a reduced amount of $370 at age 60.

2 A fully insured person dies, leaving a husband age 52. If her average monthly wage was $800, her PIA is $389. The husband will receive a lump-sum benefit of $255, but he will not receive any monthly income for 13 years, at which time he will begin to receive $389. He could, however, elect to receive a reduced monthly benefit of $278, beginning at age 60. However, if the husband had remarried before age 60, he would not receive the income benefit at any age.

3 A fully insured worker dies, leaving a wife, age 35, and two children, ages 8 and 13. If his average monthly wage was $1,200, his PIA is $517. The lump-sum benefit of $255 will be paid to the wife, and the family will receive at first a monthly benefit of $922. The computed initial benefit is (0.75 + 0.75 + 0.75) $517, or $1,164, but the maximum family benefit rule applies. This benefit will gradually be reduced to $776 after 3 years when the oldest child reaches age 18, and to $388 after 8 years , when the youngest child reaches age 16. The income stops 2 years later when the youngest child reaches age 18 until the widow becomes eligible for $517 a month when she reaches 65 years of age. If she elects a reduced benefit beginning at age 60, the monthly benefit will be $370.

Loss of Benefits

Benefits are *terminated* for several reasons, most of which have been implied in the preceding discussion. A mother's or father's benefit stops if for any reason she or he no longer has a child under 16 entitled to benefits. A child's benefit stops when he or she reaches 18 or marries. A widow or widower (unless married after age 60), or a surviving parent loses the benefit if he or she remarries. However, remarriage to another survivor beneficiary does not result in the termination of benefits. A wife's or husband's benefit continues only so long as the beneficiary remains married to the insured, unless at the time of a divorce the marriage has lasted for at least 10 years. Death, of course, terminates the benefit of any deceased person as of the preceding month.

There is one very important reason why the monthly payments may be *reduced.* If in 1982 a retired worker under 72 years of age (age 70 starting in 1983) earns more than $6,000 ($4,440 if under age 65) in any calendar year in covered or uncovered employment, the total family benefits are reduced by an amount equal to one-half of the amount earned in excess of $6,000. For example, $1,000 is withheld if the earnings are $8,000, $3,000 if the earnings are $12,000. As a result, if taxes and any extra expenses associated with working are ignored, the beneficiary always gains by working.

The rule also states that the first year the worker receives retirement benefits these shall not be reduced for any month during which a worker earns $\frac{1}{12}$ of the earnings limit or less in wages or does not render substantial services in self-employment, even if annual earnings exceed the earnings limit. The major purpose of this provision is to make it possible to pay benefits beginning with the first month of retirement.

The rule with respect to the earnings of dependent beneficiaries is the same except that only the dependent's benefit is affected. For example, if a widow, age 35, with two children under 16 should earn more than $4,440, only her benefit would be affected. In 1983 the $6,000 and $4,440 limits will be increased by the same percentage as average earnings increased from 1980 to 1981. Similar adjustments will be made thereafter.

The purpose of the earnings test is to pay benefits only to those workers and their families whose earnings have been stopped or reduced substantially by reason of retirement or death. It also cuts the total cost of the program significantly.

Other less common reasons for suspending payment are employment outside the United States in noncovered employment on seven or more calendar days, deportation because of illegal entry or conviction of crime, and conviction of treason, sedition, sabotage, or espionage.

Benefits are not duplicated, the largest being paid. For example, as stated earlier, the spouse of a retired worker may be eligible for a lifetime income based on his or her own earnings record in addition to a dependent's benefit based on the spouse's record. He or she will receive, in effect, only the higher of these two benefits.

Any benefits a spouse receives as a dependent of a retired worker or as a survivor will be reduced by any pension the spouse receives for his or her service under a federal, state, or local retirement system whose members are not also covered under OASDI. This provision does not become fully effective until December 1982.

OPERATIONAL TRENDS

Since its establishment in 1935 OASI has been considerably liberalized by enlarging the scope of covered employment, reducing the requirements for insured status, adding new benefits, and increasing their amount. A consideration of some major amendments made in the past may suggest some changes to be expected in the future.[12]

Covered Employment

Under the original Social Security Act only 6 out of 10 gainfully employed persons were in covered employment. Excluded were agricultural laborers, domestic employees, employees of federal, state, and local governments, casual laborers, employees of nonprofit charitable, religious, scientific, literary, or educational institutions, and self-employed persons. The arguments advanced in favor of these exclusions were similar to those cited earlier in the chapter, but administrative difficulties seemed much more important in 1935 than now. For example, in 1935 the inclusion of any agricultural laborers, domestic workers, or self-employed seemed administratively impossible. The 1950, 1954, and 1956 amend-

[12]A historical outline of the provisions of OASI is provided in the *Annual Statistical Supplements* to the *Social Security Bulletin*.

    The *Social Security Bulletin* usually contains a discussion of the legislative history and final provision of each set of amendments. For example, see John A. Svahn, "Omnibus Reconciliation Act of 1981: Legislative History and Summary of OASDI and Medicare Provisions," *Social Security Bulletin*, XVIV, No. 10 (October, 1981), 3–24.

ments reduced the exclusions considerably. The 1965 amendments added self-employed doctors of medicine and interns, an important group who had been previously excluded because the American Medical Association had maintained that the earnings test would deprive most doctors from receiving retirement benefits until age 72. The exemption of certain religious sects was another change. At present more than 9 out of 10 gainfully employed persons are eligible for coverage. This fraction may eventually become unity.

Insured Status

Under the original Act, a worker age 65 was entitled to retirement benefits if he or she had (1) worked in covered employment on at least one day in each of five years between December 31, 1936, and his or her 65th birthday and (2) earned at least $2,000 in covered employment. No survivorship benefits were available. This eligibility requirement was restrictive, and no benefits would be payable until 1942 (even though it could be met early in 1941).

In 1939 the eligibility requirements were liberalized because it was believed that the existing provisions were too strict in connection with retirement benefits and not entirely suitable for the newly added survivor benefits. The quarters of coverage concept was introduced with $50 as the minimum amount needed to earn a quarter of coverage.

The number of covered employments was greatly increased by the 1950 amendments and the starting date for measuring fully insured status was moved up to January 1, 1951, to make it easier for new entrants to qualify at an early date. The 1960 amendments substituted one-third for one-half as the required proportion of quarters of coverage to achieve fully insured status. The fraction was further reduced to the present one-fourth (or number of elapsed years) in 1961.

In 1977 Congress raised the minimum earnings for a quarter of coverage from $50 a quarter to $250 a year, effective 1978, with annual adjustments in the dollar amount thereafter.

Benefits

Until 1939 the only benefit was a monthly income for a retired worker based on the total wages on which an OASI tax should have been paid. The formula was as follows:

$\frac{1}{2}$% of the first $3,000

$+ \frac{1}{12}$% of the next $42,000

$+ \frac{1}{24}$% of the excess.

The formula recognized both the level and duration of earnings.

The maximum benefit was $85; the minimum was $10. No benefit was payable for any month in which the worker was engaged in "regular" employment. If a worker died before he or she had received at least 3.5% of his or her total taxed wages, the difference was returned to his or her estate. If the worker failed to qualify for monthly benefits at 65, 3.5% of the total taxed wages was returned in a lump sum. This return was considered to be a return of the worker's contributions plus interst.

The 1939 amendments made extensive changes in the benefits. First, the benefit formula was changed. The new benefit depended on average taxable earnings over the base period instead of total taxable earnings. This procedure increased the benefits available to those persons who were approaching retirement age at the time the formula was introduced.

The formula also favored low-income groups relatively more than did the old formula. The benefit was recognized more as a floor of protection than as a savings program. The formula continued to reflect the number of years of service. No benefit was payable for any month in which the claimant earned at least $15 in covered employment.

The second important 1939 change was the addition of new retirement benefits —the wife's and children's benefits, and survivorship benefits—the widow's, mother's, children's, and parent's benefits and the lump-sum benefit.

No more significant changes were made until 1950, when the increment for years of coverage was omitted. In 1954 the earnings test was restated in terms of annual earnings, and in computing average monthly earnings some years of low earnings were omitted for the first time.

The 1956 amendments lowered from 65 to 62 the age at which female workers, wives, widows, and female dependent parents could draw benefits. In 1961 men were also permitted to retire as early as age 62.

The 1965 amendments made extensive changes. Benefits for dependent children were continued to age 22 if they were full-time students attending an accredited school. The definition of "child" was broadened and the conditions under which a divorced wife could receive benefits were liberalized. Widows were permitted to elect reduced benefits as early as age 60, and to receive reduced benefits if they remarried after they reached age 60.

The July 1972 amendments increased benefits by 20%, which far exceeded the rise in prices. These amendments also provided for automatic increases in the benefits and benefit base in the future as prices and wages rise. The October 1972 amendments made several additional changes, including a much higher minimum benefit for long-term workers, a liberalization of the earnings test, and increased benefits for those who delay their retirement.

In order to correct an extremely important technical error (see later in this chapter) in the 1972 automatic benefit adjustment provisions, December 1977 amendments introduced the concept of indexing earnings (the AIME), effective 1979. The earnings test was also further liberalized.

The Omnibus Budget Reconciliation Act of 1981 eliminated the minimum

PIA, terminated the mother's and father's benefits when the youngest child attains age 16, not age 18, eliminated the benefits for post-secondary students, and eliminated lump sum death benefits when there is no eligible surviving spouse or child. The age at which a person becomes exempt from the earnings test was dropped to 70 effective 1983, not 1982 as scheduled under the 1977 amendments. As will be explained in Chapter 4, these changes reflected increasing concern over the program's financial condition.

OPERATIONAL DATA

Coverage

Old-Age and Survivors Insurance is by far the most important insurance operation in the country. In December 1977 total covered employment was estimated at 89 million, about 94% of the total paid employment. Most of the noncovered employees were federal civilian employees and employees of state and local governments. Over 106 million persons worked in covered employment sometime during 1977. At the beginning of 1979 about 133 million living workers, about 85% of the total, had already achieved fully insured or currently insured status, and millions of nonworkers were entitled to benefits as dependents of covered workers.

The increases in the number of insured living workers, the number of workers with taxable earnings, the number of new entrants, the amount of taxable earnings, the average taxable earnings per employee, and the number of employers reporting taxable wages are indicated in Table 3.4. All of the "sudden changes" appearing in Table 3.4 can be attributed to amendments to the Social Security Act and to the impact of World War II. The effect of the 1950 amendments, which greatly extended the scope of covered employment, is the most noticeable. The number of living workers insured at the end of 1961 increased markedly over those insured at the end of 1959 because of the 1960 and 1961 liberalizations in the requirements for fully insured status. Increases in wage levels and in the maximum amount taxed have caused the average taxable earnings per worker to increase substantially, especially in recent years.

Among the 133 million insured living workers at the beginning of 1979 about 80 million were permanently fully insured, 52 million were fully insured, but that status was not permanent, and less than 2 million were currently insured only.

Benefits

The number of persons receiving monthly benefits at the end of each five-year interval between 1940 and 1980 and the total monthly benefits received are shown in Table 3.5. The data are also classified by type of benefit. The increase in the number of beneficiaries and in monthly benefits for each type of benefit, except

Table 3.4 Old-Age and Survivors Insurance: Insured Living Workers, New Entrants, Workers With Taxable Earnings, and Employers Reporting Taxable Earnings, 1937–1979

Year	Living Workers at Beginning of Year (In Millions) Insured	Living Workers at Beginning of Year (In Millions) Uninsured	New Entrants (In Millions)	Workers With Taxable Earnings During Year (In Millions)	Taxable Earnings Total (In Billions of Dollars)	Taxable Earnings Average per Worker ($)	Employers Reporting Taxable Wages (In Millions)
1937	22.9	17.8	32.9	32.9	30	900	2.4
1939	27.5	23.4	4.4	33.8	30	881	2.4
1941	34.9	30.5	6.4	41.0	42	1,021	2.6
1943	40.3	32.1	7.3	47.7	62	1,310	2.4
1945	43.4	34.0	3.5	46.4	63	1,357	2.6
1947	45.7	35.1	2.7	48.9	78	1,602	3.2
1949	62.8	25.2	2.0	46.8	82	1,748	3.3
1951	71.0	22.1	6.0	58.1	121	2,078	4.7
1953	71.4	27.2	3.1	60.8	136	2,233	4.7
1955	77.0	26.8	4.8	65.2	158	2,416	4.9
1957	79.7	27.7	3.4	70.6	184	2,569	5.9
1959	89.1	22.1	3.2	71.7	202	2,822	5.5
1961	92.0	23.6	3.0	72.8	210	2,879	5.9
1963	95.8	25.5	3.5	75.5	226	2,986	6.0
1965	101.2	26.7	4.6	80.7	251	3,108	6.1
1967	106.9	26.6	4.5	87.0	330	3,791	5.9
1969	109.8	26.1	5.2	92.1	403	4,373	5.8
1971	114.8	26.1	4.5	93.3	430	4,574	5.8
1973	114.8	25.8	5.7	100.0	562	5,628	5.8
1975	121.4	24.0	4.2	100.4	665	6,634	5.7
1977	127.2	23.7	5.0	106.1	814	7,672	5.9
1979	132.9	22.8	n.a.[a]	n.a.	n.a.	n.a.	n.a.

Source: Social Security Bulletin, Annual Statistical Supplement, 1977–1979, pp. 84 and 99.

[a] n.a. = not available.

Table 3.5 Old-Age and Survivors Insurance, Number of Beneficiaries Receiving Benefits at End of Year and Monthly Benefits Received, 1940–1980 (Numbers in Thousands, Amounts in Millions of Dollars)

Year	Total		Retired Worker		Wife or Husband		Child[a]		Widow or Widower		Mother or Father[a]		Parent		Special Age 72 Benefits	
	Number	Amount	Number	Amount	Number	Amount	Number	Amount	Number	Amount	Number	Amount	Number	Amount	Number	Amount
1940	222	4	112	3	30	b	55	1	4	b	20	b	1	b		
1945	1,288	24	518	13	159	2	390	5	94	2	121	2	6	b		
1950	3,477	127	1,771	78	508	12	700	19	314	11	169	6	15	1		
1955	7,961	412	4,474	274	1,192	39	1,276	46	701	34	292	13	25	1		
1960	14,157	888	8,061	597	2,269	88	1,845	89	1,544	89	401	24	36	2		
1965	19,128	1,396	11,101	932	2,614	114	2,535	142	2,371	175	472	31	35	3		
1970	23,564	2,386	13,349	1,577	2,668	163	3,234	246	3,227	328	523	45	29	3	534	24
1975	27,732	5,048	16,588	3,437	2,867	302	3,562	457	3,889	748	582	86	21	4	223	15
1980	30,937	9,432	19,583	6,686	3,018	519	3,251	715	4,415	1,360	563	139	15	4	93	9

Source: Social Security Bulletins.

[a]The child's benefit column includes payments to children of deceased or retired workers. The mother's or father's benefit column includes only survivorship benefits; benefits paid to the mothers or fathers of retired workers' children are listed under the wife's or husband's benefit column.

[b]Less than 0.5 million.

for the parent's benefit and the special age 72 benefit, and for all benefits combined is the most important fact revealed by Table 3.5. Retirement beneficiaries and benefits have become a more important part of the total beneficiaries and benefits as the number of persons eligible for these benefits has increased. The mother's and the child's benefits, which are generally survivorship benefits, have become less important, partly because death benefit rolls reach maturity more quickly than the number and amount of old-age benefits. Indeed the number of such beneficiaries has declined in recent years, reflecting lower birth rates and changes in life styles. Not shown in Table 3.5 is the important fact that about 61% of the retired worker benefits paid in December 1980 were reduced benefits because the worker retired prior to age 65.

Table 3.6 shows how improved benefits and rising wages have increased the average monthly benefit of each type, especially during the 1970s.

Although the number and amount of OASI benefits have continually increased, certain individuals have had their benefits withheld or terminated. At the close of 1980 about 1 million benefits were being withheld. The reason for withholding about 73% of these benefits was the employment or self-employment of the beneficiary or a retired worker on whose earnings the benefit was based. Another 15% were withheld because of a government pension offset or the receipt of public assistance. Over 3 million benefits were terminated in 1980. As would be expected, death was the most important cause of termination, except in the case of the children's and mother's or father's benefits, where the child's turning 18 was the most important reason. Another important reason for the loss of mother's or father's benefits was remarriage.[13]

Table 3.6   Average OASI Monthly Benefit Being Received at End of Year, 1940–1980 (In Dollars)

Year	Retired Worker	Wife or Husband	Child	Widow or Widower	Mother or Father	Parent
1940	22.60	12.13	12.22	20.28	19.61	13.09
1945	24.19	12.82	12.46	20.19	19.83	13.06
1950	43.86	23.60	27.68	36.54	34.24	36.69
1955	61.90	33.07	36.40	48.69	45.91	49.93
1960	74.04	38.72	48.04	57.68	59.29	60.31
1965	83.92	43.63	55.94	73.75	65.45	76.03
1970	118.10	61.19	79.92	101.71	86.51	103.20
1975	207.18	105.19	128.22	192.33	147.25	171.86
1980	341.41	171.95	219.95	308.12	246.20	276.07

Source: Table 3.4.

[13]*Social Security Bulletin,* March, June, September, and December issues.

MAJOR ISSUES

Although Old-Age and Survivors Insurance is designed primarily to achieve a social objective—a floor of protection for all participants on a quasicontractual basis—it possesses some modified private insurance characteristics. Except for some special benefits for certain persons age 72 or over, benefits under the system are related to some extent to earnings and contributions instead of being related entirely to presumed need. On the other hand, the benefits are a larger proportion of low average earnings and are directly related to the number of dependents.

The objective of a protective floor makes it impossible to relate benefits exactly to contributions, because the lower-income groups and those with many dependents cannot afford to pay the entire cost of their own benefits. On the other hand, it has been considered desirable to maintain some relationship between benefits and earnings on which contributions are paid because this relationship emphasizes the distinction between OASI benefits and charity, appeals to most Americans, serves as a check on unjustifiable liberalizations, is assumed to encourage enterprise, initiative, and self-reliance, and produces a benefit that varies with the recipient's cost and standard of living.

The merger of these two concepts, however, has produced many misunderstandings concerning the nature of the system and has increased administrative costs. In addition, there is much disagreement concerning whether the two concepts have been combined in the correct proportions and, in some instances, whether they should have been combined at all.[14] This is a danger associated with all compromise solutions. In reading the discussion on specific issues that follows it is important to keep in mind the system's compromising nature and the basic disagreements over the blend of individual or private equity and social adequacy. The position one takes on this fundamental point can determine one's views on specific issues.

Only the issues associated with coverage and benefits will be discussed in this chapter. Chapter 4 will discuss the issues associated with administration and financing. Our goal is to discuss each issue as objectively as possible by presenting opposing arguments on each issue. We will defer until the end of Chapter 4 the sets of recommendations made in 1981 by the National Commission on Social Security, the President's Commission on Pension Policy, The Reagan Administration, and the House Subcommittee on Social Security. Deferring these recommendations will simplify the exposition, provide a useful review of the issues discussed in both Chapters 3 and 4, and present in one place the best clues to how OASI is most likely to change in the next few years. The reader will discover a substantial overlap between these most recent proposals on coverage and benefits and some of the proposals discussed in this chapter.

---

[14]See, for example, the proposal discussed later in this chapter.

Coverage

Although OASI covers most employments, there are still some important exclusions. Because some jobs are not covered, many workers spend some but not all of their work careers in covered employment. "In-and-out" employment of this sort may cause two major problems. Some workers just miss having enough quarters of coverage to qualify for OASI benefits though they have paid OASI taxes. Others qualify for minimum benefits on the basis of relatively short periods of covered employment and relatively small total contributions. Some of these persons may in addition already qualify for adequate benefits under some other program.

Persons who never work in covered employment do not qualify for the important benefits provided by the system. Some may be forced to seek public assistance as an alternative. On the other hand, by not participating, persons with relatively high wages or no dependents avoid sharing the costs of the social adequacy feature of the system.

For these reasons, as long as the system has existed there has been substantial support for expanding the types of employment covered and for liberalizing the conditions under which a covered person can attain insured status. Because the system now covers almost all types of employment, the pressure for increasing the kinds of workers covered under the system has lessened substantially. However, because federal government employees covered under the Civil Service Retirement System constitute one of the most important groups still outside the system and because, it is argued, there is no reason for this special treatment of federal employees, there is a strong movement to include these workers.[15]

State and local government employees who are not yet covered, about one-fourth of these employees, constitute an even larger number of excluded employees. Some local governments have terminated coverage for their employees under a section of the present law that permits state and local employers to pull out of the system after giving the Secretary of HEW two years notice. Many persons believe that these employees should be covered and that state and local governments should not have the right to terminate existing coverage agreements.

A third group whose exclusion is more frequently questioned today is the 10% of the employees of nonprofit institutions who are still not covered because either they or their employers have elected not to be covered.

The 1979 Advisory Council on Social Security recommended that all newly hired federal employees and employees of nonprofit organizations be covered on a mandatory basis. An alternative approach for federal employees would be an

---

[15]According to a recent study, about two out of five Federal civil service retirees received OASDHI cash benefits in 1975. About two-thirds of the retirees not currently receiving OASDHI benefits had worked in covered employment during their work careers. Daniel N. Price and Andrea Novotny, "Federal Civil-Service Annuitants and Social Security, December 1975," *Social Security Bulletin,* XL, No. 11 (November 1977), 3.

exchange of credit plan similar to the OASDI–railroad retirement system interchange. According to the Council, the primary reasons for extending coverage to these groups are to extend the benefits of OASDI to these workers and to protect some short-term workers from windfalls explained earlier. Removing these windfalls would, the Council estimated, save the OASDI system about 0.42% of taxable payroll.[16]

The Advisory Council would also eliminate the right of state and local governments to terminate existing coverage agreements. If this recommendation is not acceptable to Congress, the Council would require a vote of the affected workers before an agreement could be terminated.

Because the Council's recommendation applies only to newly hired employees, many present government employees and employees of nonprofit organizations would not be covered. They might still earn windfall OASDI benefits through short-term employment. The Council, therefore, recommended two plans for reducing or eliminating these benefits. For example, under one approach a PIA would be computed based on covered and noncovered earnings. A second PIA would be computed based on noncovered earnings only. The difference between the two PIAs would be the OASI benefit. This benefit would be less than the PIA based on covered earnings only because the PIA formula applies smaller percentages to earnings in excess of stated amounts.

The Advisory Council also recommended that all earnings of farm workers be taxed and credited if the farm operator spends at least $2,500 annually for farm labor. Their objective was to cover more low-pay farm workers.

The Council stated that by 2010 about 98% of the jobs should be covered. Absolute universal coverage, it argued, is not desirable nor administratively feasible. Casual work such as occasional babysitting was mentioned as a job that would probably remain uncovered.

In March 1980 a Universal Social Security Coverage Study Group, authorized under the 1977 amendments to the Social Security Act, completed an extensive two-year study of the feasibility and desirability of covering under OASDHI federal workers and noncovered employees of state and local governments and private nonprofit legal organizations.[17] The study group determined on the basis of legal, administrative, fiscal, and transition criteria that it would be reasonable to extend OASDHI coverage to these noncovered employees. They noted, however, that some constitutional questions may arise in extending coverage to employees of state and local government and nonprofit organizations. Many pension plans would have to be redesigned, and pension costs would rise for many state and local governments and nonprofit organizations. In the long run the Social

---

[16]*Reports of the 1979 Advisory Council on Social Security* (Washington, D.C., 1979), Chapter 7.

[17]*The Desirability and Feasibility of Social Security Coverage for Employees of Federal, State, and Local Governments and Private Nonprofit Organizations: Report of the Universal Social Security Coverage Study Group* (Washington, D.C.: Department of Health, Education, and Welfare, March 1980). An executive summary of this report appears in the June 1980 issue of the *Social Security Bulletin*.

Security Administration estimates that mandatory coverage would make possible a 0.5% reduction in the OASDHI tax rates. The study group also determined that covering these groups was more desirable than alternative means such as adjusting OASDI benefits for persons with noncovered employment to remove or reduce windfall benefits or providing for the transfer of credits between OASDHI and other retirement systems.

A more extreme suggestion, restated in 1965 by a task force of the Chamber of Commerce of the United States, is that some OASI benefits should be granted immediately to all aged persons.[18] In a surprise amendment to a 1966 bill increasing taxes because of the Vietnam conflict, Congress moved in this direction when it made certain persons age 72 or over eligible for some minimum benefits even though they had never worked in covered employment. The Chamber of Commerce and other supporters of "blanketing in" all aged persons argue that this would provide a better current indication of the final costs of the system, eliminate or at least lower the cost of the old-age assistance programs, and remove an important inequity under the system—the loss that some uncovered persons suffered simply because they had no opportunity to contribute to the system during their working years.

On the other hand, extensive blanketing-in would have serious ramifications. It would be inconsistent with the contribution–benefit relationship principle and would raise some difficult questions. For example, what benefit should these blanketed-in people receive? Should it be the same in all areas? Should it equal the current average public assistance benefit? If so, should this benefit become the minimum OASI benefit for all recipients? (In its 1966 action Congress adopted a uniform benefit substantially less than the average public assistance benefit or the minimum OASI benefit, but many members of Congress favored a payment equal to the OASI minimum.) How should these benefits be financed?

Partly because of these and other problems, the absence of a strong lobbying effort, and the increased concern, discussed in Chapter 4, over the financial condition of the system, blanketing-in is not an active issue.

From time to time the question is raised as to whether participation in the OASDHI program should be voluntary.[19] Those favoring a voluntary program argue that it would expand economic freedom, provide greater flexibility or choice among benefits, restrict the encroachment of government on private enterprise, and end the ways in which the present program is alleged to be unfair to younger workers, a charge that will be explored in more detail in Chapter 4. Those opposed argue that there would be adverse selection against the program (i.e., those who would elect to join would be those most likely to benefit from joining), social adequacy would be more difficult to achieve, the present program

[18]*Poverty: The Sick, Disabled, and Aged,* Second Report by the Task Force on Economic Growth and Opportunity (Washington, D.C.: Chamber of Commerce of the United States, 1965), pp. 71–73.

[19]For a comprehensive description of three arguments for and against voluntary participation see George Rejda, *Social Insurance and Economic Security* (Englewood Cliffs, N.J.: Prentice-Hall, 1976), pp. 26–33.

would be financially disrupted, some persons would be unable or unwilling to purchase private insurance, and the cost of administering OASDHI would rise. According to the report of the 1975 Advisory Council on Social Security,

> It is clear that a choice today between compulsory and voluntary coverage is really a choice between having or not having a social security program. Without compulsory participation, the present social security program could not exist.[20]

A final issue is the coverage of homemakers on the basis of the imputed value of their services. This issue is discussed below.

Benefits

Suggested benefit changes involve (1) the benefit level and structure, (2) taxation of the retirement benefits, (3) the automatic adjustments, (4) the relative treatment of males and females, and (5) the earnings test.

The Benefit Level and Structure

Issues surrounding the benefits level and structure are the minimum monthly benefit, the manner in which benefits above the minimum level are related to average monthly earnings, the way in which AIMEs are calculated, the maximum earnings base and benefit, and the amounts paid to dependents.

The stated objective of OASI is a "floor of protection" on which most families can be expected to build a private insurance and savings program. The floor rises, though not proportionately, with increases in past average monthly earnings.

Until the 1981 amendments the system provided a minimum PIA scheduled to remain forever at $122 a month. It is doubtful that a person receiving only this benefit could even meet today's bare subsistence needs. The person's annual income would be well below the poverty threshold established annually by the Social Security Administration and the guaranteed minimum income paid under Supplemental Security Income—a welfare program for the needy aged. On the other hand, many workers who qualified for this minimum benefit received more than their average indexed career earnings. Usually such persons had spent only a small portion of their careers in covered employment. Some of these persons had spent most of their lives in other employments that provided a pension that supplemented their OASDI pension. Sometimes this other pension by itself provided them with a generous retirement income. Others were not so fortunate: they spent most of their lives unemployed or worked for employers who had neither a pension plan nor a plan that pays low benefits. The 1979 Advisory Council's arguments against raising the minimum benefit for these persons are typical of the prevailing opinion. The same arguments were presented in favor of its termi-

---

[20]*Reports of the 1975 Advisory Council on Social Security* (Washington, D. C., 1975), p. 13. The Council also noted the opportunities for windfall profits for state and local employees because of the special provisions that permit state and local government groups to terminate their participation.

nation. First, persons who did not rely solely on covered earnings for support during their working lives should not expect OASDI benefits to be their sole support in retirement. Second, to provide a higher benefit to persons with less than a full-time attachment to the labor force would be inconsistent with the generally accepted principle that benefits should be related to wages. Third, program costs would be increased. Fourth, public assistance programs such as Supplemental Security Income are a more appropriate way of providing a reasonable floor of protection to those who are needy because they do not have other ways of supplementing their minimum OASDI benefits.[21]

Most observers, however, do not believe that the same arguments apply to persons who work most of their lives in covered employment at low wages. In October 1972 Congress established the special minimum benefit for long-service workers that was described earlier. The 1979 Advisory Council recommended that workers with at least 30 years of service should receive a benefit that will keep them out of poverty. Accordingly, because the Social Security Administration's 1979 monthly poverty line was $237, the Advisory Council recommended that the $11.50 per year factor in the then current special minimum benefit formula be raised to $13.65. For a single person with 30 years of service the special minimum benefit in January through May 1979 would have been (30 − 10) ($13.65) = $273 instead of $230. Like the $11.50, the $13.65 would be increased each June as the cost of living increases. The Council also recommended that for years before 1975 the earnings level required for a year of service be reduced from one quarter of the maximum taxable earnings that year to one quarter of the average wages. From 1975 to 1984 the earnings required would be gradually increased until it equalled one quarter of the maximum taxable earnings base. Their reasoning was that until recently the federal minimum wage was much lower and many low-wage jobs were not covered either by the federal minimum wage or OASDI. Some observers, on the other hand, believe that the present special minimum benefit is overly generous.

Instead of providing a higher benefit for higher average monthly earnings, the system could provide the same benefit for all workers. The rationale would be that the purpose of OASI is to provide a specified minimum standard of living for all beneficiaries. Persons who wanted more protection could do so by private means. A flat benefit system of this type would require fewer records and be much easier to administer than the present system. However, because such an approach completely ignores the relationship between benefits and prior earnings or standards of living, it has received little support. For example, the 1979 Advisory Council unanimously rejected proposals that would pay all persons a benefit having little relation to their prior earnings.

At the other extreme benefits could be made proportional to earnings. This

---

[21]Three members of the Council noted that many migrant and other farm workers, domestic workers, and other low-pay workers have through no fault of their own worked only part-time. Yet they have not sought public assistance during most or all of their working lives. They should not have to do so following retirement.

approach would substantially reduce the benefits paid persons with lower average earnings or with dependents. This approach also has little support. The 1979 Advisory Council unanimously rejected such a proposal because it would substantially increase the fraction of the beneficiaries who would require public assistance. Instead the Council endorsed the traditional principle that OASI benefits reflect a balance between social adequacy and individual equity.

Differences of opinion center on the *extent* to which benefits should be wage related and the standard of living they should be designed to maintain. The formula adopted affects not only the redistribution of income among covered persons but also the need for private or other public supplementation at various income levels. Under the 1982 PIA formula the earnings replacement rate is about 90% of the first $230 of the AIME, 32% of the next $1,158, and 15% of the earnings in excess of $1,388. The dollar values in the formula are adjusted each year as earnings increase. Both the percentages and portion of the average monthly earnings to which they apply could be modified in numerous ways. For example, each of the percentages could be increased by 10%, to 99, 35.2, and 16.5%. The result would be a 10% increase in all benefits paid, but the benefits payable for a specified AIME would continue to have the same relationship to the benefits payable for any other amount of earnings. On the other hand, if the first percentage were increased to 100%, the other two percentages remaining the same, the benefits payable to those with lower earnings would be increased relatively more than the payments to those with higher earnings. Increasing the earnings amount to which the 90% applied, but not the point at which the 15% applied, would also change the benefit to earnings ratio in favor of lower earnings. Raising the 15%, but neither the 90 nor the 32%, would produce higher benefits only for those with higher earnings. The possible variations are almost unlimited.

The 1979 Advisory Council recommended an important change in the PIA formula. The Council unanimously agreed that as a worker's earnings rise, the present value of the increase in future benefits should at least equal the present value of the increased taxes they (not their employers) must pay on those earnings. In Chapter 4 we will discuss the present value of benefits relative to the present value of employee taxes for various categories of beneficiaries. As one might expect from studying the present benefit structure, this ratio is lowest for the young male worker who earns the highest amount taxable under OASDI and never marries. For such a person increased earnings currently create additional taxes with a higher present value than the additional benefits because of the tilt in the present PIA formula. The Council proposed instead a formula that would guarantee even these young high-pay workers that as their earnings rise the present value of their additional benefits (assuming an interest rate equal to the rate of inflation plus 2.5%) will equal the present value of their additional contributions. The Council formula would be a two-bracket formula, instead of the present three-bracket formula, as follows:

61% of the first $442 of AIME
+ 27% of the AIME in excess of $412.

The $412 would have been adjusted each year, starting in 1980, as average wages increased. This formula would produce the following:

1 A PIA equal to the poverty level for those persons who worked full-time during their careers at the federal minimum wage.
2 Lower PIAs than the present formula for persons who are not long-service employees eligible for the new special minimum benefit described above and whose AIME is substantially less than the AIME of a person who worked full-time during his or her career at the federal minimum wage.
3 Little change in the PIAs of workers with average wages.
4 Higher PIAs for workers earning the maximum taxable amount.

The Advisory Council estimated that this recommendation, plus the one presented earlier that would increase the special minimum benefit, would change the PIA's in January, 1982 as follows:

		PIA		Percent
AIME		1979 Law	Proposed	Change
Federal minimum wage earner	$ 459	$319	$348	9
Career average earner	847	476	481	1
Career maximum earner	1,258	606	622	3

In a thought-provoking book published in 1968, Pechman, Aaron, and Taussig suggested that OASDI be divided into two systems because, in their opinion,

> The United States has attempted to solve two problems with one instrument—how to prevent destitution among the aged poor and how to assure to people, having adequate incomes before retirement, benefits that are related to their previous standard of living.[22]

In their total reform proposal, the prospects of which they considered dim, they would replace the present program with two systems. One, a guaranteed minimum income program of the type discussed in Chapter 16, would provide a minimum subsistence standard of living for families of all sizes. What is currently OASI would become a strictly wage-related earnings replacement program, which the replacement rate being roughly the same (say, 50%) at all earnings levels between a subsistence level and the median earnings level. Each beneficiary unit would receive the more advantageous of the two benefits. This dual system, they argue, would be efficient and flexible. The cost of performing the two distinct functions of the system would be identifiable; each could be altered without affecting the other, except at the margin. A strictly wage-related program would

[22]Joseph A. Pechman, Henry J. Aaron, and Michael K. Taussig, *Social Security: Perspectives for Reform* (Washington, D.C.: The Brookings Institution, 1968), p. 215.

be a legitimate government activity because of the following: (1) shortcomings in the individual savings decisions (e.g., widespread shortsightedness with respect to retirement needs, complexity of invstment decisions, and inflation); (2) inadequacies of private pension plans, to be examined in Chapter 6; and (3) the cost to other members of society if a person makes inadequate provision for retirement.[23] The Advisory Council rejected a closely related "double-decker" plan that would have paid (1) a flat amount (the $122 minimum PIA) to each aged person, disabled person, and surviving child plus (2) 30% of the AIME to persons eligible to receive OASDI benefits based on their own earnings. The first deck would be financed from general revenues, the second from payroll taxes. Those opposing this proposal argued mainly that such a radical change would alter the benefit and financing structure in ways they considered undesirable and would create some important risks. For example, they noted that benefits would be reduced for many dependents and survivors, that the system would impose a heavy claim on general revenues.[24] and that increases in the flat amount over time were unlikely despite the need for such increases.

Benefits are currently based upon average indexed career earnings since age 21 less earnings in the lowest five years. Many would favor basing benefits instead on the highest 5 or 10 years of earnings. Private pension plans usually relate the retirement benefit to "final" earnings because workers tend to judge the adequacy of a pension by its relationship to earnings just prior to retirement. Indexing earnings adjusts earnings for changes in average national earnings during the worker's career, but many workers receive greater than average salary increases.

Indeed one way of measuring the adequacy of OASI retirement benefits is to determine the "replacement ratio," or the retired worker's benefit during the first year of retirement divided by the worker's wages the year prior to retirement. Listed below are the replacement ratios for various 1980 wages and years of retirement, assuming a 5% annual increase in these wages, a 4% increase in the maximum taxable wage base, and a 3% increase in the CPI.

Year of Retirement	1980 Wages		
	$10,000	$20,000	$30,000
1982	0.45	0.33	0.22
1985	0.43	0.31	0.22
1990	0.40	0.30	0.21
1995	0.39	0.29	0.20
2000	0.38	0.28	0.20
2010	0.36	0.27	0.20
2020	0.35	0.26	0.18

[23]*Ibid.,* pp. 60–65.

[24]Some objected to using any general revenues to finance OASDI. This issue is discussed in detail in Chapter 4.

The ratios are higher in 1982 and 1985 in part because, as explained earlier, persons who reach age 62 prior to 1984 will receive a benefit under the old formula if it is higher. For persons with dependents these ratios would be higher.

The 1979 Advisory Council rejected any substantial increase in the number of dropout years, but it did recommend a change in the present practice. The Council observed that permitting all persons to drop out their five years of lowest earnings favors young disabled workers and their survivors over older retired or disabled workers and the survivors of older deceased workers. The reason is that five years is a larger fraction of the years in the AIME computation period for younger persons. Consequently the effect on their AIMEs and, therefore, their PIAs will be higher, other things being equal. When this provision was introduced in the mid-1950s, the intent was to help the large number of newly covered persons who did not have any opportunity to establish a covered earnings record prior to 1956. The relative effect on older and younger workers was apparently not considered. Consequently the Council majority recommended that workers be allowed to disregard one year of earnings for each six years elapsing between the end of the year in which they reached age 21 and the year in which they became eligible for benefits. The minimum number of dropout years would be one, the maximum six.

Once the benefit formula is determined, the maximum benefit depends on the maximum average monthly earnings included in the calculation. Most persons agree that there should be some maximum because (1) persons with higher incomes should have some individual responsibility for protecting themselves and their families and (2) public funds are more sorely needed elsewhere. What that maximum should be, however, is unclear.

Under the original $3,000 base, 92% of the covered payroll was taxed and 98% of the covered workers had all of their earnings covered. Because increases in the base did not keep pace with increases in average earnings, the proportion of earnings taxed dropped to a low of 74% in 1965. The 1972 amendments prescribed automatic adjustments as average earnings increased. The December 1977 amendments established ad hoc increases for 1979–1981 that were expected to exceed the automatic adjustments, thus raising the proportion of the taxed payroll in covered employment from 85% in 1978 to about 91% after 1980.

Pechman, Aaron, and Taussig favored using family earnings instead of individual earnings and limiting these earnings to the median family income in the United States. In 1968 former Secretary of HEW Wilbur Cohen recommended a higher standard that would make OASI the basic system of economic security for persons at all earnings levels. Private pensions, he believed, have too many shortcomings to provide a satisfactory substitute.[25]

The July 1972 amendments were criticized in many quarters for raising benefits much more than the cost of living, raising the benefit base too high,

---

[25]Wilbur J. Cohen, "A Ten-Point Program to Abolish Poverty," *Social Security Bulletin,* XXXI, No. 12 (December 1968), 7–8.

imposing additional heavy costs on business, and threatening the development and even the existence of private pension plans. In the words of a highly respected business periodical,

> In a real sense, that legislation—tucked in as an amendment to the debt ceiling bill —took Social Security over the watershed. The scope of the program today and the basic principles on which it is financed bring it much closer to a universal pension system than a supplementary insurance plan, a system which could eventually absorb and replace private pension plans. Whether this will in fact occur depends upon whether current trends continue or the system stabilizes, and upon the success of the private sector in extending coverage and improving the benefits provided by employee-benefit plans.[26]

Several changes in dependents' benefits have been suggested. Many people are surprised to find that a widowed parent receives benefits only until the youngest child entitled to benefits is 16 and that a widow's or widower's benefit does not begin until age 60. Some suggest the elimination of this gap, but to do so would substantially increase the cost of the system. It would also mean that widows or widowers could claim benefits at a much earlier age than workers, a situation that some would consider unfair.

According to Pechman, Aaron, and Taussig, who studied budgets prepared by various agencies, if the objective of OASI is to provide equivalent living standards for families of all sizes, for each additional family member the family benefit should be increased by only 30% of the income of a single person. These authors also argued that a case can be made for making dependents' benefits the same for all AIMEs. In their opinion, except for the maximum family benefit, which is too harsh, the present system treats workers with dependents too generously.

The 1979 Advisory Council made no recommendation concerning the "gap" in survivorship benefits. They did, however, reject several Carter administration proposals that would have reduced or eliminated certain benefits. Some of these proposals are now law as a result of the 1981 amendments passed with Reagan Administration support. For example, instead of recommending that the lump-sum death benefit be payable only to needy persons, they recommended that this benefit be continued and, by a narrow majority, that the benefit be increased from $255 to three times the PIA or $500, whichever is less. As noted earlier, the amount is still $255 and payable only to a surviving spouse or child. The Council also rejected proposals that would stop children's benefits at age 18, stop payments to mothers caring for nondisabled children after the youngest child reached age 16, and eliminate survivorship income benefits for currently insured workers. Student benefits, it argued, are an essential form of wage replacement, particulalry for low-income families. Although the Council agreed that changing dependency patterns may alter prevailing opinion on how old a child should be before a parent

[26]"The Forces Reshaping Social Security," *Business Week,* July 15, 1972, 54, 82–91.

should receive payments for child-care responsibilities, it argued that for the present parents who need the money should not be forced to seek outside work. Elimination of the currently insured status survivorship benefit, it noted, would deny such benefits to the survivors of women who reenter the labor force after some period as a homemaker. As noted earlier, as a result of the 1981 amendments, children's benefits will soon stop at age 18 and mother's or father's benefits stop when their youngest child reaches age 16.

The Council also suggested some changes in dependents' benefits that will be discussed under the section that follows on the relative treatment of men and women.

Taxation of Retirement Benefits

Taxation of OASDI retirement benefits has been advocated on the grounds that (1) these benefits would be taxable if treated in the same way as private pensions and (2) taxing these benefits would have little, if any, effect on beneficiaries whose only income was from OASDI. For example, a majority of the 1979 Advisory Council recommended that half of the OASDI retirement benefit be included in a beneficiary's taxable income. Under a private pension plan the proportion of the pension that is taxable is roughly unity minus the ratio of the worker's total contributions to the total benefits that will be received if the retirement period equals the life expectancy. Under OASDI the payroll taxes paid by workers are usually far less than half the benefits they can expect to receive. (The difference is supplied mainly by employers and future generations of employees.) Consequently the private pension analogy would suggest a higher percentage subject to tax. However, the actual percentage is difficult to calculate and taxing more than 50% would probably be unacceptable. Not taxing OASDI retirement benefits at all most favors those persons who have other sources of income after retirement. Some Council members who favored such a tax believed that it should be phased in gradually.

Automatic Adjustments

The principle of automatic adjustments in taxable wages and benefits now seems well established, but this matter was discussed at great length prior to its adoption in 1972.[27] Some questions still remain regarding its implementation.

The December 1977 amendments corrected an important technical error in the way the 1972 amendments stated that benefits were to increase as prices rise. Prior to those amendments there was no indexing of earnings. Instead of calculating the AIME for a worker who was retiring or deceased, the Social Security Administration calculated his or her average monthly earnings. The procedure was the same except that the past earnings were not indexed. Instead, to adjust for inflation, each June the PIA corresponding to each average monthly earnings was

---

[27]For a discussion of the arguments, see J. G. Turnbull, C. A. Williams, Jr., and E. F. Cheit, *Economic and Social Security,* 4th ed. (New York: Ronald Press, 1973), pp. 110–111.

increased by the change in the CPI. The net effect was that ultimately the PIA would exceed the average monthly earnings to which they were related. Under what were considered to be reasonable wage and price increase assumptions in 1972 this relationship was not particularly disturbing, because the "replacement ratio" described earlier would remain about the same over time. Under what now seem to be the most plausible assumptions this ratio would have increased over time. Future beneficiaries would receive a far greater adjustment for inflation than was originally intended (the ratio would have exceeded 100% eventually) and the financial impact was highly adverse. Chapter 4 discusses this technical error and its effects in more detail.

The adjustment was too great because inflation affected the worker in two ways: first, the worker's average monthly wage was higher because at least part of the salary increases received over time could be attributed to inflation; second, the PIA corresponding to each average monthly earnings figure was being adjusted each year for the CPI increase. As explained above, under certain wage and price assumptions this method worked, but it proved to be highly sensitive to wages and price changes. The 1977 amendments "decoupled" this computation by substituting an AIME for average monthly earnings and freezing the PIAs relative to their respective AIMEs.

Some persons argue that the PIA calculation is still too generous, especially considering the financial condition of the program. Instead of indexing earnings to completely reflect changes in average earnings, one suggestion is that the index reflect only part of the change in the average standard of living. Another suggestion is that the index adjust for price increases instead of wage increases.

The CPI has also been questioned as a way of measuring changes in the cost of living for most OASDI beneficiaries as well as for the general population. Critics claim that this index overstates the increase in living costs because, for example, it is influenced by increases in mortgage rates, which do not affect most beneficiaries. A recent report by the Social Security Administration, however, suggests that the CPI index has increased by about the same amount as the cost of living for the elderly.[28] Starting in 1983 the CPI itself will be revised.

Because inflation is a much more serious problem now than in 1972, the Advisory Council recommended that benefits be increased twice a year—in March and September if the cost of living has increased by at least 3% since the last adjustment. A counter argument is that benefits should be adjusted to reflect only part of the CPI increase. The wages of many workers, it is argued, have not kept pace with price increases. One suggestion is that the increase be limited to the increases in average wages when wages increase less than prices. Some would oppose this suggestion unless it included a provision that would permit OASDI beneficiaries to catch up what they lost when their increases were limited to the increases in average wages and later wages rose faster than prices.

[28]Benjamin Bridges, Jr., and Michael D. Packard, "Price and Income Changes for the Elderly," Social Security Bulletin, XLIV, No. 1 (January 1981), 3–15. For a description of the proposed changes in the CPI see "The New Math on Inflation," *Newsweek,* November 9, 1981, 69.

Treatment of Men and Women

Several steps have been taken to treat men and women equally under OASI. Until recently the time span over which the worker's average monthly earnings was calculated ended just before the 65th birthday year for men and the 62nd birthday year for women. For men and women reaching age 62 after 1974 the treatment is the same for both sexes.

Until recently men also had to meet tighter requirements to qualify for dependents' benefits. For example, to receive a husband's or widower's benefit the husband of a retired or deceeased female worker had to prove that he was receiving at least one-half of this support from his wife when she retired or died. This practice was considered to be discriminatory against women workers as well as men dependents because a female worker's contributions did not purchase the same protection for her dependents.

Even more noteworthy was the fact that until recently there was no father's benefit for a widower left with the children of a deceased female worker or for the husband of a retired woman worker who had dependent children.

Several important differences in treatment, however, still exist. The 1979 Advisory Council reported that they spent more time on these issues than on any other. As a group, they maintained, women get a better return on the taxes they pay then do men for two reasons: their average wages are lower and the system favors lower AIMEs; they also live longer than men, which substantially increases the cost of their retirement benefits. The Council noted, however, that in several respects the treatment of women is inadequate or inequitable. For example, the system makes homemakers economic dependents of men, many women do not earn additional benefits by working, women who stop work to raise children are penalized, widow's benefits are generally inadequate, and divorced women maintaining a separate household receive a benefit that is inadequate when one considers the higher cost of maintaining a separate household than living with a spouse.

The Council recognized that the death, disability, or retirement of homemakers, usually women, who are not paid for their services does not trigger any OASDI benefits for themselves nor for their dependents or survivors. One solution would be to impute earnings for these services and have the homemaker pay taxes on these imputed earnings. The Council rejected this solution on the grounds that (1) it would be difficult to distinguish between full-time and part-time homemakers, (2) the earnings level to be credited would be highly arbitrary, (3) under any reasonable imputed earnings level the aged widow's benefit based on the spouse's earnings would almost always be higher, and (4) it is not clear how much, if any, homemakers should pay for these benefits.

Women are also the ones who must usually choose between a dependent's benefit and one based on their own earnings. When the dependent's benefit is larger, they give up the benefit based on their own earnings. According to the Council, a wife who earns one-sixth or less of a couple's total earnings will find that her benefit as a dependent exceeds her PIA. One solution would be to permit the worker to claim both benefits, but this solution would substantially increase costs and create different inequities. The 1979 Advisory Council, however, considered and rejected a closely related proposal that would permit the spouse with lower earnings to receive 100% of the higher of the two benefits plus 25% of the lower benefit. The Council found this proposal far less satisfactory than the earnings-sharing concept discussed next. It would reduce but not eliminate the disparity in benefits for one- and two-earner couples with the same total income; it would increase the disparity in benefits for two-earner couples and single workers; it would not provide disability benefits for homemakers; and homemakers would continue to be economically dependent on their spouses.

The Council concluded that the most promising approach is to base separate OASDI benefits for husbands and wives on half the couple's combined covered earnings, with two modifications.[29] To illustrate, suppose that the combined AIME for a couple is $2,000. Separate PIAs would be calculated for both the husband and wife, assuming an AIME of 0.50 ($2,000) = $1,000. Because the PIA formula favors lower PIAs, the separate PIAs would together exceed the single PIA based on a $2,000 AIME. Two problems with this approach are that (1) the benefit paid a surviving spouse would be only half the couple's benefit— too little to maintain the prior standard of living—and (2) the benefits of a higher-pay spouse who became disabled or retired would be based on only part of the actual wages lost. Consequently the first modification would pay the surviving spouse benefits based on 100% of the couple's combined earnings. The second modification would permit a higher-pay earner who retired or became disabled before the lower-pay spouse to receive a benefit based on his or her full earnings, not on half the couples' combined earnings. After the lower-pay earner retired or became disabled both spouses would receive benefits on half the combined AIME.

In favor of such an approach, the Council cited several advantages, including the following:

1   Marriage would be recognized as an economic partnership.
2   Each person would be insured for retirement and disability benefits in their own right.
3   Benefits for couples with same combined AIME would be the same regardless of how these earnings were divided among the spouses.
4   The earnings of a working wife would increase the size of the retained benefits received by her and her husband.

[29]In determining the couple's combined earnings for any year the separate earnings would be covered up to the maximum taxable wage base. Thus if in 1981 the husband earned $40,000, and the wife $20,000, the combined earnings for that year would be the maximum taxable wage base for the husband, or $29,700, plus $20,000 for the wife. If the husband and wife consistently earn the same incomes, their two PIAs would be the same as at present.

5   If the wife is out of the labor force for a few years to bear and raise children, she will still be credited with half of her husband's earnings during those years.

6   Many widows would receive higher benefits than at present.

7   Divorced wives would receive a more logical, generally higher benefit. Their benefits would be based on half the couple's combined earnings during the marriage and all of their own earnings after or before that time. The 10-year requirement would be eliminated.

This approach, however, is not without its problems. For example, benefits for one-earner couples would be reduced relative to two-earner couples with the same combined income. Benefits for married women would generally be higher, but benefits for married men would generally be lower. Divorced high earners, at present generally men, and their dependents in any subsequent marriage would receive less than under the present law. The plan assumes that benefits for children and young surviving parents will continue to be determined as at present, but the Council acknowledged that it took this position without considering whether some other strategy would be better. Finally, single persons would not benefit from any of the proposed changes, despite the fact that they would share their increased cost, estimated at 0.35% of the payroll over the long run.

Because these issues are so complex and deserve further analysis, most of the Council members recommended that Congress and other interested groups carefully examine the concept of shared earnings, giving special attention to the specific plan described above. They emphasized that some of the most basic institutions and traditions of American life (marriage, the family, and care of dependents and survivors) could be affected by the change.

A narrow majority recommended immediate implementation of two parts of the proposed plan. First, persons divorced after 10 years of marriage would be eligible for retirement benefits based on shared earnings. Second, aged widows or widowers should receive benefits based on the couple's combined earnings.

The Earnings Test

The earnings test is another highly debatable feature of OASI. Those who favor granting retirement benefits to all eligible persons past the retirement age, regardless of their earnings, maintain that these persons have a proprietary interest in the benefit that is being denied and that the test reduces national output and OASI contributions by forcing benefit recipients out of the labor force. The latter argument becomes more persuasive as the proportion of the aged in the population increases. Finally, it is argued, the test most adversely affects those low-income workers who do not have access to private pensions or savings to supplement their OASI benefit. The contrary view is that the benefit is designed to be paid only to those persons who have retired from full-time employment; none of the present retirement beneficiaries can claim that they have paid for all the benefits to which they would be entitled except for the earnings test; and removing the test would increase the cost substantially in order to meet a relatively unimportant need. In addition, according to this view, the earnings test causes only a relatively small loss of national output because the current sliding-scale approach permits a reasonable amount of partial employment and persons who are otherwise inclined to continue full-time employment are not likely to retire simply to receive retirement benefits that are much less than their current full-time earnings. The sliding-scale approach also benefits most those with lower earnings.

In response to demands for liberalizing the test, in 1977 Congress increased the annual exempt amounts for persons age 65 and over for 1978–1982. Furthermore, beginning in 1983 the age at which the test will no longer apply will drop to 70.

After reviewing similar arguments the 1979 Advisory Council recommended no change in the earnings test except that it saw no reason why the exempt amount should be less for younger beneficiaries. It specifically supported continued application of the test to earnings only, not to profits, rents, interest, and pensions. It argued that to extend the test to these sources of income would discourage private supplementation and in effect impose a needs test on the receipt of benefits.

Retirement Age

Pressures exist to change the normal retirement age of 65 in both directions. Until recently the strongest pressures were to lower this age. Automation and the resulting unemployment of many older workers, combined with (1) the desire of many older workers to retire early because of health problems, desire for more leisure time, or inability to keep pace with the pressures of their jobs, and (2) high unemployment rates among younger workers who are anxious to replace those older workers, continue to generate such pressures. The fact that almost two-thirds of the former workers receiving OASI retirement benefits retired early also supports the argument for a lower retirement age. Because paying *unreduced* OASI benefits at age 62 or earlier would increase the cost of the system substantially, Congress has been reluctant to consider this suggestion seriously.

Some authorities believe that permitting *reduced* retirement benefits at age 62 is a questionable way of handling the problem of workers forced out of the labor force by poor health or deteriorating employment opportunities because the benefits to which these people are entitled are likely to be inadequate in the short and long runs. They urge further consideration of more liberal disability, pension, and extended unemployment benefits for this group.[30]

On the other side of this issue the higher benefits introduced in 1972 and

---

[30]Margaret S. Gordon, *National Retirement Policies and the Displaced Older Worker,* Reprint No. 250 (Berkeley, CA: Institute of Industrial Relations, University of California, 1965), p. 599. Although this source is dated, the recommendation is still timely.

increased in 1977 for those who delay their retirement beyond age 65 are significant because they may encourage some later retirements. Public Law 95-256, which raised the minimum compulsory retirement age under private pension plans to 70, is another force in this direction.

A 1979 Advisory Council majority recommended consideration of some modest increase in the retirement age from 65 to, say, 68 early in the 21st century. It argued that expected advances in health care and longevity would produce about the same number of retirement years starting at age 68 as at present for a person retiring at 65. Labor shortages may develop if more aged do not work and many older workers would be healthier and happier if they did continue to work. A major argument is that if the retirement age is not increased at that time, the payroll tax rates will have to be substantially increased over the rates presently scheduled. Some members, however, opposed any such increase. They argued that to raise the age would break faith with younger persons currently covered and reduce benefits at all ages prior to 68, that most workers prefer early retirement, that many workers, especially those with physically demanding jobs, are unable to continue working after age 65, that the cost projections for the next century are subject to considerable error, and that the increased cost of supporting the aged will be offset in part by a substantial reduction in the cost of supporting children.

The Council recommended continuation of the present provisions allowing retirement with an actuarial reduction as early as age 62. It also recommended consideration of a special program that would pay long-term unemployment benefits to persons approaching the normal retirement age who are able and willing to work but unable to find a job. For these persons and those who are disabled, early retirement is forced, not voluntary. The disabled should receive Disability Insurance benefits.

The Council rejected proposals to increase the delayed retirement credit percentages, because it considered other benefit liberalizations to be more important. Increasing these credits, it believed, would most help those with higher earnings.

SUMMARY

Old-Age and Survivors Insurance is a social insurance program established under the Social Security Act of 1935. Unlike the public assistance programs, OASI is entirely federally supported and administered.

Except for some special benefits payable to persons turning 72 before 1968 who may never have worked in covered employment, in order to receive OASI retirement or survivorship benefits a person must be either "fully insured," or "currently insured." Fully insured persons are eligible for most of the survivorship and retirement benefits, whereas currently insured persons are eligible only for some of the survivorship benefits.

The basic benefit is a retirement benefit for an insured person at age 65, with reduced benefits available as early as 62. The formula used to determine this benefit reflects a compromise between the desire to provide a floor of protection for all families and the desire to preserve some relationship between taxable earnings and benefits. At present several formulas, all of which incorporate this principle, are used, depending on when the worker reaches or will reach age 62. For those reaching age 62 in 1984 or later the Decoupled Formula Method will be the only formula used. Under this formula the benefit is 90% of a specified portion of the worker's average indexed (taxed) monthly earnings, 32% of the next specified portion, and 15% of the excess. After the worker retires the benefit is adjusted each June to match increases in the Consumer Price Index.

The benefits for the dependents of a retired worker are a life income to the spouse after age 62, income to the spouse until the youngest child is age 16, and income until age 18 for children.

The death benefits are a life income for a widow or a dependent widower after age 60, income to a widow or widower until the youngest child reaches age 16, income for children until age 18, a life income to dependent parents of the deceased after age 62, and a lump-sum death benefit.

Although OASI covers most employments, there are still some important exclusions. The latest Advisory Council on Social Security recommended that all newly hired federal employees and employees of nonprofit organizations be covered on a mandatory basis. Suggested benefit changes involve the benefit level and structure, taxation of retirement benefits, the relative treatment of males and females, and the earnings test. For example, the latest Advisory Council recommended a two-tier benefit formula to replace the present three-tier formula (61 and 27% to replace 90, 32, and 15%), taxing half the OASI retirement benefit, serious consideration of an approach that would base separate OASDI benefits for husbands and wives on half the couple's combined earnings, and applying the same earnings test to beneficiaries of all ages. Pressures exist both to raise and to lower the normal retirement age of 65. The Advisory Council recommended some modest increase to, say, age 68 soon after the turn of the century. Chapter 5 will summarize some important sets of recommendations made in 1981 by some special commissions, the Reagan Administration, and the House Subcommittee on Social Security.

SUGGESTIONS FOR ADDITIONAL READING

See suggestions for Chapter 4.

Chapter Four

Old-Age and Survivors Insurance: Financing and Administration

This chapter concludes the discussion of OASI started in Chapter 3. Whereas Chapter 3 described the provisions, operations, and issues concerning coverage and benefits, this chapter deals with the financing and administration of the program.

FINANCING

With two exceptions explained below, OASI benefits and the expenses of administering the OASI program are financed by earmarked payroll taxes paid by workers and their employers. The exceptions are (1) the special benefits payable to persons age 72 before 1972 (1970 for women) and (2) wage credits granted for military service in addition to those earned by virtue of regular coverage of the armed services under the program.

Workers have been required to contribute because (1) the problems created by death and old age are not entirely caused by employment, (2) what employers might reasonably be asked to contribute alone would not provide adequate benefits, (3) employee contributions encourage individual responsibility and an awareness of the benefits and costs of the program, and (4) an employee contribution strengthens the employee's claim for a voice in the program. Although the law and Congressional intent are silent on this point, the benefits and contributions have been designed to give most workers at least as much protection over time as their own contributions would purchase from private insurers.[1] Employers have been required to contribute because they have (1) a moral obligation and business interest with respect to their own employees and (2) a social obligation with respect to the entire system. The cost of protecting their employees against the problems of death and old age is considered a proper charge against business operations and, presumably, part of this charge can be shifted to consumers. Part of the charge might also be shifted to the workers through reduced wages.

[1] This "money's worth" concept is examined in more detail later in this chapter.

102

Contribution Schedule

In 1982, to support both OASI and Disability Insurance but not Medicare, the employee and employer each pay 5.40% on the first $32,400 of the employee's earnings. Of this 5.40%, 0.825% is allocated to Disability Insurance. A self-employed person pays 8.05% on net earnings up to $32,400 Of the 8.05%, 1.2375% is for Disability Insurance. The 8.05% figure is a compromise betwen an employee rate and a combined employer–employee rate.

Wages include all payments in cash or in kind, with certain exceptions such as the employer's OASDI and unemployment compensation contributions or payments in kind to domestic and farm workers. Tips are not included as wages unless they exceed $20 in a month, in which case they are reported by the employer, but the employer contribution is paid only on the excess of the federal minimum wage over the actual wages paid. Net self-employment earnings do not include interest, dividends, and rent unless the self-employed person receives them in the course of business as a real estate or securities dealer.

The wage base is automatically adjusted each year in units of $300 to match changes in the average annual earnings of all workers, both covered and uncovered. To allow for time to gather the data the adjustment cannot be based on the change in average earnings during the preceding two years. Instead the base period is the two years ending one year before the adjustment year. For example, if average annual earnings increase by 10% from 1980 to 1981, the 1983 contribution base will be 1.10 × ($32,400) rounded to the nearest multiple of $300.

The employee and employer tax rates are scheduled to rise in 1985 and thereafter as follows:

> 1985–1989   5.70 (0.950 for Disability Insurance)
>
> 1990 on   6.20 (1.100 for Disability Insurance)

All persons in covered employment must contribute, even if they derive no benefit from the payment. For example, a fully insured person who could retire with a maximum benefit must contribute if he or she works in covered employment.

Each employer withholds the contribution from the covered employees and sends twice this amount to the District Director of Internal Revenue, with a detailed report on the employees covered. Self-employed persons pay their tax in connection with their income tax return.

The Trust Fund

The OASDI funds collected less the Disability Insurance contributions are appropriated to the Old-Age and Survivors Insurance Trust Fund. The disability contributions are placed in a separate fund. The Secretary of the Treasury is the Managing Trustee of the Fund, with broad powers over it. The other members of the Board of Trustees are the Secretary of Labor and the Secretary of Health and Human Services. The part of the Fund not needed to pay benefits and administrative costs is invested in (1) interst-bearing U.S. Government obligations or securities guaranteed as to principal and interst by the United States or (2) special public bonds created exclusively for the Trust Fund. The interest on the special bonds must equal the average market yield on all the federal debt outstanding that will mature four or more years after the date of the special issue.

The Fund does not represent a legal policy reserve of the type required to be established by private life insurers. A private life insurer must carry as a liability item on its balance sheet the difference between the present value of future benefits promised under its contracts in force and the present value of future premium payments for these contracts. The private insurer could (and may be forced to) stop selling contracts at any time. If its interest and mortality assumptions are correct, future premiums plus an amount equal to this liability item accumulated at interest would be sufficient to pay all future claims. The OASI Trust Fund is not nearly this large. On the assumption that the system will operate indefinitely, the objective is to set the contribution schedule such that the current amount in the Fund plus future contributions and interest on the assets of the Fund will be sufficient to pay all future benefits and administrative expenses as they come due over the next 75 years and still leave a small amount in the Fund. This feature of the OASI Trust Fund is explored in more detail later in this chapter. The assets in the Fund thus offset a small part of the cost through interest earnings and serve as a contingency fund in years when expenditures exceed income. Under current rules the financing is arranged so that the Trust Fund assets are never expected to be more than a few year's expenditures.

ADMINISTRATION

Old-Age and Survivors Insurance is administered by the Social Security Administration, which is part of the Department of Health and Human Services. The Social Security Administration has hundreds of regional and district offices located throughout the country.

Each worker covered under OASI has a social security number, which is used to keep a record of his or her earnings. Benefits are computed on the basis of this earnings record, which is kept by the Social Security Administration at its central office in Baltimore, Maryland. Insureds are encouraged to check their accounts from time to time by sending to the Baltimore center a postcard form available at local offices.

To receive benefits, a worker, dependents, or survivors must file an application at a local Social Security Administration office. If the applicant believes that there has been an error in the earnings record or in computing the benefit, he or she may ask the Social Security Administration to reconsider the case. If the applicant is dissatisfied with the decision resulting from this reconsideration, he or she may request a hearing before a hearing examiner of the Bureau of Hearings and

Appeals. The hearing examiner's decision may be appealed to the Appeals Council of the Social Security Administration. Further appeal, if necessary, may be made to the federal courts.

OPERATIONAL TRENDS

Although the use of earmarked payroll taxes to finance OASI benefits has remained the same since the system started, there have been numerous changes in the contribution structure (tax rate and wage base) and the size of the Trust Fund.

The Contribution Structure

In 1937 the employer and employee were each asked to contribute 1% on the first $3,000 of the worker's earnings. This contribution was scheduled to increase by 0.5% every three years until 1949, when it would have reached 3%. The purpose of this gradual increase was to lessen the impact of the required contribution on the economy.

Because a tax increase is unpopular and many persons questioned the necessity for an increase, the original rates were not increased as scheduled. However, it was not until 1947 that this original schedule was abandoned. Since that time the maximum taxable earnings and contribution rates have been increased periodically.

The 1972 amendments made significant changes in the contribution structure. Provision was made for automatic adjustments in the contribution base, starting in 1975, as average earnings increased. The 1977 amendments made two changes in response to a worsening financial situation: for 1979, 1980, and 1981, the wage base was increased substantially above what the automatic adjustments would have produced; the tax rates were also increased, and will increase, significantly, especially prior to 2011.

In 1980, when it became apparent that the OASI Trust Fund would soon be temporarily exhausted, Congress increased for 1980 and 1981 the proportion of the combined OASDI rate that was allocated to OASI. The 1981 benefit reductions were inspired by continuing financial difficulties to be explained later.

The Trust Fund

Until 1940 the excess of income over expenditures was kept in an Old-Age Reserve Account, which was administered by the Secretary of the Treasury. The balance was invested in special 3% government bonds. On January 1, 1940, the monies in this account were transferred to the Old-Age and Survivors Insurance Trust Fund, which was to be administered by a Board of Trustees. The monies were to be invested in public issues bought on the open market or in special bonds bearing the average rate of interest on the public debt. Later amendments changed the rate on the special bonds several times before the present rate was enacted.

The intent behind the original tax schedule was to accumulate a sizable trust fund as soon as possible so that the interest on the assets might be used to pay a substantial proportion of the costs. For example, by 1980 the interest on these assets was expected to equal about 40% of the disbursements. From the beginning, however, it was assumed that the Fund need not be as large as that required of a private insurer because it was assumed that the system would operate indefinitely into the future. Strong opposition to the philosophy supporting a sizable trust fund had existed prior to its adoption, but this opposition later became more outspoken and effective.

In 1939 a much more liberal benefit schedule was being studied, and it was recommended that the government contribute to the cost. The intent of the changes actually made is unclear. A tax increase scheduled for 1940 was postponed, but no increase was recommended in later years to make up for this reduction. As a result the Trust Fund's progress was slowed down considerably, particularly since the benefits were substantially liberalized by the same amendments. On the other hand, the federal government did not pledge itself to participate in the program. The Board of Trustees was asked to report immediately when the Fund balance was unduly low or would probably exceed three times the highest annual expenditures during the ensuing five years. This appeared to set a maximum limit on the Fund, but the maximum was exceeded almost immediately and Congress did nothing except to continue postponing tax increases.

The result of the freezes was that a larger share of the financial burden was passed on to future OASI taxpayers. It also became apparent that the tax schedule was not sufficient to make the system self-supporting.

The Revenue Act of 1943 authorized Congress to make direct appropriations when necessary to finance the benefits provided.

In 1950 Congress reversed itself and declared that the system was to be self-supporting. It adopted a higher contribution schedule, and for the next two decades tended to increase contribution rates whenever it liberalized the program. As a result, by 1972 the Trust Fund was not nearly as large as intended in 1935, but it was more than a contingency fund and, according to Congress, should be sufficient with future contributions to pay all benefits and expenses for the next 75 years. The contribution schedule in the 1972 amendments was based on a new concept for the Trust Fund. Future contributions plus the trust fund were still supposed to be sufficient to pay all benefits and expenses for the next 75 years, but the contribution schedule was derived using less conservative actuarial assumptions than in the past. The program thus moved closer to a pay-as-you-go system, with the trust fund serving primarily as a contingency fund. The 1977 changes in the contribution structure did not change this concept; they merely provided more monies to keep the system solvent, assuming this objective. As noted earlier, in 1980 and 1981 some of the contribution rate scheduled for the Disability Insurance (DI) fund was placed in the OASI fund. The 1981 amendments made no change in the contribution schedule.

OPERATIONAL DATA

The income and expenditures of the OASI Trust Fund since 1937 are shown in Table 4.1. The income includes taxes, transfers from the Railroad Retirement Account,[2] Congressional appropriations from general revenues to meet the costs of certain special benefits or military wage credits, and interest on the Trust Fund's invested assets. The income exceeded the expenditures each year until 1957, when the relationship was reversed, causing the Fund assets to decline for several years. Tax schedule increases enacted in 1958 and 1961 reversed this trend

Table 4.1 Receipts, Expenditures, and Assets of OASI Trust Fund, 1937–1980 (In Millions of Dollars)

	Receipts		Expenditures		
Year	Net Tax Contributions[a]	Interest[b]	Benefit Payments[c]	Administrative Expenses	Total Assets
1937	765	2	1	[d]	766
1941	789	56	88	26	2,762
1945	1,285	134	274	30	7,121
1949	1,670	146	667	54	11,816
1953	3,945	414	3,006	88	18,707
1957	6,825	558	7,347	162	22,393
1961	11,285	548	12,194	239	19,725
1965	16,017	593	17,173	328	18,235
1967	23,216	818	19,976	406	24,222
1969	28,390	1,165	24,701	474	30,082
1971	34,210	1,667	34,027	514	33,789
1973	46,416	1,928	46,528	647	36,487
1975	57,241	2,364	59,499	896	36,987
1977	70,185	2,227	74,328	981	32,491
1979	88,477	1,797	92,021	1,112	24,660
1980	103,996	1,845	106,525	1,154	22,824

Sources: Social Security Bulletin, Annual Statistical Supplement, 1977–1979, 80 and *Social Security Bulletin,* LXIV, No. 5 (May 1981), 43.

[a]Includes Congressional appropriations in 1946–1951 and since 1966 to meet the cost of benefits for certain World War II veterans and for military wage credits and special transitional benefits, respectively.

[b]Includes interest on amounts held in the Railroad Retirement Account to the credit of the OASI Trust Fund during 1954–1957.

[c]Includes transfers to the Railroad Retirement Account in 1958 and each succeeding year. The transfer in 1980 was $1,442 million.

[d]Administrative expenses before 1940 were in effect deducted from contributions before the latter were credited to the Fund.

[2]The purpose of these transfers is to put both funds in the position in which they would now be if railroad employment after 1936 had been covered under OASI.

in 1962. During 1975–1978 expenditures again exceeded income and total assets declined. The tax increases resulting from the 1977 amendments were expected to produce income in excess of expenditures by 1980, but adverse economic conditions (inflation and unemployment, as explained later) caused large deficits to continue.

Until 1960 the total assets were always at least twice the annual benefits. Until 1955 interest on invested assets exceeded 10% of the benefit payments; interest now is less than 2% of the annual benefits. The effective annual rate of interest earned by the assets of the OASI Trust Fund during fiscal year 1980 was 8.3%.

Long- and Medium-Range Actuarial Projections

Each year Social Security Administration actuaries report to the Board of Trustees which in turn reports to Congress on how the OASI system is likely to fare financially during the next 75 years.[3] The "maximum remaining lifetime" of current OASI participants is 75 years.

1981 Projections

Table 4.2 summarizes the major findings of the 1981 Board of Trustees report, which examined the financial health of the system preceding the enactment of the 1981 amendments that reduced some of the benefits. Table 4.2 reports the findings for OASI, DI, and OASI and DI combined. Because these cash benefit programs are so closely related, it is customary to evaluate the financial health of both OASI and DI at the same time and in the same way.

Based on a number of assumptions explained below, the actuaries first calculated for each of the 75 years the contributions to be received from workers and their employers, expressed as a percentage of the covered payroll in that year. The contribution percentage in Table 4.2 is the arithmetic average of the 75 annual contribution percentages. Next they calculated for each of the 75 years the benefits and administrative costs, expressed as a percentage of covered payroll that year. The expenditure percentage in Table 4.2 is the arithmetic average of the 75 annual expenditure percentages. The difference between the average contribution percentage and the average expenditure percentage is called the actuarial balance. If negative, this balance represents the amount by which contributions must be increased or costs decreased (or some combination of these changes) if the system is to remain self-supporting over the next 75 years. If the balance is positive, the benefits can be increased or the contributions decreased within limits and the system will remain self-supporting. This analysis ignores the present trust

[3]For example, see *1981 Annual Report of the Board of Trustees of the Federal Old-Age and Survivors Insurance and Disability Insurance Trust Funds,* 97th Congress, 1st Session, House Document No. 97–66, July 2, 1981. For the highlights of the 1980 annual report see Dwight K. Bartlett III, "Current Developments in Social Security Financing," *Social Security Bulletin,* XLIII, No. 9 (September 1980), 10–20, 35.

Table 4.2 Projected Average Tax Rates and Expenditures, OASI, DI, and OASDI, 1981–2055, Under Intermediate Assumptions (As a Percentage of the Taxable Payroll)

	OASI	DI	OASDI
Intermediate A Assumptions			
Taxes	10.10	2.15	12.25
Expenditures	11.71	1.47	13.17
Balance	−1.61	0.68	−0.93
Intermediate B Assumptions			
Taxes	10.10	2.15	12.25
Expenditures	12.54	1.52	14.07
Balance	−2.44	0.62	−1.82

Source: 1981 Annual Report of the Board of Trustees of the Federal Old-Age and Survivors Insurance and Disability Insurance Trust Funds, 97th Congress, 1st Session, House Document No. 97–66, July 2, 1981.

fund assets and any interest earnings on these funds, which are relatively small.

According to Table 4.2, despite the substantial increase mandated by the 1977 amendments in the scheduled contributions, under two sets of intermediate assumptions to be explained later, from 1981 to 2055 the projected expenditures would exceed the projected contributions. Under the intermediate A assumptions the result would be an actuarial deficit of 1.61% of the taxable payroll for OASI, but an actuarial gain of 0.68% for DI. Under the intermediate B assumptions these two balance would be −2.44% and 0.62%. In recent years the system has been considered to be in "close actual balance" if the average tax rate is within 5% of the average cost rate. Neither OASI nor OASDI satisfies this standard under either set of intermediate assumptions.

For the three 25-year periods included in these 75 years the actuarial balances under the intermediate assumptions, starting in 1985, would be as follows:

	OASI	DI	OASDI
Intermediate A Assumptions			
1981–2005 (%)	0.47	0.80	1.27
2006–2030 (%)	−1.26	0.58	−0.67
2031–2055 (%)	−4.03	0.64	−3.38
Intermediate B Assumptions			
1981–2005 (%)	−0.31	0.74	0.43
2006–2030 (%)	−2.01	−0.54	−1.47
2031–2055 (%)	−5.00	−0.59	−4.41

Under the intermediate A assumptions for the first 50 years the total system would be approximately in balance; for the last 25 years the projected deficit would be substantial. Under the intermediate B assumptions the total system would experience more than a 1% deficit in the second 25 years.

Under the intermediate A assumptions the combined trust funds were expected to reverse their decline later in the 1980s as contributions exceeded expenditures for the first time in recent years. Early in the next century, after reaching a peak of almost four times annual expenditures, the combined Trust Funds were again expected to decline; by 2040 they would be exhausted. The OASI Trust Fund would be exhausted earlier, by 2030, but the DI fund would still be growing at the end of the 75 years. Under the intermediate B assumptions the combined trust funds would be exhausted in 2025. The OASI Trust Fund would be exhausted in 1984 and never recover. All of the calculations presented thus far are based on "intermediate" assumptions, which are the ones on which most policy decisions are made. The intermediate A and B assumptions share the same demographic assumptions but different economic performance assumptions. Some of the major assumptions were as follows:

1   Mortality rates declining gradually to 2055 levels that will be 36% less on the average than 1978 levels.

2   A fertility rate that increases slowly to 2.1 children per woman by 2005 and remains level thereafter.

3   Disability incidence rates rising gradually to an ultimate level in 2000 that is about 15% greater than the 1978–1980 level.

4   Annual wage increases in covered employment declining under the intermediate A assumptions to 7.1% by 1985 and 5.0% from 1995 on. The corresponding intermediate B assumption percentages were 8.1% and 5.5%.

5   Annual increases in the Consumer Price Index declining under the intermediate A assumptions to 4.7% by 1985 and 3.0% from 1990 on. Intermediate B assumptions were less optimistic, these two percentages being 7.4% and 4.0%, respectively.

6   Unemployment rates declining to 5.9% under the intermediate A assumption by 1985 and 5.0% from 1995 on. Under the intermediate B assumptions these rates were assumed to decline to 6.8%, by 1985 and 5.0% from 2000 on.

Many other assumptions dealt with such variables as labor-force participation rates for men and women, timing pattern of fertility, marital status, insured status, administrative expenses, and interest rates, which affect the growth of fund assets.

Estimates were also developed based on two other sets of assumptions: optimistic assumptions and pessimistic assumptions. Table 4.3 compares the calculations under these two alternative sets of assumptions with the calculations under the intermediate assumptions. The optimistic assumptions show no deficit for

Table 4.3 Projected Average Tax Rates and Expenditures, OASDI, 1981–2055, Under Alternative Assumptions (As a Percentage of the Taxable Payroll)

	Optimistic Assumptions	Intermediate A Assumptions	Intermediate B Assumptions	Pessimistic Assumptions
Taxes	12.25	12.25	12.25	12.25
Expenditures	10.99	13.17	14.07	18.50
Balance	1.25	−0.93	−1.82	−6.25

Source: See Table 4.2.

OASDI, the pessimistic assumptions a higher deficit. For OASI alone the optimistic assumptions produced a positive balance of only 0.30%. Under the pessimistic assumptions the OASI deficit was 6.51%. Some of the key assumptions for 2000 and later years under each set of assumptions are the following:

Ultimate Values	Optimistic	Intermediate A	Intermediate B	Pessimistic
Fertility rate	2.4	2.1	2.1	1.7
Annual average earnings increase (%)	4.5	5.0	5.5	6.0
Annual consumer price increase (%)	2.0	3.0	4.0	5.0
Unemployment rate (%)	4.0	5.0	5.0	6.0

Lower fertility rates, higher unemployment rates, and price increases that are closer to earnings increases than the intermediate assumptions indicate would increase the deficit. The opposite relationships would reduce the deficit.

Pre-1981 Projections

Until 1972, when automatic adjustments in benefits and the contribution base were introduced, the actuarial balance was calculated using a more conservative methodology, which is described in earlier editions of this book. The methodology was more conservative principally because it assumed that average earnings would not increase over the next 75 years. Because increases in average earnings increased contributions more than it did benefits, the calculation produced an actuarial balance that was almost certain to be exceeded. Nevertheless, in 1971, according to the intermediate cost assumptions contained in that year's report the actuarial deficiency was only 0.06 for OASI and 0.10 for DI. All reports prior to the 1981 report contained only one set of intermediate assumptions. As noted earlier, in 1972 benefits were increased by 20% across the board without increasing scheduled contributions nearly as much. Changing the wage increase assumption was the principal reason this move seemed feasible.

In 1974 the actuarial report to the Board of Trustees indicated a worsening situation with an OASDI actuarial deficiency, under intermediate assumptions, of 2.98%. As noted earlier, in 1975 the combined OASDI Trust Fund assets began a decline that was expected to continue. From 1974 through 1977 the projected deficit increased, reaching 8.20% in the 1977 report. The yearly estimates are summarized below:

	1974	1975	1976	1977
Average contributions (%)	10.91	10.94	10.97	10.99
Average expenditures (%)	13.89	16.26	18.93	19.19
Actuarial balance (%)	−2.98	−5.32	−7.96	−8.20

According to the 1977 report the deficit would be 2.34% from 1977 to 2001, 7.67% from 2002 to 2026, and 14.57% from 2027 to 2051.

Why is there this sudden change in the present and projected financial health of the system? The short-run deficits were explained by the following: (1) a much higher inflation rate than anticipated coupled with the failure of average earnings to keep pace with, let alone grow faster than, prices; (2) higher unemployment rates than expected; and (3) higher than expected disability costs. In other words, inflation, unemployment, and more and longer disability claims were the culprits.

The projected long-range deficits were explained by substantial changes in some significant assumptions. For example, the fertility rate assumption was decreased. Under the 1977 assumptions the proportion of the population that is aged was expected to increase more rapidly, especially after 2010. The ratio of OASDI beneficiaries to workers was expected to increase from about 30% in 1978 to 35% in 2000, over 50% in 2025, and 49% in 2050. Whereas in 1978 there was one beneficiary for every three workers, during the last 25 years of the 75-year projection it was assumed that there will be one beneficiary for every two workers. A second major change in assumptions involved wages and prices. In 1972 cost studies the actuaries assumed wage increases of 5% and consumer price increases of $2\frac{3}{4}$%. The 1977 intermediate assumptions were annual wage price increases of 4%, producing a smaller assumed increase in real wages. The effect of this change was particularly significant before the correction of the technical error in the way benefits were automatically adjusted for price increases. These adjustments, it was discovered later, were particularly sensitive to the assumptions concerning wage and price increases. With a $5\frac{1}{4}$–2% set of assumptions a male with median earnings retiring at age 65 from now until 2050 would receive in the first year a benefit equal to about one-half of the worker's covered earnings the last year before retirement. With $5\frac{3}{4}$–4% assumptions the replacement ratio would rise gradually to 70% by 2050; with $6\frac{1}{4}$–5% assumptions the ratio would be 100% by 2050. Logically and equitably the replacement ratio should be the same regardless of the date the worker retires, unless Congress takes direct action to change the ratio. Furthermore, this substantial rise in replacement ratios under the new wage–price increase assumptions was extremely costly. For each of the three sets of assumptions used in the 1977 report the effect of the technical error or overindexing was as follows:

	Actuarial Balance (%)	
Assumption	With Error	With Error Corrected
Optimistic	−3.88	−3.26
Intermediate	−8.20	−4.46
Pessimistic	−16.09	−6.52

Correcting this error, therefore, eliminated almost one-half of the projected 8.20% deficit. If the pessimistic assumptions turn out to be correct, the effect of the decoupling would be even greater.

As noted earlier, in response to these threats to the financial solvency of the OASI and DI Trust Funds in 1977 Congress (1) eliminated the technical error by relating the primary insurance amount to average indexed monthly earnings and (2) substantially raised the contribution rates and the maximum payroll tax base. Consequently, when the Board of Trustees submitted its report in 1978, the situation was much improved.[4] The projected actuarial balances under the intermediate assumptions for the next 75 years and the three 25-year components were as follows:

	1978–2052	1978–2002	2003–2027	2028–2052
OASI (%)	−1.26	0.79	−0.76	−3.80
DI (%)	−0.14	0.23	−0.36	−0.30
OASDI (%)	−1.40	1.02	−1.11	−4.10

The demographic assumptions were close to those described earlier for the 1981 report except that the disability incidence assumption was much less favorable. The 1981 economic performance was assumed to be less favorable than under the intermediate A assumptions but more favorable than under the intermediate B assumptions. In the short run these assumptions were much more favorable.

For the 75-year period the 1980 report projected a slightly larger actuarial deficit, −1.52%, than did the 1978 report for the combined OASDI program. For the first 25 years, however, the results were expected to be slightly more favorable than was expected in 1978. For the OASI program the expected 75-year deficit increased from 1.26 to 2.16. For the DI program, the expected deficit of 0.14 became an actuarial gain of 0.64. As will be indicated in the next section, however, the short-range projections disclosed some immediate cash-flow problems.

[4]A. Haeworth Robertson, "Financial Status of Social Security Program After the Social Security Amendments of 1977," *Social Security Bulletin,* XLI, No. 3 (March 1978), 21–30.

Short-Range Actuarial Projections

In addition to these long-range and medium-range projections, each year Social Security Administration actuaries prepare short-range projections covering a five-year period. The 1980 report covering the period 1980–1984 showed that under intermediate assumptions the OASI program expenditures would exceed income in each of these years. For the DI program, on the other hand, income would exceed expenditures substantially, but not enough to offset the OASI deficit. The projected yearly surpluses or deficits in billions of dollars were as follows:

	OASI	DI
1980	−5.8	2.2
1981	−10.4	4.1
1982	−12.4	5.7
1983	−14.2	7.8
1984	−16.2	10.0

By 1983 the OASI deficits were expected to exhaust the OASI Trust Fund.

Based on these short-range projections the Board of Trustees recommended that the OASI Fund be temporarily permitted to borrow from the Disability Insurance and the Hospital Insurance funds (see Chapter 9). The loans would be repaid with interest later. Such loans, the Trustees argued, would make it possible for the combined OASI, DI, and HI funds to remain self-supporting until the 1990s, when the OASI program itself would again become self-supporting under intermediate assumptions. As noted earlier, in 1980 Congress did reallocate some of the 1980 and 1981 contributions scheduled for DI to OASI. As will be noted later, many persons favor financing Hospital Insurance (HI) with general revenues and diverting part or all of its taxes to the OASDI system. The 1978 report expected both OASI and DI to operate at a deficit until 1981, when the higher contribution rates and maximum wage bases would begin to produce substantially more income. Why did the 1980 report produce a much more pessimistic picture for OASI and a more optimistic picture for DI? Both programs were affected by unfavorable economic developments during 1978 and 1979 and resulting changes in the 1980 intermediate assumptions for 1980, 1981, and 1982. These factors are summarized below:

	1978 Assumptions (%)	Actual Actual (%)	1980 Assumptions (%)
1978			
Wage increase	7.2	8.1	
CPI increase	6.1	7.6	
Unemployment rate	6.3	6.0	

1979		
Wage increase	7.9	8.3
CPI increase	6.1	11.5
Unemployment rate	5.9	5.8

1980		
Wage increase	7.9	9.6
CPI increase	5.7	14.2
Unemployment rate	5.4	7.2

1981		
Wage increase	7.4	9.5
CPI increase	5.2	9.7
Unemployment rate	5.0	7.9

1982		
Wage increase	7.4	10.9
CPI increase	5.0	9.0
Unemployment rate	4.8	7.3

In 1980 real wages were expected to decline during the five-year period rather than increase, thus increasing the expenditures relative to income. Unemployment rates were also projected to be higher.

The DI program's actual and projected status was improved by a dramatic reduction in disability incidence rates and an increase in termination rates after 1977. The reasons for this rapid change are not understood, but some of the change is attributed to (1) a tightening of the administrative process for determining disability and (2) a reduction in the number of persons who, when applying for Supplementary Security Income (see Chapter 15), found that they were eligible for DI benefits. The DI program's actuarial balance was also improved because the Disability Insurance Amendments of 1980 lowered the maximum family benefits to be paid to disabled workers and introduced some other cost-saving measures.

In 1981 the Board of Trustees reported a worsening situation, mainly because of continuing inflation and high unemployment. This report differed from earlier reports in that it estimated short-run operations of the trust funds under five alternative sets of assumptions—the four already mentioned plus a "worst case" assumption that was more pessimistic than the pessimistic assumptions. To illustrate, the assumptions concerning some key variables in 1981 and 1985 were as follows:

	Assumptions				
	Opti-mistic	Inter-mediate A	Inter-mediate B	Pessi-mistic	"Worst Case"
1981: Annual average earnings increase (%)	10.6	10.2	10.2	11.5	12.8

Annual consumer price increase (%)	10.7	11.1	11.1	12.6	10.6
Unemployment rate (%)	7.7	7.8	7.8	7.9	8.3
1985:					
Annual average earnings increase (%)	6.8	7.1	8.1	11.5	10.6
Annual consumer price increase (%)	4.1	4.7	7.4	12.6	12.8
Unemployment rate (%)	5.7	5.9	6.8	7.9	8.3

Under these assumptions, the projected yearly deficits in OASI operations in billions of dollars were as follows:

	Assumptions				
	Optimistic	Inter-mediate A	Inter-mediate B	Pessi-mistic	"Worst Case"
1981	−3.3	−3.7	−3.7	−3.0	−4.3
1982	−10.1	−11.8	−12.1	−13.1	−15.3
1983	−12.7	−15.1	−17.0	−24.1	−29.3
1984	−13.1	−16.9	−23.2	−31.8	−38.6
1985	−6.3	−11.5	−22.7	−34.5	−40.9

Under all five sets of assumptions, including the optimistic assumptions, the OASI Fund would be exhausted late in 1982. On the other hand, under all five sets of assumptions the assets in the DI Trust Fund would increase rapidly during this period. The combined OASDI funds were projected to be exhausted in 1984 under the two sets of intermediate assumptions, in 1983 under the pessimistic and "worst case" assumptions. A trust fund, however, is considered to be "depleted" before it becomes exhausted. Because of differences in the cash flow of income and outgo during a month, income becomes insufficient to pay benefits when at the end of any month the assets fall to less than about 9% of the following 12 months of disbursements.[5] Using this standard, the combined funds will be depleted under all five sets of assumptions in late 1982 or sometime during 1983.

If the Hospital Insurance Trust Fund, to be explained in Chapter 9, is combined with the OASI and DI Trust Funds, interfund borrowing would prevent the depletion of the trust funds during the next decade under the optimistic and intermediate A assumptions. Under the intermediate B assumptions the combined funds would be depleted in 1985, exhausted in 1988. Under the pessimistic

---

[5]Benefits are usually payable on the third day of the following month. Income is received more or less uniformly during the month.

assumptions, these two events would occur in 1984 and 1986, respectively, under the "worst case" assumptions in 1983 and 1985.

On the basis of this analysis the Board strongly urged Congress to deal promptly with both the short range and long range financial problems. August 1981 amendments are expected to reduce the long-range actuarial deficit under intermediate B assumptions from 1.82% to 1.65%. Half of the reduction would result from the phasing out of postsecondary student benefits. In December 1981 Congress authorized Interfund borrowing but only during 1982.

MAJOR ISSUES

The manner in which OASDI should be financed is one of the most debated questions in the nation. Major issues involve (1) the use of general revenues, (2) the role of the trust funds, (3) whether workers receive their money's worth from the system, (4) the effect of OASDI on private savings, and (5) the trade-offs between increasing the contribution base and increasing its rate. The cost and quality of the administration are also questioned in some quarters.

Financing

General Revenue Financing

Since OASI benefits the entire population directly or indirectly and the vast majority are directly affected, it has been argued that the government should pay the entire cost of the program out of general revenues. According to this view, the individual income tax, which would probably be increased to provide the necessary revenue, is superior to the payroll tax because of the following: (1) it takes into account the size of the taxpayer's family, personal deductions, and income other than wages and salaries; and (2) it is a progressive tax, thus imposing a relatively greater burden on high-income groups. Payroll taxes, on the other hand, increase proportionately with earnings up to the wage base and are regressive beyond this point. To the extent that employers bear payroll taxes, they are inclined to use labor-saving devices and pay overtime rather than hiring additional workers. Because the income tax is more responsive to changes in income than to those in the payroll tax, it is also a better automatic stabilizer.

Supporters of present payroll tax financing believe that the direct benefits of the program to beneficiaries are so much more important than the indirect benefits that it would not be equitable to tax nonparticipants. Furthermore, they argue, payroll tax financing is superior to general revenue financing in that it identifies and emphasizes the cost of the benefits, thus encouraging a careful review of proposed liberalizations. Finally, although these supporters admit that the payroll tax may be regressive for incomes above the tax base, they observe that no benefits are paid on average monthly earnings above this base and that the benefit structure clearly favors low-income families and those with dependents.

Milton Friedman, the noted economist, has made the interesting observation that, despite the weighted benefit structure, poorer workers, as a group, receive lower benefits per contribution dollar than those with higher earnings. He reasons that higher-income workers start work later, pay taxes for a shorter period, and live longer than the poor, thus enabling them to receive benefits for a longer period. The tax-free nature of OASI benefits also favors the more highly paid.[6]

A much stronger argument can be made for using a government contribution to pay *part* of the cost, reducing the payroll tax to the amount that would be necessary if the system were to begin operations now and only new entrants into the labor force participated. If this suggestion were adopted, general revenues would provide about one-third of the financing. Present payroll taxes could be reduced or, alternatively, benefits increased. Some of the arguments against complete general revenue financing would lose some of their force, but opponents still believe that cost controls would be weakened and that pressures would soon be exerted to increase the share financed by general revenues.

Support for some contribution from general revenues has increased in recent years as more and more people have questioned the desirability of further increases in payroll taxes. The realization that early in the next century there will be one beneficiary for every two workers has caused more people to consider this possibility. The substantial increases in payroll taxes scheduled under the December 1977 amendments were opposed by many who favored some use of general revenues.

General revenues have already been used to finance part of the OASDHI medical expense programs and to pay the cost of the special cash benefits to persons turning 72 before 1972 (1970 for women) who had not worked enough in covered employment to have earned any insured status.

The 1979 Advisory Council on Social Security recommended that HI be financed through general revenues and that, beginning in 1980, part of its payroll tax be reallocated to OASI and DI.[7] They agreed that when benefits are related to a person's earnings, they should be financed through a tax on these earnings, but HI provides the same protection for all. To make the cost of HI visible, however, it should be financed by an earmarked portion of the personal income tax and a matching payment from corporation income taxes.

The Council would have dropped the total (OASI, DI, and HI) contribution rate from 6.13% in 1979 to 5.60% in 1980 and reduced the scheduled increase in the wage base. On the other hand, to remove doubts about the future solvency of the system it recommended scheduling a 7.25% contribution rate, starting in

---

[6]Cited in "The Forces Reshaping Social Security," *Business Week,* July 15, 1972, 58.

[7]See "Social Security Financing," *Social Security Bulletin,* LXIII, No. 5 (May 1980), 18–29 for a detailed discussion of the Advisory Council's recommendations regarding financing. The 1975 Advisory Council made a similar recommendation.

2005. The Council recommended, however, that the decision to alter benefits or contribution rates not be made primarily on the basis of projections more than 50 years in the future. The 75-year benefit projections, however, should be continued because they shed light on the long-run financial consequences of benefit promises and alert Congress to important long-run trends.

Finally the Council recommended that general revenue payments be made to the trust funds during periods of high unemployment. Such payments would be made only if trust fund balance was less than 60% of annual expenditures. The trust funds should also be authorized to borrow from the U.S. Treasury if reserves fall below three months' expenditures. This recommendation, the Council argued, would reduce the chance of payroll taxes having to be raised during a recession. It introduces, but limits, the use of general revenues.

The Trust Fund or Pay-As-You-Go System

In 1972 the role of the trust fund was reduced and OASI moved closer to a pay-as-you-go system. Those who would prefer the stronger reserve system in effect up to 1972 or an even larger trust fund argue that collecting more contributions now than are needed to meet current benefits and expenses reduces the tax burden of future generations, encourages more honest accounting concerning the cost of proposed benefit increases, increases the moral obligation of future Congresses to continue benefits equal to at least the current level, and more adequately preserves the contribution principle in the system.

Those persons favoring the present, more complete pay-as-you-go system oppose a large trust fund because they believe that a large fund has been and would continue to be used as an argument in favor of further liberalization in the law. Opponents of a large trust fund also consider such a large accumulation of monies to be an unnecessary complication in a program that is expected to operate indefinitely and is backed by government taxing power. Moreover, they fear that the taxes necessary to accumulate more than a contingency fund would increase a "fiscal drag" upon the economy. OASDHI contributions, they observe, have reached the point where their fiscal impacts are highly significant. In 1980 OASDHI contributions totaled almost $144 billion. These contributions amounted to over half the receipts from individual income taxes and almost twice the receipts from corporation income taxes. Because of their magnitude, a rise in OASDI contributions can easily offset a decrease in federal income taxes designed to stimulate the economy. These pay-as-you-go advocates counter the argument of a trust fund reducing the burden on future generations in three ways: first, they claim that the trust fund makes it possible for the government to borrow instead of taxing the present generation more heavily in other ways; second, many of the public expenditures financed by the present generation (for example, those for national defense and education) will benefit future generations; and third, reducing the tax burden of future generations is not the only objective of a trust fund. If the payroll tax is lower in the future than it would be without a large trust fund, but there are no more goods and services than there would be under a pay-as-you-go plan, the sole effect of the trust fund would be to slightly improve the position of the taxpayer relative to that of OASDI beneficiaries. A large trust fund makes a real contribution to the economic welfare of future taxpayers only if it transfers funds from current consumption to investment, thus increasing production in the future. How effective a larger trust fund would be in this respect is a matter of conjecture.

Some people believe that the trust fund approach leads to double taxation. With the size of the trust fund being much less today, this view has become less important, but it is still worth repeating because of the common misunderstanding on this point. The argument is as follows:

1   The government taxes employers and employees covered under the OASI program. But assume that it taxes more than is needed to meet current out-payments. Therefore a reserve (a trust fund) is built up and by law invested in U.S. government securities. This is the first taxation stage—single taxation.

2   The securities held in the reserve (trust fund) are interest bearing. In order to pay the interest on these obligations, the government taxes the general public. This is the second or "double" taxation stage, which is viewed as "fraudulent" by certain critics.

A variety of minor rebuttals has been made to this argument: if the excess of taxes over out-payments were invested in private rather than in government securities, we would have government ownership of private industry (and hence "socialism"); or, the contention might have some merit if the excess receipts caused the government to spend more than it otherwise would.

But these rebuttals do not get at the core of the false reasoning involved in this type of argumentation. That there are two stages of taxation is obviously the case. But this is not double taxation, nor is it fraudulent. Assume that taxes were just sufficient to meet present benefit requirements, as they tend to be at present, and hence that there were no trust fund. As the percentage of the retired aged increased, those actively covered under the system would have to pay increased taxes to meet the obligations imposed by the given benefit structure. Disregarding discount complexities, one can show that the interest paid on the trust fund and raised by taxation would equal the increase in taxes that would be required to meet obligations in the absence of such a fund. Thus there is no "double taxation." There might be some legitimacy to the criticism that the taxes are paid by different groups and that in the case of a trust fund the "general public" helps support the OASI beneficiary, whereas on a pay-as-you-go approach the OASI group finances itself. But this is not the same as double taxation or fraud.

The 1979 Advisory Council recommended that the OASI and DI trust funds be combined. OASI and DI benefits and costs should be analyzed separately, but

Congress should not have to readjust taxes when one fund has problems and the other does not. The Council also recommended that the trustees notify the appropriate committees of Congress whenever the trust fund is expected to fall below 75% of outlays or if it is expected to go considerably above that level. If the Council's recommendations for countercyclical general revenues and borrowing authority are adopted, the Council would reduce the 75% standard in the recommendation to 60%.

The "Money's Worth" Question

One of the most frequently asked questions about OASDI is whether a covered worker will receive his or her "money's worth" from participating in the program, that is, whether the worker's benefits will at least equal his or her contributions. The answer to this question is important because it will greatly influence the extent to which the public supports the program and the likelihood of the system operating indefinitely, an assumption that is crucial to current financing plans. For example, if younger workers will not receive their money's worth, they may in time support termination of the system. The answer may also influence decisions by those workers for whom coverage is voluntary or who have the option to withdraw from the system.

Even if younger workers do not receive their money's worth, however, it may be argued that instead of pressing to abolish the program, they would favor improved benefits, general revenue financing, or both. Furthermore, the social adequacy features of OASDI, which is one reason why some workers may not receive their money's worth, reduces public assistance costs and income taxes. If OASDI were abolished, welfare costs would rise, thus exposing workers perhaps to a different higher tax burden.

Instead of limiting the comparison of benefits to the worker's contributions, many argue that if the worker is to receive his or her money's worth, the benefits should equal or exceed the combined employer–employee contributions. Because, they claim, the employer matches the employee contribution, it is the combined contribution that measures the cost of the worker's benefits. The opposite view is that although the employer's contribution is determined by the employee's total contributions, at least part of the employer's contributions pay not for particular workers' benefits but for the social adequacy features of the program.

For some workers the answer to the money's worth question based on either comparison is clearly yes, for others clearly no. For example, low-pay, long-service employees who qualify for the special minimum benefit will receive benefits considerably in excess of their own and their employer's contributions. Spouses who qualify for dependents' benefits that are more liberal than the benefits based on their own earnings will receive benefits based on their own earnings that are considerably less than their own contributions.

For most workers the answer depends on the methodology used and the assumptions made. The Social Security Adminsitration recently compared the *present value* of a worker's expected benefits with the *present value* of his or her contributions based on certain worker characteristics and actuarial assumptions.[8] The present value of the benefits (or contributions) is the amount that, when invested at a specified rate of interest, would provide out of principal and interest enough money to pay the benefits (or contributions) for the average worker with specified characteristics. Possible benefits (or contributions) are adjusted for (1) the likelihood that the possible benefits (or contributions) will be paid (for example, by mortality rates) and (2) the timing of the payment that permits an interest discount similar to that described in Chapter 2.

Table 4.4 summarizes the main findings. A "future value" ratio of 2.00 or more indicates that the present value of the benefits is at least twice the present value of the contributions, that is, the benefits exceed the combined contributions. A ratio of 1.0 or more but less than 2.0 indicates that the employee will receive his or her money's worth with respect to the employee contribution but not the combined contribution. A ratio of less than 1.0 indicates that on a private equity basis the worker can expect to receive less in benefits than his or her contributions.

Table 4.4 shows that for most workers in the categories studied the ratios exceed 2.0, sometimes substantially. The highest ratio, 11.78, is for a worker with dependents and very low earnings who entered the system on January 1, 1978, at age 52. The lowest ratio, 0.92, is for an unmarried male worker with maximum earnings who entered the system at age 22. Only one ratio out of the 105 shown is less than 1.0. Of the 105, 23 are below 2.0. All 23 are for unmarried workers; 17 of the 23 apply to workers with high or maximum earnings. This analysis suggests that most workers will receive benefits that are worth more than their own contributions; many will receive more in benefits than the combined employer–employee contributions. Workers with high earnings and no dependents will receive the least for their contributions.

The findings are sensitive to the assumptions made. Some of the key assumptions in the Social Security Administration study are as follows:

1 Unmarried workers will remain unmarried.

2 Married workers are male with a nonworking wife of the same age and two children, 25 and 27 years younger than the parents, who will remain eligible for children's benefits until age 22.

3 Annual percentage increases in earnings will decline from 7.80% in 1979 to 5.75% in 1983 and later years. Annual percentage increases in consumer prices will decline from 5.20% in 1979 to 4.00% in 1982 and later years.

4 The interest rate will be 6.6%.

[8]O. R. Nichols and R. G. Schreitmueller, "Some Comparisons of the Value of a Worker's Social Security Taxes and Benefits," *Actuarial Note No. 95*, April 1978, HEW Publication No. (SSA) 78-11500.

Table 4.4 Worker Becoming Covered in 1978: Illustrative OASDI Worker's Future Value Ratios

Age on January 1, 1978	Very Low Earnings	Low Earnings	Median Earnings	High Earnings	Maximum Earnings
		Unmarried male worker			
22	2.81	1.75[a]	1.41[a]	[a]	0.92[b]
27	3.25	2.02	1.62[a]	1.33[a]	1.06[a]
32	3.49	2.25	1.78[a]	1.49[a]	1.18[a]
37	3.60	2.49	1.92[a]	1.65[a]	1.32[a]
42	3.81	2.84	2.12	1.79[a]	1.51[a]
47	4.15	3.38	2.45	2.02	1.79[a]
52	5.27	4.30	3.08	2.48	2.14
		Married male worker with dependents			
22	6.33	3.95	3.20	2.62	2.10
27	7.64	4.77	3.87	3.17	2.52
32	8.06	5.21	4.12	3.47	2.75
37	8.25	5.70	4.39	3.78	3.02
42	8.59	6.44	4.81	4.07	3.43
47	9.22	7.58	5.50	4.54	4.01
52	11.78	9.47	6.83	5.48	4.74
		Unmarried female worker			
22	3.80	2.37	1.90[a]	1.56[a]	1.25[a]
27	4.42	2.75	2.21	1.82[a]	1.45[a]
32	4.79	3.09	2.45	2.05	1.62[a]
37	4.92	3.40	2.62	2.26	1.80[a]
42	5.14	3.84	2.89	2.44	2.06
47	5.49	4.55	3.31	2.73	2.42
52	6.80	5.73	4.12	3.31	2.87

Source: O. R. Nichols and R. G. Schreitmueller, "Some Comparisons of the Value of a Worker's Social Security Taxes and Benefits," *Actuarial Note No. 95,* April 1978, HEW Pub. No. (SSA) 78-11500, Table 1.

[a]Indicates ratio of 1.00 to 2.00.

[b]Indicates ratio below 1.00.

5 The mortality and disability rates will be those used in the 1977 Board of Trustees report.

6 The worker will retire at age 65.

The Social Security Administration warns that the ratios would have been lower if the assumptions had been changed in any one of the following ways:

1   The wife is older than the husband.

2   There are fewer children per married couple.

3   The parents are younger when the children are born.

4   Children leave school before age 22.

5   The annual percentage increases in earnings and the Consumer Price Index are low.

6   The annual percentage increase in a given worker's earnings are higher than the annual percentage increase in general wage levels.

7   The interest rate is higher.

8   Mortality rates are higher.

9   Disability rates are higher.

10   Disability termination rates are higher.

11   The retirement age goes up.

A change in the opposite direction for any of these variables would increase the ratios in Table 4.4.

If the scheduled contributions were increased or benefits lowered to reduce the actuarial deficiency explained above, all of these ratios would, of course, be reduced somewhat. As noted earlier, 1981 amendments have since lowered benefits.

Table 4.5 shows in some detail how 12 of the ratios in Table 4.4 were derived. Table 4.5, which allocates the benefits by category, is instructive because it illustrates how the benefits vary by (1) the peril involved, (2) whether there are dependents, and (3) the sex, age, and earnings of the worker. Retirement benefits are more costly than death and disability benefits. Dependents' benefits more than double the cost for married males. Unmarried female workers get more in benefits for their contributions than do unmarried males. Older entrants fare better than younger entrants; lower-pay workers better than higher-pay persons.

The Effect of OASDHI on Private Savings

Does OASDHI reduce private savings and capital formation? In 1974 Professor Martin Feldstein published a study in which he claimed that OASDHI reduces private savings by 38%.[9] He reasoned that private savings are less because OASDHI reduces the need to accumulate assets for retirement. Because OASDHI is financed on a pay-as-you-go basis, contributions to this program do not result in capital accumulation.

Professor Dennis Logue has questioned this conclusion.[10] He notes that plant

[9]For a recent statement see Martin Feldstein, "Social Security," Chapter II A in Michael J. Boskin (Ed.), *The Crisis in Social Security: Problems and Prospects,* 2nd ed. (San Francisco, Calif.: Institute for Contemporary Studies, 1978).

[10]Dennis E. Logue, "Social Security and Capital Formation," *Tuck Today,* June 1978, 16–19.

and equipment expenditures as a percentage of the gross national product have been fairly stable since 1950. He argues that people are clever enough to grasp the long-run impossibility of a system in which the present value of benefits exceeds the present value of taxes. To ease the burden on future generations, they either save more to offset future OASDHI taxes or make greater investments in human capital through education, technology, and so forth. What OASDHI *has* done is to permit individuals to achieve a target standard of living by investing in lower-risk, lower-return investments.

Four major empirical studies using U.S. time-series data to investigate the effects of OASDHI on private savings were recently reviewed by the Social Security Administration.[11] Professor Feldstein, for example, used the following basic equation:

Consumer
expenditures
$$\text{in year } t = a + b_1 \text{ (disposable personal income, year } t)$$
$$+ b_2 \text{ (disposable personal income, year } t - 1)$$
$$+ b_3 \text{ (gross retained earnings, year } t)$$
$$+ b_4 \text{ (net worth of households, year } t - 1)$$
$$+ b_5 \text{ (unemployment rate, year } t)$$
$$+ b_6 \text{ (social security wealth—present value of expected benefits, year } t)$$
$$+ \text{ an error term.}$$

According to the Social Security Administration, the empirical results for 1929–1971 suggest that OASDHI decreased savings only when the unemployment rate was excluded, but no justification exists for this exclusion. After also examining studies by Alicia Munnell, Robert Barro, and Michael Darby, the Social Security Administration concluded that either "(1) the analysis of U.S. time-series data cannot isolate the effect of the social security program on private saving or (2) the program does not have a significant effect on private saving."[12]

In May 1979 the four authors were given an opportunity to comment on this review in the *Social Security Bulletin*.[13] Martin Feldstein observed that more recent data supported his conclusion more strongly and reduced the ambiguity introduced by unemployment. Robert Barro agreed that many problems of economic conception, structural theory, and data severely limit the reliability of

[11]Louis Esposito, "Effect of Social Security on Saving: Review of Studies Using U.S. Time-Series Data," *Social Security Bulletin,* LXI, No. 5 (May 1978), 9–17.

[12]Ref. 10, p. 17.

[13]"Social Security and Private Saving: Another Look," *Social Security Bulletin,* XLII, No. 5 (May 1979), 33–40. See also Michael J. Boskin and Marc Robinson, "Social Security and Private Saving: Analytical Issues, Econometric Evidence, and Policy Limitations," *Special Study of Economic Change, Vol. 8: Social Security and Pensions: Programs of Equity and Security,* Studies Prepared for the Use of the Joint Economic Committee, Congress of the United States, 96th Congress, 2nd Session, pp. 38–64.

Table 4.5 Worker Becoming Covered in 1978: Components of Certain Figures Shown in Table 4.4 (Dollar Figures Are Present Values on January 1, 1978)

	Worker Becoming Covered at Age 22		Worker Becoming Covered at Age 42	
	Median Earnings	Maximum Earnings	Median Earnings	Maximum Earnings
I Male worker				
A Worker's covered earnings ($)	329,414	830,730	186,318	463,722
B Worker's OASDI taxes				
1 Amount	19,557	49,439	10,701	26,726
2 Percentage of covered earnings	5.9	6.0	5.7	5.8
C Benefits payable to unmarried worker				
1 Old-age ($)	20,856	34,635	19,652	35,105
2 Disability ($)[a]	6,648	11,003	3,076	5,302
3 Total benefits (1 plus 2) ($)	27,504	45,638	22,728	40,407
4 Worker's future value ratio (C.3 divided by B.1)[b]	1.41	0.92	2.12	1.51
5 Replacement Cost (C.3. as % of A) (%)	8.3	5.5	12.2	8.7
D Additional benefits payable to dependents of married worker				
1 Old-age (to spouse and surviving spouse) ($)	25,084	41,658	22,611	40,390
2 Disability ($)	1,313	1,924	21	44
3 Death before retirement ($)	8,708	14,477	6,145	10,946
4 Total benefits (1 + 2 + 3) ($)	35,105	58,059	28,777	51,380
E Total benefits payable to married worker and dependents				
1 Total benefits (C.3 + D.4) ($)	62,609	103,697	51,505	91,787
2 Worker's future value ratio (E.1 divided by B.1)[b]	3.20	2.10	4.81	3.43
3 Replacement cost (E.1 as % of A) (%)	19.0	12.5	27.6	19.8

II Unmarried female worker

A Worker's covered earnings ($)	343,465	866,737	195,307	486,749
B Worker's OASDI taxes				
1 Amount ($)	20,421	51,654	11,249	28,129
2 Percentage of covered earnings	5.9	6.0	5.8	5.8
C Benefits payable to unmarried worker				
1 Old-Age ($)	32,187	53,453	29,466	52,636
2 Disability ($)[a]	6,713	11,138	3,039	5,226
3 Total benefits (1 + 2) ($)	38,900	64,591	32,505	57,862
4 Worker's future value ratio (C.3 divided by B.1)[b]	1.90	1.25	2.89	2.06
5 Replacement cost (C.3 as % of A) (%)	11.3	7.5	16.6	11.9

Source: O. R. Nichols and R. G. Schreitmueller, "Some Comparisons of the Value of a Worker's Social Security Taxes and Benefits," "Actuarial Note No. 95, April 1978, HEW Pub. No. (SSA) 78-11500, Table 3.

[a]Includes lump-sum death benefit value.

[b]Indicates that figures are also shown in Table 4.4.

estimates of the effect of social security on saving and capital formation. No present evidence exists, however, in his opinion, that supports the view that the expansion of OASDHI has curtailed capital formation in the United States. Michael Darby argued that the empirical results *do* support the hypothesis that OASDHI decreased private saving. If someone starts out with the strong belief that OASDHI reduced private saving, he observes that the data do not lead to a rejection of that hypothesis. Indeed the data support that hypothesis more strongly than the hypothesis of unaffected saving. Finally, Alicia Munnell expressed her current view that OASDHI has probably not had a major impact on saving. She noted that saving was reduced by OASDHI benefits exceeding the level of intrafamily transfers they replaced. However, this reduction was probably offset by an induced retirement effect that encouraged individuals to save more over a shorter working life for a longer retirement. In the future, however, she expected OASDHI to have a discernible negative impact on saving. OASHI benefits have increased substantially in recent years, far exceeding the level of intrafamily transfers that would have otherwise occurred. In addition, in the future workers will probably have longer working lives, enabling them to reduce their saving rate over this period.

Contribution Rate or Base Changes?

Contributions can be increased by raising either the contribution rate or the contribution base; the impact of the increase is different, however, because lower-pay workers and their industrial employers are much less affected by an increase in the earnings base. Another consideration is that as the wage base rises the amount of additional revenue produced by further increases becomes less and less. Some additional views on the optimum size of this base have already been presented in the benefit evaluation section in Chapter 3.

The 1977 amendments raised the contribution bases for 1979–1981 to a higher level than automatic adjustments were expected to develop. The expected result was to subject about 91% of the total covered payroll to tax after 1980. A Senate-passed proposal, not adopted by a conference committee, would have raised the base for *employer* contributions to $50,000 for 1979–1984, and $75,000 from 1975 on. Early in the next century the employee contribution base would have risen enough to reachieve parity. The Carter Administration proposed no limit on the employer contribution base by 1981.

The 1979 Advisory Council recommended that instead of the legislated ad hoc increases in 1980 and 1981 the 1979 base for employers ($22,900) should be increased only by the percentage increase in average national earings. In their opinion a higher base would extend OASDI coverage to a level where forced savings are unnecessary and where workers should rely on private pensions and savings. A narrow majority would be willing to consider having the *employer* tax based on the entire wage, but not in the near future because of the inflationary effect of such a change on employers.

Administration

OASI administrative expenses are about 1.3% of the benefits paid, 0.11% of taxable payroll. The administration of the system is highly mechanized and efficiently conducted. In addition, death and old-age benefits are relatively easy to handle, the system incurs no selling expenses because it is compulsory, the program enjoys huge economies of scale, and the Social Security Administration escapes some of the taxes and other expenses incurred by private insurers.

The National Commission on Social Security

As indicated in Chapter 3, all of the issues discussed above plus others have also been reviewed by a National Commission on Social Security established by the December 1977 amendments. This bipartisan Commission included five members, one of whom was the chairman, appointed by President Carter, and four members appointed by Congress. The Commission was charged with studying the coverage, benefits, and financing of OASDHI plus alternative programs and the integration of OASDHI with private programs. The Commission's major recommendations concerning OASI coverage, retirement age, benefits, financing, and administration, which were released in 1981,[14] are presented below. In addition to summarizing the views of this Commission this listing provides a useful review of Chapters 3 and 4.

COVERAGE

1   Coverage should be extended in 1982 (on a mandatory basis) to all governmental employees not now under a retirement system.

2   Coverage should be extended in 1982 (on a mandatory basis) to the President, the Vice President, members of the Cabinet, the Commissioner of Social Security, and members of Congress. Civil Service Retirement benefits and contributions for these officials should be reduced by the OASDI benefits accruing and the OASDI taxes, respectively.

3   Coverage should be extended in 1982 (on a mandatory basis) to all employees of nonprofit organizations (except that any such organization operated by a religious sect opposed to public insurance could opt out).

4   Coverage should be extended in 1985 to all new governmental employees in positions covered by a retirement system now in existence.

5   The option for state and local governments and nonprofit organizations to withdraw from coverage that had previously been elected should be eliminated after a one-year grace period.

6   The portion of windfall benefits accruing for governmental employees with

---

[14]*Social Security in America's Future,* Final Report of the National Commission on Social Security, Washington, D.C., 1981.

future periods of noncovered governmental employment should be eliminated.

7   A Federal Employee Benefit Protection Board should be created to review and make recommendations to the President and Congress on the implementation of coverage for federal employees and the way in which existing government employee plans should be modified and coordinated with OASDI and Medicare. The Board should include representatives of federal employee organizations.

8   The minimum earnings requirements for coverage should be increased as follows: domestic workers, from $50 per quarter to $150; casual labor, from $100 per year to $150 per quarter; and self-employed persons, from $400 per year to $600. (The test of $150 per year for farm workers should be retained, but the alternate test of 20 days per year of work for one employer should be eliminated.)

9   All payments made directly by an employer to an employee on account of sickness should be considered as wages, but only for periods up to six months after the last month worked.

RETIREMENT AGE

1   Beginning in the year 2001, the minimum age at which unreduced retirement benefits are available should be increased gradually from 65 to 68, reaching 68 in 2012. The corresponding minimum ages for other types of benefits (including those for spouses, widows, and widowers) should similarly be increased, and this should also be done in tandem for persons claiming reduced benefits at earlier ages.

2   Larger increases in benefits should be available for persons who delay retirement beyond the normal retirement age. (Those reaching 65 before 1982 would not qualify, because under present law they are more favorably treated in the computation of benefits with regard to earnings after 65.)

BENEFITS

1   The special minimum benefit, applicable to persons with long periods of coverage and low earnings, should be changed by increasing the maximum number of years creditable therefor from 30 to 35 and permitting up to 10 years of child care (for care of children under six years of age) to be counted as creditable years for these purposes.

2   Widow's and widower's benefits for persons who are widowed before age 60 (and before the deceased spouse reached age 60) should be computed by indexing the earnings record of the deceased worker by wages during the period between the worker's death and the time benefits are payable. (At present such indexing is done by prices.)

3   The automatic benefit increases resulting from changes in the CPI should be

limited when, over a two-year period, the CPI has risen more rapidly than wages. (The increase should then be reduced by the excess of the two-year average annual rise in the CPI over that in wages.) This procedure should only be used when the benefit increase that would be based on the CPI rise is 5% or more. There should be a retroactive "catch up" in future years, if wages rise more rapidly than the CPI, to make up for such reductions.

4   The automatic benefit increases resulting from changes in the CPI should be based on the CPI for all urban consumers, rather than on that for urban clerical and manual workers only.

FINANCING

1   The tax rate schedule for OASDI should be changed so that the program is adequately financed over the next 75 years and maintains, on the average, a contingency reserve of at least one year's outgo.

2   One-half of the cost of the HI program should be financed from general revenues, beginning in 1983.

3   The other half of the HI program should be financed from payroll taxes. The payroll tax rate schedule for HI should be revised so that the program is adequately financed over the next 75 years and maintains, on the average, a contingency reserve of at least one year's outgo.

4   In general, the reduction in the HI payroll tax rates (as described in recommendations 2 and 3 should be utilized for the purposes of financing the OASDI program (as described in recommendation 1).

5   In recognition of the general revenues cost for reducing the employee tax rate for HI, a $2\frac{1}{2}\%$ surcharge should be added to the federal personal income tax.

6   The combined employer–employee tax rate for OASDI and HI combined should not exceed 18%—9% for employers and 9% for employees. When this would otherwise occur, the excess over 18% should be financed from general revenue payments to OASDI.

7   The tax rate for the self-employed should continue to be $1\frac{1}{2}$ times the employee rate for OASDI and the same as the employee rate for HI.

8   The maximum taxable earnings base for both OASDI and HI for both 1985 and 1986 should be maintained at its 1984 level (estimated to be $39,000) and then automatically adjusted thereafter.

9   Borrowing should be authorized among the OASI, DI, and HI trust funds, on a permanent basis, repayable with interest.

10   As an emergency measure only, borrowing should be authorized by any of the trust funds from the U.S. Treasury until the end of 1985, the loans to be repayable with interest.

11   The operations of the OASI, DI, HI, and Supplementary Medical Insurance

trust funds should be removed from the unified budget of the U.S. government.

12 The chief actuarial officers should provide a certification in the annual Trustees' Reports as to the assumptions and methodology used in preparing their actuarial cost estimates and valuations.

13 No changes should be made in the financing of the Supplementary Medical Insurance program, because it is now adequately funded.

14 Payments to the Railroad Retirement Account under the financial interchange provisions between the Social Security and Railroad Retirement programs should not be made in those cases where the Railroad Retirement program does not pay benefits to the individuals for whom such payments are made (e.g., divorced widows).

ADMINISTRATION

1 An independent government agency should be established to administer the OASDI, Medicare, Supplemental Security Income, and Medicaid programs.

2 Additional resources should be made available to improve the administration and delivery of services to beneficiaries. Arbitrary limits on personnel and resources for the administration of these programs should be eliminated.

3 The W-2 income tax forms should provide more specific information as to the meaning of terms and the allocation of the OASDI and HI payroll taxes.

4 A new OASDI court should be established to take over the functions of the federal district courts in appeals of OASDI cases.

5 A special index to measure price changes for the elderly should be constructed and considered for use in indexing OASDI benefits. Separate indexes should not be used for every beneficiary group.

6 The windfall portion of benefits arising from future periods of noncovered government employment (due to the weighted benefit formula) should be eliminated.

7 Benefits payable to children age 18–21 attending school should be suspended when the beneficiary is not attending school full-time, and greater efforts should be made to collect overpayments of these benefits.

8 When either spouse elects to receive a separate benefit check, the total benefit payable to the two spouses should be divided equally between them.

9 Marriage and remarriage should be eliminated as terminating events for benefit entitlement.

EARNINGS TEST

1 The earnings test, which measures whether a worker has retired, should be retained.

2 The age at which the earnings test no longer applies, which is scheduled to

be lowered from 72 to 70 in 1982, should be left at age 72 (until 2001, when it should move up in tandem with the minimum age for unreduced retirement benefits).

3 To partially offset the effect of the earnings test in withholding tax-free OASDI benefits a refundable credit under the federal income tax should be provided, increasing with the age of the individual. (This would not be available to those reaching age 65 before 1982.)

Reagan Administration and Congressional Proposals

Two other indications of how OASDI might be changed in the future are the early 1981 proposals of (1) the Reagan Administration and (2) the House Subcommittee on Social Security that have not yet been adopted by Congress.

Reagan Administration Proposals

Among the President's proposals that were not adopted, the most controversial was a reduction in early retirement benefits. For example, workers retiring at age 62 would receive 55% of their unreduced benefit instead of the current 80%. Opponents were particularly upset about the fact that this reduction would become effective immediately, thus upsetting the plans of many workers who had planned to retire early in the next few years. A second proposal that would further reduce early retirement benefits would move from age 62 to age 65 the end of the time span over which the AIME is calculated. A third related proposal would eliminate dependents' benefits for the children of early retirees. No change was proposed in the retirement age, but to encourage later retirements the earnings test limit would be increased gradually to $20,000 in 1985 and eliminated thereafter.

A major proposal that attracted less attention than one might expect would until 1987 increase the bend points in the PIA formula less than the amounts indicated by the increase in average national earnings. The effect of this change would be to reduce for most workers the currently scheduled PIA relative to the AIME. Under current law the wage replacement ratio for an average worker retiring at 65 is about 41%. This proposal would reduce the replacement rate by 1987 to about 38%. Because all other benefits are expressed as a percent of the PIA, they would also be reduced accordingly.

The Administration would also defer cost of living adjustments in OASI benefits to October's checks instead of July's. Also, instead of basing the adjustment on changes in the CPI from the first quarter of the previous year to the first quarter of the current year the President would calculate the change from the end of June in the previous year to the end of June in the current year.

Under another Administration proposal workers who spend part of their career in non-OASI covered employment would have their OASI benefits reduced by benefits they receive from their noncovered employment.

Still another proposal would apply the special family maximum applied since 1980 to disability benefits to retirement and survivor benefits as well. The President would also have eliminated completely the $255 lump sum death benefit.

Currently, sick leave pay is not subject to OASDHI taxes. The Administration would tax this pay and include it in the calculation of the AIME.

House Subcommittee on Social Security

The House Subcommittee on Social Security, headed by Representative Pickle, is a subcommittee of the Ways and Means Committee. The major recommendation in a bill introduced by Representative Pickle, but not yet endorsed by the Subcommittee, is one not proposed by President Reagan. Starting in 1990 Representative Pickle would over a 10 year period raise the normal retirement age from 65 to 68, with early retirement being possible at age 65 with reduced benefits.

Like the President, Representative Pickle would reduce OASI benefits by the amount of benefits from noncovered employment and defer cost of living adjustments to October payments.

The Pickle bill would prohibit covered groups of state, local, and nonprofit employees from withdrawing from OASDHI.

Under this bill, divorced wives whose marriage had lasted at least 25 years would at the time of the divorce be credited with half the combined earnings of the husband and wife during the course of their marriage.

Representative Pickle did not yet recommend but the Subcommittee has been considering a plan to reduce the early retirement at 62 benefit from 80% to 70% of the age 65 level. Instead of reducing these benefits immediately, however, this proposal would gradually phase in this change beginning in 1990, thus giving potential early retirees time to adjust. Another proposal under consideration would raise the benefit for those retiring at age 68 to 140% of the age 65 level.

A final proposal would base cost of living adjustments on a Personal Consumption Expenditure index rather than the CPI. This index is not expected to increase as rapidly as the CPI index.

The Robertson Freedom Plan

One of the most radical proposals for changing OASI has been advanced by A. Haeworth Robertson, who was Chief Actuary of the Social Security Administration from 1975 to 1978. Although this proposal is generally considered to have little chance of being adopted, we discuss it here because it is thought-provoking and presents a substantially different point of view.[15]

Robertson argues that old age can be anticipated and financial plans made accordingly. The only reason for the government to be involved in any way is the following contingencies—inflation, extraordinary life spans, and misfortunes out-

[15]A. Haeworth Robertson, *The Coming Revolution in Social Security* (McLean, Va.: Security Press, 1981), Chapters 27 and 29.

side the control of an individual in planning for old age. Similarly, an individual should be able to anticipate and prepare through personal saving and private life insurance for the needs of his or her family and estate in the event of his or her death. The federal government should protect the person against inflation, poor planning, and genuine misfortunes.

For everyone who will be age 45 and over on July 4, 1984, the program would remain unchanged. For younger persons, however, Robertson would establish a four-part old-age and survivorship program:

1 A mandatory Senior Citizen Benefit program. At age 70 each person who had been a resident citizen for at least 25 years would receive a monthly pension sufficient to provide a minimum level of support ($250 a month, say, if this benefit had been available in 1980). This amount would be increased each year following retirement to match increases in some cost of living index. This benefit would be financed through appropriations from general revenues.

2 Individuals would be permitted to invest up to 10% of their earnings in Freedom Bonds. These bonds would pay no interest, but their value would be indexed to maintain their purchasing power. At retirement age these bonds could be exchanged for a pension that would be indexed.

3 The government would provide cost of living supplements to workers receiving private pensions, none of which are ever likely for cost reasons to increase pensions following retirement to match increases in living costs.

4 There would be no death benefits except that survivors could receive the face value of the Freedom Bonds.

5 A welfare program would continue as a supplement to the Freedom Plan to provide benefits to needy survivors of deceased persons who had not made adequate financial arrangements.

The President's Commission on Pension Policy

In early 1981 a President's Commission on Pension Policy, appointed by President Carter, submitted its final report on public and private pension plans. The major recommendations of this Commission, many of which apply to OASDI, are summarized at the end of Chapter 5.[16]

SUMMARY

Except for the special benefits for some persons turning 72 before 1968, OASI benefits are financed entirely by contributions paid by the worker and the em-

---

[16]*Coming of Age: Toward a National Retirement Policy* (Washington, D.C.: President's Commission on Pension Policy, 1981).

ployer. The 1982 OASDI contribution rate on each is 5.40% (including 0.825% for DI) on the first $32,400 of the employee's earnings. Self-employed persons pay 8.05% (1.2375% for DI). The employee and employer tax rates are scheduled to rise gradually to 6.20% (1.10% for DI) from 1990 on. The wage base will be adjusted each year to match increases in average national earnings.

The OASDI funds collected less the DI contributions are appropriated to the OASI Trust Fund. The fund balance is invested in long-term government obligations.

OASI is administered by the Social Security Administration, which is part of the Department of Health and Human Services.

According to 1981 actuarial projections, using two sets of intermediate assumptions, over the next 75 years OASI benefits and administrative costs, expressed as a percentage of covered payrolls, will on the average exceed contributions expressed as a percentage of payroll by 1.61 or 2.44. The actuarial balance was estimated to be 0.47% or −0.31% the first 25 years, a 1.26% or 2.01% deficit the next 25 years, and a 4.03% or 5.00% deficit the last 25 years. The ratio of OASDI beneficiaries to workers was expected to increase from about one-third in 1980 to over one-half in 2025.

According to 1977 actuarial projections the 75-year deficit was an alarming 8.20%. The 1977 amendments corrected a technical error in the automatic adjustments, which explained almost half of that deficit. They also raised the tax rates and the wage base.

The 1981 short-range projections showed that during each of the next five years OASI program expenditures would exceed income, causing the OASI Trust Fund to be exhausted by late 1982.

Major financing issues involve (1) the use of general revenues, (2) the role of the trust funds, (3) whether workers receive their money's worth from the system, (4) the effect of OASDHI on private savings, and (5) the trade-offs between increasing the contribution base and increasing the contribution rate.

SUGGESTIONS FOR ADDITIONAL READING

1981 Annual Report of the Board of Trustees of the Federal Old Age and Survivors Insurance and Disability Insurance Trust Funds, 97th Congress, 1st Session, House Document No. 97–66, July 2, 1981.
This 1981 report explains the methodology used to make long-, medium-, and short-range actuarial projections for the OASI and DI trust funds.

Ball, Robert M. *Social Security, Today and Tomorrow.* New York: Columbia University Press, 1978.
A clear, comprehensive description and analysis of OASDHI plus recommendations for change by the Commissioner of Social Security under Presidents Kennedy, Johnson, and Nixon.

Boskin, Michael J. (Ed.). *The Crisis in Social Security: Problems and Prospects,* 2nd ed. San Francisco, Calif.: Institute for Contemporary Studies, 1978.
A thought-provoking collection of papers by authors with different viewpoints defining the major issues and policy options.

Brinker, Paul A. *Economic Insecurity and Social Security.* New York: Appleton-Century-Crofts, 1968.
Chapters 3 and 4 deal with OASI.

Brittain, John A. *The Payroll Tax for Social Security.* Washington, D.C.: The Brookings Institution, 1972.
An in-depth analysis of the method of financing OASDHI.

Campbell, Rita Ricardo. *Social Security: Promise and Reality.* Stanford, Calif.: Hoover Institution Press, 1977.
An analysis of OASDHI by a member of the 1975 Advisory Council on Social Security.

Chen, Yung-Ping. *Social Security in a Changing Society.* Bryn Mawr, Pa.: McCahan Foundation, 1980.
Chapters, 2, 4, and 5 of this highly readable short volume cover the OASDI program.

Coming of Age: Toward A National Retirement Income Policy. Washington, D.C.: President's Commission on Pension Policy, 1981.
The final report of the Commission appointed by President Carter to study both public and private pensions.

Derthick, Martha. *Policymaking for Social Security.* Washington, D.C.: The Brookings Institution, 1979.
An analysis of the reasons why so little political conflict accompanied the development of OASDHI during its first four decades. The author cites the competence of the program executives, the technical knowledge required, and the attractiveness of the program because it was incremental, promised specific benefits in return for taxes, and contained many compromises and ambiguities. The author urges more serious partisan debates in the future.

Munnell, Alicia H. *The Future of Social Security.* Washington, D.C.: The Brookings Institution, 1977.
A comprehensive review and analysis of OASDI and its relationship to other sources of retirement income.

Myers, Robert J. *Social Security.* 2nd ed. Homewood, Ill.: Richard D. Irwin, 1981.
Chapters 2 through 10 provide an authoritative discussion of OASDHI by the 1947–1970 Chief Actuary of the Social Security Administration. Mr. Myers is now the Administration's Deputy Commissioner for Policy. Chapter 10 presents the methodology for OASDHI actuarial cost estimates.

Pechman, Joseph A., Henry J. Aaron, and Michael K. Taussig. *Social Security: Perspectives for Reform.* Washington, D.C.: The Brookings Institution, 1968.
A comprehensive, thought-provoking analysis of OASDHI. Professor Aaron served later as Chairman of the 1979 Advisory Council on Social Security, of which Dr. Pechman was a member.

Rejda, George E. *Social Insurance and Economic Security.* Englewood Cliffs, N.J.: Prentice-Hall, 1976.
Chapters 5 through 7 of this comprehensive book discuss OASDI coverage, benefits, financing, and administration.

Report to the President of the Committee on Economic Security. Washington, D.C.: Government Printing Office, 1935.
The committee report that led to the passage of the original Social Security Act.

Reports of the 1979 Advisory Council on Social Security. Washington, D.C.: Government Printing Office, 1979.
This report of the latest Advisory Council is valuable reading not only for the recommendations made but for its discussion of present provisions and operations.

Robertson, A. Haeworth. *The Coming Revolution in Social Security.* McLean, Va.: Security Press, 1981.
In addition to presenting the author's Freedom Plan, this book describes clearly, comprehensively, and interestingly the OASDHI program.

Social Security in America's Future, Final Report of the National Commission on Social Security. Washington, D.C., 1981.
The final report of the Commission established by December 1977 amendments to the Social Security Act.

Social Security and Medicare Explained. Chicago, Ill.: Commerce Clearing House, latest edition.
A complete, easy-to-read description of OASDHI.

U.S. Department of Health, Education, and Welfare. *Annual Report.* Washington, D.C.: Government Printing Office, latest edition.
Comments on the current operations of OASDHI.

Chapter Five

Employee-Benefit Plans and
Other Private Approaches
to Death and Old Age

OASI provides a floor of protection against the financial losses caused by premature death and old age. Most families, however, particularly those in the middle- and upper-income groups, seek to supplement this compulsory coverage with private insurance and savings.

A family's insurance program usually includes three layers of protection: (1) OASI, (2) employee-benefit plans, and (3) individual life insurance and annuities. This chapter addresses itself to the top two layers in this program. Because this text focuses primarily on social insurance, the discussion of these private supplements will be much less detailed than that on OASI. After describing the development of modern employee-benefit plans and the reasons for their phenomenal growth, their principal characteristics and operations will be explained.

The treatment of individual life insurance will be limited to a discussion of the principal types of contracts and their uses, some major contract provisions, and the ways in which individual life insurance might be combined with employee-benefit plans and OASI to develop an integrated protection program.

The chapter concludes with an evaluation of these two layers of protection.

EMPLOYEE-BENEFIT PLANS

The Social Security Administration defines an employee-benefit plan as

> . . . any type of plan sponsored or initiated unilaterally or jointly by employers and employees and providing benefits that stem from the employment relationship and are not underwritten or paid directly by government (Federal, State, or local). In general, the intent is to include plans that provide in an orderly predetermined fashion for (1) income maintenance when regular earnings are cut off because of

death, accident, sickness, retirement, or unemployment and (2) benefits to meet medical expenses associated with illness or injury.

This definition, which will be used in this book, excludes nondirect-wage compensation such as paid holidays, jury and voting pay allowances, Christmas bonuses, and purchase discounts. It also excludes the newly developed employee-benefit plans described later in this chapter that provide automobile and home-owners' insurance. This chapter will focus on the death and retirement benefits provided by these plans.

Scope and Growth

Data on two aspects of employee-benefit plans—persons covered and contributions paid—illustrate their present scope and growth. Table 5.1 shows the proportion of wage and salary workers who in 1976 had some protection against death and old age. For comparison purposes, Table 5.1 presents similar information for other types of benefits. Data are not available for later years.

Over three-fourths of all wage and salary workers were covered under death benefit plans. Almost half of all private employees (62% of full time workers age 25 and older) under retirement plans. Coverage under both types of plans has increased substantially since 1950; the rate of growth was much greater in the 1950s than in the 1960s and 1970s.

In 1976 employers and employees contributed about 0.59% of their total wages and salaries to death benefit plans, and 4.73% to retirement plans. Both contribution percentages depend on the number of employees covered, the be-

Table 5.1 Estimated Coverage of Wage and Salary Workers Under Employee-Benefit Plans, 1976

Type of Benefit	Percentage of Employed Wage and Salary Workers
Private and public employees	
Life insurance and death benefits	77.5
Accidental death and dismemberment	54.6
Hospitalization	71.0
Surgical	68.7
Nonsurgical physician's care	68.8
Major-medical expense	36.4
Private employees only	
Temporary disability	47.0
Long-term disability	16.8
Pension	46.0
Supplemental unemployment	2.8

Source: Social Security Administration.

Table 5.2 Estimated Total Employer and Employee Contributions Paid Under Employee-Benefit Plans, As a Percentage of All Wages and Salaries, 1950, 1960, 1970, and 1976

Type of Benefit	1950	1960	1970	1976
Private and public employees				
Life insurance and death benefits	0.34	0.54	0.68	0.59
Accidental death and dismemberment	0.01	0.03	0.04	0.04
Hospitalization	0.40	0.96	1.44	1.86
Surgical				
Nonsurgical physician's care	0.21	0.49	0.76	1.20
Major-medical expense	—	0.18	0.44	0.78
Private employees only				
Temporary disability	0.41	0.53	0.71	0.76
Long-term disability	—	—		
Pension	1.67	2.46	3.25	4.73
Supplemental unemployment	—	0.05	0.03	0.04
Total				

Source: Same as Table 5.1.

nefits provided, and the budgeting patterns over time. As indicated in Table 5.2, these percentages have increased substantially since 1950.

According to the latest annual survey of 922 firms by the Chamber of Commerce of the United States, in 1979 employee-benefit plans, broadly defined, averaged 36.6% of the payroll of these employers.[1] These firms covered a broad spectrum of sizes and industries, with the number of employees ranging from fewer than 100 to more than 5,000. The Chamber's broad definition includes any arrangement for compensation other than direct wages. Consequently, in addition to the types of benefits included in Tables 5.1 and 5.2, the Chamber definition includes legally required payments for employee security such as OASDHI contributions and non-security-related payments such as payments for holidays not worked, vacations, Christmas bonuses, and suggestion awards. The legally required payments for employee benefits totaled 9% of the payroll. Private employee benefits, as more narrowly defined in this text, were almost 15% of the payroll, or more than one-third of the total employee-benefit payments.

Development

Employee-benefit plans have clearly played an increasingly important role in the average worker's search for economic security. The characteristics of these plans

[1] *Employee Benefits 1979* (Washington, D.C.: Chamber of Commerce of the United States, 1980), p. 8. Private employee-benefit payments included pensions, payments in case of death or poor health, paid sick leave, dental expense benefits, separation or termination pay allowances, and contributions to profit-sharing and employee thrift plans plus non-security-related benefits.

are discussed later in this chapter, but first we shall look at their historical background.

At the turn of the century the social and economic status of the average worker was far from utopian.[2] Most workers were expected to solve the problems caused by death, disability, and old age on their own, but few were financially able to do so. Some workers, however, belonged to mutual benefit associations, which provided small benefits in case of death or disability. These associations included the employees of a given firm or the members of a trade union. Participation was almost always voluntary, and many workers did not join even though they were eligible. Employees usually managed the plans, with the employer contributing directly to the cost in about one-third of the plans. The employer contributed indirectly to the cost of other plans by performing some of the administrative duties or permitting employees to handle them on company time.[3]

Very few employees, aside from railroad workers, received company pensions when they retired. Most of the pension plans that did exist were informal plans, with the amount and duration of each pension being determined by the employer at the date of retirement. Pensions were paid out of current income and varied with that income. There were a few formal pension plans that contained a formula for determining the benefit, but there was no guarantee that the given pension might not be discontinued. Since these pension funds also operated on a pay-as-you-go basis or, at best, with a partial reserve, the discontinuance or reduction of these benefits was a distinct possibility, and often happened.

Because each of the mutual benefit associations and pension funds covered a small number of persons, the benefit payments tended to vary greatly from year to year. This was especially noticeable in the case of death and disability, and many of the mutual benefit associations either failed or faced financial difficulties because of adverse loss experience in a single year.

In 1910 Montgomery Ward and Company decided to increase the death and disability benefits provided by its mutual benefit association. The company was concerned about possible unstable loss experience and thought that this risk could be eliminated by insuring the benefits with a commercial insurer. The negotiations with insurers were lengthy because the idea was novel, but a group insurance contract was finally issued in 1912.[4] All employees in Chicago and Kansas City who had worked for the company for at least six months were covered, regardless of their individual insurability status. The company paid the entire premium. Because of the savings involved in wholesaling the benefits, the cost of the group protection was less than that of equivalent individual insurance contracts.

During this period employers were becoming increasingly interested in provid-

[2]See Louise Wolters Ilse, *Group Insurance and Employee Retirement Plans* (Englewood Cliffs, N.J.: Prentice-Hall, 1953).

[3]L. W. Ilse, *Group Insurance and Employee Retirement Plans* (Englewood Cliffs, N.J.: Prentice-Hall, 1953), p. 24.

[4]See Ref. 3, Chapter 2 for a more detailed discussion.

ing death and disability protection for their employees, and the new group life insurance and group health insurance contracts appealed to them. Several reasons have been advanced to explain this employer interest in welfare benefits: some argue that employers became more humanitarian and wanted to improve the lot of the workers for unselfish reasons; others believe that selfish motives predominated. According to the latter, employers began to realize that a worker is more productive if he or she does not have to worry about the possible or actual financial losses caused by death or poor health; he or she becomes more loyal to the firm and is less likely to leave it or to strike against the employer. Still others believe that employers were aware of the growing power of the labor movement and attempted to wrest the initiative from labor leaders. Certainly not all employers had the same motives, and many were probably motivated by all three factors. Part of the movement can also be credited to the salesmanship of the insurance industry.

Labor unions initially opposed the new group insurance idea as an example of paternalism that would destroy the union movement. Fraternal associations and a large segment of the commercial insurance industry also questioned the soundness of the idea, because there was no individual underwriting. They also argued that the contracts were discriminatory, threatened the continued existence of individual insurance, and emphasized term insurance,[5] which they considered to be unsatisfactory except in special instances. The press and the general public, however, were generally sympathetic to the plan.

In order to assure sound underwriting and placate opposition in the insurance industry, many states passed legislation that limited the conditions under which group insurance could be written and listed certain provisions, the sense of which had to be included in every group insurance contract. Unions generally remained opposed to employer-sponsored benefits, but in the 1920s many unions began to insure their own members under group insurance plans, in some cases forming their own insurance companies to underwrite the plans.

In 1926 the Amalgamated Association of Street and Electric Railway Employees became the first union to introduce life and disability insurance into a collective bargaining agreement.[6] Although collective bargaining agreements were to become an important force in the growth of group insurance in later years, until the 1940s most unions preferred to press directly for higher wages, shorter hours, and improved working conditions, and not for these "fringes."

The pension movement also grew, but much less rapidly. Over 200 new plans, all self-insured, were established between 1910 and 1920. Pension costs, of course, were much higher than the cost of other fringe benefits. The growth in pension plans that did occur was due to the increased employer interest already discussed.

---

[5]Insurance payable if death occurs within the specified term. No cash values are accumulated under this type of insurance (see later in this chapter).

[6]L. W. Ilse, *Group Insurance and Employee Retirement Plans,* (Englewood Cliffs, N.J.: Prentice-Hall, 1953), p. 339.

However, in connection with pensions, two additional reasons for this employer interest should be added to the list: first, pension plans made it possible to retire older persons in a more graceful fashion when their usefulness declined; second, promotion lanes were continually being opened for younger employees, and their incentives increased as a result.

Shortly after 1920 some employers, impressed by the success of the group life insurers, agreed to insure their pension plans on a group basis with commercial insurers. The major advantage to be gained through such an approach was the contractual guarantee of the insurer.[7] In the late 1920s insured pension plans became popular, and during the 1930s and early 1940s most of the new pension plans were insured plans.

During World War II there was a tremendous increase in the importance of employee-benefit plans. Wage increases were limited under the wartime government stabilization program, but death, retirement, and other security benefits customarily were not. Therefore many employers, on their own or, more commonly, through collective bargaining, substituted insurance benefits for wage increases. The high excess profits tax structure reduced the actual cost to employers. Employees also benefited taxwise because the employer's contributions to a plan qualified with the Internal Revenue Service were not considered taxable income to the employees.[8]

This growth continued after the war as many of the larger unions pressed for and obtained welfare benefit clauses in their collective bargaining agreements. Pensions were highlighted in these union demands. Some unions argued that the depreciation and obsolescence of manpower are proper charges on industry. (This argument has been attacked on the ground that a person ages even if he or she does not work.) A more common and powerful argument advanced by the unions held that pensions were deferred wages. Current wages were reduced in order to provide pension benefits. However, unions were willing to accept plans under which the employees lost their deferred wages if they terminated their employment prior to retirement age. This concession was probably a wise tactic at the time because it reduced the cost of pensions to employers. Coverage under self-insured plans also began to grow more rapidly than coverage under insured plans because of the greater flexibility they permitted with respect to benefit formulas, budgeting arrangements, and types of investments.

An important bench mark in the pension movement was the establishment of the United Mine Workers Retirement Plan, which became effective in 1947. The plan initially provided, in addition to certain death and accidental injury and sickness benefits, a pension for workers age 60 with 20 years of service. The fund is administered by trustees representing the union, the public, and the coal operators, and it is financed entirely by the operators through the payment of a "royalty" rate per ton of coal mined.

[7]The relative merits of insured and self-insured pension plans are discussed later in this chapter.
[8]This point is more extensively discussed on page 147.

Two years later the U.S. Supreme Court rendered two important decisions. In 1946 the Inland Steel Company of Chicago had refused to bargain with the United Steel Workers on the issue of a compulsory retirement age in an existing retirement plan. The National Labor Relations Board (NLRB) ruled in 1948 that pensions were a form of wages and that the provisions of a pension plan were conditions of employment. Therefore the company was required to bargain with the union on company pension plans. The NLRB issued a similar ruling concerning group life insurance benefits in the same year. Both rulings were sustained by the Supreme Court in 1949, and union interest in welfare benefits soared, now that the legal status of collective bargaining on these benefits had been clarified. The United Steel Workers and the United Automobile Workers negotiated important retirement plans during the same year.

Strong union and employer interest in employee-benefit plans has continued till the present time. Many new plans are established each year and benefits in existing plans are improved. The most important reasons for the current interest in these plans are (1) the tax incentives provided by the federal government, (2) the savings in insurance costs made possible by marketing and servicing groups of employees instead of individual employees, and (3) the expectation by most prospective and present employees that their employer will provide and their union will bargain for an attractive package of insurance benefits.

The strong trend to self-insured pension plans has been halted because, as explained later in this chapter, insured plans have become more flexible and hence more competitive. On the other hand, self-insured death benefit plans have become somewhat more popular among large employers.

In 1974 Congress enacted the Employee Retirement Income Security Act (ERISA), which placed some important constraints on pension plans and, to a lesser extent, other employee-benefit plans. ERISA, also known as the Pension Reform Act, applies to most pension plans except for governmental and church plans and union plans that do not provide for employer contributions. Some of its most important constraints will be discussed later in this chapter.

A recent major development has been the addition of automobile insurance and homeowners' insurance to employee-benefit plans. Most of the present programs are "mass merchandising" plans under which individual policies are sold to the employees on a payroll deduction basis. Employees pay the entire premium; the employer makes the necessary arrangements and deducts the premiums from wages. "True" group property and liability insurance, like the group life insurance discussed in this chapter, is characterized by group selection and a uniform average rate for all employees. Only a few such plans have been established.

Many employees find these plans attractive because their premiums are lower, they can pay their premiums through periodic salary deductions, and they expect group pressure to improve their chances of obtaining and retaining insurance coverage and receiving sympathetic claims treatment. Others would at present receive little or no premium reduction, and in automobile insurance, where the quality of service is important, they prefer their present insurers. Some employers fear that they will be blamed if the employee is unhappy with the handling of claims and that they will be asked to pay part or all of the premiums. The concept, however, is becoming more popular and such plans are expected to increase in importance. The rate at which they will grow will depend mostly on (1) employer willingness to pay part of the cost, (2) whether Congress will provide some tax incentives similar to those that encourage group life and health insurance, (3) and insurers' ability to reduce costs through the group concept.

Classifications of Employee-Benefit Plans

Before turning to a detailed discussion of the death and retirement benefits provided under employee-benefit plans it is instructive to view some of the ways in which employee-benefit plans can be classified.

First, the plans may differ according to the type of group insured. The group may consist of the employees of a single employer or the employees of two or more employers in an industry, an area, or an industry within an area (called a multiemployer group). Multiemployer groups usually include the members of a labor union or certain labor unions. Sometimes they include employees of employers belonging to an employers' association.[9] From this point on we shall restrict our attention primarily, but not exclusively, to plans covering the employees of a single employer.[10] These plans include about 75 to 90% of the covered employees, depending on the type of benefits.

Second, employee-benefit plans can be classified according to whether they were established unilaterally by the employer(s) or in accordance with some collective bargaining agreement. Over half of the plans fall into the latter category.

Third, employee-benefit plans may be administered by the employer(s), by an employee organization(s), or jointly by an employer–employee board of trustees. More than four-fifths of the plans are administered by employers.

Fourth, the plans may be financed by employers, employees, or both. Employers pay the entire cost in well over half the plans, especially in pension plans. The trend is toward noncontributory (employer-pay-all) plans. The major advantages of a noncontributory plans are as follows:

---

[9]Insurers do not restrict group coverages to employer groups. Other types of groups, which are becoming more important, are members of professional associations, college alumni association members, debtors of a common creditor, and persons owning savings or investment accounts.

[10]A survey of group life insurance in force by type of group covered at the end of 1978, exclusive of dependent coverage, credit life insurance, the federal employees' group plan, and the Servicemen's Group Life program, showed that groups related to members' employment or occupation accounted for about 96% of the insurance in force. Single-employer groups covered through master contracts issued to their employers accounted for 88% of the amount of insurance in force on employees. See *1980 Life Insurance Fact Book* (Washington, D.C.: American Council of Life Insurance, 1980) p. 31. For more information on multiemployer pension plans see Daniel F. McGinn, *Joint Trust Pension Plans* (Homewood, Ill.: Richard D. Irwin, 1978).

1 The employee does not have to pay an income tax on the premiums paid by the employer if the group insurance expenditures by the firm are "reasonable." Premiums paid for group life insurance in excess of $50,000, however, are taxable. Premiums paid for disability insurance are not taxable, but the benefits are except under certain conditions. In the case of pensions the employee can defer and in some cases escape the tax if the pension plan is qualified with the Internal Revenue Service. To be qualified a pension plan must, among other things, be for the exclusive benefit of the employees and must not discriminate in favor of certain classes of highly paid employees.

2 All eligible employees are insured.

3 The administrative costs are lower because there is less record keeping.

The principal advantages of a contributory plan are the following:

1 The plan can provide larger benefits if both the employer and employees contribute.

2 The employee may take a greater interest in the plan and may as a result derive more satisfaction from the protection.

3 The plan is less likely to be discontinued.

Tax considerations and the inclusion of insurance benefits in collective bargaining agreements are the primary factors favoring the current trend toward noncontributory plans.

Fifth, the plans may be classified according to whether they are self-insured by the administrator or insured with an outside agency. Because most *death benefit* plans are insured, a study of these plans is almost entirely a study of group life insurance underwritten by commercial insurers, and our analysis will be limited to this subject. On the other hand more than half of the pension participants are covered under self-insured plans.[11] Our analysis must therefore include both self-insured plans and those insured by commercial insurers. We now turn to these more detailed analyses.

Group Life Insurance

Group life insurance is insurance of a group of persons bound together by some common interest. The contract is issued to the head of the group—an employer, a labor union, or the trustees of a welfare fund. The participating members receive individual certificates.

Group underwriting is substituted for individual underwriting. If the group is acceptable to the insurer, all members of the group are acceptable even if they would be unable to pass the individual underwriting standards. The cost is

[11]See Table 5.4.

relatively low because of the reduction in administrative expenses due to the wholesaling principle and the fact that the head of the group usually performs some of the administrative duties. Moreover, the head of the group usually pays part or all of the cost.

If an insurer limits group life insurance protection to those groups that have an expected mortality rate approximating that underlying the premium charged, group insurance is feasible. As a rule the expected mortality rates are assumed to differ among groups only because of differences in the age composition.

To avoid adverse selection against the insurer and to maintain a low stable premium, insurers first sought groups possessing the following characteristics:

1   Insurance should be an incidental purpose of the group.
2   Membership in the group should require a certain minimum degree of physical activity and health.
3   New entrants should be required to show a minimum grade of health.
4   There should be a continuous withdrawal of aged and impaired lives and a steady inflow of young and healthy lives.

The most insurable type of group, according to these criteria, is a group of employees under a common employer. Insurers have become much more liberal with respect to the types of groups they will underwrite.

Of course, not all groups of an acceptable type are eligible for insurance. The group must consist of a certain minimum number of persons; for a group of employees of a single employer, this is usually 10. The major purpose of this requirement is to reduce the overhead expense per insured. Moreover, underwriters feel that the proportion of impaired lives in an eligible group decreases as the size of the group increases.

If the members of the group do not pay any of the cost, all members of an eligible class must be covered. If the members pay part of the cost, all members of a specified class must be eligible to participate, and in individual employer groups at least 75%, say, of those eligible must participate. If it were not for this requirement, the proportion of impaired lives among the employees might be abnormally high. Many insurers have relaxed this requirement.

The group insurance contract itself contains some additional underwriting safeguards. First, eligibility requirements are stated. What constitutes membership in the group is clearly defined; a probationary period of membership may be required in order to avoid the high cost of insuring "floaters"; and there may be a requirement that the member be actively at work or able to present some other evidence of reasonably good health. If the insurance is voluntary, eligible members must usually apply for the insurance within 30 days after the date of their eligibility if they wish to obtain the insurance without evidence of insurability.

Second, the amount of insurance is determined automatically by the member's earnings, position, years of membership, debt, or some other criterion. It may be a flat amount for all group members. The earnings basis has proved to be the most satisfactory for the employee group, and the amount of group life insurance is usually some multiple of annual earnings. If the amount of insurance were not automatically determined, those persons in poor health would tend to purchase the largest amounts of insurance. Many current plans give the employee an option of purchasing a limited amount of additional protection. The employee may also have the option of purchasing a small amount of insurance on the lives of dependents.

Third, there is a minimum and maximum amount of insurance per person. A minimum is usually established in order to avoid unduly high administration expenses. The maximum amount is a function of the total insurance in force and, in a few states, some legal restrictions. Setting a minimum and maximum amount in this way produces a safer distribution of insurance amounts from an underwriting point of view; otherwise the insurer might have too many eggs in too few baskets.

Group Renewable Term Insurance

Most group life insurance in force is one-year renewable term insurance. From the member's point of view the insurer will pay the face amount to the beneficiary if the employee dies while insured as a member of the group, but there is no cash value if he or she leaves the group. The proceeds are payable in a lump sum or in periodic installments.

The major disadvantage of individual one-year renewable term insurance is that the premium rate increases each year and the premium becomes prohibitive for most older people. Fortunately, however, the total premium rate for a group does not change unless the age and benefit composition of the group changes.[12]

If no new members join the group and coverage is continued on all the old members, the total premium rate will increase over time. However, if the older members are dropped from the group after a certain age and younger members take their place, the total premium rate will be fairly constant over time. Note that it is the age composition of the group that must remain fairly constant, not the average age. It costs more to insure two people, ages 30 and 50, than two people both age 40, but the average age of the two groups is the same.

If the plan is contributory, each member's share of the cost is usually kept constant during his or her period of participation and seldom exceeds 60 cents per month per $1,000 of insurance. In this case the head of a group with a fairly stable age composition pays the almost constant additional cost per $1,000 of protection. The amount paid by the youngest employees may exceed the premium for individual term insurance, but after a few years the amount paid will be much less. If the plan is voluntary, some of the younger members may wait until the

---

[12]The total premium, but not necessarily the premium rate, would change if the size of the group or the benefit levels increased or decreased.

group protection is cheaper than the individual contract, but they may become uninsurable in the meantime and be unable to participate.

In calculating the total initial premium the insurer recognizes that its selling and servicing expenses do not increase proportionately with the size of the group. Furthermore, the actual cost of the protection will probably be less than the computed premium, for participating insurers return dividends to policyholders and nonparticipating insurers make retroactive adjustments of the premium. The sizes of the dividends and retroactive adjustments depend partly on the experience of the particular group. Insurers pay more attention to the experience of the particular group when that group includes many persons.

An insured who terminates his or her connection with the group has the right to purchase an individual life insurance contract up to the amount of the group coverage without evidence of insurability. Application for this coverage must be made within 31 days and the premium is that in effect for standard lives at the age attained at the date of termination. Term insurance coverage is sometimes granted for one year, but usually the converted contract must be some form of nonterm insurance. If the insurer or the employer terminates the group insurance, members who have been insured for five years (sometimes three) may convert their insurance under the same conditions, but the converted amount may not exceed $2,000. This conversion privilege is extremely important if a terminating member becomes uninsurable or insurable only at substandard rates while a member of the insured group, but there is no premium advantage for standard lives.

A new concept in group renewable term insurance is survivor income insurance. Under one common version the surviving spouse receives some percentage of the employee's monthly pay until the worker would have reached 65 or, if earlier, until the spouse dies or remarries. The income is guaranteed for a certain minimum period, such as five years. If there are surviving children, additional benefits may be paid until the child reaches, say, age 18. Note that unlike traditional benefit formulas, which tend to provide higher benefits for older workers, this formula favors younger workers with dependents. The similarity to OASI survivorship benefits is apparent. What is even more interesting, however, is the fact that the original Montgomery Ward group contract was based on similar principles, taking into account family conditions as well as salary status.

Other Forms of Group Life Insurance

A major problem with group term insurance is that the conversion privilege is of little value to members retiring at an advanced age, because the premiums on the individual contracts are very high. For this reason insurers also underwrite two additional forms of group insurance: group paid-up insurance and level-premium group permanent insurance. In the description of these forms we shall assume a group of employees under a common employer.

A group paid-up plan combines term insurance with paid-up insurance. Paid-up insurance is lifetime protection paid for by a single premium payment. The total amount of insurance for each employee is determined in the same way as under a group term insurance plan, but the composition of the total differs. Usually small units of paid-up insurance are purchased annually during the insured's participation under the plan; term insurance provides the remainder of the coverage. If the total amount of protection is constant, the paid-up insurance represents an increasing portion of the total, whereas the term insurance decreases. If none of the paid-up insurance was purchased by employer contributions, the employee is entitled to the paid-up protection when he or she leaves the group. If the employee prefers, he or she may surrender the contract for its accumulated cash value. In addition, the usual conversion rights apply to the term insurance portion of the protection. However, if the employer has contributed to the cost of the paid-up insurance, he or she may establish certain *vesting* conditions that must be satisfied before the employee may claim that portion of paid-up insurance purchased with employer contributions. (Vesting conditions are discussed more fully later in this chapter.

Group permanent or level-premium life insurance plans emphasize the retirement aspects of insurance more than group paid-up plans. In fact, they are more often used as pension plans instead of life insurance plans because of the sizable cash values available at retirement age and some tax factors. Straight life, limited payment life, endowment, or retirement income contracts (all described later in this chapter) are issued to individuals on a group basis. A withdrawing employee's claim to any cash values or equivalent paid-up insurance accumulated under this insurance will depend on vesting conditions of the type mentioned in the preceding paragraph.

The most common solution to the problem of retired employees, however, is to continue their insurance in a reduced amount under the regular group term contract. Monies are commonly accumulated in advance in a retired lives reserve fund to pay for this continued protection.

Under present interpretations of the Age Discrimination in Employment Act an employer can reduce the level of group life insurance benefits on account of age if the cost of providing these lower benefits is at least as high as the cost of the benefits provided younger workers. No benefit need be provided at age 70 or later.

Trends

Important trends in group insurance include the extension of group insurance to new types of groups and smaller groups, dependents' coverage, an increase in the maximum amount of group insurance written on a single life and in the average size of a group certificate, liberalization in the conversion privilege by permitting the insured to convert the group protection to term insurance for at least one year, survivor income insurance, and more attention to the continuing life insurance needs of retired employees.

Group Life Insurance in Force, 1912–1980

The tremendous increase in the amount of group insurance in force since its introduction in 1912 is shown in Table 5.3. As a comparison of Tables 5.3 and 5.9 will reveal, there is less group life insurance in force than individual insurance, but group insurance is becoming relatively more important.

Group Pension Plans

The amount of group life insurance in force is less than the individual life insurance in force, but group pension plans provide much more protection against old age than do individual annuity contracts. These pension plans may be formal or informal. Since almost all the important pension plans are formal, the discussion will be limited to this type.

We shall further limit our detailed discussion to those plans that cover the employees of a single employer, but as a result of collective bargaining, pooled welfare funds covering the employees of more than one employer are also common, especially among craft unions that include members working for a large number of small employers. Examples are the plans of the United Brotherhood of Carpenters and Joiners of America, the International Brotherhood of Electrical Workers, and the United Mine Workers of America. These multiemployer plans are usually entirely financed by employer contributions based on some measure such as the number of hours worked or tons of coal mined and they are jointly administered by employers and unions. One noteworthy characteristic of these plans is that an employee's pension status is not lessened by movements from one employer to another included under the same plan.

Table 5.3 Group Life Insurance in Force in the United States, 1912–1980

Year	Amount (In Millions of Dollars)[a]
1912	13
1920	1,570
1930	9,801
1940	14,938
1950	47,793
1960	175,903
1970	551,357
1980	1,579,355

Source: *1981 Life Insurance Fact Book* (Washington, D.C.: American Council of Life Insurance, 1981), p. 18.

[a]Does not include credit life insurance on loans of ten years' or less duration.

Retirement Benefits

Retirement benefits are determined in one of two ways: under a defined contribution plan or under a defined benefit plan.

Under a *defined contribution plan* the benefit is the amount that can be provided on the basis of specified annual contributions to the plan. Among plans of this type it is customary to express the contributions as a percentage of the employee's earnings. This approach is used mainly by public bodies and nonprofit organizations. One disadvantage to the employee is that the benefits cannot easily be explained and they decrease rapidly as the age of the entrant increases. Furthermore, the benefit depends more on the earnings in the early years than on those in the later years because the early contributions are credited with compound interest over a longer period of time. The advantage to the employer is that the cost is known and it varies with payroll. Employees also sometimes see this definite cost as an advantage because the benefits they have earned at any point in time are secure; they do not depend on future employer contributions. Another benefit to employers is that defined contribution plans are subject to fewer constraints under the Employee Retirement Income Security Act.

Under a *defined benefit plan* the benefit is a flat amount for all retirants or a specified function of earnings, service, or both. The contribution is the amount necessary to provide the benefit. Examples of defined benefit formulas include $600 per month for all eligible retirants, 50% of final earnings, 50% of average earnings over the past five years, $15 per month for each year of service, 2% of earnings during the final five years for each year of service, and 2% of average earnings during the five consecutive years of highest earnings for each year of service. Most plans use a formula based on length of service and average earnings during the final five or five highest-earnings years of service. Retirants, past and future, tend to judge plans on the relationship between their pension and their final earnings, not their average earnings; and over most earning careers final earnings are much greater than average career earnings. During periods of inflation they are markedly so.

Whenever length of service is a factor in determining the amount of the benefit, as it is in most plans, a distinction is made between services rendered prior to and after the installation of the pension plan. Most plans count at least part of the past service in addition to the future service; otherwise employees approaching retirement age at the time the plan was introduced would receive a very small benefit. If the benefit depends on career earnings, it is customary to assume for administrative reasons that the annual earnings prior to installation of the plan were equal to the earnings at the time the plan is installed. Because this assumption almost always results in an overestimate of past earnings, a smaller percentage is applied to past earnings than to future earnings to determine the benefit.

Because most employees will receive OASI retirement benefits, which the employer has paid for in part, the benefits under most private pension plans are affected in some way by OASI.[13] It is customary to (1) deduct benefits actually received from the private pension benefit, (2) exclude earnings under the maximum OASI earnings base from the private pension plan, or (3) apply a smaller rate of benefit to those OASI taxable earnings. When the last two methods are used, the usual objective is to produce a maximum total benefit (OASI plus private pension benefit), expressed as a percentage of earnings, that decreases as the earnings increase to the maximum OASI earnings base and remains approximately the same for all higher incomes.

A commonly accepted target of pension planners is an initial retirement income, including the OASI worker's benefit, equal to 60–75% of the earnings of the five highest-pay years for employees with 30 to 35 years of service. The 75% applies to those with lower incomes, the 60% to those earning the OASI maximum earnings base or higher.

ERISA requires unless the employee elects otherwise, that the plan pay an income for the lifetime of the employee plus at least half that amount to a surviving spouse. The plan may permit the employee to elect instead a higher income that is paid only during the lifetime of the employee. Another popular option would pay an income during the employee's lifetime, but in no case for less than n years.

Since the post-World War II period there has been considerable interest in the effects of inflation on pension benefits. Increases in the cost of living during the employee's working years and after retirement can drastically reduce the purchasing power of a pension benefit. Basing the benefit on the employee's five final or five highest-earnings years' salary is one way of recognizing increases in the cost of living during the worker's earning career, but this approach does not solve the problem after retirement. Another solution is to adjust the monthly benefit after retirement, and sometimes before, according to changes in the CPI, usually subject to a specified maximum adjustment per year. A third solution is to allow the monthly benefit paid at and after retirement to rise and fall with the value of the investments in the pension fund, the changes in which are presumed to correspond roughly with the changes in the cost of living. This third solution has been introduced in many pension plans through the variable annuity described later in this chapter. Because common stocks are not currently as highly regarded as a hedge against inflation, this approach is not as popular today as in the 1960s. The most common solution is final-salary plans with ad hoc adjustments from time to time in the pensions already being paid.

Qualification for Retirement Benefits

To qualify for retirement benefits an employee must first have been eligible to participate under the plan. Participation may be limited to those employees

---

[13]The integration with OASI must not discriminate in favor of the more highly paid employees, or else the Internal Revenue Service will not qualify the plan.

satisfying one or more of the following types of criteria: minimum age, maximum age, minimum length of service, minimum earnings, type of remuneration (hourly wage or salary), and type of work. For example, one plan may cover all employees over 20 years of age with at least one year of service. Another may cover all salaried employees earning over $20,000 a year. The minimum age and service requirements cut the cost of administration by excluding temporary employees; the maximum age limitation excludes those employees for whom it would be very expensive to provide pensions. ERISA requires that at the minimum the plan cover all workers age 25 with at least one year of service. ERISA permits a defined benefit plan to exclude employees hired five years or less before their normal retirement age. The minimum earnings requirement is designed to integrate the plan with OASI in the manner described earlier. The other requirements may be used to cut the cost or they may arise out of the special circumstances surrounding negotiated plans.

To receive full retirement benefits employees must almost always have attained a *normal* retirement age, usually 65. Sometimes there is also a minimum service requirement. As explained in Chapter 2, however, the mandatory retirement age cannot be less than 70. Under present interpretations of the Age Discrimination in Employment Act the benefit payable to workers who elect to defer their retirement may be no higher than the amount payable at the normal retirement age. The most liberal adjustment would recognize the extra service, the earnings if this would produce a higher wage base, and an actuarial adjustment factor. The actuarial adjustment factor would recognize the extra interest earnings made possible by the later retirement age and the expected shorter pay-out period.

Early Retirement, Termination, and Death Benefits

Some plans do not allow an employee to retire prior to the normal retirement date; others make an exception only in the case of total and permanent disability. However, most plans permit early retirement if the retirant meets a minimum age or minimum age and service requirement. The employer's consent may or may not be required. For example, the plan may permit an employee to retire with the employer's consent if he or she has attained age 55. Another may require that a person reach age 55 and complete 10 years of service. If early retirement is permitted, the benefit is usually the actuarial equivalent of the normal retirement age benefit. This actuarial equivalent is much less than the benefit at the normal retirement age because fewer contributions are made to the plan, the period of compound interest earnings is much less, the cost of providing an income beginning at an earlier age is much higher, and many of the early retirants are persons in poor health who would not have attained the normal retirement age.

If an employee withdraws from employment prior to the normal or early retirement age, he or she is entitled to the employee's contributions to the plan, with or without interest. The vesting provisions of the plan determine the employee's right to the benefits provided by employer contributions. The vesting may be immediate or, as is usually the case, there may be certain service or age and service requirements; once the worker is entitled to vested benefits the initial vesting may be full or partial; and the vested amount may be returned in cash or as a paid-up annuity. For example, one plan may provide for immediate full vesting, but the employee must take his or her own and the employer's contributions in the form of a paid-up annuity. Another plan may entitle the employee to 50% of the employer's contributions in cash or as a paid-up annuity after five years of service, 75% after 10 years, and 100% after 15 years. A third plan may provide full vesting of the employer's contributions as a paid-up annuity for all eligible employees with 10 years of service. ERISA requires that the vesting provision be at least as liberal as one of the following three standards: (1) 100% vesting after 10 years; (2) 25% after five years of service, increasing by 5% for each of the next five years and by 10% for each of the next five years [earlier vesting than (1), but 100% not required until after 15 years of service]; or (3) 50% vesting after five years of service when age plus service totals 45 (e.g., age 40 or more with five years of service, age 39 with six years of service). For each of the next five years the percentage vested must rise by 10%. Most employers have elected to satisfy the first minimum standard (100% vesting after 10 years), but many plans are more liberal.

If the employee dies before retirement, the beneficiaries are entitled to a return of his or her contributions, with or without interest. Sometimes a widow's benefit provides a lifetime income, expressed as a percentage of the employee's pension, for widows of long-service, older employees. Survivor income insurance, described earlier in this chapter, is sometimes used to supplement a pension plan. ERISA requires that persons who have reached early retirement age but have not retired be given the opportunity to purchase a pre-retirement death benefit.

Actuarial Cost Methods

The subject of actuarial cost methods, that is, the ways in which pension costs are budgeted over time, is too complex a subject to be covered in detail in this book. The alternatives range from a pay-as-you-go approach, similar to OASI financing, to full advance funding. If a fully funded plan is terminated, enough monies will have been accumulated to pay all benefits earned up to that date by active and retired participants. A common intermediate position would be to accumulate enough assets to continue benefits for those persons who have already retired and to pay some but not all earned benefits to active workers. Arguments in favor of substantial advance funding are that this advance action increases the likelihood that the benefits will be paid, apportions the cost of the pension plan more equitably over time, and, because of interest earnings, reduces the total dollar outlay for the employer. Possible disadvantages are that the employer might be able to earn a better return by investing the funds in the business, a sizable fund might encourage undue benefit liberalizations, and a funded plan could be more complicated and expensive to administer. Because of the serious hardships suffered by persons who work for a business with a partially funded pension plan that is terminated, ERISA requires that plans be fully funded within 30 years after they are started. This deadline may be extended if benefits are liberalized or if mortality interest or other assumptions are changed for good reason.

Funding Agencies and Instruments

As stated earlier, the pension plan may be self-insured by the employer or insured with an insurer. Under a self-insured trusteed plan a consulting actuary advises the employer, who transfers funds periodically to a trustee such as a bank. The trustee invests the money and commonly sends out the pension checks at the direction of the employer. The plan is highly flexible with respect to the benefit formula that can be used, the budgeting arrangements that can be selected by the employer, and the investments that can be made. The primary disadvantage of a self-insured operation is that no third party such as an insurer has absorbed any of the risks. There is no guarantee that the contributions by the employer will be sufficient to pay the benefits.

Under an insured plan the contributions are paid to an insurer, who administers them in one of the following ways. Small firms usually use an *individual policy arrangement* under which the employer transfers funds to a trustee who purchases an individual level-premium retirement annuity or retirement income annuity contract for each eligible employee. Each contract is designed to provide the pension the employee is expected to earn at retirement. If future circumstances cause this estimated pension to rise, the employer purchases additional contracts to provide the extra income. Until recently larger firms used *group annuity plans* under which the employer purchases a number of paid-up deferred group annuities from an insurer each year. Usually the benefit is expressed as a percentage of earnings for each year of service, and the annuity purchased in any year is sufficient to provide this benefit at the retirement date. The benefit payable at retirement is usually the same percentage of career earnings multiplied by the years of service. Under either of these plans the insurer guarantees performance under the contract purchased. The plans, however, are relatively inflexible and until the 1970s the yield on the invested funds was lower than that on the self-insured funds because life insurers are generally required by law to place most of the funds they receive in connection with these contracts in fixed obligations.

Today insurers emphasize three more flexible plans—*deposit administration plans, immediate participation guarantee contracts,* and *separate account contracts.* Under a deposit administration plan annuity contracts are not purchased until an employee retires. Annual employer contributions to the insurer are accumulated at a guaranteed minimum rate of interest and may be used to purchase an annuity at a price fixed at the time of the contribution. Employee contributions, if any, are accumulated at interest in individual accounts or used for immediate purchases of deferred annuities. The employer contributions are made on the basis of an actuarial estimate by the insurer's actuaries or a consulting actuary, but there is no guarantee that they will be sufficient to provide the benefits specified under the plan. The insurer guarantees the benefits for retiring employees only. The deposit administration plan has become quite popular because of the flexibility in financing it affords the employer and because it may be used to fund the more popular five final or five highest-pay years type of benefit. The principal differences between this plan and the self-insured one are that the deposits must be invested in legal investments for insurers and the benefits for retired persons are guaranteed by a third party.

Immediate participation guarantee contracts are even more flexible in that the insurer administers the retirement fund as if it were a self-insured trusteed fund, but the insurer reserves the right to convert the plan into a deferred group annuity plan should the fund drop to the level where it is just sufficient to provide the benefits for retired workers. In this way the retired workers receive a guarantee that their income will not be disturbed.

A separate account contract is basically a deposit administration or immediate participation contract with one additional feature. Part or all of the employer's deposit fund is allocated to one or more separate accounts, which are held separately from all other assets of the insurer. The funds in a separate account may be invested solely in common stocks, in some other type of investment, or in some combination of investments. Although an individual separate account may be established for a large employer, most separate accounts pool the funds of many policyholders. This approach to pension funding was impossible until 1960, when Connecticut became the first state to pass the necessary enabling legislation.

Trends

The important trends in group pensions include an increase in the number of persons covered, a reduction in age and service eligibility requirements, higher retirement benefits, more death benefits, new benefit formulas including cost of living adjustments and variable annuities, a movement from inflexible insured plans to more flexible insured plans and self-insured trusteed plans, more liberal vesting provisions, early retirement provisions, and the growth of industry-wide negotiated plans. Collective bargaining and ERISA have played a significant role in these developments.

Pension Plans, 1930–1980

Table 5.4 shows the rapid growth of pension plans since 1930 and the more rapid relative growth of self-insured pension plans from the end of World War II until the middle 1960s, when insurers developed separate account plans permitting equity investments. The Self-Employed Individuals Tax Retirement Act (HR10 —Keogh legislation) also provided some tax deferral incentives in the late 1960s for the establishment of insured plans by self-employed persons and their em-

Table 5.4 Private Pension Plan Coverage in the United States, 1940–1980

Year	Employees Covered (In Thousands)	
	Insured	Self-Insured
1940	695	3,565
1945	1,470	5,240
1950	2,755	7,500
1955	4,105	12,290
1960	5,475	17,540
1965	7,040	21,060
1970	10,580	25,520
1975	15,190	30,300
1980	26,080	n.a.

Source: *1981 Life Insurance Fact Book* (Washington, D.C.: American Council of Life Insurance, 1981), p. 50.

ployees. Similar but more liberal tax shelters have been available for more than a decade to employees of certain nonprofit organizations. ERISA liberalized the Keogh legislation and made possible Individual Retirement Accounts for employees not covered under a pension plan. Tax law amendments in 1981 further increased the individual pension monies that can be sheltered under these two plans. These amendments also make it possible for persons covered under a pension plan to establish also an IRA.

The number of insured plans of each type in 1980 and the number of persons covered under each type are presented in Table 5.5. Deposit administration plans, which include separate account plans, are the fastest growing type of group plans. Individual policy pension trusts and other individual pension arrangements expanded rapidly in the 1960s and 1970s, primarily because, as explained above, Congress liberalized the tax laws applying to Keogh plans covering self-employed persons and their employees and to Individual Retirement Accounts of employees without pension plans.

Table 5.5 Number of Insured Pension Plans and Number of Persons Covered, 1980

Type of Plan	Number of Plans	Thousands of Persons Covered[a]
Group annuities	91,370	19,225
Individual policy pension trusts	204,300	2,150
HR10 Keogh Plans	n.a.	480
Tax-sheltered annuities	n.a.	1,810
Individual Retirement Accounts	n.a.	1,100
Other	n.a.	1,315

Source: Same as Table 5.4, p. 54.

[a]Includes about 2.1 million pensioners.

INDIVIDUAL INSURANCE

Most of the private insurance in force today is purchased by persons acting as individuals. The responsibility for purchasing the insurance and paying the premiums is almost always the insured's. Ideally the protection is tailor-made to meet the insured's needs and desires.

Types of Life Insurance Contracts

Individual insurance contracts may protect the insured or dependents against financial losses caused by premature death, old age, or both.

Term insurance is the simplest form of life insurance. If the insured dies during the term of the policy, the face amount of the policy is paid to his or her beneficiary. If the insured does not die, the insurer pays nothing. The period of a term insurance policy may be any number of years, such as 1, 5, 10, or 25 years, or the number of years to age 65.

Because there is no savings element in the term policy, the premium is relatively low. For this reason term insurance is an excellent temporary form of protection against premature death. For example, term insurance may be purchased so as to complete the payments on a mortgage should the insured die before the mortgage has been paid off. A person who will be currently insured under OASI in a few months may purchase term insurance to protect his or her family in the interim. A young person with excellent prospects but little current income may purchase term insurance to protect his or her family in the early years of marriage.

One of the major disadvantages of term insurance is that the protection terminates at the end of the period. This would not be important in the first and second examples cited above, but it could be extremely important in the third example if the need for protection continues and the insured becomes uninsurable before the end of the term. However, term insurance policies that are renewable at least once without evidence of of insurability are available. Each time the policy is renewed the premium is increased because the probability of death increases. The premiums charged by one nonparticipating life insurer[14] for five-year renewable term insurance contracts are presented in Table 5.6.

---

[14]Almost 50% of the life insurance in force is written by mutual insurers, while about one-seventh of the insurance issued by stock insurers is written on a participating basis. This means that under about 57% of the life insurance in force, dividends to policyholders must be subtracted from the premiums paid in order to determine the actual cost of continuing the insurance in force.

Participating insurers typically charge a higher initial premium than do nonparticipating insurers, but the dividends will determine whether the actual cost of continuing the contract will be more, the same, or less.

The premiums charged by a nonparticipating insurer are quoted in this book because they are actual cost figures. If participating premiums had been quoted to show the actual cost, it would have been necessary to include divident estimates as well as initial premiums.

As indicated later in this chapter, the premiums charged by life insurers for basically the same protection vary greatly.

Table 5.6   Annual Premium Rates Charged Males by One Nonparticipating Life Insurer for \$40,000 Five-Year Renewable Term Insurance[a]

Age	Premium per \$1,000 (\$)
20	2.83
25	3.06
30	3.31
35	3.88
40	5.11
45	6.99
50	9.80
55	14.90

[a]The minimum policy amount issued is \$10,000. Premium rates decrease as the policy amount increases. Females pay lower rates.

At advanced ages the premiums are so high that the policy will probably be dropped or at least reduced. However, if the term insurance is also convertible, it may be converted within a specified period to a nonterm contract as of the original date of issue or at the attained age.

The basic nonterm contracts are *the straight life contract, the limited payment life contract,* and *the endowment contract.* Under the first two contracts, called whole-life contracts, the insurer promises to pay the face amount when the insured dies. The two contracts differ from one another in that under the straight life contract the insured pays premiums until death, whereas under the limited payment life contract the insured pays premiums until death or the expiration of a stated period, if earlier. Examples of limited payment contracts are 20-payment, 30-payment, and "paid-up at 65" contracts. Under an endowment contract the insurer promises to pay the face amount immediately if the insured dies within the endowment period *or* at the end of the period if the insured is still living. Examples of endowment contracts are 20-year endowments, 30-year endowments, and endowments at age 60. Table 5.7 shows premiums charged for four principal nonterm contracts by the same nonparticipating insurer whose term insurance rates were quoted in Table 5.6.

If a male insured continues the protection from age 25 to 60, he will pay out \$11,810 to protect his family under a \$40,000 five-year renewable term insurance policy issued by the insurer cited above; the premiums on a straight life policy would total \$15,512. However, this comparison is unfair, for possible interest earnings are ignored. If the premiums could have been invested at 6% interest after taxes, compounded annually, the true cost of continuing the term protection is \$23,185, while the straight life policy would cost him \$52,351.

On the other hand, there is one very important difference between nonterm and term insurance contracts. Under nonterm contracts the insurer accumulates at a guaranteed interest rate the differences between the level premium and the insured's yearly share of the expected death benefits and administrative expenses. This accumulation process accomplishes two objectives.

First, the cost of paying death benefits does not increase as rapidly as the

Table 5.7 Annual Premium Rates Charged Males by One Nonparticipating Life Insurer for $40,000 Straight Life, Limited Payment, and Endowment Contracts[a]

	Type of Contract ($)			
Age	Straight Life	20- Payment	Paid-Up at 65	20-Year Endowment
20	9.39	20.21	12.02	42.53
25	11.08	22.61	14.13	42.64
30	13.41	25.17	17.13	42.73
35	16.46	28.59	21.33	42.83
40	20.38	32.24	27.39	43.87
50	31.63	42.87	51.83	48.12
60	50.66	59.11	—	61.37

[a]Rates decrease as the amount of insurance increases. Females pay lower rates.

mortality rate because the increasing accumulations are part of the face amount paid the beneficiary and the "net amount at risk" (the face amount less the accumulation) decreases. In fact, except during the first year or two, when the administrative expenses are high, the level premium less the insured's share of the expenses plus the interest credited for the year is always more than enough to pay the insured's share of the expected benefits for that year. Consequently the accumulations continue to grow.

Second, the insured may claim these accumulations (called nonforfeiture values) at any time. For example, he or she may elect to retire at age 65 and use the accumulations to help finance retirement. There are usually three nonforfeiture options. The insured may elect to take the accumulations in cash, use them as a single premium to purchase paid-up insurance, or use them as a single premium to purchase extended term insurance. The paid-up insurance is a policy of the same type as the original contract in a reduced amount. The extended term insurance provides the original amount of protection for a limited number of years.[15] For example, under the $40,000 straight life policy for which the premium has been quoted, the insured may, at age 60, stop paying premiums and obtain $20,000 in cash, have $31,200 of insurance protection continued for life, or have $40,000 of insurance protection continued for about 16 years.

The cash value at the end of each policy year depends on the type of contract, the age at issue, and the actuarial assumptions made by the insurer. Under all nonterm contracts the cash value continues to grow throughout the life of the contract, but the pattern of growth differs according to policy type. Under a straight life contract the cash value usually grows steadily until it equals the face value at this age, for insurance actuaries typically assume in their premium calculations that no one will live beyond age 100.

[15]If the original contract is an endowment contract, the extended term insurance does not run beyond the maturity date of the original endowment contract. If the cash value is more than the premium required for term insurance to the maturity date, the excess is used to purchase a promise that some reduced amount will be paid to those who live to the maturity date.

Under a limited payment life contract the cash value grows more rapidly during the premium-paying period because the premiums are higher. The cash value continues to grow after the premium-paying period but at a less rapid pace, because the interest on the cash value is more than is required to pay the insured's share of the benefits the insurer expects to have to pay to the beneficiaries of the deceaseds. At age 100 the cash value equals the face value for the reason already cited.

Under an endowment contract the cash value grows very rapidly and equals the face amount at the end of the endowment period. In a sense, the straight life and limited payment life contracts are endowments at age 100.

Thus, in addition to providing protection against financial losses caused by premature death, all nonterm insurance contracts help the insured to acquire a retirement fund through a systematic savings plan.

Methods of Paying Proceeds

The death proceeds under life insurance contracts are payable in a lump sum or according to some settlement option selected by the insured or a beneficiary. Most insurers also permit the insured to select some settlement option if he or she wishes to surrender the policy for cash before death.

The four most common settlement options are the following:

1 *Interest option* The proceeds are left with the insurer for some specified period and interest payments are made to the beneficiary. The beneficiary may or may not have the right to withdraw part or all of the principal.
2 *Fixed amount option* The beneficiary receives a specified monthly income for as many months as the proceeds and the interest on the unpaid balance will afford.
3 *Fixed period option* The beneficiary receives for a specified period a monthly income of whatever amount the proceeds and the interest on the unpaid balance will afford.
4 *Annuity option* An annuity payable under this option may take one of several forms: it may be a straight life annuity under which the insurer promises to pay the beneficiary a monthly income for life; usually, however, it is either an installment refund annuity, or an annuity with a period certain.

Under an installment refund annuity, the payments are continued during the lifetime of the beneficiary, but if the annuitant should die before the annuity payments have equalled the proceeds, the payments are continued to another beneficiary until this equality is achieved. A cash refund annuity differs from the installment refund annuity only in that on death of the beneficiary the difference, if any, between the proceeds and the sum of the monthly payments is paid in cash to another beneficiary. Under an annuity with a period certain, the insurer promises to pay a monthly income for life, but the income is guaranteed for at least a specified period.

For proceeds of a given amount the monthly income differs depending on the option selected because of the differences in the guaranteed amounts and the loss of interest for varying periods. The annuities with some guaranteed amounts are a wise choice when dependents may survive the beneficiary, but the price is a reduced monthly income for the beneficiary.

Table 5.8 presents settlement options appearing in one insurance contract: the values are the *minimum* amounts this insurer promises to pay; actual payments may exceed these amounts, depending on the insurer's investment experience. These options are useful because they enable the insured to have the proceeds paid in the manner he or she deems best. The insured may or may not give the beneficiary the right to change the program set up. If the insured does not elect any options, the beneficiary may usually elect them. The options provide a safe investment, with at least a guaranteed rate of interest and no management problems. The present tax code also favors their use. Only the interest portion of the income is taxable and, except under the interest option, spouses have a $1,000 federal income tax exemption applicable to this interest.

If the settlement option privilege also applies to cash values, the insured may usually elect a joint and survivorship annuity. This annuity provides a specified income per month during the lifetime of two beneficiaries, plus a reduced income during the lifetime of the survivor. For example, a husband and wife receive $100 a month, with $66.67 a month being paid to the surviving spouse.

When the settlement options may be applied to both death proceeds and living benefits such as cash values and matured endowments, nonterm insurance contracts provide comprehensive protection against the financial problems associated with both premature death and old age. For example, an insured may purchase a straight life contract to protect his or her family, and at retirement age have the cash value converted into a lifetime income. When the options may not be applied to living benefits, the only contribution to old-age protection is the accumulation of a retirement fund.

Table 5.8   Settlement Option Values Used by One Insurer

Fixed Installment Options		Monthly Life Income per $1,000 Proceeds			
Number of Years	Monthly Income per $1,000 Proceeds ($)	Age		10 Years Certain ($)	15 Years Certain ($)
		Male	Female		
5	17.91	35	40	3.85	3.84
10	9.61	40	45	4.10	4.08
15	6.87	45	50	4.42	4.39
20	5.51	50	55	4.84	4.78
		55	60	5.40	5.29
		60	65	6.18	5.94

Settlement Options and Planning an Insurance Program

One of the important uses of a table of settlement options is the determination of the amount of insurance needed to carry out the desires of the insured. A highly simplified example follows. Assume that a husband and wife, both age 35, both work. If either the husband or the wife should die, they estimate that the surviving parent and son would need the following in addition to the important OASI survivorship benefits:

$10,000 for taxes and funeral expenses.

$800 a month for the surviving parent and child until the child reaches age 18.

$500 a month for life for the surviving parent after the child reaches age 18.

To simplify the problem assume that all of the family needs are to be met through the purchase of new private insurance. In actual practice the benefits provided under employee-benefit programs, existing individual private insurance, and other resources such as savings accounts are deducted from the family needs in order to determine the need for new individual private insurance.

One way of paying out life insurance proceeds that would provide the desired benefits is the following:

$10,000 in a lump sum.

$500 a month according to the settlement option that provides a lifetime income for the surviving spouse beginning at age 50.

$800 a month during the 15 years following death, with payment composed of (1) interest payments until age 50 on the amount held at interest to provide the lifetime income beginning at that age and (2) the remainder, provided according to a fixed installment option.

If the settlement option values in Table 5.8 are applicable[16] and the monthly amount payable under the interest option is $2.50 per $1,000 of insurance, the following amounts of insurance will be needed in addition to the $10,000 lump sum:

$$\frac{\$500}{\$4.39} \times \$1,000 = \$114,000,$$

approximately[17]; and since $114,000 at interest provides $285 a month during the 15 years following death, a remainder of

---

[16] The reader is reminded that these values are *minimum* amounts.

[17] Theoretically, a straight life annuity would be sufficient instead of a life annuity with 10 years certain, but this form is not provided by this insurer, and in any event the difference would be small.

$$\frac{\$800 - \$285}{\$6.87} \times \$1,000 = \$75,000,$$

approximately. The total insurance required for each parent is close to $189,000.

In actual practice the problem is far more complicated, and the solution much more thorough. It is necessary to recognize changes over time in the family situation, inflation, retirement needs, tax factors, existing social insurance, private insurance and noninsurance assets, and many other factors. Several solutions are possible and the particular circumstances and desires of the insured determine which one is best. Considerable skill is required in order to construct a satisfactory program.

Annuity Contracts

Life insurers issue individual annuities as separate contracts in addition to those issued as supplementary contracts under the settlement option provisions. The emphasis in these contracts is on financial preparation for old age.

Annuity contracts can be classified according to several characteristics. One classification distinguishes the straight life annuity from the other forms defined earlier in this chapter.

A second classification divides annuities into immediate and deferred annuities. Under an immediate annuity the annuitant pays the insurer a lump sum and receives a monthly income for life under one of the annuity forms discussed in connection with settlement options. The savings may be accumulated through some method other than insurance.

The more common type of annuity is the deferred annuity, under which a person normally pays premiums from the issue date to the retirement date, at which time the insurer begins to pay a monthly income according to the terms of one of the various annuity forms. Under a pure deferred annuity no benefit is paid if the insured dies prior to reaching retirement age, but few contracts of this type are issued. Usually the premiums or, if higher, the cash value is refunded in case of death.

The final classification depends on whether the insurer promises to pay periodically (1) a fixed number of dollars or (2) a fixed number of units, the value of which will depend on the changing market value of a portfolio of equities or some other investments. Contracts of the first type are called fixed-dollar or conventional annuities; contracts of the second type are termed variable annuities. Introduced in 1952 by an insurer that restricts its contracts primarily to college educators—College Retirement Equities Fund, affiliated with the Teachers Insurance and Annuity Association—variable annuities are now sold by many leading insurers in most states.

Insurers and Equity Products

Like other fixed-dollar investments, such as corporate bonds and savings accounts, standard life insurance cash values and fixed-dollar annuities do not provide any opportunity for capital appreciation. From World War II until a few years ago, when interest rates paid on long-term fixed-dollar investments rose rapidly, consumers directed an increasing proportion of their savings into equities because (1) they were interested in capital gains and (2) they believed that in the long run the value of a diversified portfolio of common stocks would tend to rise when prices rise, thus preserving real purchasing power. Particularly noteworthy was the increased interest in mutual common stock funds, which permit an investor to participate in a diversified, managed portfolio of securities. Because of this shift in consumer sentiment, term insurance, which does not include a savings element, became more popular relative to cash value life insurance, and fixed-dollar annuities became less attractive to consumers.

To counter this trend many insurers established an organization to market and manage a new mutual fund, acquired an existing organization for this purpose, or affiliated themselves with an independent mutual fund broker-dealer. Regardless of the technique employed, the result was that some or all of their agents could sell both life insurance and mutual funds.

Variable annuities were developed for the same reasons. The variable annuity usually blends the characteristics of a mutual common stock fund with those of an annuity. Like a mutual fund, the variable annuity produces a return that varies with the performance of an invested portfolio of securities. Unlike a mutual fund, the variable annuity can provide a lifetime income. Because of this latter feature, the variable annuity is superior to a mutual fund as a retirement vehicle. On the other hand, a mutual fund is a superior way of accumulating funds to meet short-term needs or to create an estate to be passed on to survivors. Rising interest rates on money market funds and other fixed-dollar instruments have resulted in some new variable annuities based on the returns on these instruments.

Variable life insurance, another product spurred by the interest in equities, is discussed later in this chapter.

After the rapid rise in interest rates on fixed-dollar investments life insurers encountered a weaker market for their mutual common stock funds and variable life insurance and annuities. Cash value life insurance became more attractive relative to common stocks, but term insurance continued to grow more rapidly as insureds became more interested in protection in their early years and many preferred other forms of fixed-dollar investments. For more on insurance as an investment, see later in this chapter.

Special Life Insurance and Annuity Contracts

Numerous modifications and combinations of term insurance contracts, basic nonterm insurance contracts, and annuities are sold by insurers. The reader is referred to any standard text on life insurance for a detailed discussion of these contracts and life insurance in general.[18] However, a few special contracts are so important in the search for economic security that they merit a brief description here:

1   Under a *modified life contract* the protection is for life, but the premium is less in the first three or five years and higher thereafter.

2   A *family income contract* is a whole-life contract plus decreasing term insurance. If the insured dies within some specified family income period, such as 10 or 20 years, the insurer will pay a monthly income of usually $10 or $20 per $1,000 of whole-life protection until the expiration of what remains of that family income period. The face value of the whole-life policy is payable at the end of the period. If the insured lives to the end of the family income period, the decreasing term insurance expires and the policy continues as a whole-life policy. The family income policy is especially designed for a young person with a family whose need for protection is greatest when the children are young.

3   A *family policy* covers all members of a family under one contract. The most common combination is $5,000 of whole-life or endowment insurance on the husband or wife, $1,000 or $1,250 term insurance to age 65 on the spouse, and $1,000 term insurance to age 21 on the children, including children born after the contract becomes effective.

4   A *joint life policy* covers two or more persons under one contract. The face amount is payable on the death of the first insured. Joint life policies have become more common with the growth of two-earner families.

5   A *retirement income annuity* is a deferred annuity plus decreasing term insurance. For each $10 of monthly income provided at retirement age by the annuity there is a promise that $1,000 will be paid to the beneficiary if this amount exceeds the cash value.

6   *Preferred risk policies* or *specials* are usually straight life contracts or contracts paid up at some very advanced age that are sold at reduced rates because applicants must meet superior underwriting standards or, what is more likely, because they are sold only above certain minimum amounts with subsequent expense savings.

7   A *guaranteed insurability rider* attached to a life insurance policy gives the insured the right to purchase additional insurance at specified ages at standard rates. In other words, the insured is protected against loss of his or her insurability.

---

[18]For example, see R. I. Mehr, *Life Insurance: Theory and Practice,* rev. ed. (Austin, Tex.: Business Publications, 1977); S. S. Huebner and K. Black, *Life Insurance,* 10th ed. (Englewood Cliffs, N.J.: Prentice-Hall, 1981); and D. McGill, *Life Insurance,* rev. ed. (Homewood, Ill.: Richard D. Irwin, 1966).

8   Several insurers have introduced *variable life insurance* contracts under
which the insurer is permitted to purchase each year, without proving insurability, additional one-year term insurance that will preserve the purchasing
power of the face amount of insurance. The annual term insurance offer
expires at age 65 or, if earlier, the first year the offer is not accepted. Other
variable contracts adjust both the face amount and the cash value according
to (1) some index or (2) the performance of some separate investment account. Variable life insurance is a natural development following the matura-
tion of the variable annuity concept.

9   *Adjustable life insurance,* sometimes known as "life cycle" insurance, permits the insured to change the face amount and the premium each year as
his or her needs, capital accumulation objectives, and ability to pay the
premium changes. For example, using the plan issued by the insurer that
introduced this insurance in 1971, the insured states initially the amount of
insurance and the annual premium desired. Depending on the relationship
between the face amount and the premium, the policy may provide only
level-premium term insurance for five years, term insurance for a longer
period, straight life insurance, or limited payment life insurance with a
payment period as short as five years. If the insured later changes the
premium, but not the face amount, the type of insurance changes. If the
premium is increased (reduced) and the existing insurance was term insurance, the term is increased (reduced); if the premium increase is large
enough, the term insurance is converted into straight life insurance or limited
payment life insurance. If the existing insurance was straight life or limited
payment life insurance, the premium-payment period is shortened (lengthened. If the premium reduction is large enough, the straight life or limited
payment life insurance is converted into term insurance.) Instead of, or in
combination with, changing the type of insurance, a premium increase (reduction) may be used to increase (reduce) the amount of insurance. Increases
in the face amount are subject to evidence of insurability, except that every
three years the face amount can be increased without proving insurability by
the percentage increase in the CPI, subject to a maximum increase of 20%.
A guaranteed insurability rider, for which there is an additional charge,
would permit the insured to increase the face amount without proving
insurability on specified option dates. The policy can also be extended for an
extra premium to provide protection similar to the family policy described
above.

10 The most recent innovation is *universal life insurance,* which can assume
many forms. Basically, universal life is adjustable life carried one step further
to enable the insured to share in the insurer's current return on the investment portion of the contract. The insurer typically invests these monies in
high-interest-yielding money market securities.

Branches of Individual Insurance

The most important branch of individual insurance sold by commercial insurers is ordinary insurance. These policies are written in amounts of $1,000 or more; premiums are designed to be paid annually but may be paid semiannually, quarterly, or monthly; and all premiums other than the first are paid directly to the branch or home office of the insurer. The preceding discussion or individual insurance has been oriented toward ordinary insurance.

One branch of commercial life insurance that is declining rapidly in relative importance is industrial insurance. "Industrial" policies have provisions that differ slightly from those in ordinary policies and are usually written in amounts of $1,000 or less. In most cases premiums are collected weekly or monthly at the home of the insured. The premiums are higher than the premiums for equivalent ordinary insurance, primarily because of the collection service. This insurance is designed mainly for low-income families.

Contracts similar to those sold by commercial insurers are issued by fraternal societies in all states and by mutual savings banks in Connecticut, Massachusetts, and New York.

Insurance in Force, 1971–1980

The spectacular growth in the total amount of private individual life insurance and the increasingly important role played by commercial ordinary insurance are illustrated by the data in Table 5.9.

At the end of 1980 about two-thirds of the population had some form of private life insurance. The average amount of life insurance in force per family was $41,500, or about two years' total disposable personal income. The average amount per insured family was $48,300. The ratio of insurance in force to total disposable income has remained fairly stable for more than a decade.

Almost all individual annuity contracts are sold by commercial insurers. The amount of annual income then payable or to be provided at maturity date under individual commercial annuity contracts increased from $375 million in 1935 to about $622 million in 1954. Individual annuities then declined in importance until 1961, when the annual income at maturity was reduced to $564 million. This decline, compared with the rapid growth of life insurance in force, was due in part to the tremendous increase in group annuities and and the threat of inflation. Since 1961 individual annuities have gradually regained their popularity as insurers increased the rate of return earned on their invested funds. At year-end 1971 the annual income at maturity under 1.8 million individual annuities in force was $1.4 billion. By year-end 1980 the number of annuities had increased to 5.4 million, and the annual income at maturity to $8.2 million. This growth has been largely attributed to purchases of annuities for individual tax-sheltered pension plans.

Table 5.9   Individual Life Insurance in Force in the United States, 1910–1980 (in Millions of Dollars)

| Year | Commercial Insurance[a] | | Fraternal Societies | Mutual Savings Banks[b] |
	Ordinary	Industrial		
1910	11,783	3,125	8,596	1
1920	32,018	6,948	10,500	15
1930	78,576	17,963	9,539	77
1940	79,346	20,866	6,676	203
1950	149,116	33,415	8,811	580
1960	341,881	39,563	14,235	1,243
1970	734,730	38,644	24,377	4,116
1980	1,760,474	35,994	58,306	13,344

Sources: *1981 Life Insurance Fact Book* (Washington, D.C.: American Council of Life Insurance, 1981), pp. 18, 102; U.S. Department of Labor, Bureau of Labor Statistics, "Operation of Savings Bank Life Insurance in Massachusetts and New York," *Revision of Bulletin 615,* 1941; Alfred M. Best, *Best's Life Insurance Reports* (New York: Alfred M. Best, 1941, 1946).

[a]Individual credit life insurance issued through a lending agency to cover payment of a debt in case of death is not included in these data.

[b]Insurance in force for mutual savings banks includes some group insurance in recent years.

Types of Contracts in Force

In 1977 about 48% of the ordinary life insurance in force was straight life insurance, 13% limited payment life insurance, 4% endowment insurance, 2% retirement income insurance, and 33% term insurance. In 1962 term insurance was only 24% of the total; endowment and retirement income insurance combined were about 10%.

Uninsurability

An individual must be insurable from the viewpoint of the insurer before he or she can obtain a policy. The sources of information consulted by an insurance underwriter are the prospective insured's application, the agent's statement, an inspection bureau's report, and, in about two out of three cases, the results of a medical examination. If there is no medical examination, a detailed nonmedical form must be completed. Personal history, family history, physical condition, and personal habits are considered in making the underwriting decision.

No one knows how many persons fail to apply for insurance because they or their agents know that they are uninsurable, but data are available that indicate the number of applicants refused insurance because of underwriting requirements. Only 3% of the applications received for ordinary life insurance are declined; about six % are rated substandard, chiefly because of physical impairments or hazardous occupations, and as a result these applicants usually pay higher premiums than do standard lives. Over the years underwriting restrictions have been liberalized.

INSURERS AS FINANCIAL INSTITUTIONS

Private life insurers and self-employed pension plans are important sources of funds for investment because a constant flow of new money makes it generally unnecessary to liquidate existing assets to pay claims. In 1980 life insurers provided 8.7% of the $393 billion used in the American money and capital markets.[19] Self-insured pension plans provided 6.4%. Because life insurers and self-employed pension plans favor long-term investments while other important agencies such as commercial banks specialize in short-term funds, life insurers and self-employed pension plans are an even more important source of investment funds than of total funds used in the money and capital markets. Life insurers accounted for 10.9% of these funds, and self-insured pension plans for 9.3%.

Table 5.10 shows how the premiums, total income, and assets of U.S. life insurers have increased since 1940. In 1980 the assets far exceeded the balance in the OASDHI trust funds. The premium income was substantially less than OASDHI contributions, but the total income (premiums increased mostly by investment income) was much closer to the total income of the OASDHI program. Of each $1 received by life insurers in 1980, $0.49 was spent on benefits, $0.28 to increase reserves to meet future claims on outstanding policies, $0.03 to increase surplus funds, $0.15 to pay operating expenses, $0.03 to pay taxes, and $0.01 to pay dividends to stockholders of stock life insurers.

Table 5.10 Premiums, Total Income, and Assets of U.S. Life Insurance, 1940–1980 (In Billions of Dollars)

| | Premiums | | | | Total | |
Year	Life Insurance	Annuities	Health Insurance	Total	Income	Assets
1940	3.5	0.4	—	3.9	5.7	30.8
1945	4.6	0.6	—	5.2	7.7	44.8
1950	6.2	0.9	$ 1.0	8.2	11.3	64.0
1955	8.9	1.3	2.4	12.5	16.5	90.4
1960	12.0	1.3	4.0	17.4	23.0	119.6
1965	16.1	2.3	6.3	24.6	33.2	158.9
1970	21.7	3.7	11.4	36.8	49.1	207.3
1975	29.3	10.2	19.1	58.6	78.0	289.3
1980	40.8	24.0	29.4	94.2	132.5	479.2

Source: 1981 Life Insurance Fact Book (Washington, D.C.: American Council of Life Insurance, 1981), pp. 56, 70.

[19]*Credit and Capital Markets 1981* (New York: Bankers Trust Company, 1981), Tables 1 and 2.

THE IMPACT OF PRIVATE INSURANCE

Private life insurers have made sizable contributions to the economic security of our population. Most American families look to private life insurance and annuities as their major supplement to the floor of protection provided by OASDHI.

The commercial insurer is by far the most important underwriter of private insurance. In this evaluation of private insurance, therefore, we shall discuss primarily the types of protection afforded, the amount of protection, and the premium structures of commercial insurers. A concluding section will briefly summarize the 1981 report of the President's Commission on Pension Policy.

Types of Protection Afforded

Commercial insurers issue a wide variety of life insurance and annuity contracts. Numerous combinations of protection against premature death and a systematic savings plan are obtainable from most leading insurers. New contracts such as adjustable life insurance represent attempts by the industry to make its products more flexible.

Very few persons question the advantages of life insurance as financial protection against premature death, but the following advantages of life insurance and annuity contracts as a systematic savings plan are less widely understood and appreciated:

1 Life insurance is a secure investment. Few insureds have suffered losses because their insurers became insolvent.
2 Because insureds are reluctant to skip premium payments or to borrow against or claim their cash values, they are likely to complete their savings plans. On the other hand, the availability of this asset is a valuable feature in emergencies.
3 The insured does not have to be concerned with investment decisions.
4 The cash values in the contract guarantee the insured a minimum rate of return that increases with the duration of the contract.
5 Actual interest returns compare favorably with returns on other investments of similar quality. This observation is discussed in more detail below.
6 In case of death the investment passes to the beneficiaries directly, thus avoiding the expense and delays of probate action.

Because the premium paid for a cash value life insurance policy purchases a package of decreasing protection and increasing savings, the return on the savings element in a life insurance contract is a complicated concept. One widely used approach calculates the rate of return one would have to make on some alternative investment program to achieve the same results over a specified period at the same cost as the purchase of the nonterm insurance contract for which the rate of return is being sought. More specifically, assume that a person, age 35, is considering the purchase of a $1,000 straight life insurance contract for which the cash value at the close of the 20th policy year is about $300. Instead of buying this policy he or she could buy decreasing term insurance and invest the difference between the premium for the straight life insurance and that for the decreasing term insurance in a savings account, mutual fund shares, or some other medium. The face value of the decreasing term insurance must be such that it equals $1,000 when added to the increasing investment. In this way if the insured dies prior to the expiration of the 20th year, the beneficiary receives the same amount whether the insured purchases the straight life insurance or the separate term insurance investment plan. The rate of return on the life insurance savings element is assumed to be that one would have to make on the separate investment fund for it to equal the $300 cash value at the close of the 20th year.

In 1979 Consumers Union applied this method to determine the rates of return on the savings components of 277 "cash value" policies (straight life or paid up at some advanced age) sold by over 100 insurers.[20] In each case Consumers Union determined the cost of the alternative term insurance using "low-cost" term rates developed by the Society of Actuaries, a professional association of life insurance actuaries. Higher term rates would have produced higher yields; lower term rates would have produced lower yields.[21] For the median $100,000 policy issued to a 35-year-old male by a participating insurer (an insurer that pays dividends to its policyholders) the annual yield over a 29-year period was 4.7%. The 9-year annual yield was only 1.2%, the 19-year annual yield 4.5%. For the median $100,000 policy issued to a 35-year-old male by a nonparticipating insurer the 29-year yield was 3.48%. The yields varied greatly among insurers; they also differed according to the issue age and the amount purchased. For example, for $100,000 participating life insurance policies issued at age 36 the annual yields over a 29-year period ranged from 8.07 to 2.24% among insurers. The best 29-year yields available from participating insurers ranged from 7.64% for a $100,000 policy issued at age 25 to 8.93% for a $25,000 policy issued at age 45.[22]

In evaluating these returns it is important to remember that these returns are substantially tax sheltered. No federal income taxes are payable on the investment return on the straight life insurance until the person cashes in the contract. Moreover, at that time only the excess of the cash value over the total premiums paid (less dividends) is taxable. As a result most persons will pay little or no tax.

---

[20]"Life Insurance: Part 2 of a Special Two-Part Report," *Consumer Reports,* XLV, No. 3 (March 1980), 163–188.

[21]For example, insureds who can obtain lower-cost association or group term insurance would not have to earn as much on the separate investment to accumulate a sum equal to the cash value.

[22]Similar returns were reported in a recent Federal Trade Commission staff report. See *Life Insurance Cost Disclosure,* Staff Report to the Federal Trade Commission by the Bureau of Consumer Protection of the Bureau of Economics, July, 1979, Tables II-7 and II-8. Unfortunately, a press release on this study suggested that the rates of return were much lower than suggested by these tables.

If the insured's combined federal and state income tax bracket is 50%, a taxable investment would have to earn 12% to equal 6% tax free.

On the negative side, in the short run the return on life insurance savings is small and commonly negative. Also, like other fixed-dollar investments, cash value life insurance provides no protection against long-period inflation and no opportunity for capital appreciation. As explained earlier, insurers have as a result added variable annuities, variable life insurance, and mutual funds to their product lines.

Some insurers have recently developed new life insurance and annuity products designed to provide with certain tax advantages about the same rates of return as short-term money market funds. Interest in such products is growing.

Life insurance contracts contain many liberal provisions. For example, if the insured dies two or more years after the life insurance contract is issued, the insurer cannot refuse to pay the death claim because of misrepresentations by the insured at the time he applied for the contract, even if fraud is involved. The contracts are also flexible, as evidenced by the nonforfeiture and settlement options.

The promises of life insurers are secure. State regulatory bodies restrict the investments of commercial insurers to high-grade securities and require them to establish a policy reserve item on the liability side of their balance sheets. This policy reserve is equal to the difference between the present values of estimated future benefits and of expected future premium payments under contracts already in force. The policy reserve differs from the OASI Trust Fund in that an indefinite operation is not and cannot be assumed. If a commercial insurer sold no new contracts, the premium payments under the contracts in force plus assets corresponding to the policy reserve amounts should be sufficient to discharge the obligations of the insurer.

However, many persons have not received the optimum protection for their premium dollars. One of the most common failings is an overemphasis on the savings feature of life insurance at a time when protection against premature death is the most important need. Unfortunately, some insurers and agents fail to recommend term insurance in many situations where it would appear to be the best choice. For example, many young workers with dependents have 20-payment life contracts in situations where renewable and convertible term insurance would seem more appropriate. On the other hand, the authors do not agree with the fairly common suggestion that most persons would be better off if they limited their life insurance programs solely to pure term insurance contracts.

This less-than-optimum protection in individual cases may be ascribed to many factors, the most important of which are (1) a lack of knowledge and appreciation of basic insurance principles by insureds and (2) the poor advice provided by what is fortunately a small proportion of insurance agents or other advisers. Both situations are being rectified, though much remains to be done. Insureds have more opportunity than ever before to learn the basic principles of life insurance. Journals and magazines print more feature articles on insurance;

competent authors have written helpful books on the subject.[23] As for the caliber of the average insurance agent, it has greatly improved: agents are required to know more about insurance contracts, law, rates, and reserves than in the past. Life insurance programming—a survey of private insurance needs followed by the selection of the best insurance contracts and settlement options to meet those needs—and estate planning have become common procedures. Some excellent training and educational programs have been established, one of which leads to the professional designation of Chartered Life Underwriter (C.L.U.).

In 1976 the National Association of Insurance Commissioners, an organization of state insurance commissioners that promotes uniformity in state legislation and regulations affecting insurance, adopted a model life insurance solicitation regulation. Many states have adopted this regulation or a similar one. Under this model disclosure bill the agent must give the buyer (1) a Buyer's Guide and (2) a Policy Summary Sheet. The Buyer's Guide describes types of life insurance policies, dividends, cash values, and how to determine the cost of life insurance using the interest-adjusted cost indices described in the section below on premium structures. The Policy Summary Sheet shows the type of policy, the annual premiums, cash values, dividend projections, interest-adjusted cost indices, and other data for policies purchased or to be purchased.

Amount of Protection

Relatively few persons are unable to purchase private individual life insurance because they are uninsurable. Another relatively small group can purchase only substandard insurance, which is either more expensive or more restricted than the contracts issued to standard lives. A very small number of persons will always be uninsurable, and contracts may on rare occasions have war and aviation exclusions, but individual underwriting procedures have been continually liberalized.

Group insurance provides relatively inexpensive protection for all participants and is especially valuable to persons who are uninsurable by individual insurance standards. Many families with no individual insurance, particularly among those with low incomes, have group insurance protection. On the other hand, over 20% of the wage and salary workers are not covered under death benefit plans. Furthermore, the protection is not tailor-made for the individual and, although the protection is convertible when the member leaves the group, the conversion cost is sometimes more than the member can afford. The continuation of group insurance on covered workers is an encouraging development.

---

[23]See the life insurance texts cited in footnote 18 of this chapter. For a different viewpoint, see consumer education books such as the one published by Consumers Union, *The Consumers Union Report on Life Insurance,* 4th ed. (Mount Vernon, N.Y.: Consumers Union, 1980).

Premium Structures

Private insurance premiums should not, on the average, exceed the expected losses and expected reasonable expenses plus a reasonable margin for contingencies and profit. In addition, they should distribute the cost equitably among insureds. The manner in which premiums vary among insureds has been discussed at various points in this chapter. The premium variations are equitable in the sense that they are supported to a large extent by differences in costs. A few additional facts concerning the general level of rates should be noted here.

The initial cost of a life insurance or annuity contract is determined by the insurer's expected mortality rates, interest rates earned on invested assets, and expenses. If the actual experience is more favorable than the expected one, the policyholders may gain because, as indicated previously, over half the life insurance in force was issued on a participating basis. Moreover, competition forces the nonparticipating insurers to make their estimates as realistic as possible.

Mortality rates have decreased, thus reducing life insurance costs and increasing annuity costs. Interest rates declined from about 5% in 1930 to 2.88% in 1947, but since that date they have increased to about 8.1% in 1980. Most life insurance investments are limited by choice and by statute to debt obligations whose yield has been greatly affected by the monetary and fiscal policies of the federal government. Expenses average about 15% of total income. Increasing mechanization, group coverages, and high-minimum policies tend to reduce the expenses, but increasing wages, rents, taxes, and other costs operate in the opposite direction. The expense ratio varies greatly among contracts and branches of insurance. All these factors plus mortality and investment experience vary among insurers. Many insureds underestimate the resulting variation in premium rates among insurance companies.

Consumers who wish to compare the premiums charged by leading insurers can consult one of several publications.[24] "Net cost" calculations were formerly used to compare insurers with respect to cost. The "net cost" is the sum of the premiums for some period, usually 20 years, less the projected dividends and the cash value at the end of the period, the difference being divided by the number of years in the period. These comparisons were criticized because they ignore the loss of interest on the premiums paid, differences in settlement options and other policy provisions, and differences in the ranking of insurers depending on the type of policy, age, and period selected for the comparison. Several other methods, too complex to discuss here, have been suggested to avoid some of these difficulties. The most popular of these methods is the interest-adjusted method, endorsed by the National Association of Insurance Commissioners and required in many states, which takes into account the time value of money and the way in which the cash values increase during the policy term.

---

[24]For example, *Flitcraft Compend* (Morristown, N.J.: Flitcraft, annual), or *Cost Facts on Life Insurance* (Cincinnati, Ohio: The National Underwriter Company, annual). See also the Consumers Union report cited in Ref. 23 of this Chapter.

Under the interest-adjusted cost method two indexes are calculated: an interest-adjusted cost surrender cost index and an interest-adjusted payments index. The surrender cost index, which assumes that the contract is surrendered at the end of the period, is determined as follows: first, calculate the accumulated value of the premiums at the end of, say, 20 years on the assumption that these premiums are invested at, say, 5% interest. Second, deduct the accumulated value of the dividends paid over these 20 years. Third, deduct the cash value or special termination dividend paid at the end of 20 years. Fourth, divide the remainder by the accumulated value of $1 invested at the beginning of each year for 20 years.[25] The result is the amount the insured would have to invest each year at 5% to accumulate a sum equal to the premiums less dividends accumulated at 5% less the cash value at the end of 20 years. For example, assume a nonparticipating (no dividends) straight life insurance policy for which the annual premium is $22 and the 20-year cash value $335. The 20-year interest-adjusted surrender cost index is

$$\frac{\$22(34.719) - \$335}{34.719} = \$12.35.$$

The interest-adjusted payments index does not assume surrender of the contract. This index is calculated in the same way, except that the cash value or special termination dividend is ignored. Using the example above, the index is

$$\frac{\$22(34.719)}{34.719} = \$22.$$

Although a substantial improvement over the traditional net cost method, this method must also be used with care. The cost ranking of insurers may vary depending on the time period and policy studied and the interest rate assumed. Furthermore, insurers frequently change their premiums and dividends. Finally, the policies issued by different insurers may vary with respect to settlement option guarantees and other features.

Another way of comparing costs on cash value policies is to compare the yields one would have to make on an alternative investment to achieve the same results over a specified period. These yields have already been discussed in the section on types of protection offered.

The President's Commission on Pension Policy

In 1977 President Carter appointed a President's Commission on Pension Policy to study public and private pension plans and recommend what Congress might do to improve these plans. The Commission's research, progress, and final (1981)

[25]$1.05^{20} + 1.05^{19} + \ldots + 1.05 = 34.719$.

report have received considerable attention because of the growing concern about problems of the aged, the high cost of pensions, and their economic effects (for example, their effect on the mobility of labor and private savings). Many observers also remembered that a report by a similar commission established by President Kennedy in 1962 was largely responsible for the 1974 passage of ERISA.

Private Pension Plans

The major recommendations of the President's Commission on Pension Policy with respect to private pension plans were as follows:

1 Every employer should be required to have a pension plan covering workers age 25 or older with one year or more of service. The minimum benefit would be a defined contribution of 3% of annual wages. This benefit would be fully and immediately vested. Firms starting new plans would be given tax credits to cushion the cost impact. Immediate reactions suggest that the prospects for this proposal are dim.

2 More study is needed on the effects of raising the minimum mandatory retirement age to 70 before any attempt is made to increase this age. The Commission did recommend, however, that private plans, like OASDI, gradually raise the normal retirement age.

3 Because of cost considerations, no change should be made in present minimum vesting standards. In an interim report the Commission had recommended liberalization of these standards.

4 Low- and moderate-income workers should receive tax credits for contributions to private pension plans. Higher-pay workers should be able to deduct their contributions in determining their taxable income.

5 All employers should provide death benefits for surviving spouses. These survivors benefits could be provided through group life insurance or a portion of vested pension benefits.

Public Plans

The Commission's recommendations on public plans covered (1) OASDI, (2) pension programs for federal employees, and (3) an ERISA for public plans.

   OASDI   In the short run the Commission recommended (1) permitting the OASI Fund to borrow from the DI and HI trust funds, (2) raising the 1982 employee tax rate to the 1985 level, (3) stopping state and local employees from withdrawing from the program, and (4) if necessary, permitting OASDI to borrow funds from the U.S. Treasury.

   The major long-term recommendations were to (1) gradually raise the normal retirement age from 65 to 68 by 1990, (2) eliminate the earnings test for persons age 65 or over, and (3) tax OASDI benefits but make the contributions tax deductible,

Pension Programs for Federal Employees   The Commission concluded that pension programs for federal employees were too liberal. They would gradually increase the earliest age at which a federal employee could collect a full retirement benefit from 55 to 65 in 1990, and to 68 in 2002. Benefits would be increased only once a year, not twice, because of price increases; the adjustment could not exceed the increase in average federal wages that year. All new federal employees would be covered under OASDHI.

ERISA for Public Plans   The Commission favored a federal law for public pension plans similar to ERISA for private plans.

A Comment on Some Economic Issues

The existence of private insurance has important economic consequences. The overall effect of private insurance is to increase the fund of savings available for investments in the economy. Annuity premiums and the portions of life insurance premiums that are used to build up cash values represent a type of forced savings, which insurers must invest, thus increasing production in the future when the insureds plan to retire. Private pension plans apparently not only result in forced savings but encourage savings in other ways. The term portions of the premiums probably also lead to an increase in available short-term investment funds, for the insurer can invest these amounts for the period elapsing between the payments of the premiums and of the expenses and benefits. If investment opportunities are not available, private insurance may simply reduce current spending and hence national income.

Once important consequence of private programs is their effect on labor mobility, as affected particularly by group insurance. The effect of group life insurance is slight because the employee's only loss in moving from one employer to another may be a period of no coverage during the waiting period. As already noted, group pensions are a more important factor, especially when the vesting provisions are a function of the length of service. Older workers are more likely to be affected by this consideration than are younger workers. It should also be remembered that seniority carries with it other advantages, which the worker must also consider. Group insurance exerts its greatest influence when the proposed movement is from a firm with group insurance to one with no group insurance.

SUMMARY

The typical family's insurance program for dealing with the financial problems associated with death and old age includes three layers of protection, (1) OASI, (2) employee-benefit plans, and (3) individual life insurance and annuities.

Over three-fourths of all wage and salary workers are covered under death benefit plans arranged by their employers; almost half of all private workers are covered under retirement plans, almost two-thirds of full-time workers, age 25 or over.

Group life insurance, the most common form of death protection, was first written by a commercial insurer in 1912 for Montgomery Ward employees. Commercial insurers entered the group pension field in the 1920s. Self-insured group pension plans were also important by that time. Almost all the early group plans were employer initiated, but group insurance benefits are now an important issue for collective bargaining.

Each member of an eligible group is eligible for group life insurance, even if he or she is not individually insurable. Another advantage to the insured is that the cost is lower than the that of equivalent individual insurance.

Most group life insurance is yearly renewable term insurance. An insured who leaves the group may replace the group protection with an individual life insurance contract without proving insurability.

Group pension benefits are computed according to either a defined benefit or a defined contribution formula. The most common benefit is a specified percentage of a worker's average salary during his or her five highest-earnings years times the number of years of service. The benefits are specified in terms of one annuity form, but usually other forms may be elected. An increasing number of plans adjust the benefit after retirement to reflect changes in the cost of living or the value of the investments in the pension fund.

Benefits available to employees terminating their employment at an early date depend on the vesting provisions. Death benefits are usually limited to a return of the employee's contributions.

The Employee Retirement Income Security Act of 1974 placed several constraints on pension plan design and administration. Among the constraints are age and service coverage requirements, minimum vesting standards, and minimum funding standards.

The pension plan may be a self-insured plan or an insured one. Insured plans include a pension trust, a group annuity plan, a deposit administration plan, an immediate participation guarantee plan, and a separate account plan. Most pension plans are insured, but the self-insured ones cover more employees.

Most new group insurance plans are noncontributory, primarily because of the tax advantages and collective bargaining.

The basic types of individual life insurance contracts are term insurance contracts and nonterm contracts, including the straight life, limited payment, and endowment contracts. Term insurance provides temporary protection against death losses only. Nonterm contracts combine protection against death losses with a systematic savings plan.

Death proceeds are payable in a lump sum or according to some settlement option selected by the insured or his beneficiary.

The savings fund under nonterm contracts may be used to continue some life insurance protection if the insured wishes to stop paying premiums. If the insured prefers, he or she may receive the savings fund in a lump sum or according to some settlement option.

Annuity contracts are primarily designed to protect the insured against the problems of old age. The basic annuities may be classified as immediate or deferred annuities and as straight life, installment refund, or cash refund annuities. Annuities may also be classified according to whether they provide fixed or variable benefits.

Many insurers have added to their product lines several equity-based products: variable annuities, mutual funds, and variable life insurance. Universal life and adjustable life are the two most recent innovations.

SUGGESTIONS FOR ADDITIONAL READING

Coming of Age: Toward a National Retirement Income Policy. Washington, D.C.: President's Commission on Pension Policy, 1981.
The final report by a national commission appointed by President Carter to study private and public pension plans.

The Consumers Union Report on Life Insurance, 4th ed. Mount Vernon, N.Y.: Consumers Union, 1980.
An educational report on individual life insurance by a leading consumer organization.

Contemporary Benefit Issues and Administration. Brookfield, Wisc.: International Foundation of Employee Benefit Plans, 1979.
A description and analysis of the leading issues involving employee-benefit plans.

Gregg, Davis W., and Vane B. Lucas (Eds.). *Life and Health Insurance Handbook,* 3rd ed. Homewood, Ill.: Richard D. Irwin, 1973.
A handbook of current practices and procedures in the life and health insurance fields.

Huebner, S. S., and Kenneth Black. *Life Insurance,* 10th ed. New York: Prentice-Hall, 1981.
A popular, comprehensive book on life insurance.

Ilse, Louise Wolters. *Group Insurance and Employee Retirement Plans.* Englewood Cliffs, N.J.: Prentice-Hall, 1953.
Chapters 1 through 6, 12, and 13 are particularly relevant.

Mehr, Robert I. *Life Insurance: Theory and Practice,* rev. ed. Austin, Tex.: Business Publications, 1977.
A popular, comprehensive treatment of life insurance.

Melone, Joseph J., E. T. Allen, Jr., and J. S. Rosenbloom. *Pension Planning,* 4th ed. Homewood, Ill.: Richard D. Irwin, 1981.
A comprehensive book on pensions.

McGill, Dan Mays. Fundamentals of Private Pensions, 4th ed. Homewood, Ill.: Richard D. Irwin, 1979.
An excellent description and analysis of the fundamentals of group pension plans.

McGinn, D. F. *Joint Trust Pension Plans.* Homewood, Ill.: Richard D. Irwin, 1978.
A comprehensive discussion of multiemployer plans.

Public Policy and Private Pension Programs. A Report to the President on Private Employee Retirement Plans, by the President's Committee on Corporate Pension Funds and Other Private Retirement and Welfare Funds. Washington, D.C.: Government Printing Office, 1965.
A report by a special committee appointed by President Kennedy to study pension and welfare plans. This report led eventually to the Employee Retirement and Income Security Act of 1974.

Rosenbloom, Jerry S., and G. Victor Hallman. *Employee Benefit Planning.* Englewood Cliffs, N.J.: Prentice-Hall, 1981.

A comprehensive, clearly written text on the objectives and characteristics of employee-benefit plans.

Snider, H. Wayne (Ed.). *Employee Benefits Management.* New York: Risk and Insurance Management Society, 1980.
An informative compilation of 14 essays by specialists in the field of employee benefits.

Spencer, Bruce F. *Group Benefits in a Changing Society.* Chicago, Ill.: Charles B. Spencer 1978.
A well-illustrated description of group life and health insurance benefits and practices.

1975 Study of Industrial Retirement Plans. New York: Bankers Trust Company, 1975.
A study of recent trends in retirement plans and a tabulation of the provisions of over 200 retirement plans.

Chapter Six

The Problems of
Poor Health

Poor health may cause a person to incur medical expenses or become disabled. The person may be ill because of an accidental injury or a sickness; the cause may or not be job-related. Poor health is the subject of the next five chapters. In this chapter we shall first discuss the types of losses caused by accidental injuries and sickness, their frequency and severity, the prices and supply of medical services, and the total costs of illness. A general discussion of the various private and public methods of attacking the economic problems created by poor health will be followed by a presentation of some data on the economic status of disabled persons.

Chapters 7 through 10 contain a more detailed discussion of workers' compensation insurance, other social insurance programs protecting insureds against loss of income caused by disability, social medical expense insurance, and private health insurance, respectively.

LOSSES CAUSED BY ACCIDENTAL INJURY AND SICKNESS

Nature and Importance

An accidental injury or sickness may cause a financial loss through medical expenses and loss of income. The potential loss of income may be estimated in the manner outlined in Chapter 2 for computing the income loss caused by death, but the cost of maintenance should not be subtracted and the income loss may be partial or temporary. The income loss caused by total and permanent disability will exceed the income loss caused by death because the maintenance cost continues. A prolonged disability may also cause a worker to be a less attractive employee after he or she recovers, because the skills the worker possessed may have become rusty or technologically obsolete. In addition, even if a person was never occupationally disabled or recovered from such a disability, the illness may restrict his or her personal life: for example, he or she may be unable to play tennis or travel to certain places. Medical expenses take the form of hospital bills, physicians' and surgeons' charges, nurses' fees, and medicine and appliance costs. The loss potential is great.

Probability of Accidental Injury or Sickness

The probability of an accidental injury or sickness loss is much more difficult to state than the probability of death for at least three reasons.

First, it is relatively easy to tell whether a person has suffered an accidental injury, but it is almost impossible to determine whether certain individuals are sick. Some persons will claim for various reasons that they are sick while they are apparently not. Others are sick, but they will not admit it.

Even if this problem did not exist, what is poor health? Is a slight cold a sickness? Is a minor cut on a finger an accidental injury? Someone has stated that we are all ill; it is just a matter of degree. Furthermore, because of differences in character or occupation, we must recognize that the same illness may disable one person but not another.

Second, a person may be ill more than once during a year, and each illness may last for a different period. The probability structure would be a complex one to describe even if the exact probabilities were known. Furthermore, the economic loss depends not only on the frequency and duration of the illness, but also on its seriousness in terms of income loss and medical expenses.

Third, births, deaths, and certain illnesses are reported on a regular basis to public authorities, but most injuries and sicknesses have not been so reported until recently, and the only information on the health status of our population came from several local studies and some special-purpose surveys, most of which were conducted many years ago.

Despite these handicaps and limitations, two studies have added greatly to our knowledge of potential disability income losses and medical expenses. In 1956 Congress authorized a *continuing* National Health Survey by the Public Health Service of the civilian, noninstitutional population. The survey develops statistics on sickness, accidental injuries, disability, the use of hospital, physicians', dental, and other services, and other health-related topics at least once a year. These statistics are based on data from a carefully selected nationwide sample, which typically includes about 120,000 persons from 41,000 households.

In 1966, 1972, and 1978 the Social Security Administration (SSA) conducted major surveys of the number of noninstitutionalized disabled persons age 18–64 in the population and their characteristics. The 1978 survey, like the 1966 and 1972 surveys, is also based on a sample, in this instance including about 12,000 persons.

Data from the National Health Survey and the 1978 SSA survey will be used to indicate the frequency and severity patterns of disability income and medical expense losses.[1]

---

[1] Unless otherwise noted, the data cited in this chapter are from the National Center for Health Statistics, *Current Estimates from the Health Interview Survey: United States—1978,* U.S. Department of Health, Education, and Welfare, Public Health Service, Series 10, No. 130 (November 1979)

Prevalence of Poor Health

According to the National Health Survey, in 1978, a fairly typical survey year, the average person was forced to restrict his or her activity on about 19 days and had to remain in bed most of the day on about seven days. The average worker, age 17 and over, lost about five complete workdays. The variations in these average disability days by age and sex are presented in Table 6.1.

The average person sustained about 2.2 acute conditions that year, acute conditions being defined as those involving either medical attention or at least one day of restricted activity and lasting less than three months. The incidence of acute conditions declined with age, the average incidence being about 3.9 conditions for children under 6 and 1.3 conditions for adults 45 and over.

On an average day in 1978 over 30 million persons, or 14% of the civilian noninstitutional population, had their activities limited to some degree by a chronic condition—one that had lasted at least three months. Approximately 23 million, or 11% of the population, were limited in the amount or kind of *major* activity they could perform. Major activities include working, keeping house, or engaging in school or preschool activities. The proportion of persons with some activity limitation due to a chronic condition increased with age (3.9% for persons under 17, increasing to 45.0% for persons 65 or over). Males had somewhat higher disability rates than females in all age groups.

According to the 1978 Social Security Administration Survey of Disabled and Nondisabled Adults, slightly more than 17% of the civilian noninstitutionalized population, age 20–64, considered themselves disabled that year because of a chronic health condition or impairment.[2] Severely disabled persons—those who

Table 6.1 Disability Days per Person, by Age and Sex, United States, 1978

Years of Age	Restricted-Activity Days		Bed-Disability Days		Work-Loss Days[a]	
	Male	Female	Male	Female	Male	Female
Under 17	10.7	11.8	4.9	5.6	—	—
17–24	10.5	14.0	4.1	6.8	4.2	4.9
25–44	13.9	18.3	4.5	7.1	4.4	6.0
45–64	23.2	28.1	7.3	10.1	6.2	5.9
65 and over	35.1	43.9	14.2	14.8	2.9[b]	6.5[b]
All ages	16.3	21.1	6.0	8.2	4.9	5.7

Source: National Center for Health Statistics, *Current Estimates from the Health Interview Survey: United States—1978,* U.S. Department of Health, Education, and Welfare, Public Health Service, Series 10, No. 130 (November 1979).

[a]For currently employed persons age 17 or older.

[b]Data not reliable.

[2]*Work Disability in the United States: A Chartbook* (Washington, D.C.: U.S. Department of Health and Human Services, Social Security Administration, Office of Research and Statistics, December 1980).

were unable to work either regularly or at all—comprised about 50% of the disabled and 8% of the population. Occupationally disabled individuals—those who were able to work regularly but not full-time nor doing the same work as before the disability commenced—totaled about 4% of the population. The third group of disabled persons, about 5% of the population, had secondary work limitations. They were able to work full-time, regularly, and at the same work, but they were limited in the kind or amount of work they could perform. Women who were limited in keeping house but not in their outside work were included in this category.

According to this survey, disability prevalence rates were slightly higher for women than for men. A considerable larger proportion of women (10%) than men (7%) were *severely* disabled. This higher prevalence of severe disability rates among women was attributed to differences between the sexes in the types of impairment, perceptions of disability, work requirements, work availability, and motivation for work.

Disability rates increased with age, rising from about 7% for young adults age 18–34 to over 36% for the oldest age category, 55–64. *Severe* disability rates rose even more sharply with age, from under 3% for the youngest age group to 25% for the oldest category.

Disability rates were also higher for blacks than for whites, for divorced and widowed persons, for persons with less education, and for persons living in rural areas.

None of these data indicate the probability of a person becoming disabled. The data on the incidence of acute conditions do indicate their frequency of occurrence, but acute conditions do not always result in disability, even for a day. The other data indicate the prevalence of a certain condition at a specified time or the average loss per year. If, say, 5% of the population is disabled on the survey date, the probability of being disabled within a year may be more or less (probably more) than 5%. Some persons disabled on the date were first disabled years ago; some persons not disabled on that date will be disabled within the year. If, say, the average person is disabled 6 days a year, this could result from a 50% chance of being disabled 12 days, a 25% chance of being disabled 24 days, a 50% chance of being disabled twice (each time for 6 days), or many other frequency and severity combinations. Insurance data, however, do shed some light on the probability of insured persons being disabled 90 days or longer.[3] Some sample data are presented below:

	Age 27	Age 37	Age 47	Age 57
Probability of being disabled for at least 90 days within the next year	.00667	.00981	.01676	.03110

[3]Health Insurance Association of America, *1964 Commissioners Disability Table* (New York: HIAA, 1965), Vol. III, p. 13.

Probability of dying
within the next year,
U.S. total population   .00130   .00187   .00467   .01092

Because the insured population is presumably healthier than is the general population, the chance of being disabled is probably higher for the average person in the United States. However, even these figures show that at every age the probability of being disabled for at least 90 days within the next year substantially exceeds the probability of death. The probability of a person in his or her 20s being disabled for at least 90 days prior to age 65 is about $\frac{2}{3}$.

We now turn to potential medical expenses. According to the National Health Survey, in 1978 over 10% of the population had one or more short-stay hospital episodes. About 1.4% had two episodes, and 0.5% three or more stays. The average length of stay was 9.7 days. Females were hospitalized more often than males, but their average stay was shorter. Persons 65 and over were hospitalized more than three times as often as young persons under 17, and their average stay was more than twice as long.

In the same year the average person made about 4.8 visits to a doctor. Females made more visits than males, 5.4 visits compared with 4.0 visits. Persons 75 and over made the most visits—6.4. Over half the population had visited a doctor within the last six months.

Causes of Disability

According to the National Health Survey, in 1978 acute conditions were responsible for about 9.9 days of restricted activity per person, over half of the average number of restricted-activity days reported. The number of days of restricted activity associated with the five major classes of acute conditions were as follows:

Respiratory conditions	4.4
Injuries	2.2
Infective and parasitic conditions	0.9
Digestive system conditions	0.5
All other acute conditions	1.8

Among chronic conditions, the following cause the most important limitations of activity:

Arthritis and rheumatism.

Heart disease.

Impairments of back or spine.

Mental and nervous conditions.

Impairments of lower extremities and hips.

Impairment of vision.

Hypertension without heart involvement.

In the 1978 Social Security Administration survey of disabled adults two-thirds of the severely disabled persons reported a musculoskeletal disorder. Over half reported a cardiovascular problem.

Note that injuries account for only a small fraction of the restricted-activity days associated with acute conditions. Another fact that emphasizes the much more important role of sickness is that of the 2.2 acute conditions affecting the average person, only about 0.3 were injuries. Adding the restricted-activity days caused by impairments due to previous injuries raises the estimated number of restricted-activity days per person due to injuries to 3.4, still a small number relative to the total 18.8. For persons age 17–64 work injuries caused about 0.9 restricted-activity days per person. Clearly, nonoccupational illness is a much more frequent problem than is occupational illness. However, in the 1978 Social Security Administration survey over 20% of all disabled adults reported impairments caused by job injuries; another 12% reported a condition caused directly by bad working conditions (noise, heat, or smoke).

A Special Note on Job-Connected Injuries and Sickness

Although job-connected injuries and sickness may be less frequent than nonoccupational illnesses, they still disable about 2.3 million workers each year.[4] About 13,200 workers die each year from work-related causes. Per 100,000 workers there were 2,374 disabling injuries in 1979, compared with 2,798 in 1970. The 1979 fatality rate was 13.6 per 100,000 workers, compared with 17.6 in 1970.

Around the turn of the century jobs were much less safe than they are today and occupational injuries became the first threat to economic security to inspire social insurance legislation in the form of workers' compensation. The exact magnitude of occupational accidents at that time cannot be accurately determined. The few data available are not comprehensive and are largely estimates. Farm work was by no means "safe." Hours were long and the work was strenuous and subject to natural physical hazards. Yet its hazards were relatively few compared with those introduced by mechanized work (including mechanized work on farms). Power-driven machines, and machine tools in particular, created new and serious accident hazards.

It would be inaccurate, however, to attribute the rising accident rate to mechanization alone. Each industry, because of its environment or operations, had its own peculiar hazards. Cave-ins and explosions in the coal mines, moving locomotives, lead poisons, overhead cranes, the pace of the new industrial tempo —all contributed to the employment hazards. So, too, did the interdependence

[4]*Insurance Facts, 1980–81 Edition* (New York: Insurance Information Institute, 1980), p. 62.

of employees in the factory system.[5] In addition, there were the problems of the fatigue of long hours, child labor, the use of "cheap" immigrant labor, and the failure of the large factories, which today produce the most enviable safety records, to assume much responsibility for the injured.[6] Somers estimates that the

> . . . peak in the industrial accident rate was reached during the first decade of the century, probably about 1907–1908. In the year ending June 30, 1907, 4,534 workers were killed in railroading alone; 1907 was also the blackest year in mining: 2,534 men were killed in bituminous mines alone.[7]

Frederick L. Hoffman of the Prudential Life Insurance Company, whose estimates for early accident experience are as good as any available, guessed the total occupational 1908 death toll at between 30,000 and 35,000.[8] A more conservative estimate by Dr. E. H. Downey numbered occupationally caused deaths at 25,000, permanent disabilities at 25,000, and temporary disabilities lasting over three days at 2 million.[9] Frederick Lewis Allen writes that

> . . . in the single year 1901, one out of every 399 railroad employees was killed; and one out of every 26 was injured. Among engineers, conductors, brakemen, trainmen, etc., the figures were even worse than this: In that single year, one out of every 137 was killed.[10]

Occupational injuries and diseases also received and continue to receive special attention simply because they are job connected. The value judgments of our society have been such that we believe our obligations to be greater to a person injured on the job than to a person engaged in some other activity. Occupational diseases tend to be understated by reported occupational injury data, since many evolve over long periods of time. The list of illnesses that come as a natural consequence of employment is nearly inexhaustible:

> The fisherman's rheumatism, the waiter's fallen arches, the surgeon's hypertension, the miner's silicosis, the boilermaker's deafness, the bus driver's peptic ulcer, the

[5]See Crystal Eastman, *Work Accidents and the Law* (New York: Russell Sage Foundation, 1916); reprinted in Paul H. Douglas, Curtice N. Hitchcock, and Willard E. Atkins (Eds.), *The Workers in Modern Economic Society* (Chicago, Ill.: University of Chicago Press, 1923), pp. 401–412.

[6]Arthur H. Reede, *Adequacy of Workmen's Compensation* (Cambridge, Mass.: Harvard University Press, 1947), p. 345.

[7]Reprinted by permission from Herman M. Somers *and* Anne R. Somers, *Workmen's Compensation* (New York: John Wiley and Sons, 1954), p. 9.

[8]Frederick L. Hoffman, "Industrial Accidents," *Bulletin of the Bureau of Labor Statistics,* September 3, 1908, 418. Quoted in Philip Taft, *Economics and Problems of Labor,* 3rd ed. (Harrisburg, Pa.: Stackpole, 1955), p. 123.

[9]Taft, *ibid.*

[10]Reprinted with permission from Frederick Lewis Allen, *The Big Change* (New York: Harper and Row, 1952), p. 56.

housemaid's bursitic knee are all, like a thousand other complaints, more or less directly attributable to the environmental conditions under which their victims work.[11]

But, in cases of occupational disease, the causal relationship between disabling disease and the occupation in which the individual is engaged is often more obscure than in the case of a traumatic injury.

Employers currently have a legal responsibility under workers' compensation laws for the wages lost and medical expenses incurred by a worker who is injured on the job or incurs a job-related disease. Less apparent costs to the employer are the other losses, often called indirect losses, which may equal or exceed the payments to employees.[12] Illustrations of such costs are wages paid to workers who were not injured but lose working time because of an accident; the cost of repairing, replacing, or straightening materials or equipment damaged in an accident; and the wages paid supervisors for time required for activities necessitated by an accident.

One result of the Occupational Safety and Health Act (OSHA), to be discussed in Chapter 7, is much more accurate data on occupational injuries and sickness. According to the most recent survey of about 200,000 sample units by the Bureau of Labor Statistics of the Department of Labor, during 1979, per 100 full-time equivalent workers in private industry there were 9.5 "recordable cases"—all job-related deaths and sickness and all injuries resulting in one or more of the following: loss of consciousness, restriction of work or motion, transfer to another job, and medical treatment other than first aid. Because some workers developed more than one recordable case per year, a somewhat smaller proportion, say, 9%, were injured or became sick at least once during the year. Of the 9.5 recordable cases, 4.3 were fatalities or disabilities causing lost workdays, defined as days away from work (3.3) or days of restricted work activity. Lost workdays averaged 67.7 per 100 full-time workers and 16 days per lost workday case. Because the survey reports only those days lost in the year in which the case is diagnosed and recognized as work related, the average number of days lost per case may be much higher than 16. The wide variation in the frequency and severity of job accidents and sickness among industries is shown in Table 6.2. The incidence rates also vary according to the size of the firm. Rates are lowest for firms employing less than 20 or over 2,500 workers. Firms employing between 50 and 1,000 workers have the highest rates.

---

[11]Berton Roueché, *The Incurable Wound and Further Narratives of Medical Detection* (Boston, Mass.: Little, Brown, 1957), p. 72.

[12]R. H. Simonds and J. V. Grimaldi, *Safety Management,* 3rd ed. (Homewood, Ill: Richard D. Irwin, 1975), pp. 397–402. For the pioneering discussion of these extra costs see H. W. Heinrich, *Industrial Accident Prevention,* 3rd ed. (New York: McGraw-Hill, 1950), p. 50.

Table 6.2 Occupational Injury and Sickness Frequency and Severity: Selected Industries, 1979 (Per 100 Full-time Equivalent Workers)

Industry	Recordable Cases	Lost Work day Cases	Lost Workdays
Agricultural, forestry, and fisheries	11.7	5.7	83.7
Construction	16.2	6.8	120.4
Manufacturing	13.3	5.9	90.2
Transportation and public utilities	10.0	5.9	107.0
Wholesale and retail trade	8.0	3.4	49.0
Finance, insurance, and real estate	2.1	0.9	13.3
Services	5.5	2.5	38.1
Mining	11.4	6.8	150.5
Private sector	9.5	4.3	67.7

Source: Occupational Injuries and Illnesses in 1979: Summary, Bulletin 2097 (Washington, D.C.: U.S. Department of Labor Bureau of Labor Statistics, April 1981).

Cost and Supply of Medical Services

Two problems associated with poor health that deserve special notice are the increasing cost of medical services and alleged inefficiencies in the allocation and use of hospital beds, physicians, dentists, and nurses.

Medical costs have increased faster in the past decade than any other major category of personal expense. One reason is the Medicare program, which began operating in 1966. Table 6.3 shows how the cost of each of the major medical care components has increased relative to each other and to prices in general. Hospital room rates showed the greatest increase: 631% from 1960 to 1980 and 452% from 1965 to 1980. Physicians' fees ranked second in this regard, and dentists' fees third. Only one component—prescription drugs—increased less in price than did the Consumer Price Index.

The quality and cost of medical services in the United States is affected by the quantity of facilities and personnel available, their distribution relative to the demand for their services, the efficiency with which the facilities are managed, and the training, experience, and attitudes of medical personnel. Only a few summary comments are possible here:[13]

1 In 1978 6.7 million persons were employed in the health care industry, nearly 60% more than in 1970. The total number of employed people in the U.S. economy rose by only 20%.

2 Of the 6.7 million people employed in this industry in 1978, 3.8 million worked in hospitals, 1.0 million in convalescent institutions, 1.1 million in offices of physicians or dentists, and the remainder at other health care sites.

3 By 1978 the number of medical and osteopathic physicians numbered

[13]This section is based on *Health, United States, 1979* (Washington, D.C.: U.S. Department of Health, Education, and Welfare, Public Health Service, 1980), Part B, Sec. 3.

424,000, 51% more than in 1970. The 91% of those physicins who were professionally active provided almost 18 physicians per 10,000 population, compared with a 1970 ratio of less than 16 physicians per 10,000 population. Most of these physicians care for patients, but a small proportion are engaged in teaching, research, administration, or some other activity. By 1990 the number of physicians is expected to increase to 594,000, or more than 24 per 10,000 population. These projections have stimulated concerns that there may be a physician surplus in 10 years or so.

4   In 1978 there were 1.1 million registered nurses, compared with 0.8 million in 1970. Dentists numbered 117,000, compared with 91,000 in 1970. Projections for 1990 suggest that these two professions may also be oversupplied in the future if current programs continue.

5   The proportion of active physicians in primary care as opposed to some medical specialty remained about 40% during the 1970s, but within this group there was a shift toward internal medicine and pediatrics.

6   In 1977 the number of active nonfederal physicians per 10,000 population varied from 20.4 in the Northeast to 14.5 in the North Central Region. The ratios

Table 6.3   Consumer Price Index and Medical Care Price Indexes, 1960–1980 (1967 = 100)

Year	Consumer Price Index	All Items	Hospital Daily Service Charges	Physicians' Fees	Dentists' Fees	Prescription Drugs
1960	88.7	79.1	57.3	77.0	82.1	115.3
1961	89.6	81.4	61.1	79.0	82.5	111.5
1962	90.6	83.5	65.3	81.3	84.7	107.1
1963	91.7	85.6	68.6	83.1	87.1	104.5
1964	92.9	87.3	71.9	85.2	89.4	103.1
1965	94.5	89.5	75.9	88.3	92.2	102.0
1966	97.2	93.4	83.5	93.4	95.2	101.8
1967	100.0	100.0	100.0	100.0	100.0	100.0
1968	104.2	106.1	113.6	105.6	105.5	98.3
1969	109.8	113.4	128.8	112.9	112.9	99.6
1970	116.3	120.6	145.4	121.4	119.4	101.2
1971	121.3	128.4	163.1	129.8	127.0	101.3
1972	125.3	132.5	173.9	133.8	132.3	100.9
1973	133.1	137.7	182.1	138.2	136.4	100.5
1974	147.7	150.5	201.5	150.9	146.8	102.9
1975	161.2	168.6	236.1	169.4	161.9	109.3
1976	170.5	184.7	268.6	188.5	172.2	115.2
1977	181.5	202.4	299.5	206.0	185.1	122.1
1978	195.4	219.4	332.4	223.1	198.1	131.6
1979	217.4	239.7	370.3	243.6	214.8	141.8
1980	246.8	265.9	418.9	269.3	240.2	154.8

Sources: Social Security Bulletins.

also varied considerably by specialty. However, these geographic variations were slightly less than in 1970. Many rural and inner-city areas still have far too few physicians.

7   Most physicians are in individual or solo practice, but the trend is toward group practice. Almost one-fourth of the active nonfederal physicians practiced in medical groups in 1975, compared with 18% in 1969.

8   Short-stay hospitals, for which the average length of stay is less than 30 days, had about 1.1 million beds in 1977, not much more than they had in 1972. On the other hand, their share of the total beds rose from 62% in 1972 to 80% in 1977.

9   About 90% of the short-stay hospitals are "community" hospitals, that is, nonfederal hospitals that provide general medical services or concentrate in certain specialities such as eye, ear, nose, and throat, rehabilitation, or children's diseases. About 56% of these hospitals are nonprivate institutions, 30% are run by state or local governments, and the remainder are proprietary.

10   Stimulated by the Hospital Survey and Construction Act of 1946 (the Hill–Burton Act) the number of community hospital beds per 1,000 population rose to 4.6 in 1977, a 44% increase over 1940. Funds were allocated to areas with bed shortages, but in 1977 the bed–population ratios still varied considerably among the states (from 7.2 in the District of Columbia to 2.4 in Alaska). Some of this difference, however, can be explained by the fact that some hospitals serve residents of other states. Also, in Alaska Indian Health Service hospitals are not counted as community hospitals. According to the National Health Guidelines for Health Planning issued in 1978 by the Secretary of Health, Education, and Welfare, the bed–population ratio should be less than 4.

11   In 1977 the ratio of full-time equivalent employees to the number of patients in a community hospital on an average day was 3.7, compared with 2.2 in 1960. This increase has been explained primarily by the increasing technical complexity of medical care.

12   In 1977 almost 19,000 nursing homes provided about 1.4 million beds. In 1973–1975 15,700 homes provided 1.2 million beds. In 1963, before Medicare and Medicaid, nursing homes provided only about 0.6 million beds. In 1976 there were 61.7 nursing home beds per 1,000 person 65 years and over, compared with 58.6 in 1971. These ratios vary greatly among the states.

13   The current health delivery system has been judged to be inefficient by many observers. Too much emphasis on hospital care, too little use of paramedical personnel to handle routine matters, the lack of incentives to reduce operating costs, and inadequate attention to the prevention of illness are among the most important criticisms.

Some proposed solutions to these problems will be presented in Chapter 9. A brief listing of some of the more important proposals or actions already taken would include a review of hospital plans to increase the number of beds or to purchase highly specialized equipment that may duplicate existing unused facilities, the greater use of paramedical personnel, incentives for the development of health resources in areas where shortages are acute, the development of nursing care facilities or home care programs that will reduce the burden on hospitals, and the reorientation and reorganization of facilities and personnel so that ill persons may be housed in an intensive care unit with access to special equipment and constant attention.

TOTAL COSTS OF POOR HEALTH

The Social Security Administration and the Health Care Financing Administration make periodic estimates of (1) the aggregate loss of earnings caused by temporary nonoccupational disability and (2) private expenditures for medical care. To these we will add rough estimates of the income lost because of nonoccupational long-term disabilities and occupational accidents and diseases.

Temporary nonoccupational disability includes all disabilities lasting six months or less and the initial six months of disabilities that last longer. It is estimated that this form of disability causes the average worker to lose about seven work days a year. On this basis the estimated income loss due to nonoccupational short-term illness in 1978 was $32.9 billion. In 1970 the estimated loss was $16.7 billion.[14]

At least an equal amount of income is probably lost because of total disabilities extending beyond six months and partial disabilities that do not totally prevent the person from working but impair job performance.[15] Consequently the total nonoccupational disability income loss in 1978 was probably at least $66 billion.

Personal medical care expenditures in 1979 totaled $189 billion, or 9.8% of disposable personal income, or $838 per person.[16] In 1972 the estimated expendi-

[14]Daniel N. Price, "Income Replacement During Sickness, 1948-'78," Social Security Bulletin, XLIV, No. 5 (May 1981), 19.

[15]The following three estimates of the proportion of aggregate income loss contributed by short-term total disabilities illustrate the wide range of judgments available:

For an estimate of one-fifth, see the Commission on Health Needs of the Nation, Building America's Health, Vol. IV (Washington, D.C.: Government Printing Office, 1952), p. 303.

Dickerson suggested 40–45% based in part on a crude rate of occurrence of long-term disability of 10 per 1,000 workers exposed and an average duration of three years beyond the six-month qualifying period. See O. D Dickerson, Health Insurance, 3rd ed. (Homewood, Ill.: Richard D. Irwin, 1968), pp. 17–18.

Berkowitz and Johnson calculated a total income loss to the working age population of $21 billion in 1967 by aggregating transfer payments made because of disability (insurance payments, for example) and inflating each type of transfer payment to the level of income these transfers were designed to replace. Short-term losses calculated by the Social Security Administration for that year were 60% of this total. However, the Berkowitz–Johnson estimate excludes the young and the aged and is in their own opinion a conservative estimate. See Monroe Berkowitz and William G. Johnson, "Toward an Economics of Disability: The Magnitude and Structure of Transfer and Medical Costs," Journal of Human Resources, V, No. 3 (Summer 1970), 271–297.

[16]Robert M. Gibson, "National Health Expenditures, 1979," Health Care Financing Review, II, No. 1 (Summer 1980), 1–36.

tures were about $80 billion, or 8.5% of disposable personal income, or $378 per person. About 66% of the increase in total expenditures since 1972 was caused by price increases, 7% by population growth, and 28% by changes in service intensity.

Of the $189 billion spent in 1979, about 45% was for hospital services, 22% for physicians' services, 7% for dentists' services, 2% for other professional services, 9% for drugs and drug sundries, 2% for eyeglasses and appliances, 9% for nursing home care, and 3% for other health services. This distribution of expenditures has been fairly stable in recent years.

For at least three reasons the aggregate loss to the economy is much greater than these two estimates suggest. First, productivity is less because of inefficiencies generated by absenteeism and its threat. Second, national health care expenditures exceeded personal medical care expenditures by over $23 billion, distributed as follows: $7.7 billion retained by health insurers for administrative expenses, profits, and reserves, $6.0 billion for government public health activities, and $9.8 billion for research and the construction of medical facilities. Third, the National Safety Council estimates 1979 economic losses due to work accidents at about $25 billion. About $3.3 billion of this total consisted of medical expenses already included in the $189 billion personal medical care expenditures.[17] The remainder, however, consisted of such items as wage losses, production delays, damage to equipment and materials, and time lost by workers not involved in the accident.

METHODS OF ATTACKING THE PROBLEMS OF POOR HEALTH

Both the private and public methods used to attack the problems created by accidental injuries and sickness include loss control and alleviation measures.

Loss Control

The methods used to control losses caused by premature death also help reduce the number and duration of accidental injuries and sicknesses. Since these methods were discussed in Chapter 2, they need not be repeated here.[18] One loss control method that was not discussed in Chapter 2, but which reduces the wage loss due to permanent disability, is vocational rehabilitation. Individuals, private non-profit agencies, insurers, employers, unions, and the government have all been active in this area, as will be indicated in Chapter 7, but much remains to be done. The principal program is the one operated by state divisions of vocational rehabilitation, which is supported to a large extent by federal grants. This program provides without cost to the client the services of a counselor, vocational

---

[17]*Insurance Facts, 1980–81 Edition* (New York: Insurance Information institute, 1980), p. 62.

[18]Medical expense programs are considered to be alleviative programs in this discussion, but they clearly have control aspects as well.

aptitude and interest tests, and any special training that seems desirable. Special maintenance allowances during retraining are payable to needy clients. The special workers' compensation and OASDHI rehabilitation provisions will be discussed in Chapters 7 and 8.

Alleviative Methods

The increasing industrialization of our society and the loosening of family ties have had an even greater effect on the role of the sick and injured than they have had on the dependents of deceased persons and the aged. The sick and injured can seldom be easily absorbed into some relative's household. They must either assume the loss themselves, collect insurance payments, or accept aid from outside sources.

Retention is the most economical and satisfactory way to meet losses that are small relative to a person's income, but insurance or outside aid is essential when the economic impact of the illness is serious.

Voluntary private insurance is by far the most important private method of alleviating the financial burden of nonoccupational illness. This method and the degree to which it provides protection against income losses and medical bills will be considered in detail in Chapter 10.

Public alleviative methods were limited until recently to one social insurance program—workers' compensation, to be discussed in Chapter 7—and to public assistance programs based on need, the provision of medical facilities to deal with certain illnesses such as tuberculosis and mental disease, and programs benefiting special groups such as the armed services, veterans, Indians, and prison inmates. Until the 1954 authorization of the OASDHI disability "freeze" and the 1956 addition of limited OASDHI disability income benefits, which were liberalized in 1960 and 1965, the only social health insurance program covering the general public was that established by temporary disability insurance legislation in four states. The 1965 amendments to the Social Security Act also established two public medical expense insurance programs for the aged: Hospital Insurance and Supplementary Medical Insurance. Under a 1972 amendment these programs were expanded to include the long-term disabled. Strong pressures exist for creating a national public medical expense insurance program covering all citizens. These present and proposed public programs will be discussed in Chapters 8 and 9.

Of the $32.9 billion income loss from short-term disability in 1978, about 36% was covered by some form of insurance. Employee-benefit plans in private industry covered 18% of the loss, sick leave plans for government employees 14%, and individual insurance 4%. Of the $189 personal health expenditures in 1979, third parties paid 68% of the total. The private third party share was 27%, the public share 40%. Of the public share Medicare paid 39%, Medicaid 28%, the Veterans Administration 7%, the Department of Defense 5.3%, workers' compensation 4%, state and local hospitals 10%, and all other programs 6%.

ECONOMIC STATUS OF THE DISABLED

Despite the wide array of public and private measures designed to alleviate the financial impact of disability, the family incomes and assets of the disabled are substantially reduced by the earnings they lose and the medical expenses they incur.

According to the 1978 Social Security Administration survey, the 1977 median family income of the severely disabled was $9,128. About 28% of these families had incomes under $5,000. About one-fourth were poor. The median family income reported that year for the nondisabled population was $17,246; about 11% had incomes under $5,000.

About 7.8 million severely disabled adults, almost three-fourths of the total, received some public income maintenance such as Disability Insurance or Supplemental Security Income. The importance of this public support is underscored by the fact that among the severely disabled families with such support 26% were poor. Among the severely disabled families without such support about 74% were poor.

The percentage of income these severely disabled families received from five different sources varied as follows, depending on whether the family received any public income maintenance:

	With Public Income Maintenance	Without Public Income Maintenance
Respondent's earnings	11	21
Other family earnings	35	69
Asset income	5	4
Public income maintenance	43	—
Other private sources including private insurance	6	6

Although the economic status of the severely disabled was ameliorated by the introduction of Disability Insurance and Medicare, to be discussed in Chapters 8 and 9, the financial condition of many disabled persons remains unsatisfactory.

SUMMARY

The average person must restrict activity about 19 days a year because of an accidental injury or sickness; the average worker loses about five workdays. About one-seventh of the population have been disabled for at least three months; one-half of these disabled are unable to work regularly. The probability of being disabled for at least 90 days prior to age 65 substantially exceeds the probability of death prior to that age.

Over 10% of the population has one or more short-stay hospital episodes a year. The average person visits a doctor about five times a year.

Age, sex, race, income, employment status, residence, marital status, and the season of the year influence the probability of being disabled or incurring medical expenses. Acute conditions account for over half of the restricted-activity days, injuries about one-fifth. Among persons age 17–64, work injuries caused about one restricted-activity day per person.

Work injuries were the first illness to be covered under a social insurance program because of much higher injury rates around the turn of the century and the special obligation our society believes it owes to persons injured on the job.

Medical costs have increased faster in the past two decades than has the Consumer Price Index. The fastest growing component has been hospital room rates.

In 1977 active doctors of medicine totaled about 18 per 10,000 population. Short-term hospital beds averaged about 5 per 1,000 population. The distribution of medical personnel and facilities is less than optimum. Many other criticisms have been leveled against the current health delivery system.

In 1978 temporary nonoccupational disability losses cost almost $33 billion. In 1979 personal expenditures for medical care were $189 billion, or $838 per person.

Efforts to control the number and duration of accidental injuries and sickness include vocational rehabilitation. Voluntary private insurance is the most important private alleviative method. Social health insurance includes workers' compensation, Disability Insurance, and Medicare.

In 1977 families with a severely disabled adult had a median income of about $9,100, compared with $17,200 for nondisabled families. About one-fourth of these families were poor. Among severely disabled families who did not receive any public income maintenance, about 74% were poor.

SUGGESTIONS FOR ADDITIONAL READING

Brinker, Paul A. Economic Insecurity and Social Security. New York: Appleton-Century-Crofts, 1968.
Chapter 9 of this text deals with health problems in the United States.

Dickerson, O. D. Health Insurance, 3rd ed. Homewood, Ill.: Richard D. Irwin, 1968.
Chapters 1 through 3 contain an excellent analysis of the costs of poor health.

National Commission on the Cost of Medical Care, 1976–1977. Monroe, Wisc.: American Medical Association, 1978.
A three-volume report of an independent commission established by the American Medical Association to provide a comprehensive review of health care costs and possible approaches toward solutions.

Rejda, George E. Social Insurance and Economic Security. Englewood Cliffs, N.J.: Prentice-Hall, 1976.
Chapters 8 and 9 of this comprehensive text analyze in detail the problems of health care and some solutions.

U.S. Department of Health and Human Services, Public Health Service. *Current Estimates from the Health Interview Survey,* annual.
An annual summary of the major findings of the continuing National Health Survey by the Public Health Service.

U.S. Department of Health and Human Services, Public Health Service. *Health, United States,* annual.
An annual report on the number and distribution of medical facilities and personnel and other health matters.

Chapter Seven

Workers' Compensation

Occupational injuries and diseases became a serious threat to economic security when, in the late 19th century, our nation's workplace shifted from agrarian to industrial grounds. It was the first hazard to economic security to inspire social insurance legislation in the United States. Injuries and sickness from nonwork causes began to come under private and public insurance systems much later. In this chapter we discuss why and how workers' compensation was introduced and its present status.

To the worker whose arm is amputated in a revolving cutter, the dollar costs, the pain and suffering, and the problems of physical and occupational rehabilitation are no different from those of another worker losing a leg as a result of a fall in a friend's home. For a long time public policy in the United States made no distinction between these two types of injuries. To recover money damages for the injury, either worker had recourse only in the common law of liability. If the worker could prove that the injury stemmed directly from the negligence or fault of the factory or homeowner, he or she could recover money damages. With the greater risks of occupational disability that accompanied industrial development during the late 19th century, however, and in response to this growing hazard to the economic security of the nation's workers, social policy began to distinguish between accidents and sickness caused by the work environment and those that were not. This recognition took three forms: (1) employer-initiated safety programs, which, though unimportant at first, have today become significant factors in holding down the toll of industrial injuries; (2) the industrial hygiene movement aimed at industrial sickness; and (3) workers' compensation legislation (which seeks through insurance to redistribute part of the costs of occupational disability), in which fault or negligence is not an issue.

EMERGENCE OF THE PROBLEM OF OCCUPATIONAL INJURIES AND DISEASES

American history from the Civil War through the close of the nineteenth century is a story of rapidly expanding industrial capitalism. In a single generation the

United States changed from an agrarian country, which had to import most of its manufactures from abroad, into an industrialized nation exporting products all over the world.

Rail transport expanded rapidly; coal, iron, and petroleum resources were exploited vigorously; and the manufacture of cotton, iron, steel, and other products increased phenomenally. In 1980, for the first time in this country's history, the wealth created by manufacturing surpassed that created by farming. By external measures, too, industrial growth was phenomenal. In 1860 the United States ranked fourth among nations in the volume and value of factory goods; in 1894 it ranked first, with factory production worth more than that of Germany and Great Britain combined.[1]

To operate the factories turning out this record production, employers recruited to the cities more and more workers—many of them women and children —from farms and abroad. With the growth of industrial cities came new problems in the mode and character of life, particularly in the economic and social life of the worker. During the first 15 years of the 20th century much of the country's energies, particularly at local levels, were directed toward adjusting public policy to the needs of the new economic environment. A concentrated attack was launched on the political, social, and economic problems created by an industrial society—child labor, slums, growing health and accident hazards, to name a few —and the results were remarkable. More social legislation (including workers' compensation) was enacted during this period than during any previous time in American history.

Professional concern for occupational health and safety can be traced back to 1837, when the first U.S. report on occupational health was issued, long before the movement for legislative reform got under way. Between that time and 1900, over 50 discussions and state reports on occupational health and accident hazards appeared, and by 1910 the industrial health movement had gained support from magazines, state agencies, and professional associations.[2]

In 1867 Massachusetts enacted legislation providing factory inspection services; two years later the first Bureau of Labor Statistics was created in that state to study the accident problem; and in 1977 the Massachusetts legislature acted to insure that employers safeguard hazardous machinery. In 1892 a safety department was established in the Joliet Works of the Illinois Steel Company, where the United States industrial loss control movement was subsequently born.[3]

As stated in Chapter 6, the exact magnitude of the occupational health hazards of the period cannot be accurately determined, but the data available indicate that the situation was much worse than it is today.

[1]For a statistical summary of this economic revolution, see Arthur M. Schlesinger, *Political and Social Growth of the American People, 1965–1940* (New York: Macmillan, 1941), p. 43.

[2]John R. Commons and associates, *History of Labor in the United States, 1896–1932,* Vol. III (New York: Macmillan, 1935), pp. 359–370.

[3]Ronald P. Blake (Ed.), *Industrial Safety* (Englewood Cliffs, N.J.: Prentice-Hall, 1943), pp. 12–22.

The Common Law of Industrial Accidents

With the sharp rise in the number of occupational injuries, the costs of disability and medical expenses became an acute problem. The physical losses, of course, were borne by the injured worker in all cases. But what of the financial burden? Was this also to be the private responsibility of the worker?

Before 1841 there were no rules of law or court decisions to answer this question, although recourse to the law was available to the occupationally and nonoccupationally injured alike. As job injuries became increasingly frequent and severe, the courts were called on to decide how the financial burden of this disability should be distributed.

In retrospect the body of common law of employers' liability that emerged from these cases seems unduly harsh. The small-scale industrial organization, frictionless labor market, and close employment relationship between owner and worker—on which the law of employers' liability was based—were all casualties of the economic revolution.

Under common law an employee injured in an accident in the course of work could recover damages only through a personal injury suit against the employer. Although a master owed his or her servants due care (the violation of which was negligence), the employee still had to prove that the employer was in fact negligent. He or she frequently encountered reluctance on the part of fellow employees to testify, probable loss of employment, and a serious (often insurmountable) financial burden.

Second, and even more onerous, was the array of common-law rules of master and servant that blocked the path to easy recovery for industrial injuries. The oldest of these was the defense of contributory negligence, which was always available in suits based on a claim of negligence. This tenet had been introduced into the common law of England in 1809.[4] In operation it defeated an employee's claim to damages if he or she had in any way also been negligent.

Two further defenses grew out of later cases. In 1842 the leading American case involving master–servant relations was decided. In *Farwell versus Boston and Worcester R. R. Co.,* a Massachusetts court denied an engineer's claim for damages based on the negligence of a switchman and established "fellow-servant" and "assumption of risk" defenses in America. The court held that

> . . . since the engineer was not in the relation of a stranger to the railroad, the employer's liability, if any, was governed by the implied contract of employment entered into with the engineer at the time of hiring and that such a contract does not extend to indemnify the servant against the negligence of anyone but the master himself.

[4]In the case of Butterfield versus Forrester, 11 East 60 (K.B. 1809) cited in Walter F. Dodd, *Administration of Workmen's Compensation* (New York: Commonwealth Fund, 1936), Chaps. 1 and 2.

Two important concepts were implied in this holding. First, servants were now denied recovery for injuries arising from a fellow servant's negligence. This was an exception to the well-established tort doctrine of respondeat superior, which held a master responsible to third persons for injuries inflicted by his or her agents. The second principle—the assumption of risk doctrine—made the hazards of an occupation noncompensable. For many years hence cases consistently holding to the assumption of risk defense partially justified this position on the theory that the wage rate of an occupation reflected its hazards. This quite painful application of Adam Smith's principle of equal net advantages together with the contributory negligence and fellow-servant defenses were the cornerstones on which was built the laissez faire approach of the common law to occupational disability.[5]

Enactment of Employers' Liability Laws

With occupational injury and death rates reaching alarming proportions, the continued application of these common-law rules was producing tragic results. The vast majority of the occupationally injured or their survivors realized either inadequate damage awards or, all too frequently, no awards at all. In the face of the wastes, uncertainties, delays, and high costs of lawsuits, widespread dissatisfaction arose with this approach to industrial injuries or diseases. In the late part of the nineteenth century many legislative attempts were made to find a new remedy. These took the form of employers' liability legislation, which was patterned, in part, after earlier attempts made in England to mitigate the effects of common-law defenses to injury claims. Between 1885 and 1910 most of the states enacted such employer liability legislation.

The first of the three common-law defenses to come under legislative attack was the fellow-servant rule. Next, by stating that an employee's knowledge of safety violations is no bar to a suit for recovery, the assumption of risk doctrine was weakened. The contributory negligence defense, however, which also applied to other negligence suits, yielded reluctantly under the more liberal legislative (and judicial) attitudes.

In addition to modifying the three common-law defenses, employers' liability laws sought to bring relief to injured workers in two ways.[6] The first of these was a legal denial of the right to "contract out" of liability. Contracts in which

---

[5]Smith observed that where there was liberty, wages would make the advantages and disadvantages of occupations equal. See Adam Smith, *The Wealth of Nations,* Modern Library ed. (New York: Random House, 1937), p. 99: "The whole of the advantages and disadvantages of different employment of labour and stock must, in the same neighborhood, be either perfectly equal, or continually tending to equality. If in the same neighborhood there was any employment evidently either more or less advantageous than the rest, so many people would crowd into it in the one case, and so many would desert it in the other, that its advantages would soon return to the level of other employments."

[6]See Commons, Ref. 2, p. 567.

workers agreed not to hold their employers liable for injuries sustained at work would no longer be binding. And, secondly, the right to sue was extended to death cases.

Employers' liability laws, following one or more of these three forms, were enacted in almost all the states by the time accident tolls were reaching their peak (1907–1908). But they did not provide an adequate solution to the problem of job-related injuries or diseases.

The Rise of Workers' Compensation Legislation

While the United States was experimenting with legislation designed to modify the results of the common-law rules of employers' liability, a far-reaching experiment was taking place in some European countries: the establishment of workers' compensation. Germany took the lead in the early 1880s, and by 1910 virtually all the countries of Europe had adopted some system of workers' compensation.

These events did not go unnoticed in the United States. The Department of Labor took official notice in its 1893 publication of a report on compulsory insurance in Germany. Shortly thereafter bills following the European models were introduced in several states (but they failed to gain passage). It became apparent through the unsuccessful attempts of several states to enact workers' compensation legislation that a thorough study was necessary to determine the needs of compensation systems, their requirements, the ways in which they might relate to our legal system and, important to employers, what their costs might be. Intensive commission investigation of the problem of occupational disability was the next step.

Some 31 investigatory commissions were established between 1909 and 1913; 9 others were in operation in the next six years. These investigating bodies, through joint conferences, hearings, and intense study, unanimously recommended that employers' liability be abolished. From these investigating committees emerged (1) a severe indictment of the record of employers' liability legislation and (2) the foundation for recommendations that later evolved into workers' compensation laws. Their recommmendations were supported by the American Association for Labor Legislation, the National Civic Federation, the American Bar Association, the American Federation of Labor, and a poll of the National Association of Manufacturers.

Failures of the Employers' Liability Statutes

Committee data documenting the failure of employers' liability systems aroused considerable public concern. They showed that (1) contrary to their purpose, employers' liability laws were not enabling workers to recover damages for injuries. Damage awards were sparse and uncertain, and when they were granted, they came long after the disability, were usually inadequate, and bore no rational relation to the injury. (2) Since employers' liability was still a system based on lawsuits, it was costly and produced ill will between employers and employees, thus failing to produce any stimulus for safety programs. The emphasis still tended to be toward concealing accidents rather than studying them frankly and attempting to reduce them. In short, it was little better than the inadequate, uncertain, and costly remedy under common law. A new approach was needed to the problem of occupational injury and disease. It was found in workers' compensation.

Workers' compensation laws were enacted in 10 states in 1911, followed by 10 more states in 1912 and 1913. After 1920, only six states (each of which later enacted systems) did not have workers' compensation legislation; today such laws are in effect in all states and under all federal jurisdictions. During the 1970s workers' compensation laws were considerably liberalized, largely as a result of the 1972 report of the National Commission on State Workmen's Compensation Laws; Congress established this commission under the Occupational Safety and Health Act of 1970 to study and evaluate state programs.

Liability Without Fault

New York was one of the first states to take the lead in the movement toward workers' compensation. In 1910 it enacted a compulsory law covering 12 specified occupations wherein employers were made liable for specified compensation payments to their injured workers, whether or not the injury stemmed from employer fault. The extent of this departure from the traditional common law of employers' liability is nowhere better dramatized than in the language of the New York Court of Appeals, which declared the law unconstitutional the following year. Said the New York court in this case,

> This is a liability unknown to the common law and we think it plainly constitutes a deprivation of liberty and property under the Federal and State Constitutions . . . if the legislature can say to an employer, "You must compensate your employee for an injury not caused by you or by your fault," why can it not go further and say to the man of wealth, "You have more property than you need and your neighbor is so poor that he can barely subsist; in the interest of natural justice you must divide with your neighbor so that he and his dependents shall not become a charge upon the state?[7]

A popular referendum and, later, state and U.S. Supreme Court decisions and legislative devices[8] overcame constitutional objections, however, and today all

---

[7]*Ives versus South Buffalo Railway Co.,* 201 N.Y. 271 (1911). Quoted and discussed in Harry A. Millis and Royal E. Montgomery, *Labor's Risks and Social Insurance* (New York: McGraw-Hill, 1938), pp. 194–196.

[8]Stefan A. Riesenfeld and Richard C. Maxwell, *Modern Social Legislation* (Brooklyn, N.Y.: Foundation Press, 1950), pp. 153–162.

states have workers' compensation laws based on the principle of "liability without fault." Yet, while the constitutional barrier in the Ives case did not deter the movement toward workers' compensation, it indirectly weakened the laws of a majority of jurisdictions. Over two-thirds of the states gave employers an "election" of being covered by workers compensation or remaining exempt—but without full protection of common-law defenses. By year-end 1971 the laws of 19 states still had some form of elective provision. By mid-1980 only three states had elective laws.

The principle of liability without fault is quite simple. The employer bears the compensable costs of job-connected illnesses of employees not because he or she was negligent or otherwise responsible for them, but simply because of social policy. The premise that behind every disability there is a negligent party has been discarded. Under modern industrial conditions the employment relationship itself is reason enough for having the employer compensate injured employees. Since the employment of labor involves the risk of injury or disease, by social policy the employer must defray its costs.

But while the interpretation of liability without fault is clear enough, its theoretical justification has raised some questions. For one thing, if considered apart from its consequences, the common-law principle that an employer should be responsible only for accidents stemming from fault has an appeal of justice and fair play. Some early acts applied only to hazardous occupations, holding the employer responsible for operating a hazardous business. But as workers' compensation laws were extended to most kinds of work, liability without fault could be justified only by reference to broader norms.

Many norms have been formulated.[9] An important early theory was that of the "trade risk." This theory held that the employer must bear the costs of the risks of the trade and, implicitly, that these costs would be shifted forward in the product price. (A slogan attributed to Lloyd George proclaimed that "the cost of the product should bear the blood of the workingman.") The implications of this justification (among them that workers are relieved of all accident costs) have been sharply criticized, and a more thorough formulation has been that of the "least social costs" principle, contending that economic losses to society were reduced to a minimum by workers' compensation legislation.[10] These theories, and particularly some of the legal justifications, were important to the acceptance and subsequent broadening of workers' compensation laws.

The policy of protecting the economic security of the workers by making employers liable for job-connected disability is not a radical policy from the viewpoint of the economics of the labor market. In fact, it can be interpreted

[9]Discussions of these norms can be found in E. H. Downey, *Workmen's Compensation* (New York: Macmillan, 1924), pp. 19–20; in Clarence W. Hobbs, *Workmen's Compensation Insurance* (New York: McGraw-Hill, 1939), pp. 61–62, See also Riesenfeld and Maxwell, Ref. 8, pp. 138–140.

[10]Edwin E. Witte, "The Theory of Workmen's Compensation," *American Labor Legislation Review,* XX, No. 4 (December 1930), 411–418.

simply as a more efficient result, economically, than would be the case in a perfectly competitive labor market. Let us examine this point.

The Compensation Principle

If all that is implied in the principle of equal net advantages were empirically descriptive of labor supply and demand conditions, the employers' common-law defense of assumption of risk would be economically persuasive. For under this condition, wage rates for individual occupations would fully reflect their relative advantages and disadvantages, including the risk of an occupational injury or disease. It would follow that, other things being equal, employments where accident rates are relatively high (say, agriculture, where the death rate is three times that of manufacturing) would pay correspondingly higher wage rates than less hazardous jobs requiring similar skill and training. Large numbers of workers would be attracted to the better jobs (tending to keep the wage rate down) and employers would have to bid up wages to attract workers to the less attractive (and more hazardous) jobs.

But do wage rates in fact reflect differences in job hazards? To some extent, yes. Structural steel workers, for example, may be paid a higher wage when working on high construction, where the danger from falls is great; test pilots receive a high wage that reflects their hazardous work; seamen receive additional pay for duty in war zones. In fact, in any business organization wage structures based on standard methods of job evaluation will, to some measure, be influenced by the relative hazard factor of working conditions. But wage differentials generally bear very little relation to the relative attractiveness of work; and no one today would seriously contend that wage rates include a "risk" portion reflecting the value of an occupation's injury risk.

In the actual labor market perfect competition does not exist. Employees do not adequately perceive occupational hazard differentials nor would they be willing or able to accept more attractive alternative job opportunities if they did know about them. Employers have an incentive not to pay the full risk rate, because their competitors cannot be expected to follow suit, and the greater portion of the cost of an injury or disease is borne by the worker. The employers' private cost of the full "risk" wage exceeds the benefits that would be received from paying this wage.

Under these circumstances, if injuries are to be compensated, it is necessary for government action to assess a social cost that will pay for the full needed social benefits. This could take two forms: wage rates in hazardous occupations could be adjusted by legislation or employers could be made liable for the cost of injuries to employees. Of these two approaches the latter (workers' compensation) can be shown to be economically more efficient in principle.

Legally forcing employers to pay a risk wage rate for hazardous jobs would result in a small increment in the wage rate. Even if this increment were large enough to compensate the worker for his or her expected or average loss, in the long run it would provide less protection for the worker in the event of an occupational injury or sickness than would an insurancelike payment, withheld and paid at the time of the loss. For, in accordance with the principle of diminishing marginal utility,[11] the disutility of one great loss would more than offset the added utility of small increments in the wage rate. Providing each employee with enough money to buy an individual insurance policy covering occupational hazards, instead of requiring employers to provide such protection, could also be justified in this way, but employer protection is less expensive because of the administrative savings made possible by insuring a group of employees or self-insuring. Hence liability without fault is not an expensive social reform but rather a more efficient method, in principle, of achieving what the labor market would achieve were it perfectly competitive.

The Current Importance of Common Law and Employers' Liability Statutes

The emergence of the workmen's compensation principle, however, has not eliminated case law from the field of industrial illness. Wholly aside from the vast numbers of cases interpreting the compensation laws, there are wide areas where liability is determined through litigation.[12] These include employees and, to a lesser extent today, job-related injuries or diseases not covered by the compensation acts.

THE OCCUPATIONAL SAFETY AND HEALTH ACT OF 1970

Before turning to present workers' compensation laws some mention should be made of the Williams–Steiger Occupational Safety and Health Act of 1970, called by J. D. Hodgson, then Secretary of Labor, "the most significant legislative achievement of the year, perhaps the decade, for the American worker."[13] Although many observers are less effusive about its significance, the Act has had important implications for loss control programs and workers' compensation.

Loss Prevention and Reduction Programs

The major purpose of the Act is to provide workers with as safe and healthful working conditions as possible. The basic approach is standard setting and enforcement.

---

[11]A good brief discussion of the law of diminishing marginal utility applied to insurance is presented by Paul A. Samuelson, *Economics,* (8th ed. (New York: McGraw-Hill, 1970), pp. 410–411.

[12]Railroad employment is the most important example. See Chapter 13 for a discussion of the Federal Employers' Liability Act.

[13]"The Safety Act's Hidden Bite," *Business Week,* January 9, 1979, p. 19.

Coverage

The law applies to any employer engaged in a business affecting interstate commerce.[14] Federal, state, and local government employers are exempt, but they are included under other programs. Similarly, working conditions protected under other federal occupational safety and health laws (such as the Federal Coal Mine Health and Safety Act) are excluded.

Safety and Health Standards

It is the general duty of employers to furnish employment free from recognized hazards causing, or likely to cause, death or serious physical harm. They have a specific duty to comply with safety and health standards promulgated under the Act. Employees are also expected to comply with these standards.

Numerous detailed standards have been promulgated that deal with such matters as walking and working surfaces, means of egress, and general environmental controls. Most of those standards were previously developed as voluntary guidelines by private business associations such as the American National Standards Institute; others are federal standards that existed prior to OSHA; and many are new or revised standards. Proposed new or revised standards must be published in the *Federal Register.* Interested parties have 30 days in which to request an informal learning. Also, the validity of such standards may be challenged within 60 days after their promulgation by petitioning the U.S. Court of Appeals.

In those situations where it is determined that employees are exposed to grave danger emergency temporary standards may also be established merely by publication in the *Federal Register.*

An employer may apply for a temporary variance from a standard to gain time to meet it. Employees must be made aware of this application and be given an opportunity to appear at the hearing.

Enforcement

To enforce the standards Department of Labor safety inspectors are authorized to enter, without notice but at reasonable times, any covered establishment. The employer and a representative authorized by the employees may accompany the inspector during the tour through the premises.

An employee who believes that a serious violation of a standard exists may request an inspection by sending a signed written notice to the Department of Labor. The name of the complaining employee need not be given to the employer.

If an inspector discovers a violation, he or she is directed to issue a written citation describing the nature of the violation. The citation must be posted near the place where the violation occurred and the employer is given a reasonable

---

[14] The products of the firm need not be shipped across state lines. Mere communication across state lines is enough to establish interstate effects.

time to correct the situation. Notices may be issued instead of citations for de minimis violations.

The employer has 15 days to appeal the citation. A hearing commissioner acting on behalf of the Occupational Safety and Health Commission will hear the case and make a decision; the Commission will also hear the case and make a decision. The Commission, composed of three members appointed by the President, may review the decision if one member wishes to do so. Commission orders may be appealed to the U.S. Court of Appeals.

Citations issued for serious violations, that is, where there is substantial probability that death or serious physical harm could result, carry mandatory monetary penalties up to $1,000 per violation. Nonserious violations may also result in monetary penalties in the same amount. Failure to correct violations within the time prescribed may result in a penalty up to $1,000 for each day the violation continues.

Willful or repeated violations of the Act's requirements may result in a penalty of $10,000 per violation. A willful violation that results in the death of an employee is punishable by a fine of $10,000 or imprisonment up to six months; a second conviction doubles the penalties.

State Participation

States that submit an approved plan for the development and enforcement of occupational safety and health standards may assume responsibility for administering the Act. The state standards must be at least as effective as the federal standards they replace. If a state plan is accepted, the Secretary may continue to check enforcement with federal standards until it is determined that the state plan is operating satisfactorily. The state plan cannot be fully certified until at least three years after its acceptance. Following this certification the Secretary must continue to evaluate the performance of the state plan and withdraw approval, if necessary, to protect workers in that state. States whose plans are rejected can appeal the Secretary's decision to the U.S. Court of Appeals. The Secretary can make grants to states for experimental and demonstration projects or for administering approved plans. The federal and state government share the costs of the state plans equally in most respects.

In 1980 almost half the states had plans that had been accepted by the federal government. Only a few of these plans, however, had been fully certified. Several other states had requested that their plans be accepted; a few have terminated their plans, primarily because of the costs involved.

Other Provisions

Employers of eight or more employees are required to maintain accurate records and make periodic reports on their compliance with the law and on work-related deaths, injuries, and diseases. An annual survey must be posted for the information of employees that shows separately for injuries and each of the seven occupational disease codes (1) the number of fatalities, (2) the number of lost workday cases, (3) the number of lost workdays, (4) the number of nonfatal cases without lost workdays, and (5) the number of cases involving transfer to another job or termination of employment. Occupational safety and health statistics have been substantially improved by these records.

A National Institute for Occupational Safety and Health, established within the Department of Health and Human Services, carries out research and educational functions assigned to that department.

Issues

OSHA has been one of the most vigorously debated activities of the federal government. One point of view holds that the program has not been enforced as vigorously as intended, partly because the initial enthusiasm about the program has dampened or because the necessary funds have not been appropriated. It is argued that there have been too few inspections, that the inspections have not been as thorough as they should be, and that the penalties in many cases have been too small. The other point of view holds that the standards have been far too numerous, unnecessarily detailed, frequently unrealistic, and often at odds with standards issued by other federal or state agencies. It is argued that the cost of compliance with the standards in terms of productivity or dollar outlays is excessive relative to the benefits involved. Small businesses in particular have complained about the way in which the program has affected their costs. These critics argue, apparently with increasing support, that OSHA should concentrate its limited resources on firms with higher hazards or poor loss experience.

Workers' Compensation

The Act established a 15-member National Commission on State Workmen's Compensation Laws to evaluate state workers' compensation laws and report its findings and recommendations by July 31, 1972. The report of the Commission is summarized later in this chapter. This provision was added because the Senate Labor Committee had some serious questions concerning the adequacy of state laws.

PRESENT WORKERS' COMPENSATION PROGRAMS

Today in each of the 50 states, the District of Columbia, and Puerto Rico workers' compensation is the major economic security program for occupational injuries and disease. The laws of all states are based on the principle of liability without fault, but because they are individual state laws, their benefit and coverage provisions vary widely from jurisdiction to jurisdiction. This section describes these laws as of October 1, 1980.

Qualification for Benefits

Although the benefits an occupationally disabled worker receives under workers' compensation vary widely from state to state, the right of a worker to these benefits is determined under all jurisdictions by three basic elements[15]: (1) the worker must be an "employee" working in a "covered employment"; (2) the worker can receive benefits only for injuries and disease, the nature and origin of which are compensable under the law; and (3) the disability must have resulted from employment. Let us examine these in detail.

An "Employee" in "Covered Employment"

The question of who is an "employee" has prompted considerable litigation, particularly in the case of casual employees and those working for independent contractors, but this element of coverage is now fairly well established. An independent contractor controls the manner, methods, and details of the work in which he or she is engaged. The employer controls the work of an employee. Borderline cases, however, still arise.

The interpretation of the term "covered employment" is more varied from state to state. Initially most states excluded small employers; 14 still do. All states exclude some types of employment. For example, most laws exclude or impose special wage or service requirements on domestic servants, farm laborers, and the so-called casual employees whose work is not in the usual course of the trade of the employer. Many states exclude a few specified employees such as professional athletes or employees of charitable organizations. As explained in Chapter 13, federal civil service employees and railroad workers are covered under special programs. In three states—those with elective laws—the employer may accept or reject the Act, but rejection means loss of the three common-law defenses. In actual practice the vast majority of employers in those states elect to comply with the workers' compensation provisions. In addition, some employers exempted from either compulsory or elective coverage voluntarily bring their employees under the law. Self-employed persons are eligible for voluntary coverage under some laws.

Compensable Injuries

"Employees" working in "covered employments" can receive benefits only for disabling injuries and sickness, the nature and origin of which are compensable by statute. In adopting from English law the phrase "personal injury by accident," a majority of American jurisdictions embraced the concept of injury as associated with a traumatic occurrence. The rigor of this definition became troublesome, however, in cases where disabilities emerged from gradual deterioration

---

[15]Stefan A. Riesenfeld and Richard C. Maxwell, *Modern Social Legislation* (Brooklyn, N.Y.: Foundation Press, 1950), pp. 162–291.

of a bodily member due to work causes or repeated accidents. U.S. courts have developed a liberal definition of the concept of an "accident" so as to compensate cases such as these. In revising the laws legislatures are increasingly discarding the word "accident." The battle over compensability has largely shifted to the requirement that the injury be traceable to the employment.

Legislative coverage of occupational diseases developed much more slowly than did injury coverage. Massachusetts pioneered in this area in 1910 when it provided "blanket" coverage for all occupational diseases, along the lines of the Federal Employees' Compensation Act explained in Chapter 13. Other states developed the "schedule" system, providing coverage only for diseases specified by law. Today blanket or full coverage is provided by all jurisdictions.

Employment-Connected Disability

To be compensable the covered employee's injury or disease must have resulted from employment, again as specified by statute. The requirement that there be a proper relationship between the employment and the injury or disease has become a thorny legal question and policy issue. Almost every state law, again borrowing from England, extended coverage to accidents "arising out of and in the course of employment." This phrasing was intended to reduce to a minimum questions on the origin of the injury, but litigation concerning the interpretation of these words is almost endless.[16]

Two types of issues arise. First, should an admittedly compensable injury or disease be compensated when it occurs under "unusual" circumstances? Typically, should workers be covered while traveling for their employer? After or before working hours? Off duty, going to and from work? Or, at work when a worker takes a devious route? And so on. For the most part, court interpretations of these issues have tended to take a liberal view of what is "in the course of employment."

Second, and perhaps more important as far as policy is concerned, are injuries and diseases where the link with employment is not clear. That is, did the injury "arise out of" the employment? Conditions such as nontraumatic loss of hearing, coronary and pulmonary afflictions, and radiation diseases may be caused by employment, but they are also associated with nonwork hazards of life. Back injuries have proved especially troublesome because (1) they are so easy to feign and (2) they may have occurred off the job. Allocating liability for these conditions presents serious policy issues, perhaps the major ones facing workers' compensation today.[17] Let us now turn to the question of the benefits paid to an eligible disabled employee.

---

[16]For detailed discussions of these and other legal issues, see Arthur Larson, *The Law of Workmen's Compensation* (Albany, N.Y.: Matthew Bender, 1968, updated periodically).

[17]See Chapter 12 of the National Commission on State Workmen's Compensation Laws, *A Compendium on Workmen's Compensation* (Washington, D.C.: Government Printing Office, 1972). This book is referred to hereafter as *A Compendium.*

Types and Amounts of Benefits

The two basic types of benefits provided by workers' compensation laws are (1) cash or indemnity payments and (2) payments for medical services. Although rehabilitation services, which are an important recent development, consists partly of medical services, ideally they should extend well beyond these. Hence they are considered separately here.

Cash or Indemnity Payments

Cash benefits are payable to disabled workers in all jurisdictions only after a "waiting period" that ranges typically from three to seven days after the injury and is designed to reduce compensation costs and discourage possible malingering. If the time lost typically exceeds a specified period, 14 or 21 days, the worker receives benefits for this waiting period. Although the overwhelming majority of job-caused disabilities are of very short duration and hence do not involve cash benefit payments (because of the waiting periods), they do account for substantial aggregate medical benefits.

Disability extending beyond the waiting period is classified for benefit purposes into "temporary" and "permanent." Temporary total disability payments are made to a worker who cannot work at his or her usual occupation during the period of recovery. Cash benefits for temporary total disability are usually weekly payments calculated at two-thirds of the average weekly wage at the time of the injury, subject to a specified weekly maximum and minimum. About one-third of the states limit the number of weeks during which benefits will be paid or their total amount. For example, if the worker was earning $240 a week and the maximum weekly benefit was $250, he or she would receive two-thirds of $240, or $160 a week. If the worker's wage had been $480, the maximum benefit of $250 would be paid. All but one-fifth of the states adjust the maximum benefit annually as the state average weekly wage increases. There are 26 states that set the maximum at 100% of the state average weekly wage. Five states set a higher level, the highest being the District of Columbia's 200%. The lowest percentage, found in six states, is $66\frac{2}{3}$. Nine states pay additional amounts when there are dependents. Two of these states, however, only increase the minimum benefit when there are dependents.

Over 70% of the disabling occupational injuries result in only temporary disability, but these injuries account for only 25% of the cash payments.

Permanent disabilities resulting from more serious injuries are classified by the severity of the disabling condition into minor permanent partial, major permanent partial, and permanent total disability. Permanent total disability, for example, involves injuries that, except for cases of successful rehabilitation, prohibit further employment. Permanent total disability benefits typically consist of two-thirds of the wage lost, subject to a specified weekly maximum and minimum. In about one-third of the states benefits are limited to a stated number of weeks or dollar amount. In about one-fourth of the states permanent total disability benefits, once paid, are adjusted annually to maintain the disabled worker's standard of living or purchasing power. Usually, however, the adjustment in any one year is limited to some maximum, such as 6%. As was true for temporary total disability, about nine states pay extra amounts for dependents.

Since it is extremely difficult to determine the exact degree of permanent partial disability, most acts set forth "schedule disabilities" that list the duration of compensation payments for specific injuries. These benefits are intended to make up a portion of the anticipated future reductions in earnings caused by the disability. They do not depend on whether the injured person returns to work. Thus, in addition to temporary total disability benefits during the healing period, a permanent partial disability payment "schedule" might provide the following payments (using but two examples, ranging from one extreme to the other): (1) for the loss of a little finger, $66\frac{2}{3}$% of the daily wage at the time of injury, subject to a specified weekly maximum and minimum, for 15 weeks; (2) for the loss of one arm and one leg, $66\frac{2}{3}$% of the daily wage at the time of the injury, subject to the specified weekly maximum and minimum for 400 weeks. The duration of payments for a given disability varies greatly among the states. Some states adjust the duration for factors such as the worker's age. States also disagree on the relative duration of payments for different disabilities. In addition to scheduled permanent partial disabilities, the Act usually provides benefits for nonscheduled permanent partial disabilities that replace part of the actual earnings lost.

Florida recently introduced a wage-loss approach to permanent partial disabilities that is being observed with great interest. Instead of making scheduled permanent partial disability benefits regardless of whether the injured person returns to work, Florida pays 95% of the difference between 85% of the employee's average monthly wage and the wage he or she is able to earn after reaching maximum medical improvement. The payment, however, cannot exceed two-thirds of the employee's average wage at the time of the injury. The maximum payment period is 525 weeks.

Death benefit payments to survivors are also an important benefit provision, and, like disability payments, they vary greatly from jurisdiction to jurisdiction. In over half the jurisdictions these payments to dependents are limited both in time and amount. Both the weekly benefit and duration commonly depend on whether there are minor children. As is true for permanent total disability benefits, about one-fourth of the states adjust the benefits paid annually to match all or part of the increase in prices or wages. In addition to these income replacement benefits, all states pay burial allowances ranging from $300 to $2,500.

Payments for Medical Services

During the early development of workers' compensation laws, little or no provision was made for medical benefits. Today, however, all states cover all medical expenses. This liberalization in medical benefits has been characterized as the greatest single improvement in workers' compensation.

Medical benefits account for about one-third of total benefit payments under workers' compensation.

Rehabilitation Services

The most promising of the recent benefit developments is the growth of provisions for physical and vocational rehabilitation.[18] Under early workers' compensation laws, after the limited medical care called for by law had been provided the disability was "fixed" as it stood; and when treatment ran out or no further benefit from it was apparent, permanent total disability was often presumed. With the advances in physical medicine, paramedical services, and vocational training facilities, permanent total disability can no longer be presumed.

But far too few injured workers receive the medical or vocational rehabilitation needed to reduce their disabilities to a minimum and restore them to full economic usefulness. Provisions for making effective rehabilitation services available have developed slowly in workers' compensation laws.

Today about two-thirds of the jurisdictions make some provision relating to rehabilitation, usually offering added indemnity or maintenance allowances during retraining. Federal, state, or private facilities are usually utilized for rehabilitation services. Five jurisdictions operate rehabilitation facilities directly under their workers' compensation program.

Second Injury Funds

Employers have avoided hiring handicapped workers for many reasons, one being their fear that further injury could result in a total disability claim. In a well-known case in Oklahoma in 1925,[19] it was held that an employee who had previously lost sight in one eye could bring a claim against his employer for permanent total compensation for loss of the other eye in the course of his employment. "Seven thousand one-eyed, one-armed and one-legged workmen were fired overnight in that state. Oklahoma employers were unwilling to take on handicapped workers for fear that additional injury would cost them permanent total disability awards."[20]

Second-injury funds have been adopted to meet this situation in all states but Georgia. Money for these funds is usually collected by a moderate assessment on employers or their insurers (in most states, for death cases where there are no dependents eligible for benefits; in a few states, in cases of serious disability). In theory the second-injury fund protects an employer from any additional financial

---

[18]For further information on rehabilitation, see "Rehabilitation of Disabled Workers and Employment of the Handicapped," *Report of the National Workshop on Rehabilitation and Workmen's Compensation* (Washington, D.C.: National Institute on Rehabilitation and Health Services, 1971), pp. 55–104, and Chap. 11 of *A Compendium . . . , Ref. 17.*

[19]*Nease versus Hughes Stone Co.,* 244 Pac. 778.

[20]Address of Under Secretary of Labor Arthur Larson, "Highlights of the Proposed Model Workmen's Compensation Law," November 17, 1955, U.S. Department of Labor Press Release No. 1360.

losses under the workers' compensation law if a handicapped worker suffers a second injury. In principle, employers are made liable only for the disability of the second injury and the fund pays the rest of the benefits. In practice, it is not always possible to determine how much of the disability was caused by the second injury. Consequently, the employer may in many cases be made responsible for the first, say, 104 weeks of disability. The state fund pays the excess.

This device, if broad enough in its coverage, reduces an important disincentive to employ handicapped workers. Moreover, it has generally proved to be relatively inexpensive, since, except under the most comprehensive funds, there are relatively few claims against the state fund.

However, the effectiveness of this program has fallen far short of its potential. Many employers are still unaware of its existence. At the same time various restrictions and limitations imposed on these funds in most states have served to sharply limit their application. For example, most states either limit their fund to (1) workers with a few handicaps—almost always those who previously lost one hand, arm, foot, leg, or eye—or (2) workers whose second injury, combined with their previous impairment, results in permanent total disability. Most observers believe that until these statutes are broadened and their application more clearly understood, unnecessary barriers to meaningful employment will continue to confront the handicapped worker. Some persons, however, believe that the importance of these funds has been overrated. Handicapped persons, they argue, face far more serious barriers to employment than the possible adverse effects on workers' compensation costs. They would abolish such funds or limit their scope to impairments that constitute clear barriers to employment.

Security Requirements

Because of the wide fluctuations in workers' compensation obligations for most employers from year to year, because of the long-term nature of some of the payments that must be made, and because state legislatures wanted to be certain that employers could meet their worker's compensation obligations, all states except Louisiana require employers to insure these obligations or demonstrate their ability to self-insure.[21]

The District of Columbia and 31 states require private employers to purchase protection from private insurers. In all of these states, except Texas, employers may request permission to self-insure their obligation. Louisiana employers also choose between private insurance and self-insurance.

Six states[22] plus Puerto Rico have exclusive state funds that underwrite all of

[21]C. A. Williams, Jr., *Insurance Arrangements under Workmen's Compensation,* U.S. Department of Labor, Bureau of Labor Standards, Bulletin 317 (Washington, D.C.: Government Printing Office, 1969), p. 17. For a more recent study see *Workers' Compensation: Analysis of Insurer Operations,* an October 1977 report prepared by Teknekron, Inc., for the U.S. Department of Labor, published in *Research Report of the Interdepartmental Workers' Compensation Task Force,* Vol. 4 (Washington, D.C.: U.S. Government Printing Office, 1980).

[22]Nevada, North Dakota, Ohio, Washington, West Virginia, and Wyoming.

the workers' compensation insurance in those states. Four of these jurisdictions —Nevada, North Dakota, Puerto Rico, and West Virginia—do not permit any private employers to self-insure.

The remaining 12 states[23] have competitive state funds. Employers in these states can self-insure, if they demonstrate their ability to do so, purchase private insurance, or buy protection from the state fund.

In 1979, excluding payments under the federal "black lung" program described later, private insurers paid about 61% of total workmen's compensation benefits, state funds about 23%, and self-insurers about 16%.[24] These proportions have remained about the same for many years, but because of rapidly increasing costs during the 1970s more large employers have recently started to self-insure.

Because of their dominant position, only the pricing practices of private insurers will be discussed here. About 60% of employers (the smaller ones) are class rated, but these insureds pay less than 15% of the total premiums. Their payroll is divided into classes on the basis of the type of industry, the occupation of the employee, or the industrial operation performed. Generally the entire payroll falls into one class determined by the industry, except for clerical office employees, drivers, and certain other "standard exceptions." In most states all insurers charge the same initial premiums, but they may return different dividends to their policyholders.

Most of the remaining employers (those whose annual premium would otherwise be at least $750) are experience rated. Under experience rating the class-rated premium is increased or decreased according to (1) how the particular employer's past loss experience compares with the experience of the average employer of the same size in the same class and (2) the statistical reliability of that experience. The larger the employer, the more reliable that experience becomes because of the operation of the law of large numbers. Consequently, little credibility is assigned to the experience of employers who barely qualify for experience rating; extremely large employers may be rated solely on the basis of their own experience.

Employers whose premiums exceed $2,000 are technically eligible for retrospective rating, but most insurers limit such rating to employers paying a premium of $25,000 or more. The retrospective premium equals the actual losses and expenses of the insured during the policy period plus a small net insurance charge, but the premium is not permitted to exceed a specified maximum nor fall below a specified minimum. The net insurance charge is necessary because of the maximum premium feature. Retrospective rating permits quasi-self-insurance, with the insurer providing loss control and loss adjustment services.

---

[23]Arizona, California, Colorado, Idaho, Maryland, Michigan, Montana, New York, Oklahoma, Oregon, Pennsylvania, and Utah.

[24]Daniel N. Price, "Workers' Compensation Payments and Costs, 1979," *Research and Statistics Note No. 5* (Washington, D.C.: Office of Research and Statistics, Social Security Administration, U.S. Department of Health and Human Services, July 27, 1981).

All employers paying premiums in excess of $1,000 receive premium discounts reflecting expense savings on larger insureds. Acquisition and general administrative costs are a smaller proportion of larger premiums than of small ones.

Private insurance premiums may therefore depend on the industry to which the employer belongs, the employer's loss experience relative to that of other employers of the same size in the same industry, and the size of the business.

Private insurers can reject applicants they consider undesirable. In most competitive-fund states the state fund is obligated to accept these rejected employers. In the other states private insurers have formed assigned risk plans on a compulsory or voluntary basis to insure these employers. Under these plans applicants are either assigned to individual insurers in proportion to their market shares or insured by a pool consisting of all insurers. Most of these plans impose a surcharge on the rates the employer would otherwise pay.

THE FEDERAL COAL MINE AND SAFETY ACT OF 1969

The Federal Coal Mine and Safety Act of 1969 was the federal government's first major incursion into the state workers' compensation system. This Act provides benefits to employees who are totally disabled by pneumoconiosis and to their dependents in the event of death. The basic rate is 50% of the minimum monthly payment under the Federal Employees' Compensation Act to a disabled federal employee in the first step of grade GS-2. This basic rate is increased when there are dependents, the maximum family benefit being twice the basic rate. Benefits are automatically increased when federal salaries increase. The benefit amount is reduced by any unemployment compensation benefit or by any workers' compensation benefit being paid for pneumoconiosis. The Social Security Administration is responsible for most claims filed prior to 1974, the Department of Labor for most claims from 1974 on. Until 1977 amendments, if an individual coal miner operator could be identified as responsible for the claim, that operator had to pay for the benefit. The costs not attributable to individual employers were financed through general revenues. Under the 1977 amendments, for miners whose last employment was before January 1, 1970 and for those for whom no responsible coal-mine operator can be identified, benefits are paid out of a trust fund supported by an excise tax paid by all coal operators except where the Secretary of Labor has certified that the state law provides adequate coverage.

The Reagan Administration has proposed a tightening of the eligibility requirements for this program. The General Accounting Office reported in 1980 that thousands of dubious claims were being certified because of the 1977 liberalization in the eligibility requirements. For example, current employment in a mine cannot be used as conclusive evidence that a miner is not totally disabled if his or her job has changed in a way that indicates a reduced ability to perform his or her usual coal-mine work. Miner recipients claim that economic pressures, not recovery from their disability, force them to return to work. The Reagan Administration also seeks an increase in the coal excise tax, which has proved insufficient to keep the trust fund solvent.

Operations

In 1979 almost 90% of the wage and salary workers were covered under workers' compensation programs. The others must prove negligence on the part of the employer. Benefits *paid* were $11.9 billion. Benefits incurred that would recognize payments to be made in the future because of injuries or diseases which occurred in 1979 would be larger. Of this total about 29% were medical payments, 60% disability benefits, and 11% survivor benefits. Table 7.1 shows how coverage, benefits, and employer cost have increased since 1940. Note the fairly stable employer cost as a percentage of payroll from 1940 through 1970 followed by a rapid increase during the 1970s. Benefits paid increased 22% from 1978 to 1979; one explanation is that The Black Lung Benefits Reform Act of 1977 allowed many miners and survivors to claim benefits for the first time.

APPRAISING WORKERS' COMPENSATION

Protection against the economic losses caused by occupational injuries and disease was the objective of the first social insurance programs both here and abroad. During the first decade after its introduction in the United States coverage under the programs expanded rapidly and benefits were substantially liberalized. For the next 50 years progress was much less rapid; indeed, in some ways the programs became less liberal. By 1970 critical concern with the role and success of this pioneering social insurance was greater than it ever had been. Among the methods of greatest concern were the exclusion of many employees, the failure of maximum weekly benefits to keep pace with increases in state average weekly wages, the handling of permanent partial disability cases, the time or duration limits placed on permanent total and death benefits, limits on medical care, inadequate rehabilitation services, the proportion of litigated cases, delays and other administrative problems, the level and allocation of program costs, and the wide variations among states in coverage, benefits, and costs. As indicated earlier, in that year Congress established a National Commission on State Workmen's Compensation Laws.

National Commission on State Workmen's Compensation Recommendations

In its 1972 report the National Commission identified five major objectives of workers' compensation[25]:

[25] *The Report of the National Commission on State Workmen's Compensation* (Washington, D.C.: Government Printing Office, 1972).

Table 7.1 Workers' Compensation Coverage, Benefits, and Costs,[a] 1940–1979

Year	Millions of Workers Covered	Benefits Paid Total in Millions of Dollars	Percentage Paid For Medical Expenses	Disability	Survivorship	Cost to Employer as Percentage of Payroll ($)
1940	24.2–25.0	256	37	50	13	1.19
1950	36.5–37.2	615	33	58	9	0.89
1960	44.8–45.0	1,295	34	58	8	0.93
1970	59.0–59.3	3,031	35	58	7	1.11
1975	67.0–67.4	6,598	31	58	11	1.32
1979	78.2–78.9	11,872	29	60	11	1.93

Source: Daniel N. Price, "Workers' Compensation Payments and Costs, 1979," *Research and Statistics Note No. 5* (Washington, D.C.: Office of Research and Statistics, Social Security Administration, U.S. Department of Health and Human Services, July 27, 1981).

[a]Includes in addition to state programs the federal system for federal employees and federal black lung program.

1 *Broad coverage of employees and of work-related injuries and diseases* Protection should be extended to as many workers as feasible, and all work-related injuries and diseases should be covered.

2 *Substantial protection against interruption of income* A high proportion of a disabled worker's lost earnings should be replaced by workers' compensation benefits.

3 *Provision of sufficient medical care and rehabilitation services* The injured worker's physical condition and earning capacity should be promptly restored.

4 *Encouragement of safety* Economic incentives in the program should reduce the number of work-related incentives.

5 *An effective system for delivery of the benefits and services.*

In the judgment of the National Commission state laws should possess the following characteristics; the 19 starred recommendations were deemed essential:

1 *Covered employments*
  (*a) Coverage should be compulsory, with no waivers permitted.
  (*b) Numerical exemptions should be eliminated.
  (c) Coverage should be extended to all occupations and industries, without regard to the degree of hazard.
  (*d) Farmworkers should be covered as of July 1, 1975.
  (*e) Household and causal workers should be covered as of July 1, 1975, at least to the extent to which they are covered under OASDI.
  (*f) Coverage should be mandatory for government employees.
  (*g) There should be no exemption for any class of employees such as professional athletes or employees of charitable organizations.
  (h) Employers, partners, and self-employed persons should be eligible for coverage on an optional basis.
  (i) Workers should continue to be eligible for benefits from the first moment of their employment.
  (*j) Injured employees or their survivors should have the choice of filing a claim in the state where the injury or death occurred, where the employment was principally localized, or where the employee was hired.

2 *Injuries and diseases covered*
  (a) The "accident" requirement should be dropped as a test for compensability.
  (*b) Full coverage should be provided for work-related diseases.
  (c) The "arising out of and in the course of employment" test or some more generous one should be used to determine coverage.

(d) The etiology of a disease, being a medical question, should be determined by a disability unit under the control and supervision of the
workers' compensation agency. For deaths and impairments apparently caused by a combination of work-related and non-work-related
sources, issues of causation should be determined by this disability unit.
If the work-related factor was a significant cause of the impairment or
death, full benefits should be paid.

3 Relationships to other remedies

(a) Workers' compensation benefits should continue to be the exclusive
remedy of the employee against his or her employer for work-related
injuries or diseases.

(b) Suits by employees against negligent third parties should generally be
permitted, but not against third parties performing the normal functions of the employer.

(c) Benefits of other insurance programs should be coordinated with workers' compensation. In general, workers' compensation should be the
primary source of benefits for work-related injuries and diseases.

(d) Workers' compensation benefits should not be reduced by the amount
of any payments from a welfare program or other program based on
need.

4 Temporary total disability benefits

(a) The waiting period should not exceed three days; benefits should be
retroactive after no more than 14 days.

(*b) Temporary total disability benefits should, subject to the maximum
weekly benefit, be at least 80% of the worker's *spendable* weekly earnings. Spendable earnings are basically savings plus employee-benefit
costs minus taxes. Higher-pay workers and those with no dependents
would have spendable earnings that were substantially less than their
gross earnings plus supplements because of our tax structure. However,
until the state maximum exceeds 100% of the state average weekly
wage, the replacement ratio should be at least two-thirds of the
worker's *gross* weekly wage.

(*c) The maximum weekly benefit should be at least the following fraction
of the state average weekly wage:

As of July 1	Percentage
1973	$66\frac{2}{3}$
1975	100
1977	$133\frac{1}{3}$
1979	$166\frac{2}{3}$
1981	200

(Only the 1975 objective was deemed essential.)

5 *Permanent disability benefits*

(*a) Permanent disability should be defined as a permanent impairment that makes it impossible for a worker to engage in any substantial activity for a prolonged period, if not for life.

(*b) Benefits should be subject to the same wage replacement percentages as temporary disability benefits.

(*c) Benefits should be subject to the same maximum weekly benefits as temporary disability benefits.

(d) Permanent total disability benefits should be increased through time by the same proportion as increases in the state average weekly wage. This recommendation is designed to protect long-term disability cases against erosion in the value of the benefits.

(*e) Permanent total disability benefits should be paid for the duration of the worker's disability without any dollar or time limitations.

(f) The disability insurance portion of OASDI should continue to reduce payments for those workers receiving workers' compensation benefits.

(g) States should undertake a thorough examination of permanent partial benefits, and the federal government should sponsor a comprehensive review of present and potential approaches to permanent partial benefits.

6 *Death Benefits*

(*a) Death benefits should be subject to the same wage replacement rate as temporary and permanent total disability benefits.

(*b) Death benefits should be subject to the same maximum weekly benefit as temporary and permanent total disability benefits.

(c) To protect beneficiaries against the value-eroding power of inflation, death benefits should be increased through time by the same proportion as increases in the state's average weekly wage.

(*d) (1) Death benefits should be paid to a widow or widower for life or until remarriage; (2) if remarriage occurs, two years' benefits should be paid in a lump sum to the widow or widower; (3) benefits for a dependent child should be continued at least until the child reaches age 18 or beyond; (4) if the child is a full-time student, benefits should be continued at least until age 25.

(e) Workers' compensation death benefits should be reduced by the amount of any OASDI benefits.

7 *Medical care and rehabilitation benefits*

(a) The worker should be permitted the initial selection of his or her physician, either from among all licensed physicians in the state or from a panel of physicians selected or approved by the workers' compensation agency.

(*b) There should be no statutory time or dollar limits on medical care or rehabilitation services.

(c) The workers' compensation agency should have the discretion to determine the appropriate medical rehabilitation services in each case.

(*d) Once a worker receives medical benefits, with rare exceptions he or she should be able to file a claim for further medical care at any time.

(e) Every workers' compensation agency should have a medical rehabilitation division with authority to supervise medical care and rehabilitation services and with specific responsibility for making certain that every worker who could benefit from vocational rehabilitation services is offered these services.

(f) Employers should pay all authorized vocational rehabilitation costs.

(g) Special additional maintenance benefits should be provided a worker during the period of his rehabilitation.

(h) Each state should establish a broad second injury fund financed by assessments on insurers and self-insurers or by appropriations. These funds should be publicized and interpreted liberally to encourage employment of the handicapped.

8 Safety incentives

(a) A standard workers' compensation reporting system should be devised that will mesh with the forms required by the Occupational Safety and Health Act of 1970 and permit the exchange of information among federal and state safety agencies and state workmen's compensation agencies.

(b) Insurers should be required to provide loss control services, and the workers' compensation agency should carefully audit the services provided by insurers and self-insurers. Revocation of the right to insure or self-insure may be necessary if the insurer or self-insurer is not providing an effective safety program.

(c) Subject to sound actuarial standards, experience rating should be extended to as many employers as practicable.

9 Administration

(a) A workers' compensation agency should administer the program. It should include an administrator, an informal procedures unit, a medical and rehabilitation supervision unit, a disability evaluation unit, an audit unit, and a statistical analysis unit.

(b) Members of the appeals board and the chief administrator, who in most cases should not belong to the appeals board, should be appointed by the governor, subject to confirmation by the legislature. All employees of the agency should be full-time civil service employees.

(c) An advisory committee in each state should conduct a thorough examination of the state's workers' compensation law in the light of the Commission report.

(d) The workers' compensation agency should be financed by an assessment on insurance premiums or benefits paid plus an equivalent assessment against self-insurers.

(e) States should be free to continue their present insurance arrangements or to permit private insurance, self-insurance, or state funds where any of these types of insurance are now excluded.

(f) Procedures should be established in each state to provide benefits to employees whose benefits are endangered because of an insolvent insurer or because an employer fails to purchase required insurance.

The Commission endorsed the basic concept of a separate workers' compensation program, but reached the "inescapable conclusion . . . that state workmen's compensation laws in general are inadequate and inequitable."[26] It noted that as of 1972 only 9 of the 50 states met 13 of the 16 standards published earlier by the Department of Labor, even though these standards were conservative compared to the Commission recommendations. There were 10 states that met four or fewer recommendations.

The Commission urged states to comply with their essential recommendations as of July 1, 1975. It recommended that Congress check the degree of compliance as of that date and, if necessary, act to guarantee compliance with these recommendations with no further delay. Congress has not yet acted on the Commission report. It has, however, since the early 1970s, been considering various versions of a bill that would establish federal standards which, if not satisfied within a state by a specified date, would apply these standards to occupational injuries and diseases in that state. The first bill lost expected support because it included standards tighter than the Commission recommendations and gave the Secretary of Labor the authority to promulgate additional standards. The most recent version, being much closer to the Commission's wishes, has a much higher probability of being approved, but some new opposition has surfaced largely because of recent rapid increases in workers' compensation costs.

Because Congress has not yet acted, the July 1, 1975, deadline was not as important as the Commission had intended. The effect of the Commission report, however, has been considerable. Coverage has been expanded and benefits liberalized in many ways. Nevertheless, most states fell considerably short of meeting all 19 standards by mid-1975. Table 7.2 shows the scores for each recommendation as of October 1980 for the 50 states and the District of Columbia. If all 51 jurisdictions satisfied all 19 recommendations, the total score for all jurisdictions

---

[26]See Ref. 25. One finding that supported this exclusion is that as of January 1, 1972, the maximum weekly benefit for temporary total benefits in more than half of the states did not reach the poverty level for a nonfarm family of four persons. In about 20 jurisdictions the unemployment insurance weekly maximum was higher.

Table 7.2 Compliance With the National Commission on State Workers' Compensation's 19 Essential Recommendations, October, 1980

Standard	Number of Jurisdictions Meeting Standard	Standard	Number of Jurisdictions Meeting Standard
Coverage		Permanent total disability	
Compulsory	48	Defined	50
Waivers	28	$66\frac{2}{3}\%$	48
Number of employees	36	Maximum benefit	29
Farmworkers	14	Duration	33
Household, casual workers	1	Death	
Government employees	30	$66\frac{2}{3}\%$	32
Special classes	17	Maximum Benefit	25
Filing option	27	Life of widow	18
All diseases	51	Remarriage	11
Cash benefits		Child	19
Temporary total disability		Student	8
$66\frac{2}{3}\%$	49	Medical benefits	
Maximum benefit	31	No limits	51
		No termination of rights	45

combined would be 969. Instead, the 51 jurisdictions had compiled a score of only 620, or 64%. No jurisdiction complied with all the recommendations. One, New Hampshire, met all but one-half of one standard. Only 5 programs had scored 15 or more points; 13 satisfied 10 or less standards. On the other hand, this performance was much better than that in 1972. Also some standards are more important than others and a jurisdiction is not given any credit for moving closer to satisfying a standard. Finally, many states have met other important Commission standards such as the automatic annual adjustments in permanent total and death cases.

Interdepartmental Workers' Compensation Task Force

One of the recommendations of the National Commission was that the President appoint a follow-up commission to provide encouragement and technical assistance to the states and examine more closely the areas of permanent partial disability and the delivery system. The President did establish an Interdepartmental Policy Group, which included the Secretaries of Labor, Commerce, and Health, Education, and Welfare, (HEW) and the Federal Insurance Administrator. In May 1974 this group published a *White Paper on Workers' Compensation,* which (1) supported the National Commission's 19 essential recommendations, (2) stressed the need for automatic cost of living adjustments in long-term benefits, (3) called for improvements in state data systems, and (4) recommended the formation of a task force, reporting to the Policy Group, to provide technical assistance and conduct an extensive research program. The Task Force was created and in January 1977 the Policy Group sent a report on its efforts[27] to the President and Congress. The main conclusions were as follows:

1 No program nor combination of programs seems likely to replace or outmode workers' compensation.

2 Although the states have not yet met the National Commission's recommendations, they should have more time to strengthen their programs. A program requiring so much interaction with claimants and so affected by local conditions is probably best handled at the state level.

3 The federal government should assist and monitor state progress. The technical assistance effort should be increased significantly and grants made to states interested in improving their data systems or administrative reforms.

4 The performance of the state system in the handling of claimants with no disability (medical expenses only) or temporary disability has been satisfactory, but not the handling of permanent disability, death, and occupational disease cases. While constituting only about 5% of the cases, these troublesome areas account for half of the benefit dollars. The problems are excessive litigation, long delays in payment, low disability termination rates, and little relationship between the benefits awarded and the actual wage loss.[28] Benefits are not related to wages largely because of (a) compromise and release "lump-sum" settlements by insurers and (b) statutory lump-sum or weeks of benefits for permanent partial disability benefits. According to a special survey conducted for the Task Force, in 1973 half of the permanent partial cases, half of the death cases, and almost three-fourths of the permanent total cases were settled by compromise and release under which the insurer paid the worker a lump sum in exchange for a release from any further responsibility. Too often the amounts paid bear little relationship to the wage loss developed in the future. Statutory scheduled permanent partial benefits also may bear little relationship to actual future wage losses.

To correct this problem the Policy Group recommended that compensation for wage loss be separated from any compensation for the impairments themselves and that replacement benefits be paid only as wage loss accrues.

In 1978 Dr. John Burton, who served as Chairman of the National Commission, proposed a modification of this recommendation.[29] The pure wage loss approach, he argued, would channel benefits to those who experience actual disability. However, the cases would have to be kept open for long periods, it

---

[27] *Workers' Compensation: Is There a Better Way?*, Report to the President and the Congress of the Policy Group of the Interdepartmental Workers' Compensation Task Force, January 19, 1977.

[28] According to the Task Force, 39% of the permanent partial cases and 52% of the permanent total cases are litigated. In contested cases the average delay between the start of payment is about 134 days. See Ref. 27, p. 16.

[29] John F. Burton, Jr., "Wage Losses From Work Injuries and Workers' Compensation Benefits: Shall the Twain Never Meet?," paper presented to the 64th Annual Convention of the International Association of Industrial Accident Boards and Commissions, Quebec City, Quebec, September 12, 1978.

would be difficult to determine whether a worker's reduced earnings were due to the injury or the many other factors that may affect earnings, and relating benefits to actual wage loss might create disincentives to work. He advocated two sets of benefits: Type I, presumed disability benefits, would be based on rating standards emphasizing objective factors such as limited motion (rather than subjective factors such as pain), adjusted for several factors such as age and education, which usually influence the extent of work disability. The benefit would be two-thirds of the preinjury wage, subject to a weekly maximum. The higher the adjusted rating, the longer the Type I benefits would be paid. Type II benefits, which would be 80% of potential earnings, would begin after Type I benefits had expired. No state has yet adopted this recommendation or that of the Task Force. However, as explained earlier, Florida has adopted a complete wage-loss concept for permanent partial disability benefits.

5   Although states should comply with the 19 essential recommendations of the National Commission, they need to undertake further reforms, many of which, but not all, are included among the Commission's other recommendations. For example, although all states now provide full coverage of occupational diseases, many states still limit their compensability in various ways. The disease must be "peculiar to the worker's occupation," the worker must have been exposed to the hazard over a specified minimum period of time—sometimes in that state—or the worker must notify the employer within some time period after the hazard was encountered, even though the condition may remain latent for many years. The Task Force would remove these limitations. They would establish in each state a panel of experts to determine the compensability of occupational disease cases whose findings would be binding as to all questions of fact or causation except for questions of law.

The strong position of the Task Force favoring replacement of lost earnings as they accrue has already been noted. In addition, the Task Force favored a maximum weekly benefit of twice the state average weekly wage and an annual increase in long-term wage replacement benefits equal to the increase in the state average weekly wage. In addition to replacing lost wages, employers should be required to continue OASDI pension, and health insurance coverage on disabled employees. At retirement age workers' compensation benefits would stop and retirement benefits start.

States might also want to pay additional amounts for impairments that are not related to wage losses. For example, there may be 10 classes of impairments for each of which a stated dollar amount would be paid.

The state workers' compensation agency should oversee rehabilitation and reemployment, which should become a major thrust of the program. The employer should have the primary responsibility for developing and implementing a rehabilitation plan and should be liable for all costs, including maintenance, travel, and other expenses. The employer should make every effort to return the employee to the same job, an equivalent job, or one within the employee's capacity. If no such jobs are available, the employer and insurer should help the worker find a new job. If the worker is actually engaged in searching for a new job, up to 60 days of additional workers' compensation should be paid, but the worker should be required to choose between this benefit and unemployment compensation. If suitable employment is available and the employee refuses to return to work, the employer should be able to petition the state agency to terminate the wage replacement benefits.

Broad second injury funds should be enacted in all states to support the reemployment of injured workers.

Experience rating of insurance premiums should be extended to small as well as large employers. Dividend plans should also reflect the loss experience of employers. Insurers should increase and improve their loss control efforts.

Employers should be encouraged to self-insure or merge with non-work-related coverage the first few hundred dollars of medical expenses and the first few days of disability.

State agencies should take on a much more active role and considerably strengthen the administration of workers' compensation. To illustrate, a unit within the agency should initiate contracts with the worker after receiving the first report of injury or disease, tell the worker how the system works, and help file a claim. Employers or their insurers should be required to begin payments within 15 days or explain why this was not done.

Workers eligible for both workers' compensation and OASDI disability or survivorship benefits should receive the higher of the two. If the OASDI benefit is higher, the worker should be paid the workers' compensation benefit plus an OASDI supplement. At age 65 OASDI benefits should become primary. If the workers' compensation benefit is higher, workers' compensation should supplement OASDI up to the workers' compensation level.

The Problem of Increasing Cost

In recent years the cost of workers' compensation has increased dramatically. According to Social Security Administration estimates, in 1979 the cost of workers' compensation insurance and self-insurance to employers was 1.93% of covered payrolls.[30] In 1970 the cost was 1.11%. In recent years, in some states workers' compensation premium rates have increased by more than 30% in one year. The result has been intense employer concern and the establishment in several states of commissions charged with reviewing the law and its administration.

One reason for the increasing cost is the liberalizations in coverage and benefits designed to meet the recommendations of the National Commission and the Interdepartmental Task Force. The greater the need for reform in the state law, the greater the increase in cost.

Inflation is another important cause. The cost of workers' compensation is

[30]Price, "Workers' Compensation Payments and Costs, 1979," *op. cit.*

directly affected by the rapid rise in the cost of medical care, by higher wages, and by higher administrative costs.

Other charges are that the state agencies have become too liberal in deciding whether an injury arose out of and in the course of employment, in determining whether a disability is permanent, in reopening closed claims, and in retraining workers for positions for which they are not qualified or for which there is no demand. Critics also note that as the benefits are improved more workers tend to claim disability or to delay their return to work. Higher federal and state income taxes also make the compensation benefit look more attractive. Some of these additional claims are justified, but others, it is argued, are not. As explained in more detail below, the relatively high unemployment rates during the 1970s may have also contributed to higher disability rates and lower recovery rates. In some instances workers are compensated more than once for the same disability. To illustrate, in at least one state until 1981 a worker could receive a permanent partial disability benefit while still receiving a temporary total disability benefit. If the disability were later judged to be permanent total, the employer would not receive any credit for the permanent partial disability benefit already paid. As another example, consider the case of a worker who, because of an automobile accident not related to work, had been previously 25% disabled, for which he or she had been paid no-fault benefits or a tort liability settlement. If this worker is injured on the job in such a way that the disability is increased to 30%, in most states he or she will receive benefits as if the job accident caused a 30% disability. Some would argue that except for claims covered under a second injury fund, the employer should be given full credit for any preexisting condition (e.g., chronic arthritis or heart disease), regardless of whether the worker was previously compensated for that condition. In short, although major emphasis has been placed on correcting inadequacies in coverage and benefits, there is also strong support for tightening the program in other respects. As program costs have increased, these pressures have intensified.

Workers' compensation costs vary greatly among industries. Class rates in a given state may range from, say, 20 cents per $100 of payroll to over $100 per $100 of payroll. Furthermore, since insurance can be provided more efficiently to larger companies, and since the price may reflect safety records, premiums may vary widely among individual employers in the same industry. Insurance costs vary from state to state, too, depending on the benefit provisions of the law and the distribution of employments in a given area.

Allocating costs in this fashion alerts society to the cost of each business in terms of workers' injuries. In some instances society may be persuaded to forgo the use of costly products, and individual employers who are unable to force consumers to bear their high costs may be forced to close their doors. Another advantage of this pricing objective is that industries and individual employers who are experience rated or retrospectively rated have some incentive to improve their loss experience. The private insurer system, however, does not distinguish among small employers in a given industry; inadequate or illogical (e.g., permanent partial disability schedules) benefit structures distort both the cost allocation and loss control objectives; workers' compensation costs are such a small proportion of payroll costs for most employers that even substantial percentage changes may have little effect on consumer interest in the product or on employer actions; safety programs involve considerable fixed and indivisible costs, thus reducing the incentive effect of changes in workers' compensation costs; and employers may reduce losses not by preventing accidents but by fighting claims. The system also favors larger firms.

At the time workers' compensation laws were first being enacted, a major opposing argument was that they would put home industry at a competitive disadvantage, deter the location of industry within the state, and possibly even drive business firms away. Although all states have workers' compensation laws today, the argument is still an important one in legislative debates over the liberalization of laws.

Do interstate cost differentials in fact produce such undesirable economic effects?[31] Most persons appear to agree that workers' compensation costs, averaging 1% of payrolls (in contrast, e.g., to the estimated 37% spent for all fringe benefits), are not significant enough to play an important role in location decisions or in competitive advantage in the short run. Long-run effects, too, are probably exaggerated. Yet it must be recognized that along with other factors such as taxes, power resources, and labor, employers take workers' compensation costs into account when deciding where to locate their firms. Also some industries may be more affected than others and workers' compensation costs have risen dramatically in recent years.

Another phase of workers' compensation insurance costs—one that is not so wholly related to the benefit level and distribution of industry—has raised questions about their economic impact. That is, these costs seem to move countercyclically. With rising employment and prosperity, costs tend to go down; with declining levels of employment, they tend to rise. This movement is sometimes attributed to abuse of the system. It is argued that workers have an incentive to malinger when benefits may restore much of their lost earnings and reemployment opportunities are few; and they may be helped in this process by dishonest physicians, who, during periods of economic decline, are willing to prolong the treatment of compensation cases when payment is assured by the compensation for injuries (real or feigned) incurred during employment.

Insurance costs are often criticized as being excessive for the amount of benefits paid by workers' compensation. The exact proportion of private insurance premiums that reaches disabled workers is the subject of some disagreement. How

---

[31]In a careful study of interstate variations in employers' costs, Dr. John F. Burton, Jr., concluded that these differentials should not influence plant location decisions. J. F. Burton, Jr., *Interstate Variations in Employers' Costs of Workmen's Compensation* (Kalamazoo, Mich.: W. E. Upjohn Institute for Employment Research, 1966), p. 73. See also John Burton, "Workers' Compensation Costs for Employers," *Research Reports of the Interdepartmental Workers' Compensation Task Force,* Vol. 3 (Washington, D.C.: U.S. Government Printing Office, 1980), 9–32.

much of every premium dollar collected is paid out to workers in the form of indemnity and medical benefits? Insurance sources estimate 75 cents; labor sources contend less than 50 cents.[32]

Even if the insurer estimate is correct, some questions remain. Is workers' compensation being insured efficiently? Or, more directly, do the acquisition and administrative costs of workers' compensation put an unreasonable cost burden on the social insurance program? In assessing insurer expense rates it is important to keep two facts in mind. First, expense rates vary greatly among individual insurers. Second, insurers pay a state premium tax of about 2% on their premium income and spend part of the expense allowance on direct services to policyholders such as loss control, claims adjustments, and certain services provided by agents and brokers (e.g., analyzing their exposure and answering questions on coverage). Third, many stock insurers and most, if not all, mutual insurers return in dividends to policyholders part of the premiums they collect. Fourth, insurer expense ratios have been steadily declining. Nevertheless, the Achilles heel of private workmen's compensation insurers is their expense ratio.[33]

The issue is made far more complex when the alternatives are private insurers on the one hand and state insurance on the other; for, in addition to the difficulties of measuring the many variables involved (such as service to policyholders and claimants, safety engineering, and other components of insurance costs), ideological preferences tend to make the issue more political than economic. Private insurance, as we have seen earlier, is the dominant method by which workers' compensation liabilities are insured today, although 12 jurisdictions offer the state fund alternative, and seven (including Puerto Rico) have state insurance exclusively.

Periodically jurisdictions without state funds question whether they should have one; some with exclusive state funds investigate whether their funds should be competitive; and others with competitive state funds consider whether their fund should be converted to an exclusive fund or abolished. Few of these investigations have changed the existing situation. The last exclusive state fund was established in 1919, the last competitive fund in 1933. No jurisdiction with a state fund has ever terminated its operations. However, in 1965 critics of the Oregon exclusive state fund succeeded in passing legislation to permit competitive private insurers. In 1969 the Arizona competitive fund was required to alter its operations in ways that favored private insurers.

The arguments were essentially the long-standing ones: on the one hand, a state fund has smaller administrative and supervisory expenses[34]; and, on the

---

[32]Insurers relate losses paid in a given year, plus the increase in the reserve established for future payments on injuries already incurred, to premiums actually earned. Labor relates only losses paid to all premium income, regardless of whether it was earned during the policy period.

[33]See Ref. 21, p. 207.

[34]According to the Teknekron study for the Interdepartmental Task Force, p. II–2, private insurers allocated about 28% of their earned premiums to expenses during 1972–1974. State fund expenses in 1974 ranged between 8 and 27%, *Ibid.*, Table II–E. Expenses per lost time claim for private insurers were about $900; state fund expenses ranged from $268 to $1,714.

other hand, private insurers, on the average, rank ahead of state funds in servicing their insureds. The cost differences have not been sufficiently high to induce any state without a competitive state fund to establish one in many decades. Similarly, state funds have performed well enough to defeat any movement to abolish them.[35]

Neither the National Commission nor the Interdepartmental Task Force recommended private insurers over state funds or vice versa. They did, however, urge both types of insurance to improve certain aspects of their operations, such as loss control. The recent escalation of workers' compensation costs has caused some state commissions to reexamine the possibility of a state fund.

PROPOSALS FOR INTEGRATION WITH OTHER PROGRAMS

Some persons are so unhappy with workers' compensation that they would abolish it as a separate system. They are particularly disturbed by the litigation and delays that arise out of the requirement under workers' compensation that the injury or disease arise out of or in the course of employment. They also question why a person should have different protection against work injuries and deaths than against nonwork occurrences. Finally, they have little hope of correcting the inadequacies and heterogeneity of present state laws.

One suggested alternative approach would integrate workers' compensation into existing or proposed systems.[36] The medical care benefits would be provided by a comprehensive national medical expense insurance program. The permanent total disability and death cash benefits would become part of a liberalized OASDHI system. Indeed, the OASDHI system might be revised to include temporary disability and permanent partial disability benefits in addition to the long-term total disability benefits.

Another version would require all states to establish temporary disability insurance programs similar to those now found in five states, but these would pay the same benefits to persons disabled on and off the job. The long-term disability, death, and medical expense benefits would be paid under the two federal programs described in the preceding paragraph.

A third alternative would differ from the second only in that unemployment compensation would deal with income replacement for all short-term disabilities.[37]

Critics of these alternative approaches note the extensive legislative and ad-

---

[35]For a more extensive discussion of these arguments see Ref. 21, Chap. 7.

[36]For two descriptions of such approaches see the following: Monroe Berkowitz, *Workmen's Compensation: The New Jersey Experience* (New Brunswick, N.J.: Rutgers University Press, 1960), pp. 272–273; also, John F. Burton, *The Significance and Causes of the Interstate Variations in The Employers' Costs of Workmen's Compensation,* unpublished doctoral dissertation, 1965, Ann Arbor, Mich.: University of Michigan, pp. 29–32.

[37]Merton C. Bernstein, "The Need for Reconsidering the Role of Workmen's Compensation," *University of Pennsylvania Law Review,* CXIX (1971), 1001.

ministrative changes that would be necessary to implement them and the many uncertainties associated with these changes. More importantly, they argue, workers should receive higher benefits for work-incurred injuries. Years ago workers traded their right to sue their employers for what they anticipated would be adequate workers' compensation benefits. If they are to receive no more favorable treatment under a social insurance program for work-incurred injuries, their right to sue their employers for negligent acts should be restored, with possibly unsatisfactory consequences. Moreover, they argue, on ethical grounds an injured employee deserves better treatment for work-incurred losses. Also, supplementing workers' compensation with, say, OASDHI would (assuming present financing arrangements) shift the funding of benefits for job-related injuries from employers to payroll taxes paid by employers and employees. Furthermore, the loss control incentives and resource allocation advantages claimed for workers' compensation industry and experience rating would be lost. There exists, of course, the possibility of retaining special experience-rated contributions for the occupational disability portions of more comprehensive programs, but most supporters of comprehensive programs do not contemplate such an approach. Indeed, they deny that workers' compensation pricing has that much effect on safety programs or resource allocation. They believe that alternate methods such as fines and penalties would be at least as effective. Finally, critics oppose some integration proposals because these would remove what they consider to be the advantages of private insurer involvement.[38]

A quite different approach would retain workers' compensation as a separate system, but permit the worker to claim that the employer was negligent and sue for supplemental benefits (e.g., wage losses in excess of workers' compensation benefits and pain and suffering). Such a dual system would permit some workers to secure higher benefits, but it would increase litigation and impose on employers an extra cost that they would certainly oppose. Permitting this alternative might also reduce pressures to improve the "no-fault" benefits. Following the example set by certain automobile no-fault compensation plans, the right to sue might be limited to persons suffering economic losses in excess of some stated amount or some scheduled physical impairments.

The National Commission rejected both of these approaches in their deliberations. The Interdepartmental Task Force also supported a separate workers' compensation program. Although the basic concept will continue to be questioned by some observers, principally because of the necessity of proving the work relationship, attention is presently concentrated on improving the current system.

---

[38]For the reasons noted in this paragraph, no nations except the Netherlands and New Zealand have completely eliminated the distinction between work injuries and nonwork injuries. Furthermore, none of the national health insurance proposals discussed in Chapter 12 would replace workers' compensation. See Chapters 6 and 19 of Ref. 17.

SUMMARY

Unemployment caused by occupational disability is a less serious aggregate problem in economic security than is unemployment due to labor-market causes. But work-connected injuries and sickness are costly noneconomic barriers to employment and tend to present a serious threat to individual economic security. Disability shuts off earnings (sometimes permanently) and brings with it extensive medical costs.

Although work has always produced injuries and sickness, the rate of these occurrences began to rise in this country as industrialization began in the late nineteenth century. Early interest in combating the problem resulted in scattered safety legislation, a few individual employer safety programs, and eventually an industrial hygiene movement aimed at preventing industrial illness. But during the period of the peak rates of occupational disability injured workers had as their chief recourse a lawsuit at common law in which recovery required demonstrating the employer's negligence as a cause of disability.

This system, which permitted employers to defend on the grounds of contributory negligence, negligence of fellow employees, or assumption of the risks of employment by the claimant, produced serious hardships. Lawsuits were costly, time consuming, produced serious antagonisms, and only infrequently resulted in adequate recoveries. Dissatisfaction with this approach to the problem led to the widespread enactment of employers' liability laws, which weakened employers' common-law defenses. But, since lawsuits were still required for recovery, they were but a small improvement over the common law. Against this background state legislatures turned to a German legislative experiment: workers' compensation laws, which provided benefits to injured workers on an insurance basis without the need of a lawsuit or proof of fault. The liability without fault principle of workers' compensation was first enacted early in the twentieth century, and today all states have these laws, though they differ widely in their coverage, benefits, and effectiveness.

The Occupational Safety and Health Act of 1970 has important implications for both industrial safety and workers' compensation. Under this act federal or approved state safety standards are being established and enforced. The Act also established a National Commission on State Workmen's Compensation Laws, whose 1972 recommendations have had a profound impact on state workers' compensation laws.

To qualify for workers' compensation a worker must be an employee working in covered employment who suffers an injury or disease arising out of and in the course of his employment.

Cash benefits for temporarily disabled workers are usually weekly payments, following a short waiting period, equal to two-thirds of the worker's average weekly wage, subject to a specified maximum. If a worker is permanently and totally disabled, these payments are usually continued for life. Permanent partial disability usually entitles the worker to temporary total disability benefits during the healing period, plus a specified amount tied to the type of impairment. Cash benefits are also provided survivors of deceased workers. Most states now automatically adjust the maximum weekly benefit for increases in average wages or the cost of living. Some states make similar adjustments in the benefits paid long-term disabled or survivors.

All state laws cover all medical expenses incurred by the worker. Most also provide some indemnity or maintenance allowances for workers undergoing vocational rehabilitation.

All states except one require employers to insure their worker's compensation obligations or demonstrate their ability to do so. State funds write all the insurance in 7 jurisdictions and compete with private insurers in 12 others. Employers pay private insurance premiums that vary according to their industry, their own experience, and their size.

Workers' compensation programs have been greatly improved since 1972, when the National Commission on State Workmen's Compensation Laws found existing programs inadequate and inequitable. The Commission made numerous recommendations for improvement, 19 of which were deemed essential. These essential recommendations included compulsory coverage with no occupational or size exemptions, full coverage of work-related diseases, a maximum weekly cash benefit by July 1975 of at least 100% of the state average weekly wage, and full medical care and rehabilitation services. As of October 1980, despite the standards noted above, no jurisdiction satisfied all 19 standards, 13 met 10 or less standards. The Commission had urged federal action to guarantee compliance if the standards were not satisfied by July 1975, but Congress is still considering a model standards bill that would implement this suggestion. An Interdepartmental Task Force on Workers' Compensation, set up in response to one of the National Commission's recommendations, recommended in early 1977 that the states be given more time, but it endorsed the Commission's recommendations and added some of its own, particularly with respect to the handling of permanent partial disability claims, occupational disease cases, and rehabilitation. The rapidly rising worker's compensation costs since 1972 have also caused many employers to argue that the administration of the system needs to be tightened, and some overly liberal provisions changed.

Some radically different approaches have also been suggested. For example, one approach would absorb workers' compensation into a revised OASDHI system and a new national medical expense insurance program. Another approach would permit workers to sue for their uncovered economic and intangible losses in those cases where employers are negligent. The major thrust at present, however, is on improving workers' compensation.

SUGGESTIONS FOR ADDITIONAL READING

Barth, Peter S., with H. Allan Hunt. *Workers' Compensation and Work-Related Illnesses and Diseases.* Cambridge, Mass.: MIT Press, 1980.
A comprehensive analysis of the special workers' compensation programs asocciated with occupational diseases.

Berkowitz, Monroe. *Workmen's Compensation: The New Jersey Experience.* New Brunswick, N.J.: Rutgers University Press, 1960.
The most thorough of the individual state studies of workmen's compensation.

Cheit, Earl F. *Injury and Recovery in the Course of Employment.* New York: Wiley, 1961.
A book-length evaluative study of the performance of workmen's compensation, especially its effectiveness in restoring economic losses of disabled workers. This book includes a comparative study of employers' liability systems, together with policy proposals for the future of workmen's compensation.

Cheit, Earl F., and Margaret S. Gordon (Eds.). *Occupational Disability and Public Policy.* New York: Wiley, 1962.
A symposium of many leading scholars and practitioners in this field expressing their diverse views, including a discussion of foreign experience.

Dodd, Walter F. *Administration of Workmen's Compensation.* New York: Commonwealth Fund, 1936.
A classic on workmen's compensation administration, containing many still timely generalizations and insights.

Downey, E. H. *Workmen's Compensation.* New York: Macmillan, 1924.
Long considered a classic, this volume is a basic work in the field of early workmen's compensation philosophy and development.

Kulp, C. A., and J. W. Hall. *Casualty Insurance,* 4th ed. New York: Ronald Press, 1968.
See especially Chapters 7–9, 21, and 22. Chapters 7 and 8 are good discussions of occupational injuries and workmen's compensation. The other chapters present the various aspects of workers' compensation insurance and rate making.

Larson, Arthur. *The Law of Workmen's Compensation.* Albany, N.Y.: Matthew Bender, 1968, updated periodically.
A comprehensive, updated set of volumes on the legal issues in workers' compensation.

National Commission on State Workmen's Compensation Laws. A Compendium on Workmen's Compensation. Washington, D.C.: Government Printing Office, 1972.
The most recent comprehensive discussion of workers' compensation laws, administration, and issues.

National Commission on State Workmen's Compensation Laws. Supplemental Studies. Washington, D.C.: Government Printing Office, 1972.
In-depth analyses of many workers' compensation topics.

Reede, Arthur H. *Adequacy of Workmen's Compensation.* Cambridge, Mass.: Harvard University Press, 1947.
A detailed examination of the development of workers' compensation coverage and benefits during the first half of its existence.

Rejda, George E. *Social Insurance and Economic Security.* Englewood Cliffs, N.J.: Prentice-Hall, 1976.
Chapter 12 of this comprehensive text deals with workers' compensation.

Report of the National Commission on State Workmen's Compensation Laws. Washington, D.C.: Government Printing Office, 1972.
The report of the 15-member Commission appointed by the President under the Occupational Safety and Health Act of 1970 to study and evaluate state workmen's compensation laws.

Somers, Herman M., and Anne Ramsay Somers. *Workmen's Compensation.* New York: Wiley, 1954. Comprehensive analysis of workmen's compensation and an excellent treatment of benefit adequacy, insurance, and rehabilitation. See especially Chapters 3–8.

State Compliance With The 19 Essential Recommendations Of The National Commission On State Workmen's Compensation Laws, 1972–1980. Washington, D.C.: U.S. Department of Labor, Employment Standards Administration, Office of Workers' Compensation Programs, January 1981.
A detailed analysis of how the states have responded to the National Commission's 19 essential recommendations.

Williams, C. A., Jr. *Insurance Arrangements Under Workmen's Compensation. Bulletin 317.* U.S. Department of Labor, Bureau of Labor Standards. Washington, D.C.: Government Printing Office, 1969.
An analysis of the security requirements of workmen's compensation laws and the operations of private insurers, state funds, and self-insurers.

Workers' Compensation: Is There a Better Way? Reports to the President and the Congress of the Policy Group of the Interdepartmental Workers' Compensation Task Force, No. 39, February 10, 1977, Part II published by Commerce Clearing House, Chicago, Ill.
This report of the Policy Group of the Interdepartmental Workers' Compensation Task Force updates and expands on the Reports of the National Commission on State Workmen's Compensation Laws. The Task Force also issued during 1977–1979 nine volumes containing valuable research reports and technical assistance reports.

Chapter Eight

Social Disability
Income Insurance

This chapter examines the two most important social insurance programs providing protection against nonoccupational loss of income, namely, (1) the Disability Insurance part of OASDI and (2) temporary disability insurance legislation in five states. Social medical expense insurance is discussed in Chapter 9.

OASDI DISABILITY BENEFITS

Disability benefits were included under OASDI for the first time in 1954 and extended or limited through a series of later amendments to the Social Security Act. Many persons had recommended their inclusion as early as in the 1930s. These disability benefits are the disability freeze, disability income payments, income payments for disabled children, and survivorship benefits for disabled widows and widowers.

The Disability Freeze

To qualify for the disability freeze a person must satisfy certain insured status requirements and be disabled for at least five months by an impairment that is expected to result in death or continue for at least 12 calendar months.

The worker must usually be fully insured and have at least 20 quarters of coverage out of the last 40 quarters, including the quarter in which he or she became disabled. Persons disabled before they reach age 31 qualify if half the quarters elapsing between the quarter in which they attained age 21 and the quarter in which they were disabled are quarters of coverage. In order to maintain a minimum requirement of six quarters, persons becoming disabled before age 24 must have quarters of coverage in half the 12 quarters preceding the quarter of disability. Blind persons must be fully insured, but they need not satisfy the test of recent attachment to covered work. The insured status requirements, therefore, are in most instances more restrictive than those for survivorship benefits.

A person is considered disabled only if the physical or mental impairment is of such severity that he or she is not only unable to do his or her previous work but cannot, considering age, education, and work experience, engage in any other kind of substantial gainful work that exists in the national economy. Blindness is assumed to cause disability even if the person is able to work. In the test applied to other impairments the work must be for remuneration or profit. It need not be full-time, and it need not exist in the immediate area in which the person lives. A specific job vacancy need not exist, and there need not be any assurance that the person would be hired if he or she applied for work. However, such jobs must exist in significant numbers either in the region where the person lives or in several regions of the country. In other words, one's inability to do one's previous work is not a sufficient condition to be considered disabled. Age, education, and work experience will be considered in determining what other type of work the person might reasonably be asked to do. The individual will not be considered disabled if he or she refuses to move to a region where such work is available or if he or she would not be hired for some reason other than disability. The purpose of these conditions is to distinguish between persons who are out of work because of their impairment and those not working for other reasons.

In practice, determinations focus on the more objectively determinable factors —primarily the presence of a severe medical impairment.[1] Almost 80% of the awards are made to applicants who (1) have one or more impairments described or equivalent to one listed in federal regulations and (2) either are not working or are earning less than a specified amount that the Social Security Administration believes constitutes substantial gainful activity ($300 a month in 1980). The other awards are made to persons with less severe impairments whose physical capability and experience match those combinations of vocational considerations that Social Security Administration regulations say justify a disability finding. Under these regulations persons age 55–64 who are unable to perform work requiring a medium amount of strength and endurance and have no transferable skills or relevant work experience are eligible for benefits even though they may be physically able to perform less demanding work. Persons age 60–64 with this degree of impairment are usually found to be disabled if they are unable to find jobs they have recently performed, even if they have transferable skills.

The disability freeze benefit protects a fully or currently insured worker against losing this status or having retirement or survivorship benefits reduced as a result of a long period of total disability. In determining whether a person is fully or currently insured, any calendar year, part of which falls in a period of disability, may be excluded. These years of disability are also ignored in determining the time span for calculating the average indexed monthly earnings (AIME). However, in both determinations the exclusions are made only if this will benefit the applicant.

To illustrate the application of these requirements and rules, consider the following example. Assume that a woman worker reaches age 65 in February

[1]*Reports of the 1979 Advisory Council on Social Security.* Washington, D.C., 1979, p. 143.

1982. In order to be fully insured on that date she must have 28 quarters of coverage (i.e., quarters of coverage equal to the number of years elapsing between December 31, 1950, and January 1, 1979, the year in which the worker reached age 62). If this worker had worked in covered employment since January 1965 and earned four quarters of coverage each year but became totally disabled on January 1, 1970, she would have earned only 20 quarters of coverage. If it were not for the disability freeze, she would not be entitled to any retirement benefits in 1982. However, she does qualify for the freeze because at the time of her disability she was fully insured and had at least 20 quarters out of the last 40 quarters. Because of the freeze, she is entitled to retirement benefits, since the nine years between December 31, 1969, and January 1, 1979, do not count as elapsed time. She has 20 quarters of coverage, but only 19 years have elapsed. Moreover, because of the freeze, the average indexed monthly wage will be computed on the basis of the time span between December 31, 1955, and January 1, 1970.[2]

Disability Income Payments

To qualify for disability income payments a person must satisfy the same eligibility requirements as for the disability freeze, except that blindness is not assumed to cause total disability. However, a blind person between the ages of 55 and 65 is considered disabled so long as he or she is unable, because of blindness, to engage in substantially gainful activity requiring skills or abilities comparable to those required in former occupations.

Like the primary insurance amount (PIA) used to determine survivorship benefits, the disabled worker's monthly income payments are determined by the Decoupled Formula Method. Until recently the first step was to calculate the AIME for the time span extending from the end of the year in which the person became 26 years of age (or 1955 if later) to the beginning of the year in which the worker became disabled. The Social Security Disability Amendments of 1980, however, made one important change in this time span for workers who became disabled prior to age 47. As indicated in Chapter 3, starting the computation period at the end of the 26th birthday year (or 1955 if earlier) permits a worker to drop out the five years of lowest earnings after the end of his or her 21st birthday year (or 1950 if earlier). The 1980 amendments limit the dropout years for disability income claimants to one-fifth of any elapsed years after their 21st birthday year (or 1950 if earlier), but not exceeding five. Fractions are disregarded in this calculation. Consequently, any claimant age 26 or younger cannot drop out any years; claimants age 27–31 can drop out one year. Claimants age 47 or over, who incur most of the disabilities, can drop out five years.[3]

[2]Because this worker was more than 47 years old when she was disabled, she is entitled to the maximum number (five) of dropout years. See the discussion of dropout years in the next section.

[3]Subject to a maximum dropout of three years, the claimant can in addition drop out those years in which there was a child under age 3 in the same household and the disabled worker did not work that year.

The second step is to apply the Decoupled PIA Formula for that year to the AIME. For example, for persons who become disabled in January through May 1982 the PIA is equal to

90% of the first $230 of the AIME,

+32% of the next $1,158 of the AIME,

+15% of the AIME in excess of $1,388.

For persons disabled in June through December 1982 the PIA determined by this formula will be increased by the 1982 CPI adjustment granted to persons awarded disability income benefits earlier.

The monthly payments start at the end of the first month after the completion of a five-month waiting period. The payments stop at age 65, when the person qualifies for retirement benefits, or if earlier, two months after the end of the month in which the disability ceases. Dependents' benefits are paid under essentially the same conditions and in the same amounts as the benefits paid to the dependents of retired workers. However, as a result of the 1980 amendments there is a special family maximum equal to the lesser of (1) 85% of the AIME or, if greater, the PIA or (2) 150% of the PIA. Table 3.3 presents some illustrative examples.

If the claimant was not permitted to drop out five years in calculating his or her disability income PIA, the PIA is recalculated at age 65 to reflect the five dropout years allowable for retirement benefits. Otherwise, the retirement benefit simply continues the disability income benefit. Like the OASI monthly benefits, these disability income benefits are increased each June to match CPI increases.

Several provisions are aimed at removing deterrents to the rehabilitation of disabled beneficiaries. First, all applicants are to be promptly referred to their state vocational rehabilitation agency and benefits are withheld if an applicant refuses without good cause to accept services offered by that agency. Second, persons who return to work under any kind of rehabilitation plan or are rehabilitating themselves are paid benefits during a nine-month trial period as long as they do not recover medically from their disability. If after the close of the trial period the worker demonstrates an ability to engage in substantially gainful activity, benefits terminate three months later. Because of 1980 amendments, if in the next 12 months the workers' earnings should drop below the substantially gainful activity level, he or she is automatically returned to active status. Third, the five-month waiting period requirement does not apply to persons who again become disabled within five years after the termination of disability insurance benefits or an earlier period of disability. Finally, state vocational rehabilitation agencies have since 1965 received payments from the Disability Insurance Trust Fund for the cost of rehabilitation services furnished to selected disability income recipients. The 1981 amendments limited these federal reimbursements to cases where the services have resulted in the beneficiary's performance of substantial gainful activity for a continuous nine-month period. If a state is unwilling to participate under these conditions or does not have an acceptable vocational rehabilitation plan, the Commissioner of Social Security may contract for such services with other public or private organizations or individuals.

If a disabled worker is also entitled to workers' compensation benefits because of an occupational injury or disease or, since 1981, disability benefits provided under most government programs, the Disability Insurance benefit is reduced in those months in which the total combined Disability Insurance and other public disability benefits otherwise payable to the workers' family would exceed 80% of the worker's average monthly earnings prior to the disability, subject to an adjustment for changes in national earnings levels. If these combined benefits would exceed this percentage, the OASDI benefits will be reduced by the excess. For this purpose the workers' average monthly earnings are defined as the largest of three amounts, (1) average monthly earnings during the five consecutive years of highest earnings after 1950, (2) the one year of highest earnings in a period consisting of the period of disablement and the five preceding years, and (3) the average monthly earnings used to compute the disability benefits. Needs-tested benefits and Veterans Administration benefits are not included in this calculation.

Income Payments to Disabled Children

If a child has been totally disabled since before reaching age 22, is unmarried, and either (1) is dependent upon a parent, stepparent, or adopting parent entitled to OASDI retirement benefits or (2) was dependent on a parent and was entitled to OASDI survivorship benefits, the child may receive the appropriate OASDI child's insurance benefit even though he or she may be now 18 years of age or more. The mother's or father's benefit would also be continued.

For example, a fully insured male worker, age 32, has a wife age 30, and a son, age 6, who is totally disabled. Effective August 1982, if the worker should die during the next year, the mother and son would both receive survivorship benefits until the son reached age 16. The son's survivorship benefits would continue for two more years until the son was age 18. Because of the disability provisions, the son's benefit would then be continued for life and the mother's benefit would be continued as long as he remained in her care. On the other hand, if the father should live to age 65 and retire, the son would receive a child's benefit at that time, although he would then be 39 years of age. If the mother was still living and the child was in her care, there would also be a mother's benefit for two years (until she qualified for a spouse's benefit at age 65).

Survivorship Benefits for Disabled Widows and Widowers

A disabled widow or widower is entitled to a widow's or widower's survivorship benefit as early as age 50 if the disability started before seven years after the spouse's death. A widow or widower who was not disabled when the spouse died, but who received a mother's or father's survivorship benefit following the spouse's death, qualifies for a widow's or widower's survivorship benefit if she or he becomes disabled within seven years after the mother's or father's benefit has stopped.

The disability test for these survivors is more stringent than the one described earlier. Their physical or mental disability must be sufficient to preclude them from engaging in any gainful activity.

For each month a disabled widow or widower receives a survivorship benefit prior to age 65 the survivorship benefit is reduced. For each month in which benefits will be received at ages 60 through 64 the reduction is the same as for a regular widow's benefit—$\frac{19}{40}$ of 1%. For each month benefits are received at ages 50 through 59 there is a further reduction of $\frac{43}{240}$ of 1%. Thus, if the benefit starts at age 50, the reduction is $(60 \times \frac{19}{40}) + (120 \times \frac{43}{240})$, or 50%.

Financing and Administration

The OASDI payroll tax covers the costs of these disability benefits. To meet the cost of the income benefits for disabled workers, their wives, and their children the OASDI contribution rates applied to the first $32,400 earnings include a 0.825% tax on employees and employers and a 1.2375% tax on self-employed persons. As indicated in Chapter 3, the contribution base will increase each year as average wages increase. In 1985 the disability portion of the OASDI contribution rate paid by employers and employees is scheduled to rise to 0.950%; from 2011 on the rate will be 1.100%. The corresponding self-employer rates are 1.425 and 1.650%.

The additional taxes collected for this purpose are appropriated to the Disability Insurance Trust Fund, which operates in essentially the same fashion as the OASI Trust Fund discussed in Chapter 4.

The most important problem in the administration of disability benefits is determining whether the applicant is totally disabled and whether this disability is likely to last at least 12 months. Almost all disability determinations are made by state agencies (where possible, state vocational rehabilitation agencies) under agreements between the states and the Secretary of Health and Human Services. The Social Security Administration makes determinations only for persons living outside the United States and a few other cases specifically excluded from state jurisdiction. State agencies are used most often because it is assumed that these agencies have had more experience in this area than the federal agency and to facilitate rehabilitation contacts with the disabled persons.

In order to promote uniformity among the states, the Social Security Administration sets standards to guide the state agencies; it also reviews a sample of state determinations for consistency and conformity with the national standards and checks on such matters as age, insured status, and dependency status. Workers can appeal decisions to the Bureau of Hearings and Appeals of the Social Security Administration. Decisions at this level may in turn be appealed to the federal courts.

Until the 1980 amendments federal examiners reviewed only 5% of the state determinations. Only decisions favorable to the worker could be reversed. Because of those amendments the sample determinations were increased to 15% in 1981, 35% in 1982, and 65% from 1983 on. Decisions favorable or unfavorable to the worker can be reversed.

Trends

When disability benefits were first added to OASDI in 1954, they were limited to the disability freeze. Furthermore, only disabilities that were expected to result in death or to continue for a long and indefinite period qualified a person for this benefit. The disability income payments and the income payments to disabled children were added in 1956, but no disability income payments were made until the worker was at least 50 years of age. Workers' compensation benefits, if any, were deducted from the disability insurance payments. Dependents of disabled workers first became eligible for benefits under the 1958 amendments and at the same time the deduction of workers' compensation benefits was eliminated. The requirement that the disabled worker be at least age 50 before benefits started was dropped in 1960. The 1965 amendments shortened the required expected duration of disability to one year and introduced the current treatment of workers' compensation benefits. In 1967, the definition of disability was expanded as indicated earlier, the insured status requirements for persons 31 or younger were liberalized, and survivorship benefits were provided for disabled widows and widowers as early as age 50. In 1972 the waiting period was reduced from six to five months. The Social Security Disability Amendments of 1980 reduced the number of dropout years for younger workers, introduced the special family maximum for disability income benefits, added 12 months in effect to the trial period, and increased the percentage of state determinations reviewed by the Social Security Administration. The 1981 amendments limited federal payments to states for rehabilitation services to successful cases and modified the workers' compensation offset to include disability benefits provided under most government programs. The elimination of the $122 minimum benefit and the other changes in OASI benefits noted in Chapter 3 also affected Disability Insurance benefits.

Operations

Because of the rapid introduction of new and more liberal benefits described above, the increases in the number and amount of benefits since 1960 have been substantial. Table 8.1 shows the rapid growth during 1957–1978 in the number of disabled workers and their dependents receiving OASDI disability income benefits. From 1978 to 1980 the number of beneficiaries declined slightly but the dollar benefits continued to increase. Table 8.1 does not include benefits paid to disabled children, widows, and widowers. The shortening, in 1965, of the required expected duration of disability to one year increased the number of persons

Table 8.1 Number of Disability Income Beneficiaries at End of Year, Total Monthly Benefits Received, and Average Monthly Benefit, by Type of Recipient, 1957–1980

Year	Disabled Workers			Dependent Spouses			Dependent Children		
	Number in Thousands	Total Amount of Benefits in Millions of Dollars	Average Monthly Benefit ($)	Number in Thousands	Total Amount of Benefits in Millions of Dollars	Average Monthly Benefit ($)	Number in Thousands	Total Amount of Benefits in Millions of Dollars	Average Monthly Benefit ($)
1957	150	11	73	—	—	—	—	—	—
1960	455	40	89	77	3	34	155	5	30
1965	988	97	98	193	7	35	558	18	32
1970	1,493	196	131	283	12	43	889	34	39
1975	2,489	562	226	453	30	67	1,411	87	62
1976	2,670	655	245	474	35	73	1,480	101	68
1977	2,834	752	265	494	39	79	1,525	115	75
1978	2,880	830	288	492	42	86	1,497	125	83
1979	2,870	924	322	475	46	96	1,431	136	95
1980	2,861	1,061	371	462	51	110	1,359	150	110

Sources: Social Security Bulletins.

eligible for benefits, but the increase was not as dramatic as many had expected. From 1970 to 1975 the number of disability awards relative to the number insured increased from 4.84 per 1,000 to 7.11 per 1,000. Termination of disabilities also declined from 100.4 per 1,000 cases in force in 1970 to 75.2 per 1,000 in 1975. Social Security Administration actuaries attributed these results to increasingly attractive benefit levels, high unemployment rates, an apparent increase in the acceptance of program benefits, and a reduction in the extent of the federal review of state determinations during that period. The establishment of Supplemental Security Income in 1974 also acquainted many persons with the existence of Disability Insurance and their eligibility for benefits.[4] As already noted in Chapter 4, starting in 1978 these trends were reversed. Why this happened is not clear, but two contributing factors were a tightening of disability determinations and a reduction in the number of Supplemental Security Income applicants who in the process discovered they were eligible for Disability Insurance benefits. The Disability Amendments of 1980 are expected to reduce both the total dollar payments and the number of beneficiaries. The reduction in the number of drop-out years for younger workers, the new special family maximum, and the increase in federal reviews of disability determinations should work in this direction. The 1981 modification of the workers' compensation offset and the benefit reductions should also cut costs.

The progress of the Disability Insurance Trust Fund since its formation is shown in Table 8.2. The decline in the trust fund assets from 1961 to 1965 occurred because benefits were not terminated by death or recovery as rapidly as had been originally assumed. Consequently the Board of Trustees recommended and Congress agreed that the contributions allocated to this trust fund be increased. Some of the increase, of course, was also necessitated by the liberalizations in the disability provisions as a result of those same amendments. Further liberalizations in 1967 caused the two rates to rise again, as did the substantial benefit increase in 1972. Except for the changes in the actuarial assumptions described in Chapter 3, contributions would have had to be increased much more than they were. For reasons already noted in in Chapter 4 the financial situation worsened considerably shortly thereafter, particularly with respect to Disability Insurance. The Disability Trust Fund faced depletion in late 1978 or 1979. Scheduled contributions were increased substantially by 1977 amendments. By 1980 Disability Insurance experience had improved considerably and Congress transferred to OASI some of the 1980 and 1981 contributions that had been scheduled for Disability Insurance.

Actuarial estimates of the progress of the Disability Insurance Trust Fund under the present system and proposed changes are prepared periodically. The 1981 methodology, assumptions, and findings have already been summarized in

---

[4]Francisco R. Bayo, Stephen C. Gross, and Samuel S. Weissman, *Experience of Disabled-Worker Benefits Under OASDI, 1972–1976,* Actuarial Study No. 75, Social Security Administrative Office of the Actuary, June 1978.

Table 8.2 Receipts, Expenditures, and Assets of Disability Insurance Trust Fund, 1957–1980 (In Millions of Dollars)

	Receipts		Expenditures		
Year	Net Contributions[a]	Interest	Benefit Payments[b]	Administrative Expenses	Total Assets
1957	702	7	57	3	649
1960	1,010	53	568	36	2,289
1965	1,188	59	1,597	90	1,606
1970	4,497	277	3,096	164	5,614
1975	7,530	502	8,534	256	7,354
1976	8,336	422	10,082	285	5,745
1977	9,266	304	11,546	399	3,370
1978	13,554	257	12,629	325	4,226
1979	15,232	358	13,816	371	5,630
1980	13,396	487	15,515	368	3,629

Sources: Social Security Bulletin, Annual Statistical Supplement 1977–1979, p. 81; Social Security Bulletin, LXI, No. 5 (May 1981), p. 44.

[a]Includes transfers from the Railroad Retirement account to the Disability Insurance Trust Fund in 1959 and 1960, and transfers for military service wage credits starting in 1966.

[b]Includes transfers from the Disability Insurance Trust Fund to the Railroad Retirement account starting in 1961 and reimbursements for state rehabilitation services starting in 1966.

Chapter 4. Administrative expenses are about 1.5% of the benefits paid, 0.16% of the taxable payrolls.

Major Issues

Because the disability insurance portion of Old Age, Survivors, and Disability Insurance covers the same employments as OASI, uses some of the same insured status requirements, employs basically the same benefit structure, and, like OASI, is financed by payroll taxes, much of the OASI evaluation in Chapters 3 and 4 could be repeated here. The 1977 correction in the automatic benefit adjustment was particularly important. Instead, only the unique features of the Disability Insurance provisions will be considered.

The addition of disability benefits to OASI in 1954 was a historic occasion because for the first time this social insurance system included a peril whose existence was not relatively easy to determine. Perhaps because of its limited scope, but also because of the nature of the problem it solved, the disability freeze was almost universally acclaimed. The disability income benefits, on the other hand, were opposed in many quarters as an unwise venture into an area that would be difficult to administer. Many who did not oppose the original limited income benefits have expressed concern about the effects of later liberalizations in the age and expected duration of disability requirements and benefit levels.

On the other side are those who would favor reducing still further the 12-month requirement to, say, 6 or even 3 months and liberalizing the "any substantially gainful activity" requirement. They note that the present OASDI requirement is more severe than that used in private long-term disability insurance, which usually pays benefits (1) during the first few years if the insured cannot work at his or her own occupation and (2) thereafter if the insured cannot do any job for which he or she is suited by education, training, or experience. They also observe that most "severely disabled" persons identified in the 1972 Social Security Administration Survey of Disabled and Nondisabled Adults did not qualify for OASDI benefits. Pechman, Aaron, and Taussig have argued that in order to lessen the use of permanently reduced early retirement benefits under OASDI, eligibility for disability benefits should be liberalized progressively with increasing age.[5]

As noted above, the Social Security Administration already uses more liberal criteria for workers age 55–59 and still more liberal criteria for workers age 60–64. A narrow majority of the 1979 Advisory Council on Social Security recommended that the criteria now applicable to claimants age 60–64 be extended to workers age 55–59.[6] On the other hand, the Council majority rejected a proposal that would have further liberalized the definition of disability. For example, under the rejected proposal most *skilled* workers would have been presumed to be disabled if they could not longer perform jobs requiring a medium amount of strength and endurance.

Part of the growth in awards to 1977 was attributed to changes in program administration. The Social Security Administration originally reviewed all state determinations; starting in 1972 it used a 5% "quality reassurance" stratified sample. It also stopped returning questionable allowances to the state agencies. Concern has also been expressed about the variations in program administration among the various states. As already indicated, the 1980 amendments will increase the federal presence by soon requiring that it review two-thirds of the state determinations.

The 1979 Advisory Council made several recommendations designed to encourage disabled people with residual work capacity to return to work. Work expenses, they argued, should be deductible from the earnings used to determine whether the worker is engaged in substantial gainful activity; the substantial gainful activity level used by the Social Security Administration should be specified in the law and indexed to match increases in wage levels; and workers who complete trial work should have their benefits reinstated if their earnings drop below this level in the following 12 months. This last recommendation was

[5]J. A. Pechman, H. J. Aaron, and M. K. Taussig, *Social Security: Perspectives for Reform* (Washington, D.C.: Brookings Institution, 1968), pp. 141, 211, 226–227.

[6]*Reports of the 1979 Council on Social Security* (Washington, D.C., 1979), Chap. 6.

implemented by the 1980 amendments. The Council also favored more periodic reviews of past awards to see whether they are still justified. The 1980 amendments mandated a review every three years of all cases except those where the disability is believed to be permanent.

The emphasis on rehabilitation in the system is highly commendable, but a much smaller proportion of disabled persons than actually expected receives rehabilitation services. A large proportion claim that they are not aware of the existence of such services. The situation has improved somewhat since trust fund monies were made available for rehabilitation services. In 1976 about 20,000 beneficiaries were being rehabilitated each year, about half as a result of the trust fund program.[7] On the other hand, only about 40% of these rehabilitated leave the benefit rolls and about one-quarter of these return within a few years. In 1974 the Social Security Administration reported that savings due to benefit terminations had exceeded costs by 2.5 to 1, but the General Accounting Office contends that a better estimate is 1.15 to 1. Congressional funding is dependent on savings at least matching costs. The General Accounting Office has also criticized the Administration's tendency to continue benefits unless the worker dies or voluntarily returns to work.

The preceding paragraphs have been concerned with eligibility requirements. Benefit levels, however, have attracted the most attention. Before the DI Amendments of 1980 some disabled workers, especially those with dependents, received DI benefits that exceeded the after-tax income they would receive from working. Many received benefits that were considered sufficiently high to create a disincentive to seek rehabilitation and a return to work. High benefits also created an incentive for workers with marginal claims to apply for benefits. The existence of high DI benefits discouraged the development of private long-term disability insurance, especially for lower-income workers whose monthly DI payment was a substantial fraction of their former income. Principally because of the high expenditures under this program during most of the 1970s, in 1980 Congress limited the maximum family benefit to the amounts specified earlier.

The 1979 Advisory Council on Social Security agreed that family benefits under DI should be less than the OASDI limit. A narrow majority, however, recommended that the DI limit be 90% of the five consecutive highest-earnings years of the worker's wage-indexed earnings. This cap would then be increased each year at the rate at which average wages (not prices) increase. If wages increase faster than prices, this special limit would eventually exceed the OASI limit, which is increased to match price increases. However, the DI limit would never be permitted to exceed the OASI limit. This limit was patterned after what was at that time the limit on combined DI and workers' compensation benefits. Few beneficiary families would have been affected by this limit. A substantial minority favored a stricter cap that, in a slightly modified form, was included in

[7]Mordechai E. Lando and Aaron Krute, "Disability Insurance: Program Issues and Research," *Social Security Bulletin,* XXXIX, No. 10 (October 1976), 11.

the 1980 amendments. Most of the Council also recommended that the limit be applied to all federal disability insurance programs combined, not just DI. Other programs that would be affected would include the black lung program, the Railroad Retirement System, the Civil Service Retirement System, and the programs for members of the uniformed services.

The Advisory Council also repeated for DI its recommendation, reported in Chapter 3, that workers be permitted to drop out one year for each six years after age 21 in the calculation of their AIME. The 1980 amendments permit disability claimants to drop out one year for each five years after age 21, subject to a maximum of five years.

One benefit liberalization favored by the Advisory Council, but not adopted by Congress, would have reduced the waiting period from five to three months. They considered eliminating the waiting period completely, but rejected this option because of its high cost, the difficulties encountered in determining the duration of disability soon after it starts, and the existence of short-term sick leave and disability payments. The Council also recommended that disabled widows and widowers, regardless of age, should receive unreduced benefits. They would also extend spouses' benefits to disabled spouses of disabled or retired workers, regardless of age.

The removal of the deduction for workers' compensation benefits in 1958 generated a storm of protest from many quarters. The major reason for the elimination of this deduction was the widely supported belief that the worker should not lose the benefits to which he or she had contributed and that in most states the combined benefit would still be considerably less than the income loss. However, as a result of the removal of this deduction it became possible in many cases for a seriously injured worker to receive combined benefits that would exceed wages prior to the disability. With the liberalized definition of disability now in effect, this problem could have become more significant in the years ahead. Some observers also feared that by overlapping workers' compensation benefits the federal OASDI system was encroaching upon state workers' compensation programs and might eventually supplant the state systems, an outcome they considered undesirable.

The reinstatement of this deduction in 1965, whenever the combined OASDI and workmen's compensation benefits exceed 80% of the worker's average monthly earnings prior to disability, represents a compromise approach to this problem. When the disabled person's savings in taxes and work expenses are considered, the maximum possible benefit might still be attractive relative to wages, but the seriously disabled person may incur many extra expenses. The 1981 modification of this offset to include disability benefits from most government programs reduces the relative attractiveness of the DI benefit to many workers.

At the end of 1977 about 66,000 families with a disabled worker had their DI benefit reduced or withheld because of the workers' compensation offset. Less than 1,200 families lost their benefit completely. The average offset, however, was substantial, reducing the average monthly family benefit from $439 to $261. As workers' compensation benefits are further liberalized (see Chapter 7) this offset should become more important.

A more basic issue is whether workers' compensation should not be supplanted by expanded disability and medical expense insurance benefits under OASDHI. The arguments made for and against such a change have already been presented in the evaluation of workers' compensation.

National Commission on Social Security

Chapter 4 summarized the 1981 recommendations of the National Commission on Social Security regarding OASI. Many of these recommendations also apply to DI. Listed below are the Commission's other recommendations relating specifically to DI.

1   For the purpose of determining continued eligibility for disability benefits the dollar amount of substantial gainful activity should be raised to the exempt amount under the retirement earnings test for persons under age 65.

2   The dollar amount used in determining whether a month is included in the trial work period should be indexed for future years by changes in average wages.

3   The maximum family benefit for disability cases should be increased, so that it is the smaller of (a) 80% of the five consecutive years of highest earnings (indexed) or (b) the maximum applicable to retirement and survivor benefits.

4   Social Security Administration District Offices should have at least one specialist in disability cases and also staff trained to provide information about Medicare, and efforts should be made to tell beneficiaries that such information is available.

5   In disability cases applicants should be informed of their right to have their treating physician comment on the findings of consultative examinations ordered during the adjudicative process.

6   Administrative law judges should hold prehearing conferences when requested by disability applicants who are represented by counsel.

Reagan Administration Proposals

President Reagan has proposed several major cost-saving changes in DI. First, only medical factors would be used to determine eligibility for disability benefits. Age, education, and work experience would no longer be considered. Second, the disability would have to be expected to last 24 months instead of the current 12 months. Third, instead of requiring that at least 20 of the last 40 quarters be quarters of coverage, the President would raise this requirement to 30 of the last 40, including 6 of the last 13. Fourth, the waiting period before benefits start would be increased from five months to six months.

House Subcommittee on Social Security Proposals

Representative Pickle, chairman of the House Subcommittee on Social Security, would direct the Secretary to establish guidelines governing disability determinations that he would expect to be tighter than current rules. He also proposed that the federal government finance training of doctors in the evaluation of medical impairments. Finally, he would require the HHS Secretary to review a portion of all cases decided on appeal by an administrative law judge who, some observers claim, too often favor the claimant.

The Robertson Freedom Plan

The Robertson Freedom Plan was described in Chapter 5 as a radical alternative to the present system's provisions for death and old age. This plan assumes that an individual should be able to anticipate and prepare for his or her family needs in the event of disability except for inflation, unusually long-term disability, and genuine misfortunes outside the control of the individual.[9] For persons 45 or over on July 4, 1984 the present system would continue. For younger persons the plan would be as follows:

1 Benefits would be payable only to adult resident citizens
   (a)   who were totally and permanently disabled and who had been so disabled for 12 full months,
   (b)   who satisfied minimum requirements of recent attachment to the paid work force and perhaps a minimum residency requirement, and
   (c)   who agreed to participate in a qualified rehabilitation and retraining program.
2 The monthly cash benefits would equal the then current Senior Citizen Benefit described in Chapter 4. This benefit would be financed by earmarked general revenues.
3 Medicare benefits would be provided during the period when cash benefits were paid.
4 A welfare program would supplement this plan for hardship cases.

TEMPORARY DISABILITY INSURANCE LEGISLATION

Only five states—Rhode Island, California, New Jersey, New York, and Hawaii —have laws providing cash payments for employees who are temporarily disabled because of an accidental injury or sickness.[8] This legislation is aimed primarily

[9]A. Haeworth Robertson, *The Coming Revolution in Social Security* (McLean, Va: Security Press, 1981), Chapter 29.

[8]The federal law covering railroad workers is discussed in Chapter 13. Puerto Rico enacted legislation in 1968 patterned after the California law.

at the economic problems associated with nonoccupational illnesses, but all states except New York pay benefits in certain cases when the illness is job connected.

The basic emphasis is different, however, from both unemployment and workers' compensation. The latter is an economic security program providing protection against job-connected illness. The former, through its "able to work" and "available for work" requirements to be described in Chapter 12, provides indemnification for the healthy person who is unemployed.

Historical Development

Rhode Island adopted the first law of this type in 1942. California passed its act in 1946, New Jersey in 1948, New York in 1949, and Hawaii in 1969. Interest in this type of legislation dates back, however, to the 1915–1920 era, when workers' compensation was being introduced.[10] Bills advocating the passage of temporary disability income legislation were debated in many states, but none were passed. During the 1920s interest in the subject waned.

The Depression years saw a renewal of interest in this type of coverage, and many persons felt that temporary disability insurance should be provided under the Social Security Act. The problems of unemployment and old age seemed much more important at the time, however, and the opposition to the inclusion of any form of health insurance was strong. As a result, the Act as passed contained no reference to disability insurance.

However, in its deliberations the Committee on Economic Security considered the matter of health insurance and suggested further study of this problem. It pointed out that it might be desirable to coordinate unemployment insurance and temporary disability insurance. A similar recommendation was made in 1939 by the President's Interdepartmental Committee to Coordinate Health and Welfare Activities.

In 1939 the late Senator Robert Wagner introduced a bill that provided, among other things, for federal grants-in-aid to states having approved temporary disability insurance legislation. The bill was not reported out of the Senate Committee on Education and Labor, but it received much publicity and many states began to study the problem seriously.

Most of those who favored the passage of temporary disability insurance legislation felt that this insurance should be combined with unemployment insurance for several reasons. First, unemployment insurance provides protection against loss of income due to lack of work but not due to disability. Therefore temporary disability insurance is a natural extension of unemployment insurance. Furthermore, the two systems should be related because it is logical to continue

[10]Alfred M. Skolnik, "Temporary Disability Insurance Laws in the United States," *Social Security Bulletin,* XV, No. 10 (October 1952), 11–24. Much of the material that follows is based on this article and a comprehensive analysis by Grant M. Osborn, *Compulsory Temporary Disability Insurance in the United States* (Homewood, Ill: Richard D. Irwin, 1958).

the checks of an unemployed person on the same basis if he or she becomes disabled after the date of unemployment. Second, some states had required employees to contribute to the cost of unemployment insurance and had discovered that these taxes were not needed. In these states the cost of temporary disability income insurance could be met through the diversion of part or all of an existing tax instead of through the imposition of a new tax. And third, administrative expenses would be reduced if the two programs were integrated.

For these reasons Rhode Island, California, and New Jersey patterned their temporary disability insurance plans along the lines of their unemployment insurance plans. Several states, including Hawaii, did not pass temporary disability income laws, but amended their unemployment insurance laws as a partial solution to the problem. The amended laws guaranteed that unemployment insurance benefits would not be terminated simply because an unemployed worker was disabled after filing a claim and registering for work.

Washington passed a temporary disability insurance law in 1949 that was similar to those in New Jersey and California, but it was defeated in a public referendum in 1950.

New York, on the other hand, passed a law patterned after its workers' compensation act. Those who favored this approach argued that temporary disability is more closely related to occupational disability than to unemployment. Furthermore, since New York employees did not contribute to the cost of unemployment insurance, a new tax would be required in any event.

Hawaii, the most recent state to adopt such legislation, replaced its earlier approach noted above with a program that, for active workers, is independent of both its unemployment compensation and workers' compensation programs.

The discussion devoted to this subject in this book is not justified by the number of persons directly affected by this legislation nor by the likelihood that this number will substantially increase. The programs, however, represent interesting and diverse attempts to deal with an important problem, and the lessons to be learned from an analysis of these programs may point the way to better solutions.[11]

Coverage

The employments covered under the Rhode Island, California, New Jersey, and Hawaii acts are almost the same as those covered under their unemployment insurance acts. The employments covered under the New York act differ in several respects from those covered under either its unemployment compensation or workers' compensation insurance programs.

[11]Many of the important detailed provisions of these laws have been omitted for the sake of brevity and clarity of exposition. For a detailed summary of the laws, the reader is referred to an updated looseleaf edition of *Comparison of State Unemployment Insurance Laws* (U.S. Department of Labor, Unemployment Insurance Service), Sec. 600–630.

The types of employees excluded under all five laws are interstate railroad workers who have their own temporary disability insurance program, most government employees, and some employees of some nonprofit institutions. Domestic employees are excluded except in Hawaii and New York. Agricultural workers are covered only in California and Hawaii. Self-employed persons may elect coverage in California.

New York excludes work for employers who do not employ at least one worker on each of 30 days in a calendar year.

Qualifications for Benefits

In addition to working in covered employment, a person must satisfy the following types of requirements.

Qualifying Wages

In Rhode Island a worker must have earned either $1,200 or at least $20 for 20 weeks in the base period, which is the 52 weeks ending with the second week immediately preceding application for disability benefits.

A California worker must earn $300 during the base period, which is approximately the first four of the last five calendar quarters preceding application for unemployment or disability benefits.

A New Jersey worker must have earned either (1) $15 or more from one employer in each of 17 weeks during, roughly, the 52-week period preceding the week the disability began or (2) $2,200 total wages during this period. If unemployed, however, the requirement is earnings of $30 or more from one employer in each of 30 weeks during the 52 weeks preceding a valid claim for either disability or unemployment benefits.

An employed New York worker must have completed four or more consecutive weeks of employment for one employer or 25 days of regular part-time employment prior to the disability. If the worker terminates employment, in most cases he or she will retain eligibility for four weeks. Unemployed workers must either qualify for unemployment insurance benefits, except for their disability, or satisfy a similar wage requirement.

In Hawaii a worker must have earned at least $400 and been employed for at least 20 hours in each of 14 weeks during the four completed calendar quarters preceding the first day of disability.

Labor Force Status

The purpose of the temporary disability insurance legislation is to make income payments to those persons who cannot work or cannot seek work because of disability. The wage qualification does not always accomplish this objective, because a person may qualify on the basis of a past employment record. Therefore all states require that claimants who have been unemployed for more than a few weeks prove their continued attachment to the labor force.

Definition of Disability

In general, a person is assumed to be disabled if he or she is unable to perform his or her regular or customary work because of a physical or mental condition. New Jersey requires that unemployed workers be unable to perform the duties of any occupation. Unemployed workers in New York must be unable to perform in any employment for which they are reasonably qualified by training and experience.

New York is the only state that specifically limits the coverage to nonoccupational illnesses, but, as indicated below, workers' compensation benefits usually reduce the disability benefit in the other states.

Disqualifying Incomes

The purpose of temporary disability insurance legislation is to replace income that has been lost. For this reason the states may disqualify a claimant whose earnings continue despite physical disability or who receives other income because of disability.

Until 1946 workers' compensation benefits were ignored in Rhode Island, but at present disability benefits are not paid to workers receiving workers' compensation for the same disability. In California only the difference between the disability benefits and a temporary workers' compensation benefit is paid, but full disability benefits are paid even if the worker is receiving workers' compensation cash payments for permanent disability. No disability benefits are payable in Hawaii or New Jersey if the claimant is receiving workers' compensation benefits other than permanent partial or total benefits for a *prior* disability. The same rule applies in New York, except that only permanent *partial* benefits for a prior disability are ignored.

Rhode Island and Hawaii do not reduce disability payments if the worker's wage is continued under a formal or informal paid sick leave plan. In California and New Jersey wages that are continued plus the disability benefit may not exceed the worker's wage prior to the disability. New York reduces the disability benefits by any wages paid unless they are supplementary benefits paid pursuant to a collective bargaining agreement. New Jersey is the only state that deducts retirement plan benefits.

Other Disqualifications

All states disqualify a person who is receiving unemployment insurance benefits.

Except in Rhode Island, if a person is ineligible for unemployment compensation for such reasons as involvement in a labor dispute or discharge for misconduct, he or she is usually ineligible for disability benefits.

Benefits

The benefits are determined by three factors: the benefit amount, the duration of the benefits, and the waiting period.

Benefit Amounts

Weekly benefits in Rhode Island are 55% of average weekly wages[12] during the base period, plus $3 for each dependent child under 18 or disabled child, the maximum dependents' allowance being $12. The minimum weekly benefit, exclusive of dependents' allowances, is $12; the maximum benefit is 50% of the average weekly wage in covered employment during the preceding calendar year.

In California the weekly benefit is a function of the total earnings during the base period quarter of highest earnings. For almost any earnings amount the benefit will be higher than the corresponding unemployment insurance benefit. In 1980 the minimum weekly benefit was $30, the maximum $154. Until January 1, 1979, the California Act also provided hospital benefits of $12 a day for 20 days.

New Jersey distinguishes between employed and unemployed workers. In New Jersey the disability benefit for employed workers is a function of the average weekly wage during the eight weeks preceding the disability. Weeks in which the employee earned less than $15 from one employer are excluded. For unemployed workers the same formula, but a longer and more distant base period, is used. Under this formula the weekly benefit ranges from $10 to two-thirds of the statewide average weekly wage.

The New York benefit is one-half the average weekly wage during the last eight weeks in covered employment. In 1980 the minimum benefit was $20 or the worker's average weekly wage, if less. The maximum benefit was $95.

In Hawaii, except for a worker with an average weekly wage of $25 or less, the benefit is 55% of the average weekly wage. The maximum benefit is two-thirds of the state average weekly wage. Thus all states except California and New York have flexible maximum benefits tied to the state average weekly wage.

The Duration of Benefits

In Rhode Island and New Jersey benefits can be paid for up to 26 weeks in a 12-month period, but the benefit duration depends on the number of weeks the claimant worked in the base period.

In California the benefits are payable for 39 weeks for any one period of disability or until the claimant has received three-quarters of his or her base period wages. In New York and Hawaii the uniform limit is 26 weeks in any 52-week period, except that in Hawaii unemployed workers receive benefits only for 26 weeks after they first receive unemployment insurance benefits.

The Waiting Period

A waiting period reduces the cost of the program by eliminating the frequent small losses that add up to a large total. Claims adjustment expense and the

---

[12]The average weekly earnings equal the total earnings divided by the number of weeks in which the worker earned $20 or more.

temptation to feign claims are also reduced. All five states require a waiting period of seven consecutive days at the beginning of each uninterrupted period of disability. California, however, requires no waiting period for hospitalized patients or if the worker is unemployed and disabled for more than 49 days. New Jersey pay benefits for the waiting period after benefits have been paid for three consecutive weeks.

Types of Insurer

Four different methods have been used to insure these benefits. All eligible employers in Rhode Island are insured under a monopolistic state fund. In California and New Jersey all eligible employers are insured under a competitive state fund until the appropriate agency approves a self-insured or privately insured plan. New York requires that the employer purchase approved benefits from either a competitive state fund or a private insurer unless the employer can satisfy the appropriate agency that this obligation can safely be self-insured. Hawaii resembles New York, except that there is no competitive state fund. Disability benefits for unemployed workers formerly covered under a private plan and for persons working for an employer who failed to purchase the required insurance are paid by a special state fund in New York and Hawaii and by the state disability fund in California and New Jersey.

California will not approve a private plan unless it is more liberal than the state plan in at least one respect and at least equal in all other respects. Furthermore, a majority of the employees must consent to the private plan. Even if the plan is approved, those employees who prefer to retain their membership in the state plan may do so. A regulation effective in 1963 (reinstating a provision in effect from 1947 through 1954) prevents private insurers from selecting only employee groups whose sex, age, and wage level composition would leave the state fund with only the less desirable groups. Self-insured plans are not subject to this regulation, which is designed to prevent adverse selection against the state fund.

New Jersey requires that approved private plans be as liberal as the state plan in all respects. A majority of the employees must agree to the plan if it is contributory. If the majority agrees, all employees are automatically covered.

New York approves a private plan if it provides benefits that are at least as favorable actuarially as the state plan. The temporary disability income benefits must be at least 60% of the statutory benefits. If these benefits are less than 100% of the statutory benefits, there must be other benefits such as medical expense benefits to make up the difference.

The New York employer decides how to insure the obligation. No majority vote of employees is necessary. Workers who terminate their employment are insured under the private plan for four weeks after they leave covered employment.

Hawaii, like New York, permits deviations from the state plan if the private plan benefits are actuarially the same or better.

Financing

Rhode Island requires that employees pay a tax of $1\frac{1}{2}\%$ on the first $6,000 of wages to finance the disability benefits. Employers pay nothing. Prior to the enactment of temporary disability income legislation Rhode Island had required its employees to contribute to the cost of unemployment insurance. The disability tax was at first a diversion of part of this unemployment tax. At the present time there is no unemployment tax on employees.

In 1946 the Federal Unemployment Tax Act was amended to permit states that had required employee contributions for unemployment insurance to recover these contributions for the purpose of financing disability income plans. Rhode Island, California, and New Jersey benefited from this amendment.

California levies a 1% tax on the first $14,900 of earnings of employees covered under the state plan. Employers pay nothing. Self-employed persons, who can elect coverage, pay $1\frac{1}{2}\%$ of wages which in all cases is considered to be $3,525 a quarter.

A California worker insured under a private plan is not permitted to contribute more toward the cost of this plan than the rate for coverage under the state plan. The total cost may be more or less than 1%, because private insurers, unlike the state insurer, take into account the underwriting characteristics and loss experience of the group in determining the premium. However, because of the underwriting restrictions that became effective in 1963, the cost is likely to be higher. Also, the benefits under the private plan must be more liberal, and this affects the total cost.

The state fund pays all the benefits to qualified workers who have been out of covered employment for more than 14 days. These benefits are financed out of a portion of the statutory tax rate and assessments on private plans. Private plans are also assessed for the cost of the added administrative work caused by their existence.

The New Jersey plan is financed in essentially the same way as the California plan except for the following important differences: (1) an employee covered under the state plan pays a tax of $\frac{1}{2}\%$ on the $6,200 of wages, while the employer pays a tax of $\frac{1}{4}\%$; (2) the employer's contribution to the state plan is subject to modification through a form of experience rating. The employer's rate may range from 0.1 to 1.1% on the basis of the employer's experience and the total balance in the state fund. Benefits for unemployed workers are financed out of interest earned on the employee contributions withdrawn earlier from the federal trust fund and by assessments on employees.

In New York employees may not pay more than $\frac{1}{2}\%$ on the first $60 of weekly earnings toward the cost of the plan, unless there is a special agreement to the contrary approved by the state in recognition of superior benefits. The employer pays the additional cost, if any. Both the state fund and private insurers use premiums that reflect in approximately the same way the underwriting characteristics and loss experience of each insured group. Consequently, adverse selection against the state fund is much less likely. Benefits for unemployed workers are financed by assessments, as needed, on the New York state fund, self-insurers, and private insurers and by interest earned on a fund created by special contributions during 1950.

Employee contributions in Hawaii cannot exceed half the total cost or, if less, $\frac{1}{2}\%$ of weekly earnings up to the annually computed taxable wage base—two-thirds of the state average weekly wage. Assessments, as needed, on insurers and self-insurers sustain the Special Disability Fund from which benefits are paid during unemployment.

Administration

In Rhode Island, California, and New Jersey the unemployment insurance agency administers the law, while in New York the Workers' Compensation Board is the administrator. The unemployment insurance agencies in the first three states both administer the law and operate the state fund. In New York the Workers' Compensation Board exercises general supervision over private insurers, self-insurers, and a separate state fund. Hawaiian law is administered by a newly created Temporary Disability Insurance Division of the Department of Labor and Industrial Relations. In all five states, under both private and public plans, provision is made for appeal to several administrative boards and eventually to the courts if a claimant is dissatisfied with the award he or she receives.

The state funds are operated essentially on a pay-as-you-go basis. However, some monies have been accumulated because the employee contributions, interest earnings, and recoveries from the Federal Unemployment Trust Fund have exceeded the benefits and administrative expenses. These amounts are invested in interest-bearing government securities, and the interest and principal can be used to reduce the current tax, improve the benefits, or serve as a contingency fund.

Operations

In 1978 over 16 million workers, more than one-fifth of the workers covered under state unemployment insurance programs, were covered under these state laws.

In California about 7% of the covered employees were insured under private plans, most of which were self-insured. The regulation against adverse selection, coupled with the requirement that the private plan be superior to the state plan, has been cited as the reason for the drastic decrease in the proportion of employees covered under private plans from over 30% in 1960 to 7%. In New Jersey the proportion covered under private plans was 31%, which is also less than the 60% reported in 1960. The requirement that the private plan be at least as good as the state plan in all respects and the experience rating approach used by the state plan may explain the increasingly important role of the state plan. In New

York, on the other hand, over 90% of the covered employees were insured under private plans. In both New Jersey and New York most private plans were insured plans. Hawaii has no state plan; few employers self-insure.

Cash benefits under these five temporary disability insurance laws were $1.1 billion in 1979 compared with $0.7 billion in 1970 and $0.3 billion in 1960.

Private plans tend to be more liberal than public plans in terms of the average weekly benefit. This result is not unexpected, because of the criteria established for the approval of private plans.

Evaluation

Temporary disability insurance legislation was designed to provide a minimum income during periods of temporary disability (primarily nonoccupational) to persons who were attached to the labor force, that is, employed or temporarily unemployed at the time they were disabled. The general objective of this legislation has been achieved without any apparent serious adverse economic effects. The original Rhode Island legislation had many obvious defects, but these have been corrected, at least in part.

Numerous issues have arisen in connection with temporary disability insurance legislation, only a few of which can be discussed here. The basic issue, of course, is whether any public program is needed in this area. The arguments here usually center on the adequacy of private employee-benefit plans, which now provide equivalent protection for almost half of the wage and salary workers in private industry. In some states the proportion is much higher, and in other states much lower. In this connection it is interesting to observe that the passage of the legislation in the first four states contributed to the growth of private insurance elsewhere because interstate employers often extended the same protection to all their employees, labor unions often pressed for such uniform coverage, and insurers learned how to deal with small groups. The interest of labor unions in this legislation has been somewhat reduced by the success they have experienced in private negotiations with employers on similar protection. Private arrangements, they have discovered, are more flexible. Furthermore, the role of the union in improving the protection is more direct and obvious to the union's membership.

Eligibility requirements and benefit formulas have been subject to the type of criticism that, as will be explained in Chapter 12, has been directed at unemployment insurance. Lack of coordination with unemployment insurance and worker's compensation has led to some adverse selection against the program with the most liberal benefit schedule. Like the maximum benefits under these two older programs, the temporary disability insurance maximums have also tended to lag behind increases in statewide average wages, but three states now relate their maximum benefits to the state average weekly wage.

Mention was made earlier of the arguments favoring the attachment of a temporary disability income program to unemployment insurance or worker's compensation. Some persons favoring the unemployment insurance approach and the adoption of temporary disability insurance legislation in all states would levy a federal tax, similar to the federal unemployment tax, against which the employer would be permitted to offset any contribution to a state program. Others would make temporary disability insurance a part of OASDI. They believe that OASDI should provide comprehensive protection against the financial losses associated with death, retirement, or poor health. Opponents believe that federal action should be limited to long-term disability. A federal short-term disability program would involve extensive administrative machinery that, in their opinion, would be less satisfactory than either private insurance or state funds.

One of the most debated issues is the role of private and public insurers. Many of the arguments are similar to those presented with respect to workers' compensation. Private insurers, it is argued, incur more administrative expenses and the state incurs extra supervisory costs. On the other hand, private insurers claim greater efficiency and effectiveness and argue that decreased benefit costs will offset increased administrative costs. However, because of the unique nature of the temporary disability insurance programs, a few additional arguments are presented on both sides.

In favor of a state fund of *some* type it is argued that there must be some way to handle payments to persons who become disabled while temporarily unemployed. Those favoring a *compulsory* fund support their position by observing that employees contribute to the cost; the plan under this system would be easier to explain to employees, and it would be possible to charge all groups a uniform rate, which they consider to be socially desirable. A competitive state fund cannot successfully charge a uniform rate because of the adverse selection problem encountered in California, which has been only partially solved through the special regulation noted earlier, and which in itself introduces administrative complications. Opponents of *any* state fund suggest that payments to unemployed persons should be handled directly by unemployment insurance systems. They do not agree that there should be a compulsory state fund because the employees contribute and they do not consider state plans to be more easily understood. Uniform pricing, they believe, is unfair and provides no stimulus for loss control. Finally, they argue, with a private insurer the temporary disability insurance benefits can be made a part of a "package" plan providing death, medical expenses, and disability benefits that cuts costs and improves employee satisfaction. They also fear that a compulsory state fund in this area would interfere with the development of all forms of private health insurance.

In states where temporary disability legislation seems advisable, the New York plan offers a compromise between varying objectives. Eligibility requirements and benefit levels are a compromise between equity and administrative ease. Joint financing recognizes that the employer and employee both benefit from the program. Private insurers are given the maximum opportunity to develop their own coverages, but the state plan is an ever-present fair yardstick. Costs are distributed partly on the basis of pooling and partly on the basis of the experience of the individual group. The case for experience rating is weaker than under workers' compensation because the employer has less control over the conditions that determine the loss potential, but it does allocate the losses on the basis of the best estimate of that loss potential.

One basic question is whether temporary disability insurance legislation of the current type, although extremely important, makes the best use of our limited resources. Many would argue that relatively more attention should be directed, on the private and public levels, toward long-term disability insurance.

SUMMARY

The two most important social disability income insurance programs are Disability Insurance under the Social Security Act and temporary disability legislation in five states.

Disability Insurance provides a disability freeze, disability income payments, income payments for disabled children, and survivorship benefits for disabled widows and widowers.

To qualify for the disability freeze a person must satisfy certain status requirements and be totally disabled for at least five months by an impairment that is expected to result in death or continue for at least 12 calendar months. The freeze protects a fully or currently insured worker against losing this status and having survivorship or retirement benefits reduced as a result of his or her disability. Following a five-month waiting period, the program also provides income payments for the disabled person and his or her family calculated in the same way as retirement benefits. Several provisions are designed to encourage rehabilitation.

Disability Insurance is financed through earmarked payroll taxes. The Social Security Administration administers the program, but almost all disability determinations are made by state vocational rehabilitation agencies.

Some critics fear that Disability Insurance has been liberalized too much and too fast. Others would reduce the waiting period and further liberalize the definition of total disability. The rehabilitation services are valuable, but need to be extended to more disabled persons. Much attention is focused on the integration of Disability Insurance and disability benefits provided under other government programs.

The Social Security Disability Amendments of 1980 reduced for many workers the number of years they can drop out in calculating their average indexed monthly earnings, lowered the maximum family benefits, tightened federal administration, and extended the trial work period. The 1981 amendments reduced some benefits and modified the workers' compensation offset to include disability benefits from most government programs.

Temporary disability insurance legislation in five states protects workers against short-term disability income losses. Three of the states coordinate temporary disability insurance with unemployment insurance; a fourth regards it as a supplement to workers' compensation. The fifth state has a program that is not related to either of these other programs. One state requires insurance in a monopolistic state fund; three states permit private insurers to compete with a state fund; and the fifth has no state fund. Two states tax the employee only; the other three tax both the employer and the employee.

SUGGESTIONS FOR ADDITIONAL READING

Ball, Robert M. *Social Security, Today and Tomorrow.* New York: Columbia University Press, 1978. A comprehensive, clear description and analysis of OASDHI plus recommendations for change by the Commissioner of Social Security under Presidents Kennedy, Johnson, and Nixon.

Brinker, Paul A. *Economic Insecurity and Social Security.* New York: Appleton-Century-Crofts, 1968.
Chapter 11 of this book describes and evaluates disability insurance and compulsory temporary disability insurance.

Campbell, Rita Ricardo. *Social Security: Promise and Reality.* Stanford, Calif.: Hoover Institution Press, 1977.
An analysis of OASDHI by a member of the 1975 Advisory Council on Social Security.

Compensation Systems Available to Disabled Persons in the United States. Washington, D.C.: Health Insurance Association of America, 1979.
An excellent analysis and description of the public and private insurance and public assistance programs providing benefits for disability.

Dickerson, O. D. *Health Insurance,* 3rd ed. Homewood, Ill.: Richard D. Irwin, 1968.
Chapter 4 describes disability insurance and nonoccupational disability legislation. Chapter 16 analyzes the place of social insurance in the total economic security scheme.

Munnell, Alicia H. *The Future of Social Security.* Washington, D.C.: Brookings Institution, 1977. A comprehensive review and analysis of OASDI and its relationship to other sources of retirement income.

Myers, Robert J. *Social Security,* 2nd ed. Homewood, Ill.: Richard D. Irwin, 1981.
Chapters 2 through 10 of this book by the 1947–1970 Chief Actuary of the Social Security Administration discuss OASDHI in detail. Mr. Myers is now the Administration's Deputy Commissioner for Policy.

Osborn, Grant M. *Compulsory Temporary Disability Insurance in the United States.* Homewood, Ill.: Richard D. Irwin, 1958.
A comprehensive discussion of the early problems arising in connection with the temporary disability insurance programs in four states and the federal program for railroad workers.

Rejda, George E. *Social Insurance and Economic Security.* Englewood Cliffs, N.J.: Prentice-Hall, 1976.
Chapter 10 of this comprehensive text covers Disability Insurance, Medicare, and temporary disability insurance.

Reports of the 1979 Advisory Council on Social Security. Washington, D.C., 1979.
Chapter 6 of this report describes in detail the Disability Insurance program as of 1979 and recommends several substantial changes in the program.

Robertson, A. Haeworth. *The Coming Revolution in Social Security.* McLean, Va.: Security Press, 1981.

In addition to presenting the author's Freedom Plan, this book provides a lucid explanation of OASDHI.

Social Security in America's Future. Final Report of the National Commission on Economic Security, Washington, D.C., 1981.
The final report of the Commission established under the 1977 amendments to the Social Security Act.

Chapter Nine

Medicare and National Health Insurance Proposals

Despite the heavy financial burden imposed by medical expenses, with two exceptions social nonoccupational medical expense insurance did not become part of the general U.S. economic security system until 1965. The two exceptions were the hospital benefits provided until recently under the California temporary disability insurance legislation and the medical expense benefits provided under some of the plans established under the corresponding New York law. The other general health insurance programs, other than workers' compensation, froze the eligibility status of the insured for death and retirement benefits or paid a disability income, but did not pay medical expenses or provide medical services. In 1965 Congress established the Medicare program, which provides medical expense benefits for the aged and, since a 1972 amendment, the long-term disabled. More recently Congress has been seriously considering several proposals that would create a medical expense program covering most citizens.

After briefly reviewing events leading to the passage of the historic 1965 legislation, this chapter summarizes the major provisions of the two Medicare programs—Hospital Insurance and Supplementary Medical Expense Insurance—and evaluates their performance to date. The remainder of this chapter describes the pressures for a more extensive federal medical expense program and the major characteristics of the leading proposals plus the plans four states have already established.

HISTORICAL DEVELOPMENT OF MEDICARE

Although Hospital Insurance and Supplementary Medical Insurance are recent additions to our economic security program, interest in social medical expense insurance has been intense during most of this century, particularly in the 1930s and 1940s.[1] Compulsory medical expense insurance first attracted widespread

---

[1]For an interesting, detailed discussion of Medicare, see Peter A. Corning, *Evolution of Medicare . . . from Idea to Law,* U.S. Department of Health, Education, and Welfare, Office of Research and

public attention in 1912 following the enactment in a few states of the first workers' compensation legislation. Several state legislatures considered bills that would have required most employers to provide medical expense insurance for their employees, but none passed. The issue continued to attract attention until the 1920s, when it was almost dropped.

Early Recommendations

In 1929 the Committee on the Costs of Medical Care was formed in response to increasing dissatisfaction with medical costs and medical resources. This Committee, which was privately financed, included a distinguished group of leaders in the fields of medical practice, public health, and the social sciences. The Committee report emphasized the uneven incidence of medical expenses, but the majority of the Committee felt that, although compulsory medical expense insurance "may ultimately be necessary and desirable in some states, . . . for most states and probably for almost all of them at the present time, it is much more desirable . . . to develop voluntary insurance for medical care." The Committee approved the group practice principle and suggested grants-in-aid to increase the medical resources in certain areas.

The Depression intensified public interest in the problem because the average family was hard pressed if there were *any* medical expenses. In 1935 President Roosevelt's Committee on Economic Security concluded that health insurance, including medical expense insurance, should be included as part of a federal social insurance system, but the Committee made no specific proposals, and the Social Security Act itself contained no reference to health insurance.

The year 1935 marked the beginning of a National Health Survey and the appointment by the President of an Interdepartmental Committee to Coordinate Health and Welfare. As noted in Chapter 6, the National Health Survey produced some extensive information on the frequency and severity of disability and medical care. The Interdepartmental Committee submitted a report that was largely responsible for the 1939 Wagner bill, already mentioned in connection with temporary disability insurance.

The Wagner bill provided for federal grants-in-aid to states having approved disability insurance programs and medical expense plans. The bill emphasized the provision of medical care for the needy, but it also stated that temporary disability insurance plans would not be approved unless all those covered under temporary disability insurance were also covered under an approved compulsory medical expense insurance plan. Although the bill died in committee, it was widely discussed.

Statistics, Social Security Administration Research Report No. 29 (Washington, D.C.: Government Printing Office, 1969). For a report on the development of Medicare written by the former Chief Actuary of the Social Security Administration, see Robert J. Myers, *Medicare,* McCahan Foundation Book Series (Homewood, Ill.: Richard D. Irwin, 1970), pp. 1–84.

The Wagner–Murray–Dingell Bills

The appearance of the Beveridge Report in England in 1942 was the next stimulus, and in 1943 Senators Robert Wagner and James Murray introduced a bill that would have created a "unified" national social medical expense insurance program. Representative Dingell introduced the same bill in the House. A second Wagner–Murray–Dingell bill was introduced in 1945. Both bills called for a federal system of medical expense benefits and compensation for temporary disability. President Truman recommended the passage of a National Health Act in November 1945, and the third Wagner–Murray–Dingell Act was introduced to carry out his recommendations. This third bill was the high point in the movement for compulsory medical expense insurance for citizens of all ages until the movement was revived in the late 1960s.

Senator Robert Taft and others were opposed to the Wagner–Murray–Dingell bill, but they felt that some action was necessary. They sponsored proposals that, in effect, would have provided federal grants-in-aid to states, with approved plans providing medical care for the indigent and medically indigent. These bills and the successors to the Wagner–Murray–Dingell bill all failed.

The Forand Proposals

During most of the 1950s interest in social medical expense insurance was considerably diminished. Many bills were introduced in Congress that would have added medical expense benefits to OASDI, but they attracted only scattered support. In 1954 the Eisenhower Administration introduced a bill that would have created a federal reinsurance pool, the purpose of which was to encourage the extension of private insurance plans, particularly with respect to aged persons, substandard lives, and catastrophe losses. This bill and its amended versions of 1955 and 1956 either were defeated or died in committee as a result of the combined efforts of those who were disturbed by the vagueness of the proposals, those who believed that the bill was a weak solution to the problem, and those who felt that it provided an opening wedge for "socialized medicine." Private insurers feared the federal controls they thought would accompany any subsidy under the plan.

In 1958, at public hearings before the House Ways and Means Committee on some proposed amendments to the Social Security Act, new interest was generated in social medical expense insurance when Representative Forand proposed an extension of the OASDI program to include hospitalization, nursing home, and surgical service benefits *for aged and survivor beneficiaries only.* The concept of limiting medical expense insurance to OASI beneficiaries had been proposed earlier (e.g., in 1937 by Surgeon General Thomas Parron of the Public Health Service and in 1944 by Merrill Murray, an official of the Social Security Administration), but had attracted little attention. By 1958 it had become apparent that a more limited approach might have more success of enactment.

Toward Medicare Legislation

In 1960, a presidential election year, social medical expense insurance *for the aged* was one of the most important issues considered by Congress. After concentrating mainly on a revised Forand bill and counterproposals by Senator Javits and the Eisenhower Administration, in June the House Ways and Means Committee reported out a bill sponsored by Representative Mills, Chairman of the Committee. Instead of establishing a social medical expense insurance system, this bill, passed quickly by the House, liberalized the medical expense provisions under Old Age Assistance, at that time the public assistance program for the aged. It also established Medical Assistance for the Aged, a public assistance program for the *medically* indigent aged, aged who did not qualify for Old Age Assistance cash benefits but who needed help in paying their medical expenses. Senator Kerr sponsored this measure in the Senate and a few weeks later the Senate approved the Kerr–Mills program.

During the 1960 presidential campaign medical care insurance for the aged was a key issue. Following his inauguration in 1961, the late President Kennedy pressed strongly for a program based on the same principles as the Forand proposal. Consequently several bills were introduced that would have extended the OASDI system to provide medical care for the aged, but until 1965 these bills also failed.

Early in 1965 several new bills were introduced. The prospects for passage of this legislation were now much improved because the 1964 presidential election results favored candidates pledged to support hospital insurance for the aged, the composition of the House Ways and Means Committee had changed, and Chairman Mills had adopted a more favorable attitude toward the new proposals.

Three proposals commanded most of the attention of the Ways and Means Committee during early 1965. First, companion bills introduced by Representative King and Senator Anderson would have provided hospital care, posthospital extended care, home health services, and out-patient diagnostic care. No doctors' care was included. Second, an Eldercare proposal, introduced by Representatives Herlong and Curtis and supported by the American Medical Association, would have amended the Kerr–Mills bill to extend additional federal support to states providing medical assistance for the aged, blind, and disabled in the form of private health insurance. In support of this proposal, it was argued that limiting the program to those who need assistance would cut the cost sharply and that for this more limited group the benefits would be more adequate because they would not be limited to hospital services. The third proposal, introduced by Representative Byrnes with strong Republican support, would have established a voluntary federal health insurance program covering all types of medical expenses. Participants would pay a premium that varied directly with their OASDI benefits, but Congress would also have to appropriate some funds from general revenues. This insurance program would involve private insurers as servicing agents.

In March 1965 the Committee introduced its own bill, which embodied some of the characteristics of all three proposals. First, it proposed hospital insurance benefits similar to those supported by Representative King and Senator Anderson; but unlike their proposal, the Committee established a separate program supported by a separate tax. This position was consistent with Chairman Mills's desire that the hospital insurance benefits not threaten in any way the established OASDI system. Second, in order to plug the gaps in the benefits provided by this system, the Committee established a voluntary physicians' care insurance program supported by participants' premiums and government general revenues. Third, the Committee also approved liberalization of the medical assistance program. Although the Committee's total proposal was much more far reaching than even supporters of social medical expense insurance had reason to expect one year earlier, essentially this proposal became Public Law 89–97 on July 30, 1965.

In October 1972 amendments to the Social Security Act extended coverage to the long-term disabled. Two other important sets of amendments, in 1980 and 1981, will be described at various points later in this chapter.

HOSPITAL INSURANCE

The major features of Hospital Insurance (HI) can be summarized according to the ways in which they affect coverage, benefits, financing, and administration of the system. HI is also known as Medicare Part A.

Coverage

Covered employment under this program includes all employments covered under OASDI plus railroad employment.

HI benefits are payable only to aged or long-term disabled persons. The eligible aged are those age 65 or over who are eligible for any type of OASDI or Railroad Retirement System monthly benefit. For example, a person may be eligible as a retired worker, a dependent spouse, or a surviving spouse. Also eligible are those persons who would qualify for OASDI benefits except for the fact that their annual earnings cause them to lose all of their monthly benefits under the earnings test. Because a considerable portion of the aged (about 10%) were not covered under OASDI at the time the program was established and because it was deemed desirable to include these persons under this program, all other individuals turning 65 before 1968 were made eligible for benefits if they were (1) citizens or (2) aliens lawfully admitted for permanent residence who had resided in the United States for at least five consecutive years. Not eligible under this transitional provision were retired federal employees or their dependents who were covered or could have been covered under the Federal Employees Health Benefits Act of 1959.[2]

[2]Under this act the federal government contributes toward the cost of medical expense benefits for its employees and their dependents.

The provision of full benefits for persons who had not made any contributions toward the program constituted a distinct departure from the social insurance philosophy that had prevailed in the United States up to that time. However, this transitional provision applies to a diminishing group of people. Another transitional provision permitted persons reaching age 65 after 1967 but before 1974 to qualify on the basis of fewer quarters of coverage than were required for cash benefits.

Aged persons who do not otherwise qualify for HI can voluntarily enroll by paying the full cost of coverage, which is $89 a month for the 1981–1982 fiscal year. This premium is increased each July 1 by the same percentage as the hospital benefit deductible explained below had been previously increased. Applicants must also enroll in the Supplementary Medical Expense Insurance program.

DI beneficiaries and disabled railroad retirement annuitants become eligible for these benefits after they have been entitled to disability benefits for at least 24 months. DI beneficiaries include disabled workers, disabled widows and widowers between the ages of 50 and 65, and disabled children. A 1980 amendment permits an individual who becomes reentitled to cash disability benefits within five years (seven years for adult disabled children, widows, and widowers) to have previous months of disability benefits entitlement counted toward the 24-month waiting period. A second 1980 amendment, which is related to the 24-month trial work provision noted in Chapter 8, continued Medicare protection during this trial period plus an additional 24 months for those workers who do not recover medically during this period.

Special coverage is extended to fully or currently insured persons and their dependents or survivors with chronic kidney disease who need dialysis with kidney machines or transplants. Coverage begins three months after a course of treatment is begun and ends 12 months after the transplant or termination of the dialysis.

Benefits

The types of benefits to be provided include (1) hospital benefits, (2) skilled nursing facility benefits, and (3) home health services benefits.

The system covers the cost of almost all types of hospital services normally furnished to in-patients, including such items as room and board, operating facilities, laboratory tests and x-rays, drugs, dressings, general nursing services, and the services of interns and residents in training. Not covered are the services of private duty nurses or hospital-employed physicians such as radiologists, anesthesiologists, or pathologists. Only the cost of semiprivate accommodations is covered, unless a private room is medically necessary. Except in emergency situations, the service must be rendered by a participating hospital that has met certain standards described below.

Duration limits and deductible and cost-sharing provisions (called "coinsurance" provisions in law) affect the amount of benefits provided. There are two duration limits. First, benefits are covered up to 90 days in a single "spell of illness," which is defined as the period beginning with the first day of hospitalization and ending after the person has not been an in-patient in a hospital or a skilled nursing facility for 60 consecutive days. Second, each person also has a "lifetime reserve" of 60 additional benefit days that can be used to supplement the 90 days provided for each spell of illness. Each time this reserve is used the number of reserve days remaining is reduced by the number used. Under the deductible provision, in each spell of illness the patient must bear the first $260 of the cost, plus the charges, if any are incurred, for the first three pints of blood. Under the cost-sharing provision the patient must bear in addition a cost of $65 per day for all days after the first 60 days in a spell of illness and $130 per day for all lifetime-reserve days.

The purpose of these provisions is to reduce the cost of the system and encourage the patient who does not need the services to forgo them. An interesting feature is that the deductible and cost-sharing amounts are adjusted annually to reflect changes in hospitalization costs. The original 1966–1968 deductible and cost-sharing amounts were $40, $10, and $20, respectively. The 1982 amounts are 550% higher. Because there are no dollar limits on the services covered, the automatic adjustment feature is necessary to keep the patient's share of the bill about the same as hospital costs rise. The 1981 amendments increased the deductible 12.5% more than the increase in hospital costs. Also, these amendments changed the cost-sharing amounts from those in effect when the spell of illness began to those in effect during the year when the services are furnished.

In-patient psychiatric hospital care is covered under the system, but there is a *lifetime* limitation of 190 days of service.

After a patient has been hospitalized for at least three days, he or she becomes eligible for posthospital care in a qualified skilled nursing facility (including a convalescent wing of a hospital). The patient must ordinarily be admitted to the skilled nursing facility within 30 days (14 days until 1980 amendments) after discharge from the hospital. A doctor must certify that skilled services are required on an in-patient basis because the beneficiary needs skilled nursing care on a continuing basis. Services must be of a type that would be covered were they furnished to a patient in a hospital. Benefits are limited to 100 days in each single spell of illness. There is no deductible provision, but the patient must bear a cost of $32.50 per day for all days after the first 20 days in a spell of illness. This amount is also subject to adjustment to reflect changes in hospital care costs. Originally it was $5.

A patient who has been hospitalized also becomes eligible for certain home health services after hospitalization. Until 1980 amendments the patient had to have been hospitalized for at least 3 days. To receive these benefits the person must be under the care of a physician; a plan calling for these services must be established within 14 days after the patient is discharged from a hospital or skilled nursing facility; the services must be provided by a qualified home health agency; and the services must be such that they would be covered if provided to a patient in a hospital. Intermittent visiting nursing care and physical, occupational, or speech therapy are examples of services covered. Although these benefits are designed for homebound persons, they may include services furnished at a hospital, skilled nursing facility, or rehabilitation center when the services require equipment that is not ordinarily taken to patients' homes. No limit is placed on the number of home health visits. Until 1980 amendments the maximum number of visits was 100 in the next 365 days after the patient was discharged from the hospital or skilled nursing facility or, if earlier, the beginning of the next spell of illness.

Out-patient hospital diagnostic services were also originally covered under HI, but the Social Security Amendments of 1967 transferred this benefit to Supplementary Medical Insurance.

Excluded under all three covered types of benefits are services obtained outside the United States (except for emergency services required in connection with an illness occurring in the United States), the extra cost of "luxury" services such as a private room or television, custodial care, hospitalization for services such as elective cosmetic surgery not required for the treatment of an illness, services performed in a federal institution such as a Veterans' Administration hospital, and workers' compensation cases.

Financing

HI benefits are financed primarily through contributions by employers, employees, and self-employed persons, computed on the same maximum taxable base as OASDI. Unlike OASDI, however, the HI system imposes the same rate on self-employed persons as on employees and employers. In 1982 all three pay 1.30% on the first $32,400 of earnings. In 1985 the contribution rate is scheduled to rise to 1.35%, and from 1986 on to 1.45%. These rates, which are lower than those scheduled prior to the 1977 amendments, will be applied to the OASDI wage base as adjusted.

The HI contributions are placed in a separate HI Trust Fund with its own Board of Trustees. Except for the fact that the Administrator of the Health Care Financing Administration serves as Secretary, the Board has the same membership as the OASI and DI trust funds and follows the same investment procedures.

Benefits for those persons age 65 before 1968 who were covered under the transitional provision are supported by general revenues.

Social Security Administration actuaries periodically calculate the level premium (constant employer–employee tax rate) that, combined with the tax on self-employed persons, will be necessary if the HI program is to remain self-supporting for the next 25 years and have a balance in its trust fund equal to the outgo for the next year at the end of the period.[3] Estimates are made for a 25-year

---

[3]*1981 Annual Report of the Board of Trustees of the Federal Hospital Insurance Trust Fund,* 97th Congress, 1st Session, House Document No. 97–67, July 2, 1981.

period instead of the next 75 years, as is true for OASDI, because it is difficult to estimate longer-range trends in medical care costs and utilization. Indeed, it is difficult to make reasonable assumptions for a 25-year period. At the time the program was established in 1965 the level-premium cost estimate as 1.23% of the taxable payroll, which was equal to the level-premium value of the scheduled contributions. According to the 1981 estimates, under the intermediate A assumptions the average expenditures for the 25-year period 1981–2005 would average 3.94% of the taxable payroll. To maintain a balance in the Trust Fund equal to half of a year's disbursements[4] would cost an additional 0.08%. Because contributions were expected to average only about 2.84%, the projected actuarial balance was −1.18%. If these intermediate A estimates are correct, the Trust Fund would be exhausted by about 1993. Under the intermediate B assumptions, average expenditures would be 4.19%. Maintaining the Trust Fund at the level of one-half year's expenditures would cost 0.09%. Because the estimated average contribution rate was 2.84%, the projected actuarial balance was −1.44%. The Trust Fund would be exhausted in 1991.

As was the case for OASDI, the actuaries also prepare optimistic and pessimistic estimates. The 1981–2005 estimates are summarized below:

	Opti- mistic	Interme- diate A	Interme- diate B	Pessi- mistic
Average contribution rate (%)	2.84	2.84	2.84	2.84
Average cost (%)	3.26	4.02	4.28	5.64
Actuarial balance (%)	−0.42	−1.18	−1.44	−2.80

Under the pessimistic assumptions the Trust Fund will be exhausted in 1989. Even under the optimistic assumptions the Trust Fund would be exhausted in 1998.

Key assumptions concerning in-patient hospital costs involve the following: (1) economic factors—increases in unit costs if hospitals face the same wage and price increases as the general economy; (2) the volume of services rendered—increases in total output as measured by hospital admissions; (3) unit input intensity—the increase in costs due to (a) wage and price increases for hospital inputs that exceed those in the general economy and (b) increases in the number of employees and the amount of supplies and equipment used to produce a unit of service; and (4) changes in the HI's share of aggregate in-patient hospital costs. The intermediate estimates assumed (1) the same wage and price increases in the general economy as in the two OASDI intermediate projections, (2) an increasing volume of services rendered (attributed after the first few years to changes in the age and sex mix in the population), (3a) a modest continuation of the higher wage in-

[4]The 1971 Advisory Council on Social Security recommended that the balance in the trust fund should be one year's expenditures to protect the fund against annual fluctuations in program experience.

creases paid hospital workers,[5] and (3b) a gradual return to pre-Medicare employer input per unit of service and nonlabor unit input intensity. Based on these assumptions, aggregate in-patient hospital costs were expected to increase each year for the next 25 years, but the annual rate of increase was expected to decline from about 17% in 1980 to 8 or 9% by 2000. The HI share of these costs was also expected to increase, but at a decreasing rate. Similar assumptions were made for the cost of skilled nursing facility and home health agency services.

Under the intermediate A assumptions HI total expenditures were estimated to be 2.27% of taxable payroll in 1981, rising to 5.80% by 2005. Under the intermediate B assumptions the expenditures in 2005 would be 6.38% of taxable payroll.

Administration

The Department of Health and Human Services administers this system through the Health Care Financing Administration, which also administers Supplementary Medical Insurance and Medicaid. Until 1977 Medicare was administered by the Bureau of Health Insurance of the Social Security Administration.

State agencies, operating under an agreement with the Secretary, determine whether a hospital, skilled nursing facility, or home health agency is eligible to participate under the program. To be eligible a hospital must do the following:

1 Be primarily engaged in providing to in-patients, by or under the supervision of physicians, diagnostic and therapeutic services or rehabilitation services.
2 Maintain clinical records on all patients.
3 Require that every patient be under the care of a physician.
4 Provide 24-hour nursing service.
5 Have a hospital utilization review committee that studies admissions, services provided, and durations of stay to establish professional norms and reviews those cases where the patient has been in the hospital for what is considered to be an extended period.
6 Meet the living standards prescribed under local or state law.
7 Meet any other requirements the Secretary deems necessary except that these requirements cannot exceed those established for accreditation by the Joint Commission on Accreditation of Hospitals.

Utilization review committees may be a hospital staff committee consisting of two or more physicians or a similar group from outside the hospital. If after

[5]The higher wage increases from 1967–1976 were attributed to the following: (1) growth in third-party reimbursement, which may have weakened resistance to wage demands; (2) increased proportions of more highly trained personnel; (3) an increased degree of labor organization and activity; and (4) the historically lower earnings of hospital employees. See Ref. 3, p. 47.

consulting with the attending physician the committee concludes that continued in-patient care is unnecessary, it so notifies the hospital. Payments under the insurance program cease three days after such notice is given. Special provisions apply to psychiatric and tuberculosis hospitals and to Christian Science sanatoria.

Participating skilled nursing facilities must do the following:

1 Have in effect a transfer agreement with one or more participating hospitals.
2 Be primarily engaged in providing in-patients with skilled nursing care and related services or rehabilitation services.
3 Have policies developed with the advice of professional personnel including at least one physician and one registered professional nurse.
4 Have a physician, a registered professional staff, or a medical staff responsible for executing these policies.
5 Require that the health care of every patient be under the supervision of a physician and have a physician available in case of emergency.
6 Maintain clinical records on all patients.
7 Provide 24-hour nursing service and have at least one professional nurse employed full-time.
8 Dispense and administer drugs and biologicals according to appropriate procedures.
9 Have a utilization review committee similar to the one described above for participating hospitals.
10 Satisfy any local or state licensing requirement.
11 Meet any other conditions established by the Secretary relative to the physical facilities or the health and safety of the patients.

Home health agencies include such institutions as a visiting nurse association, a subdivision of a local or state health department, or a department of a hospital or skilled nursing facility offering home health services. To participate in the HI program, the agency must do the following:

1 Be primarily engaged in providing skilled nursing services and other therapeutic services.
2 Have policies established by a group of professionals including at least one physician and one registered professional nurse.
3 Provide a physician or registered professional nurse to supervise the services rendered.
4 Maintain clinical records on all patients.
5 Satisfy local or state licensing standards.
6 Meet any other conditions the Secretary establishes in the interest of the health and safety of the patients.

All three types of institutions must agree not to charge any beneficiary for that portion of covered services for which payment would be made under the program.

Professional standards review organizations (PSROs) consisting of substantial numbers of practicing physicians in local areas assume the responsibility for comprehensive and ongoing review of services provided under Medicare. PSROs are responsible for assuring that institutional services (1) are medically necessary and (2) meet professional standards. A PSRO at its option and with the approval of the Secretary of Health, Education, and Welfare may also assume responsibility for reviewing noninstitutional care and services. Various safeguards are included to (1) protect the public interest, including appeals procedures, and (2) prevent proforma assumptions by PSROs in conducting their reviews. Until a 1981 amendment PSROs were required to delegate reviews to hospital utilization review committees to the extent that they were determined to be effective. Such delegation is now optional. Because many persons have questioned the cost-effectiveness of PSROs the Omnibus Budget Reconciliation Act of 1981 directed the Secretary to evaluate each organization and authorized the termination of as many as 30% of the current PSROs by the end of fiscal year 1982.

Payments for services rendered can be made directly by the government to providers of these services, but each provider can and usually has elected to receive its payments through a fiscal intermediary. Fiscal intermediaries can be nominated by associations in behalf of their members or by individual providers. The Secretary must approve the nomination. While public agencies such as a state public health agency can serve as fiscal intermediaries, most providers have nominated private agencies such as commercial insurers, Blue Cross associations, or other hospital expense insurance plans. Most hospitals have nominated Blue Cross associations, but four commercial insurers also operate nationally. A few hospital expense associations other than Blue Cross, Blue Shield, or commercial insurers perform this function, but only in a single state or part of a state.

These fiscal intermediaries determine the amount to be paid each provider and make the payments. They are reimbursed for the reasonable costs of their services.

Providers of services under HI are reimbursed on the basis of the "reasonable cost" of providing those services, not the charges typically made by the provider, unless these charges are less. If a provider has elected to deal with the government through a fiscal intermediary, that agency determines reasonable costs in accordance with the law and government regulations. The law requires that in establishing regulations the Secretary recognize both direct and indirect costs. Otherwise the Secretary is permitted considerable flexibility. For example, the regulations may provide for different methods in different circumstances. The regulations actually drafted cover the types of costs covered, and the share of these costs that can be allocated to the government program. Examples of included costs are the expenses associated with approved educational activities, depreciation, and a limited return on the equity capital of proprietary facilities. Illustrative exclusions are research costs, discounts and allowances received on the purchase of goods or services, and capital expenditures determined to be inconsistent with state or local health facility plans.

The Secretary may establish limits on overall direct or indirect costs that will be recognized as reasonable for comparable services in comparable facilities in an area. He or she may also establish maximum acceptable costs for items or groups of services such as food costs. With respect to medical supplies and equipment, the reimbursement amount cannot exceed the lowest charges at which supplies of similar quality are widely and consistently available. Amendments in 1981 lowered the reimbursement limits on several items. For example, the limit on hospital inpatient general routine operating costs was lowered from 112% to 108% of the mean costs of each comparable group of hospitals.

The Secretary may pay hospitals, skilled nursing facilities, home health agencies, or physicians in any manner mutually agreed on as long as it creates incentives for increasing the efficiency of health care delivery without adversely affecting its quality. The Secretary may undertake studies, experiments, or demonstration projects with respect to various forms of prospective reimbursement of facilities, ambulatory surgical centers, and other matters.

Health Maintenance Organizations (HMO) may be paid under a method that gives them special incentives for cost control. A HMO is characterized by (1) a comprehensive range of medical services including preventive medicine and (2) prenegotiated, fixed periodic payments by or on behalf of individuals or families entitled to these services. An illustration would be a plan that provides covered services in a hospital it owns, staffed by salaried doctors and nurses. No fees are charged for specific services rendered. These organizations, proponents claim, have an incentive to keep their patients well, be efficient, and avoid unnecessary procedures. Because they provide such comprehensive services, they also reduce the emphasis on expensive hospital care. Patients have convenient access to a wide range of services, doctors can readily consult with one another, and facilities and equipment can be more fully utilized. Some doctors prefer the regular work schedule, economic security, and working conditions of a HMO. On the other hand, patients may lose some of their freedom of choice under a HMO and the services may be overutilized by some patients. Also, some doctors prefer solo practices. The operations of existing HMOs are described in Chapter 10.

Finally, the Secretary is required to make public individual and comparative evaluations of the performance of fiscal intermediaries and state agencies under Medicare and Medicaid.

A 1977 amendment strengthened the federal government's ability to detect, prosecute, and punish fraudulent activities. This amendment increased the penalties for such actions, required providers of services and suppliers to disclose more information that make it easier to detect fraud, and made some improvements in the PSRO program. A 1981 amendment imposed a civil money penalty of up to $2,000 plus an assessment equal to twice the amount of the fraudulent claim and barred the fraudulent claimant from further participation in the program.

SUPPLEMENTARY MEDICAL INSURANCE

The second medical expense insurance program established under the 1965 amendments is Supplementary Medical Insurance (SMI), which differs in many ways from the other insurance programs under the Social Security Act. The major features of this system will be discussed under the same general headings as was HI. SMI is also known as Medicare Part B.

Coverage

A major difference between this program and the others is that participation is voluntary. Subject to a few exceptions, all aged persons can participate. More specifically, those eligible to enroll include all aged persons eligible for HI benefits and any other aged persons who are citizens or aliens lawfully admitted for permanent residence who have resided in the United States for at least five consecutive years.

DI beneficiaries, railroad retirement disabled beneficiaries, and persons needing kidney transplantation or dialysis who are eligible for HI are also eligible for SMI.

Aged and disabled persons who become eligible for HI are automatically enrolled under SMI. They must be so informed and given an opportunity to decline the coverage. Other persons must enroll during their initial enrollment period or some "general" enrollment period. A person's initial enrollment period is the seven-month period starting three months before the month in which he or she attains age 65 and meets the other requirements. Each year there is a general enrollment period from January 1 to March 31. A 1980 amendment provided for continuous open enrollment, but in 1981 Congress repealed this provision and reinstated the annual January–March enrollment period.

Once a person has elected coverage he or she can terminate participation if not an OASDI or Railroad Retirement beneficiary by failing to pay premiums when due. Otherwise he or she must specifically elect during a general enrollment period not to participate in the future. A person who terminates coverage has one opportunity to reenroll.

These enrollment procedures are similar to those used by private insurers in connection with voluntary group insurance. Their objective is to reduce adverse selection against the program.

Benefits

The far-reaching benefits under this program supplement those under HI. They include the services of physicians and surgeons in a hospital, clinic, doctor's office, patient's home, or elsewhere; home health services of the type covered under HI, but there is no requirement that the patient be previously hospitalized; out-patient hospital diagnostic services, diagnostic x-ray and laboratory tests, and other diagnostic tests performed outside a hospital; x-ray, radium and radioactive isotope therapy; physical therapy; ambulance services; surgical dressings and splints, casts, and other devices for the reduction of fractures and dislocations; the rental of durable medical equipment used at the patient's home, such as iron lungs, oxygen tents, hospital beds, and wheelchairs; prosthetic devices (other than dental) that replace all or part of an internal body organ; and braces and artificial legs, arms, eyes, and so on. Not covered are drugs, private duty nursing, dental services except under special circumstances, skilled nursing home and custodial care, routine physical and eye examinations, chiropractic services (except under limited conditions), elective cosmetic surgery, services performed by a relative, household member, or governmental agency, eyeglasses and hearing aids, and workers' compensation cases.

Payments for outside-the-hospital treatment of mental, psychoneurotic, and personality disorders are limited during any calendar year to $250, or if smaller, 50% of the expenses. Physical therapy benefits are limited to $500. Otherwise there is no maximum limitation on the benefits, but, with one exception, the patient must bear the first $75 ($50 until the 1972 amendments and $60 until 1981 amendments) of expenses incurred in a calendar year plus 20% of the excess. The $75 deductible and 20% cost-sharing percentage do not apply to (1) home health services, (2) expenses incurred for radiological or pathological services furnished a hospital inpatient by a physician, nor (3), since a 1980 amendment, to diagnostic services as an outpatient within 7 days before the patient is admitted as an inpatient. Until the 1981 amendments expenses incurred in the last quarter of a calendar year could be counted toward the $75 (then $60) deductible for that year and the next year.

Financing

Persons electing to participate in the SMI program during fiscal year 1981–1982 pay monthly premiums of $11. Because of variations in medical costs throughout the country, this premium is a bargain for some enrollees, but not for all. If a person fails to enroll during his or her initial enrollment period, the premium is increased by 10% for each full 12-month period between the close of the initial enrollment period and the actual enrollment date.

Premiums are automatically deducted from OASDI, Railroad Retirement, or Civil Service Retirement monthly benefit checks if the aged person is currently receiving such benefits. Other persons pay their premiums directly, subject to a grace period of two months.

The premiums are intended to cover one-half the average cost of insuring a person aged 65 and over. Any increase in the premium, however, cannot exceed the per unit increase in cash benefits since the last SMI premium adjustment. In December of each year the Secretary is required to announce the amount to be charged during the next fiscal year starting on July 1.

The government contributes out of general revenues an amount equal to (1) the premiums paid by insureds plus (2) twice the extra premium persons age 65 and over would have paid, except for the cash benefit increase limitation, plus (3) twice the extra amounts disabled beneficiaries would have paid if they had been charged one-half their true costs. For 1981–1982 the "adequate" actuarial premiums for persons age 65 (twice the beneficiary premium, except for the cash benefits limitation) is $22.60, for disabled persons (their true cost) $36.60.

These premiums and contributions are placed in a separate SMI Trust Fund, out of which all benefits and administrative expenses are paid. This fund, like the HI Trust Fund, has its own Board of Trustees, but this Board has the same membership as the HI Trust Fund and follows the same investment procedures. The Trust Fund assets are supposed to generate some income and guarantee the payment of premiums without sharp changes in premium rates during periods of short-run adverse fluctuations.

In its 1981 report the Board of Trustees estimated how *incurred* expenditures during 1981–1982 would compare with that year's fiscal income under four sets of assumptions—low cost assumptions, two intermediate assumptions, and high cost assumptions.[6] The expenditures estimate includes an allowance for benefits and associated administrative costs that will have been incurred but not paid. Only the results for the two intermediate assumptions are presented in the report. The results, in millions of dollars, are as follows:

	Intermediate A	Intermediate B
Income	16,655	16,657
Expenditures	14,915	14,918
Difference	1,740	1,739

Both intermediate assumptions yield about the same result, a $1.7 billion excess of income over expenditures.

On June 30, 1982, under both intermediate assumptions, the Trust Fund balance (on an incurred basis) was expected to be 9% of projected expenditures for the following year, compared with 0% the preceding year. Under low cost assumptions this percentage was 5%, under high cost assumptions −5%. Even under pessimistic assumptions the income should more than cover the claims *paid*. The program was considered actuarially sound, the 9% balance in the Trust Fund being considered sufficient to cover the impact of a moderate degree of projection error. The premiums are supposed to be adjusted each year to avoid any deficit in the fund.

[6]*1981 Annual Report of the Board of Trustees of the Federal Supplementary Medical Insurance Trust Fund,* 97th Congress, 1st Session, House Document No. 97–68, July 2, 1981.

Administration

This program, like HI, is administered by the Health Care Financing Administration.

In addition to having certification responsibilities under HI and SMI with respect to hospitals, skilled nursing facilities, and home health agencies, state agencies certify under SMI independent laboratories, suppliers of portable x-ray services, and clinics, rehabilitation agencies, and public health agencies providing out-patient physical therapy services.

As is true for HI, fiscal intermediaries determine the amounts to be paid providers of services and make the payments. Payments to hospitals, skilled nursing facilities, and home health services are handled in the same manner as under the HI program, by the same agencies, where such agencies have been nominated. Otherwise the Secretary contracts out this responsibility or makes the payments directly. Payments for other services are made by private fiscal intermediaries selected by the Health Care Financing Administration—usually Blue Shield plans or commercial insurers.

Payments for these other services may be handled under an assignment or itemized bill method. Under the assignment method the patient assigns SMI benefits to the doctor (or other supplier), who sends a claim to the local SMI fiscal intermediary. Under this approach the doctor must accept the SMI payment as the total fee. Less than half the bills are processed in this way. Under the itemized bill method the patient requests payment under the program. This request must be accompanied by either itemized bills, paid or unpaid, or by a statement by the physician, included as part of the request form. The itemized bill method is used if the patient prefers this approach or if the doctor refuses to accept an assignment. A doctor may refuse to accept an assignment because his or her fee exceeds the prevailing charge limit and he or she wishes to bill the patient for the excess.

Payments to hospitals, skilled nursing facilities, and home health agencies are usually determined on a reasonable cost basis, as under HI. Payments for other services are determined on a reasonable *charge* basis unless they are included under one of the experimental methods of reimbursement described later in this chapter. The fiscal intermediaries determine whether individual charges are reasonable, subject to standards established by the Health Care Financing Administration. To be reasonable a physician's charge must not exceed the customary charge made by the physician for similar services or the prevailing charges (those made by most physicians) in the locality for such services. The 1972 amendments set as an upper limit to prevailing charges the 75th percentile of customary charges in past years for similar services in the same locality. They also limited increases in physicians' fees for this purpose by a factor that takes into account increased costs of practice and the increase in earnings levels in an area. Because of lags in gathering data and the fact that the national economic index used to limit the annual increases in the prevailing charges has not increased as rapidly as physicians' fees, the upper limit is at present less than the 75th percentile of current charges. Prior to the 1972 amendments the Social Security Administration, which was then in charge of the program, set the standard, sometimes at higher percentiles and without using a national economic index limit. Prior to 1969 no directives defined prevailing charges and some fiscal intermediaries defined the upper limit as the 90th percentile. Fees, therefore, are more rigidly controlled today than they were in the early years of the program.

The limit on home health agency costs was formerly set by regulation at the 80th percentile of average per visit costs. In 1981 Congress enacted a 75th percentile limit and urged the Secretary, as soon as feasible, to apply this limit separately to each type of service. It also tightened some other cost controls.

OPERATION OF THE MEDICARE PROGRAM

At midyear 1978 almost 27 million persons were enrolled under the HI program, 24 million of whom were aged and 2.8 million disabled. Although SMI is voluntary, the enrollment was almost the same—26 million, of whom 23.5 million were aged.

Table 9.1 shows the number of claims approved for payment and the amounts reimbursed under HI and SMI from the start of these programs in July 1966 through 1980. It also indicates the major categories of charges and bills. The total amount reimbursed under the HI program has increased steadily since the inception of the program. Until 1972 the number of claims remained about the same, but average claim costs increased. Since 1972 the number of claims has also increased. In 1980 aged beneficiaries submitted almost 90% of the bills and collected about 89% of the amount reimbursed. Both the number and amount of SMI bills have increased steadily since this program was established. Under SMI aged persons submitted about 90% of the bills and collected about 84% of the amount reimbursed.

Claims for inpatient hospital services dominate the HI program. In 1980 the average number of covered days of care per claim were 9.8. Hospital charges were $2,893 per claim and $294 per day. HI paid 70% of the total hospital charges on submitted claims.

Physicians' services in 1980 accounted for about 73% of the SMI reimbursements. The average allowed charge was $83, of which 78% was reimbursed.

The progress of the HI and SMI trust funds is shown in Tables 9.2 and 9.3. HI Trust Fund receipts exceeded expenditures, except in 1971, and 1972, and 1977. Hospital costs and, to a lesser extent, utilization rates have exceeded the original actuarial estimates, but higher contribution rates enacted in 1967 were sufficient to keep the fund growing,[7] except in 1971 and 1972, when some impor-

---

[7]The Social Security Amendments of 1967 increased the rates paid by employers and employees by 0.1%. However, they also liberalized eligibility requirements and improved benefits.

tant amendments already discussed tightened utilization and reimbursement procedures. The 1977 deficit was small and not expected to continue. By raising the wage base, but lowering the tax rate, the 1977 amendments left this fund in about the same condition as before.

Receipts under the SMI program have usually exceeded expenditures, but Table 9.3 ignores the liabilities the program has incurred at the end of each year for services already performed but not yet paid. In only 7 of the 14 fiscal years ending June 30, 1980, have the assets exceeded these liabilities. On June 30, 1980, the assets exceeded these liabilities by 38%.[8] The steady increase in expenditures shows why the SMI premium has been increased many times over the original $4 a month. The increasing importance of general revenue transfers is also evident.

THE CONTINUING CONTROVERSY

Despite the bitter debates that preceded the passage of Medicare legislation, few people today favor abolishing the program. Numerous suggestions have been made, however, that would expand the coverage and benefits or tighten the administration.

During the past decade Congress has again considered various proposals that would establish a social medical expense program covering all or most citizens. Discussion of these proposals will be deferred until later in this chapter. Attention is directed here to more limited proposals.

The reader may recall that the 1958 Forand proposal was not limited to aged OASDI beneficiaries. Survivors of deceased workers are still not covered, but the 1972 extension of coverage to disabled persons has greatly reduced the pressures for further expansion of the OASDI beneficiaries covered under this program.

Because aged persons are more frequent purchasers of prescription drugs than are younger persons, there has been considerable support for adding drugs to the list of services covered. No action has been taken on this suggestion, mainly because the cost of such a benefit would add to the system. Avoiding the unnecessary use of drugs and establishing reasonable charges for these drugs might also prove troublesome. Some opponents argue further that although the aged spend more on prescription drugs than do the young, drug expense is a serious problem for less than one-fifth of the aged. Consequently, considering the administrative difficulties and costs, they question whether such a benefit is needed.

The deductible and percentage participation provisions have been criticized on the grounds that they impose a financial burden on the aged, discourage the aged from seeking medical care as soon as they become ill, and complicate the administration of the program. As the deductibles have increased in response to rising medical prices, opponents of cost-sharing provisions have increased in number

[8]See Ref. 6, p. 27.

Table 9.1 HI and SMI Claims Approved and Amount Reimbursed, July 1966 to December 1980

Period Claim Approved or Bill Recorded	HI				SMI		
	Total	Inpatient Hospital Service	Home Health Service	Skilled Nursing Facility Benefit	All Services	Physicians' Services	Outpatient Hospital Service
	Millions of Claims or Bills						
1966[c]	2.0	1.9	a	b	1.0	0.9	a
1967	7.1	5.4	0.3	0.8	24.4	20.2	2.5
1968	7.9	6.0	0.5	1.0	31.4	25.6	3.5
1969	7.7	6.1	0.6	0.9	39.9	33.5	3.6
1970	7.5	6.3	0.6	0.6	39.7	32.8	4.0
1971	7.4	6.4	0.5	0.5	44.9	37.1	4.5
1972	7.7	6.7	0.5	0.4	51.8	42.2	5.7
1973	8.3	7.2	0.6	0.5	43.5	34.3	5.6
1974	9.5	8.2	0.8	0.5	68.0	54.2	8.0
1975	10.3	8.7	1.1	0.5	83.1	64.5	10.5
1976	11.1	9.2	1.3	0.6	87.1	66.6	11.7
1977	11.7	9.6	1.6	0.6	111.7	86.0	14.0
1978	12.3	9.9	1.8	0.5	112.7	85.3	15.4
1979	12.8	10.3	2.0	0.5	142.7	109.6	17.5
1980	13.6	10.9	2.2	0.6	154.4	117.5	19.8

Millions of Dollars Reimbursed

Year			[b]			
1966[c]	824	821	82		63	61	n.a.
1967	3,135	2,864	23	241	1,079	1,000	n.a.
1968	3,947	556	38	348	1,342	1,220	44
1969	4,484	101	49	335	1,783	1,614	68
1970	4,844	568	47	228	1,750	1,573	85
1971	5,370	5,150	42	177	1,956	1,748	105
1972	5,916	5,710	49	156	2,227	1,975	136
1973	6,680	6,431	61	189	1,918	1,655	147
1974	8,408	8,080	94	228	3,190	2,676	304
1975	10,414	10,006	146	262	4,111	3,269	462
1976	12,789	12,287	200	301	4,564	3,497	585
1977	14,707	14,140	254	314	6,191	4,751	767
1978	16,827	16,207	309	311	6,627	4,932	909
1979	19,235	18,537	373	324	8,750	6,569	1,131
1980	22,845	22,042	460	342	10,291	7,562	1,421

Sources: *Social Security Bulletins* until 1973, *Health Care Financing Review* for later data.

[a]Less than 0.05.

[b]Not effective until 1967.

[c]July through December.

Table 9.2 Receipts, Expenditures, and Assets of HI Trust Fund, 1966–1980 (In Millions of Dollars)

Calendar Year	Receipts			Expenditures		Assets at End of Year
	Net Tax Contributions[a]	Reimbursements From General Revenues	Net Interest	Benefit Payments	Administrative Expenses	
1966	1,874	37	31	891	107	944
1968	4,170	1,044	74	4,179	99	2,083
1970	4,944	874	161	5,124	157	3,202
1972	5,792	429	182	6,319	184	2,935
1974	10,976	519	528	9,101	271	9,119
1976	12,872	141	753	13,343	336	10,605
1978	17,533	829	822	17,688	460	11,477
1980	24,088	840	1,138	25,067	476	13,749

Source: Social Security Bulletin, LXIV, No. 5 (May 1981), 45.

[a]Includes transfers from Railroad Retirement Account.

Table 9.3 Receipts, Expenditures, and Assets of SMI Trust Fund, 1966–1980 (In Millions of Dollars)

Calendar Year	Receipts			Expenditures		Assets at End of Year
	Premium Income	Transfers from General Revenues	Net Interest	Benefit Payments	Administrative Expenses	
1966	322	—	2	128	74	122
1968	832	858	21	1,518	183	421
1970	1,096	1,093	12	1,975	238	188
1972	1,382	1,389	37	2,325	290	643
1974	1,804	2,225	95	3,318	410	1,506
1976	2,060	3,810	106	5,080	542	1,799
1978	2,470	6,287	299	7,252	503	4,400
1980	3,011	7,455	408	10,635	610	4,530

Source: Same as Table 9.2, 46.

and intensity. Supporters argue that without these provisions the services would be overutilized and program costs would be much higher. Some believe that the insured should be required to pay a larger share of the cost.

Critics who would liberalize the program also favor extending the days of care in a hospital or skilled nursing facility. Present limits, they argue, do not provide sufficient protection for aged persons with lengthy illnesses.

Elimination of the SMI premium has many supporters. The frequent increases in this premium are especially burdensome on the aged, many of whom have relatively fixed incomes except for OASDHI benefits. One common suggestion is that the HI contribution rate be increased to cover the cost of SMI, which would shift the burden to active employees and their employers.

Some persons who would strongly oppose general revenue financing of OASDI favor funding Medicare from general revenues. For example, the 1975 and 1979 Advisory Councils noted that, unlike OASDI benefits, Medicare benefits are not related to wages. They favored gradually shifting part or all of the HI portion of the OASDHI tax rate to OASDI and supporting HI out of general revenues.

The most criticized aspect of the program has been its administration. Some have from the beginning opposed involving private fiscal intermediaries. They believe that the federal government could administer the program itself more effectively and efficiently. Private insurers dispute this assertion, pointing to the large costs associated with establishing a new government agency and the transfer value of their private health insurance experience. As Tables 9.2 and 9.3 indicate, administrative expenses are about 4% of the benefits paid.

Most of the attention, however, has been directed to inadequate cost controls under the system, particularly in its early years. As noted earlier, hospital charges and physicians' fees have soared since the advent of Medicare, and Medicare has been blamed for much of the increase. Private fiscal intermediaries and the government have been accused of being too generous in their payment levels.

Several Congressional reports have been highly critical of doctors and hospitals for charging excessive fees and rendering unwarranted medical attention. According to these reports, some doctors charge for services that they do not administer, hospitals allow interns and residents to administer treatments while payments go to doctors, unnecessary inoculations have been administered, and some doctors have sent two or more bills for the same services. Moreover, some doctors earn huge incomes from Medicare business.

While admitting that some doctors are guilty of abuse, the American Medical Association and others have asserted that their number is very small. Furthermore, they believe some of the government allegations to be unfair. For example, one doctor accused of obtaining several thousand dollars in fees was the billing agent for many doctors engaged in group practice. Other doctors devote all or most of their practice to the poor and for the first time are receiving adequate compensation for their services.

In response to criticism of this sort the Social Security Administration and its successor, the Health Care Financing Administration, tightened their administration and reimbursement procedures.

The steps taken to control the maximum fees paid physicians have already been noted earlier in this chapter. One unfortunate result of the tighter definition of prevailing fees has been that more of the aged are billed for the excess of the doctor's fee over the Medicare payment. For example, an SMI patient who visits a doctor may expect to pay the first $75 of his or her annual doctor's bills plus 20% of the excess. Unless the doctor accepts an assignment, however, if the doctor's charges exceed the SMI upper limit, the patient's share of the bill will be larger. The effect of the data lag and the national economic index on the SMI upper limit has already been noted. As stated earlier, less than half the SMI charges are assigned.

Utilization review committees have provided some checks on overutilization or misuse of services, but many observers believe that closer surveillance and stiffer penalties for abuses are needed. The PSRO program was established by the 1972 amendments and strengthened by a 1977 amendment as a cost control measure. In 1981, as already noted, Congress directed the Secretary to evaluate the effectiveness of each organization and to terminate ineffective groups. As already noted, 1977 and 1981 amendments also strengthen the government's capability to detect, prosecute, and punish fraudulent activities.

In recent years Congress has also considered cost-containment bills designed to hold down the future costs of health care, but the issue has proved to be complex and highly controversial.

The 1979 Advisory Council on Social Security reviewed primarily the financing of HI, which is related to the financing of OASDI. Time did not allow a careful examination of other aspects of Medicare. Because they believed that future Advisory Councils would also be hard pressed to examine all programs established under the Social Security Act, they recommended that a separate Advisory Council be appointed periodically to review both Medicare and Medicaid, the public assistance program, as well as other elements of any national health plan.

The Advisory Council listed the following areas as being in need of additional study[9]:

1 Problems health care consumers face in meeting increasing out-of-pocket costs, in obtaining available and needed services, and in being assured that the services they receive are of high quality.

2 Overall problems in the health care system affecting the organization and delivery of quality care, and access to that care at affordable prices.

3 The role the Medicare program should play in any large national health insurance plan.

[9]*Reports of the 1979 Advisory Council on Social Security* (Washington, D.C., 1979), p. 208

4   Methods of developing less costly alternatives to in-patient hospital care and of controlling hospital costs.

5   The need for reducing the 24-month waiting period for Medicare for disability beneficiaries.

6   Improved methods of reimbursing physicians and other providers under Medicare and Medicaid.

7   The financing of the programs.

8   Medicare premiums, deductibles, and coinsurance payments.

9   Coverage of outpatient prescription drugs under Medicare.

10 The need for improved coverage of the mentally ill.

11 The provision for some reimbursement of medically necessary long-term nursing home care.

12 The need to provide Medicare coverage for OASDI beneficiaries under age 65, including younger wives and husbands of beneficiaries 65 and older.

National Commission on Social Security

Chapter 4 summarized the major findings of the National Commission on Social Security concerning OASI. Chapter 8 listed some additional recommendations concerning DI. Many of these recommendations also apply to Medicare. Listed below are the Commission's other recommendations relating to Medicare.

COVERAGE

1   HI coverage should be extended in 1982, on a mandatory basis, to all governmental employees (federal, state, and local).

BENEFITS

1   The minimum age for eligibility for Medicare benefits, except in disability cases, should be moved up gradually from 65 to 68, beginning in 2001, in the same manner as OASDI retirement benefits.

2   The waiting period for Medicare benefits coverage for disabled beneficiaries should be reduced from 24 months to 12 months.

3   A catastrophic cap should be placed on a person's annual cost-sharing payments for HI and SMI. It should be $2,000 for 1982, to be indexed in subsequent years by the change in the CPI.

4   Hospital benefits should be determined on a calendar year basis, rather than on a spell of illness basis. No more than one initial deductible should be payable in any one year.

5   The daily cost-sharing percentages for hospital benefits should be changed from 25% of the initial deductible for days 61–90 (and 50% for the lifetime reserve of 60 days) to 10% for days 51–100 and 5% for days 101–150. Lifetime-reserve days should be eliminated.

6 Home health visits should be reimbursed under SMI, except for persons who have only HI, who would be reimbursed under that program.

7 The maximum benefit for outpatient psychiatric services under SMI should be increased from $250 to $375 per year.

8 Benefits should be paid for hospital care outside of the United States, which is not now covered. The maximum amount of the benefit would be at the rate of 50% of the initial deductible per day of hospitalization, less the usual cost-sharing payments.

9 The costs of laboratory services for hospital inpatients should be billed under the HI program, rather than under SMI, even when the services are provided through an outside laboratory.

REIMBURSEMENT AND HEALTH CARE COSTS

1 Experiments with negotiated fee schedules for physicians and prospective reimbursement for hospitals that would encourage efficiency should be continued and extended.

2 Medicare and Medicaid should not be used as instruments to limit the rise in health care costs. However, the programs should encourage further experimentation with groups like Health Maintenance Organizations. Federal and state governments should encourage competition in the delivery of health care services in order to restrain cost increases.

3 Hospitals participating in Medicare should retain the right to nominate intermediaries.

ADMINISTRATION

1 Hearings under the SMI program should be conducted by a federal employee, instead of a representative of the insurance carrier.

The Reagan Administration

The Reagan Administration has considered the following changes: impose the HI payroll tax on federal employees, increase the SMI premium to pay 34 percent of the costs, delay coverage to the first day of the first full month the person is eligible, index the SMI $75 deductible, limit federal reimbursements for some ancillary services not now subject to such limits, pay only 80 percent of the reasonable charges by radiologists and pathologists, and require private insurance coverage for persons working beyond age 65.

House Subcommittee on Social Security

Representative Pickle, chairman of the House Subcommittee on Social Security, has introduced a bill that would fund Hospital Insurance partially through general revenues. The Reagan Administration opposes any use of general revenues.

The Robertson Freedom Plan

The Robertson Freedom Plan, already described in Chapters 5 and 7, would continue the present Medicare program with some revisions for those age 45 and over on July 4, 1984.[10] The major revision would be an increase in the deductibles and cost-sharing amounts for relatively minor illnesses and a reduction for expensive, extended illnesses. For persons under 45 as of July 4, 1984, the program would be different. The benefit types and amounts would remain essentially the same, but eligibility requirements and method of financing would change. All resident citizens age 70 and over would be eligible but residency for at least 25 years during the period from age 35 to age 70 could be required. As indicated in Chapter 8, persons receiving monthly cash disability benefits would also receive Medicare benefits. Like the other Freedom Plan components the benefits would be financed from earmarked general revenues. A welfare plan would care for the truly needy who required care prior to age 70.

NATIONAL MEDICAL EXPENSE INSURANCE PROPOSALS

A few years after the passage of Medicare legislation, strong pressures developed for a national social medical expense insurance program covering most, if not all, citizens. Several factors, some of which have already been noted, accounted for these pressures:

1   Hospital room and board charges, physicians' fees, and the prices for other medical services soared after 1965, partly because of Medicare and improvements in employee-benefit coverage and benefits.

2   The public became aware of and more disturbed by the shortage of medical personnel, particularly in certain geographical areas, by the decline in the number of general practitioners, and by wastes and inefficiencies in the health delivery system resulting from inadequate planning, coordination, and incentives for careful management.

3   More publicity was given to the fact that despite the advanced state of medical research, technology, and equipment in the United States, life expectancy and infant mortality rates have not improved for over a decade. Furthermore, the United States ranks behind such countries as Japan, the United Kingdom, and Sweden on both scores. Critics of these comparisons point out that the United States may simply keep more accurate records and that factors other than the quantity and quality of medical care affect the results.

4   The public had become accustomed to having a portion of medical expenses handled by employee-benefit plans or Medicare. Although private benefits

[10]A. Haeworth Robertson, *The Coming Revolution in Social Security* (McLean, Va: Security Press, 1981), Chapter 28.

have been substantially improved during the past decade, their limitations have also become more apparent. Private plans were also accused of paying inadequate attention to the prevention of illness.[11]

5   Criticisms of Medicare centered not on the existence of a government program dealing with medical care, but on the limitations of the program and the lack of adequate controls over the cost and quality of the services rendered. Whereas in the debates over Medicare many had questioned whether the federal government should operate *any* social medical expense program, after Medicare was established the presence of the federal government was accepted by most parties. The new debate centered on how far and in what ways the federal government's role should be enlarged beyond Medicare.

The debate continues. Because of the rapidly increasing cost of medical care as well as other goods and services, most observers believe that the prospects for a comprehensive national medical expense insurance program are not as bright today as they were during the 1970s. On the other hand, interest in some form of national medical expense insurance continues to be strong. The principal characteristics of the major alternatives are summarized briefly below.

Principal Characteristics

National medical expense insurance proposals vary according to each of the following characteristics:

1   The persons they would cover and whether participation would be compulsory or voluntary. For example, some proposals would cover all citizens on a compulsory basis. Other proposals would make participation voluntary or cover low-income families under a different plan than other families. Some would exclude Medicare families who would continue under that program or include those families under a separate replacement program.

2   The benefits that would be provided. All proposals cover general hospital care and physicians' services, but they differ as to whether they would include dental care, vision care, prescription drugs, and other more specialized services. They have differed greatly on whether there would be an initial deductible, whether the patient would share costs in excess of the deductible, and the maximum benefit. At one extreme there would be no deductibles nor participation percentages and unlimited benefits. At the other extreme the program would cover only part of the "catastrophic" medical expenses in excess of some sizable deductible. If there would be a separate plan for low-income families, it would usually be more generous.

3   Those who would pay for the benefits and the manner in which this is to be

[11]Private health insurance is described and evaluated in Chapter 10.

done. Employers and employees would almost always be required to contribute to the cost through premiums or earmarked taxes. Under many proposals the government would be asked to use general revenues to finance some of the benefits. If there would be a separate plan for low-income families, these families would usually pay little or none of the costs, the benefits being financed by general revenues.

4   Those who would administer the plan. Some proposals would have the plan administered completely by the federal government; private insurers would not participate. Others would use private insurers as risk bearers and general administrators subject to close supervision by either the federal government or the state government. Still others would follow the Medicare example of having basically a government operation with private insurers serving as fiscal intermediaries.

Five Illustrative Plans

In a detailed Social Security Administration analysis of national medical expense insurance proposals four general approaches were identified: (1) tax credits; (2) catastrophic protection; (3) mainly public, not including tax credit or catastrophic protection plans; and (4) mixed public and private, not including tax credit or catastrophic plans.[12] To these should be added more recent proposals for (5) competitive comprehensive medical expense insurance.

Tax Credits

At one time the American Medical Association (AMA) supported a proposal that would provide credits against personal income taxes to offset the premium cost of qualified private health insurance policies. All persons under age 65 would be eligible, but participation would be voluntary. Medicare would continue for those age 65 and over.

The qualified policy would provide basic and major-medical expense benefits. As will be explained in Chapter 10, basic medical expense policies cover the first dollar of expenses incurred, subject perhaps to a $25 or $50 deductible, up to some specified limit. Major-medical expense policies pay part of the expenses in excess of a sizable deductible, the maximum dollar benefit being very large. Under the qualified major-medical expense policy the deductible would be 10% of the family's taxable income.

All families would receive a tax credit equal to the premium for the major-medical benefits. Families with no income tax liability would also be credited with the cost of the basic benefits; since they have no tax to pay, they would receive

[12]U.S. Department of Health, Education, and Welfare, Office of Research and Statistics, *National Health Insurance Proposals: Provisions of Bills Introduced in the 94th Congress as of February 1976* (Washington, D.C.: U.S. Government Printing Office, 1976).

a voucher for the premium cost. As the tax liability increased, the tax credit for the cost of the basic benefits, expressed as a percentage of the basic benefit cost, would decrease. For tax liabilities of $891 or more the tax credit would be 10% of the basic benefits cost.

Employees covered under a qualified employee-benefit plan would be permitted to report a premium equal to their own contribution plus 80% of the employer contribution.

The AMA currently supports a plan that requires employers to offer private health insurance to employees, with employers paying a specified fraction of the cost. The tax credit provisions described above would still apply to the persons not covered under an employee-benefit plan.

Catastrophic Protection

Catastrophic protection only would be provided under a bill proposed by Senator Long. After a person had spent 60 days in a hospital or had spent $3,000 in a single year ($5,000 per family) on nonhospital medical expenses the plan would cover most of the additional costs. These dollar amounts will probably be increased to reflect wage and price increases since the bill was originally introduced. This protection against only financially serious illnesses would be insured by a government insurer similar to Medicare, but employers and the self-employed could instead elect to purchase approved insurance from private insurers. Employers would pay a payroll tax of 1%, which they would be permitted to claim as a tax credit against their federal income tax. A separate medical assistance plan, financed by federal and state general revenues, would provide catastropic protection for individuals earning less than $3,000 a year. Medicare would be amended to provide catastropic protection for the aged.

Mainly Public

The Kennedy–Griffiths bill, introduced in the early 1970s and patterned after one developed by the Committee for National Health Insurance and the AFL-CIO, would cover all U. S. residents against most types of medical expenses. Most services such as care in a hospital or by physicians or home health services would be covered without any deductibles or maximum limitations such as those found in Medicare. Care in a skilled nursing facility would be limited to 120 days; dental care would be limited at first to children under age 25, but eventually the entire population would receive this benefit. Medicare would be abolished. The plan would be financed by (1) employers and employees through earmarked taxes on payrolls, (2) an earmarked tax on income, and (3) general revenues. The Department of Health, Education, and Welfare, now the Department of Health and Human Services, would administer the program through regional and local offices. No private insurers would be involved. Providers of services would not be owned nor employed directly by the government, but they would be subject to numerous service and cost controls.

In early 1979 Senator Kennedy proposed a substantially different approach—the Health Care for All Americans Act. Still the most liberal proposal with respect to benefits, instead of excluding private insurers, this bill would require employers to buy insurance for employees from private insurers. Employees would pay up to 35% of the premiums, the employers the rest. Persons not covered under employee-benefit plans would also be insured by the private sector, the premiums being shared by the insureds and the government in varying proportions, depending on the insured's need for assistance. Employers, employees, and other insured persons, it is assumed, would pay 60% of the cost; the remainder would be covered by general revenues. The plan contains several measures designed to control costs.

Mixed Public and Private

In 1981 the Carter Administration proposed a National Health Plan that would not take effect until 1983. Under Phase I of this plan employers would be required to purchase for their employees private medical expense insurance that would pay all medical expenses over $2,500 a year. Employers would pay 75% of the premiums, employees the remainder. The federal government would pay employer costs above 5% of the total payroll. Medicare and Medicaid would be combined into a new federal program called Healthcare. Healthcare, financed by general revenues and the present Medicare taxes, would provide unlimited coverage for the poor and set limits on the amounts doctors and hospitals could charge them. The aged and disabled Medicare beneficiaries who are not poor would have partial coverage on expenses below $1,250, and full coverage above that level.

Competitive Comprehensive Medical Expense Insurance

Competitive comprehensive medical expense insurance proposals rely on tax incentives to improve the quality and efficiency of employee-benefit plans. The leading bills were introduced by Senators Durenberger and Schweiker and Representative Ulman. Because these proposals do not require nor create incentives for employers to establish such plans and because they do nothing for persons not covered under employee-benefit plans, some observers do not consider these plans to be national medical expense insurance. Proponents argue, however, that this approach, if adopted, would directly benefit a large segment of the population and, through its cost incentives, many others.

Under these bills, for the employer contribution to tax-free income for the employee, the employee-benefit plan must offer two or more options, each of which is offered by a separate insurer. The Schweiker proposal would have required that at least one of the options include a co-payment feature. Representative Ulman would require that one of the options be either a HMO or low cost plan. All options must cover all annual out-of-pocket expenses in excess of some stated amount, such as $3,500. The employer would have to make the same contribution toward each option. If the employee chose a low-cost option for which the premium cost was less than the employer contribution, he or she would receive the difference in cash. This cash payment would be tax free under the Schweiker proposal. Ulman and Durenberger would instead set a tight limit on the tax-free contribution the employer could make to the plan.

Medicare and Medicaid would continue to serve their respective populations.

The Choice

National health insurance proposals are receiving serious Congressional and public attention. According to recent Gallup surveys commissioned by the AMA, about two-thirds of the civilian population favor some form of national health insurance. Reasons for this support are (1) the desire to expand access to medical care for those perceived to be underserved, (2) concern with rising health care costs, and (3) the belief that national health insurance would improve the quality of health care. Those favoring national health insurance, however, disagree on what the general approach should be.

Among the criteria that will be considered and weighted in choosing among the various proposals are the following: the extent of coverage, the preservation of individual choice, the scope of benefits, the percentage of expenses covered, preventive care availability and incentives, protection against overutilization of services, the probable effect on the cost and quality of medical care, and incentives for efficient delivery of health care. Additional factors are the extent to which the present health delivery system would be disrupted, the ability of the present health delivery system to provide the insured benefits, the total cost of these benefits, the distribution of this cost among the government, employers, employees, and non-wage earners, the effect on private health insurance, the use of private insurers as fiscal intermediaries in a program underwritten by the federal government, and the authority and identity of the central administrators.

STATE MEDICAL EXPENSE INSURANCE PLANS

While Congress has been debating the pros and cons of various national medical expense insurance programs, four states have established state medical expense plans. In 1973 Maine became the first state to enact a catastrophic medical expense plan. Rhode Island was second in 1974, followed by Minnesota in 1976. In 1974 Hawaii required all employers to have group medical expense plans for their employees.

Maine

Under its plan Maine helps pay medical costs that are "of such magnitude as to constitute a financial catastrophe" for those persons facing such costs. The plan is scheduled to terminate whenever a federal catastrophic plan becomes effective.

The plan pays the expenses a person incurs during a calendar year in excess of (1) other sources such as health insurance, Medicaid, or liability awards and (2) a substantial deductible. The deductible is the sum of the following three items: (1) 20% of the net income received during the year by the applicant (or those legally responsible for the applicant's care), (2) 10% of the applicant's (or responsible person's) net worth in excess of $20,000 that consists of cash or readily cashable assets, and (3) $1,000. All benefits are vendor payments, not cash reimbursements to applicants.

Rhode Island

The Rhode Island catastrophic health insurance plan, financed from state general revenues, pays the annual medical expenses incurred by a family in excess of a specified out-of-pocket expenditure. For a family with no private health insurance this deductible is $5,000 or, if higher, 50% of the family income (adjusted for family size). For a family with qualified private basic and major-medical expense insurance the deductible is $500 or, if higher, 10% of the family income. Separate deductibles apply to Medicare beneficiaries.

All private insurers must offer a qualified plan to all persons and employers in the state; the premiums are subject to strict regulation; insurers are permitted to form a reinsurance pool to spread the losses under qualified policies; and providers of services must be certified and charge rates in the public interest.

Minnesota

Minnesota's Catastrophic Health Expense Protection (CHEP) program pays 90% of the annual medical expenses in excess of a deductible. The deductible is 20% of the gross family income, up to $15,000, plus 25% of the next $10,000, plus 30% of the income in excess of $25,000. Expenses paid by anyone else—for example, a health insurer or a workers' compensation insurer—do not count toward the deductible. In other words, unlike Rhode Island, Minnesota applies the same plan to families with and without health insurance.

In 1978 benefits totaled $400,000. By 1980 the cost had risen to $3.8 million, causing some persons to advocate eliminating or drastically limiting CHEP. When the program started, the deductible percentages were 40, 50, and 60% and in no case could the deductible be less than $2,500. The 1979 legislature removed the $2,500 minimum and cut the percentages in half. The 1981 legislature favored restoring the program to its original form, but the governor vetoed the bill that would have appropriated monies for the program to operate on this basis. The net effect is that the program technically still exists in its more liberal form but no new applications are being accepted.

The Hawaii Prepaid Health Care Act

Hawaii enacted the first and thus far the only law that requires employers to provide group medical expense insurance for their employees.[13] All employees working 20 hours a week must have this protection and the employer must pay at least half the cost. Coverage for dependents is optional. Employers who can prove economic hardship as a result of this Act are eligible for subsidies from the state. The coverage must meet prevailing standards, equivalent to coverage held by the majority of the subscribers to the Hawaii Medical Service Association, a fee-for-service plan, or to the Kaiser Foundation Health Plan, an HMO. Benefits must include hospitalization, surgery, anaesthesia, physicians' care in and outside a hospital, and diagnostic examinations. Over 98% of the civilian population in Hawaii now have some form of medical expense insurance.

SUMMARY

Interest in social medical expense insurance has been intense for most of this century, but it was not until 1965 that this form of insurance became part of the general U. S. economic security system. Earlier attempts to develop such a program, one that would have covered all citizens, reached a peak in the middle 1940s, but the movement was considerably diminished during most of the 1950s. In 1958 Representative Forand suggested a plan that would cover only aged and survivor OASI beneficiaries. The plan was later limited to aged beneficiaries and debated at length by Congress. In 1960 Congress rejected the Forand bill, but liberalized the medical expense provisions under Old Age Assistance and established Medical Assistance for the Aged, a public assistance program for the medically indigent aged.

Attempts to revive the social insurance proposal during the early 1960s were unsuccessful, but the 1964 presidential election results favored candidates pledged to support hospital insurance for the aged.

In 1965 Congress considered the King–Anderson bill, which sought to establish such a program, plus counterproposals that would instead have improved medical assistance programs for the aged. By summer Congress had established Hospital Insurance and Supplementary Medical Insurance, the combination being more popularly known as Medicare. It also created Medicaid—a liberalized medical assistance program not limited to the aged.

The 1972 amendments extended the Medicare program to include disabled as well as aged beneficiaries.

Hospital Insurance benefits are payable to persons age 65 or over who are

---

[13]John van Steenwyk, Patricia K. Putnam, and Orlando K. Watanabe, "The Hawaii Prepaid Health Care Act: Legislating Health Insurance in the Islands," *Risk Management,* XXVIII, No. 7 (July, 1981), 26–30.

eligible for any type of OASDI or Railroad Retirement System monthly benefit, plus those persons who would qualify except for the earnings test. Special transitional coverage was granted other persons turning 65 before 1968. Also covered are Disability Insurance beneficiaries and disabled qualified railroad retirement annuitants. The benefits include hospital benefits, skilled nursing facility benefits, and home health services benefits. Duration limits (e.g., 90 days of hospital care per spell of illness plus a 60-day lifetime reserve), deductibles, and other cost-sharing provisions affect the amount of benefits provided. Because there are no dollar limits on covered services, the deductible and cost-sharing amounts are adjusted as the costs of these services rise. The benefits are financed through contributions by employers, employees, and self-employed persons computed on the OASDI wage base. The Health Care Financing Administration administers the program, with private insurers serving as fiscal intermediaries. Providers of services under this program are generally reimbursed on the basis of reasonable costs, not charges.

Supplementary Medical Insurance is a voluntary program in which all aged persons can participate, as well as Disability Insurance beneficiaries and disabled railroad retirement annuitants. The principal benefit is payment of 80% of all doctors' bills incurred in a calendar year in excess of $75. All insureds currently pay a monthly premium of $11, which is matched by the federal government out of general revenues. This program, like Hospital Insurance, is administered by the Health Care Financing Administration, with private insurers as fiscal intermediaries. Payments to doctors are determined on a reasonable charge basis.

Among the changes in the Medicare program that have received serious consideration are the following: extension to include other OASDHI beneficiaries, the addition of prescription drug coverage, elimination of all deductibles and other cost-sharing provisions, requiring insureds instead to pay a larger share of the costs, increases in the number of days of hospital and nursing home care, absorption of the Supplementary Medical Insurance premium charge into the Hospital Insurance contribution, funding Medicare from general revenues, a completely public administration, and tighter cost controls.

In 1980 Congress liberalized the program in various ways; in 1981 it moved in the opposite direction. Strong pressures have once again developed for a social medical expense insurance program covering all citizens. Factors accounting for these pressures include the following: soaring medical costs; dissatisfaction with the supply, distribution, and management of medical personnel and facilities; public acceptance of medical expense insurance; limitations of private medical expense insurance; and experience with Medicare.

Despite these strong pressures, opinions differ considerably on details. For example, proposals vary greatly according to (1) whom they would cover and whether participation would be compulsory or voluntary, (2) what benefits would be provided, including the share of the cost to be paid by the patient, (3) who would pay for the benefits and how, and (4) who should administer the plan. This heterogeneity plus rising medical costs have dampened some of the interest in this subject, but it remains a major issue.

Three states—Maine, Rhode Island, and Minnesota—have established state catastrophic medical expense plans. Hawaii requires employers to provide medical expense insurance for their employees.

SUGGESTIONS FOR ADDITIONAL READING

1981 Annual Report of the Board of Trustees of the Federal Hospital Insurance Trust Fund. 97th Congress, 1st Session, House Document No. 97–67, July 2, 1981.
This 1981 report explains the methodology used to make 25-year actuarial projections for the HI Trust Fund.

1981 Annual Report of the Board of Trustees of the Federal Supplementary Medical Insurance Trust Fund, 97th Congress, 1st Session, House Document No. 97–68, July 2, 1981.
This 1981 report explains the methodology used to determine whether the balance in the SMI Trust Fund is sufficient to cover the impact of a moderate degree of projection error.

Ball, Robert M. *Social Security, Today and Tomorrow.* New York: Columbia University Press, 1978.
A comprehensive, clear description and analysis of OASDHI plus recommendations for change by the Commissioner of Social Security under Presidents Kennedy, Johnson, and Nixon.

Blanpain, Jan, with Luc Delisie, and Herman Nys. *National Health Insurance and Health Resources: The European Experience.* Cambridge, Mass.: Harvard University Press, 1978.
An analysis of the development of national health insurance in five countries—West Germany, England and Wales, France, the Netherlands, and Sweden.

Brinker, Paul. *Economic Insecurity and Social Security.* New York: Appleton-Century-Crofts, 1968.
Chapter 10 includes a discussion of group practice plans, compulsory health insurance, and Medicare.

Burns, Eveline M. *Social Security and Public Policy.* New York: McGraw-Hill, 1956.
Chapter 6 provides an excellent discussion of the British National Health Service and other social insurance approaches to the problem of medical care.

Campbell, Rita Ricardo. *Social Security: Promise and Reality.* Stanford, Calif.: Hoover Institution Press, 1977.
An analysis of OASDHI by a member of the 1975 Advisory Council on Social Security.

Chen, Yung-Ping. *Social Security in a Changing Society.* Bryn Mawr, Pa.: McCahan Foundation, 1980.
Chapters 2, 4, and 5 of this highly readable short volume cover the OASDI program. Chapter 3 covers the Medicare program.

Dickerson, O. D. *Health Insurance,* 3rd ed. Homewood, Ill.: Richard D. Irwin, 1968.
Chapter 4 describes the Medicare program. Chapter 10 discusses several issues affecting social medical expense insurance.

Fain, Tyrus G., Katharine C. Plant, and Ross Milloy. *National Health Insurance.* New York: R. R. Bowker, 1977.
An edited volume of contemporary government documents on national health insurance; this includes a summary of the major proposals and estimates of their cost.

Feder, Judith M. *Medicare: The Politics of Federal Hospital Insurance.* Lexington, Mass.: Lexington Books, 1977.
An analysis of the reasons for and possible effects of shifting responsibility for Medicare administration from the Social Security Administration to the Health Care Financing Administration

Feder, Judith, John Holahan, and Theodore Marmor (Eds.). *National Health Insurance: Conflicting Goals and Policy Choices.* Washington, D. C.: The Urban Institute, 1980.
A comprehensive, integrated collection of essays that consider the choices to be made in designing and implementing a national health insurance program.

Friedman, Kenneth M. and Stuart H. Rakoff, (Eds.). *Toward a National Health Policy.* Lexington, Mass.: Lexington Books, 1977.
A collection of papers on the politics of health care delivered at two meetings of the American Political Science Association.

Lindsay, Cotton M. (Ed.). *New Directions in Public Health Care,* 3rd ed. San Francisco, Calif.: Institute for Contemporary Studies, 1980.
A critical evaluation of proposals for comprehensive national health insurance by 12 economists and health care specialists. This volume presents a strong case for increasing economic incentives to make the present system work more effectively.

Myers, Robert J. *Medicare.* Homewood, Ill.: Richard D. Irwin, 1970.
An in-depth treatment of the historical development, coverage, benefits, financing, and administration of Medicare and Medicaid.

Myers, Robert J. *Social Security.* 2nd ed. Homewood, Ill.: Richard D. Irwin, 1981.
Chapters 6 through 10 of this book by the 1947–1970 Chief Actuary of the Social Security Administration discuss Medicare in great detail. Mr. Myers is currently the Administration's Deputy Commissioner for Policy.

Rejda, George E. *Social Insurance and Economic Security.* Englewood Cliffs, N.J.: Prentice-Hall, 1976.
Chapters 10 and 11 of this comprehensive book discuss Medicare and national health insurance proposals.

Social Security in America's Future, Final Report of the National Commission on Social Security. Washington, D.C., March 1971.
The final report of the Commission established to study OASDHI under the 1977 amendments to the Social Security Act.

Social Security and Medicare Explained. Chicago, Ill.: Commerce Clearing House, latest edition.
A detailed, easy-to-read explanation of the most recent Medicare legislation and its administration.

Somers, Herman M., and Anne R. Somers. *Medicare and the Hospitals: Issues and Prospects.* Washington, D.C.: Brookings Institution, 1967.
An excellent discussion of Medicare, how it developed, and how it affects hospitals and doctors.

Chapter Ten

Employee-Benefit Plans and Other Private Approaches to Poor Health

Although OASDHI provides important disability income and medical expense insurance, the typical family remains exposed to many financial losses associated with poor health. Consequently most families also need and have some private health insurance obtained through employee-benefit plans or the purchase of individual contracts. This chapter is concerned with these two layers in the typical three-layer insurance program.

Employee-benefit plans are discussed before individual insurance because they provide coverage for many more persons than does individual health insurance. The principal characteristics of each of these two approaches are investigated, as well as the most significant trends in their development. This chapter concludes with an evaluation of private health insurance in general.

EMPLOYEE-BENEFIT PLANS

An employee-benefit plan has been defined in Chapter 5. Attention is directed here to the plans that meet medical expenses or replace earnings if a person is disabled.

Scope and Growth

Data on the number of wage and salary workers who have protection against poor health for themselves were tabulated in Chapter 5. In 1976, the latest year for which data are available, only 17% had long-term disability income protection. Medical expense insurance coverage was more common. About 70% of the workers had some protection against hospital bills and surgical fees, and one-third had some protection against very large medical expenses through major-medical expense insurance. Many dependents also had medical expense coverage.

Next to life insurance, medical expense insurance was the most common benefit provided by employee-benefit plans. Short-term disability income insurance was about as common as pension benefits.

In 1976 employers and employees contributed about 3.8% of total wages and salaries to medical expense plans and 0.8% to disability income plans. The higher proportion paid to medical expense plans reflects the greater number of persons insured against medical expenses as well as the higher cost of the average coverage afforded. Medical expense costs have risen more rapidly since 1950 because the number of persons covered has expanded at a more rapid rate and the prices of medical services have risen dramatically. Only pension benefits cost more than health insurance benefits.

Development

The historical development of employee-benefit plans has been discussed in Chapter 5. All that need be added here is that health insurance benefits were much less important than death and pension benefits until the 1940s. Now it is the second most common benefit because of an increasing awareness by the public of the need for this form of protection, the more frequent inclusion of these benefits in collective bargaining agreements, and the stronger interest of private insurers in the health field.

Classifications of Health Plans

In Chapter 5 employee-benefit plans were classified according to (1) the type of group insured, (2) whether the plan was established universally or in accordance with some collective bargaining agreement, (3) the persons administering the plan, (4) the proportion of the cost paid by employers, and (5) whether the plan is self-insured by the administrator or insured with an outside agency. Most plans providing benefits in case of poor health cover the employees of a single employer. Over half are covered under some collective bargaining agreement. Most are administered by employers, but some are managed by employee organizations or by joint employer–employee boards of trustees. Employers pay the entire cost in many plans. Finally, well over half the plans were insured. The proportion would have been much higher had it not been for a large number of unfunded paid sick leave plans.

Disability Benefit Plans

Disability benefit plans include sick leave plans, temporary disability insurance, long-term disability insurance, accidental death and dismemberment insurance, and supplementary workers' compensation benefit plans. Group life insurance and pension plans may also provide disability benefits.

Sick Leave Plans

Sick leave plans, which are self-insured by the employer, may be formal or informal. Only the formal plans will be discussed here, but some employers do continue the wages of disabled employees for some temporary period although they have made no formal agreement to do so.

Under formal sick leave plans the benefits may be paid according to a predetermined formula or they may be awarded on a discretionary basis at the time of need. These plans usually continue the worker's earnings in full, beginning with the first day of absence from work, for a specified number of days, usually between 5 and 15 a year. The maximum number of days of sick leave may be related to the length of the employee's service for the employer. Sometimes unused leave can be accumulated from year to year.

Public employers are much more likely than private employers to have formal sick leave plans. Furthermore, private employers with plans tend to restrict them to administrators, executives, and other salaried workers; production workers are often excluded. Private employers commonly use sick leave plans to supplement group temporary disability benefits, for example, by payments during the first week. Public employers almost always provide sick leave in lieu of any other disability income protection.

Group Temporary Disability Income Insurance

Some General Characteristics of Health Insurance

Group temporary disability income insurance, like group life insurance, is characterized by group selection and mass merchandising techniques. Several additional observations are peculiar to group health insurance, of which group temporary disability insurance is one form. First, the fact that an individual's protection cannot be canceled unless the group contract is canceled is especially valuable in health insurance. Second, because age is a much less important factor in health insurance than in life insurance, group health insurance is written on groups that would not be eligible for group life insurance. Third, group insurance is an even more important part of health insurance than life insurance. Health insurance did not become popular until the late 1940s, by which time the group concept had become generally accepted. Furthermore, group health insurance, especially group medical expense insurance, is much less likely than group life insurance and pension plans to require supplementation with individual insurance.

Like group life insurance contracts, most group medical expense insurance contracts permit a terminating group member to convert the group coverage to an individual contract without a medical exam. Some states require that the group coverage itself be extended for a specified period. Under some plans retired employees continue to be covered.

Under present interpretations of the Age Discrimination in Employment Act long-term disability benefits can be reduced on account of age if cost-justified in the same manner as group life insurance benefits. For workers covered under Medicare medical expense plans can "carve out" Medicare benefits. Alternatively, employers can supplement Medicare with a plan that would cost no less than a carve-out plan and be no less favorable overall.

Premiums depend on the percentage of females in the group and, in the case of the disability income and dismemberment coverages, on the industry. The age and income composition of the group are important in group major medical expense insurance. Premiums are adjusted partly according to the experience of the particular group and partly according to the total group experience of the insurer. In addition to the rate for employees, there may be a separate medical expense insurance rate for dependents, or one rate for one dependent and another for two or more dependents, or one rate for a spouse only, another for children only, and a third for spouse and children.

For a variety of reasons insurers have developed special rating methods applicable to group disability and medical expense plans that convert the insured plan into quasi-self-insurance. For example, under a minimum premium plan the insurer becomes liable for annual claims only after the claims total more than, say, 90% of the premium normally charged for that year. The premium charged is 10% of the normal premium, which the insurer uses to pay expenses, absorb losses in excess of the 90% threshold, and earn a profit. The advantage to the insured is that the state premium tax levied on premiums is less, the employer retains the use of substantial monies, which can be invested until needed to pay claims, and the employer is motivated to become deeply involved in claim administration. A second example is an Administrative Service Only (ASO) agreement under which the insurer in effect is merely a servicing agent for a retention program.

Temporary Disability Insurance Benefits

Group temporary disability income insurance contracts provide an income for the person who is temporarily unable to perform the duties of his or her own occupation. The insurer promises to pay a specified weekly income for a maximum period of 13 or 26 weeks, or sometimes 52 or 104 weeks. Payments usually begin with the first day of disability due to an accidental injury and with the fourth or eighth day of disability due to sickness. The weekly income is usually some fraction of the employee's weekly wage (between one-half and two-thirds) up to a maximum dollar allowance. If the plan covers occupational illnesses, workers' compensation payments are deducted from the group insurance benefits.

Group Long-Term Disability Income Insurance

Although a few insurers offered group long-term disability insurance prior to 1960, this coverage did not attract much attention nor interest until the 1960s. Long-term disability (LTD) plans typically pay a totally and permanently disabled employee an income to some advanced age, such as 65, after the completion of a waiting period. The employee is considered disabled during the first two years if he or she cannot perform the duties of *his or her* occupation. For payments to be continued beyond the initial two years the employee must be unable to engage in *any* occupation for which he or she is reasonably fitted by education, training, or experience. The income is almost always a percentage of the worker's most recent wage, subject to some maximum monthly amount. The most common waiting period is six months, which restricts payments to seriously disabled workers and avoids overlaps with sick leave or temporary disability insurance payments. A shorter waiting period such as 60 to 90 days is common when there is no temporary disability insurance.

LTD benefits are usually reduced by OASDI benefits, workers' compensation payments, or other public programs. Because OASDI has a different definition of long-term disability, workers may receive LTD benefits even if they do not qualify for Disability Insurance payments and vice versa. The standards may also differ for other public programs. In most cases, however, the programs would overlap and LTD benefits would be reduced. Lower-pay workers and workers with dependents may indeed receive little or no benefits. To solve this overlap problem a number of plans have tried other approaches to integrating LTD benefits with these public programs, but the full-offset approach remains the most common. The leading alternative does not offset any OASDI benefit unless the combined LTD and OASDI benefits exceed a high proportion of the worker's wage, such as two-thirds or 70%. Another approach is to reduce the worker's contribution on the portion of his or her salary up to the OASDI wage base.

A few LTD plans provide for periodic adjustments in the income being received by a disabled worker when prices rise. For example, the adjustment may be keyed to the Consumer Price Index, subject to a maximum annual adjustment of 3%. A more common approach is to freeze the OASDI offset at the initial level. This freeze does not change the private plan payment, but it does permit the worker to share any OASDI increases. Otherwise the increase in the OASDI benefits merely decreases the private plan payments.

Initially group long-term disability insurance was limited to the firm's higher-pay employees. This insurance has since been extended to lower-income workers, but this extension was slowed by the liberalization of OASDI disability income benefits. The case for extending LTD insurance to these workers was strengthened by the Social Security Disability Amendments of 1980.

Group Accidental Death and Dismemberment Insurance

Group accidental death and dismemberment insurance provides a lump-sum payment if the worker dies or loses a member (eye, hand, or foot) as a result of accidental means within 90 days after the accident. Because this insurance covers such a narrowly defined event, it is inexpensive and much less important than the sick leave benefits and disability income insurance discussed earlier.

Supplementary Workers' Compensation Insurance

Because maximum workers' compensation benefits in many states did not keep pace with wage levels or nonoccupational disability income benefits, some employers have established supplementary workers' compensation benefits.[1] These plans vary widely in philosophy and practice. The most common single practice is to pay the employee his or her full compensation, from which workers' compensation is deducted, for a limited period of time.

Most employers self-insure these supplemental benefits, but sometimes a sick leave plan or disability insurance program provides the extra payments. If a disability insurance program is used, the maximum benefit is that provided for nonoccupational disabilities.

Although recent data on the number of such supplementary plans are not available, one would expect the recent significant increases in workers' compensation benefits to have lessened their importance.

Group Life Insurance

Group life insurance contracts commonly guarantee that life insurance will be continued in force without charge for 12 months if a person under age 65 terminates membership because of total disability and remains totally disabled. Most new contracts, however, provide for the waiver of premiums for life in case of total and permanent disability. A few provide for the payment of the face amount in case of death or total or permanent disability.

Pension Plans

Pension plans may provide some assistance for a disabled person through their early retirement provisions. Under some plans only totally disabled persons can retire early; under others the amount of the early retirement pension is greater for a totally disabled person. Some plans include total and permanent disability income insurance as a separate feature. Usually they provide a specified income beginning within a few months after the occurrence of the disability and continuing to the date of normal retirement. Some provide waiver-of-premium benefits that enable the employee to retire at the normal retirement age with the same income that he or she would have received had he or she continued to participate in the plan at the same salary up to that time.

Medical Expense Plans Underwritten by Commercial Insurers

For discussion purposes employee-benefit plans providing medical expense benefits can be categorized according to whether they are (1) "commercial" insurance plans, (2) Blue Cross plans, (3) Blue Shield plans, and (4) other plans (called independent plans because they are not in one of the first three categories).

[1]Harland Fox, "Company Supplements to Workmen's Compensation," Chapter 12 in E. F. Cheit and M. S. Gordon (Eds.), *Occupational Disability and Public Policy* (New York: Wiley, 1962).

Commercial insurance plans are underwritten by "commercial" insurers, usually stock insurers (owned by stockholders) or mutual insurers (owned by policyholders). The "commercial" label is not a satisfactory way to distinguish these insurers from the insurers of the other plans. For example, if "commercial" implies a profit-making objective, mutual insurers should not be considered commercial. Moreover, some of the underwriters of the "other" plans are profit-making ventures. However, this terminology is in common use and no better term has been suggested. The most satisfactory alternative is to call commercial insurance plans simply "insurance plans," but this approach implies that the other underwriters' plans are not insurance plans. Legally and technically there are some important differences between commercial insurers and the other underwriters; but, according to the definition of insurance adopted in this book, all four categories provide insurance protection from the viewpoint of the worker and his or her dependents.

Commercial insurance plans can be subdivided into three classes, depending on the nature of the benefits, (1) basic benefit plans, (2) major-medical benefit plans and comprehensive benefit plans, and (3) Health Maintenance Organizations.

Basic Benefit Plans

Basic benefit plans provide "first dollar" coverage of specified types of medical expenses; that is, they cover the first dollar of costs incurred. To reduce premiums, however, insurers have increasingly included small deductibles in those contracts that exclude, say, the first $25 or $50 of expenses. Commonly covered expenses are those arising from hospital care, surgery, nonsurgical physicians' care in a hospital, doctor's office, or patient's home, and out-of-hospital x-ray and laboratory examinations. An increasing number of plans cover posthospitalization care in skilled nursing homes, home health services, prescription drugs, dental care, and vision care. The insurer typically makes a separate promise with respect to each type of covered service.

Typical group hospitalization insurance contracts promise to pay daily room and board charges up to some stated amount for a period up to some specified number of days, such as 70 or 120. The stated amount is usually less than the prevailing semiprivate room charges in the locality. There is a strong trend, however, toward paying the cost of a semiprivate room, regardless of the actual charges. Some policies pay a specified amount per day, regardless of the actual charge.

Reimbursement for other hospital expenses incurred within the covered period is limited to some multiple, such as 10 or 30, of the daily room and board allowance. Some plans, however, place no dollar amounts on these expenses. There is a trend toward sharing with the insured the loss above, say, 20 times the daily allowance.

According to a 1979 Health Insurance Institute survey of *new* group cases, 79% of the employees were covered for the full cost of semiprivate or ward accommodations.[2] About 11% were protected against hospital confinements up to 70 days, another 29% up to 100 days, 32% up to 180 days, and 28% for 180 days or more.

Not covered under a typical plan are treatment in a government hospital, unless charges are made for reasons other than the presence of insurance, workers' compensation injuries or diseases, self-inflicted injuries, or injuries caused by war. Alcoholism, drug addiction, and mental disorders are sometimes excluded, but some limited coverage is usually provided. Some states require such coverage.

Group surgical insurance contracts usually promise to pay the cost of specified surgical operations up to the limit specified in a schedule. Under new group plans issued in 1979 more than half the employees were eligible for a maximum surgical benefit of $1,000 or more. About 26% were eligible for payments on a "usual and customary" basis, a concept described in Chapter 9 and later in this chapter in the section on Blue Shield plans.

Group medical expense insurance covers doctors' nonsurgical care. This care may be covered no matter where it is provided or only in-hospital care may be covered.

Group dental insurance generally covers most types of diagnostic, preventive, and restorative dental care. The insurer typically agrees to pay 50 to 80% of the expenses in excess of some small deductible up to some maximum limit. Often the benefits for preventive care are more generous than those for restorative care. For example, the insurer may pay a larger percentage of charges for preventive care.

Dependents, including the employee's spouse and children up to some age, such as 19, or if attending school, 22, may be insured under each of these plans. These dependents usually receive the same benefits as the employee does.

Most plans include a coordination-of-benefits provision under which (1) individuals covered under two or more group contracts (say, a working spouse) are prevented from receiving combined benefits in excess of the expenses covered at least in part under any of the contracts involved and (2) rules are established for determining the order in which the insurers will pay benefits. According to these rules, the plan covering the person as an employee pays before the plan covering the same person as a dependent. A plan covering the dependents of a male pays before the plan covering the dependents of a female. If these two rules do not establish the order in which the plans should pay, the plan covering the individual for the longer period of time pays first.

Basic medical expense insurance enables the insured to budget systematically the medical expenses associated with the less costly illnesses. It does not provide adequate protection against the sizable medical expenses associated with long-term serious illnesses.

[2]*New Group Health Insurance* (Washington, D.C.: Health Insurance Institute, 1980).

Major-Medical Benefit Plans

Major-medical benefit plans typically supplement a basic benefit plan that includes at least hospital and surgical expense coverages. The basic plan may be underwritten by the same insurer or some other underwriter. This supplementation increases the worker's protection against more costly illnesses. The typical major-medical plan covers most types of medical expenses other than routine physical examination, eye examinations, and cosmetic surgery or dental care, except that required because of an accident. It pays 80% of the covered expenses in excess of a stated deductible up to a specified maximum. Requiring the insured to bear the deductible amount and a percentage of costs in excess of the deductible reduces the premium by relieving the insurer of some claims payments and the expenses of paying them and by giving the insured some incentive to hold costs down. Under an increasing number of plans, however, the insurer will pay 80% of the expenses above the deductible, up to some specified amount, plus all of the excess up to the maximum amount.

Under a *corridor deductible* the expenses must exceed basic plan benefits plus a flat amount, commonly $100. Under an *integrated deductible* the expenses must exceed the greater of basic plan benefits or some flat amount such as $500. The deductible usually applies to all expenses incurred by an insured during a calendar year, but sometimes there is a separate deductible for each injury or sickness. Usually the deductible applies separately to each covered person, except when two or more persons are injured in the same accident.

The maximum amount the insurer will pay is some large amount, such as $250,000. Under new group plans issued in 1979 about 30% provided unlimited benefits. Usually the maximum limits the total payments that will be made to the worker (or a dependent) during his or her lifetime. However, if the insured returns to work following an illness or if he or she can produce satisfactory evidence of insurability, the maximum is restored to its original limit.

Some "pure" major-medical expense benefit plans do not supplement basic benefit plans. Instead, they pay a percentage of the expenses in excess of some stated amount, such as $500. This type of major-medical expense insurance was the original concept introduced in the late 1940s. The objective is to limit coverage to "catastrophic" expenses that the insured cannot handle out of income or small savings accounts.

Comprehensive Medical Benefit Plans

Comprehensive medical benefit plans combine basic medical and major-medical expense insurances in one package. These plans can be classified into two major categories. The first is a major-medical expense contract, with a low deductible such as $50 per illness. The second commonly provides first dollar basic hospitalization and surgical expense protection up to some specified amount such as $1,000. The other expenses are subject to a deductible of, say, $100, and the insurer pays, say, 80% of the expenses in excess of the basic coverage and deductible amount. Under many current plans the insurer pays all of the expenses in excess of a specified amount. About one-third of the persons with commercial group major-medical expense insurance obtain this protection through these comprehensive plans.

Health Maintenance Organization Option

The newest development in commercial insurance plans is a concept developed by and still dominated by the independent plans to be described later. Under this approach the commercial insurer makes available a Health Maintenance Organization (HMO) option under its group plan. A HMO provides comprehensive health care in return for a prenegotiated lump-sum or periodic payment for this care. Most HMOs are closed panel or prepaid group practice plans whose salaried physicians and other professionals provide the prescribed services. Some HMOs are associations of professionals with individual practices. The insurer may assume various roles in the development and operation of affiliated HMOs. For example, the insurer may provide financial support by acquiring an ownership interest, lending money, or agreeing to share in operating losses. It may also provide marketing services. Through its regular insurance offerings it may provide out-of-area emergency coverage or other protection not provided by the HMO.

Although the concept originated in 1929, in 1970 there were still only 25 HMOs in the United States. Organized medicine opposed or discouraged group practice plans and many states passed laws that made it impossible or extremely difficult to develop such plans. This opposition declined in the 1950s and 1960s, but most people were still unfamiliar with the concept and reluctant to abandon the fee-for-service solo physician approach, with which they were more familiar.. Rapidly rising medical costs in the late 1960s caused many government officials to favor HMOs as a form of cost control. HMOs were encouraged under most national medical expense insurance proposals. By late 1979 over 200 such plans existed, of which many were affiliated with commercial insurers. The Health Maintenance Organization Act of 1973 has stimulated HMO growth in two ways. First, the act authorized grants and loans to develop new public and nonprofit HMOs and expand old ones that meet certain requirements. For example, to be certified the plan must provide certain basic health services. If it has provided comprehensive health services for at least five years or has an enrollment of at least 50,000, it must have annual open enrollment periods unless it developed a deficit in its most recent fiscal year. Also, 48 months after qualification it must charge all individuals or families the same fees under a "community rating" system. Certified profit HMOs are eligible only for loan guarantees. Second, the federal law supersedes state laws that may impede the development of certified HMOs. Third, if there is a certified HMO in the area that has not closed its enrollment, employers of 25 or more persons must offer their employees the option of joining a HMO.

Advantages alleged for HMOs include the following: (1) by joining a HMO, the subscriber obtains one-stop health care. He or she is assigned to a primary-care physician, such as a general practitioner or pediatrician, who refers the subscriber to specialists when necessary. Usually the HMO houses a team of doctors, nurses, laboratory technicians, and administrative staff in a single building. Treatment rooms for minor surgery may be provided or, in many cases, complete hospital facilities. HMOs that do not own nor contract hospital services usually arrange traditional hospital insurance for their subscribers. Out-of-area benefits are also provided in this fashion. (2) Because HMOs provide service benefits instead of cash benefits, their subscribers are protected against any increase in the cost of these services during the coverage period. (3) HMOs are efficient, cost-conscious operations. Because these organizations provide services for a fixed fee, they have an incentive not to render unnecessary services. The salaried physicians employed by the plan share this incentive, and these physicians, nurses, and other staff are subject to some control by HMO management. The comprehensiveness of the services rendered at a single location enables the plan to utilize its facilities, equipment, and staff in a most efficient manner. Finally, probably because HMO plans provide out-patient and preventive care, HMO subscribers have, according to many studies, lower hospital utilization rates and in-patient surgical procedure rates than members of other plans.

Critics argue the following: (1) HMOs may have an incentive to provide too few services; (2) subscribers must use the plan's doctors and facilities, which in some cases are quite limited in number or of low quality; (3) the medical care may be too impersonal; (4) some subscribers overutilize the plan services at the expense of others; and (5) many plans provide no out-of-area coverage. Supporters downplay the importance of these arguments.

Trends in Commercial Insurance

Group disability income insurance was first written in 1870, but this form of insurance did not make much progress until the late 1920s because both insurers and employers were directing most of their efforts toward the problems caused by premature death and old age. Meanwhile, some group life and group pension plans included total and permanent disability income protection.

The 1930s witnessed a disastrous experience with lifetime indemnity coverages, written at that time only as individual not group insurance because of a combination of inadequate premiums, inadequate reserves, inadequate underwriting, and many improper claims. Almost all insurers withdrew from this field or seriously restricted their coverage. On the other hand, medical expense insurance began to grow because the Depression emphasized the need for this form of protection and a new competitor, the Blue Cross movement, was born. Group hospitalization policies were issued for the first time in 1934, and group surgical policies in 1938.

As economic conditions improved during the 1940s, commercial life insurers cautiously reentered the individual lifetime indemnity field, and health insurers began to liberalize their coverage. These liberalizations were made on a much sounder basis than during the 1920s. Interest in medical expense coverage continued to grow rapidly, and group policies covering charges for physicians' care appeared in 1943. The most significant development was the first writing of a major-medical expense policy in 1949. This policy was written on a group basis at the request of a society of employees of the General Electric Company, which was seeking this form of protection for its members.

Comprehensive insurance was a product of the 1950s, which also witnessed the first writing of medical expense insurance for small groups of five or more persons. By the end of the decade commercial insurers had written their first group dental insurance contracts and were preparing to develop group long-term disability insurance on large scale for the 1960s.

During the late 1950s and the 1960s insurers improved their medical expense plans for the aged. In the group field they allowed retiring employees to continue the same or, more commonly, reduced protection after they left the group. After Medicare was established in 1965, insurers turned their attention to plans supplementing this program.

The most significant recent developments are the expansion of dental insurance, the liberalization of medical expense policies to cover skilled nursing home care, mental illness, and larger expenses, and the movement into HMOs.

Blue Cross Plans

Commercial insurance plans cover about half the workers with medical expense protection under employee-benefit plans. Medical expense plans underwritten by Blue Cross associations provide hospital expense insurance for most of the remainder. A Blue Cross association is a voluntary nonprofit hospital expense prepayment plan that has applied for and received the approval of the American Hospital Association. There are about 70 locally autonomous Blue Cross associations in the United States. Almost all the associations cover a state or part of a state. A few cover more than one state. The plans do not compete with each other, the plan areas being mutually exclusive. The promoters of most associations were hospitals in the plan area. Member hospitals usually elect the board of directors, whose members represent the hospitals, the medical profession, and the public. Frequently the member hospitals explicitly guarantee the plan benefits.

Blue Cross associations issue a separate contract to each subscriber. Commercial insurers contract with the employer or some other group head and give employees a certificate describing the major provisions of the contract affecting them.

Each association contracts with both its subscribers and its member hospitals. All associations do not use the same contracts, and most of them offer more than one form of contract to their subscribers.

Subscriber Contracts

A "typical" Blue Cross contract with a subscriber promises to provide certain hospital *services* in a member hospital for a stated period of time, regardless of the cost of the services. If a subscriber wants better accommodations than those provided under a Blue Cross plan, he or she receives a cash allowance based on the covered accommodations to help cover the expenses. In either case the subscriber receives no cash directly; the hospital bill is reduced.

For example, the most widely held type of contract provides the subscribers with room and board, general nursing service, use of the operating room, and a broad list of other hospital services in ward or semiprivate accommodations of *member* hospitals for some specified number of days, such as 70 or 180, in each period of separate and unrelated disability. The most liberal plans have a 365-day duration limit. Thus, if the subscriber is hospitalized for the specified number of days or less, he or she may have no hospital bill to pay except for those services not listed among the covered hospital extras. If the subscriber wants private accommodations, some specified amount, such as the hospital's usual charge for semiprivate accommodations, is allowed on the charges for room and general nursing services. All other benefits are generally provided on a full-service basis.

Until recently a major difference between Blue Cross and commercial insurers was that Blue Cross covered the entire cost of covered medical services, whereas commercial insurers paid specified dollar amounts that often were less than the actual charges. As already noted, however, commercial insurers now cover under many new contracts the actual charges, regardless of their amount.

Special benefits are provided for Blue Cross subscribers who may be hospitalized in a nonmember hospital or in an institution that belongs to a different Blue Cross plan. Not many Blue Cross subscribers are hospitalized in nonmember hospitals, because less than 10% of the nation's hospital beds fall in that category. Benefits in these nonmember hospitals are limited to some specified dollar amount per day, and the money is often paid to the insured after he or she has paid the hospital bill.

If a subscriber is hospitalized in a member institution in a different area, an Inter-Plan Service Benefit Bank Agreement makes it possible for the home plan to provide the service benefits of the plan in the area in which the subscriber may be hospitalized for the number of days to which he or she is entitled under the home plan. When a person moves from one area to another, an Inter-Plan Transfer Agreement enables the subscriber to maintain continuous coverage.

Many plans cover care in a nursing home following hospitalization. They also cover outpatient x-ray and laboratory examinations and x-ray or radiation therapy. Otherwise outpatient care is usually limited to accident victims.

The most common and important variation from this typical contract covers room and board costs up to a specified daily allowance. Other common variations are dollar limitations on some of the hospital extras, small deductibles, and partial benefits for an additional specified period.

Common exclusions are workers' compensation cases, cases for which hospitalization is provided by law, and hospitalization primarily for diagnostic studies and rest cures. Although some plans provide full benefits for services rendered in a general hospital, only limited benefits are usually provided for nervous and mental diseases, alcoholism, and drug addiction. As noted earlier, some states require such coverage. Preexisting conditions are sometimes excluded entirely or during a waiting period of 6 to 24 months.

Dependents may be covered under the contract, the coverage for children usually commencing at birth and continuing to age 19 or, if the child is attending school, to age 22.

The contracts between the associations and the member hospitals are primarily concerned with the method of determining the payment for services rendered to subscribers. Although the payment may be (1) a straight per diem (based on average charges) for each day of care or (2) all or part of the actual hospital bill, the usual procedure is to base the payment on cost statements prepared by the hospital. Some plans have used average cost statements in order to encourage efficient hospital administration. Costs are interpreted liberally to include obsolescence and depreciation, interest, and contingency allowances, but the Blue Cross association usually pays less than the charges to nonmembers. This differential has been justified on the ground that (1) billing costs are low, (2) there is no collection problem with Blue Cross subscribers, and (3) hospitals are encouraged to control costs. Because the payments to the hospitals under these contracts will no doubt be influenced by the financial condition of the association, the member hospitals are in fact, if not in name, the ultimate insurers. Under some plans the hospitals specifically guarantee the benefits.

A coordination-of-benefits provision, described earlier in this chapter, is a common feature of Blue Cross plans.

Employees terminating their employment can convert their group protection to individual coverage. The individual coverage, however, tends to be more limited, more costly, or both.

The premium structure for Blue Cross plans includes one rate for subscribers and either one rate for dependents, regardless of the number, or two dependent rates—one for a spouse only and the other for a spouse and children. Although Blue Cross associations philosophically favor community rating—the same rates for all groups—competition with commercial insurers has forced most associations to consider the actual experience of groups in excess of a certain size.

Blue Cross associations, often joined by the local Blue Shield association, also underwrite supplementary major-medical and comprehensive extended benefit plans. These plans may extend the basic contract to cover more days of hospitalization or pay 80% of the hospital charges, physicians' fees, and other expenses incurred in excess of some corridor deductible. Once the expenses exceed a specified amount, Blue Cross' share may rise from 80 to 100%.

To a greater degree than commercial insurers, but much less than independent plans, the Blue Cross associations, sometimes in cooperation with a Blue Shield association, have made available a HMO option under their group plans.

Trends in Blue Cross Contracts

Hospital expense prepayment plans have been traced back to 1880 in Minnesota and Oregon, but the modern movement is considered to have started with the Baylor University Hospital Plan in 1929. A group of teachers in the Dallas city schools who were impressed by the need for protection against hospital expenses approached the hospital administrators with the original idea. As a result of their talks, all Dallas teachers who belonged to a Sick Benefit Fund were promised 21 days of hospitalization in a semiprivate room for a premium of 50 cents a month. Other groups joined the plans as its popularity grew.

Hospital administrators throughout the country studied the plan and many of them adapted the underlying principles to their own situation. They discovered that through such plans they could provide a valuable form of protection and cut down the amount of free service they were providing. The Depression and increasing hospital services had intensified their financial problems.

The fear of excessive competition among two or more plans in a given area and the disadvantages of limiting coverage to one hospital suggested the joint participation of several hospitals in a single plan. The first joint plan was established in 1932 in Sacramento, California, and was followed in 1933 by plans in six other cities.

In 1933 the American Hospital Association (AHA) approved the principle of prepaid hospital expense and appointed a special committee to study the growing movement. The committee reported a few months later on the essentials of an acceptable plan. In 1936 the AHA established a Commission on Hospital Service as a clearing house and center for information and advice. In 1937 the Commission began to approve plans meeting their standards, and Blue Cross was born.

Contracts have been improved with the passage of time. As in the case of commercial insurers, increased competition, experience, and consumer interest are responsible for these improvements. The number of days of coverage has been increased to as many as 365 or more, the list of hospital extras has been lengthened, out-patient diagnostic service has become more common, and many plans provide nursing home coverage. Blue Cross plans now write the comprehensive version of major-medical expense insurance and commonly tailor their contracts to their client's needs and desires. The independent plans have learned to work together, and today the Blue Cross subscriber can receive service benefits in a different plan area. The community-rating concept has been replaced by experience rating.

Blue Shield Plans

A Blue Shield association plan is a voluntary nonprofit surgical and nonsurgical physician's care plan that has sought and qualified for membership in the National Association of Blue Shield Plans. The approximately 70 locally autonomous Blue Shield associations were originally organized by local medical societies, but the boards of directors commonly include some nondoctors. The daily operations of the plan are usually handled by the staff of the local Blue Cross plan.[3]

All Blue Shield contracts provide surgical benefits, most cover charges for in-hospital nonsurgical physicians' care, and some include benefits applying as well to home and office calls by a doctor. Under their "full-service" contract the association pays all doctors their "usual, customary, and reasonable" charges. As long as the doctor charges the patient the same amount as he or she charges others for the same service and as long as the doctor's charge is not unreasonably high relative to the charges made by other doctors in the area for the same service, the plan will pay the entire charge. Participating physicians agree to accept the Blue Shield benefit as full payment for their services. Nonparticipating physicians who charge more than the Blue Shield payment may collect the full amount of their bill from the patient, who will in turn collect the Blue Shield benefit directly from the association.

If the subscriber is attended by a nonparticipating doctor, the allowances may be the same or somewhat less. If the subscriber is treated by a participating physician in a different area, the full benefits are payable, and although no formal promise is made, the participating physician usually accepts the benefits as full payment for patients who would be entitled to service benefits at home.

Usually dependents may be covered under the contract, although the benefits may be less liberal. Coverage for children usually extends from birth to age 19, 22 if the child is attending school.

The exclusions and limitations in Blue Shield contracts are similar to those in Blue Cross contracts.

The associations pay the participating physicians the allowances in the contracts, but the physicians would no doubt accept some modification of these payments if the Blue Shield association encountered financial difficulties. Most of the plans are in fact specifically underwritten by the participating physicians.

Like Blue Cross associations, Blue Shield plans grant terminating employees conversion rights.

The Blue Shield rate structure closely resembles that of Blue Cross associations.

Blue Shield associations, like Blue Cross associations and often in conjunction with them, also write extended benefit or supplementary major-medical insurance. They have also cooperated with Blue Cross associations in HMO projects.

Trends in Blue Shield Contracts

Medical society-sponsored prepayment plans covering surgical fees and charges for physicians' care date back to 1929 in Washington and Oregon. They were an outgrowth of earlier prepayment plans controlled by lay persons that started in the 1880s when employers entered into contracts for the provision of service to

---

[3]Some Blue Shield plans include hospital benefits, and some Blue Cross plans include surgical and physicians' care benefits. In a few such instances Blue Cross plans compete with Blue Shield plans. In Minnesota a few years ago the Blue Shield association was merged into the Blue Cross association.

workers injured on the job. Because physicians found that the lay associations were forcing the doctors to compete for their subscribers on a price basis, county medical societies organized their own medical service bureaus.

The movement did not grow rapidly until 1939 when the California Physicians Service was established on a statewide basis by the California Medical Association. The governor of California had proposed a social medical expense insurance bill and the doctors resolved to prove that a voluntary plan would work. Soon plans were being formed in other areas.

Blue Cross plans encouraged the movement, for their subscribers were requesting coverage against doctors' bills, and commercial insurers were providing this protection. In 1942 the AMA approved the principle of prepayment plans sponsored by medical societies. During the next three years the Council on Medical Service and Public Relations coordinated the existing plans and gave guidance to local medical societies that were interested in establishing new plans. Some plans began to display the Blue Shield symbol. In 1946 a definite set of standards was made public and the formal approval program, which is now controlled by the National Association of Blue Shield Plans, was started.

The coverages have gradually been liberalized. Physicians' care in a hospital, doctor's office, or at home is being provided in more contracts; there are fewer exclusions; and the full-service contract has become the usual approach. Blue Shield plans now issue extended benefit or supplementary major-medical expense insurance.

Independent Medical Expense Plans

Independent medical expense plans include a wide variety of insurers not classified as commercial insurers, Blue Cross associations, or Blue Shield associations. Most of the persons covered under independent plans belong to industrial plans that serve defined groups of employees or union members. The most popular of these industrial plans are welfare funds covering members of a single union and jointly managed by employers and employee representatives. An example of such a plan is the program of the United Mine Workers of America Welfare and Retirement Fund, which almost completely covers the services provided miners and their dependents by approved hospitals and physicians.

Industrial plans covering the employees of a single employer are more properly regarded by the employer as retention instead of insurance, the employer's motive usually being a desire to avoid the expense loading of the insurer and to administer his or her own claims. In addition, many employers provide limited plant facilities, which usually consist of the services of an industrial nurse or first-aid attendant and a full-time or part-time physician. The purpose of these facilities is generally to administer preliminary and other physical examinations, render emergency treatment, and, less commonly, consult with the employees with respect to temporary minor illnesses. As a rule, the services and facilities increase with the size of the firm.

The leading nonindustrial independent plans include plans sponsored by a community or private group clinic. Community plans, which are open to most individuals or groups in the community, including employee groups, are usually sponsored by a local consumer organization and operated on a nonprofit basis. Private group clinic plans are prepayment plans operating under the direction, control, and ownership of a group of doctors or dentists, depending on the services rendered. Dental society plans are nonprofit prepayment dental care plans resembling Blue Shield plans. Examples of large nonindustrial community plans are the Health Insurance Plan of Greater New York and the six Kaiser Foundation Health Plans. The Ross-Loos Medical Clinic on the West Coast is the largest private group clinic. The Delta Dental Plan of Minnesota illustrates the dental society approach.

The benefits provided under these plans vary greatly, but most of them provide fairly complete protection for their members against most types of medical expenses, including those for preventive care. Physical examinations and immunization shots, for example, are often included among the benefits. Over half the persons covered under independent plans are covered under programs that provide at least one type of medical service through salaried physicians, nurses, and others or through contractual arrangements with community hospitals or clinics. These group practice arrangements were the original HMOs and still dominate that field. Thus independent plans have exerted a much greater influence on current trends in medical expense insurance than their share of the enrollment would suggest.

Trends

Although these independent plans insure relatively few persons, their influence on medical expense insurance has been substantial. Commercial insurers and Blue Cross and Blue Shield associations have adopted many of their practices, which in turn has made these insurers more attractive to persons formerly enrolled under the independent plans. A case in point is the recent addition by these insurers of HMO options. In the meantime independent plans continue to venture into new areas such as vision care, nursing home care, and the provision of prescription drugs. The operating methods and costs of various group practice arrangements are being intensively studied as a possible model for other public or private insurers.

INDIVIDUAL INSURANCE

Although employee-benefit plans provide most of the health insurance in force, individual health insurance still plays an important role. Some persons are not members of eligible groups; others wish to supplement their group coverage with individual policies tailored to their special needs. Because commercial insurers write most of the individual insurance in force, only their practices will be considered here.

Individual insurance contracts may be divided into two classes: those that protect insureds against loss of income and those that protect insureds against medical expenses.

Disability Income Contracts

Disability income contracts may in some instances also provide medical expense protection, but they are designed primarily to provide income coverage. Because of the many variations that exist in practice, disability income contracts are difficult to summarize. Most contracts, however, fall within the general framework described below.

Benefits

Disability income policies usually cover either accidental injuries alone or both accidental injuries and sickness combined. In the latter type of policy it is common practice to issue a separate contract covering each of the two perils because of the differences in the protection afforded against them.

The *accident* policy or the accident portions of a combined policy generally provides protection against loss "resulting directly and independently *of all causes* from *accidental bodily injury* occurring while this policy is in force." Under this provision the result, but not the means, must be accidental. For example, an insured may strain his back while lifting a heavy object. The requirement that the loss result independently of all other causes is supposed to cut out claims where some preexisting impairment or sickness causes the accident and to reduce claims where the preexisting condition significantly increases the severity of the loss. In practice, the full loss is usually payable if the accident is the dominating cause, even if it is not the sole cause.

Certain types of accidents are excluded; for example, losses caused by war, suicide, and intentionally inflicted injuries, injuries while in military service during wartime, and injuries sustained while a crew member of an aircraft or a student pilot.

Most disability income policies are schedule policies permitting the insured to select the types of benefits he or she wishes to purchase. Sometimes, however, the contract provides only one or a few of the possible coverages; sometimes the contract is a package including all or most of the common coverages. The following discussion is directed toward the schedule policies.

The most important benefits included in the schedule are the total and partial disability income benefits. The total disability income provision provides a stated weekly or monthly benefit for a specified number of weeks or months (e.g., 60 months) if the injury within a short period following the accident (commonly 100 days) completely prevents the insured from engaging in his or her regular occupation. Some insurers consider persons totally disabled up to age 65 or even for life if they cannot work at their own occupations. The requirement that the disability commence shortly after the accident eliminates claims of doubtful origin that occur later, but it may also eliminate some legitimate claims. The payments will generally be continued after the expiration of the "own occupation" benefits, either for life or for some stated number of years, as long as the insured is prevented from engaging in any gainful occupation for which he or she is reasonably fitted by education, training, and experience. A common proviso is that in no case is a person to be considered totally disabled if he or she engages in any occupation for remuneration or profit.

The partial disability provision, which is often omitted, provides a specified weekly or monthly income (commonly two-fifths or one-half of the total disability income benefit) for a specified number of weeks or months (e.g., six months) if the injury within a short period following the accident, or immediately following a period of total disability, renders the insured unable to perform one or more but not all the duties of his or her occupation.

The determination of total or partial disability depends on the physical capacity of the insured, not the loss of wages. The fact that the insured's employer may continue his or her wages does not reduce the insurance benefit.

Some insurers now provide "residual" benefits if the insured returns to work, but his or her income is reduced by 20% or more because of the disability. The benefit is the total disability benefit times the percentage by which the insured's income is reduced by the disability.

Another important disability benefit is provided by the dismemberment and loss-of-sight provision. A "capital sum" such as $10,000 or 208 times the total disability weekly indemnity is payable for the loss of both hands, both feet, the sight of both eyes, one hand and one foot or either hand or foot, and the sight of one eye of the loss occurs within specified times (e.g., 90 days or during a period of compensable total disability) following the accident. Lesser amounts are provided for other dismemberment and sight losses and a separate provision may provide similar benefits for various fractures and dislocations. This provision may be worded in several ways, some of which favor the insured, while others actually restrict the benefits.[4] For example, the dismemberment benefits may be in addition to total disability income payments, or they may establish a minimum number of such payments. On the other hand, the dismemberment benefits may in rare cases be in place of total disability income payments.[5]

The contracts also commonly contain an accidental death benefit, which is a limited kind of life insurance. Another provision doubles the amount payable under the benefits described to this point if the injuries result from *specified types* of accidents, such as those occurring while the insured is a passenger in or on a public conveyance, except aircraft, or as a result of the collapse of the outer walls or the burning of a building if the insured is in the building at the time of its collapse or at the commencement of the fire. The comments made in the last

---

[4]O. D. Dickerson, *Health Insurance,* 3rd ed. (Homewood, Ill.: Richard D. Irwin, 1968), p. 207.

[5]This provision is restrictive only if the insured would have received more in total disability income payments.

chapter with respect to the double indemnity clause in life insurance could be repeated here, because the value of this clause is even more questionable than the double indemnity rider. Other "fringe" benefits may also be included.

The *sickness* portion of the policy generally provides protection against loss resulting from sickness first manifesting itself after the effective date of this policy. Preexisting sicknesses, in other words, are excluded.

Usually the only disability income benefit under the sickness portion provides a total disability income.[6] If the insured is completely unable to engage in his or her regular occupation, the insurer will, usually after a waiting or so-called elimination period of one or two weeks, pay a specified weekly income for a stated period, say, two or five years. Longer-term benefits are available, but seldom beyond age 65. When the maximum duration of benefits is more than a short period such as two or five years, the test of disability is often changed after that period to inability to engage in any occupation for which the insured is fitted by education, training, and experience. As was true for accident benefits, however, some insurers continue the "own occupation" definition of total disability for longer periods.

The elimination period in sickness insurance contracts, which may be much longer than the one cited above (e.g., six months), serves the same purposes as the deductible in property and liability insurance—to cut costs of unimportant losses and morale hazard. Accidental injury benefits may also be subject to an elimination period, but their use there is much less common.

If a disabled person recovers but is later disabled from the same cause, a question often arises as to (1) whether a new elimination period applies before benefits start and (2) whether benefits already paid are subtracted from the maximum amount to be paid. Contracts usually handle this problem by stating that if the insured recovers for at least, say, six months, the second disability will be considered a new one.

Standard Provisions

The contract provisions discussed to this point are not covered under the 1950 Uniform Individual Accident and Sickness Policy Provisions Law, which all states have enacted. One important uniform provision prohibits the insurer from contesting a claim for loss commencing three years or later from the date of issue of the contract on the ground that the condition existed prior to that date, unless the condition is specifically excluded in the contract. Other required provisions deal with a time limit beyond which the insurer cannot contest the contract because of a misrepresentation by the insured in applying for the contract, reinstatement, a grace period, claims notices, claim forms, proofs of loss, claims payments, beneficiary change, physical examinations and autopsies, and time limits on legal actions.

---

[6]Partial and residual disability benefits, however, are becoming more common.

Common optional provisions deal with the adjustments to be made in the amounts paid because of changes in occupation during the policy term or misstatements of age in the application. An optional provision dealing with duplicate insurance states that the insurer will pay only that proportion of the benefit for which it would otherwise be responsible that the benefits provided by all policies of which the insurer had notice prior to the loss bear to the total of all benefits applicable to the loss. For example, an insurer providing a benefit of $400 a month would pay only two-thirds of that amount if the insured had another $200-a-month policy in force and failed to tell the insurer about this duplicate insurance. Other optional provisions deal with the deductibility of unpaid premiums from claim payments, the necessity of conforming to state statutes, and the exclusion of losses caused by the commission of a felony, an illegal occupation, or the illegal use of intoxicants and narcotics. The important optional standard provisions that give the insurer the right to cancel the contract are discussed next.

Cancellation and Renewal Provisions

An important consideration in purchasing disability income insurance is the right of the insured to continue the coverage at his or her option for many years, regardless of the insured's health. Formerly, many insurers included a cancellation provision in their contracts that allowed the insurer to cancel the contract at any time after a stated number of days' notice. This practice is rare today. Many contracts still give the insurer the right to refuse to renew the contract after the original term expires, but this right is often restricted to reasons specified in the contract. Over half the contracts written currently are more liberal noncancellable and guaranteed renewable policies. Noncancellable policies are renewable at the option of the insured till some advanced age such as 60 or 65. Guaranteed renewable contracts, which are less common in disability income insurance, differ from noncancellable policies in one important respect: the insurer reserves the right to change the table of premium rates applicable to outstanding policies in the same series, but not with respect to a single insured. In other words, the insurer cannot raise the rate for a single insured merely because his or her attractiveness as an insured decreases unless it raises the rate for all insureds in the same class.

Some Special Features of Noncancellable and Guaranteed Renewable Policies

Disability income contracts that are noncancellable or guaranteed renewable may contain some provisions not found in contracts that are conditionally renewable or renewable at the option of the insurer. For example, a benefit usually found in long-term noncancellable and guaranteed renewable contracts, but not other contracts, is the waiver or premiums payable under the contract if the insured is totally disabled for more than a specified period of time.[7]

---

[7]The waiver may be limited to the time during which monthly income benefits are payable.

A provision permitted by law only in noncancellable or guaranteed renewable contracts is an average earnings clause. Under this clause, if the total monthly income benefits payable under all valid coverages (not including workers' compensation or employee-benefit plans unless specified) exceed the greater of (1) the insured's monthly earnings at the time disability commenced or (2) his or her average monthly earnings for the two preceding years, the insurer is liable only for that proportionate part of the benefits under the policy that the higher earnings figure bears to the total of the valid coverages. This clause, however, cannot reduce the benefits under all valid coverages below $200 or, if less, the total benefits under all such coverages. The portion of the premium paid during the past two years for the benefits not paid because of this provision is returned to the insured. To illustrate, assume that an insured's gross monthly earnings at the date of the disability were $400, while average monthly earnings during the past two years were $300. A contract with an average earnings clause and benefits of $200 a month would pay only 40% of $400, or $160, if another contract provides benefits of $300. Such a clause is important in noncancellable and guaranteed renewable contracts because of the potential fluctuations in earnings over the long run.

In recent years insurers have added some interesting benefits to traditional noncancellable and guaranteed renewable insurance. One applies the family income concept developed by life insurers. The insurer promises to pay a monthly income to a totally disabled insured for the remainder of a stated period that commences when the policy is issued. Under a guaranteed insurability rider the insured can purchase certain additional disability income protection at specified option ages without providing insurability. The insured may wish to increase the protection because his or her income increases, the cost of living rises, or he or she wishes more adequate protection. Some insurers will attach an inflation rider that will tie the benefits to the Consumer Price Index, subject to some maximum percentage adjustment.

Premium Rates

The premium rates for disability income insurance depend on the benefits offered, the cancellation and renewability provision, and the occupation, age, and sex of the insured. To illustrate, one insurer sells only to persons in relatively safe occupations a contract that is noncancellable till age 65 and guaranteed renewable thereafter till age 72. The policy provides total disability, dismemberment, and waiver of premium benefits. The total disability income benefits would be continued for one, two, three, or five years or to age 65, depending on the duration purchased by the insured. Possible elimination periods for illnesses caused by sickness are 7, 14, 30, 60, 90, 180, or 365 days; accident benefits may start immediately or after 7, 14, or 30 days. For a policy with a 14-day elimination period applicable to both accidents and sickness the premium rate per $10 a month for a male age 30 with a professional or office job is $4.18. For a male age

50 the rate is $9.11. Women would pay as much as 75% more than men the same age in the same occupational class.

Some insurers now market modified premium plans under which the insured initially pays a lower premium than would otherwise be the case with one or two upward adjustments being made at later ages. Two other special arrangements provide cash values similar to those found in life insurance. Under one plan the insurer will pay the total premiums less any claim payments to an insured who surrenders his or her policy or to the beneficiaries of a deceased policyholder. Some of these policies mature at a specified date, when the insured turns such as 65. Under a second plan the insurer returns the premiums paid during 10-year periods if there are no claims. If there are claims but they are less than a stated percentage of the premiums, the insurer will return part of the premiums paid.

Riders on Life Insurance Policies

Two major disability benefits that may be added to life insurance contracts are (1) a waiver of premium and (2) a disability income. Both benefits are commonly provided by means of riders attached to life insurance contracts, but the waiver of premium benefits is often included in the life insurance contract itself. All life insurers issue waiver of premium insurance, although not on all types of contracts. Many insurers also offer a total disability income rider. The waiver of premium may be purchased without the disability income benefit, but the opposite is not possible.

The waiver of premium benefit guarantees that if the insured, as a result of either accidental bodily injury or disease, is totally and (presumably) permanently incapable of engaging in any occupation for wage or profit (interpreted by most courts to mean any occupation for which he or she is fitted), the insurer will waive the payment of premiums on the contract during the continuance of the disability. The disability must occur, however, prior to some advanced age, such as 55 or 60, and must not have resulted from intentionally self-inflicted injury, war, or a violation of the law. Before the disability is presumed to be permanent, it must usually have lasted at least six months, but the waiver is retroactive. Blindness and double dismemberment, however, are considered immediately as having caused total and permanent disability.

The disability income rider replaces the income lost because of the disability. This rider usually pays $10 a month per $1,000 to a totally and (presumably) permanently disabled person, as defined above in connection with the waiver of premium benefit.[8] The income is payable during the continuance of the disability until age 60 or 65, at which time the rider converts the life insurance contract into a matured endowment contract. No payment is usually made, however, for

---

[8]Average earnings clauses similar to those used in noncancellable and guaranteed renewable contracts are seldom found. The most interesting and apparently successful attempt to reduce the overinsurance problem is the practice of one insurer that, in addition to an average earnings clause that provides only enough income to bring the benefits from all contracts up to 75% of the formerly earned income, defines total disability as a reduction in earned income of at least 75%.

the first five or six months of disability, the first payment being made at the end of the sixth or the seventh month.

The disability income rider is appealing because on a guaranteed renewable basis and for a relatively attractive price made possible by the packaging concept the insurer promises to pay a disabled person an income to an advanced age or for life, regardless of whether the cause of the disability is accidental injury or sickness. The major drawback is the required relationship between the rider and a life insurance contract.

The premiums for life insurance waiver of premium and disability income riders are level over the premium-payment period of the life insurance contract or until the coverage under the rider ceases, whichever comes first. The rates for standard lives depend primarily on the issue age and sex of the insured. Applicants rated substandard for reasons of occupation or health may be denied this coverage or charged a higher premium rate.

Medical Expense Contracts

Most individual medical expense insurance is written by commercial insurers. Medical expense insurance is sometimes included in the individual disability income contracts discussed above, but most insureds buy their medical expense insurance separately. This insurance can be classified as either (1) basic or (2) major-medical expense insurance.

Illustrative of the *basic medical expense insurance* contracts, which are more numerous than individual major-medical expense policies, is one providing the following benefits:

$100 per day hospital room and board coverage up to 120 days.

Miscellaneous hospital expenses up to 20 times $100 for inpatient services, 10 times $100 for outpatient services.

Surgical fees up to scheduled amounts, the maximum amount being $1,000.

In-hospital visits by a physician up to $10 per day for up to 60 days of hospital confinement.

Recently hospital "indemnity" benefits have become increasingly popular. Under this approach the insurer pays a specified amount per day, week, or month for hospital confinement, regardless of the actual charges incurred.

In general, individual contracts tend to be less liberal than group plans with respect to the types of expenses to be covered and the maximum benefits. More conditions and diseases tend to be excluded or made subject to special restrictions.

Under individual *major-medical expense insurance* contracts, the insurer usually promises to pay 75 to 80% of eligible expenses in excess of a stated deductible up to some specified maximum. Sometimes the insurer pays all the excess expenses, but there are limits on hospital daily room and board charges, surgical fees, and other named services. The policy may permit upward adjustment in these limits at a later date. Some insurers pay 75 to 80% of the expenses up to a certain amount, 100% of the excess up to the stated maximum. Some individual major-medical expense contracts are purchased with sizable deductibles (say $15,000) to supplement group protection.

Most individual medical expense contracts are guaranteed renewable to some specified age, such as 60 or 65. The right the insurer reserves under guaranteed renewable policies to change premiums for a policyholder class is especially important to an insurer of medical expenses because these expenses are subject to inflationary pressures. The guaranteed renewability feature, however, does protect the insured in case his or her health deteriorates. This protection is not present in those policies that permit the insurer to cancel the contract during the policy term or refuse renewal at the end of each term.

NAIC Minimum Standards Regulation

In 1974 the National Association of Insurance Commissions (NAIC) adopted a minimum standards regulation applicable to individual health insurance policies that goes far beyond the standard provisions described above. The following examples illustrate the scope of the regulation, which covers both disability income and medical expense insurance:

1   Under a noncancellable or guaranteed renewable policy covering the insured and spouse, if the insured dies, the spouse must become the insured.

2   Under family policies, coverage for mentally retarded or physically handicapped children must be continued beyond the normal termination date if such children are not employable.

3   As noted earlier, after three years from the date of issue of the contract an insurer cannot deny a claim on the ground that the condition existed prior to the date of the claim, unless the condition is specifically excluded under the contract. The new regulation says that a condition cannot be so excluded unless (a) the condition manifested itself within five years prior to the effective date of the coverage in such a manner as to cause a prudent person to seek diagnosis, care, or treatment, or (b) medical advice or treatment was recommended or received within that five years.

4   Daily room and board charges insured under a basic hospital expense insurance policy must be covered either for 80% of semiprivate room charges or not less than $30 a day; miscellaneous hospital expenses must be covered for either 80% of the charges insured up to at least $1,000 or not less than 10 times the daily room and board charges.

5   Aggregate maximum limits under major-medical expense insurance policies must be at least $10,000; the participation percentage must not exceed 25%; and the deductible must not exceed 5% of the aggregate maximum limit unless the policy complements some basic coverage.

Several states have adopted minimum benefit standards based in part on these principles.

OPERATIONS OF PRIVATE HEALTH INSURERS

The past three decades have witnessed a remarkably rapid increase in voluntary private health insurance. Two factors are evidence of this progress: the number of persons insured and the percentage of income losses and medical expenses paid by private health insurance benefits.

Number of Persons Insured

The Health Insurance Institute, a private commercial insurer association, reports annually on the number of persons covered under private insurance contracts. The figures do not include persons covered under workers' compensation insurance, total and permanent disability riders on life insurance contracts, nor contracts covering accidental injuries only. The figures do include workers covered under private plans in the five states with temporary disability insurance legislation.

Table 10.1 compares data on the number covered at the close of 1950, 1970, and 1978. The data indicate the following: a tremendous growth since 1950 in all forms of coverage, especially physicians' care and major-medical expense coverage; the greater popularity of medical expense coverage as compared with loss-of-income coverage; the dominant role of commercial insurers and the Blue Cross–Blue Shield associations; and the greater importance of group insurance relative to individual insurance.

Proportion of Illness Losses Covered by Insurance

Another yardstick used to measure the effectiveness of private health insurance is the percentage of the total nonoccupational short-term disability income losses and medical expenses covered by private insurance benefits. Table 10.2 summarizes the record of private insurance according to this measure in 1950, 1970, and 1978.

The growth of all forms of private health insurance is impressive. The percentage of medical expenses covered in 1950 was considerably less than the percentage of disability income losses covered, but medical expenses are now more fully covered than disability losses. Hospital bills are the most nearly completely covered type of expense.

Of the insurance benefits covering income losses, 61% were paid by sick leave plans (38% by government sick leave plans), 33% by commercial insurers and self-insurers, and 6% by publicly operated cash sickness funds. OASDI payments during the sixth month of long-term disability covered about 0.5% of the loss.

Table 10.1 Number of People Protected Under Private Health Insurance, Year-End 1950, 1970, and 1978

	1950	1970	1978	1978 Percentage Increase Over	
				1950	1970
Loss of income					
Short-term disability					
Commercial group insurance	15,104	27,876	30,747	104	10
Commercial individual insurance	13,067	14,901	17,606	35	18
Paid sick leave[a]	8,900	15,900	22,318	151	30
Other[a]	2,900	2,400	2,700	(7)	12
Net total[a]	37,793	58,089	70,378	86	21
Percentage of civilian population	25	29	33		
Long-term disability					
Commercial group insurance	—	6,954	12,635	—	82
Commercial individual insurance	—	4,012	6,465	—	61
Net total[a]	—	10,966	19,100	—	74
Percentage of civilian population	—	5	9		
Hospital expenses					
Commercial group insurance	22,305	80,505	92,286	314	15
Commercial individual insurance	17,296	26,658	36,051	108	35
Blue Cross, Blue Shield, and medical society plans	38,822	75,055	85,816	121	14
Independent plans	4,445	8,131	17,271	189	112
Net total[a]	76,639	158,847	181,464	137	14
Percentage of civilian population	51	79	84		

Surgical expenses					
Commercial group insurance	21,219	81,549	94,698	346	16
Commercial individual insurance	13,718	17,961	16,742	22	(7)
Blue Cross, Blue Shield, and medical society plans	19,690	66,042	74,604	279	13
Independent plans	3,760	10,532	20,770	452	97
Net total[a]	54,156	151,440	172,499	219	14
Percentage of civilian population	36	75	80		
Physicians' care expense					
Commercial group insurance	5,587	74,899	90,797	1,525	21
Commercial individual insurance	2,714	10,283	14,043	417	37
Blue Cross, Blue Shield, and medical society plans.	11,428	62,273	70,517	517	13
Independent plans	2,873	[b]	20,350	608	[b]
Net total[a]	21,589	138,658	164,145	660	18
Percentage of civilian population	14	69	76		
Major-medical expense					
Commercial group insurance	96	81,962	108,872	[c]	18
Commercial individual insurance	12	5,414	6,890	[c]	27
Blue Cross, Blue Shield, and medical society plans	[b]	24,905	39,317	[b]	48
Independent plans	[b]	[b]	14,084	[b]	[b]
Net total[a]	[b]	103,544	141,538	[b]	37
Percentage of civilian population	[b]	51	65		

Source: Source Book of Health Insurance Data, 1979–1980 (Washington, D.C.: Health Insurance Institute, 1980), pp. 13–16, 21.

[a]Net figures after adjustment for duplication of other coverage.

[b]Not available.

[c]Extremely large because of very small 1950 base.

Table 10.2 Private Insurance Benefits in Relation to Disability Income Losses and Private Consumer Expenditures for Medical Care, 1950, 1970, and 1978 (In Millions of Dollars)

	1950			1970			1978[b]		
	Loss	Insurance Benefits	Percentage of Loss Covered by Insurance	Loss	Insurance Benefits	Percentage of Loss Covered by Insurance	Loss	Insurance Benefits	Percentage of Loss Covered by Insurance
Disability income loss[a]	4.8	0.9	20	16.8	5.9	35	32.9	11.5	35
Medical expenses									
Hospital services	1.8	0.7	37	13.7	10.0	73	31.0	24.6	79
Physicians' services	2.6	0.3	12	10.2	4.9	48	23.7	12.5	53
Other services	3.7			15.2	0.8	6	36.7	4.5	12
Total	8.1	1.0	12	39.0	15.7	40	91.4	41.6	46

Sources: Daniel N. Price, "Income Replacement During Sickness, 1948–78," *Social Security Bulletin*, XLIV, No. 5 (May, 1981), 23; and Marjorie Smith Carroll and Ross H. Arnett III, "Private Health Insurance Plans in 1977: Coverage, Enrollment and Financial Experience," *Health Care Financing Review*, I, No. 2 (Fall 1979), 14, 21.

[a]Short-term non-work-connected disability (lasting not more than six months) and the first six months of long-term disability.

[b]1977 for medical expenses.

These data emphasize the liberal individual payments under the sick leave plans, because relatively few people are covered under these plans. Of the medical expense benefits about 30% were paid by Blue Cross associations, 12% by Blue Shield associations, 47% by commercial insurers, and 11% by independent insurers.

In interpreting these data we should remember that insurers may consider complete coverage impossible or undesirable for underwriting reasons. Many consumers may not find complete coverage a good buy. They may prefer to pay a smaller premium for partial coverage (such as major-medical expense insurance) and meet the uncovered losses out of income or savings. Finally, many do not feel *any* need for health insurance because (1) they do not have to pay for the care they receive (uniformed service personnel, for example), (2) their religious views make them opposed to insurance, or (3) their income is so high that they prefer to meet all their expenses out of current income or savings.[9]

The Social Security Administration recognizes that complete coverage may not be a fair bench mark. Consequently, with respect to disability income losses they also compute insurance benefits as a percentage of the income loss that may be considered insurable or compensable under prevailing insurance practices. First they recognize that insurance plans are not designed to cover the first few days or first week of disability. Eliminating the first three days cuts the income loss by 30%; eliminating the first week reduces the loss by 45%. They also exclude the income losses of those workers who are covered exclusively under paid sick leave programs, which on the average cover 77% of the income losses of those workers. In 1950 insurance benefits met 15% of the income loss, excluding the first three days, and 20% of the income loss, excluding the first seven days. In 1978, the last year for which this type of analysis is available, the percentages were 25 and 32, respectively, about the same as a decade earlier.

The Social Security Administration further recognizes that insurers prefer to compensate the disabled person for less than the total insurable loss in recognition of the fact that a disabled person's nonmedical expenses including taxes are reduced and that there must be some incentive to return to work. The Social Security Administration assumes that two-thirds of the wage loss is a reasonable standard. On this basis the percentage of the income loss covered by insurance benefits in 1950 was 23, excluding the first three days, and 29, excluding the first week. In 1978 the respective percentages were about 37 and 47. No reliable data are available on private protection against long-term disability income losses, but the percentage is much smaller.

With respect to medical expenses, consumer expenditures include some items that are not covered by medical expense insurance, such as nonprescribed drugs, some drug sundries, and sunglasses. Most medical expense insurance does not cover the difference in cost between private and semiprivate accommodations, but consumer expenditures include this difference. If expenditures of this sort were

[9] J. F. Follman, Jr., "Some Medico-Economic Trends," *The Journal of Insurance,* XXVII, No. 2 (June 1960), 49.

excluded from the expenditures base, the proportion of consumer expenditures covered would be three or four percentage points higher. Moreover, full coverage may not be the goal. As we have already seen, the federal Medicare program does not provide full coverage.

A recent private study reported that in 1977 the proportions of individuals with adequate public and private protection for selected benefits were as follows[10]:

In patient hospital care	91%
Inpatient psychiatric care	91
Inpatient laboratory and x-ray services	96
Inpatient physician visits	53
Physician office and home visits	43
Nursing home care	48
$250,000 or more catastrophic protection	62

Protection was generally considered to be adequate if at least 80% of the expense of covered services would be borne by a third party, except for inpatient psychiatric services, for which any protection was considered adequate.

Unfortunately, these data do not tell us to what extent some families benefited more than others from private insurance. The benefits may have a large percentage of their losses covered. Furthermore, there is no information on the types of benefits paid. It makes a difference both to the family and to society whether the benefits were used to pay for a few serious losses or for many nonserious losses.

According to the Health Interview Survey, in 1975 out-of-pocket health expenses per capita were $182, not including insurance premiums paid ($245 including those premiums).[11] Of this $182, $30 was spent for hospital care, $63 for doctors' services, $41 on dental work, $31 on prescription drugs, $15 for eyeglasses, contact lenses, or optometrists' services, and $6 on other medical expenses. These expenses varied widely among families as follows:

Expenses per Capita ($)	Percentage of Total Families
Under 50	28
50–99	15
100–249	29
250–499	17
500–999	8
1,000 or more	3

[10]Stephen G. Sudovar and Patrice Hirsch Feinstein, *National Health Insurance Issues: The Adequacy of Coverage* (New York: Health Issues, 1979). This study is one in a series of studies and reports made possible by a grant from Roche Laboratories, a division of Hoffmann-La Roche, Inc.

[11]*Personal Out-of-Pocket Health Expenses, 1975,* Data from the National Health Survey, Series 10, No. 122 (Washington, D.C.: U. S. Department of Health, Education, and Welfare, Public Health Service, National Center for Health Statistics, November 1978).

The per capita expenditure ranged from $90 for persons under 17 years of age to $344 for persons 65 years and over. Adjusted for age, it ranged from $135 for families with income of less than $3,000 to $231 for families with incomes of $25,000 or more.

CURRENT ISSUES

Private health insurance has expanded significantly, but many problems remained to be solved. The many proposals for a national medical expense insurance program are ample testimony to this fact. In this section we consider separately the protection afforded, underwriting practices, the problems of overutilization and overinsurance, premium structures, and the types of control effected.

Protection Afforded

Private insurance contracts are available to protect insureds against long-term disability income losses, short-term disability income losses, and medical expenses.

Disability Income Policies

Under most individual disability income policies the insurer will pay lifetime benefits for a total disability caused by accidental injury. If the disability is caused by sickness, however, many policies limit the benefit duration to a few years, although benefits to age 65 can be purchased from most insurers. Partial disability payments are usually limited to a relatively short period. Some insurers include in their policies a "residual" benefit that continues a partial payment for a person who recovers enough from a total disability to return to work but at a reduced income.

During the 1960s long-term disability insurance became a much more common feature of employee-benefit plans, but the proportion of the population with this coverage on either a group or individual basis is still small. Liberalizations since 1965 in OASDI eligibility requirements and benefit amounts caused many insurers to look less favorably on this field, particularly with respect to low-income workers, but the Social Security Disability Amendments of 1980 may cause insurers to renew their interest in insuring these workers.

Temporary disability income benefits are readily available from commercial insurers on an individual or group basis and under paid sick leave plans. The cause of the disability may be an accidental injury or sickness.

Medical Expense Policies

Until insurers introduced major-medical expense insurance, medical expense insurance was primarily a device for budgeting over a number of years the cost of the *less* financially serious illnesses. Major-medical and comprehensive insurance now provide substantial protection against the financially *more* serious injuries. Ideally there should be no amount nor duration limits. Such protection is now available.

Insurance against the costs of nonsurgical care by a physician, in the physician's office or the patient's home, nursing home care, various forms of home care, dental services, drugs, and similar needs are being more fully developed and marketed, but most persons still do not have this form of protection. Studies indicate that hospital utilization is reduced when nonhospitalized illness is covered under the same plan. In addition, chronic illnesses are becoming increasingly important for a variety of reasons, including the growing proportion of the aged in our population. This trend has increased the demand for and supply of more comprehensive benefits. Independent plans have often pioneered in these and other areas, and their activities should not be hindered by artificial barriers. The addition of HMO options by commercial insurers and Blue Cross–Blue Shield plans is a positive development.

The exclusions under medical expense contracts are more numerous and more important than those under disability income contracts, but they are being reduced. Group insurance contracts tend to be more liberal than individual contracts. Treatment for mental and nervous disease is still usually more limited than treatment for physical problems. For the insurer coverage of these conditions poses special problems, but from the patient's point of view there is no reason to treat them differently. Comprehensive mental health benefits, however, are now included in some employee-benefit plans and individual contracts.

The aged formerly had little or no protection against medical expenses, but Medicare and private supplementary coverage have greatly relieved, though far from solved, this problem. Employee-benefit plans and individual insurance policies commonly pay all or part of the expenses that the Medicare recipients incur, because of the deductibles, cost-sharing percentages, and duration provisions under that program. Unfortunately, the individual insurance policies and marketing practices of some insurers have proved to be misleading. The Social Security Disability Amendments of 1980 established some guidelines for these so-called Medi-gap policies. Under a voluntary program, to become effective in July 1982, insurers can request the federal government to certify that their Medi-gap policies meet or exceed the policy and marketing standards established by the NAIC.

Opinions as to the adequacy of the present plans vary, depending on the standard desired. Those who believe that the plans should provide complete protection against all types of medical expenses consider the present plans inadequate. Ideally, private health insurance should be available that would pay all the losses that the insured family cannot handle out of its current income and small savings accounts. On this score private insurance rates fairly high and its record is improving, but there are still some important gaps and weaknesses to be overcome.

Underwriting

A larger percentage of applicants is ineligible for private health insurance than for private life insurance. Advanced age and poor health are the principal reasons for the rejections. Moreover, individual contracts may be renewable only at the option of the insurer; some allow the insurer to cancel during the policy term.

Much more attention is now being paid to substandard lives and the rural population. As noted above, although the aged are now eligible for extensive medical expense benefits under HI and SMI, private insurers sell contracts supplementing this government protection. Most leading insurers also sell disability income and medical expense insurance on a guaranteed renewable or noncancellable basis under which they relinquish their right to cancel or refuse to renew the contract till some advanced age. Most medical expense contracts are now guaranteed renewable, in many cases for life.

Group insurance is another solution to the problem of individual uninsurability, because all members of an eligible group are insurable. Although group protection cannot, for underwriting reasons, be extended to cover all persons in the population, insurers have broadened their concept of eligible groups to include smaller groups and new types of groups such as trade associations, professional associations, employer associations, and unions. One version of group insurance is the "mass enrollment" technique offered by several insurers, under which aged persons in an area are invited to enroll during a specified period for protection supplementing HI and SMI. Eligibility for individual medical expense insurance is also increased through group insurance, because under most noncommercial plans and an increasing number of commercial insurance plans terminating members are permitted to purchase individual insurance contracts without proving insurability.

A few states require that insurers provide protection through a pool for those individuals who cannot secure protection through normal channels.

There will always be some persons who will be ineligible for private insurance. Others will not choose or be able to afford the protection, and the protection purchased will probably always be incomplete for many others. Most persons agree that, for these reasons, unless a more extensive social health insurance program is established, there will be a continuing need for public assistance programs covering the expenses of medical care for all age groups. Many believe that these gaps will result in an extension of existing social disability income and medical expense insurance programs.

Overutilization and Overinsurance

The twin problems of overutilization and overinsurance have received considerable attention in recent years. Overutilization of medical services consists of a more frequent use of these services than necessary, the use of more expensive or extended services than required, and unreasonable charges by suppliers. Various studies have indicated that insured persons are more likely to overutilize health services than are noninsureds. Hospitals, physicians, insurers, and patients have all contributed to this overutilization, but all four groups would gain from some improved controls. Only insurer approaches will be considered here. However, it should be recognized that only physicians can determine whether medical services are being overutilized. Hence there is great need to perfect the operations of medical society review committees, hospital review committees, and similar groups that check on the practices of individual doctors and hospitals. Such committees have already been described in connection with the Medicare program. Their operations should be extended to include all age groups.

Insurers can exercise some control through investigation of applicants' moral qualities, but the right of individual selection is relinquished under group insurance, and moral qualities are difficult to evaluate. Insurers may also attempt to control overutilization through policy provisions that force the insured to share part of the loss, for example, certain types of expenses such as hospital room and board; or the policy may contain a deductible or a percentage participation provision. These provisions, however, should not exclude nor limit coverage of expenses against which it is reasonable to insure. They should also not discourage insureds from seeking early treatment or obtaining adequate treatment for extended illnesses.

A special problem that affects both disability income and medical expense insurance is overinsurance, resulting from duplicate insurance protection. In the past it has been customary to assume that the possibility of overinsurance had been considered prior to issuance of the policy and that the insured was entitled to collect from all insurers with whom he or she had policies. However, overinsurance may result from narrow coverages that apply only in certain instances (such as automobile medical payments insurance), from later enrollment under a new group plan, or from later liberalizations in an existing group plan. Moreover, as benefits have been improved, it has become more likely that a person with two or more contracts is overinsured. Consequently, more insurers are inserting provisions in their policies providing for some sharing of the losses with duplicating insurance. Noncancellable and guaranteed renewable disability income insurers are for similar reasons making more frequent use of a provision that limits total recoveries from all insurers to the insured's prior earnings.

A new concept, incorporated in one of five types of national health insurance proposals presented in Chapter 9 and already used in some private plans, is to pay cash to persons who elect less comprehensive coverage or whose claims total less than some specified amount.

Premium Structures

As stated in Chapter 5, private insurance premiums should not, on the average, be excessive and they should distribute the cost equitably.

Cost Levels

One indication as to whether the premiums are excessive, on the average, is the benefit ratio or ratio of benefits incurred to the earned income. Other things being equal, a high ratio is favorable, for it indicates that most of the premiums are being returned to policyholders in the form of benefits.

Table 10.3 lists the 1975–1977 average benefit ratio of each type of insurer. Paid sick leave plans are not included. The benefit ratios were higher for medical expense insurance than for disability income insurance. Among the medical expense insurers the average 1975–1977 benefit ratio was at least 89% in each case, except for commercial individual insurance. Because the insured receives more individual attention under this form of insurance, the cost of selling and servicing the protection is greater. Since these benefit ratios vary somewhat over time, slight differences among the ratios should be ignored. A high benefit ratio may be associated with an underwriting loss that may cause the insurer to raise its prices the following year to correct the imbalance. For example, commercial group insurers had the highest average three-year benefit ratio, but they also had

Table 10.3 Benefits, Operating Expenses, and Net Underwriting Gain as a Percentage of Earned Income, 1975–1977 Average

Benefit and Type of Insurer	Benefits	Operating Expenses	Net Underwriting Gain
Loss of income[a]			
Commercial insurers			
Group insurance[b]	71.2	c	c
Individual insurance[d]	43.8	c	c
Other	70.1	c	c
Medical expenses			
Commercial insurers			
Group insurance	98.3	13.3	−11.6
Individual insurance	52.5	46.2	1.3
Blue Cross associations	96.2	5.3	−1.4
Blue Shield associations	89.5	11.0	−0.5
Independent plans	96.3	7.0	−3.4

Sources: Daniel N. Price, "Cash Benefits for Short-Term Sickness, 1948–1976," *Security Bulletin,* LXI, No. 10 (October 1978), 106; Marjorie Smith Carroll and Ross H. Arnett III, "Private Health Insurance Plans in 1977: Coverage, Enrollment, and Financial Experience," *Health Care Financing Review,* No. 2 (Fall 1979), 20.

[a]1974–1976 for loss of income insurance.

[b]Includes private insurance written in connection with temporary disability insurance legislation.

[c]Not available.

[d]Excludes self-insured unfunded employer-administered plans in states without temporary disability insurance legislation.

the largest underwriting losses. The income these insurers earned from investments (made possible because they receive premiums before they are needed to pay losses and some expenses) may have offset some, perhaps all, of these underwriting losses. The combined underwriting and investment profit, however, may still have been less than the level they considered acceptable.

Operating expense ratios are another more stable measure of insurer efficiency. Table 10.3 shows that Blue Cross associations had the lowest average 1975–1977 expense ratio among medical expense insurers; commercial individual insurers had the highest ratio. In comparing these ratios, however, it is important to first remember that taxes, primarily a 2–3% state tax on premiums, constitute a larger percentage of the expenses for commercial insurers than for other types of insurers. Second, operating expense ratios for hospital coverage tend to be less because the premiums are higher, the number of claims per enrollee are less, and the coverage is administratively less complex.

The Distribution of Costs

There are two schools of thought concerning the equitable distribution of insurance costs. One school maintains that it is socially and economically desirable to use an average premium for all insureds, regardless of their age, sex, and group experience. The objective of this community-rating school is the widest possible pooling of risks and extension of coverage. The other school argues that a uniform distribution of the costs is not a fair distribution. Premiums should vary among insureds according to their expected losses and expenses. The members of this school also believe that a uniform premium will work only if the insurer has a monopoly or if all insurers charge the same uniform premium, because otherwise the insureds will seek out the insurer charging the lowest premium. Even if the premium were uniform, it might be higher than some of the healthier insureds would be willing or able to pay. Hence compulsion and possibly some subsidy might be necessary if these people are to be insured.

Types of Control

Except in small plans in which members have the right to attend meetings and vote, the insured usually has little or no direct control over the types of contracts offered. Stockholders, the present management, physicians, or hospitals control most of the plans. However, this lack of control by the insureds is not too important as long as competition forces the plans to experiment and to liberalize their coverage.

Service benefit plans are generally considered to have greater opportunities of controlling the cost and quality of the services rendered because of the close relationship between the insurers and the purveyors of the services. Group practice plans, particularly those that own and operate their own facilities or are served by doctors with no other practice, are supposed to have the most opportunity and incentive for such controls. This is perhaps the major reason why so many of the current national medical expense proposals would encourage the development of HMOs. On the other hand, supporters of indemnity plans argue that the controls associated with service plans are more apparent than real and that outside review committees of physicians and similar groups can be equally effective in controlling costs and quality.

Although the Employee Retirement Income Security Act, mentioned in Chapter 5, was aimed primarily at pension plans, it also affects the administration of employee-benefit plans providing disability, medical expense, or death benefits. For example, plan participants must receive a description of the plan written in a manner that the average participant can understand. The plan administrators must file with the U.S. Department of Labor an annual report providing detailed financial information concerning the plan's operation. Persons who exercise discretionary authority or control over the management of the plan or its assets must discharge their duties in the interest of the participants.

A CONCLUDING NOTE

The most obvious characteristic of private health insurance is at the same time a strong point and a weakness. The multitude of contracts available, with their heterogeneous benefits and costs, gives the insured considerable freedom of choice. Moreover, the competition among insurers has produced many important improvements. On the other hand, the wide variety of options available makes it extremely difficult for the average person to make intelligent choices.

Clearly, despite impressive advances during the past three decades, existing private medical expense insurance falls far short of providing truly comprehensive coverage for the entire population. Over 20% of the population still have no protection against medical expenses. Most contracts in force cover only certain types of services, limit the amount or duration of these services for all or certain illnesses, or exclude some conditions entirely. Some of these restrictions may be necessary to avoid overutilization of services. Others are cost-cutting devices designed to keep the premiums within "affordable" limits. Until comprehensive insurance is brought within the reach of most families, pressures for social medical expense insurance of some kind will continue but, as noted in Chapter 9, opinions vary widely on what form such a program should take. Some would rely on improved private health insurance.

SUMMARY

Private health insurance provides protection against the loss of income caused by disability and medical expenses.

Health insurance is one of the most common benefits included in employee-benefit plans. Paid sick leave plans, which are usually self-insured by the employer, and group temporary disability insurance, underwritten by commercial insurers, pay income to workers disabled for a short period. Long-term disability insurance typically continues part of a totally disabled worker's income to age 65.

The medical expense insurance provided under employee-benefit plans is underwritten by four major classes of insurers, namely, (1) commercial insurers, (2) Blue Cross associations, (3) Blue Shield associations, and (4) independent plans. Commercial insurers write basic medical expense insurance, major-medical expense insurance, and comprehensive medical expense insurance. More recently many of these insurers have also made available a Health Maintenance Organization option.

Blue Cross and Blue Shield associations are the most important competitors of the commercial insurers. There are many types of Blue Cross contracts, but the typical contract provides a specified number of days of service in ward or semiprivate accomodations of member hospitals. The subscriber receives dollar benefits if hospitalized in a nonmember hospital.

The typical Blue Shield contract pays the usual, customary, and reasonable charges of doctors for surgical and nonsurgical care in the hospital. Member physicians agree to accept these charges as full payment for services rendered.

Although Blue Cross and Blue Shield plans originally emphasized basic protection, they now sell in addition supplementary major medical or extended benefit coverage. Many make available a Health Maintenance Organization option under their group plans.

The independent insurers include the nonindustrial insurers (community plans, private group clinics, and dental society plans) and the industrial insurers (unions, employers, and groups of employees). Benefits under these plans tend to be comprehensive. A distinctive feature of many of these plans is the provision of services through a Health Maintenance Organization.

Although employee-benefit plans provide most of the health insurance in force, individual health insurance is still important. Most of this insurance is written by commercial insurers.

Individual disability income insurance can be classified as the following: (1) insurance that can be renewed only with the consent of the insurer; (2) noncancellable insurance, which is guaranteed renewable at the same rate to some advanced age; or (3) guaranteed renewable insurance, which permits the insurer to adjust the rates, but only for an entire class of insureds. The income benefits vary depending on whether the disability is partial or total and whether the disability is caused by an accidental injury or sickness.

Individual medical expense contracts, like their group counterparts, can be classified as basic, major-medical, or comprehensive insurance. These contracts are usually guaranteed renewable, subject to adjustable class premiums.

SUGGESTIONS FOR ADDITIONAL READING

Compensation Systems Available to Disabled Persons in the United States. Washington, D.C.: Health Insurance Association of America, 1979.
An excellent analysis and description of public and private disability insurance.

Contemporary Benefit Issues and Administration. Brookfield, Wisc.: International Foundation of Employee Benefit Plans, 1979.
A description and analysis of the leading issues involving employee-benefit plans.

Dickerson, O. D. *Health Insurance,* 3rd ed. Homewood, Ill.: Richard D. Irwin, 1968.
A dated, but still highly useful book on health insurance.

Eilers, Robert D. *Regulation of Blue Cross and Blue Shield Plans.* Homewood, Ill.: Richard D. Irwin, 1963.
A dated, but still informative, analysis of Blue Cross and Blue Shield plans, as well as their regulation.

Follman, J. F., Jr. *Medical Care and Health Insurance.* Homewood, Ill.: Richard D. Irwin, 1963.
An authoritative account of the development of private health insurance up to the early 1960s.

Gregg, Davis, W. and Vane B. Lucas (Eds.). *Life and Health Insurance Handbook,* 3rd ed. Homewood, Ill.: Richard D. Irwin, 1973.
A handbook of current practices and procedures in the life and health insurance fields.

Huebner, S. S., and K. Black, Jr. *Life Insurance,* 10th ed. New York: Appleton-Century-Crofts, 1981.
This leading book contains chapters on individual and group health insurance.

Ilse, Louise Wolters. *Group Insurance and Employee Retirement Plans.* Englewood Cliffs, N.J.: Prentice-Hall, 1953.
Chapters 1, 2, and 7 through 10 of this book describe the historical development of group health protection underwritten by commercial insurers and Blue Cross–Blue Shield associations.

Life, Health, and Other Group Benefit Programs. Brookfield, Wisc.: International Foundation of Employee Benefit Plans, 1978.
A compilation of articles covering all phases of life and health employee-benefit programs.

MacIntyre, Duncan M. *Voluntary Health Insurance and Rate Making.* Ithaca, N.Y.: Cornell University Press, 1962.
A detailed analysis of the methodology, relative merits, and effects of experience rating and community rating.

Mehr, Robert I. *Life Insurance: Theory and Practice,* rev. ed. Dallas, Tex.: Business Publications, 1977.
This leading book contains chapters on individual and group health insurance.

Rosenbloom, Jerry S. and G. Victor Hallman. *Employee Benefit Planning.* Englewood Cliffs, N.J.: Prentice-Hall, 1981.
A comprehensive, clearly written text on the objectives and characteristics of employee-benefit plans.

Snider, H. Wayne (Ed.). *Employee Benefits Management.* New York: Risk and Insurance Management Society, 1980.
An informative compilation of 14 essays by specialists in the field of employee benefits.

Somers, Herman M., and Anne R. Somers. *Doctors, Patients and Health Insurance.* Washington, D.C.: Brookings Institution, 1961.
A penetrating analysis and evaluation of the organization and financing of medical care.

Spencer, Bruce F. *Group Benefits in a Changing Society,* rev. ed. Chicago, Ill.: Charles D. Spencer, 1978.
A well-illustrated description of group life and health insurance benefits and practices.

Chapter Eleven

The Problems of Unemployment

Unemployment is defined and interpreted in many different ways in economic literature; for our purposes we shall simply note it as enforced idleness among persons who are willing and able to work. Unemployment has many causes and is uneven in its impacts on the various sectors and individuals in our economy. Unemployment, as we define it, was not a serious problem until the development of modern industrialism. Prior to the Industrial Revolution most people lived in rural areas. Their wants were simple and they satisfied most of these directly through their own efforts. They were their own farmers, butchers, bakers, and candlestick makers. They generally produced little more than they needed for themselves. Some manufacturers and traders hired workers for a wage, but most people who produced goods for others worked for employers in small towns or, more frequently, in their own homes. These operations tended to provide fairly stable employment; masters tended to develop close relationships with their journeymen and apprentices and be concerned about their continued employment. The Industrial Revolution produced a more complicated, interdependent, impersonal society that (1) made more persons dependent on the continuation of a money wage (in the United States today some 85% of us work for others) and (2) made that continuation more uncertain.

In previous chapters we analyzed unemployment associated with poor health or old age; here we will deal with "involuntary economic" unemployment—unemployment that involves a relative or absolute reduction in the demand for labor. Even if one looks only at the economic consequences of this unemployment, one cannot help being influenced by its significance.The authors' generations were all severely affected by the post-1929 Depression. And 50 years later unemployment is still a major threat. (And, as these lines were written in mid-1981, the picture was again worsening.)

This chapter treats three major topics: (1) the concepts of employment and unemployment; (2) their measurement; and (3) certain ways in which society has sought to control ("minimize") unemployment, whether through public or private approaches. Chapter 12 deals with public alleviative measures, of which unemployment insurance is the most important example.

348

THE NATURE OF UNEMPLOYMENT

The economist has been traditionally concerned with "involuntary" unemployment—the case where, at a give wage level and with a given set of working conditions, there are more job seekers than jobs available. We use this easily understood concept here even though more advanced economic analysis treats the topic in much more complex ways.

Multiple factors are at work in creating such unemployment: first, the impersonal operation of the labor market, reflecting differences between growth-gap or cyclical aggregate demands for, and supplies of, labor; second, labor-market maladjustments illustrated by the more selective though still impersonal factors of frictional or structural unemployment; third, personal factors such as discrimination in hiring practices. We discuss these topics more fully below.

Unemployment is not an easy term to define precisely nor to quantify, either conceptually or empirically, let alone in terms of the above three-fold classification.[1] We have focused on involuntary unemployment, on the basis that voluntary unemployment, by its very definition, has no relevance for the problem of economic insecurity. But, "voluntary" is an elusive term: an individual may be "voluntarily" idle in the sense that search for work has been discouraging and the person has temporarily removed himself or herself from the labor force or in the sense that he or she is only interested in work if a certain type of job comes along. How much of this "involuntary voluntarism" exists is a matter of some debate; estimates for 1970–1980 indicate that if "discouraged workers"—those no longer looking for employment—were counted as unemployed, the unemployment rate would be 15 to 25% higher, depending on the year in question. (If the unemployment rate were 4%, for example, and "discouraged workers" were 25% of that, the "total" unemployment rate would be 5%—an increase of one *percentage point*. We return to this issue below.)

"Partial" employment poses another problem. In 1978 there were 88,880,000 persons "at work," but 21,441,000, or 24.1%, worked fewer than 35 hours per week.[2] Table 11.1 highlights these data. Not all this partial employment has an equivalent unemployment counterpart. Thus, for example, many housewives may be able and may prefer to work only on a part-time basis. To the degree that this is true, productive capacity is expended by any participation in the labor force on their part, and theirs is not involuntary unemployment. However, among these part-time employees there are those who are only "partially" employed and would prefer a longer workweek. In 1978, of the 21, 441,000 part-time workers noted above, one-third desired full-time work.

---

[1] The reader interested in a detailed discussion is referred to *The Measurement and Behavior of Unemployment,* A Report of the National Bureau of Economic Research (Princeton, N.J.: Princeton University Press, 1957).

[2] The number of persons "at work" is smaller than the number "employed," since a fraction of those employed are not at work because of vacations, illness, and so on.

Table 11.1   Persons at Work and Hours Worked, 1978

Number of Hours at Work	Number of Persons (In Thousands)	Percentage Distribution
Total	88,800	100
1–34	24,441	24.1
1–4	792	0.9
5–14	4,065	4.6
15–29	10,541	11.9
30–34	6,043	6.8
35 and over	67,439	75.9
35–39	6,301	7.1
40	36,725	41.3
41 and over	24,413	27.5
Average Hours, total at work	39.0	—
Average Hours, workers on full-time schedules	43.2	—

Source: U.S. Department of Labor, Bureau of Labor Statistics, "Employment and Unemployment During 1978: An Analysis," *Special Labor Force Report 218,* Table 32.

Except for Table 11.2 all other tables in this chapter are based on this source. We have deliberately used 1978, since the unemployment rate was 6%—about midway between the "better and poorer" rates of the 1970s. The reader is urged to think about the differential impacts on various groups and categories as unemployment increases or decreases from this 6% level. All data are for persons 16 years and over. In this and other tables percentage figures may not add to 100 because of rounding off.

"Disguised" unemployment is a further problem that is both conceptually and realistically important, though quantifying it is an extremely difficult task. This type of unemployment occurs when persons are not placed in jobs where their capacities are utilized to the fullest. Such "underunemployment" implies that a norm or standard of employment is not being met. Examples of such underutilization are common: excess numbers of persons in given industries such as agriculture, or in given regions such as the South, who would make a greater contribution to national productivity if labor mobility operated so as to place them elsewhere. Or, in a given company an individual may not be producing to capacity because of imperfections in the placement process. The college graduate driving a taxi is a familiar current stereotype.

As noted earlier, in this chapter we shall be concerned essentially with involuntary and total unemployment. Partial and disguised unemployment will receive some attention, the former in the general discussion on unemployment, the latter in a more special way. However, any detailed analysis of and prescription for disguised unemployment not only raises broad issues of economic policy, but leads to a consideration of education, counseling, placement, and other topics far beyond the scope of this book. Partial unemployment, while involving some specialized characteristics, is of such a nature as to permit more general treatment.

THE MEASUREMENT OF UNEMPLOYMENT: AGGREGATE DATA

Not until 1940 was comprehensive and continuous information available on the extent of unemployment. Census data were available in earlier years in the form of gross figures on those totally unemployed during the census survey week. But these data are not entirely comparable from one census to another, and of course they did not constitute continuous annual series. And, ad hoc surveys, usually not comparable, were made from time to time. Table 11.2 presents information on unemployment starting with the late 1920s: the "labor force" measurements of 1940 were carried back to the 1920s. Particularly noteworthy are the high unemployment rates in the 1930s (the peak rate was 24.9% in 1933) and the relatively high rates in recent years.

The relevant definitions in this labor force conceptual framework are as follows[3]:

1 *Employed.* Employed persons comprise those who during the survey week were either one of the following: (a) "at work"—those who did any work for pay or profit, or worked without pay for 15 hours or more on a family farm or business; or (b) "with a job but not at work"—those who did not work and were not looking for work but who had a job or business from which they were temporarily absent because of vacation, illness, industrial dispute, bad weather, or because they were taking time off for various reasons.

2 *Unemployed.* Unemployed persons include those who during the survey week did either of the following: (a) did not work at all and had looked for work within the past few weeks; or (b) did not work at all and (i) were waiting to be called back from layoff, (ii) were waiting to report for a new job scheduled to begin in the next 30 days, or (iii) would have been looking for work but were temporarily ill.

3 *Labor force.* The civilian labor force comprises the total of all civilians classified as employed or unemployed in accordance with the criteria described above. The total labor force also includes members of the armed forces stationed either in the United States or abroad.

These concepts have been criticized for counting some persons as unemployed who should not be and not counting other persons who should be. For example, it is contended that many workers choose jobs that are seasonal in nature or subject to periodic layoffs. Such jobs sometimes pay high wages and the layoff period is short. Counting people who are waiting to report for a new job within 30 days classifies as unemployed many persons who are not. Treating unemployment among secondary wage earners in the same way as unemployment among primary wage earners has also been criticized as overstating the unemployment

[3]See the U.S. Department of Labor, Bureau of Labor Statistics, "Concepts and Methods Used in Labor Force Statistics," *Report No. 62*, (1979).

Table 11.2 Employment and Unemployment, 1928–1978 (In Thousands)

Year	Total Labor Force Including Armed Forces	Civilian Labor Force Total	Employed	Unemployed Number	Unemployed Percentage
		Persons 14 Years of Age and Over			
1928	47,367	47,105	45,123	1,982	4.2
1930	50,080	49,820	45,480	4,340	8.7
1932	51,250	51,000	38,940	12,060	23.6
1934	52,490	52,230	40,890	11,340	21.7
1936	53,740	53,440	44,410	9,030	16.9
1938	54,950	54,610	44,220	10,390	19.0
1940	56,180	55,640	47,520	8,120	14.6
1942	60,380	56,410	53,750	2,660	4.7
1944	66,040	54,630	53,960	670	1.2
1946	60,970	57,250	55,250	2,270	3.9
		Persons 16 Years of Age and Over			
1948	62,080	60,621	58,344	2,276	3.8
1950	63,858	62,208	58,920	3,288	5.3
1952	65,730	62,138	60,254	1,883	3.0
1954	66,993	63,643	60,110	3,532	5.5
1956	69,409	66,552	63,802	2,750	4.1
1958	70,275	67,639	63,036	4,602	6.8
1960	72,142	69,628	65,778	3,852	5.5
1962	73,442	70,614	66,702	3,911	5.5
1964	75,830	73,091	69,305	3,786	5.2
1966	78,893	75,770	72,895	2,875	3.8
1968	82,272	78,737	75,920	2,817	3.6
1970	85,903	82,715	78,627	4,088	4.9
1972	88,991	86,542	81,702	4,840	5.6
1974	93,240	91,011	85,936	5,076	5.6
1976	96,917	94,773	87,485	7,288	7.7
1978	102,537	100,420	94,373	6,047	6.0
1980	106,821	104,719	97,270	7,448	7.1

Sources: Historical Statistics of the United States: Colonial Times to 1970, Part 1 (Washington, D.C.: U.S. Department of Commerce, Bureau of the Census, 1975), 126–127, 135; and *Employment and Earnings* (Washington, D.C.: U.S. Department of Labor, Bureau of Labor Statistics). Figures for varying years may not correspond exactly with those of previous years because of changes in concepts or measurement techniques. The variations are minor, however.

problem. On the other hand, the present system does not count as unemployed "discouraged workers" who have taken themselves out of the labor force because they do not believe they can ever get a job. Partial unemployment is also ignored.

Another limitation is that the rates are estimates based on a sample of over 56,000 households conducted once each month. The results are therefore subject to sampling errors, particularly for unemployment rates among certain segments of the population. Furthermore, the annual rates are the average of the 12 monthly rates. Consequently, they do not tell how many people were unemployed in a year. To the extent that some of the unemployed in July, say, were not among the unemployed in June, the number of persons unemployed some time during the year is larger than the annual rate indicates.

Over the years numerous changes have been made in the way unemployment is defined and the manner in which data are gathered. The National Commission on Employment and Unemployment Statistics conducted an exhaustive study on how this information might be made more accurate and more useful. Particular emphasis was being placed on improving local estimates, because under many programs federal funds are distributed to localities on the basis of their unemployment rate. The Commission's report, *Counting the Labor Force*, was completed in 1979 and will undoubtedly influence future trends. One basic recommendation was that the "hidden unemployed" (or the "discouraged" workers) should continue to be excluded from the official unemployment count.

Possibly the most basic disagreement over the unemployment "count" and "rate" relates to the purpose for which the data are to be used. One view is that even if the rate is higher today than in, say, 1970, it is because of the unemployment of secondary and tertiary workers in the household. Hence human welfare is not as adversely affected as would be true if "the rate" were for primary breadwinners: "the rate" does not measure hardship. The opposing view is that "the rate" relates to economic performance, and if that rate is "high," performance is not what it could be. (There are also less objective considerations: a "high" rate may trigger in additional unemployment insurance benefits or may provide for additional revenue sharing.) Calculations of rates based upon different labor force characteristics do produce different rates. *But,* whatever the method, the rate structures over time tend to move together. Hence measurement over time is not affected, so that, from this point of view, any rate could be used to get at relative performance.[4]

Data are also available on the proportion of workers covered under unemployment compensation who are receiving benefits. This proportion is considerably less than the unemployment rate because of the eligibility requirements for benefits. State agencies frequently provide local estimates on aggregate or sector unemployment.

---

[4]For a good discussion see Glen G. Cain, "The Unemployment Rate as an Economic Indicator," *Monthly Labor Review,* 102, No. 3 (March 1979), 24–35.

The Measurement of Unemployment: Specialized Data

Unemployment has dimensions other than weekly, monthly, or annual aggregates for the economy. Data—detailed in some cases, fragmentary in others—are available for various of these other dimensions and are discussed below. To a considerable extent these data can be fitted into the previously noted "selective" and "personal" categories of unemployment. A knowledge of these dimensions is important because attempts to deal with unemployment must recognize them. The problem is more complex than merely finding a given number of additional jobs for the economy as a whole.

Unemployment by Regions

Unemployment tends to vary by geographic regions. Such unemployment may result from various causes: resource depletion, changes in demand for the products turned out by industries in the region, natural catastrophes such as floods, and so on. Regional unemployment may persist for relatively long periods, as was the case for textiles in New England or coal mining in West Virginia, or it may be more short lived, as was true for automobiles in Detroit, steel in Pittsburgh, or aerospace industries in Los Angeles and Seattle. Short lived may, however, become longer lived: What is, as of 1980, the future of automobiles in Detroit? Steel in various localities? Readers can undoubtedly provide their own examples. Labor-market area unemployment does differ from one market to another.

Unemployment by Occupation and Industry

Unemployment also varies by occupation and industry. The occupational breakdown in 1978 is shown in Table 11.3.

These differences can be explained by demand and supply and the forces behind them, for example, changing consumer preferences, changing technology, the nature of the occupation and skills it requires, its seasonality, and the "fixed" versus "variable" cost nature of differing vocations, as well as the impacts of foreign competition (witness automobiles and steel in 1980).

Other variations are also found. Thus industrial employment may decrease at a given time, but nonindustrial may increase. Or one may find the construction industry with a high percentage of unemployment, the self-employed with a low, and others in between. In part, the self-employment figures may be misleading, since many of the self-employed may continue in marginal businesses, as their own "bosses," rather than look for employment elsewhere, working for others.

Unemployment by Worker Characteristics

Unemployment varies according to age, race, sex, whether the person is a full-time or part-time worker, and other worker characteristics. Table 11.4 shows how

Table 11.3   Unemployed Persons, by Occupation of Most Recent Job, 1978

Occupation	Persons (In Thousands)	Unemployment Rate (%)
Total, 16 years and over	6,047	6.0
White-collar workers	1,717	3.5
Professional and technical	381	2.6
Managers, officials and proprietors	214	2.1
Clerical workers	256	4.1
Sales workers	866	4.9
Blue-collar workers	2,323	6.9
Crafts and kindred workers	603	4.6
Carpenters and other construction craftsmen	322	7.9
All other	281	3.2
Operatives except transport	960	8.1
Transport equipment operatives	195	5.2
Nonfarm laborers	566	10.7
Construction laborers	172	16.1
All other	394	9.3
Service workers	1,029	7.4
Private household	63	5.1
All other	966	7.6
Farm workers	110	3.8
No previous work experience	868	—
16–19 years	652	—
20–24 years	142	—
25 years and over	73	—

Source: U.S. Department of Labor, Bureau of Labor Statistics, "Employment and Unemployment During 1978: An Analysis," *Special Labor Force Report 218,* Table 11.

unemployment rates varied in 1978 among selected classes of workers. Note that although the aggregate unemployment rate was 6%, nonwhite male teenagers faced a 34.4% rate and females, 38.4%. The psychological, political, and sociological implications of this are obvious: Watts in the 1960s, Miami in 1980.

Unemployment by Reason for Unemployment

Persons may be unemployed because they lost their last job, voluntarily left their last job, have reentered the labor force, or are looking for their first job. According to Table 11.5, in 1978 only 41.5% had "lost" their last job, and of these, one-fourth were on layoff—not terminated. About 14.3% were looking for their first job. Question for the reader: does the voluntary quit rate vary directly or inversely with the unemployment rate?

Table 11.4 Unemployment Rates Among Selected Classes of the Population, 1978

Class	Rate (%)
Total	6.0
Teenagers, 16–19 years	
Male	15.7
Female	17.0
Nonwhite	
Male	10.9
Female	13.1
Nonwhite teenagers, 16–19 years	
Male	34.4
Female	38.4
Married men, spouse present	2.8
Married women, spouse present	5.5
Women who head families	8.5
Full-time workers	5.5
Part-time workers	9.0
Blue-collar workers	6.9

Source: U.S. Department of Labor, Bureau of Labor Statistics, "Employment and Unemployment During 1978: An Analysis," *Special Labor Force Report 218,* Tables 3,8,9,10.

Unemployment by Duration

While short-term unemployment has its adverse consequences, it is the individual who is unemployed for a long time and exhausts the right to unemployment compensation who faces the greatest problems. Fortunately, as Table 11.6 indicates, 46.2% of the unemployed in 1978 were out of a job for less than five weeks. On the other hand, 10.5% were unemployed for over 26 weeks, and the picture was worse for some segments of the population.

Table 11.5 Unemployed Persons, by Reason for Unemployment, 1978

Class	Percentage of Total
Job losers	41.5
On layoff	11.5
Other job losses	30.0
Job leavers	14.1
Reentrants	30.0
New entrants	14.3
Total	100.0

Source: U.S. Department of Labor, Bureau of Labor Statistics, "Employment and Unemployment During 1978: An Analysis," *Special Labor Force Report 218,* Table 13.

Table 11.6 Unemployment Duration, 1978

Duration (weeks)[a]	Percentage of Total
Under 5	46.2
5–14	31.0
15–26	12.3
Over 26	10.5
Total	100.0

Source: U.S. Department of Labor, Bureau of Labor Statistics, "Employment and Unemployment During 1978: An Analysis," *Special Labor Force Report 218,* Table 14.
[a]Average duration was 14.3 weeks.

FULL EMPLOYMENT: CONCEPTS AND HISTORICAL PATTERNS

If one views unemployment, as just discussed, as an indicator of economic malfunction, and if one accepts the maintenance of a high level of employment as a desirable goal of society, then it may be instructive to measure past performance of the economy with this yardstick. A "high level of employment" may, of course, be interpreted in different ways. In turn, the performance record will vary depending on the standard selected.

At one extreme is the criterion of "full employment." Defined in its more rigorous sense the concept has been interpreted as

> . . . having always more vacant jobs than unemployed men . . . [with] the normal lag between losing one job and finding another . . . very short.[5]

A somewhat less rigorous definition, though not necessarily incompatible with the one above, is found in an early United Nations report:

> We define full employment as a situation in which unemployment does not exceed the minimum allowances that must be made for the effects of seasonal and frictional forces.[6]

A yardstick that appears still less exacting was given in the 1953 *Economic Report of the President:*

> . . . it is assumed for purposes of this study that unemployment, which during the past two years has been below the two-million mark, could rise to as much as $2\frac{1}{2}$ million by 1955 without presenting a general unemployment problem. Such an

[5]See William H. Beveridge, *Full Employment in a Free Society* (New York: W. W. Norton, 1945), p. 18. (One could, of course, have more vacant jobs than unemployed "men" if the unemployed lived in the wrong areas or did not possess the requisite skills and so on.)
[6]*National and International Measures for Full Employment* (Lake Success, N.Y.: United Nations, 1949), p. 13.

unemployment figure in a considerably larger labor force would not depart so markedly from the Nation's legislated objectives of "maximum employment" as to call for new counteracting public measures . . ..[7]

Out of a labor force of 68.6 million, $2\frac{1}{2}$ million (the 1955 projection) would amount to an unemployment rate of 3.6%. Various other views of "high-level" unemployment were found in the 1950s and 1960s, ranging up to unemployment levels of 5% or so. (In some cases a range of percentages is used with variations for seasonal and frictional factors.) While 5% was a "popular" figure in the 1950s, 4% was more frequently heard during the Kennedy and Johnson Administrations. This became tempered during the Nixon Administration as inflation pressed hard upon the economy. The Humphrey–Hawkins Act, passed in 1978, set twin goals of 4% unemployment and 3% inflation by 1983 (0% inflation by 1988). Steps taken to reduce inflation, however, are not supposed to impede achievement of the unemployment goal; this may be a pious hope in these days of "stagflation."

If one views "full employment" (or "high-level employment") as involving 4% unemployment, then using the data cited earlier, in 53 of the 80 years in this century to date unemployment has been higher. Moreover, 12 of the years in which unemployment was lower were war years. The last year in which unemployment was 4% or less was in 1969.

With both major political parties committed to some type of full employment policy, it is not likely that we shall see in our lifetime a duplication of the experiences of the 1930s. But the reduction of unemployment is not cost free, particularly if rising prices are viewed as a "cost." To a considerable extent, as we moved along in the 1970s the preoccupation of economists was less with the *definition* of full employment, and much more with trying to approach high-level employment while keeping a rein on inflation. Most economists believe that to achieve full employment today the inflation rate has to be higher than in the past.

The above paragraphs have been retained from earlier editions as they provide a useful historical backdrop. New and challenging analytical developments have taken place since the last edition (1973), and it is to these that we now turn.

The "Phillips Curve" and Unemployment and Inflation

The Phillips Curve was named after the late A. W. Phillips, who first introduced it in 1958.[8]Phillips propounded an inverse relationship between the rate of unem-

---

[7]*The Economic Report of the President* (Washington, D.C.: Government Printing Office, 1953), p. 83.

[8]A. W. Phillips, "The Relation Between Unemployment and the Rate of Change of Money Wage Rates in the United Kingdom, 1962–1957," *Economica*, 25 (November 1958), 283–299. The literature on this topic is so vast that we cannot begin to do it justice here. The best general "reader" on this subject, given our judgment, is Thomas M. Humphrey, *Essays on Inflation* (Richmond, Va.: Federal Reserve Bank of Richmond, 1980). The entire volume is most useful, but here see the two essays under "Inflation and Unemployment."

ployment and the rate of wage price change. The lower the level of unemployment, the greater the increase in wage rates and hence in prices. Phillips did not seek to "define" full employment. But the relationship he developed purportedly offered an array of "trade-offs" (and hence policy choices) between unemployment and inflation.

The relationship Phillips spelled out for the United Kingdom seemed to hold also for the United States in the decade after World War II and into the early 1950s, but shifted outward after that. And in the 1970s the correlation broke down, with scatter points all over the chart.

The "Natural Rate" of Unemployment

This hypothesis, first suggested by Milton Friedman and since expanded by other economists, contends that there is, in effect, a "natural rate of unemployment" for the economy as a whole. In the abstract this is the rate that would be ground out by the economic system as it worked itself out to an equilibrium position.

What this rate is numerically is not specified. That, however, is not the important point. What is relevant, according to the proponents of this point of view is that there exists no permanent trade-off between unemployment and inflation. In the long run, "real" economic variables tend to be independent of "nominal" ones as the system moves toward equilibrium. Under certain conditions, however, a short-run trade-off *may* exist. And, it does no good to set a "target rate" of unemployment as being consonant with "full" employment; the system produces its own "natural" rate.

"Expectations"

The third strand involves new developments involving "expectations": how economic agents view future trends. "Adaptive" expectations can be visualized as a rear-view mirror approach and the use of the "Past" as a basis for predicting the future. The new and challenging concept of "rational" expectations takes a different tack. It postulates that economic agents assimilate and take into account *all* relevant information concerning the future. Hence, except for random shocks, price expectations will always be correct. Given this view, even short-run trade-offs are not possible: economic agents "anticipate" and hence thwart remedial policies.

Tying the Threads Together

What do these three concepts have to do with full employment as previously discussed? The essential points appear to be the following:

1   It is not feasible to talk of full employment in terms of a target rate such as, say, 4%. There is a "natural rate" toward which the economy will inexorably

move. This rate may vary with differing circumstances, but for a given system
it is "fixed."

2   If this is the case, then in the long run there is no trade-off between unemployment and inflation, although in the short run it may exist.

3   Add rational expectations and the short-run trade-off also disappears. Hence
the only way in which economic policy can be used to, say, bring unemployment down is if it "surprises" economic agents. If such agents anticipate the
consequences of policies, they will undertake actions that will nullify or
thwart such policies.

4   One can visualize a Non-Inflationay Unemployment Rate (NIUR)—a rate
that will not sanction wage increases of a magnitude such as to "push" up
costs (and hence prices). Views today suggest that such a rate may be in the
6–7% range.

5   Wage and price controls and income policies are no solution except for
temporary use, as in war periods; experience attests to this. Distortions are
created and when the controls are lifted, the system goes awry.

Where does all this leave us? In one respect it sounds completely fatalistic:
nothing can be done. (This is in contrast to the buoyant enthusiasm of the early
1960s, when it was believed by many that the economy could be "fine tuned" so
as to minimize unemployment with, in turn, only "minimal" price increases.)
While there is no unanimity among economists regarding these new developments, it *is* true that the performance of the U.S. economy in the 1970s was not
one likely to breed optimism as concerns full employment. We still do not have
a good analytical and policy-oriented approach to the problem of "stagflation."

THE IMPACTS OF UNEMPLOYMENT

Thus far we have talked about the nature and dimensions of unemployment
without specifying in any detail why it is an undesirable phenomenon. In one
respect the answer may appear obvious; in others it may be well to be more
specific.

Impacts on the Economy

Unemployment impacts negatively and obviously on the level of economic activity in the national economy, the region, or the locality. (We make no distinction
here as to "cause" and "result.") The experiences of the United States in the
1930s, of various textile mill areas in the North for a longer period, or of the
western "ghost town" historically illustrates this point. The impact on industries
and firms and on other businesses in various areas is also clear, as is the influence
on future supplies of skilled labor. And most apparent is the "foregone produc-

tion" that is forever lost; this is what is emphasized by those who would hold to the construct that provided the "highest" unemployment rate at any given time.

While aggregate unemployment has been less in the last two decades than in earlier periods, selective unemployment persists and has become chronic in some regions. It has been said that unemployment frequently serves a useful "corrective" economic function. This may have a grain of truth to it, but the process is still inherently "cruel" and in many cases of selective unemployment it does *not* provide the necessary adjustment.

Impacts on the Individual and His Family

The direct income loss impacts are obvious. But there are indirect and noneconomic consequences. While it is hard to quantify these impacts, or even estimate their seriousness in some cases, there seems to be little doubt that they are undesirable in nature. In protracted unemployment there appears to be some loss of skill, a worsening of mental outlook, some increase in delinquency and crime, physical debilitation, very frequently of children in the family, and some deterioration of the family unit.[9]

Impacts on Social Institutions

Unemployment reaches beyond the individual, the family, and economic forces to affect society as a whole. It erodes social institutions, changes the direction toward which political parties move, institutes new beliefs and new groups, and realigns the structure of society.[10] Witness the concern in 1980 as to the "political" implications of rising unemployment; witness also the unrest of the minorities most adversely affected by it.

Whether such social changes can be held to be essentially undesirable (as were the impacts on the individual and his family) is a matter of opinion. Certainly, however, unemployment in the past has been an important instrumentality of change. Unemployment may have been, to be sure, only a symptom of deeper-lying causes, yet there is little doubt that it was one of the symbols seized on in

[9] Several useful, though older, sources that discuss this problem are Philip Klein, *The Burden of Unemployment* (New York: Russell Sage Foundation, 1923); Stuart A. Rice, "The Effect of Unemployment upon the Worker and His Family," *Business Cycles and Unemployment* (New York: McGraw-Hill, 1923); and *Men without Work, A Report Made to the Pilgrim Trust* (Cambridge, Mass.: Cambridge University Press, 1938). Areas of interest change, and we have relatively little research of this type today as compared with a quarter-century ago, perhaps because the last big wave of data concerns the physical and mental condition of members of the armed forces in World War II and the relation of such conditions to economic experiences in the post-1929 period. There appears, however, to have been some increase in interest following recent recessions; in the summer of 1980 one could find many articles dealing with the negative psychological aspects of unemployment.

[10] For interesting early analyses, see Robert S. Lynd and Helen M. Lynd, *Middletown in Transition* (New York: Harcourt Brace Jovanovich, 1937); and Frederick Lewis Allen's two books *Only Yesterday* and *Since Yesterday* (New York: Harper and Row, 1931 and 1939, respectively).

the pressures of social change: look only for an example in the Franklin D. Roosevelt days.

"TYPES" AND "CAUSES" OF UNEMPLOYMENT

In order to analyze policies and programs designed to combat unemployment it is necessary to look at "types" of employment and "causal" factors involved in the phenomenon.

A useful classification system for this purpose is the following[11]:

	Long Term	Short Term
Inadequate demand	"Growth-gap" unemployment	Cyclical unemployment
Labor-market maladjustment	Structural unemployment	Frictional unemployment

Let us look at each of these in turn.

Growth-gap unemployment can be visualized in two ways. First, the economy simply does not grow at a rate sufficient to absorb all those (new entrants, reentrants) who want jobs. Why it does not is a complex question that is beyond the scope of our competence and hence our discussion. But, as a "fact" it exists. Second, while the "gap" can be viewed in annual terms, it is essentially a secular (long-run) concept.

Cyclical unemployment can be superimposed upon the growth-gap version. The economy *does* grow, but in the process—as time passes—one gets cycles of prosperity and depression. And in a depression (or even in a milder version, a recession) the level of economic activity falls and unemployment increases.

Frictional unemployment is a kind of "residual" unemployment. Unless all persons were locked into a job, it is bound to exist. For example, it takes time (and effort) to find a job. This is true for a new entrant, a reentrant, and one who has quit a job to look for a new one, or, similarly, one who has been discharged. Until the new job is located, unemployment exists for the individual. "Job search" takes time; a whole new body of analysis has developed around "search theory." "Seasonal" unemployment is frequently regarded as an "extended" type of frictional unemployment. Other "irregularities" are also customarily included under the frictional umbrella.

Structural unemployment is a newer concept as concerns types or causes. It first surfaced as a major issue in the early 1960s, during the debate over whether the major cause of unemployment at that time was a structural matter or resulted from a deficiency of aggregate demand. (It has been generally concluded that the

[11]Adapted from Eleanor Gilpatrick, "On the Classification of Unemployment: a View of the Structural-Inadequate Demand Debate," *Industrial and Labor Relations Review,* 19, No. 2 (January 1966), 201–212.

structuralists lost the debate.) This type of unemployment can result from a number of causal factors. Three examples may suffice as illustrations. Consumer tastes change, a given product goes out of favor, and the company shuts down. Workers from that company—particularly older ones—with specialized skills and living in a given area may find it very difficult to find another job elsewhere. Or significant technological change takes place and given workers find that they are technologically obsolete. Again unemployment is the result. Workers here may well not be "between" jobs—hence the long-run aspect. A third variant arises in cases where a natural disaster, or imports, or the closing of a government base (to cite but three examples) adversely effects employment in an area or industry. This is a somewhat specialized application of the structural type.

We may add to the above another variant that is relevant in terms of "causes" —unemployment that results from "personal" factors. On the demand side, employers may discriminate against certain groups. If this is widespread, members of these groups may find it very difficult to secure employment. On the supply side, given individuals may not possess marketable skills (for a variety of reasons, such as deficient education), may have poor work habits, and so on. Again, except in very tight labor markets where employers are desperate for employees, unemployment is the consequence.

APPROACHES TO THE PROBLEM OF UNEMPLOYMENT

Until the Great Depression individuals were generally forced to bear the economic consequences of unemployment themselves. Indeed, the prevailing public attitude was that, except during serious depressions, it was the worker's fault if he or she became unemployed. If the person's resources were not sufficient for support during the period of unemployment, he or she could in most cases turn only to friends or relatives for support. Other sources that aided some of the unemployed were (1) private charities, (2) local public relief, and (3) (very limited) private employee-benefit plans.

The Great Depression changed attitudes toward unemployment significantly and stimulated the development of new and improved alleviative measures. Other approaches have been developed since that time. In this chapter we shall concern ourselves essentially with noninsurance public policy measures and, briefly, private approaches, reserving for Chapter 12 a discussion of the chief public alleviative measure (unemployment insurance). We will discuss public policy measures in terms of the previously outlined diagram of the "types" of unemployment.

Inadequate Demand: Growth-Gap Unemployment

As noted previously, this is a long-run phenomenon: the economy does not grow "rapidly" enough to provide jobs for all the members of the growing population who want them. If one refers back to Table 11.2, one finds in the quarter-century between 1954 and 1978 that there were 34,260,000 more people employed in the latter year; in effect, economic growth had generated that many "new" jobs. Yet there were $2\frac{1}{2}$ million more *un*employed in 1978 than in 1954.

Why? Why did the economy not grow "sufficiently" so as to provide sufficient additional job opportunities to take up this slack? Note, however, that the unemployment rate in 1978 was only one-half of a percentage point greater than in 1954. Hence one could say that on a relative basis the "slack" was no greater in the latter year. This is of little comfort to those unemployed. And it does not indicate optimal performance for the economy as a whole.

We (at least the authors) do not know the answer to this growth rate question.[12] Historically it simply seems to be the case that growth *has* provided jobs, but there is always a "residue" of unemployed over and above cyclical, frictional, and structural levels; this is the growth-gap element of unemployment.

With the relatively poor growth performance of the United States in recent years, new attention is being paid to this problem. The following are views proposed of late to accelerate growth, though they hardly merit claim to any kind of synthesized growth theory.

1   Increasing the rate of savings in the economy so that investment in plant and equipment can also be increased. This, it is suggested, would increase employment, yield improvements in output and hence from "supply-side economics" help control inflation, and in general make for more efficient production. (Comparisons are frequently made between the United States, West Germany, and Japan: the latter two economies, with much higher savings rates, are performing much better.)

2   Increasing investment incentives by methods such as investment tax credits, accelerated depreciation, and lower capital gains taxes.

3   Increasing the emphasis on research and development, which would in turn increase the efficiency of production.[13]

4   Utilizing a higher degree of worker participation so as to enhance productivity.

In the 1930s "growth" was an important issue: Keynesian economics attest to this. Since World War II much more attention has been devoted to the "cycle"

[12]For a very useful "empirical" analysis see Edward F. Denison, *Accounting for United States Economic Growth 1929–1969* (Washington, D.C.: Brookings Institution, 1974). See also the U.S. Department of Labor, Bureau of Labor Statistics, "Patterns of U.S. Economic Growth," *Bulletin 1672* (Washington, D.C.: U.S. Government Printing Office, 1970). This interesting bulletin (with useful bibliographies) develops 1980 projections for final demand, output, employment and so on. It also illustrates the pitfalls of projections: labor force, employment, unemployment figures, for example, are quite wide of 1980 realities.

[13]As an example at the industry level see *The Wall Street Journal,* July 2, 1980, p. 8, where the headline reads, "Study Urges Steelmakers to De-Emphasize Dividends, Increase Research Spending." The article cited a study showing that steel would be increasingly vulnerable to foreign competition unless, among other things, it changed its attitude toward research.

and its impacts on the economy and employment. But in the 1980s we are likely to reemphasize growth, and "supply-side" economics may well turn out to be one of the major thrusts.

Inadequate Demand: Cyclical Unemployment

As we have already noted, along a growth line prosperity and depression (or recession) are superimposed. Hence there is a cycle of ups and downs, and in the latter phase unemployment increases. Most of our attention for the last 35 years (and, indeed, prior to 1929) has focused on this cycle and particularly depressions: causes and cures.

Two questions are relevant in addressing the issue of cyclical unemployment:

1 At what point does the level of unemployment come to be viewed as "critical"? That is, critical in the sense that specific measures are taken to combat it. In part this appears to be a political matter: one can hardly view an administration as being indifferent to unemployment in an election year. But unemployment increasingly has an economic (and another political) component: if remedial measures are undertaken, what might be their impact on the price level? The politician today has no easy set of answers; to reduce unemployment may imply increasing inflation.

2 If the decision is made to introduce measures designed to lessen unemployment, what types of programs are available? What type should be used? They generally fall into two categories: (a) "automatic" devices, wherein a lowering of economic activity (and hence an increase in unemployment) calls forth its own compensatory actions; and (2) discretionary and consciously planned measures.[14]

Automatic Stabilizers

The first category of devices noted above includes what have come to be called "built-in stabilizers." A number of these are presently existent in the economy, some linked directly to employment, others not. Among the principal stabilizers are the following.

Unemployment Insurance and Other Welfare Payments

An increase in unemployment does not curtail purchasing power by an equivalent amount, because unemployment insurance shores up in part the purchasing power of the covered unemployed. This program is planned to be countercyclical in nature, collecting more (less) in taxes than is paid out in benefits in prosperous

[14]For a useful discussion see the article in *Policies to Combat Depression,* a Report of the National Bureau of Economic Research (Princeton, N. J.: Princeton University Press, 1956).

(unprosperous) times. (The program may not turn out to be entirely countercyclical, insofar as "experience rating" modifies this characteristic.) Other transfer payments, such as public assistance, play an important role.[15]

Graduated Income Tax

Under the present tax structure a given increase (decrease) in income occasions a greater (less) than proportional increase in tax receipts. Thus, as economic activity lessens and incomes decrease, the income tax decreases more than proportionately. With given consumption patterns, this stabilizer also is countercyclical. By the 1980s, however, as inflation moved nominal incomes continually upward—and into higher tax brackets—this flexibility (in a downward sense) was more apparent than real.

Other Measures

Other types of built-in stabilizers include farm-aid programs, in which compensatory payments tend to move in direction opposite to that of the cycle, and corporate and family savings, which tend to exhibit the same tendency (although this latter phenomenon has been erratic in the 1970s).

While these built-in stabilizers are of some countercyclical importance, they do not, for obvious reasons, replace all of the purchasing power lost. Furthermore, as a specific example, unemployment insurance benefits may be exhausted. Finally, in the same way as automatic stabilizers tend to check rising unemployment rates, they may retard recovery in various ways.

Consciously Implemented Programs

The two most important consciously planned actions are public works and monetary and fiscal policies.

Public Works

As countercyclical devices, public works have been exhaustively analyzed, discussed, and utilized.[16] It will be useful, however, to comment briefly on such measures even though their use is much more limited today than it was a generation or two ago.

[15]For an excellent discussion of built-in economic security stabilizers see Ida C. Merriam, "Social Security Programs and Economic Stability," *Policies To Combat Depression,* a Report of the National Bureau of Economic Research (Princeton, N.J.: Princeton University Press, 1956).

[16]For useful summaries of public works in the 1930s, see Arthur D. Gayer, *Public Works in Prosperity and Depression* (New York: National Bureau of Economic Research, 1935); and J. M. Clark, *Economics of Planning Public Works* (Washington, D.C.: Government Printing Office, 1935). The Public Works Acceleration Act of 1962 provides an example of the use of this technique. In the early 1970s discussion continued on the use of "public" works and "public" jobs to combat high levels of unemployment. By the 1980s less and less was heard of the "public" work aspect of this dual approach.

The rationale of the public works approach is simple. Since various public projects—roads, airports, dams, office buildings, schools—must be undertaken from time to time, why not undertake such projects (or the majority of them) when the economy is operating below capacity? Two purposes would be served by such an approach: first, "excessive" construction, adding fuel to the flames, would be avoided in prosperous times; second, the economy would be shored up by the introduction of such construction in depressed times.

Various problems are raised by such an approach. One is planning. For the system to be sound there should be advance planning, so that construction undertaken returns the greatest possible yield per dollar of investment. On this basis "useful" projects are preferable to those that merely seek to get money into circulation. This in turn implies that the program should not seek to maximize direct employment at the expense of efficiency, and, conversely, that public works employees should be regarded as bona fide workers, not as relief clients, and should be paid going wages. And planning is not easy: when is the next recession due?

Another problem is timing. The public cannot postpone all projects indefinitely. Construction may have to be undertaken in prosperous times, defeating in part the countercyclical process. The school-building program since World War II illustrates this point. Again, while it is not likely that the public will "run out" of projects, some problems of this type might develop locally. Hence again advance planning is required. Still another difficulty is deciding not only when to turn them on, but also when to turn them off. Turning them on may be easier than turning them off; thus, if a "critical point" of $x\%$ unemployed is reached, a program may be set in motion. But since projects require a definite construction period, it may not be so easy to curtail the program if and when unemployment falls to the point where labor markets are tight.

Also, such projects may be of limited usefulness at the local level if they are financed and administered essentially at that level. One study concluded that even if state and local public works programs had been stabilized to the greatest degree practicable in the period 1920–1939, they would have changed the gross national product in the average year by only a fraction of 1%.[17] The study further raised serious doubts as to the potency of timed public works for alleviating the consequences of cyclical contractions. But it was also noted that if federal money were made available on a sufficient scale, 25% of the unemployment slack could be taken up by public works. Hence there is a useful role to be played by such programs, though they may not be the primary measures they were once thought to be.

---

[17] See W. E. Upjohn Institute for Community Research, *Public Works and Employment From the Local Government Point of View* (Chicago, Ill.: Public Administration Service, 1955). A critical reader of the first edition of our text wondered why local dollars are of any less value than federal dollars. They are not; it is just that there are so many more of the latter.

Monetary and Fiscal Policy

The two major tools used to expand the aggregate demand for labor and thus reduce aggregate unemployment are monetary policy and fiscal policy. Monetary policy is implemented by the Federal Reserve Board. If the Board wishes to stimulate demand, it can expand the money supply through various techniques. The Board can reduce the reserves that banks must maintain in Federal Reserve Banks or in cash in their own vaults to support a given volume of loans; it can reduce the rate banks must pay to borrow money from the Federal Reserve banks, and it can buy government bonds in the open market, thus raising their prices and lowering interest rates.

Fiscal policy is determined by Congress, often acting on recommendations by the President. To stimulate the economy Congress can reduce taxes, thus encouraging more private consumption and investment, and increase government spending, even though this may create a deficit in the federal budget. The 1979–1980 policies of the "Fed" and Congress highlight such approaches and attendant problems; they also illustrate the "politics" of political economy.

Some economists favor monetary policy; others favor fiscal policy. Both policies have worked at times, but both have their limitations. (And, there are serious differences today between the monetarists—the Friedmanites—and the fiscalists—the Hellerites.) First, the two may sometimes work at cross-purposes, expansionary fiscal policies leading to more government borrowing and higher interest rates, which may make a monetary policy more difficult. As noted earlier, most economists believe that expansionary policies are almost certain to raise prices and that to achieve full employment today the inflation rate has to be higher than it was in the past. Since our economy is so large and complex, the nature and timing of the effects of expansionary policies cannot be predicted with precision. And, given newly developing theories of "expectations," many economists conclude that such policies will be successful only if they "surprise" economic agents. If such policies are "anticipated" in terms of their inflationary thrust, economic agents will undertake measures that will, in effect nullify the intent of the policies. Finally, these policies may affect some sectors of the economy more than others. For example, low interest rates may stimulate the construction industry more than most others. (Or, as in 1980–1981, high interest rates will seriously and adversely affect the same industry.) Despite these limitations, however, these policies remain important weapons in the fight against aggregate unemployment, though their "magic" is more controversial than it was a decade ago.

Until the last decade most policies that focused on a deficiency of aggregate demand (as it related to unemployment) made relatively little distinction between growth-gap and cyclical cases. Currently, however, attention is being directed separately to both variants.

Frictional Unemployment

The two categories of unemployment noted above tend to be impersonal in nature, in that they deal essentially with "numbers." But the labor market functions in a personal way: individuals try to get their first jobs, individuals become unemployed, given employers offer jobs, and so on. And in order for individuals to know of jobs and facts about them, and for employers to know of job applicants, it is necessary that the labor market maximize its flow of information. In providing such a two-way flow of information the labor market not only makes it easier to secure the first job but also facilitates the individual employment readjustments necessitated by both aggregate and selective unemployment. This labor-market procedure may be developed in two ways: first, by "structuring" an unstructured market and, second, by increasing the flow of information in a structured market.

An unstructured labor market may be viewed as one in which the only "link" is cash.[18] Structuring introduces other considerations into the market: occupational groupings, attachments to employers of given types of employees and vice versa, developing a flow of information about the job market, using rational techniques in job marketing. While certain of these structural characteristics impose restraints on the market, others help improve its operation. The entry of a union may assist in structuring a labor market through the introduction of job classes, wage "rationalization," information on job availability, and other procedures.

The employment exchange or service is the major mechanism by means of which the structured market increases the flow of information. Information and job search analysis, as related to this problem, is currently the subject of considerable research in the field of labor economics. In the United States two principal types of agencies, the private and public employment services, are found. While private employment agencies have had a checkered past, public regulation has been imposed, and many of them today perform a useful function, bringing together job offerers and job seekers in clerical, secretarial, professional, and other fields. Many employers and unions have maintained various employment services: the hiring hall, preferential hiring, and maintenance of job opportunity lists. Some such methods may be discriminatory, as in the case of the preferential treatment given union members; it is probable that the net result has been to increase the structured operation of the labor market.

Although the public employment service approach has a history dating back at least to the early 1900s, it was not until 1933, with the passage of the Wagner–Peyser Act, that the system was fully formalized. This act set up a federal–state system of public employment offices, the purposes of which were to structure the

[18] For a more sophisticated treatment, see Clark Kerr, "The Balkanization of Labor Markets," *Labor Mobility and Economic Opportunity* (Cambridge, Mass.: Technology Press, 1954), particularly p. 95.

labor markets and to bring together those seeking and those offering jobs.[19] The system was federalized in 1942 as part of the war manpower program and was returned to the states shortly after 1945.

The employment service performs a number of functions, including (1) seeking to match workers and jobs through the local employment service office, (2) acting as a service arm of the unemployment insurance system in that those who have applied for unemployment insurance are required to register at such an office, and (3) performing broader service functions such as providing counseling and testing services and making labor-market surveys.

The employment service is thus, in a major way, a meeting place for buyers and sellers. An unemployed individual may register for work. An employer may list job openings, specifying in some detail relevant job information. When a job request is received, the employment service provides a referral service by sending applicants to the job. There is no pressure on the individual to accept the job (except the implicit incentive that exists in the case of an applicant drawing unemployment insurance).

The role of the public employment service has become increasingly important in the United States. Not only has the abstract objective of increasing the efficiency of labor markets been influenced, but the concrete goal of job placements has increased annually. The employment service operates under a number of difficulties: the frequent use of the service by "marginal" employers and employees, the problem of securing all the relevant information about jobs and applicants, pressures from both job seekers and job offerers who each want "something better," and the stigma of a political operation. While the quality and quantity of results vary from one state to another, it may be generally said that the service has tended to be increasingly accepted by employers and applicants, that it has become more effective in placement operations, particularly in the blue-collar job category, and that it has had a positive effect in increasing the rational economic operation of the labor market. It still has a way to go, however, before its operation can be called "optimal," however this term is defined.

The Manpower Services Act of 1966 was a step in the direction of improving the service. Among other things, it provided for a network of multi-job-market clearance centers, better trained counselors, and labor-market forecasting. Its purpose was to aid job hunters at all occupational levels. Additional developments of various types have occurred since then; the accomplishments on a cost benefit basis are, however, not easily calculated.

Structural Unemployment

This type of unemployment is customarily classified under the "Labor-Market Maladjustment" heading. There is logic to this, although it may verge on "selective" aggregate unemployment. And it is also true that a healthy economy with

[19]For a general summary see William Haber, "The U.S. Employment Service in a Changing Economy," *Studies in Unemployment,* prepared for the Senate Special Committee on Unemployment, Eugene J. McCarthy, Chairman (Washington, D.C.: U.S. Government Printing Office, 1960).

a high level of employment (and hence job opportunities) would help reduce the problem.

As noted previously, this type of unemployment can be illustrated in a variety of ways; the three examples noted previously should suffice. One is the case of the worker whose skills have become obsolete. Another involves employees "immobilized" in areas where the impacts of changing demand patterns have left their mark. The shutdowns of automobile assembly plants and steel mills in 1980 exemplify this.

There are two major approaches to this type of unemployment. One is "retooling" the worker, preparing him or her for other occupations. This technique operates on the labor supply side. The other is shoring up demand for the products of a "disadvantaged" industry; here the focus runs from product demand through to labor demand.

Retraining and Relocation Approaches

One major retooling approach to this type of unemployment has been through retraining as exemplified by the earlier Manpower Redevelopment and Training Act and the current Comprehensive Employment and Training Act (discussed below). (In contrast, however, to various European countries, "mobility allowances" as another technique designed to relocate displaced employees have not been used extensively in the United States. This is true at the public policy level, although many private employers do assist employees in relocating geographically if a plant is shut down.)

For the older worker, however, such unemployment may well be a haunting experience; getting prematurely thrown on the "industrial heap" is all too frequently the outcome. Frictional unemployment is short run; structural unemployment may not only be prolonged but, as the last sentence notes, "permanent."

The leading current example of the training or retraining approach is the Comprehensive Employment and Training Act (CETA) of 1973. Until drastically reduced in 1981, the Act also provided public service employment for the long-term structurally unemployed. Authorized employment and training services included, but were not limited to, job search assistance, skill training, on-the-job training, work experience, and supportive services. To be eligible for these programs a person had to be (1) on or eligible for welfare or from a family with an income below the Bureau of Labor Statistics' lower living standard and (2) unemployed, underemployed, or in school.

However, the program also provided occupational upgrading and retraining programs for employed persons. The public service employment, which was targeted at the entry level, was combined with training and designed to lead to regular employment and was usually provided by local governments using federal funds in accordance with a master plan approved by the federal government. The private sector, however, also participated. The eligibility requirements were tighter for public service employment than for training. To be eligible for public service employment the person had to be either on welfare or unemployed for at least 15 weeks and be from a low-income family. In this respect CETA was a program designed also to tackle "personal" unemployment, discussed below.

CETA also authorized programs for special groups, some of which existed previously. Examples are the following: services to Indians, migrant workers, veterans, the handicapped, older workers, offenders, and persons with limited English-speaking ability; the Job Corps for youths; and the Young Adult Conservation Corps.

A new program added in 1978 stated the intent of Congress to deal with countercyclical unemployment as well as other types of unemployment. The goal was to provide temporary jobs equal in number to one-fifth of the number of unemployed in excess of 4% of the work force; if the unemployment rate exceeded 7%, however, the one-fifth rose to one-fourth. Eligibility was limited to persons unemployed for at least 10 of the preceding 12 weeks and those from families with incomes at or below 100% of the Bureau of Labor Statistics lower living standard. Whereas specific funding was provided for the structural unemployment programs, the funding of the other specific programs was left open.

CETA had been severely criticized prior to its 1978 extension. Widespread misuse of funds, patronage, and waste in public service jobs were the principal concerns as well as the ineffectiveness of some of the training and the long-term employment of some persons on CETA payrolls. The 1978 amendments gave the Labor Department increased authority to find and root out corruption, prohibited the use of funds to support jobs that the local governments would have ordinarily financed themselves, limited the time for which individuals could hold public service jobs and the wages they could receive, and restricted participation to the economically disadvantaged and unemployed. Under the Omnibus Budget Reconciliation Act of 1981 Congress abolished the public service job program and reduced drastically the funds available for other CETA programs.

"Demand"-Oriented Approaches

Employment in geographic areas, industries, and, in some cases, occupations may be adversely effected by natural disasters (drought, floods, volcanic eruptions), import competition, government action (as in closing military bases), and a variety of other factors. The result may be what is frequently considered a variant of structural unemployment.

There are a number of methods by which this selective type of structural unemployment can be attacked. First, employers and unions can seek to anticipate and adjust to changes in demand for a given product or service; assist in readjustment where plant shutdowns and/or job severance is involved, to rationally plan the introduction of new equipment, and develop employment and wage guarantees where feasible. All these private methods are discussed later in this chapter. The private sector frequently cannot successfully combat such unemployment: the magnitude of the problem is simply too great. Hence it may be necessary for the government to step in; among its methods are the following.

Allocation of Government Defense or Other Contracts

If a labor-market area is classed as an excess labor supply area and if it has certain types of productive facilities, the government may specifically allocate contracts to it, and indeed this approach has been used at various times. The usefulness of this method in reducing selective pockets of unemployment is obvious. The danger is that it may simply become a political pressure issue with all the attendant consequences. This is pointedly illustrated in a converse situation: the closing of certain Army and Navy installations. News of defense contract awards or installation closings or other factors affecting regional or local employment can be found daily.

Nonemergency "Financial" Relief Afforded to Industries or Regions

The following mechanisms come to mind: stockpiling programs; accelerated depreciation allowances as for defense industries; changes in credit terms as for housing, automobiles, and home appliance producers; direct subsidies for various industries, such as shipbuilding; tariff changes, as for the watchmaking and bicycle industries; and so on. The current Federal Trade Adjustment Assistance Program is a good example of a specific public policy. It provides "assistance money" to workers who lose their livelihood because of foreign competition resulting from liberalized U.S. trade policy. These selective measures may be disadvantagious to specific consumers (such as by "increased" taxes to make the above-noted payments to displaced workers disadvantaged by foreign competition), but there is a benefit (to the displaced worker) along with the tax "cost."[20]

Direct Emergency Assistance

In the case of natural or other disasters—droughts, floods, hurricanes, tornadoes —government agencies may seek to assist the restoration of business activity (and employment) by direct loans, emergency grants, and similar measures. Drought —and disaster—areas and federal assistance in 1980 illustrate this.

Relief and Reclamation of Depressed Areas

Both public and private bodies have developed various types of depressed-area proposals.[21]

---

[20]In 1980 the U.S. auto industry suffered a marked slacking off of demand. In some cases assembly plants were permanently closed, and layoffs were sizable (more than 250,000). *The Wall Street Journal* (July 9, 1980, p. 6) took note of President Carter's program to help that industry; this program eased emission standards, temporarily halted major vehicle safety rules, and speeded up depreciation, among other aids. How much this will ease the impact of foreign competition remains to be seen at this date.

[21]See the various *Economic Reports of the President;* many of those issued to date are valuable sources of information on this topic.

The Government as Employer of Last Resort

There is no single integrated program of this type at either the federal or state level. But there is a multiplicity of specific "client-oriented" programs usually involving federal funding, with some state and local financing, and, in general, state and local administration. Given the nature of the clientele, such programs are more usefully discussed under "personal" unemployment and are treated below.

The advantages of all the above procedures are obvious. The dangers are twofold. First, government assistance may be based primarily on partisan political considerations. Second, the assistance may perpetuate an already uneconomical situation. Thus governmental measures to maintain farm employment opportunities would be open to serious debate, since one of the logical solutions of this problem in the past has been increasing mobility *from* the farm. Yet these measures can assist in minimizing the readjustment problems associated with selective unemployment.

Let us make one side note in conclusion here. Much is made these days of cost benefit analysis, a very useful technique. Even granted difficulties in application, we would like to see greater application of it with respect to the various approaches noted above.

"Personal" Unemployment

This topic is discussed in greater detail in Chapter 14. But a brief comment may be made here. One note at the outset: all unemployment is "personal" in the sense that it is the "individual" who is without a job (irrespective of the fact that the effects of joblessness may spread to others, such as the family). We do not focus on this obvious characteristic, but rather on the "hard to employ" (the hard-core jobless), who find it difficult to obtain gainful work for whatever reason. Revenue sharing may be envisaged as a "job-producing" program.

On the labor demand side "discrimination" (for whatever reason) is one of the most prevalent factors "causing" unemployment (or underemployment) for various categories of individuals. Public approaches are the only tenable "preventive" method. Such approaches take the form of statutes involving specific civil rights and equal employment opportunity legislation. Private employer compliance is found in such phrases as "affirmative action employer." But securing compliance and invoking enforcement is a horrendously complex matter: witness the many test cases that have proceeded through judicial channels to the U.S. Supreme Court. And the end is nowhere in sight.

On the demand side also, one recurring proposal suggests making the government the employer of last resort. There is no single integrated program here akin to, say, the Fair Labor Standards Act and minimum wages, but there are many specific client-oriented programs that do provide employment, in particular when that employment is combined with job preparation and training of one type or another. These are discussed next.

On the supply side individuals may be unemployed (or even unemployable) because of lack of skill, poor work habits, inability to secure transportation and so on. While the government has not adopted a comprehensive program to provide jobs for those, say, out of work because of a recession, it has developed many specific programs combining work with training. A comprehensive list and description of these would take up a chapter in itself, but some of the better known programs would include the following. CETA has already been discussed. For youth one finds the Job Corps and Summer Job Programs for Youth. For women, particularly those with children, who may be on welfare there is the Work Equity Program (WEP) and the Work Incentive Program (WIN). Cost benefit studies of such programs have generally shown positive results, although a hardheaded critic might question the study techniques utilized.

In addition, there are many programs that seek to assist in youth education of various types so as to inculcate traits which will make employment at a later date easier to obtain.

AN EVALUATION

Major strides have been made in the United States in the last 40 years in the identification and measurement of employment and unemployment. While a critic might not necessarily agree that the labor force concept and the currently used definitions of employment and unemployment are the most economically useful, this approach is a great improvement over that a half-century ago; and it is likely that continuing improvements will be made, increasing the accuracy of concepts and measurement.

The approach to the unemployment problem increasingly requires a concurrent approach to the inflationary pressures that may be generated by "full-employment" policies. The American economy became so deflationary conscious during the 1930s and 1940s that it may well be that the opposite possibility is the greater future threat. There may be more truth than sophistry to the "Uneasy Triangle" argument that a society can have *no more* than any *two* of the following three objectives: free collective bargaining, full employment, and stable prices.[22] In the last three decades we have chosen the first two, and the burden has fallen on those whose incomes did not rise as fast as the average increase in prices. If the recent past presages the future, then the possibility of high unemployment with double-digit inflation may pose a real dilemma.

All the techniques we have examined here—monetary and fiscal policies, public works, selective emergency measures, and employment exchanges—seem capable of performing useful, if sometimes limited, roles in the control of unemployment. In general, the performance record has been good where these policies

[22]See "The Uneasy Triangle" in *The Economist,* issues of August 9, 16, 23, 1952, 322–323, 376–378, and 434–435, respectively. This trilogy was propounded earlier in this country by C. O. Hardy. For skepticism about its validity, see the paper by Milton Friedman in *The Impact of the Union,* edited by D. McC. Wright (New York: Harcourt Brace Jovanovich, 1951), particularly pp. 226ff.

have been applied, including even the emergency "alphabet" agencies of the New Deal. But there seems to be little doubt that some measures may produce undesirable economic consequences. Thus measures to prevent "high-level" unemployment may lead to accelerating inflation. Emergency measures designed to reduce unemployment in critical areas may be successful, but they may also perpetuate uneconomic situations instead of, say, encouraging the labor mobility necessary to rectify the situation.

In conclusion, the unemployment–inflation problem increasingly appears to be one of delicate balance. There is no necessary guarantee that the market mechanism will automatically achieve and maintain this balance for society. And if the government, broadly defined, seeks to assist in maintaining equilibrium, it has powerful tools at its command, but it also has several pressing problems. First, it may well have to make some hard choices with respect to the alternatives that are open to society, namely, free collective bargaining, full employment, and stable prices. Second, it must administer its policies so as to achieve the alternative it selects. This requires establishing criteria of various "levels" of employment, securing a continuous flow of information thereon, choosing the correct policy, and timing the actions carefully; and if we accept the rational expectations view, it will require much good fortune. Given this, the best we can probably hope for is achievement within a limited range. There is little doubt that we can avoid the debacle of the 1930s. But, given a dash of wisdom and a little courage, and perhaps considerable luck, we should be able to avoid the opposite extreme.

PRIVATE APPROACHES TO UNEMPLOYMENT

Private approaches to unemployment, although limited in their potential, are no less important today than they were in the first four editions of this text. But such approaches currently appear to have a lower profile; there is much less of a focus, for example, on guaranteed employment plans than was the case a decade or two ago.

It is difficult to discern the reasons for this shift. In part it appears to result from the continued belief of employers in many industries—for example, automobiles, housing, and steel—that the preventive approach, employment stability, is beyond their control. In part it also seems true that employers have become somewhat more sophisticated and, where possible, implicitly seek to utilize stabilization methods. On the alleviative side, programs such as Supplementary Unemployment Benefits, discussed below, have not exhibited any growth in the last decade or two.

Preventive Approaches

Conceptually, such programs are easily described: employers simply operate their businesses so as to minimize the possibility of severing employees from the work force for economic reasons. "Employment stabilization" is a term frequently used to describe such programs. This approach is more feasible when seasonal factors are involved; in cyclical or secular cases the situation tends to be well beyond the control of a given firm.

Employment stabilization requires a multiple attack on the factors contributing to instability. From the product–production side the employer can utilize various techniques such as the following: developing multiple product lines (such as coal and ice as an often used older example) to minimize seasonal variations; producing for stock is another method. Technology may play an important role: in construction techniques have been developed so as to permit year-round activity. No longer is it necessarily the case that work shuts down for winter months in cold climes. In marketing the firm may work out arrangements with its customers to regularize deliveries, thus avoiding production peaks and valleys with attendant employment problems.

Personnel administration techniques—in the area of manpower planning—are useful. Instead of a work force surplus or shortage pattern, a more rational use of manpower can help considerably. Interesting and relatively recent developments in labor-market analysis have produced new insights in this area. Many types of firms are visualized as having skill-specific jobs peculiar to those firms. Training for such jobs is of the on-the-job variety, with the employer bearing the major costs. The employer thus has an investment in his employees; he does not desire a turnover pattern that requires the continuous training of new workers. In the language of this newer analysis there is an "implicit contract" between employer and employee; one economist has characterized it as the "invisible handshake."[23]

Such contracts are formally viewed today as extending essentially to wages, hours, and working conditions rather than to employment guarantees. But implicitly the guarantee may also extend, insofar as feasible, to employment. No employer wishes to have an image that turns away applicants or causes him to lose valuable workers. Hence the contract "buys" a type of employee loyalty that has considerable value in tight labor markets. It is presumed to enhance employee morale, which reflects itself in many ways, not the least of which is improved productivity.

No hard data are available as to the extent and consequences of such contracts. One suggested consequence of this practice is that it, of necessity, makes wages rigid downwards. If employers are viewed as behaving in their best self-interest, widespread use of such contracts must certainly be the case, resulting wage rigidities or not. The times are not what they used to be: who among you readers has ever taken a wage cut?

Yet, as the year 1980 indicated, underlying forces may be so powerful that the

---

[23]For a good account see Arthur M. Okun, "The Invisible Handshake and the Inflationary Process," *Challenge*, 22, No. 6 (January–February 1980), 5–12. "Implicit contracts"—for which the "Invisible Handshake" is another name—are the subject of considerable current labor economics research.

employer cannot maintain work force stability, desire it though he might. The permanent closing of selected assembly plants in the automobile industry or of mills in the steel industry attest to this. (How much this problem was a result of employer "mistakes," and how much from "outside factors" such as imports, is an issue not readily quantified.) One result, however, has been the increased ethical conviction that sufficient advance notice should be given to affected employees in such cases. Unlike various Western European economies, the United States does not have formalized "redundancy" programs.

In some cases stabilization may lead to a situation in which the employer is willing to institute wage and/or employment guarantees. The Procter & Gamble, Hormel, and Nunn-Bush plans provide examples.[24] For whatever reason or reasons, emphasis has shifted away from this approach, and there has been no marked introduction of new programs.[25]

Work Force "Rationalization"

Some industries have been plagued with excessive labor forces. One example is bituminous coal, where product demand dropped markedly after World War II, given the increased use of competing sources of energy. A second example is longshoring, characterized by irregular work opportunities and an oversupply of casual labor. In addition, such industries were constrained, by collective agreements or otherwise, from introducing technological changes that would reduce costs, since such changes would further reduce labor needs.

Hence a variant of the stabilization approach has been utilized in a number of these cases, a variant that called for a work force reduction and steadier work for the remainder.

In the case of coal John L. Lewis, then the president of the United Mine Workers, negotiated collective agreements after World War II, which gave the coal operators a free hand in introducing technological change and provided a variety of economic cushions—early retirement, severance pay—for displaced miners. Lewis contended that mining was a dangerous and dirty occupation and that it would be more sensible if, say, half the work force, at higher wages, mined the necessary coal. Employers subsequently greatly increased their capital investment, wages went up markedly with increased productivity, and the work force shrank by possibly 50%.

A more comprehensive approach was utilized on the West Coast waterfront, when in 1960 the International Longshoremen's and Warehousemen's Union and

[24] See the fourth edition of this text, pp. 254–256, for details.

[25] Current rough estimates suggest that some 0.5 million employees have some type of weekly guarantee under collective bargaining agreements, and perhaps 15,000 under annual guarantees. For useful historical analysis see W. A. Berridge and C. Wolfe, *Guaranteed Employment and Wage Plans* (New York: American Enterprise Association, 1948) and Murray W. Latimer (Research Director), *Guaranteed Wages,* Report to the President by the Advisory Board (Washington, D.C.: Government Printing Office, 1947). Little new material has appeared in the last 25 years.

the Pacific Maritime Association concluded a far-reaching stabilization agreement. As in the Mineworker's program, waterfront employers were, in effect, given a free hand in the introduction of new machinery and work methods. But worker protection was more comprehensive than in mining. For employees registered in the "full-status" category there were to be no layoffs; either an earnings guarantee or early retirement would go into effect. If it became necessary to reduce the size of the work force, early retirement (then at the figure of $320 a month and since then more than double) *from the top* was invoked. Man-hour reductions in work operations were very large: from 80 men in warehouse operations involving sugar in sacks to 8 men handling the commodity in bulk.[26]

Other plans of a similar nature (though with variations) were found in the Kaiser Steel Corporation–United Steelworkers of America agreement and via an arbitration award (and subsequent legislation) on U.S. railroads.

What can one say in evaluating these diverse preventive approaches? Insofar as they increase employer operating flexibility and provide employment protection for the worker (and economic cushions for those displaced), the judgment would be in the affirmative. One can, however, raise the question as to the waste of manpower and the psychological impacts on the employees of such early retirement. The majority of American workers have no such protection, however, and it is doubtful—apart from the merits of the case—whether American employees will ever have a proprietary interest in their jobs as is the case in, say, Japan.

Hence it is no accident that interest has developed in alleviative approaches, to which we now turn.

Alleviative Approaches

The major alleviative approach is public unemployment insurance, to be discussed in the Chapter 12. Various private-sector alleviative techniques have been developed, however, although on a much more limited basis than is the case with premature death or illness group insurance programs sited at the work place.

So far as we know, unemployment insurance, written on an actuarial basis by a commercial insurer, never existed in this country, although some carriers were working on such policies in the 1920s. Conditions (actuarial) for the creation of such insurance do not exist. Trade union plans were found as far back as 1831, but they never covered more than a total of 35,000–60,000 employees. Some company plans existed and at least 13 were paying benefits in the early 1930s.

At present the two alleviative program types that exist are severance pay (or dismissal compensation) and Supplementary Unemployment Benefits (SUB).

Severance pay plans originally centered on the salaried employee who was permanently separated through no fault of his own. Their use has widened:

[26]See Otto Hagel and Louis Goldblatt, *Men and Machines* (San Francisco, Calif.: International Longshoremen's and Warehousemen's Union and Pacific Maritime Association, 1963).

current plans have wider coverage, and in some limited cases payments are made in the case of "temporary layoffs," though not if discharged for cause. These plans customarily require a minimum length of service—such as 10 years—and then pay a fraction—such as one-half—of the terminal-year salary (or the 10-year average). Most plans call for a lump-sum payment, although some use a periodic payout.

SUB plans have received much more attention in the 25 years since their introduction. Because of the cyclical nature of industries, unions in automobiles and steel had long been interested in some form of employment stabilization. The previously cited Latimer *Report* concluded that conventional guarantee plans, which operated primarily by keeping employees at work, were not feasible for cyclically affected industries. But the *Report* suggested that other innovative plans, such as additional income protection for the laid-off worker, merited consideration.

One such plan was put on the Auto Workers' bargaining agenda in the early 1950s, and in 1955 a historic agreement was signed between Ford and the United Auto Workers, and with General Motors shortly thereafter. Similar plans were subsequently negotiated in the remainder of the automobile industry, women's apparel, glass, maritime, rubber, and steel industries and certain retail cases. Workers covered have averaged between 2.5 and 3 million. The plans have not been extended beyond the above-noted industries; the bargaining priorities of other unions have apparently lain elsewhere.[27]

The major characteristics of such plans are as follows:

1 *Qualification for benefits* Customarily one year of service is required; in several industries it is two.

2 *Types of benefits* All plans pay a weekly unemployment benefit to wholly unemployed workers. Most provide special or short-week benefits to the partially employed. About half provide for selected separation and moving allowances. Only a minority cover the temporarily disabled. In the glass industry the eligible employee is given a vested right to the employer's contribution; this is tantamount to a "savings account" plan. All plans relate length of service to the building up of wage credits; the majority stipulate that the employee shall receive "credit units" at a rate such as one-half unit for each week in which pay was received.

3 *Benefits* "Regular" benefits are computed as follows. Workers must qualify for state unemployment benefits. The SUB plans then pay the difference between unemployment insurance (UI) benefits and some "maximum." The majority of plans pay (when combined with UI benefits) 80–85% of wages; in the automobile industry and a few other cases it runs to 95% of the take-home pay minus the sum (such as $12.50 a week) the employee would

---

[27]An excellent description of the "birth, anatomy, and experience of SUB" is found in Joseph M. Becker, S. J., *Guaranteed Income for the Unemployed* (Baltimore, Md.: Johns Hopkins Press, 1968).

have spent had he worked. The maximum total runs to as high as $160–$180 total. Refusal to accept other work if recalled is a cause for cancellation. Most plans provide for up to 52 weeks of benefits. Special weekly benefit provisions are found in most plans.

4 *Costs and financing* All plans are financed solely by the company; the majority requires contributions to be paid into a separately maintained trust fund. Examples of benefit payments are 2–5 cents per hour; contributions may vary with the size of the fund. (SUB plans illustrate an interesting type of intraunion organizational bargaining. Company SUB payments can be viewed as foregone wages, payments that would have otherwise gone into here-and-now wage increases. Long-service workers would not likely benefit from such plans, yet they were willing to go along.)

5 *Experience under the plans* An initial problem encountered was whether payments under such plans would disqualify an employee from UI benefits; legal determination was that they would not.

The plans had their first baptism under fire in the 1957–1958 recession, and they fared well. Benefits in the period 1960–1967 varied between $64.2 million (1965) and $131.3 million (1961). In the subsequent decade the figures increased appreciably. In automobiles and steel particularly, the plans have, however, exhibited a type of prince-and-pauper character. The funds are readily built up during prosperity but run close to depletion in recessions; the 1974–1975 downturn—the most serious one since World War II—required selected short-run suspension of payments. As these lines are written in mid-1981, the verdict is not yet in as to what will result from the severe shake-out experience in automobiles and steel; at least one automobile maker is in serious difficulty. And on July 2, 1980, another automobile maker announced that payments would dry up for workers with less than 10 years' service.

Private Approaches: A Concluding Note

While private approaches resemble a patchwork system, we would conclude that much useful experimentation has been undertaken, and useful results achieved. The approach *is* consistent with our pluralistic society. And we have not been able to discern any pattern impacting negatively on the economy, that is, no major misallocation of resources, adverse incentive effects, nor worsening inflation. Nor do we feel that the worsening competitive position of automobiles and steel was a consequence of these private "unemployment" systems. But private approaches are by their very nature unable to cope with major economic employment difficulties.

SUMMARY

1   Unemployment continues to be a major economic security problem, notwithstanding basic accomplishments of the last 50 years.

2   The major problem—pointed out in the first and succeeding editions of this book and becoming much more acute in the last decade—is how to attain high levels of employment without also experiencing untenable inflation rates. The old wisdom of "curing" inflation by letting unemployment float upwards no longer works: an increasing body of analysis suggests not only is there no long-run Phillips curve trade-off, but it may not even exist in the short-run. "Stagflation" persists and economists do not have a satisfactory "remedy." Letting the unemployment rate rise to, say, 25% might be a "cure," but it would kill the patient in the process, causing human misery, lost production, and political upheaval. Pessimistic? Yes, but we have no comforting words.

3   Private approaches do play their part, and a not unimportant one at that. But they are swamped by macroeconomic aggregates, and cannot do the job themselves.

In conclusion, should another edition of this volume appear, the most important questions for discussion may well be not whether Old-Age, Survivors, and Disability Insurance is bankrupt nor whether we have National Health Insurance. Rather they will be whether we have been able to resolve those twin problems of unemployment *and* inflation.

SUGGESTIONS FOR ADDITIONAL READINGS

There is much new material on the nature and measurement of unemployment, and also an abundance of analysis on topics such as the Phillips curve, the "trade-off," the Natural Rate of Unemployment, expectations (adaptive and rational), and so on. Much of this analysis, however, is couched in highly technical language. We have included several readings here that can be read profitably even though the reader may not have been exposed to more advanced economic theory. Contrary to the above, we have not been able to uncover many new items relating to private approaches.

Becker, Joseph M., S. J. *Guaranteed Income for the Unemployed: The Story of SUB.* Baltimore, Md.: Johns Hopkins Press, 1968.
An excellent historical analysis of the birth, anatomy, and experience of SUB.

Chernick, Jack. *A Guide to the Guaranteed Wage,* Bulletin No. 4. New Brunswick, N.J.: Rutgers University, Institute of Management and Labor Relations, 1955.
A historically useful analysis of old- and new-style guarantees, with a focus at the level of the individual firm.

Doeringer, Peter B., and Michael J. Piore. "Unemployment and the 'Dual Labor Market,' " *The Public Interest,* No. 38 (Winter 1975), 67–79.

An interesting analysis of "primary" (good job) and "secondary" (poor job) labor markets and the relative impacts of unemployment therein.

Feldstein, Martin. "The Economics of the New Unemployment," *The Public Interest,* No. 33 (Fall 1973), 3–42.
An incisive account of unemployment as affected by unemployment insurance and other support programs.

Hawkins, Everett D. *Dismissal Compensation.* Princeton, N.J.: Princeton University Press, 1940.
While historically dated, Hawkins provides a comprehensive and useful treatment of all phases of such plans.

Humphrey, Thomas M. *Essays on Inflation.* Richmond, Va.: Federal Reserve Bank of Richmond, 1980.
For the interested lay reader, a superb exposition of unemployment and inflation. Humphrey is a most gifted writer. See particularly the essays "Changing Views of the Phillips Curve" and "Some Recent Developments in Phillips Curve Analysis."

Levitan, Sar A., Garth L. Mangum, and Ray Marshall. *Human Resources and Labor Markets,* 2nd ed. New York: Harper and Row, 1976.
A detailed and very useful analysis of manpower problems *and* programs.

Meyer, Laurence H. *Macroeconomics: A Model Building Approach.* Cincinnati, Ohio: Southwestern Publishing, 1980.
Technical: requires some exposure to intermediate economics as well as quantitative training. But Chapters 3 and 16–18 provide a good analysis of modern unemployment and inflation theory.

Okun, Arthur M. (Ed.). *The Battle Against Unemployment.* W. W. Norton, 1965.
A series of readings on the nature and consequences of unemployment, the problems of employment and price stability, and policy types and uses.

Phelps, Edmund S. (Ed.). *Microeconomic Foundations of Employment and Inflation Theory.* New York: W. W. Norton, 1970.
Part I, while technical, contains much relevant analysis.

Rejda, George E. *Social Insurance and Economic Security* Englewood Cliffs, N.J.: Prentice-Hall, 1976
Chapters 14 and 15 of this comprehensive book discuss the problems of unemployment and several solutions to these problems.

Shiskin, Julius. "Shiskin on the Unemployment Numbers." *New York Times,* Jauary 18, 1976, Sec. 3, p. 14.
The then Commissioner of Labor Statistics addresses (1) problems involved in emphasizing employment or unemployment and (2) seven alternative measures of unemployment.

Shiskin, Julius. "Employment and Unemployment: The Doughnut or the Hole?" *Monthly Labor Review,* 99, No. 2 (February 1976), 3–10.

Slichter, Sumner H., James J. Healey, and E. Robert Livernauh. *The Impact of Collective Bargaining Upon Management.* Washington, D.C.: Brookings Institution, 1960.
Chapter 16 on income security and severance pay plans provides detailed information on such practices, although the material does not deal with the last 20-plus years.

U. S. Department of Labor. *Employment and Earnings* (monthly), *The Monthly Labor Review,* and special reports.
"Services," reports, and other publications of the Bureau of National Affairs, Inc., the Commerce Clearing House, and the Conference Board provide a wealth of data for many items discussed in this chapter.

Chapter Twelve

Unemployment Insurance

The major public program in the United States for the alleviation of the undesirable consequences of unemployment is the unemployment insurance (or compensation) system, which was established as a result of the Social Security Act of 1935. In addition to this basic system there are a number of special programs, as, for example, for railroad employees. These are discussed in Chapter 13.

The terms "unemployment compensation" and "unemployment insurance" as used above are commonly employed interchangeably. In the early days of the program "compensation" was used. After 1937, when the Social Security Act was declared constitutional, there was a tendency to use the term "insurance." Since "compensation" and "insurance" are both found in ordinary usage, we shall follow this custom here.

As was noted in Chapter 11, there are various ways in which society can approach unemployment problems. Loss control approaches, public and private, and private alleviative approaches have been discussed in Chapter 11. This chapter will focus upon the remaining major area—public alleviative programs, of which unemployment compensation is the outstanding example.

DEVELOPMENT OF THE PRESENT SYSTEM

If one accepts the premise that the unemployed are a fixed cost to society, though they may be a variable cost to the employer, the question that must be answered is how society will provide for this overhead item. Various alternatives are to be found. At one extreme is the case where society lets the unemployed take care of themselves through private means, namely, personal resources, relatives, friends, and private charities. Where public assistance was provided, it was commonly done under the "poor relief" or "work relief" doctrine.[1] At the other extreme would be some complete public "cradle to the grave" system. The trend in the United States has changed from the almost completely private approach to one with a significant degree of public intervention.

[1]For a useful summary see Florence Peterson in D. D. Lescohier and E. Brandeis, *History of Labor in the United States, 1896–1932,* Vol. III (New York: Macmillan, 1935), Chaps. 11 and 12.

Early Unemployment Compensation Laws

Early attempts at governmental unemployment insurance were made on a state basis, in Massachusetts in 1916 and in Wisconsin, with the Huber bill, in 1921. On a federal basis, resolutions or bills were introduced in Congress in 1916, 1928, 1931, and 1934. Nothing developed from these sources, however, in no small measure because of the opposition of labor organizations. Such opposition arose because of a fear of government as such and a further fear that a system of this type could be turned against employees on strike. By 1932 the forces of economic necessity diminished labor opposition, and in that year Wisconsin passed the first unemployment compensation law in the United States. The law was a deferred statute, however, not to go into effect for two years. Four other states passed unemployment insurance laws prior to the Social Security Act of 1935, but only the New York law became effective.[2]

Social Security Act of 1935

The insurance approach was crystallized in the Social Security Act of 1935. One of the several major components of that Act related to unemployment compensation. As noted in Chapter 3, in 1934 a national Committee on Economic Security had been created; out of its deliberations had come a series of recommendations, including a national system for old-age insurance and a federal–state system in the unemployment field. Preference for a federal–state tax-offset plan rather than for a national system or a tax-rebate plan was based on the following: in part, the belief that such an approach would be the most likely to survive the test of constitutionality; in part, the fact that the Committee included among its influential members persons who were responsible for the Wisconsin plan; in part, disputes between adherents of different types of funds, which disputes could be resolved by letting each state try its own approach; and, in part, the belief that a faster job could be done if each state were encouraged to act on its own. We shall examine this 1935 Act, with subsequent modifications, after commenting on the compensation principle and its application in this field.

THE COMPENSATION PRINCIPLE

If the labor market operated so that the principle of equal net advantage were fully applicable, one would expect that wage rates for individual occupations would reflect their relative advantages and disadvantages, so that the final wage rate would equalize the advantages and disadvantages among all occupations.[3] And it would therefore follow that, other things being equal, occupations in

---

[2]See Harry Malisoff, "The Emergence of Unemployment Compensation," *Political Science Quarterly,* LIV, Nos. 2, 3, 4 (June, September, December, 1939), 237–58, 391–420, and 577–99, respectively.

[3]See Chapter 8 for a more detailed analysis of the applicability of this approach in workers' compensation.

which the incidence of unemployment was high would pay correspondingly higher wage rates than similar occupations in which this incidence was low. Demand and supply factors operating in such a labor market would work so as to bring about these optimal conditions.

Do wage rates in fact reflect such differences in the risks of unemployment? To some extent, yes. For a long period various building trade rates tended to take into account the pressures of seasonal unemployment. But these cases are few; we have little correspondence, for example, of rates with the risks of cyclical, secular, or technological unemployment.

If this is the case, what alternatives are open to society if it wishes to take positive action? One approach would be for wages to be set legislatively or administratively so as to reflect differing unemployment risks. The serious ethical implications and enormous administrative difficulties in such an approach are readily apparent.

An alternative approach is to use the compensation principle, in which the cost of production includes a charge (tax) for the specific unemployment risk. If this cost is shared by the public (through higher prices), the employer (through reduced profits), and the employee (through lower wages), the burden is distributed. The utility of the compensation payment at the time of unemployment is greater than that of incremental increases in the wage rate that would occur under wage adjustment. Thus this method is more economically rational than that of administrative wage setting, to say nothing of being more feasible operationally. Even if it is assumed that the employee bears the *full* burden of the cost, this method has merit. First, while it may be *forced insurance,* thus limiting freedom of choice, it is there and the employee can draw on it in time of need. (There is no assurance, for example, that "compensatory" wage rates would be used by the individual to provide for unemployment needs.) Second, the risk is spread through insurance, thus forcing a social sharing of the burden. (It should be noted, however, that experience rating may narrow this risk spreading significantly.) Hence there is both administrative feasibility and economic logic to the "compensation" or "insurance" principle.

UNEMPLOYMENT PROVISIONS OF THE 1935 SOCIAL SECURITY ACT

The unemployment insurance section of the federal Social Security Act had two distinguishing characteristics. First, it was an enabling act designed to encourage the states to pass their own laws. As indicated below, it quickly achieved this objective. Second, it provided a set of minimum standards for state laws, permitting the states to enact more liberal, but not more restrictive, laws. The basic elements in this federal statute, now known as the Federal Unemployment Tax Act (FUTA), are as follows.

Coverage

FUTA influences state coverage in two ways: first, employers covered under FUTA must pay a federal tax against which employers covered under an approved state plan may credit some or all of their state contributions. Second, to be approved a state plan must cover some unemployments not taxed under FUTA.

Coverage is a matter of the employer's size as well as the type of employment. Currently, except for employers of agricultural labor and domestic service, FUTA applies to employers who (1) paid wages of $1,500 or more during any calendar year or (2) employed one or more workers on at least one day in each of 20 weeks during the current or immediately preceding calendar year. Agricultural employees must have a quarterly cash payroll of at least $20,000 or employ at least 10 workers. In other words, only large farms are covered. For domestic service in a private home, local college club, or local chapter of a college fraternity or sorority the quarterly cash payroll must be at least $1,000; the number of employees has no effect on coverage.

FUTA covers all types of employment except those specifically excluded. Since 1939 railroad workers have been excluded, but these individuals are covered under the special program described in Chapter 13. Nonprofit organizations are not taxed under FUTA, but for a state law to be approved it must cover service for such organizations that employ four or more persons in each of 20 weeks in the current or preceding calendar year. The state, however, may exclude services for a church or other religious organization. Services for a state or its political subdivisions are also not taxed under FUTA, but these services must be covered under a state plan if the plan is to be approved. The state cannot place a size exemption on such services, but it may exclude certain services such as those performed as an elective official, a member of the state National Guard, or a temporary employee hired in a flood or similar emergency. The state law may also exclude service by an inmate of a custodial or penal institution or as part of an unemployment work-relief or work-training program financed at least in part by public funds. Other exclusions not covered by FUTA and not required for federal approval include casual labor not performed in the course of the employer's business and services such as those provided by a spouse, a minor child, a student for a university, or a patient for a hospital. Self-employment is not covered because it is difficult to determine for a given week whether a self-employed person is unemployed.

The original Act was much more restrictive. Employers had to employ at least eight workers to be covered, and numerous types of employment—agricultural labor, domestic service, service for nonprofit organizations, and governmental employment—were excluded. Federal government civilian employees were covered as of 1955, and in 1956 the size requirement was reduced to four employees. The Employer Security Amendments of 1970, which became effective in 1972, made the most significant changes in unemployment insurance since the program's establishment in 1935. The size requirement was reduced to the present provision and coverage was extended to certain employees of nonprofit organizations and state and local governments. Important 1976 amendments added coverage of some agricultural labor and domestics and broadened the coverage of government workers.

Why these earlier exclusions, some of which are still effective? The reasons lie in complex administrative, economic, and political circumstances. Thus there was some belief that smaller employers could handle implicitly their unemployment problems; moreover, the administrative difficulties were felt to be of such a nature that it would not be feasible to include the employer of fewer than eight. A cutoff of 20 weeks was used, since it would eliminate most seasonal employment. Certain employment classes—such as casual labor or domestic service—were excluded, partly because of administrative difficulties and, additionally in the former case, because of the belief that one should have some permanence of attachment to the labor force before one could rightly make a claim on the system. Agricultural labor was excluded, in part for administrative and political reasons and also because of the belief that the depressed farm economy could not bear the costs.

Qualifications for Benefits

The Act leaves to the states the right to determine specific qualifications for benefits, such as allowable reasons for job separations and interpretations of the terms "able to work," "available for work," and "allowable earnings" while unemployed. The federal Act does not deny compensation to an otherwise eligible applicant. It includes the stipulations that the applicant shall not be ineligible if he or she refuses to accept new work under any of the following conditions:

1 If the job opening is available because of a strike, lockout, or other labor dispute.
2 If the wages, hours, or working conditions are substantially less favorable than those prevailing for similar work in the locality.
3 If as a condition of employment the individual must join a company union, or resign from or refrain from joining a bona fide labor organization.

The logic of these specifications is clear; they are designed to prevent an undercutting of desirable labor standards and to preserve the neutrality of the state vis-à-vis employers and labor organizations.

Since 1972 benefits cannot be denied to an individual taking approved manpower training; compensation cannot be denied nor reduced because a person files a claim in another state or Canada; and there can be no denial of benefits through cancellation of wage credits (see later in this chapter) except for work misconduct, fraud, or a disqualifying income.

Benefits

Benefit levels and durations as such are not specified in the federal Act. There are, however, several indirect stipulations. First, benefits must be paid through public employment offices or other such agencies as may be approved. Second, all monies withdrawn from the unemployment fund of a state shall be used solely in the payment of unemployment compensation, with certain administrative and disability exceptions. Third, an extended benefit program, described below in the section on state programs, finances half the cost of extending benefit durations up to 39 weeks during periods of high unemployment.

Costs and Financing

The major feature of the federal Act is its financing provisions. Originally a federal tax of 3% was levied on the wages and salaries paid by covered employers, as previously defined. Up to 1939 the tax was levied on total wages; in that year an amendment set a limit of $3,000. The limitation was imposed because of the disparate relation between in-payments and possible benefits for higher-income groups.[4]

The 3% rate was selected for two basic reasons. First, it represented an "actuarial" figure that would have provided benefits at levels envisaged in a number of proposed bills for the period 1920–1932. Second, it was a compromise between "disaster relief" and "high-benefit" plan proponents.

The important "enabling innovation" in the federal Act was as follows. The specified 3% tax was to be paid to the federal government. If, however, the state in question had an approved unemployment insurance law with its own tax structure, up to 90% of the federal tax could be deducted or "offset." (Numerically, if an employer's federal tax was, for example, $3,000, then up to $2,700 of the state tax might be offset for the state.) The remaining 10% (or $300) was to be paid to the federal government for administrative costs. Beginning in 1961, the 3% was increased through the years to various levels, in part to take care of increased operational costs, in part for the repayment of monies advanced by the federal government to finance temporary extensions of unemployment insurance benefits, and in part to finance half the cost of an extended benefit period program discussed later. The underlying logic, however, remains the same. Thus at present the federal government levies a 3.4% tax on the first $6,000 of a covered employee's wages. The offset for state taxes is still limited to 2.7%. The permanent tax rate is 3.2%, but it will remain at 3.4% as long as the federal system, through its extended unemployment compensation account explained below, owes the U.S. Treasury for loans used to pay extended benefits. For more details on these

---

[4]It is interesting to note that while the OASDHI tax base has risen substantially, the federal unemployment insurance base was held at $3,000 until January 1, 1972, when it was increased to $4,200. The reader should ask why this was the case.

loans see later in this chapter. Given the "enabling" feature of the 1935 Act, a state law would, of course, "keep the monies at home" for use within the state, instead of having them go to the federal government for commingled use in various states. There was thus considerable incentive for a state to pass its own law; and this, in fact, was what happened in all the states within the short span of two years.

Technically, *all* the monies collected by a state are sent to the Secretary of the Treasury and put into an Unemployment Trust Fund, thus centralizing and safeguarding the reserve. The "title" to a state's monies is, however, retained by it, and a separate book account is maintained. The funds, other than those needed for current state withdrawals, are invested in U.S. bonds, either regular or special issues. Interest earned on these bonds is periodically added to the reserve. A state may draw on its account, but only to the limit of its balance, and only for the purpose of paying unemployment benefits. (A 1946 amendment permitted the states utilizing employee contributions to withdraw such contributions to pay disability benefits.) The federal Act does not require employee contributions, but it does not prohibit them. Although 10 states have at various times levied an employee tax, only 3 do so today.

In order to assist in providing an economic incentive for the reduction of unemployment an "additional credit" provision was incorporated in the Act. A state may write into its own program a provision whereby an employer with good unemployment experience pays a lower tax. But the federal offset applies only to such taxes as the employer pays to the state. Hence, unless a special provision were made, the employer with a reduced state tax would technically pay the balance to the federal government. Special provision, however, has been made in the law via the "additional credit" proviso. Hence the employer with a reduced state tax is permitted to deduct not only what he or she *does* pay to the state, but what *would have been paid* had he or she paid the maximum tax, subject to the federal offset. In order to prevent abuse of this tax-reduction procedure, the experience-rating provisions (that is, the provisions that permit low-unemployment employers to pay lower rates) of state acts must meet minimum federal standards. The federal standards require an experience period of at least three years, but new employers can be allowed a shorter period on a "reasonable basis."

The 0.7% federal tax monies are automatically credited to an employment security administration account in the Federal Unemployment Trust Fund. From this account Congress annually appropriates the amount necessary to meet the total cost of "proper and efficient administration" of approved state laws. A second account, the extended unemployment compensation account, is used to reimburse the states for the federal share of the cost of the federal–state extended benefit programs described in detail later. This account is financed through transfers from the administration account equal to $\frac{1}{10}$ of the federal tax monies collected. However, no transfers can be made from the administration account when the balance is equal to at least 40% of the amount appropriated by Congress that year for administration expenses. Also the extended unemployment compensation account is not permitted to exceed the greater of $750 million or 0.125% of total wages in covered employment for the preceding calendar year. A third account, the federal unemployment account, is the source of non-interest-bearing repayable advances or loans to states with low reserves in their individual accounts. As a result of the 1981 amendments, interest will be charged on the loans received between April 1, 1982 and December 31, 1987. The interest rate will be that paid by the federal government on the state balances the last quarter of the preceding calendar year but no higher than 10%. If the state repays the loan by September 30 of the year it received the advance and receives no new loans the rest of the year, it will not have to pay any interest on that loan. This federal unemployment account is also financed out of transfers from the administration account, the amount transferred being the excess not retained in the administration account nor transferred to the extended unemployment compensation account. The federal unemployment account, however, is also limited to the greater of $550 million or 0.125% of total wages in covered employment for the preceding calendar year. If after the transfers to the extended unemployment compensation account and federal unemployment account the balance in the administration account exceeds the 40% standard, then the excess is allocated to the individual state accounts in the proportion that their covered payrolls bear to aggregate covered payrolls. These allocations can be used to pay benefits or, under certain conditions, administrative expenses.

Administration

The federal law is administered by the Secretary of Labor through the Unemployment Insurance Service of the Employment and Training Administration. The states retain considerable autonomy; their major responsibility is to comply with federal specifications, but, given that, they exercise the day-to-day administration of the state laws. The federal administrative specifications require the state to do the following:

1 Administer its law in such a way as will, within reason, permit full payment of unemployment compensation when due.
2 Cooperate with state agencies administering public works or employment.
3 Provide for a review system for denied claims.
4 Make the necessary reports to the federal administration.
5 Apply the merit system to its administrative staff.

Hence there is considerable variation in the details of state administration. Administrative costs are borne by the federal government, as explained above.

STATE UNEMPLOYMENT INSURANCE ACTS

In attempting to portray the present state unemployment insurance system in the United States, one faces the same dilemma that arises in connection with most of the programs discussed in this text. On the one hand, a detailed presentation does not serve the purpose of this book, whose aim is analysis and evaluation. Moreover, a detailed presentation would become out-of-date as quickly as it was printed, so rapid are developments in this field.[5] Yet it is obvious that one cannot analyze and understand if one does not have some fund or stock of information with which to work. We shall adopt the compromise of sketching in the main informational threads without attempting in any way to suggest that this provides a definitive treatment of the full range of available data.[6]

Coverage

As was previously noted, the federal law sets a floor below which the states cannot go in restrictiveness. The states can, however, adopt more liberal provisions, and this is the trend that has developed. The following data illustrate the picture as of January 1, 1980.

First, as to the size of the firm (number of employees), except for employers of agricultural and domestic services, the Social Security Act amendments that became effective January 1, 1972, define an employer as a person who employs one or more workers in each of 20 days in a year, each day being a different week, or one who has a payroll of $1,500 in a calendar quarter. When the law read, "eight, or, after 1954, four or more workers," a state could enact a law with broader coverage by including employers with fewer than eight (or four) workers. Indeed, by 1965 half of the states had laws that covered employers with one to four employees. With a "one-employee" federal minimum, that option is closed unless a state wishes to include employers with no employees (in effect, a self-employed individual).[7] This type of extension is not likely. A state can, however, reduce the 20-day or $1,500 requirement, and almost two-fifths of the states have done so. Also, the contractual relationship of employer and employee and the location of employment have been defined in ways such as to broaden coverage. Only a few states have lower size requirements for agricultural and domestic service employers than is specified by the federal law, but about two-fifths of the states cover nonprofit organizations employing only one worker.

[5]This is even more the case in unemployment compensation than in OASDI, for in the latter instance there is only a single federal law; in the former the complex diversity of state laws is apparent. This same comment applies to workers' compensation.

[6]The source used in the following section is the U.S. Department of Labor, Bureau of Employment Security, *Comparison of State Unemployment Insurance Laws as of January 1, 1978,* with supplements.

[7]California does permit employers otherwise subject to its law to apply for self-coverage. Approval is not automatic.

Second, the federal Act excludes certain types of employment. Prior to the 1970 and 1976 amendments states tended to cover some types of employments excluded under the federal law, but today the differences are much less significant. To illustrate these continuing differences, about two-fifths of the states cover casual laborers and about two-fifths cover student nurses and interns employed by a hospital. Except in Alabama, Massachusetts, and New York, employers may request approval to cover most types of employment ordinarily excluded under the state law.

Qualifications for Benefits

Many of the complexities of state laws are to be found in the provisions dealing with qualifications for benefits. But these are complexities of detail; the underlying approach is similar. Let us look systematically at both similarities and differences.

Eligibility Conditions

Eligibility conditions represent the "affirmative statement of the risks selected for coverage under the program"; they are the "conditions *precedent*" to the risk against which the program insures.[8]

Eligibility conditions require (1) extension of unemployment beyond the waiting period (2) by a claimant who has been established as part of the labor force by having earned qualifying wages in covered employment and (3) who has a continuing attachment to the labor force (being able to work and available for work), indicated by registration for work at an employment office.

The "waiting period" is discussed below under "Benefit Levels." Let us merely note here that it is most commonly one week and that an individual must be unemployed beyond the waiting period before becoming "eligible."

"Attachment to the labor force" admits to participation in the benefits of the system only employees having a bona fide attachment. Such attachment is measured by requiring that the individual earn a specified amount of wages or work for a certain period of time within his or her base period, or both. (The "base period" or "base year" is a period of time, commonly one year, that precedes the period in which benefits start. In about two-thirds of the states the base year is the first four of the last five calendar quarters completed prior to filing a claim. For example, if the person files a claim on April 10, the base period is the preceding calendar year.) Usually the law requires the base period compensation to be equal to some multiple, such as 1½, times the wages earned during the base period quarter of highest earnings. The objective is to require wages in more than one quarter during the base period. Some states in this category set the require-

[8]We have extensively used here L. G. Williams, "Eligibility for Benefits," and P. H. Sanders, "Disqualification for Unemployment Insurance," both in *Vanderbilt Law Review*, VIII, No. 2 (February 1955), 286–306 and 307–337, respectively. (After nearly 30 years these articles still contain the most useful analysis we have seen. They are classics in their own right.)

ment at some multiple, say 30 or 40, times the weekly benefit amount, which as explained later, is $\frac{1}{26}$ or some other fraction of the high-quarter wage. Most other states require a flat dollar amount of wages or a specified number of weeks of employment.

The labor-force attachment must not only have been in the past; it must exist at present and into the future period for which the individual wishes to be eligible. Such continuing attachment is measured by the individual's being able to and available for work. Here the states set their own eligibility requirements, since there are no federal specifications except the labor standard provisions. "Able to work" implies physical and mental ability. The unemployment insurance system as presently structured is an economically oriented system; it is not set up for the purpose of providing health insurance benefits (which may be covered in part by workers' compensation or by private health plans). One evidence of ability to work is the filing of a claim and registration for work at a public employment office, which is required under all state laws, ordinarily on a weekly basis. There are 10 states, however, that do not disqualify a person who is ill. Five more have the temporary disability insurance programs, discussed in Chapter 8, which provide different benefits for these unemployed workers.

Availability for work is a more complex issue.[9] The customary interpretations of availability include (1) indication of availability as evidenced by registration at the appropriate public employment office, (2) actively seeking work or making a reasonable effort to obtain work, and (3) willingness to accept suitable work (to be defined shortly).

Disqualifying Provisions

Disqualifying provisions represent negative conditions or the "conditions *subsequent*" to the risk. "Precedent" and "subsequent" should be viewed here in terms of the *processing* of an individual's claim: eligibility conditions are first checked; then it is ascertained whether the individual is otherwise "disqualified." In terms of what the individual "does," the disqualifying action may actually be the first event in time.

A major cause of disqualification arises out of the method of job separation; certain types of separations disqualify an individual (either temporarily or permanently) from receiving benefits. The purpose of such qualifications is to restrict benefits to those who become unemployed through no fault of their own; that is, it is generally held that an employee who "voluntarily" leaves his job should take the consequences.

The series of disqualifying reasons includes voluntary separation from work, discharge for misconduct, refusal of suitable work, and unemployment due to a labor dispute. Possible penalties range all the way from postponement of benefits to cancellation of all wage or service credits earned during the base period. The

[9]For a useful analysis and discussion, see Ralph Altman, *Availability for Work: A Study in Unemployment Compensation* (Cambridge, Mass.: Harvard University Press, 1950).

theory behind postponement is that after a specified time the worker's unemployment is caused more by general conditions than by the disqualifying act. Cancelling the wage and service credits is a severe penalty because the worker must reestablish eligibility for future spells of unemployment. As noted earlier, federal law prohibits use of this penalty, except in certain cases. Other possible penalties are a reduction in the benefit duration or a denial of benefits for the current spell of employment. Less than half the states impose the same penalties for all major causes. Furthermore, in some cases the disqualification is mandatory, in others it may be left to the discretion of the administrative agency.

In general, there can be exceptions to the reasons or penalties for disqualification, depending on the circumstances involved. All states disqualify an individual for voluntarily leaving employment without "good cause." But if quitting was for "good cause," then benefits are not denied. What constitutes "good cause" becomes, of course, a complicated matter and one with which administrative agencies have to concern themselves regularly. The penalty for discharge for misconduct may be scaled down according to the type of misconduct. Thus "aggravated misconduct" may disqualify for a longer period than "lesser misconduct."

Refusal to accept suitable work also disqualifies an individual. In addition to the federal specifications on suitable work, other criteria have been developed to evaluate the suitability of an offer of work. These include the following: (1) the degree of risk to a claimant's health, safety, and morals; (2) the claimant's physical fitness, prior training, experience, and earnings; (3) the length of unemployment and local job market prospects, and (4) the distance of the job from home. It should be noted that the suitable work criteria are imposed not only as an initial test, but throughout the period of unemployment, whereas the job separation cause is a "once and forever" action. Labor dispute disqualifications, in general, last as long as the labor dispute, though there is a pattern of exceptions and qualifications for lockouts, the location of the dispute, and indirect actions. Workers not taking part in the dispute and having nothing to gain may not be disqualified. Finally, certain special groups of individuals may be specifically disqualified, for example, students not available for work while attending school and women who quit their jobs to assume marital obligations or to bear children.

Even though an individual meets all the above requirements, there are still certain factors that may prevent him or her from starting to collect benefits or continuing to receive benefits once started. Fraudulent misrepresentation not only disqualifies an individual, but all state laws contain some provision for the recovery of benefits paid. Other incomes received may disqualify an individual, usually through a reduction in benefits. Thus workers' compensation, OASDI old-age benefits, private pensions, wages in lieu of notice, or dismissal payments may restrict unemployment benefits. Partial employment does not disqualify an individual, but it may reduce benefits. Thus in 1980 all states allowed an individual to earn some sum each week without reducing benefits; the size of the sum varied from $2 to one-half the weekly benefit amount.

All the above restrictions are designed to carry out the intent of the unemployment insurance system, given its basic premises. One may quarrel with these basic premises, but if one accepts them, the subsequent regulatory framework logically flows out of the system. It is apparent, of course, that one may differ with specific regulations or their applications.

Benefit Levels

If an individual meets all the above qualifications, what benefits are paid? The following are the principal factors involved in benefit calculations.

The Benefit Year

The period in which an employee may receive benefits is called a "benefit year." This is usually a one-year period; in most jurisdictions it is an "individual benefit year," related to the date of unemployment and the filing of a claim. In other states the potential benefit year begins for all claimants on a date specified in the law, usually April 1 or the first week of July.

The Waiting Period

All but 12 states require a one-week waiting period before benefits are payable. This is an "uncompensable period" during which the employee must have been otherwise eligible for benefits. In nine more jurisdictions the waiting period becomes compensable if certain stipulations are met, such as the payment of benefits for a given number of weeks. There is only one waiting period per benefit year. Thus if a worker has two spells of unemployment during one benefit year, the waiting period applies only to the first. The purposes of a waiting period are, first, to exclude from coverage those unemployed who secure reemployment within this period; that is, it permits unemployment compensation to be applied to those who more fully need it. The belief here is that an individual should be expected to, and be able to, finance a week of unemployment. Second, like "deductible insurance," it reduces the cost or, conversely, for a given premium it allows a higher benefit.

The Weekly Benefit Amount

Numerous formulas are used to compute the weekly benefit amount, but they all base benefits on the employee's past wages (customarily during the base period or some portion thereof) within minimum and maximum limits.

Three principal methods are used in benefit calculations. About four-fifths of the states use a "high-quarter" formula, which bases benefits on wages in that quarter of the base period in which wages were the highest. Benefits are computed by applying a fraction, such as $\frac{1}{26}$, to the high-quarter wages. For workers with 13 weeks of employment in the high quarter, this fraction, used in 13 states, provides benefit restoration of 50%, subject to minimum and maximum benefit limitations. Since workers may have some unemployment even in the high quarter, almost half the states using this formula use fractions larger than $\frac{1}{26}$ ($\frac{1}{19}$ currently being the maximum).

Eight states use a weighted schedule that gives a greater proportion of high-quarter wages to lower-pay workers.

Four states use an "annual-wage" formula. A benefit "schedule" or "table" is set up that directly relates benefits to base period wages. Such schedules tend to be weighted so as to provide a proportionately higher benefit restoration for the low-wage earner.

The remaining nine states use an "average weekly wage" formula in which benefits are calculated as a percentage of average weekly wages in the base period.

In all cases there are statutory benefit minimums and maximums. All but six states specify dollar minimums; the other six express the minimum as a percentage of the state average weekly wage. In 1980 the lowest minimum was $5, the highest minimum $38. More than two-thirds of the states have flexible maximums ranging from 50 to 67% of the statewide average weekly wage in covered employment. In 1980 the highest maximum was $180, the lowest $74.

Dependents' Allowances

Dependents' allowances are provided by 13 states. A rather rigorous set of restrictions defines dependency. The weekly allowance is usually a fixed sum per dependent, but in four states the allowance depends on both the number of dependents and the worker's former earnings. All states limit the maximum dependents' allowances payable in one week, but the types of limits vary greatly. In Rhode Island and the District of Columbia the total weekly maximum is the same with or without dependents. In Massachusetts the allowance is $6 per dependent, up to a $66 maximum.

The Duration of Benefits

Nine states pay benefits for the duration of unemployment up to a stated maximum, usually 26 weeks. Most, however, limit the maximum dollar payments to a fraction, usually one-third of the base period wages. The extreme fractions are one-fourth and three-fifths. In these variable-duration states the maximum payment period is also usually 26 weeks. They range, however, from 20 to 39 weeks. In periods of "high unemployment," however, the maximum duration may be extended under a federal–state program established by the Employment Security Amendments of 1970. In 1958 and 1961, during periods of high unemployment, Congress had enacted similar temporary extended benefit programs. Until 1981 amendments "high unemployment" was considered to exist when *either* (1) the national *insured* unemployment rate equalled or exceeded 4.5% for 13 consecutive weeks or (2) the insured unemployment in the state equalled or exceeded 4% and equalled or exceeded the rate in the same period of the preceding two calendar years by at least 20%. At its option, when the 20% factor was not met, a state could still provide extended benefits when the state insured unemployment rate reached 5%. The high unemployment ceased to exist when *both* (1) the national insured unemployment rate dropped below 4.5% for 13 consecutive weeks and (2) the state unemployment insurance rate was either less than 4% or less than 20% higher than in the same period of the two preceding calendar years over a 13-week period. Under the 1981 amendments the national trigger was repealed. Only state insured unemployment rates now trigger extended benefits on or off. Extended benefit claimants are excluded in determining these state insured unemployment rates. Effective September 25, 1982 the required state rates will be increased from 4% plus the 20% factor to 5% plus the 20% factor and without the 20% factor from 5% to 6%. Also effective that date, extended-benefits claimants must have worked at least 20 weeks or have an equivalent amount of wages during the base period.

Amendments included in the Omnibus Budget Reconciliation Act of 1980 also imposed additional requirements on the states for federal participation in this program. First, this Act eliminated the federal payment for the first week of extended benefits that did not require recipients to wait a week before receiving benefits. This provision affected the 12 states noted earlier that in 1980 had no waiting period. Second, the Act denied extended benefits to unemployed persons who did not meet certain work-related rules such as willingness to accept suitable work or to actively engage in seeking employment. Third, the Act stated that no state termination of a disqualification for voluntary leaving, misconduct, discharge, or refusal of suitable work shall apply to extended benefits unless this termination was based on employment subsequent to the disqualification.

This program extends the benefit duration to the lesser of (1) one-half the total amount of regular benefits or (2) 13 times the weekly benefit. The maximum duration under both the regular and extended programs is 39 weeks. Three states have separate extended benefit programs that will pay additional benefits under conditions or terms not covered by the federal–state program.

From 1971 through 1975, in response to continuing high unemployment rates, Congress enacted or continued a series of temporary extended benefits programs that first increased the maximum duration to 52 weeks and finally to 65 weeks. These temporary programs, financed solely by federal funds, expired in 1978.

Costs and Financing

As stated earlier, the federal Act currently levies a 3.4% tax paid by employers on the first $6,000 of each employee's wage against which can be offset up to 2.7% of any state tax. State financing has been greatly influenced by this federal tax structure. Additionally, the employer can be credited with any reductions under an approved experience rating plan. No tax on employees was provided for in the Act.

Employee Contributions

Although 10 states at one time or another utilized employee contributions, only Alaska, Alabama, and New Jersey did so in 1980. (California, Rhode Island, and New Jersey utilize employee contributions for a related system of disability insurance.) The wage base is the same as for employers. The rates vary: in Alabama it is 0.5%, but employees pay only when the fund is below the minimum normal amount; in New Jersey it is 0.5%; and in Alaska it is 0.3–0.8%, depending on the rate schedule in effect.

Experience Rating

Unemployment insurance is essentially an alleviative system, but it also contains a control incentive whereby an employer who reduces unemployment (or who is so placed that his or her employment is "normally" stabilized) can have the tax reduced. The procedure used is called experience rating. All states now have in effect some experience-rating system.[10] The reason is clear: no state feels it can put its industry at a competitive disadvantage by not having such a plan. While social insurance costs are but one of many factors involved in plant location (including the attraction of new industry or the retention of present companies), state legislatures can directly exercise some degree of control over these costs.

Experience-rating formulas vary greatly among the states, but they all attempt to measure each employer's unemployment experience with some measure of exposure, such as payrolls. The worse this experience relative to the exposure, the higher the tax rate paid by the employer. Over 30 states use a "reserve-ratio" formula. Under this formula usually the total benefits received by the employer's workers since the program became effective are subtracted from the employer's contributions over that period. This balance is divided by the employer's payroll, in most cases over the past three years. The rate is determined by a schedule that states the rates for specified ranges of reserve ratios. The higher the ratio, the lower the rate. Different schedules are used, depending on the balance in the state unemployment fund. For a given reserve ratio the rates usually rise as the state fund balance declines. For example, in New York the most favorable schedule, used if the state fund balance is at least 10% of the payroll, sets a minimum tax rate of 0.3% and a maximum rate of 3.0%. The least favorable schedule, used if the state fund balance is less than 5% of the payroll, sets a minimum rate of 4.3% and a maximum rate of 5.2%.

Other approaches are the benefit-ratio formula (benefits in the past three or five years are compared with recent payrolls), the benefit-wage-ratio formula (wages paid to recently separated employees—called benefit wages—are compared with recent total taxable wages and multiplied basically by the state ratio of total benefit payments to total benefit wages), and the payroll variation plan (unemployment is measured by the decline in an employer's payroll over time).

[10]Puerto Rico and the Virgin Islands do not.

Minimum rates paid under the most favorable circumstances vary among the states from 0 (11 states) to 1.2%, the usual minimum ranging from 0.1 to 0.4%. Under the least favorable schedules the maximum rates range from 2.7 to 7.5%. The net effect of experience rating has been to reduce the average contribution rate considerably below 2.7% (for example, 1.9% in 1975).

Another result of experience rating has probably been to keep the benefit structure lower than it would otherwise have been. This may have happened for two reasons. First, given a lower tax rate, employer pressures have tended to resist any increase in benefits that would require an increase in tax rates. Second, state legislatures have been reluctant to raise rates unless such a raise were general among the states; to do so unilaterally would be to add a factor of competitive disadvantage. This should not imply, however, that there have been no benefit increases.

Other Cost-Financing Details

State laws contain various other financing features designed to make the system operate more efficiently. Let us examine the more important ones.

1 In 1980 18 states had tax bases higher than the $6,000 specified under federal law. Hawaii's base, the highest, was $11,200. All but a few states had a standard rate of 2.7%. Montana's standard rate was the highest, 3.9%. Less than half the states required a minimum fund balance before *any* rate could be less than the standard rate, usually 2.7%.

2 Half of the states permit "voluntary contributions," by means of which an employer can "buy back." That is, by making a voluntary contribution the employer can improve the reserve ratio and thus lower the experience rate. The contribution systems are structured so as to save the employer more than the amount of the voluntary contribution.

3 In all states the employer may not be charged under experience rating for certain benefits. Such noncharges are of several types. First, the employer may not be charged for benefits based on employment of short duration or for appealed cases that are reversed. Second, in discharge or voluntary quit cases, where benefits must ultimately be paid, the employer may not be charged. The intent here is to relieve the employer of charges for unemployment due to circumstances beyond his or her control. It should be noted, however, that the "system" must in some way recover the monies paid in benefits for such cases.

4 All state laws specify the conditions under which the experience record of a predecessor employer may be transferred to an employer who acquires the business. In a minority of states "total" transfer is required; in the others partial as well as total is allowed.

5 If the claimant had more than one base period employer, which employer is

to be charged for the benefits paid an unemployed claimant? The majority of states charge benefits against all base period employers in proportion to wages earned, on the basis that unemployment results from general conditions. There are 13 states that charge base period employers in reverse chronological order, while 9 charge one employer, commonly the most recent.

6 The federal law requires that nonprofit organizations be permitted to pay their benefit costs instead of paying taxes if they so desire. Governmental entities must also be given this option, but the contribution alternative need not be made available. Most states, however, allow a choice.

Administration

Since there are no specific requirements in the federal Act as to the form of the state administration or its place in the state government, a number of agency types have developed. In 1980 over half the states had established an employment security division in the state department of labor or other labor-oriented agency. Recently some states have moved the division into a human relations, human resources, or social service agency. The rest have an independent board or commission or an independent department of the state government. To some extent the form of the administrative agency is an accident of political pressure, of existing state government units, and of historical growth. But, irrespective of the form, the purpose is clear: to administer the state act in conformity with its intent as well as content.

The administrative procedure set up for the processing of claims is similar in all states. The unemployed individual files a claim for benefits following specified steps and using specified forms. This is usually done at a local public employment office, although in unpopulated areas another public official may substitute for an employment office. The claim is then centrally reviewed (locally in some states) and the benefit amount and duration determined. Benefit claimants customarily receive their checks by mail, but they must report regularly (usually weekly) at the local public employment office. All states provide an appeals procedure for the individual whose claim is denied. The appeals agency is an impartial tribunal, variously composed in different states. In all but a few states an additional appeals stage is provided. Appeal agency decisions can be reviewed by the courts, but only as to matters of law and not of fact. All but four states provide for an advisory council—usually with equal employer and union representation—whose purpose is to help in policy formulation and administrative problem solving.

As noted earlier, the administration of the state acts is financed by the federal government through grants from the general federal treasury. Most states, however, have established special administrative funds, consisting usually of interest on delinquent contributions, fines, and penalties, to meet special needs.

Administrative provision is also made for the handling of interstate claims. Eligibility and benefits are based on the worker's combined earnings in the states in which he or she had worked. These states share the costs of these benefits. In most cases the benefit depends upon the law of the state in which the claim is filed. That state pays the benefit and is reimbursed by the other states involved. If a claimant moves to a new state, the new state usually takes over the payment of the benefit, for which it is reimbursed by the original state. The advantage of this procedure in permitting desirable labor mobility is obvious.

OPERATIONAL DATA

The preceding material was designed to present an overall view of the nature of state unemployment insurance programs. This discussion now turns to some important operational data.

Coverage

Table 12.1 presents data on coverage for selected years of operation under the state unemployment insurance system. Coverage has more than tripled since 1940 and has resulted in the inclusion of a greater proportion of the civilian labor force. The Employment Security Amendments of 1970 are the major reason for the substantial increase during the 1970s.

Table 12.1 Coverage Under Unemployment Insurance—State Programs, 1940–1978

	Coverage		Payrolls Covered[a]	
Year	Number (In Millions)	Percentage of Employed Civilian Labor Force	Amount (In Billions of Dollars)	Percentage of Civilian Wages and Salaries
1940	23.1	49	32.4	65.7
1945	28.4	54	66.6	66.6
1950	32.9	56	102.8	72.5
1955	36.6	59	158.4	78.6
1960	40.5	62	209.7	80.2
1965	45.5	64	277.1	79.4
1970	52.8	67	414.3	78.8
1975	65.4	77	679.2	86.9
1978	83.2	88	756.1[b]	87.1[b]

Sources: Social Security Bulletin, Annual Statistical Supplement, 1977–1979, p. 75; 58. *Handbook of Unemployment Insurance Financial Data* (Washington, D.C.: Employment and Training Administration, U.S. Department of Labor, 1981).

[a]Taxable plus nontaxable payroll in covered employment.
[b]1977.

Beneficiaries, Benefits, and Average Employer State Tax Rates

Table 12.2 presents data on insured unemployment as a percentage of covered employment, the average weekly number of beneficiaries, the benefit amounts, the average benefit duration, the average weekly benefit, and the average employer state tax rate. The benefit data reflect periods of prosperity and recession, inflation, and program coverage extension and benefit liberalizations. The average employer tax rates reflect these factors as well as experience rating and changes in the wage base.

The Unemployment Trust Fund

Table 12.3 traces the unemployment trust fund from its inception through 1980. In most years receipts have exceeded disbursements, causing the fund balance to rise, but it declined in 1946, 1949–1950, 1954, 1959–1961, 1970–1972, and 1974–1976, periods of high unemployment. The largest decline in history occurred in 1975, when the state balances dropped from $10.5 billion to $4.6 billion.

What size should the fund be? The answer depends on how one views the fund: as a "contingency" fund, as an "earnings" fund, or as some other kind of reserve. A currently accepted view is that the fund should be between one and one-half and two times the largest amount of benefits paid in any previous 12-month period. Given this view, since 1975 the "fund" has been inadequate.

One might get the impression that the fund is a federal fund. This, of course, is not the case. The totals presented in Table 12.3 merely represent the summation of individual state funds (technically "reserve accounts"). From this fact flows a problem hidden by the fund aggregation shown above; not all states have the same unemployment experience. Some are hit much harder than others in periods of economic recessions. At different times individual state funds have approached dangerously low levels. The affected state has several alternatives open to it. While it is difficult to cut benefits, increases can be forestalled. Since there is customarily a relationship between individual state fund size and tax rates under experience rating, a lowering of the fund may call for increased tax rates. This is a second alternative and the one most commonly followed.

A third alternative is to secure a loan from the federal unemployment account that until the 1981 amendments was interest-free.[11] A state is eligible for such a loan whenever its reserves available for benefits at the end of a calendar quarter are less than the amounts of benefits paid out in the 12 months ending with that calendar quarter. Employers in states that run a deficit for two years in a row must

---

[11]This account was originally set up in 1944 as a federal Emergency Reserve, designed to handle what was expected to be the vast immediate postwar unemployment problem. It was abolished in 1952 and reestablished in 1954. Given the increase in the federal tax from 0.3 to 0.4% (as of January 1, 1961, and subsequently), additional changes were made in the structure and operation of the fund. For a useful discussion, see Robert J. Myers, *Social Insurance and Allied Government* Programs (Homewood, Ill.: Richard D. Irwin, 1965), pp. 78–82.

Table 12.2 Insured Unemployment Rates, Average Employer State Tax Rates, Beneficiaries, and Benefits Under Unemployment Insurance—State Programs, 1940–1979.

Year	Insured Unemployment Rate	Number of Beneficiaries (Average Number, in Millions)	Amounts of Benefits (In Billions of Dollars)	Average Actual Duration of Benefits (Weeks)	Average Weekly Payment for Total Unemployment ($)	Average Employer State Tax Rate
1940	5.6	1.0	0.5	9.8	11	2.7
1945	2.1	0.5	0.4	9.5	19	1.7
1950	4.6	1.3	1.4	13.0	21	1.5
1955	3.5	1.1	1.4	12.4	25	1.7
1960	4.8	1.7	2.9	12.7	33	1.9
1965	3.0	1.1	2.3	12.2	37	2.1
1970	3.4	1.5	4.2	12.3	50	1.3
1975	6.0	3.4	18.2	15.7	70	1.9
1979	2.9	2.0	15.0	13.3[a]	90	2.8[a]
1980[b]	3.9	3.3	n.a.	n.a.	100	n.a.

Sources: Annual Statistical Supplement, 1977–1979, pp. 66, 67, 75; Social Security Bulletins.

[a]1978.

[b]Estimated by author.

404

Table 12.3   The Unemployment Trust Fund—State Programs, 1936–1977

Year	Collections (In Millions of Dollars)	Interest (In Millions of Dollars)	Benefits (In Millions of Dollars)	Balance (In Millions of Dollars)	Ratio of Benefits to Collections and Interest (%)
1936	65	1	Less than $500,000	65	—
1940	861	59	517	1,805	56
1945	1,161	118	461	6,833	36
1950	1,190	146	1,342	6,948	99
1955	1,215	185	1,352	8,242	97
1960	2,300	195	2,748	6,626	110
1965	2,973	266	2,165	8,336	67
1970	2,521	610	3,900	11,846	125
1975	10,626	380	16,929	4,573	154
1977	9,846	227	11,724	5,500	116
1978	11,508	345	7,710	9,643	65

Sources: Social Security Bulletin, Annual Statistical Supplement, 1977–1979, p. 73; *Handbook of Unemployment Insurance Financial Data* (Washington, D.C.: Employment and Training Administration, U.S. Department of Labor, 1981).

pay a federal payroll tax that rises by 0.3% a year until the state has repaid its debt. Under 1981 amendments, until December 1, 1987 a cap of 0.6% (or, if higher, the level in effect in the year prior to the year the state qualifies for this cap) was placed on this federal tax credit reduction if the state has taken certain steps (e.g., tax increases or benefit constraints) designed to restore solvency to its system.

The heavy payouts during the mid-1970s caused about 20 states to use the third alternative. To repay these debts many states have increased their tax rates or disqualification penalties.

Federal Allowances and Readjustment Programs

Closely related to unemployment compensation are three programs that provide assistance or incentive payments to workers totally or partially unemployed for reasons that are not attributable to any prior employer. The federal government, not the states, finances these programs and determines their provisions.

The Disaster Relief Act of 1974 authorized the President to provide assistance to a person unemployed as a result of a disaster. The 1967 amendments set up the WIN program which, as described in Chapter 15, makes incentive payments to recipients of Aid to Families with Dependent Children who are enrolled in training programs. The Trade Act of 1974 assists workers who are unemployed or underemployed because of the adverse effects of increased imports that may result because of the trade arrangements under the Act. In addition to compensation for up to 52 weeks, the Act provides up to 26 weeks more to complete a course of training, relocation allowances, and job search allowances. In 1981 Congress tightened this law in several ways. For example, previously increased imports had to have "contributed importantly" to the layoffs. Now increased imports must be "an important cause and not less than any other cause." The Security of Labor can under certain conditions require recipients to extend their job search beyond their labor market area. If a worker exhausts regular unemployment insurance benefits and collects one or more weeks of trade readjustment assistance before unemployment insurance extended benefits are triggered "on," the combined benefit under both programs is limited to 52 weeks.

ISSUES

To illustrate the current major issues in unemployment compensation we will briefly summarize recommendations made recently by (1) Professor Martin Feldstein, (2) the National Commission on Unemployment Compensation, and (3) the Chamber of Commerce of the United States. Brief mention will also be made of a Reagan Administration proposal not yet adopted by Congress.

The Feldstein Recommendations

In 1974 and 1975 Professor Martin Feldstein published two articles calling for a major restructing of unemployment insurance.[12] Feldstein argued that three myths concerning unemployment compensation have prevented us from adopting a more rational unemployment compensation policy. First, he argues, the unemployed are not, as many believe, a hard core of employees unable to find jobs. Instead, most layoffs are temporary and brief.

Second, benefits replace a much larger fraction of a family's lost income than is commonly believed. According to Professor Feldstein, benefits replace at least two-thirds of lost *net* income. In some cases the net income might exceed the lost net income. These high rates reflect the fact that although replacement of gross wages has remained about 50% in most states (subject to maximum weekly benefit amounts) federal income taxes, OASDI taxes, and state income taxes cause net income to be considerably less than gross income. A benefit equal to 50% of the gross income is a much larger percentage of the net income after taxes. Furthermore, because families seldom lose all their income during years when they receive unemployment compensation, it is the higher marginal tax rates (under a progressive income tax structure) that determine the replacement ratio relative to the net income lost. This tax effect reduces incentives for workers to avoid and, even more strongly, to shorten spells of unemployment. Although

---

[12]Martin S. Feldstein, "Unemployment Compensation: Adverse Incentives and Distributional Anomalies," *National Tax Journal,* XXVII (June 1974), 231–244; "Unemployment Insurance: Time for Reform," *Harvard Business Review,* LIII, No. 2 (March–April 1975), 51–61.

accepting some of Professor Feldstein's arguments, other researchers such as Professor Daniel Hamermesh have emphasized that replacement ratios are not as generous as Professor Feldstein's analysis suggests.[13] First, unemployment compensation is calculated using base period earnings, which, because of inflation and career progression, are usually less than the wages lost. Second, the waiting period delays the start of the income; so do delays in filing benefits. Third, no benefits are paid after the worker has exhausted his or her benefit rights. Fourth, an unemployed worker usually loses some or all of the employee benefits associated with employment within a short time after he or she stops working.

The third myth attacked by Professor Feldstein is that most of those who collect unemployment compensation are poor or would be poor without these benefits. Instead, he observed, according to a 1966 survey adjusted to 1970 prices, the 53% of all families with incomes below $10,000 received only 48% of all dollars paid as unemployment insurance benefits. The 11% with income of more than $20,000 received 8% of the benefits. Hamermesh agrees that benefits are paid to persons at all income levels. He does not find this result surprising.[14] He asserts, however, that in the 1966 survey there was substantial underreporting of unemployment insurance benefits, probably mostly by low-income families. Also, a much larger fraction of total benefits than of total money income goes to persons with lower incomes.

Based on his analysis, Feldstein made three recommendations:

1 Tax unemployment compensation. This recommendation would reduce disincentives to work, treat families in different tax brackets more equitably, and increase tax revenues. Starting in 1979, unemployment compensation became taxable under certain conditions in whole or in part under the federal income tax. The amount that is taxable is the lesser of (a) the total unemployment compensation or (b) one-half the amount by which the adjusted gross income, including the total unemployment compensation, exceeds the worker's "base amount." For single persons the base amount is $20,000, for married persons filing a joint return, $25,000. The proportion of total unemployment compensation that is taxable may thus vary from 0 to 100%.

2 Strengthen experience rating to increase employer incentives to prevent or reduce unemployment. Eliminate the maximum rate and reduce the minimum rate to 0. Investigate the possibility of considering only recent experience and setting separate rates for the various major components of a large company.

3 Consider replacing the present program with the following:

   (a) For the first three months an unemployed worker would be able to *borrow* up to 60% of his or her previous gross wage.

---

[13]Daniel S. Hamermesh, *Jobless Pay and the Economy* (Baltimore, Md.: Johns Hopkins University Press, 1977), pp. 17–22.

[14]Daniel S. Hamermesh, *Jobless Pay and the Economy* (Baltimore, Md.: John Hopkins University Press, 1977), pp. 24–25.

(b)   For the next three months the worker would receive an insurance
benefit of 30% of the lost wage plus the opportunity to borrow up to
40% more. Only the insurance benefits would be subject to tax.

(c)   After six months the worker would receive insurance benefits for six
months or longer, equal to 60% of the lost wage. Additional funds
could be either borrowed or provided as nonrepayable benefits to
finance retraining or relocation.

In other words, under this system unemployment *insurance* benefits would
be limited to workers who were unemployed for at least three months. Loans
would replace a substantial share of the current insurance benefits.

The National Commission on Unemployment Compensation

In 1976 Congress directed that a National Commission on Unemployment Compensation be appointed to evaluate and make recommendations for improving
unemployment insurance programs. The Commission, which included 13 members representing business, labor, and the public, issued its final report in 1980.[15]
Its major recommendations, grouped according to whether they deal with coverage, eligibility for benefits, benefits, or financing, are stated briefly below. Some
of these recommendations were the result of a close vote within the Commission.

Coverage

The Commission would favor liberalizing the conditions under which two types
of employees would be covered. First, they would cover agricultural workers on
the same basis as other workers. They would remove the requirement that farms
employ 10 or more workers or have a $20,000 quarterly payroll. Second, they
would extend coverage to household workers if the employer pays $50 for such
service in a calendar quarter. Reducing this requirement from $1,000 to $50
would make unemployment compensation consistent with OASDHI.

The Commission also recommended that Congress and the Department of
Labor consider the possibility of covering homemakers through unemployment
insurance credits for equivalent work, transfer of unemployment compensation
credits earned by the spouse, and other approaches.

Eligibility for Benefits

The Commission's major eligibility recommendation would relax disqualification
conditions and penalties. They did not recommend any changes in the federal law,
but they recommended that states consider the following. First, do not disqualify
workers for leaving with good cause, including compelling family obligations and
sexual harassment. Second, limit disqualification for misconduct to misconduct

[15]*Report of the National Commission on Unemployment Compensation* (Washington, D.C., 1980).

connected with work. Third, do not impose any reemployment and earnings requirement for any disqualifying act. Fourth, disqualifications for discharge for misconduct, refusal of work, or voluntary quit should be for a variable number of weeks depending on the seriousness of the action. Fifth, do not require any reduction of benefit rights except for fraud or receipt of disqualifying income.

In addition, the Commission recommended that states eliminate "actively seeking work" availability requirements. Instead the Commission recommended that all claimants be required to demonstrate their availability for work by doing those things reasonably prudent persons would do in the same circumstances to find work.

They also recommended that individuals should be eligible for benefits if they become temporarily disabled after they file a claim, provided that they are not offered any suitable work and are not receiving disability insurance for the same disability.

Benefits

The Commission would liberalize benefits in several important respects. To accomplish this result they would establish the following federal minimum benefit standards. First, except for the weekly maximum, the unemployment insurance benefit should be at least 50% of the individual's average weekly wages based on the high-quarter or some appropriate equivalent basis. Second, the weekly maximum should be at least two-thirds of the state average weekly wage. This requirement should be phased in as follows: 55% in 1982, 60% in 1984, and two-thirds in 1986.

In addition, the Commission would eliminate the 120% factor in the state extended benefit trigger and set the state insured unemployment rate at 4.0%, seasonally adjusted for a 13-week moving average. Fearing the probability of prolonged employment for many persons in the near future, the Commission would create two additional extended benefit programs that would extend the maximum duration to 52 weeks and 65 weeks, respectively. Under the first the state trigger insured unemployment rate would be 4.5%, the national trigger 5.0%. Under the second these two rates would be set at 5.0% and 5.5%, respectively. Instead, as already noted, in 1981 Congress repealed the national trigger and raised the required state unemployment rates.

The Commission also recommended a lifetime-reserve benefit program for older workers that would provide a transitional passage from regular full-time employment, after layoff from a permanent job, to eventual retirement. To be eligible the worker would have to be currently eligible for unemployment insurance and have at least 40 OASDHI quarters of coverage. During unemployment occurring at or after age 60 these workers would receive benefits for as long as 52 weeks from regular unemployment insurance and this lifetime-reserve program.

The Commission would stop taxing unemployment benefits. They reasoned that this taxation could be offset by an equal increase in benefits, is discriminatory because not all other income is taxed, and cannot be effectively policed.

In addition to these changes in the federal law, the Commission also directed several recommendations to the states. First, the weekly benefit amount should be not less than 50%, probably 60%, of the claimant's average weekly wage. Second, the maximum weekly benefit should be at least two-thirds of the state average weekly wage. This weekly maximum should be periodically adjusted to ensure that 75–80% of the workers receive 50% of their lost wages. Third, states should adopt a partial benefit formula that provides strong incentives to accept part-time work. Fourth, the Commission urged states to carefully consider the possibility of continuing the private medical expense insurance of unemployed persons who register at the employment service for work. This protection would be financed by a small increase in the state unemployment insurance tax.

Financing

A major part of the Commission report deals with the financial problems of the system. To increase the monies flowing into the program the National Commission would increase the FUTA taxable wage base substantially. Specifically, beginning in 1983 they would set the wage base at 50% of the national average total wage in covered employment. In 1985 they would raise this percentage to 55%, to 60% in 1987, and to 65% in 1989. Unlike the present wage base of $6,000, this new wage base would increase with national average wages.

The Commissioners would reduce employer taxes under FUTA by canceling the program's indebtedness for the monies it borrowed from general revenues to finance (1) Federal Supplemental Benefits from January 1975 to March 1977 and (2) extended benefits during the recessions when the national trigger was "on" from January 1975 to January 1979. They would also reduce employer taxes under *state* programs by rebating to the states the state share of the extended benefits when the national trigger was on. The amounts involved would be $5.8 billion under the Federal Supplemental Benefits program and $6.6 billion under the extended benefits program, half of which would be rebated to the states.

The Commission was deeply concerned about the large sums several states owed the federal government. Consequently they recommended that each state develop a plan to finance benefits over a business cycle and maintain adequate reserves to accomplish that result. States should set as an objective (1) a reserve fund at the beginning of any economic downturn of not less than twice the product of (a) the state annual benefit cost rate in the highest three of the prior 15 years and (b) the state's total wages for the most recent year and (2) a capacity to generate revenues at least 30% above the expected long-run state benefit cost rate. In determining when revenues should be adjusted and whether their reserve funds are solvent, states should state the balances as a percentage of total wages, not absolute dollar amounts.

To increase state revenues the Commission recommended that FUTA require state laws to not be permitted to set the contribution rate for new employers at less than the current average contribution rate in the new employer's industry. States, in their opinion, should be free to increase their maximum taxable wage base above the federal level and encouraged to index this wage base to changes in wages covered by the state programs. No experience-rating plan should develop a zero tax rate and the maximum rate should reflect anticipated benefit costs. The tax schedules should be adjusted in relation to the wage base and the amount of tax revenues needed to keep the trust fund solvent.

The Commission would make borrowing from the federal government more expensive and difficult. They would charge interest on the monies borrowed, require acceptable state solvency provisions as a condition of borrowing, and prohibit further deferrals of repayment. On the other hand, they would permit states to repay loans for their trust funds in installments instead of through automatic increases in employer FUTA taxes. As noted earlier, in 1981 Congress ordered interest charges under certain conditions on federal loans to the states.

To protect states against unusually heavy benefit costs the Commission recommended a reinsurance plan that would pay part (not to exceed 30%) of the benefit costs in excess of 2.7% of the taxable payrolls. This plan would be financed by an employer contribution rate of 0.1% of the taxable payrolls for at least a seven-year period.

The Commission further recommended that a Board of Trustees be appointed to manage the trust funds. This board would be directed specifically to explore whether states should be permitted to invest part of their reserve funds in nonfederal obligations that earn higher rates of interest than do federal government obligations.

Administration

To make the administration of unemployment compensation more efficient the Commission recommended several changes, a few of which are the following. Allocate more federal resources to the program to improve administrative techniques and develop special procedures for the detection of fraud, errors, and tax delinquencies. Permit the Internal Revenue Service to contract with state employment security agencies to collect employer FUTA taxes jointly with state contributions. Strengthen the appeals process and the U.S. Employment Service.

The Chamber of Commerce of the United States

In the opinion of the Chamber of Commerce of the United States the National Commission's recommendations call for an expanded federal role, an easing of eligibility requirements, higher benefits for longer periods, and a weakening of experience rating. The result, in their opinion, would be higher program costs and additional incentives not to work.[16]

---

[16]Eric J. Oxfeld, *Critique of the Report of the National Commission on Unemployment Compensation* (Washington, D.C.: Chamber of Commerce of the United States, 1980), mimeo.

In the Chamber's opinion federal standards are inappropriate. Such standards would not have uniform effects because of state variances in wage levels, tax rates, cost of living, family structure, and work ethic. The higher benefits and longer duration favored by the Commission would increase costs for no identifiable social purpose. The Commission's suggestion that the taxable wage base be increased would cause astronomical increases in federal and state tax revenues. Neither the federal government nor most of the states need these additional monies. Raising the federal taxable wage base would also be inequitable because it would force high-wage employers with good experience to pay a greater proportion of the administrative costs and other uses of the federal tax. Experience rating, the Chamber believes, would be weakened under the Commission's proposals. The Chamber also criticized the Commission for giving workers incentives to draw benefits rather than working and for ignoring the effect of overlapping cash payments from other benefit programs that may produce combined benefits in excess of the take-home pay the worker received while on the job.

The Chamber itself recommended that undue federal influence through budgetary control and regulatory authority be eliminated, that there be no federal benefit standards, that experience rating be strengthened, that state loan repayment conditions be strengthened (the Commission agreed), that cost equalization and reinsurance schemes not be introduced because they are unnecessary and present too many problems, that the federal Treasury assume the pre-July 1977 $5.8 billion obligation of the Federal Supplemental Benefits program (the Commission agreed) but not the cost of the Extended Benefits program, that more dollars be spent from administrative funds to reduce fraud, abuse, and error (the Commission agreed) and stiffer penalties imposed in fraud cases, that interest be charged on future federal loans to states which should be permitted to borrow only if they satisfy certain solvency criteria (the Commission agreed), and that the federal–state Extended Benefits program be amended to eliminate the national trigger, require a one-week waiting period, and impose strict job acceptance requirements. As already noted in 1981 Congress did impose interest charges on the federal loans, eliminated the national trigger, and under certain conditions imposed a one-week waiting period.

Clearly the National Commission and the Chamber disagree on many major points.

A Reagan Administration Proposal

Like the Chamber of Commerce the Reagan Administration favored and obtained the elimination of the national trigger on extended benefits. The Administration also would require that workers unemployed for at least three months be required to seek work that provides a wage at least equal to their unemployment insurance and the minimum wage even if the employment would not be in his or her usual work.

Some Additional Observations

Some additional observations on unemployment issues involve (1) the distance of the base period, (2) the compensatory influences of unemployment compensation, and (3) the pros and cons of experience rating.

The Distant Base Period

Although none of the preceding recommendations deal with this point, some observers object to the use of a distant wage base to determine eligibility for benefits and the benefit itself. They note that a worker is eligible for workers' compensation the first day on the job and receives a benefit based on the wage being paid at the time of the injury. Unemployment compensation places more stress on the worker's proving his or her attachment to the labor force and a more established wage basis. In assessing this difference it is important to remember that workers' compensation replaced an injured worker's right to sue under the tort liability system.

Compensatory Influences

What is the economic significance of unemployment insurance? What portion of lost wages is restored by unemployment benefits?

Three conclusions appear from the investigations of Lester and others.[17] The first is that in relatively mild recessions payments to the unemployed have been important in maintaining purchasing power. Second, in more severe business recessions compensating payments may be less effective. Third, economic security programs of all types are "built-in stabilizers." They may not work as effectively as we had hoped from a countercyclical point of view, but they provide a steady stream of income payments to various classes of recipients.

Experience or Merit Rating

"The primary and announced purpose of experience rating . . . is to provide a financial incentive, in the form of a reduced contribution rate, for the individual employer to make a real effort to stablize his employment."[18] Great Britain

[17]See Richard A. Lester, "The Economic Significance of Unemployment Compensation, 1948–1959," *The Review of Economics and Statistics,* XLII, No. 4 (November 1960), 349–372. See also the other studies cited by Lester in his article. See also the paper by George E. Rejda, "Unemployment Insurance as an Automatic Stabilizer," given before the American Risk and Insurance Association, September 1965. Rejda concludes that during three post-war downswings unemployment insurance offset 24–28% of the decline in national income. He also notes that unemployment taxes are not automatic *destabilizers* as asserted in the next section.

[18]Charles A. Myers, "Experience Rating in Unemployment Compensation," *American Economic Review,* XXXV, No. 3 (June 1945), 339. This article, along with the following by Professor Myers, provides an excellent analysis of the subject. *Employment Stabilization and the Wisconsin Act* (Washington, D.C.: Social Security Board, September 1940).

experimented with this approach prior to 1920 and then abandoned it. The "merit-rating" idea was incorporated into the Wisconsin Act in 1932. Today all state laws make provision for some form of merit or experience rating. (While the two terms are technically interchangeable, the latter has become the more customary.)

However, the mere fact that all states have experience-rating plans does not mean that the approach is economically logical. This has led to the frequently repeated statement that "experience rating is indefensible in theory, but thoroughly acceptable in practice." What are the presumed advantages of experience rating? The disadvantages? The following discussion seeks to get at the more relevant issues.[19]

The major contentions for experience rating are as follows:

1 On an economywide level such a system is viewed as a way of allocating or distributing the social costs of unemployment among industries in the order in which they are "responsible" for unemployment.

2 On the individual enterprise level the purpose of experience rating is, as was noted in the opening paragraph of this section, to stabilize employment in the individual firm by providing a monetary incentive in the form of a reduced contribution rate.

The principal arguments arrayed against experience rating are the following:

1 The major criticism rests on the contention that the employment experience of a business is largely beyond its control; market forces and not employer activities are the critical causal factors. Hence experience rating is a misdirected form of social policy, since it rewards one employer for a record not of his or her doing and penalizes another on the same basis.

2 Experience rating may in part tend to be self-defeating. Employers, in attempting to secure more favorable tax rates, are likely to engage in a variety of practices (some ethically defensible, others not so) that *may* increase employment stability for a small core of employees, but which *will* greatly increase instability for another group. Experience rating may actually increase unemployment for that marginal group of employees who can stand it least. Moreover, the employer has an incentive to challenge unemployment insurance payments to individuals in specific cases; a successful challenge means a better employment record and hence a lower contribution.

---

[19]Perhaps the two best sources on this topic are still Herman Feldman and Donald M. Smith, *The Case for Experience Rating in Unemployment Compensation and a Proposed Method;* and Richard A. Lester and Charles V. Kidd, *The Case Against Experience Rating in Unemployment Compensation,* both published by Industrial Relations Counselors, New York, 1939. The analysis herein leans heavily on these studies. For a more recent study see Clinton Spivey, *Experience Rating in Unemployment Compensation,* Bulletin 84 (Urbana, Ill.: Bureau of Economic and Business Research, University of Illinois, 1958).

3 Rather than being countercyclical in nature (and hence acting as a stabilizing force), experience rating "adds fuel to the flames." In boom periods, when employment is high (for reasons inherent in the functioning of the economic system), tax rates are low (when they should be high). Conversely, in depressed periods the contribution rate is high (when it should be low). Thus the entire system operates out of phase. Because of the time it takes to introduce changes in state unemployment insurance structures, however, if the depressed period is short, the higher rates may not become effective until better times, thus exerting a countercyclical influence.

Let us take a more critical look at the first objection. Can an employer stabilize employment? What forces, operating through the market, are beyond an employer's ability to regulate?

The customary answer is that the employer has little control over total employment experience, particularly that arising from cyclical and secular causes, where market forces are more crucial, although he or she does have more control over other unemployment types. While there has been little recent empirical research in this field, earlier studies tend to support this position. Thus Charles A. Myers concludes that employers can do something by way of ironing out day-to-day or intermittent irregularities in employment or reducing seasonal unemployment.[20]

Thus some general conclusions emerge. First, the stabilization of employment is a multilayered matter. Second, over the basic and quantitatively more important employment layer (secular, cyclical) the employer has relatively little control. Third, over the layer of daily and seasonally changing levels of employment the employer has a higher degree of control. Fourth, a financial incentive may help to reduce unemployment of the latter type, though there is some doubt as to whether a continuing incentive is necessary.

If these arguments have merit, then one can in turn reach certain conclusions on experience rating as a social policy. Such a system should not be used to allocate the social costs of the unemployment included in the basic layer, since it is largely outside the employer's control. But such a system might well be used in conjunction with the secondary layer of unemployment. The relationship of this approach to commercial insurance premium structures is readily apparent. Given this approach, there would be a minimum rate that *all* employers would pay. Above that, reductions of a supplementary rate would be possible, contingent upon the employer's experience.

The organizational and administrative difficulties of such a system should not be minimized, however. Critical decisions would have to be made on the choice of the basic and supplementary rates, and this would involve a variety of interindustry and interfirm comparisons. The day-by-day administration of such a system would be far from routine.

A final criticism of experience rating in unemployment compensation is a

[20]See the previously cited works by Myers, particularly Ref. 18, p. 347.

technical one. When the concept was lifted from workers' compensation, only part of the concept was used. Workers' compensation experience-rating plans vary the rates, depending on the employers' experience relative to that of other employers in the same industry *and* the statistical reliability of that experience. Because chance alone may cause a small employer's short-run experience to fluctuate greatly around its true loss potential, small employers are not experience rated. Only very large firms are rated almost entirely on the basis of their own experience. Other firms are experience rated, but their own experience is weighted by less than 100% in determining their rates. Consequently, it has been suggested that unemployment compensation experience rating plans be amended to include a credibility factor ranging from 0 to 100% of the portion of the unemployment layer attributable to the employer.[21]

SUMMARY

The Social Security Act of 1935 encouraged the development of state unemployment insurance programs by levying a federal tax of 3% on most employers in all states against which employers could deduct up to 2.7% of their contributions to a state unemployment compensation program.

The federal statute, now known as the Federal Unemployment Tax Act, requires that, to be approved, a state plan cover some specified employment not covered under FUTA. Determining who is eligible for benefits is left to the states, except for some requirements designed to prevent an undercutting of desirable labor standards and to maintain neutrality between labor and management. Benefits must be paid through public employment offices, but the states determine the level and duration except for a federal–state extended benefits program. At present the federal tax is 3.4% on the first $6,000 of a covered employee's wage, the maximum offset for state taxes still being 2.7%. States are permitted to experience-rate employers.

Some states cover some types of employment not required by the federal statute. To be eligible for benefits an unemployed worker must have earned during a base period (usually the first four of the last five completed calendar quarters) compensation equal to $1\frac{1}{2}$ times the wages earned during the base quarter of highest earnings. He or she must also be able and willing to work. A worker may be disqualified for voluntary separation from work, discharge for misconduct, refusal of suitable work, and unemployment due to a labor dispute. The penalties range from a postponement of benefits to cancellation of all wage credits earned from past employment.

States usually require a one-week waiting period before benefits begin. The

---

[21]For an extensive discussion of such an approach and the use of a social layer, industry layer, and employer layer, see Leo Bernat, *Rate-Making in in Unemployment Insurance,* unpublished doctoral dissertation, University of Minnesota, 1967.

weekly benefit is most commonly some fraction, such as $\frac{1}{26}$, of the high-quarter wages, subject to a specified minimum and maximum. Dependents' benefits are provided by 13 states. The maximum dollar payments are usually limited to some fraction, such as one-third, of the base period wages, subject to a maximum duration of 26 weeks. Under a federal–state extended benefit program the maximum duration is increased by 50% up to a 39-week maximum, when the state insured unemployment rate exceeds a specified percentage. Amendments in 1980 and 1981 increased the requirements states must satisfy to participate in this program.

All states use experience rating. The rate varies with employer experience and the balance in the state unemployment insurance fund. The minimum rates under the most favorable state fund balances range from 0 to 1.2%. The maximum rates under the most favorable schedules range from 2.7 to 7.5%.

In 1974 Professor Martin Feldstein recommended that unemployment benefits be taxed (adopted in part by Congress effective in 1979), strengthen experience rating, and replace the present program with a combined loan–insurance program.

A 1980 report by the National Commission on Unemployment Compensation contained a large number of recommendations dealing with coverage, eligibility for benefits, benefits, and financing. For example, the Commission favored liberalizing the conditions under which agricultural workers are covered. It would relax some of the disqualification conditions and penalties. By 1986 it would set the weekly maximum at two-thirds of the state average weekly wage. It would create two additional extended benefit programs that would extend the maximum duration to 52 and 65 weeks, respectively. The Commission would raise the wage base gradually until by 1989 it was 65% of the national average total wage in covered employment. It would require states to adopt plans to maintain adequate reserves. It would establish a federal reinsurance plan that would pay part of a state's aggregate benefits in excess of 2.7% of the taxable payrolls.

The Chamber of Commerce of the United States opposed most of these recommendations. Instead it favored such measures as the strengthening of experience rating and spending more dollars to reduce fraud and other abuses.

SUGGESTIONS FOR ADDITIONAL READING

Becker, Joseph M. *Experience Rating in Unemployment Insurance.* Baltimore, Md.: Johns Hopkins University Press, 1972.
A book-length treatment of this important and controversial rating technique.

Becker, Joseph M. "Twenty-Five Years of Unemployment Insurance," *Political Science Quarterly,* LXXV, No. 4 (December 1960), 481–499.
An interesting and "unorthodox" examination of unemployment insurance.

Blaustein, Saul J. *Job and Income Security for Unemployed Workers.* Kalamazoo, Mich.: W. E. Upjohn Institute for Employment Research, 1981.

A proposal for a three-tier approach to unemployment insurance. Each tier would provide benefits for up to 13 weeks. Eligibility requirements for each tier would become successively stiffer, requiring longer work experience and broader current job search. The author, who has written extensively in this field, would also establish, as part of a Job Security System, unemployment assistance compensation for those workers who exhaust their unemployment insurance or are not covered and who meet an income test.

Haber, W., and Merrill G. Murray. *Unemployment Insurance in the American Economy.* Homewood, Ill.: Richard D. Irwin, 1966.
A comprehensive description and analysis of the various issues involved in unemployment insurance.

Hamermesh, Daniel S. *Jobless Pay and the Economy.* Baltimore, Md.: Johns Hopkins Press, 1977.
An economic analysis of the effects of unemployment insurance on unemployment and the distribution of income plus other economic issues.

Lester, Richard A. *The Economics of Unemployment Compensation.* Princeton, N.J.: Princeton University, Industrial Relations Section, 1962.
An analysis of the economic impacts of the unemployment compensation program, particularly useful in the area of benefits and income maintenance.

Levine, Louis. *The Role of Unemployment Insurance in National Manpower Policies.* Kalamazoo, Mich.: The W. E. Upjohn Institute for Employment Research, 1972.
Analyzes the modification of unemployment insurance so as to meet manpower policy goals.

Mackin, Paul J. *Benefit Financing in Unemployment Insurance: A Problem of Balancing Responsibilities.* Kalamazoo, Mich.: W. E. Upjohn Institute for Employment Research, 1978.
The last in a series of 16 studies in a comprehensive review project by the Upjohn Institute. All of these studies are worth reading.

Malisoff, Harry. *Cost Estimation Methods in Unemployment Insurance, 1909–1957.* New York: New York State Department of Labor, 1958.
A useful historical and analytical examination of the actuarial aspects of unemployment insurance.

Malisoff, Harry. *Simplifying Unemployment Insurance Objectives.* Pasadena, Calif.: California Institute of Technology, Benefits and Insurance Research Center, Industrial Relations Section, 1960.
An interesting appraisal of unemployment insurance, its objectives, and the practicalities and realities of simplification.

Murray, Merrill G. *The Duration of Unemployment Benefits.* Kalamazoo, Mich.: W. E. Upjohn Institute for Employment Research, 1974.
Analysis of the issues involved in determining the length of time during which an unemployed worker should receive unemployment compensation.

Myers, Robert J. *Social Security,* 2nd ed. Homewood, Ill.: Richard D. Irwin, 1981.
Chapter 13 of this comprehensive book discusses unemployment insurance. This chapter includes an appendix on the actuarial methodology used for making cost estimates.

Papier, William. *Research Memos.* Columbus, Ohio: Division of Research and Statistics, Ohio Bureau of Employment Services, issued periodically.
Periodic memos covering various important aspects and problems of the Ohio unemployment compensation program that are not limited in their applicability to Ohio.

Rejda, George E. *Social Insurance and Economic Security.* Englewood Cliffs, N.J.: Prentice-Hall, 1976.
Chapter 16 of this comprehensive book discusses unemployment insurance.

Report of the National Commission on Unemployment Compensation. Washington, D.C., 1980.
The 1980 report of the National Commission appointed in 1976 that contains numerous recommendations dealing with all phases of unemployment compensation.

Chapter Thirteen

Social Insurance and Related Programs for Special Groups

In addition to the social insurance programs discussed in Chapters 3, 4, 7, 8, 9, and 12, five other major systems, underwritten by governmental units, deal with death, old-age, poor health, and unemployment. These programs provide special protection for veterans, servicemen and women, railroad workers, federal civil servants, and state and local government employees.

These special programs differ in two respects from those considered earlier. First, their coverage is limited to these specific groups of workers, who usually are not eligible for at least one of the more general programs. Second, their objectives and benefit structure are usually quite different. We have omitted from this discussion some special programs such as the Merchant Marine Act, which extends to marine workers the same rights railroad workers enjoy under their Federal Employers' Liability Act, and the Longshoremen's and Harbor Workers' Act, which provides longshore and harbor employees workers' compensation benefits similar to those under the Federal Employees' Compensation Act. While important to their industries, these programs were omitted to enable a more adequate discussion of the programs that, according to the numbers of workers protected, are the most important ones applying to special groups.

In Table 13.1 these economic security measures for special groups are compared with the systems we have been discussing in terms of the exposures with which they deal and the size of their coverage and benefits. Though smaller in size, these programs provide significant benefits for the employees they cover.

VETERANS' ECONOMIC SECURITY PROGRAMS

A system of veterans' benefits has been maintained by this country since the Revolutionary War. In fact, pension precedents established at that time are still used today in appeals for veterans' pensions. In times of war, veterans' benefit programs have always been reexamined and usually extended.

Table 13.1 Payments Under Selected Social Insurance and Related Programs, 1980

Types of Benefits	Number of Persons Receiving Payment, December 1980 (In Thousands)	Annual Amount of Payments (In Millions of Dollars)[a]
Retirement, survivorship, and long-term disability benefits		
Old-Age, Survivors, and Disability Insurance	35,619	120,512
Railroad Retirement	1,015	4,867
Federal Civil Service	1,746	15,042
Other public employee retirement including uniformed services programs	[b]	25,000[c]
Veterans' programs	4,937	11,358
Workers' compensation	[b]	11,000[c]
Temporary disability benefits		
State programs for temporary disability	[b]	1,200[c]
Railroad temporary disability insurance	16	101
Unemployment benefits		
State unemployment insurance	2,937	15,013
Railroad unemployment insurance	38	179

Sources: Social Security Bulletins.

[a]Annual amounts do not include $250 million in lump-sum payments under OASDI and $214 million under the other programs.
[b]Not available.
[c]Estimated by authors.

Although the veterans' benefit programs include economic security measures protecting veterans against the hazards of death, old age, unemployment, and poor health (which are in some respects comparable to our regular social insurance programs covering these hazards), the whole system, both in scope and nature, goes far beyond the system of job-oriented economic security dealt with in this book. Some of the veterans' benefit programs that have been provided by our government over the years are the following: disability compensation to veterans and dependents; old-age pensions; aid in land acquisiton; cash bounties; domiciliary care; civil service preference; life insurance; medical and hospital care; vocational rehabilitation; an automobile or other conveyance; guardianship service; readjustment benefits (GI Bill) providing reemployment rights, education benefits, readjustment allowances, unemployment insurance, and loans. This list does not include veterans' benefits provided under state laws.

The Changing Philosophy of Veterans' Benefits

Since the American Revolution the government has always accepted the view that it is responsible in some measure for the economic security of those who served it in time of war. There has never been any question about compensating the survivors of war casualties or veterans who were disabled in the service of their country. But how to discharge this responsibility to other veterans in their best interest has been debated, not without the influence of strong political and economic pressure groups, since the Revolutionary War.

A long prevailing philosophy, particularly as evidenced by the various pension acts, was that the government ought to protect veterans from indigency, to pay them a debt of gratitude, or simply to reward them for faithful service. Basically this philosophy governed veterans' benefits until World War II. Veterans were largely left to make their own economic adjustments on return from duty to civilian life, and if they failed, the government came to their aid. Under this approach, emphasis was on picking up the pieces of economic wreckage, rather than on avoiding such wreckage, if possible.

An attempt to replace the automatic pension approach with a better program after World War I failed because of the deeply imbedded concept that something was owed to the veteran. There was no general social security system, and veterans could point to many precedents for pension benefits. But World War II changed this picture. OASI had been introduced during the 1930s and veterans and their families were a much larger segment of the population. Reacting to this changed environment, Congress introduced a new approach to veterans' benefits —one that most observers feel has worked well. The new program of benefits was designed to launch veterans in their civilian roles, and to help them compete on equal terms with nonveterans. Readjustment benefits, including education benefits, unemployment allowances, job counseling, and reemployment rights, replaced the pension approach as an attempt was made to bring the veteran into the mainstream of competitive economic activity on a forward-looking basis.

Readjustment Benefits

The Servicemen's Readjustment Act of 1944—best known as the GI Bill of Rights—was the central piece of legislation in this new philosophy of veterans' benefits programs. As amended and later applied to Korean War veterans, this act provided a variety of benefits to aid the veteran in readjusting to civilian life. In 1966 legislation extended eligibility to all veterans who had served or would serve in the armed forces at any time after January 1, 1955. Benefits were increased substantially by the Veterans' Education and Training Amendments of 1970, and again in 1972. A 1977 veterans' benefits law introduced some new approaches, which are described below.

Education Benefits

Education benefits under the first GI Bill of Rights expired on July 26, 1956, after providing educational opportunities to nearly 8 million veterans at a total cost of about $14.5 billion. An estimated 2 million veterans attended colleges and universities, and some 600,000 disabled veterans became self-supporting through the program. Similarly, eligibility for Korean War veterans expired January 31, 1965. By then, over 2 million of these had entered training.

At present, if a veteran served on active duty for more than 180 days with some part of the service after January 31, 1955, and before January 1, 1977, he or she is entitled to educational assistance for a period of one and one-half months for each month of service. The maximum benefit is 45 months. A veteran with less than 181 days of service may be eligible if he or she was released because of a service-connected disability. Eligibility for these benefits generally ceases 10 years after the veteran was released from active duty or December 13, 1989, whichever occurs first. Monthly payments for full-time institutional training range from $311 for a single person to $422 for a person with two dependents. Each additional dependent increases the monthly benefit by $26. Benefits are provided not only for college, but also for high school, farm cooperative training, and apprenticeship or on-the-job training. Veterans who first entered active duty after December 31, 1976, receive educational assistance only if they participated in a Contributory Educational Assistance Program while in service by voluntarily contributing to a special fund. If they decide to use these funds later for a program of education or training, the Veterans Administration (VA) will match their contributions at the rate of $2 for every $1. The participant's monthly contribution cannot be less than $50 or more than $75. The maximum limit on total contributions is $2,700.

In addition to receiving this educational assistance, veterans pursuing their education on at least a half-time basis formerly were eligible for VA educational loans up to $2,500 in any one academic year. Under 1981 amendments this loan program was terminated except for certain Vietnam veterans.

Loan Guarantees

A major innovation of the 1944 Act has been continued in later legislation—the loan guaranty program, which was devised as an alternative to a bonus. It was less expensive for the government and was designed to serve the veteran by providing credit to enable him to get started in farming, in a business, or in buying a home. The system also provided an investment outlet for large amounts of savings accumulated at the end of World War II.

Readjustment Allowances

Readjustment allowances—payments to unemployed or partially employed veterans—were also provided under the 1944 Act, with the purpose of providing minimum income during readjustment. Today veterans are given priority for referral to CETA programs, have certain reemployment rights with their former employer, and qualify for state unemployment insurance benefits on the basis of their service earnings. In 1981 Congress disqualified for unemployment compensation those ex-servicemembers who leave the military at the end of a term of enlistment and are eligible to, but choose not to, reenlist.

Disability and Death Compensation

Service-Connected Compensation

The VA also provides some important benefits in case a veteran is disabled or dies. Compensation for service-connected disability has existed in some form since before the American Revolution. As of early 1981 the amounts paid without regard to other incomes or resources were as follows: total disability, $1,005 per month, with rates for partial disability ranging down to $54 per month for a 10% disability. Veterans 30% or more disabled receive additional compensation for dependents. Also there are statutory awards ranging in 1981 as high as $2,536 per month for specific severe disabilities.

Dependency and Indemnity Compensation benefits are paid to survivors of veterans who die from causes related to their military service or who at the time of their death had been totally disabled for many years because of such service.

In early 1981 monthly benefits paid to surviving spouses ranged from $368 to $944, depending on the pay grade held by the veteran at the time of death. For each child under 18 there was an additional payment of $43, $95 if the child was 18 or over but under age 23 and attending school. A surviving spouse who needed aid and attendance or was permanently housebound because of disability was eligible for an additional monthly $111. If there is no eligible surviving spouse, the children of the veteran may receive benefits on their own: $186 in 1981 if there was one child, $268 if there were two, and higher amounts for each additional child. Dependent parents are also eligible for amounts that depend on their income and marital status.

In addition to this compensation for death and disability, in 1981 the VA paid up to $311 per month in educational assistance to the spouse and each child of a disabled or deceased veteran.

Nonservice Compensation

Veterans may also qualify for non-service-connected disability pensions. Because veterans age 65 or over are considered permanently and totally disabled, a small fraction of these disability pensions are actually retirement pensions. All benefits for these non-service-connected disabilities are paid on a sliding scale based on need. For this reason these pensions are more closely related to public assistance than to social insurance benefits. As of 1980, for example, single veterans received an annual pension of $3,902 less the veteran's income from other sources. For veterans with a spouse and one child the annual pension was $5,772 less the annual combined income of the veteran, spouse, and child. The pensions payable to certain veterans of World War I and veterans of earlier wars, however, are not related to need.

If a veteran dies of causes not related to service, the surviving spouse, if any, and any dependent children under 18 may receive monthly payments from the VA. In early 1981 a surviving spouse could receive annually $2,615 less the spouse's income from other sources. A surviving spouse with two children could receive $3,085 less the other combined incomes of the spouse and the children.

Other Death Benefits

The VA will also pay a $300 burial allowance for any deceased veteran who was entitled to receive a Veterans' Administration disability pension. Prior to 1981 amendments all honorably discharged veterans were eligible for this benefit. All veterans, their spouses, and their minor children may still be buried in any national cemetery in which space is available. If a veteran is not buried in a national cemetery, the VA will still pay a $150 plot or interment allowance. The VA will furnish a headstone or marker for the grave wherever the veteran is buried.

Veterans who die of service-connected causes can elect a burial allowance of $1,100 instead of any other burial benefit.

The Number and Amount of Benefits Paid

Table 13.2 lists retirement, disability, and survivorship benefits paid under the veterans' program from 1940 through 1980. About half the beneficiaries receive need-related pensions; the other half receive compensation not based on need. The number of beneficiaries has remained about the same for two decades, but dollar benefits have more than doubled since 1970. Since benefits are paid from Congressional appropriations, there are no trust funds nor actuarial reports.

Table 13.2 Compensation and Pension Benefits to Veterans and Beneficiaries, 1940–1980 (Numbers in Thousands, Amounts in Millions of Dollars)

Year	Number of Persons Retirement and Disability	Survivor	Total Benefits
1940	610	323	424
1945	1,534	698	952
1950	2,366	1,010	2,224
1955	2,707	1,156	2,746
1960	3,064	1,393	3,437
1965	3,216	1,924	4,196
1970	3,210	2,301	5,480
1975	3,244	2,259	7,668
1980	3,189	1,748	11,358

Sources: Social Security Bulletins.

Medical Care

Veterans with service-connected disabilities have first priority for admission to a VA hospital for treatment of that condition. They may also qualify for nursing home care, domiciliary care, and out-patient medical treatment of that condition, including treatment at specialized VA alcohol and drug treatment facilities.

Second priority for admission to VA hospitals is given to veterans with a service disability for treatment of a non-service-connected ailment. Third priority goes to medically needy veterans with no service disability.

If a veteran is disabled or dies because of a service-connected injury or disease, his or her spouse or child is entitled to medical care under the Civilian Health and Medical Program of the Veterans Administration (CHAMPVA). Usually this care will be provided by non-VA facilities. CHAMPVA pays 75% of the reasonable charges for approved health services. CHAMPVA, however, only covers out-patient care charges in excess of an annual deductible ($50 per person, $100 per family).

Insurance

Veterans' Life Insurance

The VA issued U.S. Government Life Insurance policies to servicemen from World War I until 1940, when National Service Life Insurance (NSLI) policies were introduced. If they wanted the coverage, servicemen and women paid for this insurance. The contract was very similar to that issued by commercial insurers, except that there was no exclusion of war deaths. The original policy was a term policy that paid only in case of death, but insureds had the right to renew the policy at the expiration of the term without proving insurability. They could also convert the term policy to a level-premium contract with a cash value at any time. Both plans provided for participation in dividends resulting from gains and savings derived from favorable mortality experience and excess interest earnings.

Because the expenses of the operation were to be paid by the government out of tax revenues, the initial premiums were low. The number of actual death claims were far less than that estimated. The mortality table used was conservative, and the insurance funds were not used to pay claims if the death occurred in service or was service connected. The subsidization of this program by the government was justified on the social ground that servicemen and women had devoted part of their lives to serving their country.

Because NSLI was an expensive operation for the government, because commercial insurers argued that coverage after service was not justified, and because of numerous administrative and personnel problems, NSLI was replaced in 1950 by the Servicemen's Indemnity Act. This act provided $10,000 of free protection to every serviceman or woman. For all except disabled veterans, the only protection that a serviceman or woman could continue following their discharge was nonparticipatory five-year renewable term insurance. The premiums charged were lower than those of commercial insurers because there was no loading for expenses. Under NSLI, however, this program paid all death claims out of the insurance funds. As a result of Congressional action in 1956, the government terminated this free insurance coverage for all servicemen and women and the right of these persons to purchase insurance following their discharge. Instead, under the Servicemen's and Veterans' Survivor Benefits Act Congress made servicemen and women covered employees under OASDI. In 1958 provisions were made for those already insured to change to a lower-price term policy, nonrenewable after age 50, and for conversion to permanent plans. These insureds were also given the opportunity to add to their policies a disability income rider providing $10 a month per $1000 of life insurance.

In 1964 new legislation reopened the NSLI program for one year to certain disabled veterans, especially those who would have difficulty obtaining private life insurance, and offered a modified life plan encouraging conversion from term policies. The cost of administering this program is borne by the insureds.

The only government-insured program still open to the new issues is Service-Disabled Veterans' Insurance, which makes $10,000 of insurance available to veterans with service-connected disabilities who are otherwise insurable and who apply within one year after being informed of their disability rating. Insureds pay standard rates, with the extra costs being paid by the government.

Servicemen's Group Life Insurance and Veterans' Group Life Insurance

Servicemen's Group Life Insurance (SGLI), basically a voluntary private group life insurance plan financed mainly by the insureds, was made available in 1965 to all servicemen and women on active duty on or after September 29, 1965.

Premiums for $10,000 protection were automatically deductible unless the serviceman or woman preferred a $5,000 policy or rejected the program entirely. In 1970 the maximum amount was revised to $15,000, and in 1974 to $20,000. At the present time the options are $20,000, $15,000, $10,000, $5,000 or $0. The insurance continues 120 days after separation and may be converted to individual policies with commercial life insurers without a medical examination. This current plan, unlike earlier plans, is administered by one private insurer and underwritten by more than 500 others. The Veterans' Affairs Administration, however, establishes the premiums and supervises the program. The government reimburses the private insurers for service-connected deaths.

Until 1974 veterans were permitted to purchase only cash value policies following their discharge. Under the Veterans' Insurance Act of 1974 they were permitted to buy five-year term insurance under Veterans' Group Life Insurance (VGLI). VGLI, like SGLI, is underwritten by private insurers and can be converted to cash value insurance at any time within the five-year term.

Operations

Table 13.3 presents some data on veterans' life insurance. In 1944 the amount of veterans' life insurance in force was almost equal to the total amount of commercial life insurance in force during that year. Apparently, many veterans did not recognize the bonus feature of the insurance, for two years later the amount of insurance in force was only about 30% of the 1944 figure. Veterans of the Korean War reacted in the same way, but with a somewhat better reason. Despite the steady decline in the amount of insurance in force, veterans' life insurance is still a sizable operation.

The VA establishes a full legal reserve on these contracts similar to those maintained by commercial insurers.

Table 13.3 Veterans' Life Insurance in Force, 1940–1979 (Numbers in Millions, Amounts in Billions of Dollars)

Year	Number of Policies	Amount
1940	1	2.6
1945	13	98.4
1950	7	45.3
1955	6	42.7
1960	6	42.0
1965	6	39.4
1970	5	37.5
1975	5	35.3
1979	5	33.0
1980	5	32.4

Source: 1981 Life Insurance Fact Book (Washington, D.C.: American Council of Life Insurance, 1981), p. 101.

Uniformed Services Programs

The uniformed services provide a liberal noncontributory retirement plan for their career members. Not all branches have exactly the same plan, but, in general, a serviceman or woman who has completed 20 years of service may retire (with the consent of his or her branch) on a monthly income for life equal to $2\frac{1}{2}\%$ of his or her highest basic pay, times the number of years in the service. Basic pay does not include subsistence allowances received for meals and quarters. The maximum annuity is 75% of basic pay. Once the pension payments begin, they are adjusted upward once each year to match increases in the CPI. Until 1981 the payments were adjusted twice each year.

Unless the member is disabled, no benefit is paid for less than 20 years of service. If the retiring member is at least 30% disabled and has at least eight years of service, he or she can receive a pension equal to 30–75% of final basic pay. This disability pay is reduced by any disability compensation the member may receive from the VA. A dollar received from the VA is more valuable than a dollar of retirement pension because the VA benefit is nontaxable.

If a serviceman or woman has a spouse or dependent children when he or she retires, he or she is automatically enrolled in a Survivor Benefit Plan (SBP). This plan will continue 55% of the pension to these survivors if the serviceman or woman dies after retirement. If the serviceman or woman wishes, he or she can elect to protect only the spouse or the children or neither. The fraction can be less than 55%. A retiring member of the Uniformed Services who has neither a spouse nor dependent children can elect such coverage for any person who has a financial interest in the member's continued life. The cost of the SBP benefit is a reduction in the retiree's pension. The federal government, however, pays a substantial part of the costs, especially for spouses and children.

If a serviceman or woman dies while on active duty, his or her family is entitled to a lump sum equal to six months' pay and the burial benefits and service-connected death compensation described above for veterans' families. In addition, if the deceased had at least 20 years of service, the spouse, if any, would qualify for the maximum SBP benefit he or she would have received were the deceased retired instead of still on active duty. The SBP benefit, however, would be reduced by any Dependency and Indemnity Compensation payment by the VA.

All these benefits, together with free medical attention, are provided without cost to the members of the Uniformed Services; they are paid out of annual Congressional appropriations. Members' dependents also qualify at no cost for the Uniformed Services Health Benefit Program (USHBP). Under USHBP these dependents may receive medical care at very low cost from the Uniformed Services medical facilities on a space-available basis. Alternatively, they may participate in the Civilian Health and Medical Program of the Uniformed Services (CHAMPUS) on a cost-sharing basis. For example, if the dependent is a spouse or child admitted to a civilian hospital, CHAMPUS pays the reasonable cost of providing the hospital services less a deductible of $25. Also eligible for USHBP, but under different conditions, are retired members and their spouses and children, deceased active duty members, or deceased retired members.

Two other benefits are provided for which the member pays at least part of the cost. First, service in the armed forces is considered covered employment under OASDI, thus making servicemen and women eligible for important death, disability, and retirement benefits under that system. Second, the member has $20,000 of protection under SGLI, which was described earlier, unless he or she declines coverage or elects a lesser amount.

PROGRAMS FOR RAILROAD EMPLOYEES

The two federal laws that established economic security programs for railroad employees are (1) the Railroad Retirement Act, covering old age, death, and permanent disability, and (2) the Railroad Unemployment Insurance Act, which covers temporary disability as well as unemployment.

Old Age, Death, and Permanent Disability

In 1875 the American Railway Express Company established the first formal private pension plan for railroad workers; by 1934, almost 90 such plans had been instituted, and the railroad industry was considered a leader in the private pension field. These plans typically provided for each year of service a pension of 1% of the worker's average salary over the 10-year period preceding retirement. Most of these plans were self-insured, and few, if any, were fully funded. Consequently, they encountered financial difficulties during the Depression. In 1934, because the orderly operation of these pension plans was essential at a time when employment opportunities for younger persons were scarce, Congress enacted legislation that created a liberal compulsory retirement system underwritten by the federal government and financed by taxes levied on the railroads and their employees.

In enacting this law Congress argued that the safety of passengers and freight was endangered by the continued employment of older workers. But the U.S. Supreme Court declared the law unconstitutional on the grounds that certain provisions took property without due process of law, and the power to regulate interstate commerce did not include the power to establish a compulsory retirement system for workers in interstate commerce. A 1935 Act creating essentially the same system was declared unconstitutional by the Supreme Court of the District of Columbia, but the decision was ambiguous and the system actually started to operate in a small way in 1936. Operations under this system and litigations concerning its operations ceased in December 1936, following a joint conference of railroads and railroad unions. At this conference the details of a mutually satisfactory compulsory retirement system were worked out, and in 1937 Congress enacted these details into the Railroad Retirement Act. This act has since been amended many times; the discussion herein is based on the system as it was amended in 1981.

The Railroad Retirement System covers employees of interstate railroads and national railway management and labor organizations. It provides four basic types of benefits: retirement annuities, annuities for total disability, Medicare, and survivorship annuities. Railroad workers are not covered under OASDI, but, as will become apparent, there is a close relationship between the Railroad Retirement System and the OASDHI program. Indeed, the relationship has been strengthened in recent years.

Retirement Annuity

Retirement annuities payable under the Railroad Retirement Act include (1) regular annuities and (2) supplemental annuities. To receive a full *regular annuity* at age 65 the worker must have completed 10 years of creditable railroad service. Workers with 30 years of service can retire as early as age 60 with a full annuity. Workers with less than 30 years of service can retire as early as age 62, but the annuity is reduced by $\frac{1}{180}$ for each month the worker retires prior to age 65.

The regular annuity is a two-tier benefit.[1] The first tier, Tier I, is the OASDI benefit the worker would receive if his or her railroad service had been covered under OASDI. This tier is reduced by any OASDI benefits the worker actually receives. The second tier, Tier II, based solely on railroad service, is similar to the private pension benefits discussed in Chapter 5. This second tier, which was greatly simplified by 1981 amendments, is equal to 0.7% of the employee's average monthly compensation for his or her 60 highest months of earnings for each year of service.

Both tiers are adjusted for cost of living increases after retirement. Tier I is subject to the same automatic adjustments as are OASDI benefits. Tier II adjustments are limited to 32.5% of the rise in the CPI.

No benefit is paid for any month the retired works for a railroad or the last nonrailroad company for which the retired worked before retirement. If a retired person, age 71 or younger, has other earnings, the Tier I benefit is reduced in the same way as OASDI benefits are reduced for earnings after retirement: $1 reduction for each $2 of earnings in excess of the exempt amounts stated in Chapter 3 for OASDI. However, the Tier I benefit cannot be reduced below what that benefit would be if it were based only on railroad service through 1974.

To receive at age 65 an additional *supplementary annuity* the worker must have at least 25 years of creditable railroad service and a "current connection" with the railroad industry. To meet the "current connection" requirement the worker generally must have worked for a railroad in at least 12 of the months in the 30 months before retirement. If the worker has at least 30 years of service,

---

[1] For some workers who were permanently under OASDHI and had some minimum railroad service prior to 1975 there is a third "windfall" component.

he or she can receive this supplement as early as age 60. Workers who retire later than at age 65 generally forfeit their right to a supplemental annuity. The supplemental annuity is $23 a month plus $4 for each year of service, subject to a maximum of $43. The supplemental annuity is subject to federal income taxes, but the regular annuity is not. The supplemental annuity is also reduced by the portion of any private pension paid for by the employer, but the regular annuity is not. In 1981 Congress terminated this benefit for employees hired after October 1981.

Spouses may also receive a full spouse annuity under certain conditions. If the worker retired at age 62 or later with *less* than 30 years of service, his or her spouse is eligible for such an annuity at age 65 or, if a wife (not husband) caring for a minor or disabled child, at any age. A reduced spouse annuity is payable as early as age 60, the reduction being $\frac{25}{36}\%$ for each month prior to age 65. If the worker retired at age 60 or later with *at least* 30 years of service, the spouse can receive a full annuity as early as age 60. The full spouse annuity is one half the worker's Tier I benefit plus 45% of the Tier II benefit. Until 1981 amendments the percentage for both tiers was 50%. Divorced wives who had been married to the employer for at least 10 years were made eligible in 1981 for Tier I but not Tier II benefits.

The total retirement benefits received by a worker and spouse are limited to half the monthly taxable limit in the year of retirement plus 80% of the difference between the employee's final average monthly compensation and half the monthly taxable limit the year of retirement.

Permanent disability

Railroad workers who are permanently disabled after at least 10 years of creditable railroad service are eligible for a full retirement annuity at any age if the disability is severe enough to prevent the worker from doing any regular work. If the disability prevents the worker from doing his or her regular job, but not other jobs, no benefits are payable until age 60, unless the worker had at least 20 years of railroad service prior to the disability. Furthermore, the worker must have had a "current connection" with the railroad industry before the disability.

A disability annuitant loses one month's benefit for each $200 earned from employment over $2,400. Furthermore, unless the annuitant earns less than $2,500 that year, he or she will not receive a check for any month in which earnings exceeded $200.

Survivor Benefits

If a railroad worker dies, his or her surviving spouse, children, and certain other dependents may receive survivor benefits under the Railroad Retirement System. For their dependents to receive such benefits the deceased worker must have had at least 10 years of railroad service and a "current connection" with the railroad industry at the time of retirement or death.

Widows or widowers receive a survivor annuity (1) at age 60 or over, (2) at any age if she or he is caring for a child under age 18 (age 22 if the child is disabled), or (3) at age 50–59 if he or she is permanently disabled because of a condition that started within seven years after the worker died or a survivor benefit based on caring for a child terminated. Other dependents eligible for a survivor annuity include (1) a child under age 18, (2) a disabled child under age 22, (3) a child age 18 or over but under age 22 if a full-time student, (4) a dependent grandchild satisfying (1), (2), or (3) if both of the grandchild's parents are deceased or disabled, and (5) a dependent parent at age 60 if dependent on the deceased for at least half of his or her support, provided that the worker did not leave a qualified widow, widower, or child. The 1981 Omnibus Budget Reconciliation Act did not change the age requirements for students or their mothers or fathers. These requirements may be changed later to achieve consistency with OASDI.

Survivors receive a two-tier benefit.[2] Tier I is equal to the OASDI benefit that would be payable if the worker's railroad service had been covered under OASDI. For widows and widowers Tier II, which was changed substantially by 1981 amendments, is 50% of the Tier II amount the employer would receive if he were still living and had retired on the date he or she died. This benefit, therefore, depends upon the employee's earnings and years of service. Children get a Tier II equal to 15% of the employee's Tier II. Parents receive 85%. The family minimum would be 35%, the maximum 80%. Divorced wives and mothers of children of the employee were made eligible in 1981 for Tier I benefits but not Tier II benefits.

All Tier I monthly survivor benefits are increased automatically each year to match increases in the CPI. Tier II adjustments are 32.5% of the increase in the CPI.

Except for the benefits paid disabled survivors, these survivor benefits are subject to the same earnings test as OASDI survivor benefits.

If a worker with at least 10 years of service in the railroad service and a current connection with the railroad industry dies without leaving a qualified dependent survivor, a lump-sum benefit of $255 is payable. For those workers who completed 10 years of service before 1975, the lump sum is close to $1,200.

OASDI Benefits

As stated above, to be eligible for retirement and disability benefits a railroad worker must have completed at least 10 years of railroad service, sometimes more. To be eligible for survivorship benefits the worker must have completed at least 10 years of railroad service and have a current connection with the railroad industry. If the worker does not meet these requirements, his or her railroad

---

[2]For some widows and widowers of deceased workers who had some minimum railroad service prior to 1975 there is also a windfall benefit.

credits are transferred to the Social Security Administration, which pays OASDI benefits based on both railroad and OASDI credits.

Financing

The benefits are financed entirely by employer and employee contributions. To pay for Tier I benefits employees pay the OASDI tax rate on the OASDI wage base. Employers pay a matching amount. Tier II benefits are financed by an additional employer contribution, equal to 9.5% based on a slightly lower wage base that increases each year with average national wages. Under 1981 amendments, pursuant to a negotiated agreement between railway management and labor, the employer tax rate will rise to 11.75% and employees will pay a new tax of 2%. Supplemental annuities are financed by an employer tax on man-hours, paid at a rate determined quarterly by the Railroad Retirement Board.

At least triennially the chief actuary of the system prepares an actuarial valuation of the system's assets and liabilities. The last valuation as of December 31, 1977, was completed in mid-1979.[3] Under the assumptions used by the OASDI Board of Trustees in its 1978 reports the system had an "actuarial balance" of 2.08% of the payroll. Under the valuation method used, the actuarial balance indicates the amount by which the payroll tax needed to result in the trust fund being 0 at the end of 75 years can be reduced (a positive balance) or must be increased (a negative balance). However, this positive balance assumed no change in the present law which, as it then stood, would cause employee and spouse Tier II benefits to become very small relative to final pay. If the law were amended, as it was in 1981, to provide an award based on years of service and final pay and cost of living increases after retirement, the system would have an actuarial deficit of 0.65–2.31%, depending on whether the postretirement adjustment was complete or partial. The valuation also showed that from 1985–2000 under all assumptions the trust fund was likely to be negative unless it obtained some special additional support.

During the fiscal year 1978–1979 the Railroad Retirement Account had receipts of $4.3 billion, $1.5 billion of which was transferred under the OASDI financial interchange agreement. The expenditures were $4.4 billion, leaving an account balance on September 30, 1979, of about $2.7 billion, over $0.1 billion less than it was a year earlier.

Under the Omnibus Budget Reconciliation Act of 1981 Congress directed the President to analyze options that will assure the long-term actuarial soundness of the system and report his findings to Congress by October 1, 1982. It also required rail labor and management to submit within 180 days separate or joint funding proposals to preserve the system. The President must also submit to Congress within the same time limit proposals to insure continued payment of

[3]*Railroad Retirement Board 1979 Annual Report* (Washington, D.C.: Government Printing Office, 1980), Part II.

the OASDI equivalent benefits and to separate the OASDI equivalents from the industry pension equivalents. Congress further announced that if a satisfactory agreement to restore financial balance cannot be reached, it intends to protect the federal government's primary responsibility for the payment of OASDI equivalent benefits even if that means the direct coverage of railroad workers under OASDI.

Under the Economic Recovery Tax Act of 1981 Congress raised the employer tax rate for Tier II benefits from 9.5% to 11.75% and added a new employee tax of 2%. This change, as noted earlier, will become effective pursuant to a negotiated agreement between railway management and labor.

Medicare

The Medicare portion of OASDI protects railroad workers on the same basis as persons covered under OASDI. The Railroad Retirement Board determines eligibility of railroad annuitants and employees for hospital benefits, and the Social Security Administration pays for the services. In addition, the Railroad Retirement Board arranges for reimbursement for hospital expenses incurred in Canada to the extent that they are not covered by provincial insurance programs.

Unemployment and Temporary Disability

As early as January 1933 the Railway Labor Executives' Association proposed a federal law designed to stabilize employment and pay unemployment compensation through payroll reserves. Their desire for a national law was based on the historical pattern of railroad labor relations. Wages, hours, and conditions of work in the railroads were not governed by state boundaries but were set for the whole industry. Experience under the state unemployment compensation acts, which originally covered railroad workers, convinced the Association that a federal approach was needed. The efforts of this Association (and others) were rewarded when, in June 1938, the Railroad Unemployment Insurance Act was passed. The law has been amended several times. Its most important amendment (in 1946) extended the system to provide cash sickness benefits, similar to those paid for unemployment, for workers temporarily unable to work because of sickness (which included maternity sickness) or injury.

Eligibility

To receive unemployment benefits the employee must be out of work, but ready, willing, and able to work. He or she must also demonstrate attachment to the labor force by having earned at least $1,000 in the calendar year preceding the benefit year. A new benefit year starts every July 1. To make certain that the employee has worked more than two months during that base period, no more than $400 of earnings can be counted in any month. A person with no railroad service prior to the base year needs at least five months of service in that base year.

A worker is disqualified for varying periods if he or she leaves work voluntarily without good cause, refuses to accept suitable work, participates in a strike in violation of the Railway Labor Act, or makes a false or fraudulent statement to receive benefits.

An employee is eligible for sickness benefits is he or she is unable to work because of either an occupational or nonoccupational illness. The employee must demonstrate attachment to the labor force by meeting the earnings requirement stated above.

Benefits

The daily benefit paid to unemployed or disabled workers is 60% of the worker's last daily rate of pay, but no more than $25. In each two-week claim period the worker can be paid for up to 10 days of employment. Because no sickness benefits are paid for the first 4 days of disability, the employee can be paid sickness benefits only up to 7 days in the first claim period in a benefit year, and up to 10 days in later claim periods.

Normal benefits are payable for a maximum of 26 weeks, but cannot exceed the worker's creditable earnings in the base year, counting earnings only up to $775 per month.

However, a worker with 10 to 14 years of service can receive extended benefits for an additional 13 weeks. A worker with 15 or more years of service can receive up to 26 more weeks of benefits. Workers with less than 10 years of railroad service qualify for an additional 13 weeks only if the insured employment rate for either the national economy or the railroad industry exceeds 4.5%. Furthermore, the extended benefits paid these shorter-term workers cannot exceed half their base period earnings.

An important feature of the sickness program is that if the worker recovers damages in a legal action, the Board is entitled to be reimbursed for the amount of the sickness benefits included in these damages.

Financing

The unemployment and disability benefits are financed by a tax on employers applied to the first $400 of each employee's monthly earnings. Unlike the federal–state unemployment programs, employers are not experience rated but the tax rate does vary from 0.5 to 8%, depending on the balance in the Railroad Unemployment Insurance Account explained next.

Taxes (other than the 0.50% placed in a separate administrative expense account) collected are deposited in a Railroad Unemployment Insurance Account. In 1978–1979 receipts were $199 million, including $194 million in contributions. Expenditures were $143 million. At the close of that fiscal year the fund had a balance of $56 million. If needed, the Railroad Unemployment Insurance Account can and has on occasion borrowed funds from the Railroad Retirement Account.

Operation of the Railroad Retirement and Unemployment Systems

Although they do not affect merely as many workers as the Social Security Act, these systems do cover all employees in an important industry. Both programs are administered through the Railroad Retirement Board, membership to which is gained by presidential appointment with Senate confirmation.

Table 13.4 shows how beneficiaries and benefit payments have increased and their distribution among the four major classes. Unlike most of the other programs studied in this book, the number of beneficiaries has remained fairly stable during the past decade. Eventually they are expected to decline, as they already have for temporary disability insurance.

Occupational Disability

As indicated in Chapter 7, work on the railroads has always been among the most hazardous occupations and once had the worst accident record. Hence it is not surprising that accident compensation should long have been a concern among railway workers. They were active in the fight for compensation legislation, and in 1908 won enactment of the Federal Employers' Liability Act which, although it has been amended many times, is the basis for occupational injury compensation on the railroads today.

It is important at the outset to stress that the Federal Employers' Liability Act is not a workers' compensation law. It does not include the principle of liability

Table 13.4 Beneficiaries and Benefit Payments Under the Railroad Retirement and Railroad Unemployment Insurance Acts, 1940–1980

Year	Retirement and Disability	Survivor	Unemployment	Temporary Disability
	Thousands of Beneficiaries (End of December)			
1940	146	3	74	—
1950	256	142	35	32
1960	553	256	102	34
1970	653	326	21	22
1980	685	330	38	16
	Millions of Dollars of Benefits			
1940	116		16	—
1950	298		60	28
1960	942		158	57
1970	1,756		39	56
1980	4,867		179	101

Sources: Social Security Bulletins.

without fault. Compensation for occupational injury on the railroads must still go through the regular court channels, and the injured employee (with some exceptions) has the burden of proof of negligence. But that burden has been considerably lightened because the common-law defenses of assumption of risk and fellow servant have been denied the employer by law. Furthermore, even contributory negligence will not wholly deny a claim, but will merely reduce it.

Injured railway workers take their claims to the courts and usually depend on jury awards for their compensation. This situation is condemned as archaic in view of the compensation principle; yet the failure until recently of most compensation laws to keep pace with rapid changes in wages and other costs, together with the liberal jury awards of recent years, have caused the railway workers to defend the system of employers' liability. If it were to be changed to a compensation system, it would be over the strenuous objection of railway unions and compensation claimants' attorneys, who are convinced that workers' compensation is not sufficiently liberal to compete with the success of jury awards.

It should be noted that the occupationally injured have two other sources of income, namely, (1) temporary disability benefits under the Railroad Unemployment Insurance Act and (2) permanent disability benefits under the Railroad Retirement Act. Should an injured worker win a damage settlement for work injury, however, he or she must, as explained above, repay any benefits received from these programs.

PROGRAMS FOR FEDERAL CIVILIAN EMPLOYEES

The federal government in its role of employer has done much to insure the economic security of its many thousands of civilian employees. Programs protecting against the perils of death, old age, and poor health have long been part of the terms of federal employment, and in 1955, for the first time, unemployment compensation was made available to federal employees.

Old Age, Death, and Disability

Actually, there are several different retirement plans covering civilian employees of the federal government and quasigovernmental agencies. Special plans cover groups such as foreign service officers. The most important of these plans is the Civil Service Retirement System, which was established in 1920. This system covers 2.7 million active workers, or over 90% of all federal civilian employees. It includes all nonelective officers and employees in the three branches of the federal government, except those excluded by an executive order (part-time workers, dollar-a-year persons, temporary employees) and those included under some other retirement plan. Special eligibility requirements and benefits apply to members of Congress and persons dealing with criminals. As noted in Chapter 3, there is a movement to bring all federal workers under OASDHI coverage. Federal employees are also eligible for important life and health insurance benefits under two employee-benefit plans underwritten by private insurers. The following paragraphs describe the Civil Service Retirement System.

Retirement Annuities

Covered employees can retire with full benefits if they are age 62 with five years of service, age 60 with 20 years of service, or age 55 with 30 years of service. There is no mandatory retirement age and no provision for retirement prior to satisfying one of the three *normal* retirement age and service requirements. However, individuals involuntarily separated from federal employment for reasons other than misconduct can receive a reduced pension as early as age 50 if they have 20 years of service, or at any age if they have 25 years of service. Any employee under age 62 with at least five years of service can, if separated for any reason, apply for a deferred annuity that begins on the worker's 62nd birthday.

The basic annuity in most cases is calculated at $1\frac{1}{2}\%$ of such pay for each of the next five years of service, plus 2% of such pay times the remaining years of service. The maximum annuity is 80% of the highest three-year average salary. The basic annuity is reduced for persons retiring earlier than age 55 or if provision is made for a survivor annuitant. An unusual feature of the reduction for the survivor annuitant is that if the person named to receive the survivor annuity is the retiring employee's spouse, the age of the spouse does not affect the reduction. After the annuity payments begin they are adjusted once a year in March to match increases in the CPI. Until a 1981 amendment payments were adjusted twice a year.

Disability Annuities

Disability annuities are payable to workers with at least five years of service who are disabled and thus unable to follow their own or similar occupations. The annuity is calculated in the same way as is the retirement annuity, except for a minimum benefit of 40% of the highest three years' average annual pay or, if less, the annuity that would be payable if the individual continued in service until age 60 with the same highest three-year average annual pay. Furthermore, there is no age reduction for persons retiring because of disability. If the disability is job related, the worker must choose between this disability annuity and workers' compensation disability payments. Like retirement benefits, these disability benefits are once each year for increases in the CPI.

Survivorship Benefits.

If a government worker with at least 18 months of service dies before retirement, his or her surviving spouse, if married at least one year or the parent of a child of the marriage, will receive a survivorship annuity. This survivorship annuity equals at least 55% of the disability annuity the deceased worker would have received if he or she had instead been disabled at the date of death. Benefits cease if the widow remarries before attaining age 60. Dependent children are also entitled to an annuity until age 18, or, if they remain in school, until age 22. Children who are incapable of self-support because of a physical or mental disability that started before age 18 remain eligible for this benefit regardless of age. If there is a surviving parent, each child receives 60% of the deceased's highest three-year average salary divided by the number of children. If there is no surviving parent, the percentage is 75. In either case there are maximum amounts for each child and for all children combined, which are automatically adjusted upward as the cost of living increases.

If a worker dies with less than 18 months of service or leaves no surviving spouse or children, there is a lump-sum benefit payable equal to the employee's contributions to the system accumulated at a specified rate of interest. If the worker has at least 18 months of service and leaves a surviving spouse or children, there is a lump-sum benefit equal to the difference, if any, between the accumulated contributions and the amount paid under the survivor annuities to these beneficiaries.

Survivors of a retired worker will continue to receive 55% of that portion of a worker's pension that the worker chose as a base for the survivor annuity. That portion may vary from 0 to 100%. Married workers are automatically assumed to have selected 100% unless they request otherwise. Like the retirement and disability annuities, these survivorship annuities are adjusted once each year to preserve their purchasing power as measured by the CPI.

Persons leaving federal employment with less than five years of service can claim the contributions they made to the system. Interest is payable on these contributions if the refund covers service of more than one year. If the persons leaving have at least five years of service, they can claim their contributions (but no interest) or leave their money in the system and claim a deferred annuity at age 62.

Financing the Civil Service Retirement System

The Federal Civil Service Retirement System is jointly financed. Employees today contribute 7% of their regular compensation. A matching contribution is made by the governmental departments for which they work. Congress has authorized the Secretary of the Treasury to meet the balance of the costs of the system. This balance includes payments for (1) interest on the existing unfunded liability of the system (see below), (2) the cost of allowing credit for military service, and (3) the cost of changes in the system since 1970.

This system also permits an employee to make deposits in addition to the regular 7% deduction if he or she wants to increase the retirement annuity. These deposits earn an interest rate of 3%, compounded annually. For each $100 in the employee's voluntary contribution account he or she would receive at age 55 an annuity of $7 a year. The yearly payment would be greater for later retirement;

the amount would not be adjusted after retirement for cost of living increases.

Each year the Board of Actuaries of the system prepares an actuarial valuation of the assets and liabilities of the Trust Fund. In their 1980 report, which valued the fund as of September 30, 1977, the Board estimated that under static assumptions, which ignore the cost of inflation, the "normal cost" to support benefits accruing on account of current service was 13.73% of the payroll.[4] Because the employee contributions are 7% of the payroll, the "normal" cost to be covered by employer contributions was 6.73%, less than the 7% annual contribution by the employing agency. Under dynamic assumptions, however, which assume a 6.5% annual salary increase and a 6.0% annual CPI increase, the normal cost of the current service benefits was 36.46% of the payroll, leaving a 29.46% employer normal cost.

In addition, the fund has a net unfunded accrued liability of $167 billion under the static assumptions, $350 billion under the dynamic assumptions.

The board recommended that the Civil Service Retirement Act be changed to require dynamic assumptions and that a level percentage of payroll financing of the unfunded liability over the next 50 (or 75) years be substituted for an existing complex, inadequate method. Thus the recommended federal contribution was 48.1% of the payroll over the next 50 years (or 42.6% over the next 75 years). The normal cost contribution would be 29.5%, the level annual cost of eliminating the unfunded liability 18.6% (13.0% if this liability is to be eliminated over a 75 year period). Under the system that they found to be inadequate the recommended annual employer contribution would be 26–29%.

Operation of the Civil Service Retirement System

Table 13.5 shows the number of persons who have received retirement, disability, and survivor benefits under the Civil Service Retirement System since 1940 and the substantial dollar increase in those benefits.

The President's Commission on Pension Policy

The President's Commission on Pension Policy studied federal pensions in depth. Their major recommendations regarding the Federal Civil Service Retirement Plan have already been reported in Chapter 5.

Other Programs

In addition to the Civil Service Retirement system benefits, federal employees are allowed 13 days of paid sick leave a year, which can be accumulated without limit and used to improve the benefit at retirement.

Under the Federal Employees Group Life Insurance Act of 1954 these workers

[4]*Board of Actuaries of the Civil Service Retirement System Fifty-Seventh Annual Report* (Washington, D.C.: U.S. Government Printing Office, 1980).

Table 13.5 Beneficiaries and Benefit Payments Under the Federal Civil Service Retirement System

Year	Retirement and Disability	Survivor
Thousands of Beneficiaries (End of December)		
1940	65	—
1950	161	25
1960	379	154
1970	697	308
1980	1,296	450
Millions of Dollars of Benefits		
1940	62	
1950	184	
1960	804	
1970	2,797	
1980	15,042	

Sources: Social Security Bulletins.

became eligible for group life insurance serviced by one major private life insurer but reinsured by over 350 other insurers.

Under the Federal Employees Health Benefits Act of 1959 federal employees and their dependents became eligible for a choice among approved commercial insurance, Blue Cross and Blue Shield, and "other" plans, typically Health Maintenance Organizations, available where they live. About 40 plans, including one underwritten by a pool of commercial insurers and another by Blue Cross and Blue Shield, have been approved. Under all plans the government pays part of the cost.

Federal employees may become eligible for Hospital Insurance through OASDI covered employment. Like all aged persons they can apply for Supplementary Medical Insurance. If they are covered under either Medicare Program, that program becomes the primary payor, with the Federal Employees Health Benefits Plan providing supplementary coverage.

Occupational Illness

The oldest of the federal programs is the Federal Employees' Compensation Act —the workers' compensation system for federal government workers. In fact, it is the oldest of the American workers' compensation systems, dating back to 1908. Since the law covers employees of all branches of the federal government, its total coverage is close to 3 million workers.

Like the state workers' compensation systems considered earlier, the federal system provides indemnity and medical benefits for disability that is causually linked to employment—due either to disease or accidental injury. The federal system differs from the state laws in several respects, particularly in benefit administration, but its most significant difference is that the federal system is generally more liberal. For example, this plan provides full medical benefits, a 75% wage replacement rate if there are dependents, a high maximum weekly benefit (over $700 in 1980) and no limit on total disability length or amounts.

The Act is financed by Congressional appropriations and administered by the Office of Workers' Compensation Programs in the Department of Labor. All administrative functions of claims adjustment and administrative supervision are conducted by the Office of Workers' Compensation.

Unemployment

Until 1955 federal employees were not eligible for unemployment compensation benefits under the state unemployment compensation laws. As of January 1, 1955, however, they gained coverage under the state laws and are eligible for benefits with the same status—for purposes of the system—as employees of private industry.

EMPLOYEES OF STATE AND LOCAL GOVERNMENTS

State and local government employees are protected by widespread economic security programs.

State and Local Government Retirement Systems

About 10 million persons, or almost 80% of the persons employed by state and local governments, are currently insured under one of several retirement programs. Although these retirement systems vary widely from one locality to another, a few generalizations can be made on their operations. In 1974, according to Robert Tilove, a noted pension expert, the "typical" plan contained the following provisions.[5] The age at which the employee could retire on normal benefits was 60 if the employee had at least 10 years of service. The mandatory retirement age was 70. The retirement benefit was the number of years of service times 1.67% of the average salary earned in the most highly paid 5 years of the last 10. After retirement the pension was increased annually, up to 3%, to match increases in the CPI. Employers with at least 10 years of service could retire as early as age 55 at an actuarially reduced benefit. The plan provided 100% vesting after 10 years, 0% for less service. If permanently and totally disabled after 10 years of service, the employee was paid a normal pension. If the employee died before retirement, his or her beneficiary received a death benefit of six months' to one

---

[5]Robert Tilove, *Public Employer Pension Funds* (New York: Columbia University Press, 1976), pp. 10–11.

year's salary. If the employee died after retirement, there was no death benefit unless the employee had selected a joint and survivor option. The employee contribution was 5% of pay, the rest of the cost being paid by the government. Pay-as-you-go financing was gradually disappearing, but there was also a softening of funding policies by some systems that had formerly set rigorous standards.[6] Employees covered under the typical plan were eligible for OASDI benefits in addition to the plan benefits.

In a January 1980 report Ebasco Risk Management Consultants summarized the features of 70 statewide plans in 44 states.[7] The age and years of service requirement for full pension benefits ranged from a low of age 55 and five years of service in California to 65 years of age and 10 years of service in Texas. For a person retiring at age 65 with 30 years of service the ratio of the plan benefit to the member's gross earnings in the final year of work ranged from 23 to 58% for employees with OASDI coverage, from 25 to 74% for employees without OASDI coverage. The usual ratio was near 50%, compared with 40% for OASDI, 54% for the Federal Civil Service Retirement System, 75% for the Federal Uniformed Services, and 31% for the private sector. Only 10 of the 44 states provide automatic cost of living adjustments. Only 1 of these 10 states matches completely increases in the CPI. Many other states have provided similar ad hoc increases out of special funds authorized by the legislature.

The estimated 10 million workers covered by these programs outnumber those covered under the Railroad Retirement and Civil Service Retirement plans combined. Table 13.6 indicates the number of beneficiaries and the amount of benefits paid under state and local retirement systems in selected years from 1960 through 1978, the last year for which accurate data are available.

The steady increases over time reflect increases in the number of plans, the number of employees, their salary and benefit levels, and the maturing of existing plans.

No national figures are available on the actuarial status of these plans, but in recent years this status has been widely questioned and debated. Many funds, however, face serious financing problems. The extent of the problem varies, depending on the funding objective adopted.[8]

As reported in Chapter 5, the President's Commission on Pension Policy has recommended the passage of a Public Employee Retirement Income Security Act.

[6]Robert Tilove, *Public Employer Pension Funds* (New York: Columbia University Press, 1976), p. 172.

[7]Austin L. Herzog, *Pension Plan Provisions of State and Federal Public Employer Retirement Systems* (New York: Ebasco Risk Management Consultants, January 1980).

[8]See, for example, the various funding standards discussed in Bernard Jump, Jr., "Compensating City Government Employees: Pension Benefit Objectives, Cost Measurement, and Financing," *National Tax Journal*, XXIX, No. 3 (September 1976), 240–256 and Howard E. Winkelvoss and Dan M. McGill, *Public Pension Plans* (Homewood, Ill.: Dow-Jones, 1979), Chapters 11–13.

For a recent comprehensive analysis see *An Actuarial and Economic Analysis of State and Local Government Pension Plans,* Report to the Chairman, Joint Economic Committee of the United States by the Comptroller General of the United States (Washington, D.C.: U.S. General Accounting Office, February 26, 1980).

Table 13.6 Beneficiaries and Benefits Under State and Local Retirement Systems. (Numbers in Thousands, Amounts in Millions of Dollars)

Year	Retirement		Disability		Survivorship		
	Beneficiaries	Benefits	Beneficiaries	Benefits	Beneficiaries	Benefits	Lump Sum
1960	535	845	55	95	70	75	63
1965	725	1,390	69	155	92	125	105
1970	1,055	2,610	95	295	122	215	150
1975	1,599	5,900	128	495	221	380	250
1978	1,959	8,636	169	711	290	508	305

Sources: *Social Security Bulletin, Annual Statistical Supplement, 1970, 29;* and "Benefits and Beneficiaries under Public Employees Retirement Systems, Calendar Year 1978," *Research and Statistics Note No. 1* (Washington, D.C.: Office of Research and Statistics, Social Security Administration, U.S. Department of Health and Human Services, February 18, 1981), p. 9.

The Social Security Act permits states to enter voluntary agreements with the federal government to accept federal OASDHI coverage for employees of the state or of its political subdivisions. As of March 1978 over 9.2 million, or about 72%, of the state and local government jobs, were covered by such agreements. In five states all such jobs were covered; in two states no jobs were covered.

As of December 31, 1979 700 government employers, including the state of Alaska, had terminated their OASDI coverage. Another 250 employers had terminations scheduled for 1980 and 1981. Local governments in California, Georgia, Lousiana, and Texas accounted for most of these terminations.

Other Programs

In mid-1980 31 states covered all their state and local government employees under their workers' compensation programs. In the other states some government employees were either not covered or covered only if their unit of government elected such coverage. Many government units whose employees are covered self-insure these obligations. As was true for federal employees, state and local government employees are commonly eligible for paid sick leave. Many states share the cost of group life insurance, group disability insurance, and group medical expense insurance plans underwritten by private insurers. The Employment Security Amendments Act of 1970 extended unemployment insurance coverage in all states to certain government employees; only a few states cover their other employees.

SUMMARY

Despite many differences among the economic security programs for special groups, all of them (with the exception of the veterans' programs) have one striking similarity. Each originally sought to provide essentially the protection that most workers engaged in private industry would have received from a combination of the Old-Age, Survivors, and Disability Insurance program and group insurance and pension plans. Inevitably, this raised the question of whether it might not have been more logical for purposes of equitable treatment and administration costs to have included the special groups under the OASDI programs and used the special programs for providing the additional coverage deemed desirable.

As we have seen, the railroad system has worked out its special form of accomodation with the OASDHI, and the state and local systems are increasingly coordinating their programs. The civilian employees of the federal government remain the last major group not to have OASDHI coverage, and several studies and recommendations have been made of possible ways to provide them OASDI protection.

Veterans programs are the most diverse. Benefits include payments in case of death or disability plus medical care and the opportunity to purchase private group life insurance. If the death or poor health is not service connected, the death, disability, and medical care benefits are paid only if the veteran or his or her survivors need financial assistance. Consequently non-service-connected benefits are more closely related to public assistance than to social insurance. Veterans may also qualify for such benefits as state unemployment insurance, federal educational assistance, and federal loan guarantees.

Persons on active duty with the Uniformed Services have a liberal pension–disability plan in addition to OASDHI coverage. They receive free medical attention for themselves plus generous protection for their dependents. If they die on active duty, their survivors receive death benefits. Active duty personnel may also purchase private group life insurance. As veterans, they qualify for the programs noted above.

Railroad workers have their own pension plan that is closely integrated with OASDHI. This plan also provides important death and disability benefits. They also have a separate unemployment and temporary disability program. Unlike most workers, they are covered not under workers' compensation but under a federal employers' liability law.

Federal civilian employees are not covered under OASDHI. Most are covered under the Federal Civil Service Retirement System, which is generally considered one of the most liberal programs covering civilian employees. These employees are also eligible for private group life insurance and private medical expense insurance. The Federal Employees' Compensation Act is the oldest and one of the most liberal workers' compensation systems in the United States. Federal employees are covered under state unemployment compensation laws.

Most state and local government employees are insured under retirement programs that vary widely from state to state. For a person retiring at age 65 with 30 years of service the benefit is usually about 50% of the worker's final gross earnings, compared with 40% for OASDHI, 54% for the Federal Civil Service Retirement System, 75% for the Federal Uniformed Services, and 31% for the private sector. Almost three-quarters of the state and local government jobs are covered under OASDHI. Most, but not all, employees are covered under workers' compensation and unemployment compensation. Many states share the cost of private group life insurance, disability insurance, and medical expense insurance.

SUGGESTIONS FOR ADDITIONAL READING

Bleakney, Thomas P. *Retirement Systems for Public Employees.* Homewood, Ill.: Richard D. Irwin, 1972.
A publication by the Pension Research Council describing prevailing public employee retirement system concepts and practices and the major influences affecting the design and development of these systems.

Cheit, Earl F. *Injury and Recovery in the Course of Employment.* New York: Wiley, 1961.
See Chapter 1 for a description of the Federal Employees' Compensation Act and Chapter 7 for the Federal Employers' Liability Act.

Federal Pension Programs. Working Papers, President's Commission on Pension Policy, Washington, D.C., January 1981.
An extremely valuable description and analysis of federal pension plans covering civilian and noncivilian federal employees.

Herzog, Austin L. *Pension Plan Provisions of State and Federal Public Employee Retirement Systems.* New York: Ebasco Risk Management Consultants, 1980.
An outline of the major provisions of the Civil Service Retirement System, the Uniformed Services Retirement System, and state public employee retirement systems.

McGill, Dan. M. (Ed). *Financing the Civil Service Retirement System.* Homewood, Ill.: Richard D. Irwin, 1979.
A compilation of papers on how the Federal Civil Service Retirement System is and should be financed.

Myers, Robert J. *Social Security.* 2nd ed. Homewood, Ill.: Richard D. Irwin, 1981.
Chapters 12 and 16 of this comprehensive book deal with the Railroad Retirement System and special programs for government employees and veterans.

Pension Task Force Report on Public Employee Retirement Systems, Committee Print, 85th Congress, 2nd Session, March 15, 1978. Washington, D.C.: U.S. Government Printing Office, 1980.
A comprehensive detailed report on the characteristics of public employee retirement plans.

Publications by the Veterans Administration, Department of the Army, Navy, and Air Force, the Railroad Retirement Board, and the Office of Personnel Management of the U.S. Civil Service Commission describing current employee benefits available to veterans, Uniformed Service personnel, railroad workers, and federal civil service employees.

Report by the Comptroller General of the United States: Need for Overall Policy and Coordinated Management of Federal Retirement Systems: Vols. I and II. Washington, D.C.: U.S. General Accounting Office, December 29, 1978.
An analysis of federal retirement systems, including many smaller plans not discussed in this chapter, and the need for a more integrated system.

Report of the President's Commission on Pension Policy. Washington, D.C.: 1981.
This report by a national commission appointed by President Carter to study private and public plans contains some important recommendations concerning pension plans for federal employees.

Robertson, A. Haeworth. *The Coming Revolution in Social Security.* McLean, Va.: Security Press, 1981.
Chapters 17 and 18 of this thought-provoking book deal with the factors affecting decisions by those who can opt into or out of OASDI.

Steiner, Gilbert Y. *The State of Welfare.* Washington, D.C.: Brookings Institution, 1971.
Chapter 7 is an interesting, informative discussion of the benefits provided needy veterans.

Tilove, Robert. *Public Employee Pension Funds.* New York: Columbia University Press, 1976.
A comprehensive study of state and local government pension plans and the major public policy questions affecting these plans.

Winkelvoss, Howard E. and Dan M. McGill. *Public Pension Plans: Standards of Design, Funding, and Reporting.* Homewood, Ill.: Dow Jones-Irwin, 1979.
This book provides some valuable guidelines or standards for public pension plans on benefit structure, funding policy, and disclosure of financial information.

Chapter Fourteen

The Nature, Measurement, and Causes of Poverty

In the preceding chapters we have examined the particular economic insecurities associated with individuals (and their families, when relevant) who have a regular attachment to the labor force on other than a marginal income basis. The logical presumption is that these individuals will be able, in the normal course of events, to provide for their own economic support. It is only when misadventure occurs —an accident at the work place, an occasional spell of unemployment—that economic security programs must provide a substitute income stream or assist with additional expenses such as medical bills.

For a sizable segment of our society these programs are niether relevant nor applicable. These persons, for a variety of reasons, do not have a regular labor force attachment, or, if they do, work only intermittently and/or at substandard wages. The reasons are numerous. The person involved may be a mother who cannot seek employment because of young children at home. Disability may preclude working. Or the individual may have only a casual attachment to the labor force, so that the kinds of economic security programs previously analyzed are not applicable. Of what value, for example, is unemployment insurance to a person who has never been able to secure a job? Or to one who has never held a job long enough to qualify for such insurance or whose earnings are insufficient for qualification, even though he has been employed "long enough" to meet an attachment requirement?

The purpose of this and the following two chapters is to analyze the nature, measurement, and causes of the "poverty" of this group and the economic security programs devised to assist them. Poverty programs are quite different from the economic security programs previously discussed.

"Poverty" is as multi-dimensioned as "insecurity." We shall not be concerned, however, with other than "economic" poverty, important though the other dimensions may be. The economic dimension of poverty can be described simply: it is the inability of an individual or a household to secure enough income to meet the requirements of a specified minimum budget. ("Inability" is an ambiguous term: at one extreme it can refer to a highly motivated individual who, for a variety of reasons "external" to himself, cannot find employment; at the other, it can be applied "internally" to a person to whom work is alien. This is discussed later.)

Poverty is also distinguished by its protracted character. Except in unusual cases, risks discussed previously, such as unemployment or occupational disability, tend to be of short duration. Economic security programs designed to meet these risks reflect the short-run incidence of the insecurity. A maximum of 26 weeks of unemployment compensation and similar programs of income protection are not applicable to the long-run economic insecurity arising out of poverty. Hence poverty is not only an income insufficient to meet a minimum budget, but an insufficiency that extends beyond the short run.

Poverty in history and approaches to it are discussed in the next chapter; here we start, as noted above, on its measurement and causes.

THE MEASUREMENT OF POVERTY

There are two issues involved in the measurement of poverty. The first is determining and specifying the income line below which poverty is held to exist: the poverty threshold. The second is the "unit" of measurement used in counting the "people" below the poverty line. We take these up in turn. (Making the actual count is, of course, another issue. But this is a "census" problem, not a conceptual one.)

The measurement of poverty starts with the construction of a minimum income budget—a poverty threshold. From a census of the population a count can then be obtained of individuals and families below the minimum income line and who, therefore, can be characterized by the term "poverty."

Many such budgets have been constructed. Perhaps the earliest one publicized was the $3,000 budget for a family of four, as utilized by the Council of Economic Advisers in the early 1960s. The most widely used current series of budgets are those developed by the Social Security Administration in the mid-1960s.[1]

Although the construction of minimum income budgets is a highly technical and complicated task, their rationale is not difficult to understand. First, a "minimum diet" budget, or an "economy food plan," is constructed for individuals and for families of varying size and age composition. This diet is then costed out at current prices for a specified period of time. The resulting "food" budget provides an indication of the minimum income an individual or family requires to purchase the foodstuffs in a minimum diet.

Studies by the U.S. Department of Agriculture (USDA) and others have shown that for families of three or more persons in low-income categories, food

[1]See Mollie Orshansky, "Counting the Poor: Another Look at the Poverty Profile," *Social Security Bulletin,* XXVIII, No. 1 (January 1965), 3–29. This article is probably the best single reference on poverty budgets.

Table 14.1   Social Security Administration Poverty Index—Economy Level, Nonfarm,
1963

Family Size	Per Capita Food Expense ($)	Poverty Income Threshold ($)
1	Not estimated	1,540
2	240	1,990
3	270	2,440
4	260	3,130
5	245	3,685
6	230	4,135
7 or more	210	5,090

Source: Mollie Orshansky, "Counting the Poor: Another Look at the Poverty Profile,"
Social Security Bulletin, XXVIII, No. 1 (January 1965), 9.

costs are roughly one-third of total costs. The USDA estimated in the early 1960s
that, minimally, food for a family of four would cost $2.73 a day, or $1,000 a year.
To determine the total minimum income budget, including shelter, clothing, and
other needs, the food budget is therefore adjusted upward by 200%. If the
minimum food budget is $1,000, the total budget is $3,000. Different percentage
adjustments can be applied for single individuals and two-member families.[2]

Table 14.1 shows an early minimum income annual budget, as constructed by
the Social Security Administration.

In 1969 several modifications in the original Social Security Administration
definition of poverty were recommended by a Federal Interagency Committee.
These related to the following: (1) retaining the base year (1963) poverty thresholds for nonfarm families, but basing annual adjustments on changes in the CPI
rather than on changes in the cost of food in the economy food plan; and (2)
raising the farm poverty thresholds from 70 to 85% of the nonfarm levels.

The reason for using the CPI to adjust minimum income budgets arose from
the fact that general cost of living increases in the late 1960s were not uniformly
matched by increases in the price of goods in the economy food plan. As to farm
poverty, a 1961 study indicated that the value of food produced by farm families
for home use amounted to about 30% of their total food budget. Although it is
not yet possible to quantify precisely all the factors that make for differences in
the cost of living between farm and nonfarm families, more recent research
suggests that narrowing the differential from 70 to 85% more closely reflects the
actual relationship.

By 1980 rising prices had increased minimum income budget amounts to the
levels shown in Table 14.2.

[2]Budgets can be developed by pricing out all budget items, including food. But the "percentage"
system noted above provides similar results with much less computational difficulty and was used by
the Social Security Administration in the initial construction of minimum income budgets in the
1960s. Some 121 specific budgets for varying groups and situations have been developed.

The poverty income threshold for farm families approximates 70% of each of the family-size categories listed in Table 14.1 and 85% of those listed in Table 14.2. Thus for a farm family consisting of an unrelated individual (a "family of one") the threshold was 70% of $1,540, or $1,078 in 1964, and 85% of $3,790 or $3,222 in 1980.

A variety of comments can be made about poverty budgets and their construction and applicability.

1 A poverty threshold budget relevant during one era is not necessarily a valid budget at a later time if the budget is adjusted only to take into account the changes (increases) in prices. Increases in productivity over a period of years have resulted in increases in the plane of living. Hence one should not expect that a family of the 1900s had at hand the same bundle of goods and services as a family in the 1980s. If the 1980 bundle was adjusted only for changes in the cost of items in the 1900 budget, it would not truly reflect the 1980 situation.

For example, Robert Hunter made the following estimates for the year 1904 in the United States.[3] A budget of $460 a year would defray the minimum necessary expenses of a family of five (parents plus three children) in northern industrial communities, and $300 would be required in southern areas. If one compares the "minimum necessary budgets" of 1904 and 1980 with increases in prices (or decreases in the value of the dollar) for the same period, one is struck by the fact that the budgets have increased by more than the prices. This simply reflects the fact that the plane of living in 1980 budgets is proportionately greater than in those 80 years earlier. A static view of the poverty threshold may be rational for the short run; however, it is not for the long run.

2 Historically, in the United States, increases in productivity have outrun increases in prices, and the "distribution" of the increases in productivity has been

Table 14.2 Weighted Average Guidelines in 1980—Poverty level, Nonfarm

Family Size	Poverty Income Threshold ($)
1	3,790
2	5,010
3	6,230
4	7,450
5	8,670
6	9,890
7 or more	11,110

Source: Press Release, April 1980, U.S. Department of Labor. Unless the adjustment method is changed, the reader can update the above by merely applying the appropriate CPI increase. There are technical limitations to this use of the CPI—a changing "market basket," inclusion of mortgage interest, and so on—but the technicalities are beyond the scope of our discussion. (In March 1981, the threshold figure for a family of four was raised to $8,450. The new levels for all family sizes average $920 higher than in 1980.)

[3] See Robert Hunter, *Poverty* (New York: Macmillan, 1907), pp. 55ff.

made in such a way that there has been a more or less continuous reduction in poverty. If one took the 1904 poverty budgets of Robert Hunter and compared them with similar 1980 budgets, one would find a reduction in poverty, increased planes of living notwithstanding. (More recent poverty trends are examined below.)

3   Poverty is, however, affected by the level of economic activity. Thus in 1980 the number of individuals and families below the poverty income threshold was greater than in 1979, and another increase was predicted for 1981. Such short-run variations need not necessarily imply longer-run trends, but nor is there any guarantee that the future would be different from the past.

4   Income distribution is, in and of itself, not correlated with poverty. There will be always a segment of the population that is at the lower 10 or 20% of the income distribution. But this should not lead to the conclusion that those at the lower end of the spectrum must necessarily be impoverished. It is more than conceivable that individuals and families at this lower end can eventually lift themselves out of the poverty stratum.

5   It has become increasingly common to decry the residue of economic growth: junked automobiles, discarded beer and soft-drink bottles, and wayside litter that results from growth, affluence, and a disregard for ecological "sanitation." There is much to such charges, but it also appears to be true that economic growth provides one way—though not necessarily the only way—by means of whic a society can seek to put all its citizenry beyond an impoverished level.

The above discussion focuses on what is defined as measuring poverty in an absolute sense. Some critics contend that poverty should be measured in a relative sense, such as all those in the lowest 10th or 20th percentile of all income recipients. In this case poverty exists whenever incomes are unequally distributed. (The interested student should refer to any principles of economics book for a discussion of Lorenz curves and Gini coefficients as they are used to measure income inequality.)

Victor Fuchs has taken a middle course on this absolute–relative issue.[4] He would use one-half of median family income as the poverty threshold. In 1980 this would approximate $10,000 for a family of four. This approach permits combining absolute and relative measures. However, it also is not problem free: what of the unit with $9,999 of income? Or an income of $10,001?

THE POOR: STATISTICS AND TRENDS

Given the poverty threshold budget, what is the unit of measurement to be used in counting the poor? The conventional unit is the "household"—whether consisting of a single person or related individuals. As social and cultural patterns

[4]Victor Fuchs, "Comment" in Lee Soltow (Ed.), *Six Papers on the Size and Distribution of Wealth and Income* (New York: Columbia University Press, 1969), pp. 198–202.

change, this measurement unit significantly affects the count. For example, parents, in their later years, no longer live with their children to the extent they once did. (Over the last 20 years "household formation" has increased at about twice the rate as population.) This suggests that if more "doubling up" took place, poverty would decline: if two households below the line were to combine, their total income could well be sufficient to put them above the poverty threshold. Thus, if aging parents lived with their children, total income could well lift the family unit out of poverty. But such "togetherness" is no longer culturally common. Hence the measurement unit recognizes today's reality.

If one takes the long view of history, there is little doubt of the reduction of poverty. But comparisons with other eras offer small comfort to families forced to live under the particularly oppressive conditions of poverty in the industrialized 1980s. There has been a traceable improvement in the numbers of those classed as poor. Table 14.3 shows the gradual progress made during the 1960s. Going back further, one finds that, using a $3,000 cutoff figure (in 1962 dollars), 32% of the population was below the poverty level in 1947.[5]

The following comments can be made on the changing quantitative dimensions of poverty.

1 Poverty threshold budgets are a reflection of value judgments, and one should not expect to find complete agreement on the dollar dimensions of such budgets. The $3,000 "boundary" poverty budget (before taxes, and expressed in 1962 prices) represented a weekly income of less than $60 for a family of four. Other analyses utilizing different market baskets, many of them costing more, resulted in higher budgets.

Under a $3,000 budget for a family of four, some $5 a week per person would

Table 14.3 Persons Below the Poverty Level, 1959–1980 (All Persons in Families and Unrelated Individuals)

Year	Numbers (In Thousands)	Percentage Below the Poverty Level
1960	39,851	22.2
1965	33,185	17.3
1966[a]	30,424	15.7
1970	25,420	12.6
1975	25,877	12.3
1980	29,272	13.0

Source: U.S. Department of Commerce, Bureau of the Census, *Current Population Reports: Consumer Income,* Series P-60, No. 120 (Washington, D.C.: Government Printing Office, 1981), Table 14.3.

[a]The marked drop during 1966 as compared with that of 1965 is in part a result of a revised methodology for processing income data.

[5]See the *Economic Report of the President* (Washington, D.C.: Government Printing Office, 1964), p. 59.

have been needed for food, an approximate total of $1,000 a year for this purpose. Of the $2,000 remaining, approximately $800 (a conservative estimate) would have been required for housing—rent or mortgage payments, upkeep, utilities, heat. This would leave only $1,200 (less than $25 a week) for *all* other expenses: clothing, transportation, schooling, home furnishings and supplies, medical care, personal care, insurance, and everything else. It does not exaggerate the problem of poverty to regard $3,000 as the boundary budget in the early 1960s, or over $8,000 (and rising steadily) today.

2   The use of a $3,000 poverty threshold budget (as against, say, $2,700 or $3,300) during a specified base period obviously influences the numbers of those below the poverty threshold.[6] What constitutes a justifiable or rational poverty threshold budget is obviously a matter that involves highly selective value judgments.

But it is important to note that whatever the budget selected, the decades since World War II have brought a reduction of those in poverty from 32% of the total population in 1947 to less than 13% in 1970, a reduction of over 60% in the numbers of those impoverished. However, the trend since 1970 has not exhibited the same degree of improvement; the poverty rate has hovered between 13.0 and 11.1%. Some critics have suggested that we are now down to the "hard-core" poverty level and that it may take other measures to further reduce the rate.

3   Economic growth tends to reduce poverty by raising family incomes above the poverty line. But it also tends to incrase poverty in a quantitative sense by sanctioning higher aspiration levels and by making it possible for the young, the old, and single individuals to maintain their own way of life, thus creating large numbers of low-income units that might not otherwise exist independently.

4   If poverty has been reduced steadily and, in the context of our discussion, markedly since 1945, why is there such current concern? A number of reasons are relevant. First, as recorded statistically, the income of the poor includes monies paid under public assistance programs from federal, state, and local sources. In 1963 this totaled some $4.7 billion; by 1980 this had more than quadrupled, and some jurisdictions, such as New York City, were laboring under almost impossible welfare costs.

Second, the "War on Poverty" has assumed a kind of class-conflict dimension between the "haves" and the "have-nots."[7] In a social context this becomes a clash between those of a presumed work-oriented disposition and those not so situated, that is, between taxpayers and welfare recipients.

---

[6]For example, if $2,000 were used as the poverty threshold in 1960, the percentage of all persons below that threshold would have been 13% instead of the 22.2% cited in Table 14.3.

[7]The reader need only refer to daily newspapers for accounts of conflicts between welfare officials and those on welfare to corroborate this.

A Postscript Note on Measurement

All the above data and comments are based on the "official" method of measuring poverty. It is important to note here that this method takes into account *only cash income,* whether earned, received via transfer payments, and so on. This measure *does not include "income in kind":* child nutrition, food stamps, housing assistance, Medicaid, and so on.[8]

In the absence of *cash* transfer payments the poverty rate would have approximated 27% in 1980. Such *cash* payments reduced the rate to 13.5%, thus cutting in half the amount of "statistical" poverty in the United States.

Now suppose that in-kind payments were included in incomes of the poor. What would be the result? It depends on whose estimates one looks at. Government data reduce the rate to 8.1% *after all transfers* and to 8.3% *after all transfers and taxes.*

A more extreme view of the reduction is taken by Edgar K. Browning.[9] Browning notes that in-kind payments rose from $42 to $657 per poor person in 1964–1973, an increase of 1,464%, whereas direct cash transfers rose by only 172%. Browning concludes that the average poor family had an income that was approximately 30% over the poverty line, and hence there was practically no poverty in the United States. He also notes that the poor consume a larger share of "public goods"—education (the poor have larger families), fire protection (more dilapidated housing), police protection (live in higher-crime-rate areas) and so on.

In the same vein, Morton Paglin analyzes poverty after transfers in kind.[10]

Paglin, assisted by Gerald Wood, "cashes out" in-kind transfers at market value and then adjusts the Census cash income poverty estimates. He concludes that the number in poverty was reduced from 17.6% of the population in 1959 to 3.6% in 1975 (compared with Census estimates of 22.4 and 12.3%, respectively).

To the contrary, the National Advisory Council on Economic Opportunity held in October 1980 that "nearly 25 million Americans still live in poverty."[11] It was noted that while those in poverty have declined by 11 million since 1964, there has been a "frightening shift" toward women, the young, and minorities. (The Council excludes in-kind transfers in its estimates.)

Whose judgment does one accept? If one includes in-kind transfers, the lower

---

[8]There are several reasons for the exclusion of in-kind payments. One is quantitative: it is difficult to evaluate such payments and secure the data. Another is qualitative: a poor person has a serious illness but is covered by Medicaid. "Philosophically" how does one view such a situation? The poor should have more illnesses, since they are "protected?"

[9]Edgar K. Browning, "How Much More Inequality Can We Afford?" *The Public Interest,* No. 43 (Spring 1976), 90–110 (especially p. 91).

[10]Morton Paglin, *Poverty and Transfers In-Kind: A Re-Evaluation of Poverty in the United States,* (Stanford, Calif.: Hoover Institution Press, 1980).

[11]Press release, October 18, 1980 (Advisory Council to the President).

figures may be more "accurate." But, this should not lead one to conclude that the poverty problem is thereby "solved."

Who Are the Poor?

Innumerable characterizations are possible, in documentaries and in fiction. But perhaps the most succinct summary is contained in the previously cited 1964 *Economic Report to the President.* This document is a classic summary in that it was the first full-fledged presentation of poverty in such a *Report* and is still valid today in portraying general patterns even though the specific figures would need considerable revision.

One-fifth of our families and nearly one-fifth of our total population are poor.

Of the poor, 22% are nonwhite; and nearly one-half of all nonwhites live in poverty.

The heads of over 60% of all poor families have only grade-school educations.

Even for those denied opportunity by discrimination, education significantly raises the chance to escape from poverty. Of all nonwhite families headed by a person with eight years or less of schooling, 57% are poor. This percentage falls to 30% for high school graduates, and to 18% for those with some college education.

But education does not remove the effects of discrimination: when nonwhites are compared with whites at the same level of education, the nonwhites are poor about twice as often.

One-third of all poor families are headed by a person over 65, and almost one-half of families headed by such a person are poor.

Of the poor, 54% live in cities, 16% on farms, and 30% as rural nonfarm residents.

Over 40% of all farm families are poor. More than 80% of nonwhite farmers live in poverty.

Less than half of the poor are in the South; yet a southerner's chance of being poor is roughly twice that of a person living in the rest of the country.

One-quarter of poor families are headed by a woman; but nearly one-half of all families headed by a woman are poor.

When a family and its head have several characteristics frequently associated with poverty, the chances of being poor are particularly high; a family headed by a young woman who is nonwhite and has less than an eighth-grade education is poor in 94 out of 100 cases. Even if she is white, the chances are 85 out of 100 that she and her children will be poor.[12]

[12]See Ref. 5, pp. 56–57.

The profile characterizations of the poor can be summarized under a series of general descriptive headings.[13]

1 *Age* Poverty falls disproportionately on the old and young. In 1978, of all persons in the United States, 11.4% were below the poverty threshold. For individuals 65 and over the rate was 14.0%; for related children under 18 in families with a female head the rate was 50.6%. Of all families 9% were below the poverty level in 1978; but when the head was under 25 years, the rate was 18.5%; over 65 and female, 12.2%.

2 *Sex* For persons in families with a male head the poverty rate in 1978 was 6.6%; with a female head it was 32.3% percent. For unrelated males 14 and over the rate was 17.1%; for unrelated females, 26.0%.

3 *Family size* Two-person families had a poverty rate of 8.0% in 1978. The rate was about the same for three- and four-person families; for five-person families it was 10.7%, and was 13.9% for six-person families and jumped to 22.8% for seven-person units. Families with no children had a poverty rate of 4.7%; those with five or more related children under 18 had a rate of 37.4%.

4 *Educational attainment of family head* For those with less than eight years of elementary education the poverty rate was 20.3%. For those with less than four years of high school it was 14.4%; with less than four years of college, 3.4%. For family heads with four or more years of college the rate was only 2.0%.

5 *Number of earners and employment status* Families with no earners had a poverty rate of 29.8% in 1978; with three earners or more the rate dropped sharply to 2.7%. For families in which the head was employed the rate was 4.9%; unemployed, 24.9%; and not in the labor force (that is, not at work or looking for work), 21.7%. If the head worked full-time in 1978, the poverty rate was only 2.4%; for heads who worked 1 to 49 weeks it was 16.4%; for those who did not work at all in 1978 it was 24.0%.

6 *Occupation of family head during longest job.* As one might expect, poverty is correlated quite markedly with one's occupation. For families in 1978 whose head was an employed professional or managerial worker the poverty rate was 2.2%. For nonfarm laborers it was 10.0%, for service workers (including private households), 15.5%, and for farmers and farm laborers, 17.7%.

7 *Race* For all categories nonwhite poverty rates are higher than white. In

[13]U.S. Department of Commerce, Bureau of the Census, *Current Population Reports: Consumer Income,* Series P-60, No. 120 (Washington, D.C.: Government Printing Offices, 1979). Data in the following paragraphs are from this publication. Such reports are issued annually, with about a 12-month lag. Year-to-year changes tend to be minimal, hence the general configuration of the 1978 data hold today.

1978 6.9% of white families were below the poverty threshold; for black families the rate was 27.5%. Where the white head of a family was a farmer or farm laborer the rate was 17.4%; for black families in a similar situation the rate was 48.7%. (The highest of all poverty rates for 1978 was the black family of five children or more headed by a female: 83.2%.) In absolute numbers, 16,259,000 whites were below the poverty threshold in 1978, compared with 8,038,000 blacks and other races.

8 *Farm–nonfarm*   For all races nonfarm family poverty rates were 9.1% in 1978, compared to 10.9% for farm families. Comparable rates for whites were 6.8 and 9.9%; for blacks, 27.4 and 36.3%.

9 *Geographic region*   In 1978, for families the poverty rate was 8.3% in metropolitan areas (12.7% inside central cities, 5.3% outside) and for nonmetropolitan areas the rate was 10.8%. For unrelated individuals the respective rates were 19.3, 21.4, 16.9, and 30.1%. For persons, area poverty rates were as follows: Northeast, 8.5%; North Central, 7.1%; South, 11.7%; West, 8.3%. For unrelated individuals the rates were 20.7, 23.5, 27.2, and 17.7%, respectively. (In the South rates for blacks were 31.0% for families and 45.3% for unrelated individuals. The respective white rates were 8.0 and 23.0%.)

These statistics, in and of themselves, tell us a good deal about the "causes" of poverty. This topic is discussed in detail below, but some conclusions are obvious concerning the relation between the incidence of poverty and its causes. Unemployment of a year's duration produces an income loss that few families can counter through the use of savings of one kind or another. Or, other things being equal, a large family poses more expenditure problems than does a small one.

Second, the data above are only the cold, hard statistics of poverty. They tell us little or nothing of the human side of poverty: the misery, the pain, the emotional wreckage. A book on economic security is not the place to detail such accounts, but the reader can find them easily in fiction and documentaries, from Steinbeck's *The Grapes of Wrath* to Harrington's *The Other America*[14] and innumerable books on life in inner-city ghettos.

THE CAUSES OF POVERTY

What "causes" poverty? What is *a* "cause"? What is *the* "cause"? If one gets into the philosophy of such questions, one finds oneself rapidly bogged down in metaphysics, with questions that are perhaps unanswerable. Yet it is not possible to avoid the queries. Whatever one may visualize as "ultimate causality," if indeed such a visualization is possible, one can seek to identify more proximate factors.

[14]Michael Harrington's book, *The Other America* (New York: Macmillan, 1963) is credited with having much to do with the origin of "war on poverty" as it developed in the early 1960s.

In an early description of the dilemma of "causality," the 1964 *Economic Report of the President* noted

> Poverty is the inability to satisfy minimum needs. The poor are those whose re-
> sources—their income from all sources, together with their asset holdings—are
> inadequate.[15]

If one asks *why* income is insufficient, one finds responses such as discrimination in employment (on the demand for labor side) or lack of education (on the
supply side). What is the cause of discrimination? One goes back a step, to
prejudice. What causes prejudice? Back another step; and so on. Where is the end?
Perhaps only the philosopher or psychologist can say. Within the limits of our
discussion let us try to determine what is "known" about the causal factors
involved in poverty.

Insufficient Income and Resources

Why do the impoverished have insufficient income and insufficient resources?
Answers to these questions operate on both the demand and supply sides of the
labor market.

On the demand side a variety of factors are at work. Insufficient aggregate
demand is one cause, preventing those able to accept jobs or working only
part-time from utilizing their capacities. (Again, "cause" rears its head: why is
there insufficient aggregate demand?) But this is only part of the answer, for many
of those "fully" employed are nevertheless below poverty levels. Why? Because
they are in industries such as farming or domestic service work, where low
productivity is the key. But then, why low productivity?

Hence one needs to turn to the supply side. Workers in these industries reflect
low productivity, which in turn results from a lack of education or training,
physical or mental disability, or poor motivation. Or, on the demand side, it may
result from discrimination or low bargaining power. Back to the supply side:
poverty may result also from an inadequate knowledge of alternative opportunities, or an unwillingness or inability to be mobile.

Let us look at all these forces in a more systematic fashion.

The Economic Setting

The Level of Economic Activity

Putting to one side for the moment secular trends in the economy—long-run
economic growth or, conversely, economic decay—one can ask the following:
what is the relationship between the level of economic activity and the extent of
poverty? Or, phrased differently, how is poverty affected by the "business cycle"?

[15]See Ref. 5, p. 62.

The answer, as one might expect, is that poverty declines in good times and increases in poor. In one study[16] the 15-year period 1948–1983 was divided into (1) years of strong economic expansion (1950, 1951, 1953, 1955, 1959, 1962), (2) years of slow expansion (1952, 1956, 1960, 1963), and (3) years of no expansion (1949, 1954, 1957, 1958, 1961). In years of strong expansion the number of poor families declined by 667,000 per year. In years of slow expansion the decline was 425,000 families per year. In years of no expansion (recession years) the number of poor families rose by 400,000 per year. Hence the difference between prosperity and depression affects over 1 million families. As noted earlier, there was an increase in the number of poor in 1970 and 1971 as a consequence of lowered economic activity. The same trends held for the 1974–1975 recession and will undoubtedly occur as these lines are being written in 1980.

The reason for this is clear. For those in low-income categories the primary source of income is through employment rather than from dividends, interest, or other nonemployment sources. What is more important, however, is the fact that lower-income persons tend to be the employees who are the first to be laid off or discharged when the level of economic activity turns downward. Moreover the nonwhite, frequently the last hired, may be the first to go, thus compounding the problem for this group. (This is generally valid, though one can find exceptions such as the incidence of unemployment among engineers and scientists in the early 1970s resulting from the decline of activity in the aerospace industry or among professionals in 1980.)

Even in periods in which the level of economic activity is high there are, of course, individuals and families below the poverty threshold. But the level of economic activity is important. For example, there were 24,260,000 persons below the poverty threshold in 1974. This was an *increase* of 1,287,000 compared with 1973. Had the level of economic activity not slackened in 1974 (as compared with 1973), there would no doubt have been a further *decrease* in the number of the impoverished. It is true that economic growth was an important factor during this period and one should not mix cyclical factors with secular. But the downturn in 1974 was cyclical and its impact on the numbers of those in poverty is apparent. The same pattern will undoubtedly occur in the 1980–1981 "recession."

One can view our economy as characterized by long-run economic growth. However, the growth trend has not been even. Superimposed on it are periods in which growth has slackened or even turned downward. The implications for poverty are clear in these periods. Poverty is a consequence of insufficient income. Those above but near the poverty threshold receive their income primarily, if not entirely, from the wages earned in gainful employment. A decline in the level of economic activity results in a decline in the number of jobs available and hence in the ability of certain individuals to maintain themselves through wages earned by working.

[16]Burton A. Weisbrod (Ed.). *The Economics of Poverty* (Englewood Cliffs, N.J.: Prentice-Hall, 1965), pp. 15–16.

Economic Growth

Three general statements can be made about the relationship between economic growth and poverty:

1   Economic growth results in an annual increase in the goods and services produced by an economy.
2   Historically, in the United States, the growth in output of goods and services has been greater than the increase in prices of those goods and services. Hence there has been growth in real terms and not merely in the price tags placed upon goods and services.
3   Also, throughout our history economic growth has risen faster than "aspiration levels." As noted earlier, if one compares a minimum income budget for 1980 with one for 1900, one finds that the increases in the former have not been caused by increases in prices alone. The 1980 budget contains items not throught of in 1900. The 1980 budget also takes into account increases in aspiration levels since 1900, but the pace of economic growth has been greater than the increase in aspiration levels. There has thus been a marked decline in poverty since the turn of the century.

The ability of an economy to grow is based on a number of factors: natural resources, physical capital, and human capital. An economy well endowed with natural resources and with high-quality human capital can find the human capital utilizing the natural resources, developing physical capital, and producing an increasing output of goods and services.

The United States is an economy well endowed with natural resources and with high-quality human capital. It has experienced continuing economic growth —not always steady (witness the post-1929 decline), but persistent over long periods. The consequences have permitted increasing numbers of people to escape from poverty. Why the economy does not grow at a rate sufficient to provide jobs for all who want them is a difficult question that we are not capable of answering, though we could spell out various factors involved.

The relationship of economic growth to the reduction in poverty is vividly illustrated by the economic experience of the United States during the 1960s. In that decade the gross national product (the measure of the production of goods and services) rose from $487.7 billion to $724.7 billion in real terms (1958 prices), or an increase of 48%. During the same period the total number of persons below the poverty threshold decreased from 39,851,000 to 24,289,000, a reduction of approximately 40%. Moreover, this was in the face of a population increase from 178,136,000 to 199,067,000. That decline in the extent of poverty may not have been a cause for complacency, but the gains were not insignificant. However, that rate of decline in poverty was not matched in the 1970s. The decrease was from 25. million in 1970 to an estimated 24.2 million in 1979—a reduction of only 4.7%. Apart from the malaise of stagflation in the 1970s, it may well be that we are reaching the plateau of hard-core poverty.

The anatomy of economic growth is an interesting subject. To explore it in detail is impossible in these pages, but a number of comments can be made. Natural resources may be a necessary condition for economic growth, but the mere existence of such resources does not guarantee growth. There must also be human beings interested in and capable of utilizing such resources to produce physical capital. Or, phrased differently, there must be humans capable of combining land, labor, and capital in such a way that goods and services are produced.

A number of other factors relate to economic growth. Growth is possible under differing systems of government: compare the United States with the U.S.S.R. Each has exhibited growth since, say, 1945.[17] But, differing systems or not, political stability of some degree is required. Anarchy is not likely to be conducive to high-level economic performance. The body politic also needs to utilize "rational" economic policies. It is doubtful that confiscatory taxation or monetary mismanagement would be conducive to growth. The system of rewards and punishments for economic performance is less capable of generalization. It appears to depend importantly on the "culture" of the economy: economic rewards may be the spur under one system, prestige or other nonmonetary factors in another.

Irrespective of the political system, the entrepreneur is important. Under one system the political bureaucracy may perform this function. Under another it may be the individual or a group of individuals. But there must be some set of persons capable of initiating and guiding economic activity.[18]

Economic growth is not an unmixed blessing. In the context of this discussion two comments can be made, both related to the central issue of poverty.

First, one source of economic growth is through improved technology, or more efficient ways of producing goods and services. Such technology frequently substitutes a machine for a worker, and the worker is displaced. The debate still continues as to the long-run employment impacts of such change. What, for example, is the aggregate employment effect of what is characterized as automation? The answer is only partially relevant here. What is important is that such technology may displace persons whose age or ability may not permit them to find employment elsewhere. Second, the tempo of technological change may, if anything, be increasing rather than decreasing. The possibility of a descent into

---

[17]We leave aside such questions as to which system is likely to produce more rapid growth, if indeed such a questions can be answered.

[18]One of the authors has long been interested in how business enterprises get started. At the most general level of discussion it appears to be a consequence of an individual or group having an "idea" for new goods or service, and being (1) capable of translating it into technologically feasible terms, (2) able to secure the necessary financing, and (3) capable of marketing the goods or service. More relevant for the discussion here is the employment opportunities opened up by the creation of such enterprises—the possibilities for people to find jobs, to earn an income, and to thus avoid poverty. The reader may wish to look around his own community and ascertain the employment opportunities created over, say, the last decade.

poverty is more than an idle threat. (In 1980 the increasing use of "robots" again brought this problem to the forefront.)

Economic growth thus permits a reduction in poverty, but it also creates other problems. Two of many may be noted here. The exploitation of natural resources in the production of goods and services can lead to an exhaustion of resources in a given area and hence to real regional poverty. Appalachia is perhaps the most striking illustration of this. An increase in the output of goods and services can also produce undesirable side effects, of which pollution is a currently outstanding example. It is probable that pollution can be reduced without severely stunting economic growth. But even if growth were to be deliberately reduced, in part through a lowering of aspiration levels, the results might not have as much of an adverse effect on poverty as might be initially concluded.

To summarize, economic growth is not an unmixed blessing, but it has permitted increasing masses of mankind to lift themselves above a poverty existence.

The Distribution of Income

The goods and services produced by an economy can be divided (or distributed) in a variety of ways: equally among all inhabitants; through authoritarian control, via the Marxian philosophy (honored more in the breach than in the practice) of "from each according to his abilities, to each according to his needs"; or via the productive principle of "to each according to his contribution to production." Capitalistic economies have utilized the last method, which is the tradition found in the United States.

Without undertaking a digression on the philosophy of these several methods, a number of comments may be made. Equal distribution of income appears to be a historical rarity. Authoritarianism has almost invariably resulted in situations in which those in authority waxed rich while the rest of the populace hovered in abject misery. (Often in an authoritarian society an equality in income distribution would put everyone on the brink of misery: the rich are so few, the poor so many, and the output so low that a transfer from the former to the latter would accomplish little.) The Marxian philosophy, like equal distribution, is a rarity. Where it has been tried in "utopian" communities, it has tended to break down because of difficulties in gauging the level of personal needs. Even in the U.S.S.R. income differentials are prevalent. Finally, income distribution based on the contribution to production may suffer from ethical difficulties about what constitutes a justifiable contribution to production and how exploitation, inheritance, and other factors distort such a distribution. A distribution system need not be heartless: the state may tax the well-to-do to assist the poor, which is the common practice in Western capitalistic economies.

If income were equally distributed in the United States, what impact would equal income distribution have on the incidence of poverty? Various income indexes might be used, but perhaps the most satisfactory is "disposable personal income." This is the income available to persons for expenditure after personal tax and nontax payments have been subtracted. That is, it is the income remaining for "disposal" after taxes and other liabilities have been taken into account.

In 1970, on a per-capita basis, disposable personal income was $3,333 in current (1970) prices. That is, if such disposable income in the United States in 1970 were divided *equally* among every man, woman, and child, each individual would receive $3,333. For a family of four this would mean a *total* family income of $13,332, for *each and every* family of four in the United States. (The 1980 numbers would differ, but the conclusions would still hold.) Such a pattern of distribution would immediately abolish poverty in this country. What it would do to incentives, to entrepreneurial activity, to the willingness to invest, and so on, and hence to income in the *future,* is a matter of conjecture. The experiment of equal distribution has not been tried, and given the philosophy of reward according to "productivity," a trial is not likely. This approach to the abolition of poverty does not appear as a feasible single-stroke alternative.

If income is not equally allocated in the United States, what is the pattern of distribution? What have been the changes over time?[19] While the share received by the top 2% of families fell between 1929 and 1949, it rose from then on till 1962 and has not lessened since. The lowest one-fifth of consumer units received 4.1% of family personal income in 1935, 5.0% in 1947, 4.6% in 1962, and an estimated 4.6% in 1980.

One may well conclude, therefore, that a *major* reduction in the inequality of income distribution is not likely, and hence it is also not likely to produce a reduction in the incidence of poverty. What is more probable is that the absolute income received by the lowest 20% will grow at rates that will permit such individuals and families to climb increasingly out of poverty. Income as such will increase more rapidly than will necessary expenditures, and poverty will decrease accordingly.[20] (The pattern of the 1970s, however, tempers this optimism.)

The Labor Market

Discrimination and the Demand for Labor

There is little doubt that employers over the years have discriminated in their hiring practices on the basis of race, color, creed, age, sex, and other variables.[21] Certain kinds of "discrimination" have a rational basis. For example, an insurance company founded and operated by a given religious group would find it difficult to employ salesmen from a quite different religion, should they choose to apply for a position with the company.

[19]See Robert Lampman, "Income Distribution and Poverty," in Margaret S. Gordon (Ed.), *Poverty in America* (San Francisco, Calif.: Chandler Publishing, 1965), pp. 102–114.

[20]For an excellent discussion on the general issues of income distribution and poverty see Edward C. Budd (Ed.), *Inequality and Poverty* (New York: W. W. Norton, 1967).

[21]One of the authors served a term as Chairman of the Fair Employment Practices Commission in a midwestern city. This account is in part based on these experiences.

However, much discrimination in employment is undeniably based on factors that are rooted in prejudice. Discrimination based on sex may have innately ethical implications, and discrimination based on age may have similar complications. But neither is likely to lead to poverty as such, although the older worker or the female may be at a disadvantage.

To the contrary, discrimination based on factors such as color or creed may pose a genuine problem as respects the ability of a given individual to secure a position enabling him to earn a living above the poverty threshold. *The Economic Report of the President* for 1966 noted

> If economic and social policies could be specifically designed to lower Negro unemployment to the current unemployment level of whites, the resulting gain in GNP would be $5 billion. Part of this gain would be in the wages of new Negro employees, and part would accrue as other forms of income. A further gain would result if all Negroes were able to obtain jobs which would better utilize their abilties and training.[22]

This kind of discrimination is so well known that detailed discussion is not necessary. (The numbers for 1980 would differ; the conclusions would not.)

The Civil Rights Act of 1964 sought to remedy discriminatory action on the part of employers. While significant improvements have been made, the problem is still extremely complex. For example, assume that women desire positions on faculties of institutions of higher learning in a ratio equivalent to the proportion of female Ph.D.'s produced in a given discipline over the decade 1960–1970. During those 10 years 10 Ph.D. degrees were granted in Arabic, only 1 of them to a woman. This would suggest that all institutions teaching Arabic should struggle for a fraction of this person.

The illustration may appear farfetched, but it is not. Increasingly the problem appears to be not so much discrimination on the demand side, but a shortage of prospective employees on the supply side. (One need only try, for example, as one of the authors did, to hire a chairman for an American Indian studies department or for a Chicaño studies department in an institution of higher learning to ascertain what the supply shortages are.) Even if barriers are breaking down on the demand side, we still have a good way to go on the supply side. It is true that discrimination in the demand for labor has accentuated poverty. But a greater social responsibility rests in the failure to prepare minority groups for the opportunities that are being opened to them.

The Supply of Labor and Poverty

Even if no employer practiced discrimination in recruiting and hiring, there is no necessary guarantee that poverty would be eliminated. As noted earlier, poverty does exist within the work-oriented sector of society. (We consider below the

---

[22]*Economic Report of the President* (Washington, D.C.: Government Printing Office, 1966), p. 110.

issues associated with the non-work-oriented segment.) Putting to one side factors such as illness, which may preclude one from working at times, the chief cause of poverty among the work oriented is found in the low rates of pay attached to certain occupations such as common labor or service work. In turn, the chief reason for the low rates of pay is low productivity.

In turn, low productivity may result from poor motivation, physical or mental disability, or lack of education or training. We come full circle: if high-wage jobs were available and employers did not discriminate, many of those below the poverty threshold would not possess the capabilities of filling such jobs. (One might ask, however, if it is not discrimination if the employer fails to hire a nonqualified applicant. Is this not discrimination on the basis of inability rather than, say, race or sex? The answer appears to be that the social belief does sanction an ability criterion in employment. Yet the "unable" person may be "unable" because of discrimination, say, in education.)

Pushing the analysis one step farther, what are the reasons for poor motivation, lack of education or training, or mental disability? An interesting "explanation" is the following.[23] The determinants of "productive intelligence"—and hence of the possibility of qualifying for "living wage" jobs—are the following: (1) Intelligence A, the individual's marketable potential at the moment of conception; (2) Intelligence B, the same potential at the moment of birth; and (3) Intelligence C, the marketable ability at any point in life after birth.

Intelligence A is a limiting concept. Those with defective genes are doomed to low or zero production. Those with low Intelligence A *cannot* rise, but those with high Intelligence A may not. Intelligence A is a broad category embracing all those characteristics that allow man to perform mentally and physically.

Intelligence A can be affected and eroded between the time of conception and the time of birth. If the mother suffers from malnutrition, for example, the results may be adverse. Certain diseases such as German measles may likewise have adverse effects. The lower the socioeconomic status of the mother, the more likely these effects will be found. In the prenatal stage a social responsibility exists to provide the necessary care for a mother who might not otherwise be able to afford it. The long-run impact of such care should be to reduce the adverse effects that the lack of care produces with respect to Intelligence B. In turn, this poverty causal factor would be reduced.

Intelligence C is the combination or interplay of hereditary and environmental factors. Two individuals with equal Intelligence A may nevertheless move through quite different patterns of experience that mold and shape Intelligence C. An individual who receives an excellent education may emerge with an "intelligence" level quite different from that of a person who receives only a limited education or attends a primitive school.

Again, the social implications are clear. Insofar as society fails to make equally available those services such as education that affect Intelligence C, then society

---

[23]See Alan B. Batchelder, *The Economics of Poverty* (New York: Wiley, 1966), pp. 73–76.

will have a subgroup incapable of getting out of poverty because of a lack of education or training. The provision of services such as education does not guarantee that individuals will always take advantage of them, but the failure to provide them will inevitably produce less of a reduction in poverty than would otherwise be the case.

A Poverty Culture?

In the discussion above we have focused on those who are able to and would be willing to work (and lift themselves out of poverty) if it were not for the handicaps of, say, inadequate education or training. Is there another group to whom work is alien and who, notwithstanding any and all opportunities offered them, would reject them in favor of perpetual welfare? The authors are not trained in the disciplines capable of generating answers to this type of question, but the evidence appears to suggest the following conclusions.

First, though it surfaces as a kind of conventional cliché, it appears that, on balance, people would prefer employment and self-support rather than idleness and external support. Hence, in the thrust toward a reduction in poverty, all those educational and employment policies and practices that will increase human potential and maximize job opportunities are socially advantageous. The success of programs such as New Careers, in which mothers on welfare were able to secure an education and employment, attest to this. But, even if she has a desire to work, the difficulties for a female who heads a family with small children are obvious. In New York City alone there are over 150,000 fatherless families.

Second, there does, however, appear to be a poverty "culture" in the sense of a preference for welfare over employment. We have not been able to ascertain their dimensions or all of their characteristics, but transitory cultures such as the "antiestablishment" groups of the 1960s would be examples.

More "permanent" types may be found. An example is the family with the absent father and the mother and children on welfare by necessity *or* choice. The number of such families appears to have increased both absolutely and relatively. The solution for this kind of poverty cause does not yet seem to be on the horizon, nor does the solution for the individual "drifter," although quantitatively this group is much smaller than the absent-father family.[24]

The above questions and discussion can be phrased in a different way, as has been spelled out perceptively by one researcher working in this field.[25] Are the "poor" an *entity* with more or less stable membership or a *category* into which

[24]We discuss "incentive" problems in Chapters 15 and 16. See also the citations for Martin Anderson in Chapter 15.

[25]See the interesting analysis by Stephen Thernstrom, "Poverty in Historical Perspective" in Daniel P. Moynihan (Ed.), *On Understanding Poverty: Perspectives from the Social Sciences* (New York: Basic Books, 1968), pp. 160–186. See also, in the same volume, "The Culture of Poverty" by Oscar Lewis, pp. 187–199.

persons fall and out of which they climb? The evidence is not at all conclusive on this question and what is available does not wholly support the entity point of view. True, available statistics suggest that some parents receiving Aid to Families with Dependent Children payments were themselves reared in families in which public assistance was received. But a high percentage of these were reared during the post-1929 depression, when at least a quarter of the American people were recipients of such assistance. And studies of vertical mobility—up or down—indicate that a significant amount occurs. People move into and out of poverty. We need to know a good deal more about the "composition" of the poor before we can accept a permanent poverty hypothesis.

Motivation obviously plays a role in such cases. The determinants of this characteristic are complex and we do not seem to know a great deal about the techniques for modifying motivation. Certainly this is a matter that has long concerned societies. Witness, for example, the many poor-relief programs that sought to differentiate between the "deserving" poor (those poor through no fault of their own) and the "nondeserving" poor (those who would not work even if opportunities were available). Perhaps such problems are inherent in any society.

The handicapped and ailing may form another type of permanent poverty culture. Much has been done to improve the employability of the handicapped, but for those not employable the fact of potential poverty still exists. These persons clearly constitute a group for which society must assume the responsibility of providing support.

SUMMARY

Economic poverty is defined in terms of an insufficiency of income—for an individual or a family—to meet a minimum budget. The minimum budget is calculated by estimating the costs of maintenance at a subsistence level.

Poverty may be transitory in nature, as in the case of an individual who becomes temporarily unemployed, is not covered by unemployment insurance, and has no assets to fall back on. But poverty may have a much higher degree of permanence for certain individuals and families.

Poverty is influenced by many factors, among which economic growth is highly relevant. Long-term economic growth has been a most important influence in reducing poverty. Growth involves an increase in the output of goods and services. The distribution of this output, even in a society in which income is based on productive contribution, has made it possible for increasing numbers to lift themselves (or be lifted) out of poverty. Short-run economic factors also play a part. Thus a recession or depression increases poverty; prosperity decreases it.

The way in which income is distributed affects poverty. If, in the United States, disposable personal income were distributed equally, poverty would not exist. The ultimate results, in regard to the output of goods and services, are a matter of conjecture. But, given a strongly ingrained philosophy of reward based on productivity, it is not likely that this country will adopt a different system. However, even if the share of family income received by the lowest one-fifth of consumer units was to decline, there is no inherent reason why this distribution pattern would preclude additional individuals and families from escaping from poverty. Irrespective of relative shares, the absolute income received by the low-income segment has in the past increased at a pace that permits a reduction in the numbers of those impoverished.

Poverty is "caused" by many factors. Causality is an elusive concept and it is probable that "ultimate causality" is incapable of definition. The first cause of poverty is insufficient income. But, in seeking a cause for insufficient income, the peeling away of successive layers of causality is necessary for a better understanding of the problem.

SUGGESTIONS FOR ADDITIONAL READING

Much of the outpouring of books and articles on poverty came in the 1960s with the "war on poverty." This list includes major works from that period, with a few additions.

Batchelder, Alan B. *The Economics of Poverty.* New York: Wiley, 1966.
An incisive and very readable volume. Contains an excellent annotated bibliography.

Budd, Edward C. (Ed.). *Inequality and Poverty.* New York: W. W. Norton, 1967.
A collection of essays that discuss in an interesting and sophisticated fashion the relation between income distribution and poverty.

Galbraith, John K. *The Nature of Mass Poverty.* Cambridge, Mass.: Harvard University Press, 1979.
Vintage Galbraith: very good reading though you may not agree with all his views. The focus is global rather than on, for example, the United States.

Harrington, Michael. *The Other America: Poverty in the United States.* New York: Macmillan, 1962.
Credited as having sparked the war on poverty.

Kershaw, Joseph A., assisted by Paul N. Courant. *Government Against Poverty.* Chicago, Ill.: Markham Publishing, 1970.
Analyzes the Economic Opportunity Act of 1964, as well as other measures designed to assist low-income groups.

Miller, S. M., and Pamela Roby. *The Future of Inequality.* New York: Basic Books, 1970.
An important analysis not only of the economic dimensions of poverty, but of a number of frequently overlooked related psychological and sociological factors.

Moynihan, Daniel P. (Ed.). *On Understanding Poverty: Perspectives From the Social Sciences.* New York: Basic Books, 1968.
An interesting series of essays on the history and culture of poverty.

Orshansky, Mollie.
See her various articles through the years in the *Social Security Bulletin.* The best single source on poverty budgets and the count of the impoverished.

Perlman, Richard. *Economics of Poverty.* New York: McGraw-Hill, 1976.
A sound and comprehensive analytical treatment of poverty, programs, proposals.

Schiller, Bradley R. *The Economics of Poverty and Discrimination,* 3rd ed. Englewood Cliffs, N.J.: Prentice-Hall, 1980.
A multidimensional approach to poverty, its causes, and appropriate policy approaches.

Stein, Bruno. *On Relief: The Economics of Poverty and Public Welfare.* New York: Basic Books, 1971
Discusses the historical evolution, politics, and economics of programs in aid of the poor.

Sundquist, James L. (Ed.). *On Fighting Poverty: Perspectives From Experience.* New York: Basic Books, 1969.
A companion volume to that edited by Daniel Moynihan and noted above, but focusing on poverty programs.

U.S. Department of Commerce, Bureau of the Census. *Current Population Reports: Consumer Income,* Series P-60, No. 77. Washington, D.C.: Government Printing Office, 1971.
A series that provides continuing data on the numbers and characteristics of those in poverty.

Chapter Fifteen

The Welfare System

The poor are currently served by a complex welfare system that includes such approaches as cash payments, Medicaid, and food and housing assistance. In the opinion of many persons of varying political persuasion, both the poor and the nonpoor are so badly served by this system that it should be replaced or reformed. Some proposals for a radical shift to a guaranteed minimum income approach are presented in Chapter 16. Other proposals, discussed later in this chapter, would reform the present system in some significant ways. Some of these proposals are now law under the Omnibus Budget Reconciliation Act of 1981. In the meantime millions of poor persons receive aid under present programs. This chapter describes the five major components of the welfare system: (1) cash public assistance, including the categorical programs and general assistance; (2) Medicaid; (3) social services and child welfare services; (4) food assistance; and (5) housing assistance. The chapter concludes with a discussion of the earned income tax credit, which is a unique form of public assistance.

SOCIAL INSURANCE: ITS USES AND LIMITATIONS

Before turning to the programs designed specifically to attack poverty in the United States, let us examine briefly the uses and limitations of social insurance programs as a tool for alleviating poverty.

Social insurance benefits raise the income of many families above the poverty threshold, thus reducing the proportion of families that are poor. Social insurance benefits also reduce the degree of poverty among those families who remain poor despite the receipt of these benefits. In 1978 social insurance benefits were received by about 31% of the poor families and accounted for about 20% of their income.[1]

Social insurance, however, is designed primarily to protect all covered persons,

[1] U.S. Department of Commerce, Bureau of the Census, *Current Population Reports: Characteristics of the Population Below the Poverty Level: 1978,* Series P-60, No. 124 (Washington, D.C.: Government Printing Office, July, 1980), pp. 162, 174.

not just the poor, against financial losses caused by death, old age, poor health, and unemployment. Although the benefit structure typically favors lower-income persons, benefits bear some relation to past wages. Furthermore, the minimum benefits are below poverty levels. Raising these minimum benefits to the poverty level would place much more emphasis on social adequacy relative to private equity. To maintain an acceptable balance between these two objectives by also raising substantially the higher-than-minimum benefits would be costly and would produce benefits for higher-income persons that most would probably consider as too high.

For these reasons programs directed solely at the problems of the poor have been developed.

CATEGORICAL CASH PUBLIC ASSISTANCE PROGRAMS

Public assistance programs provide cash benefits, medical care, and other services for persons who can demonstrate that they need such assistance. Ideally, the benefit is equal to the demonstrated need. The most important public assistance programs are cash public assistance programs designed to help certain categories of needy persons: the aged, the blind, the permanently and totally disabled, and families with dependent children deprived of parental support because either parent has died, is disabled, is continually absent from the home, or, under some plans, is unemployed.

Historical Background

To understand the present welfare program of the United States, one should have some knowledge of its history, which is traceable to the English Poor Laws.

The English Poor Laws

Prior to the 16th century the feudal system provided security (although at a low level) for a good share of the English population, and the Church assumed primary responsibility for helping others in need. With the passing of the feudal system and, to a lesser extent, the dissolution of monasteries, poverty became a more acute problem and the dissatisfactions it created worried governmental authorities. On the assumption that any able-bodied person could find employment if he or she tried, in 1531 the state concentrated its attention on a law designed to stamp out vagrancy. Under this law only the aged and the impotent were permitted to beg, and they had to restrict their activities to their own neighborhood. Relief of the poor was left to the conscience of local authorities. However, a 1536 statute, which some historians consider to be the first English poor law, made local authorities responsible for the collection of voluntary contributions to be used to employ able-bodied "paupers" and to provide direct relief for others. Poor children were to be apprenticed and all begging was prohibited. Relatives were expected to assume primary responsibility for the poor of all types. Only the larger cities developed workable programs under this law; some of these cities imposed a compulsory poor rate instead of depending on voluntary contributions. In 1572 a compulsory poor rate was imposed on a national scale.

A major bench mark was the passage in 1601 of what is popularly known as the Elizabethan Poor Law or the "Old Poor Law." Under this law parishes were made the unit of administration. With funds obtained from a compulsory poor rate, the aged poor were to be granted relief, poor children were to be apprenticed, and the able-bodied poor were to be assigned jobs. As in earlier times, relatives were held primarily responsible for supporting the poor in each of these groups. Increasingly the system of local administration caused difficulties, because the poor tended to seek out those parishes with the most satisfactory relief arrangements. As a result the parishes began to restrict benefits to established residents. A 1662 Law of Settlement and Removal legalized and strengthened this practice by permitting the overseers of a parish to petition the local justices to move back to his or her place of settlement any new resident who did not rent a fairly substantial dwelling or who could not guarantee that he or she would not become a public burden in the future. Under the Elizabethan Poor Law the aged and the sick apparently received better treatment than other poor persons. Children were often apprenticed under unsatisfactory arrangements merely to reduce the cost of supporting them on relief and only feeble attempts were made to employ the able-bodied poor.

In 1723 a general act permitted parishes to refuse relief to those who would not enter workhouses. These workhouses "everywhere rapidly degenerated into mixed receptacles of misery where every class of pauper, vicious or unfortunate, young or old, sick, well or lunatic, was dumped."[2] Increasing humanitarian concern about these workhouses resulted in a 1782 act that permitted parishes to combine resources to build institutions for all paupers except the able-bodied, who were to receive relief or to work outside the institution.

Toward the end of the 18th century a series of events causing price increases made the wages of many workers inadequate. Although one solution would have been to raise wages, such action would not have been consistent with the prevailing mercantilist obsession with maintaining a favorable balance of trade. This solution was also opposed by the ruling landowning aristocracy, who wanted a good supply of cheap agricultural labor.[3] The problem seemed to be temporary. Consequently, at a meeting at Speen in 1795 the Speenhamland system (discussed in Chapter 16) was adopted: wages were to be supplemented by relief payments if they did not provide a minimum standard of living.

---

[2] "Poor Law," *Encyclopaedia Brittanica,* Vol. XVIII, 1964, p. 218.

[3] The Law of Settlement had been supported by this English ruling class for the same reason. For an excellent analysis of the effect of prevailing economic thought on the English Poor Laws, see Vlademar Carlson, *Economic Security in the United States* (New York: McGraw-Hill, 1962), Chaps. 3 and 4.

With the advent of the Industrial Revolution and the increasing popularity of the laissez-faire philosophy espoused by Adam Smith, David Ricardo, and others, the Speenhamland system was increasingly criticized as an unjustified interference of the state with individual freedom and responsibility, an undesirable influence on the moral character of the population, a subsidy for the landowning class, and a deterrent to labor mobility. The system was also imposing an almost impossible financial burden on many parishes. Consequently, a royal commission was appointed in 1832 to study the system, and its recommendations were largely responsible for the "New Poor Law" of 1834.

The 1834 law was based on the harsh philosophy that all the poor were poor because of their own failings. Able-bodied workers and their dependents were to be granted relief only in workhouses in which they could be closely supervised and where conditions would be such that the worker would clearly prefer regular employment. Other poor persons such as the aged, the sick, and the young were subjected to the same rigid discipline. Recipients lost their right to vote and were required to wear special uniforms to indicate their second-class status.

By the middle of the 19th century public sentiment began to change and the system began to be liberalized on a piecemeal basis. Outdoor relief became more common, separate institutions were created for women, children, and the aged, and more visitors were permitted to inspect the almshouses. In 1905 a Royal Commission on the Poor Laws was appointed. Although its highly critical report in 1909 did not result in any immediate amendments to the Poor Law, it did result in a more liberal administration of that law. An Old Age Pensions Act in 1908 provided pensions for needy aged on a more humane basis, and a National Insurance Act in 1911 provided sickness and unemployment insurance benefits for some workers on a contributory basis. Because subsequent developments in England are less relevant to the United States' experience, they will not be discussed here, but it should be noted that in 1948 a new National Assistance Act was enacted that was designed to supplement a comprehensive national insurance law passed in 1944.

Early Poor Laws in the United States.

Except for the fact that their poor laws were based even more heavily on a deterrent philosophy, the experience of the American states and local communities with poor laws very closely parallels that of England.[4] Initially the local governments assumed responsibility and arranged on a limited basis for outdoor relief, indentures, and boarding out needy persons. The first poor law, which, like its English precedents, provided for local responsibility and settlement requirements, was passed by the Massachusetts Bay Colony in 1639. The first poorhouse was established in Massachusetts in 1660, but it was not until the next century that the poorhouse became the most popular approach to helping needy persons.

[4]Carlson, Ref. 3, p. 38.

Apparently the Speenhamland system had little effect on American legislation, and the poor were almost continuously regarded as inferior persons. After 1870, however, there was increasing discontent with mixed poorhouses and their administration, and legislation was enacted to provide special treatment for such indigent groups as the insane, the blind, the deaf, and the dumb.

Shortly after the turn of the century Massachusetts became the first state to establish a commission to study the problems of the aged. Other states followed suit. These commissions reflected a shift in prevailing attitudes with respect to public assistance for the needy aged and needy dependent survivors in that these groups were increasingly assumed to be more the victims of circumstances than, say, low-pay workers and the unemployed. In 1909 there was a White House Conference on the Care of Dependent Children, and in 1911 Missouri and Illinois passed laws establishing "pension" systems for needy widowed mothers. In 1914 Arizona passed a "pension" law, which also covered the aged, but it was shortly declared unconstitutional. Although Alaska passed a similar law in 1915, it was so limited in effect that a Montana law passed in 1923 is generally considered to be the first old-age "pension" law.

The 1921 recession awakened more interest on the part of the states in the needy aged and widowed mothers. Energetic social reformers wrote and talked at length about the problem. One of the most notable of these reformers was Abraham Epstein, who served as Research Director of the Pennsylvania Commission on Old-Age Pensions created in 1917, worked for the Fraternal Order of Eagles during 1922–1923 in their drive for pensions throughout the country, and in 1927 established the American Association for Old-Age Security, later renamed the American Association for Social Security. This association was probably the most effective promoter of social security legislation from its establishment until Mr. Epstein's death in 1942.[5] Although its primary concern initially was old-age pensions, it later concentrated its attention on social insurance.

In spite of this increased activity, only seven states had passed old-age assistance laws prior to the Depression, and two of these laws had been declared unconstitutional. More than half of the states had passed mothers' pension laws that provided cash payments for needy widowed mothers, but the benefits were small. The federal government itself had taken no action, although bills had been introduced in Congress at various times, beginning as early as 1909.

The Depression increased and dramatized the problem. Average monthly unemployment rates rose to about 25%; soup kitchens and bread lines became commonplace, and many conservative, thrifty, industrious workers exhausted their savings and lost their homes through mortgage foreclosures. It became clear

[5]For a more detailed account of Mr. Epstein's work, see E. Wight Bakke, "Life of Abraham Epstein: An American Epic," *Social Security,* XVI, No. 7 (September–October 1942), 3–6. Another social insurance pioneer whose name deserves mention was Dr. I. M. Rubinow, considered by many to be the father of modern social security because of his 1913 volume on *Social Insurance.* For an account of Dr. Rubinow's life, see "Dr. I. M. Rubinow Passes On," *Social Security,* X, No. 7 (September–October 1936), 3–4.

to more and more people that individuals do not always control their own destiny. Consequently, the legislative pace was quickened and over half the states had an old-age assistance law by the mid-1930s. However, these laws covered only a very small segment of the aged population because of severe age, citizenship, residence, income, and property requirements. In addition, during the depth of the Depression only about 1 out of every 10 eligibles was actually receiving a pension, primarily because of financial problems experienced by state and local government units. All but two states had mothers' aid laws, but, for financial reasons, these programs also provided less support than the laws intended. Relief for other categories of the poor was left to local communities and voluntary charities. By 1932 seven states, led by New York State in 1931, had assumed some limited responsibility for the unemployed.

The Social Security Act of 1935

As noted in Chapter 3, in 1935 Congress reacted to these conditions by enacting the Social Security Act. Among other things, this Act authorized federal grants for three state categorical cash public assistance programs: Old Age Assistance (OAA), Aid to the Blind (AB), and Aid to Families with Dependent Children (AFDC). By 1937 all states (including the then territories of Alaska and Hawaii) and the District of Columbia had OAA programs. Most states also had AB and AFDC programs shortly after they were authorized. Eight states did not have effective AB programs until 1941 or later. Alaska, Missouri, Nevada, and Pennsylvania waited until the early 1950s to establish such programs. Eight states also did not have AFDC programs until 1941 or later; Nevada was the only state to defer action to the 1950s.

A fourth federal–state program, Aid to the Permanently and Totally Disabled (APTD), was established by a 1950 amendment to the Social Security Act. Most states established such programs immediately, but Alaska, Arizona, Indiana, and Iowa did not act until the early 1960s. Nevada is the only state never to have had an APTD program.

Effective January 1, 1974, as a result of a 1972 amendment to the Social Security Act, a new federal program of Supplemental Security Income replaced OAA, AB, and APTD except in Guam, Puerto Rico, and the Virgin Islands. AFDC continues to operate as a federal–state program.

Supplemental Security Income for the Aged, Blind, and Disabled

Under the Supplemental Security Income program (SSI) aged, blind, and disabled persons are guaranteed a specified monthly income from the federal government.[6] The program's characteristics and operations are described below.

---

[6]As noted in footnote 4 of Chapter 1, SSI is considered by some authors to be a demogrant system rather than public assistance. The *Social Security Bulletin* also excludes SSI data from its table showing assistance recipients and payments. Regardless of how SSI is labeled, however, it is a welfare program aimed at the needy.

Program Characteristics

Eligible blind and disabled persons living in their own households are guaranteed a specified monthly income of $264.70. This amount is adjusted each July 1 to match increases in the CPI. If both members of a couple are eligible, the guarantee is 150% of the amount guaranteed an individual. The actual payment is this guaranteed level less the person's "countable" income.

Excluded from countable income is the first $60 in a calendar quarter of any income, earned or unearned. Unearned income includes such income as interest, rents, pensions, veterans' benefits, workers' compensation, and OASDI that is not paid directly for services rendered. Also excluded is $195 a quarter of earned income plus one-half of any earnings in excess of $195. There are also some special exclusions such as work expenses of blind persons, irregularly or infrequently received income totaling $60 or less of unearned income and $30 of earned income in a calendar quarter, any assistance based on need (cash or vendor payments) made to or on behalf of SSI recipients by state or local governments, and the value of assistance provided under certain housing programs. Because not all income other than SSI is countable income, SSI recipients can have a total income including SSI that exceeds the minimum guaranteed amounts.

When the program started in 1972, the guaranteed monthly income was $130. Congress raised this guarantee to $140 effective January 1, 1974, and to $146 effective July 1, 1974. Starting in 1975, the guaranteed level has been adjusted each July 1 by the same percentage as OASDI benefits to match increases in the CPI.

If eligible recipients live in a household not headed by themselves or their spouses, the guaranteed income is reduced by one-third. For institutionalized persons the guarantee depends on the type of institution. Eligible persons receiving care in private institutions that is not covered under Medicaid (described later in this chapter) qualify for the same guarantee as individuals living in their own households. Persons receiving care in public or private institutions, at least half the cost of which is paid by Medicaid, are guaranteed only $25 a month.

The income and resources of other family members may reduce the amount of the SSI payment. The family members whose incomes are considered are the ineligible spouse of an adult recipient and the ineligible parents of a blind or disabled child recipient under age 18. In determining the portion of the spouse's or parents' income that is added to the recipient's countable income, the spouse's or parents' income is reduced by (1) personal allocations for the spouse or parents and ineligible children in the home and (2) the exclusions cited above.

In 1981 Congress required that for the month an application is filed for SSI, both eligibility for a benefit and the amount of that benefit be determined on the basis of the applicant's income and circumstances in the current month. After the first month, however, benefit amounts should be determined on the basis of the prior month's income and circumstances. Previously both eligibility and benefit amounts were determined on the basis of expectations for the next quarter.

The 1981 amendments also made persons age 60 to 64 who were entitled to the regular OASDI minimum benefit prior to December 1981 eligible to receive a special SSI benefit when their OASDI benefit was reduced. Those persons were made eligible for SSI if they qualified under all SSI rules except their age.

A person is considered to be aged if he or she is 65 or over. Blindness is defined as (1) 20/200 vision or less in the better eye with the use of correcting lens or (2) tunnel vision of 20 degrees or less. The test for disability is the same as that described in Chapter 8 for Disability Insurance—inability to engage in any substantial gainful activity because of an impairment that is expected to result in death or last at least 12 months. If the disability is due to alcoholism or drug addiction, the person must accept appropriate treatment in an approved facility.

To be eligible for SSI payments the aged, blind, or disabled person must (1) reside within the 50 states or the District of Columbia and (2) be a citizen or an alien permanently and legally residing in the United States. An individual who is an inmate in a *public* institution is ineligible unless the institution is approved for Medicaid payments and Medicaid pays at least half the cost of the institutional services provided.

Also, for an aged, blind, or disabled person to be eligible, his or her countable resources must be $1,500 or less. For couples the countable resources must be $2,250 or less. Excluded from countable resources are the recipient's home, an automobile of reasonable value (raised in 1979 from $1,200 to $4,500), personal goods and household effects of reasonable value (raised in 1979 from $1,500 to $2,000), and life insurance with a face value of $1,500 or less. Some additional special exclusions include tools and other property essential to self-support and the assets of a blind or disabled person that are necessary to an approved plan of self-support.

The Office of Family Assistance of the Social Security Administration administers this program for the federal government. The benefits to recipients and administrative expenses are paid out of general revenues.

As noted above, SSI replaced three state programs financed in part through federal grants—OAA, AB, and APTD. One major argument in favor of SSI was the great diversity among the states in payment levels under the programs it replaced. SSI established uniform payment standards nationwide. For most states the uniform standard was higher than the state payment level; but in some states the former state program was more generous. Congress, however, did not want to reduce any recipient's benefit through the conversion to SSI. Consequently it required the more generous states to supplement the SSI benefits for those recipients who were transferred from the former state program as of January 1, 1974, to raise the combined federal–state benefit to their December 1973 income level. All states are permitted, if they wished, to supplement SSI payments for all recipients or selected categories of recipients.

The state may issue these supplementary payments and maintain the payment records itself or, if it wishes, request the Social Security Administration to administer these payments and assume the administrative costs. States that elect federal administration of their supplementary plans also benefit from a "hold harmless" provision under which the federal government assumes the difference between the supplementation required to pay all recipients the amount the state paid in January 1972 to indivduals with no income and the state's calendar year 1972 share of the costs of OAA, AB, and APTD. Through this provision the federal government continued some of the cost sharing of state payments that existed prior to SSI.

All states except Texas supplement the federal SSI benefit. Texas cannot do so because of a constitutional prohibition. The District of Columbia and 26 states (other than Texas) have elected federal administration; 23 administer their own supplements.

In all states except Massachusetts, California, and Wisconsin SSI recipients may be eligible for food stamps. Those three states have increased their supplementary payments to account for the absence of food stamps.

Operations

Table 15.1 shows the number of persons receiving SSI payments or federally administered state supplementation and the amount of the payments in December of each year from 1974 to 1980. The total number of recipients has remained fairly stable, but their composition has changed. In 1974 over half the recipients were aged. From 1974 to 1980, however, the number of aged recipients declined, whereas the number of disabled recipients increased. As a result, in 1980 the disabled constituted more than half of the recipients.

Despite the fairly stable number of recipients, the total dollar payments increased by 54% from December 1974 to December 1980, causing the average payment to increase from about $113 to $168.

Of the 4.1 million persons receiving federally administered payments in December 1980, more than 59% received only SSI payments; 29% received both SSI and a state supplement, and 11% received only a state supplement. The average SSI payment was $143, the average state supplement $99. The state payments ranged from $165 in California to $14 in Mississippi and Louisiana. The payments may be higher in one state than another because its plan is more generous, but this is not necessarily the case. An alternative explanation is that the plan is the same or less generous, but the recipients have lower incomes from other sources.

Many of the 59% receiving only SSI payments lived in states that administered their own state supplements. In December 1980, 1.3 million persons in these states received SSI payments, about one-sixth of whom also received state supplements. Of the over 250,000 receiving state supplements, about one-fifth received only a state supplement. The average state supplement was $80, which was less than the average paid in federally administered states. The average payments ranged from $191 in North Carolina to $10 in Utah.

Among those persons receiving federally administered payments, about two-thirds are women, two-thirds are white, almost half are age 65 or over, almost

Table 15.1 Number of Persons Receiving Either Supplemental Security Income or Federally Administered State Supplementation and Amount of Payments, By Reason of Eligibility, December of 1974–1980

December of Year	Number in Thousands				Payments in Millions of Dollars		
	Total	Aged	Blind	Disabled	Total	SSI	State Supplementation[a]
1974	3,996	2,286	75	1,636	451	341	110
1975	4,314	2,307	74	1,933	494	374	119
1976	4,236	2,148	76	2,012	507	386	121
1977	4,238	2,051	77	2,109	528	403	125
1978	4,217	1,968	77	2,172	547	420	126
1979	4,150	1,872	77	2,201	646	457	189
1980	4,142	1,808	78	2,256	695	528	167

Sources: Social Security Bulletins.

[a]Excludes data for state supplementation under state-administered programs.

Table 15.2 Recipients and Total Payments Under Major Public Assistance Programs, 1950, 1960, 1970, and 1980

	Number or Amount				Percentage Increase		
	1950	1960	1970	1980[g]	1950–1980	1960–1980	1970–1980
Number of December recipients (in thousands)							
SSI[a] or, until 1974, its predecessors[b]	2,956	2,781	3,098	4,142	40	49	34
AFDC							
Families	651	803	2,552	3,800	484	373	49
Recipients	2,233	3,073	9,659	11,000	393	258	14
Children	1,661	2,370	7,033	7,600	358	221	8
General assistance	866	1,244	1,056	1,000	15	(20)	(5)
Medicaid or, until 1966, its predecessors[c,d]	n.a.	n.a.	14,507	22,000	n.a.	n.a.	52
Food stamps	—	—	4,340	19,000	—	—	338
Total annual payments (in millions of dollars)							
SSI[e] or, until 1974, its predecessors[a]	1,515	1,948	2,960	7,858	419	303	165
AFDC	547	994	4,853	12,500	2,185	1,158	158
General assistance							
Cash	293	320	618	1,500	412	369	143
Medical vendor payments	46[f]	102	99	1,000	2,074	880	910
Medicaid or, until 1974, its predecessors[b]	57[f]	420	5,507	22,000	38,496	5,138	299
Food stamps	—	—	551	7,500	—	—	1,261

Sources: Social Security Bulletins.

[a]Includes recipients of federally administered state supplements only.

[b]OAA, AB, and APTD.

[c]Medical Assistance for the Aged and medical vendor payments under OAA, AB, APTD, or AFDC.

[d]Fiscal year data.

[e]Includes both federally and state-administered state supplements.

[f]1951.

[g]All 1980 data except for SSI estimated by author.

90% live in their own households, and over half (70% for the aged, 35% for the disabled) receive OASDI benefits.

In order to provide some perspective on the relative importance and growth of SSI relative to the other major public assistance programs discussed in this chapter. Table 15.2 shows the number of December recipients and the total annual payments under each program for 1950, 1960, 1970, and 1980. SSI is large and growing, but it is smaller than AFDC and Medicaid on both counts. Many more persons receive food stamps and their value is only slightly less than SSI benefits.

Aid to Families With Dependent Children

AFDC programs, which provide benefits to certain needy families with children, are the most discussed and most controversial federal–state public assistance plans. All states have such plans, but they vary widely in their eligibility and benefit provisions. Various attempts have been made to replace these programs with a guaranteed minimum income program of the type discussed in the next chapter, but they have been unsuccessful.

Federal Conditions

State AFDC programs qualify for federal financial support if and only if they assist needy families with children who are deprived of parental support or care through the (1) death, (2) physical or mental incapacity (expected to last at least 30 days), or (3) continued absence from the home of a parent.[7] Eligible children must include children under age 18, but a state can elect to cover children aged 18 if they are regularly attending a secondary or technical school and may reasonably be expected to complete the program before age 19. Until 1981 amendments a state could also cover any students age 19 or 20. Federal aid is also available under AFDC for state aid to families in which a parent is unemployed, but the state plan is not required to assist such families. Under 1981 amendments eligibility is limited to families in which the principal earner is unemployed. The principal earner is the person who earned the highest income the preceding two years.

A state can, if it wishes, also receive federal aid for emergency assistance for families with children under age 21 who have an immediate and urgent need because of an emergency (to be defined by the state) that cannot be met out of family resources. Federal support is provided only for assistance authorized during one period of 30 consecutive days in any 12 consecutive months. Eligibility can be extended to families not eligible for regular AFDC payments. If migrant families are included, they may be covered throughout the state or only in selected

[7]The Social Security Act specifies that the parent must be the father, but the U.S. Supreme Court in Califano versus Wescott, June 25, 1979, required elimination of all references to gender.

areas. The assistance may be money payments, payments in kind (such as food, clothing, or shelter), medical care, or other services specified by the Secretary of Health and Human Services.

Federal law also prescribes the relative with whom a child may live while receiving AFDC. These relatives are the father, mother, grandfather, grandmother, brother, sister, stepfather, stepmother, stepsister, stepbrother, uncle, aunt, first cousin, nephew, or niece. Some states have interpreted the federal act to include additional relatives such as persons who legally adopt a child or the parents of the child.

To receive this federal aid the state program must also satisfy the conditions listed below[8] (the logic underlying each condition is appended in parenthesis):

1 The program must cover all counties in the state, but it may be administered by local governmental units. (Otherwise certain counties could be discriminated against.)

2 A single state agency must either administer the program itself or supervise the local government units administering the program. (This promotes uniformity of treatment among localities.)

3 The state must participate financially in the program. (The state government should aid the local government units in the same way that the federal government is aiding the state.)

4 The plan must employ methods of administration necessary for proper and efficient operation of the plan. Personnel in the administrative unit must be selected and retained through the merit system. (This provision is designed to produce an efficient administration of the program in which employees are not selected on the basis of their political affiliations.)

5 The Social Security Administration is entitled to any information it may require concerning the operation of the program. (This information is used primarily to determine whether the minimum federal requirements are being met, and for informational and research purposes.)

6 All persons should be permitted to apply for assistance without delay and that assistance should be provided with reasonable promptness to all eligible individuals. (All persons should have an equal opportunity to apply and unnecessary delays should be avoided.)

7 The plan must not exclude any resident of the state, defined as any person living in the state voluntarily with the intention of making his home there and not a temporary purpose.[9] (Movement among states should not be discouraged and those who move should not be penalized.)

---

[8]U.S. Department of Health and Human Services, Social Security Administration, Office of Faculty Assistance, *Characteristics of State Plans for Aid to Families with Dependent Children,* 1980 ed. (Washington, D.C.: U.S. Government Printing Office, 1980).

[9]The Social Security Act still permits a resident requirement of (1) five out of the preceding nine years and (2) one year immediately preceding the date of application for benefits, but an April 1969 U.S. Supreme Court decision (Shapiro versus Thompson) prohibits such a requirement.

8   The plan can contain a citizenship requirement, but this requirement must not exclude any citizen of the United States. In 1973, in response to a June 1971 U.S. Supreme Court decision, the federal government issued a regulation that required any alien to be lawfully admitted for permanent residence or to claim the legal right to reside permanently in the United States.

9   Recipients should not be permitted to recover cash benefits under more than one approved plan for financial maintenance assistance. (Multiple benefits could lead to overpayments and inequities. Each plan should be completely responsible for its category of the needy.)

10   Benefits must be granted only in case of need. An applicant's income and assets must be considered in determining his needs. Under 1981 amendments, in determining eligibility for AFDC each state is directed to deduct from countable income (1) the first $75 of monthly earnings for full-time employment in lieu of itemized work expenses plus (2) the cost of care for each child or incapacitated adult up to $160 per month. In no case, however, should a family with a gross income in excess of 150% of the state's standard of need be made eligible for AFDC. Advance payments on earned income tax credits must be counted as earned income; if an eligible person has not applied for these advance credits, the amount that person could have received must be counted in their earned income. Income received in a month must be considered available as income in the month it is received and also in future months. For example, a large income one month may make a family ineligible for that month and one or more months thereafter. The incomes of all family members, including stepparents, are combined for making these determinations except for the income earned by a child who is a full-time student or a part-time student but not a full-time employee. In addition to considering a family's income each state is required to limit allowable resources to $1,000 per family excluding the home and one automobile.

In determining the benefit amount the state must disregard (1) full-time earnings up to $75, (2) child care costs up to $160 per child, and (3) during the first four consecutive months in which the family has earnings in excess of the standard work expense and child care disregards $30 plus one third of the earnings in excess of $30. On the other hand, the state is permitted to subtract from the AFDC benefit the value of food stamps or housing subsidies up to the value of the food or shelter included in the state payment standard.

As is now true for SSI, eligibility depends upon the basis of income and other factors in the month the application is filed. Except for the first month, however, the benefit amount depends upon the income and other circumstances in the previous month.

If a caretaker relative (mother or father) is on strike, no benefits can be paid. If some other relative is on strike, that individual's needs cannot be counted in determining the family benefit.

(The purpose of these provisions is to limit the program to needy persons and to provide some work incentives.) Until the 1981 amendments all reasonable work expenses and child care costs were disregarded. There was no gross income limit, earned income tax credits could be counted when they were received, eligibility and benefits could be based on the income anticipated during the coming month, stepparents' income could be counted only in states that require stepparents to support stepchildren as if they were natural or adopted children, the $1,000 limit on assets was $2,000, and the $30 disregard did not expire after four months.

11   A dissatisfied applicant must have the right to a fair hearing before the supervising state agency. (This right is regarded as essential in a democracy.)

12   A state authority must establish and maintain standards for public and private institutions housing recipients of the benefits. The federal government, however, does not participate in benefits to those persons who are inmates in a nonmedical *public* institution. (If it were not for these standards, some institutions might profit at the expense of the public assistance program. The original Act, which sought to eliminate poorhouses and payments in kind, provided for federal assistance only with respect to cash grants. Later it was recognized that for some recipients, such as the infirm aged, public institutional care has many advantages. Private institutional care was possible even under the original Act.)

13   The plan must require that each applicant or recipient assign to the state any rights he or she may have to support from any other person in his or her own behalf or on behalf of any other family member for whom the applicant is applying for or receiving aid. (This condition makes it easier for the administrative agency to identify the recipient's support rights and to act on those rights.)

14   The state must have an approved child support program as required under Title IV-D of the Social Security Act. Such programs provide child support services, including the collection of child support payments for both AFDC and non-AFDC families. (The reason for requiring services to non-AFDC families is to assure that these other families have access to child support services before they are forced to apply for welfare.) The federal government pays 75% of the state program expenditures, monitors and evaluates these programs, provides technical assistance, and in certain cases gives direct assistance in locating absent parents and obtaining support payments. The 1981 amendments tightened this program. For example, a child support obligation assigned to a state as a condition of AFDC eligibility cannot be discharged in bankruptcy. Unemployment benefits to the absent parent can be intercepted to provide child support. States can change a fee of 10%, collectible from the absent parent, on support collected on behalf of a non-AFDC family.

15   The state must promptly notify the state child support collection agency when aid is furnished to a child deserted or abandoned by a parent. (This condition, as well as conditions 14 and 16, are designed to make parents with resources responsible for supporting their children and to reduce the cost of the program.)

16   Applicants or recipients must be required to cooperate with the state in establishing paternity of a child born out of wedlock and obtaining support for a child unless the applicant or recipient is found to have a good cause for refusing to cooperate.

17   The plan must provide foster care for dependent children in child-care institutions or in foster family homes who have been removed from their homes or the homes of relatives as a result of a judicial determination that remaining in these homes would be contrary to the children's welfare. (This condition extends benefits to needy children who might otherwise be disadvantaged. It also removes an important disincentive to removing children from unsuitable homes.)

18   The plan must provide information to law enforcement officials when an AFDC child's home is considered unsuitable because the child is neglected, abused, or exploited. (This provision is necessary to enforce the foster home provision and to punish parents for child abuse.)

19   Under a Work Incentive (WIN) program created by 1967 amendments and strengthened by 1971 amendments every AFDC recipient not in a specifically excepted group must register for manpower services, training, and employment under a program administered by the U.S. Department of Labor. Excepted from the registration requirements are aged or disabled persons, children under 16 or attending elementary, secondary, or vocational school full-time, people so remote from a WIN project that they cannot participate effectively, people who must stay at home because another member of the family is incapacitated, mothers or other relatives caring for children under six, and women caring for children in homes where a father or other adult male is registered. Welfare agencies must give registered recipients the services they need to accept employment or job training, for example, health services, vocational rehabilitation, counseling, and child care. The welfare agency must also certify annually at least 15% of the registrants as ready for employment or training. Failure to do so will reduce the federal share of their welfare payments by the difference between 15% of the percentage actually certified. Recipients certified as ready who refuse to accept work or training will lose their welfare benefits. Those enrolled in training programs receive an incentive payment of $30 a month in addition to their AFDC payments.

Public service employers are also encouraged to provide jobs for AFDC recipients. Public service employers may receive up to 100% of the costs of providing employment to a welfare recipient the first year, 75% the second year, and 50% the third. The federal government pays 90% of the cost of the WIN manpower program. Employers who hire WIN participants receive an income tax credit equal to 20% of wages paid to these recipients during the first year of employment.

The Omnibus Budget Reconciliation Act of 1981 added three more work incentive programs to AFDC. First, to test alternatives to the current WIN program states are authorized to operate a three-year work incentive demonstration program. Participation criteria must be the same as under the WIN program, but the components of the program can be varied in different regions or political subdivisions. Techniques to be used can include such approaches as job training, job find clubs, grant diversion to either public or private employers, service contracts with state employment agencies, and performance-based placement incentives. Second, states are authorized to operate community work experience programs and require AFDC recipients to participate in these programs. These programs must meet appropriate health and safety standards, not displace currently employed persons or fill vacant positions, and limit the hours worked to the AFDC family benefit divided by the higher of the federal or state minimum hourly wage. Persons exempt from WIN registration are to be exempt from this "workfare" program except that parents caring for a child under 6, but not under 3, can be required to participate if child care is available. Third, with expected savings from reduced AFDC grant levels, states are permitted to provide job opportunities for AFDC eligibles or pay nonprofit and governmental entities a subsidy to cover the costs of hiring AFDC eligibles. The total amount of federal funding for regular AFDC payments and for subsidies to employers under the voluntary jobs program cannot exceed the present level of estimated AFDC spending in the state after the introduction of the other AFDC provisions in the Act.

20 The state must provide on a voluntary and confidential basis family planning services to present, former, or likely recipients of child-bearing age. Beginning in fiscal 1974, the federal share of AFDC funds is reduced by 1% if the state in the prior year fails to provide requested services.

21 Beginning in fiscal 1975, AFDC funds are also reduced by 1% if the state fails to inform AFDC recipients of the availability of child health screening services (see the discussion of Medicaid in this chapter) or if it fails to provide such services.

22 Under the WIN and child support enforcement programs the state must under certain conditions pay vendors directly for services rendered to children or make protective payments to someone other than a parent. (Protective and vendor payments are sometimes necessary to protect children against misuse of AFDC payments.) The state agency may also at its option make protective payments in other cases under specified condition. The number of protective payments may not exceed a stated percentage of the number of other AFDC recipients.

Federal Financing

If the state program satisfies the conditions just described, the federal government pays 50% of the state plan expenditures for administration. Until the 1981 amendments the federal government paid 75% of the costs of training employees of agencies adminstering AFDC. Except for foster care recipients and emergency assistance, under the *regular* formula the federal government also promises to pay the following position of the *average* monthly benefit per recipient (not per family):

$\frac{5}{6}$ of the first $18

+ 50–65% of the next $14.

The 50–65% fraction is 50% for states with above average per capita incomes and ranges from 50 to 65% for the other states. The equation used to determine the federal share, which is bounded by 50 and 65%, is as follows:

$$\text{Federal share} = 1.00 - 0.50 \left(\frac{\text{State per capita income}}{\text{National per capita income}} \right)^2.$$

States that have an approved Medicaid plan, however, may elect an *alternative* formula that has proved more attractive to most states. Under this formula the federal government pays 50 to 83% of *all* benefit costs. The actual percentage is determined by the following equation:

$$\text{Federal share} = 1.00 - 0.45 \left(\frac{\text{State per capita income}}{\text{National per capita income}} \right)^2,$$

subject to a minimum share of 50% and a maximum share of 83%. Besides increasing the federal share for the states with below average per capita income, this alternative formula places no maximum on the benefit costs to be shared.

For foster care recipients the federal portion is determined under the "regular" formula, except that the 50–65% fraction is applied to the next $82 (not the next $14).

For emergency assistance the federal share is 50%, subject to a state ceiling that depends on the state's share of AFDC caseloads and expenditures.

In 1978 Congress provided additional funds for states whose dollar error rate in AFDC payments was less than 4%. In 1981 Congress required states to take prompt action to correct both overpayments and underpayments.

Initially the federal government paid one-third of the state's expenditures, excluding monthly amounts above $18 for the first child in the family and $12 for each additional child. Adults were not covered. In 1939 the fraction was raised to one-half. The two-tier approach was introduced in 1946; one needy relative could be included as a recipient starting in 1950; in 1958 the federal matching percentage was changed from the same percentage for all states to a variable percentage that depends on the state's relative per capital income; and, starting in 1962, a second needy adult could be included as a recipient if the second adult was the spouse of either an incapacitated or unemployed parent. However, the spouse of an unemployed parent could be counted only in those states that had extended their program to cover unemployment.

State AFDC Plans

State plans vary greatly as to (1) who is eligible for AFDC, (2) what benefits they receive, (3) how the plan is financed, and (4) how the plan is administered. The characteristics of these state plans as of September 1979 are summarized below. The 1981 amendments will require some important changes in these plans. About four-fifths of the states required that the family have at least one child under 21 years of age. If this child was 18 or over, he or she must have been regularly attending high school, a college or university, or a vocational or technical training course. In the remaining states the child must have been under 18 years of age.

In about half the states the child must have been deprived of parental support or care through death, continued absence from the home, or physical or mental incapacity of a parent. Only 26 states had extended their plans to pay families in which a parent is unemployed.

A family was assumed to be needy if it had insufficient income or other resources to provide eligible children with a reasonable subsistence compatible with decency and health. In most states disregarded earnings were limited to those required for federal approval. Four states, however, disregarded an additional $5 a month of income from any source. Federal law gives the states this option. More than one-fourth of the states permitted the conservation of all or part of a child's earned income for future identifiable needs such as education, special training, and employment, which is also an option under federal law.

All states set limits on the property owned by the child and other members of the family. For example, in North Carolina ownership of real property used as a home did not disqualify an applicant. Also exempt from consideration were one essential motor vehicle, household furnishings, and personal effects. However, real property not used a home and not producing income and savings, cash values of insurance, bonds, and any other cash reserves were limited to $1,100 for an adult and one child plus $50 for a needy spouse and for each additional eligible child up to a $2,000 maximum.

Emergency assistance was available in 22 states under a variety of conditions. For example, New York provided emergency assistance when there was a natural disaster, serious injury to persons or damage to property, mass emergencies, or any situation that renders a family destitute or homeless. Other situations might also be covered. Kansas limited such assistance to civil disorders and natural disasters, potential eviction, utility discontinuence, and energy-conserving repairs for a client's home. Connecticut covered only the discontinuance of utility services for nonpayment of bills. Several states discontinued emergency assistance programs during the 1970s.

Benefits

The amount of assistance to which an eligible family is entitled is equal to the state payment standard less the family's countable income. The countable income is the actual income less the disregarded earnings noted above.

In September 1979 the payment standards for a family of two (a mother age 20–54 and one child age 3–5) ranged from $482 monthly, in Vermont, to $115, in Texas. Only two states had a two-recipient standard of $400 or more; 15 had a standard of less than $200. For a family with four recipients (a mother age 20–54 and three children ages 3–5, 9–11, and 12–14) the range was $656, in Vermont, to $187, in Texas. Only 6 states had a four-recipient standard of $500 or more; 14 had a standard of less than $300.

Only three states included in their two-recipients payment standard a food allowance that equalled or exceeded the amount the U.S. Department of Agriculture estimated the average two-person family would need to pay home food costs, assuming low food prices. In only 14 states was the payment food allowance at least 80% of the U.S. Department of Agriculture estimate; in seven states the allowance was less than half the Department of Agriculture estimate. Only Vermont included in its four-recipient payment standard a food allowance that equalled or exceeded the U.S. Department of Agriculture average low-price food cost estimate for the average four-person family. In only three states was the payment food allowance at least 80% of the Department of Agriculture estimate; in 15 states the allowance was less than half the low-cost estimate for the average family.

There were 27 states that paid at least some families less than their payment standard. Four states used the payment standard for smaller-size families, but reduce the payment for larger families. The other 24 paid all families less than their payment standard would indicate. The usual procedure is to reduce the payment standard for all families by a specified percentage. In these 20 states the reduced standard ranged from 90 to 42% of the full standard. For two- and four-recipient families all 27 states would pay families with no countable income less than the full standard would indicate. In only 10 states would two- or four-recipient families receive 80–99% of the full standard; in two states the percentage would be less than 50.

Most states did not reserve the right to recover payments made to these families. The benefits were designed primarily to aid the children in these families and were not considered a loan against future earning power.

All but seven states made protective and vendor payments in some situations in addition to those in which federal law makes such payments mandatory.

Over half the states providing emergency assistance made money or vendor payments depending on the situation. The next most common method of payment was cash, vendor payments, or payments in kind.

Financing

State governments paid costs not met by federal grants in about four-fifths of the states; state and local governments shared these costs in the other states. With a few exceptions that used earmarked revenues, states relied on general funds to finance AFDC programs.

Administration

In 33 states the state government administered the system. In the other states the state government supervised local administration of the system.

Operations

Table 15.3 shows for AFDC the number of recipients, the total money payments, and the average monthly payments for selected years between 1945 and 1980. The increase in all three measures reflects increases in the population, liberalizations in the eligibility standards and improvements in the assistance standards, social and other demographic changes in the population, the development of and changes in other social programs, a reduction in the proportion of the population that is poor, and inflation. In constant 1940 dollars the 1950, 1960, 1970, 1975, and 1980 average monthly benefits would have been only $12, $13, $18, $19, and $48, respectively. The total payments in millions of dollars would have been $322, $474, $1,752, $2,400 and $2,125, respectively. In constant dollars, therefore, AFDC costs have actually declined in recent years.

As Table 15.2 indicates, AFDC recipients are exceeded in number only by Medicaid and food stamp participants. Medicaid is the only program with larger expenditures.

California and New York account for almost one quarter of the national AFDC caseload and one-third of the total benefits paid. Seven states (California, New York, Illinois, Michigan, New Jersey, Ohio, and Pennsylvania) have about half the recipients and pay over 60% of the benefits.

Children on AFDC are currently 9–10% of all children in the United States. In 1978 this percentage ranged from over 12% in 8 states (California, 12.5%; District of Columbia, 29.3%; Illinois, 12.6%; Massachusetts, 12.7%; Michigan, 12.7%; Mississippi, 13.1%; New Jersey, 13.0%; and New York, 13.6) to under 5% in 10 states (Arizona, 4.2%; Idaho, 3.8%; Montana, 4.2%; Nebraska, 4.5%; Nevada, 3.0%; New Hampshire, 4.6%; North Dakota, 3.8%; Texas, 4.5%; Utah, 4.7%; and Wyoming, 2.5%).

Special attention has focused recently on error rates. During April through September 1978 payments to ineligible recipients and overpayments to eligible recipients were 9.4% of total payments. During April through September 1973 the error rate under a less rigorous definition was 16.5%. The 1978 ineligible error rate was 5.1%; the overpayment rate was 4.4%. In addition to these errors, almost 1% of the payments were underpayments to eligible recipients. The error rates varied greatly among the states. In six states the ineligible and overpaid error rate exceeded 15% (Alaska, 31.2%; Delaware, 16.1%; District of Columbia, 22.4%; Illinois, 17.1%; Pennsylvania, 16.3%; and Massachusetts, 15.9%). In eight states the error rate was 4% or less (California, 3.7%, Indiana, 3.7%; Minnesota, 3.4%; Nevada, 0.6%; North Dakota, 1.6%; Oklahoma, 3.2%; Utah, 2.8%; and Wyoming, 4.0%).

Emergency assistance is not included in the above AFDC data. In 1978 the total payments were small ($84 million) relative to other AFDC payments, but they were important ($191 per family) to the 32,000 recipient families. The number of recipients has been fairly stable during recent years, but the total payments have increased, largely because of inflation. AFDC families are about

Table 15.3 Aid to Families With Dependent Children: Recipients, Total Money Payments, and Average Monthly Payment, 1945–1980

Year	December Recipients (In Thousands)			Total Money Payments (In Millions of Dollars)	Average Monthly Payment ($)	
	Families	Children	Total		Per Family	Per Recipient
1945	274	701	943	150	52	15
1950	651	1,661	2,233	552	71	21
1955	602	1,661	2,192	618	86	24
1960	803	2,370	3,073	1,001	108	28
1965	1,054	3,316	4,396	1,660	137	33
1970	2,552	7,033	9,659	4,853	190	50
1975	3,568	8,106	11,404	9,211	229	72
1980[a]	3,800	7,600	11,000	12,500	280	100

Sources: Social Security Bulletins.

[a]Estimated by author.

two-thirds of the recipients. About 94% of the payments are for maintenance, the remainder for medical care.

In 1978 about 1 million persons were registered under the WIN program. About 74% were females, 56% were white, 58% had not completed high school, 53% were 25 to 39 years of age, and 17% were volunteer registrants. Almost 290,000 WIN registrants entered employment, usually on a full-time basis. Welfare cost savings were estimated at $600 million, program costs at $364 million.

During fiscal year 1979 state child support programs reported collecting more than $1.3 million, $600 million in support of about 529,000 AFDC families. Collection costs were $366 million. AFDC collections were 5.2% of AFDC payments. This collection ratio was over 10% in four states (Idaho, 10.4%; Utah, 10.6%; Washington, 11.0%; and Wisconsin, 10.1%). In five states the ratio was 2.0% or less (District of Columbia, 1.1%; Georgia, 1.4%; Illinois, 1.5%; Mississippi, 1.0%; and Oklahoma, 1.4%).

Characteristics of AFDC Families

Because of the strong interest in AFDC, some facts about families receiving assistance in March 1977 are summarized below.[10] The average AFDC family included 3.1 persons. In 85% of these families the father was absent; in 34% the father was never married to the mother. In 2.6% the father was deceased, in 5.9% the father was physically or mentally incapacitated, and in 5.1% the father was unemployed. About 93% percent of AFDC children lived with their mothers. About 51% of the mothers were under age 30; about 8% were teenagers.

In over 8% of these families the mother worked full-time; in over 5% the mother worked part-time; and in over 10% the mother was actively seeking work or in school or training. These employed mothers were usually service workers such as waitresses or beauticians. The median number of months these families had been on AFDC was 25. About 41% of the families were white, 43% black, and 12% Hispanic. About 15% lived in public housing; 75% rented private housing. About 74% participated in the food stamp program.

Compared with 1969, these AFDC families had become smaller, mothers were more likely to have full-time jobs but less likely to have part-time jobs, the median number of months on AFDC was slightly larger, and more of the families were white, lived in public housing, and participated in the food stamp program.

Issues

The categorical cash public assistance programs, especially AFDC, are under attack from many quarters. Their eligibility requirements, benefits, financing, and

---

[10]U.S. Department of Health, Education, and Welfare, Social Security Administration, Office of Research and Statistics, *Aid to Families with Dependent Children: A Chartbook* (Washington, D.C.: U.S. Government Printing Office, 1979).

administration have all been criticized. The replacement in 1974 of OAA, AB, and APTD with SSI has answered some, but not most, of the criticisms.

Eligibility Requirements

Only certain categories of the poor—the aged, the blind, the permanently and totally disabled, and certain families with dependent children—are included under these programs. Other poor persons (e.g., low-income "intact" two-person families) must turn to general assistance, which, as we will see below, will not accept many of them and will pay only limited benefits to most of those it does accept. In about half the states AFDC does not cover the families of unemployed able-bodied workers even though the federal government would finance such benefits.

The income standards in most states are well below the poverty threshold of the Social Security Administration. Consequently, many poor persons in the four favored categories are also excluded from participating in these plans. The wide variation in state income standards also means that many poor persons who are not eligible for assistance in their home state may be eligible for coverage in another state. Differences in the cost of living explain some, but by no means all, of the variation in income standards. SSI has reduced but not eliminated this heterogeneity among the states for the aged and the disabled.

The eligibility requirements for AFDC have been accused of encouraging desertion and illegitimate children. One reason the federal government extended AFDC to include families with unemployed fathers was the belief that many unemployed fathers often deserted their families in order to qualify them for AFDC. According to one study, however, desertion rates in states that added unemployed families do not differ significantly from rates in states that did not, thus shedding doubt on the hypothesis that AFDC causes desertions.[11]

Basing eligibility and the amount of the benefits on demonstrated need has been criticized on the ground that, as presently administered in many jurisdictions, the needs test invades the recipient's privacy and in addition may damage his or her self-respect. Emphasis on demonstrated need, it is agreed, may also destroy the prospective recipient's incentive to work and save. Finally, administering the test takes too much of the social worker's time, is expensive, and often conflicts with proper counseling procedures. The needs test, however, is by definition an essential part of assistance programs designed to supplement a wage-related contributory social insurance program. It also has the advantage of tailoring the assistance to the need. To remove the test completely would raise the cost and alter the entire complexion of public assistance.

Steps have been taken instead to reduce the disadvantages of the needs test without destroying the basic character of public assistance. The balance achieved is necessarily a compromise between competing goals. To cite four examples, first,

[11]Gilbert Y. Steiner, *The State of Welfare* (Washington, D.C.: Brookings Institution, 1971), p. 37.

payment standards have been developed to reduce the subjectivity and the questioning involved in applying the test. In many instances, however, as noted earlier, the payment standard is less than the need recognized by the state agency itself. Second, the disregarded earnings provisions in the federal standards and state laws give recipients some incentive to work. Furthermore, because a claimant is permitted to hold some assets and still be declared needy, he or she has some incentive to save. Third, a few years ago a simplified test of need was introduced in many states with federal encouragement and it is now mandatory. Under this simplified test, unless there is good reason to doubt the information supplied, the state agency accepts the applicant's declaration or affidavit concerning age, income, property holdings, and other factors indicating the extent of his personal need. These declarations are then spot-checked by the agency to validate the simplified approach itself and to discourage dishonest declarations. Virtues claimed for this system are that it permits faster, less expensive determinations of need, is more acceptable to the client, and permits social workers to concentrate on counseling services. Critics believe fraudulent claims increase under this system. Fourth, the SSI guaranteed minimum income approach simplifies the procedure.

The requirement that able-bodied AFDC recipients accept work or training opportunities has been applauded as a way to replace dependency with self-support and to penalize laziness. The WIN program has provided jobs for many recipients and removed others from welfare. Opponents claim that the WIN program has had little effect on welfare costs, usually secures only low-level jobs for recipients, has trained persons in skills they already possess or for jobs that do not exist, and creates additional red tape for recipients.

Benefits

The wide variation among states in AFDC benefits and their generally low level has been mentioned above in connection with eligibility requirements. The wide variation means that eligible poor families receive different treatment depending on the state where they reside. The generally low level of benefits means that most families receiving assistance must live below the poverty threshold. On the other hand, in some states AFDC families may receive benefits that exceed the income of a fully employed worker earning the minimum wage permitted by law. Some would argue that the fault in these cases lies with the minimum wage level, not the AFDC benefit. Nevertheless, the fact remains that in those states full-time workers with low incomes resent AFDC families with almost as much income.

Perhaps the poverty threshold is too ambitious a goal. If this threshold were adopted, many more families would become eligible for benefits and the average benefit would rise substantially. The other citizens would have to be convinced that the resulting additional tax burden was justified and that these additional taxes were being used in the best way. A poverty threshold may also be opposed on the grounds that it treats the poor too generously relative to the nonpoor, that it would reduce the incentive to work, or that it would have other undesirable social and economic implications.

A more modest, less questioned test of the adequacy of public assistance benefits is the relationship between the largest amount paid by the state and its payment standard, which is the amount the state believes the recipient requires to meet basic needs. We have already noted that in 1979 27 states, paid at least some families less than their payment standards.

In evaluating the adequacy of AFDC payments, however, it is important to remember that these families are typically also eligible for Medicaid, food stamps, and housing assistance. Food stamps are particularly important because food costs are a substantial part of a poor family's living expenses.

In July 1979 the median state maximum potential monthly AFDC benefit for a four-person family was $340. The median state maximum food stamp benefit was $150. A family qualifying for both benefits would receive $490 a month, or $5,880 a year. In eight states (Alabama, Arkansas, Georgia, Louisiana, Mississippi, South Carolina, Tennessee, and Texas) the food stamp benefit exceeded the AFDC benefit. For example, in Mississippi the maximum potential benefits were $120 for AFDC and $204 for food stamps. In New York, on the other hand, the two maximum benefits were $536 and $92, respectively. Because AFDC income is considered in determining the food stamp allotment, the higher the maximum AFDC benefit, the lower the maximum food stamp allotment, but the offset is not 100%.

In real terms AFDC benefits have not increased in recent years. According to one study, from 1973 to 1978 real benefits for an AFDC family with no countable income declined in 12 of 20 states.[12] The declines were 24–33% in four of these states. Combining food stamps with AFDC moderated the declines, but in 10 of the 20 states real benefits still decreased. In four of these states the decrease was 11–14%. In evaluating this analysis one must remember, however, that the wages of many workers also failed to match cost of living increases over this period.

SSI benefits are also less than the poverty threshold, but the maximum federal SSI payment for an aged couple exceeds the maximum AFDC benefit for a two-person family in over three-fourths of the states. Furthermore, all states except Texas supplement these federal payments for poor aged and disabled persons. The combined benefits also vary less among the states because of the substantial federal base. Annual adjustments in this SSI base to match increases in the CPI provide some protection against price increases. For the reasons advanced in Chapter 3 concerning the OASDI automatic benefit adjustments, many persons have questioned whether the CPI overstates the correction needed for most persons to match increases in their cost of living. Because the state

---

[12]Testimony delivered by Barry L. Friedman and Leonard J. Housman in *How to Think About Welfare Reform for the 1980's,* Hearings before the Subcommittee on Public Assistance of the Committee on Finance, U.S. Senate, 96th Congress, 2nd Session, February 6 and 7, 1980 (Washington, D.C.: U.S. Government Printing Office, 1980).

supplements are not automatically adjusted, however, for many SSI recipients benefits have not kept pace with inflation as measured by this index.

Financing

The variation among state laws and their interpretation regarding eligibility and benefits reflects not only different attitudes toward the poor but also the relative cost of assistance payments and the ability and willingness of the nonassisted to bear that tax burden. The poorer states are doubly disadvantaged in that a larger proportion of their inhabitants are needy and the taxable per capita income is low.

By providing a substantial SSI base and favoring in its AFDC formula states with low per capita income, the federal government has attempted to "equalize" the tax burden and encourage more uniformity among the states. The burden, however, remains uneven. For some states the burden is high because their per capita income is low. For others the burden is high because they have plans that are more generous.

Within a state the burden often varies substantially among localities. The residents of New York City, for example, bear an especially heavy burden, because, like other large cities, New York attracts many poor persons from other areas and New York State provides liberal benefits.

Even if the tax burdens of cities and states for the categorical programs were to be completely "equalized," some financing problems would remain. Public assistance costs keep rising at the same time that states and local communities are being asked to increase their responsibilities in certain areas such as pollution control. Compounding this problem is the fact that attempts to increase state and local taxes have met increasing resistance.

Administration

Because public assistance by its very nature requires separate consideration of each case, it is not surprising to find that administrative expenses are high relative to the benefits paid. This observation and those that follow are much more applicable to AFDC than to SSI. Because the administering agency must also pry into the personal lives of recipients and in many instances make highly subjective decisions, it is also not surprising that many clients adopt a negative attitude toward the program and believe in some instances that they have been treated unfairly. Because the administrative decisions are complex, and resources limited, error rates have exceeded acceptable levels. Payments have been made to ineligible persons, and overpayments to eligible persons.

Some steps have been taken to remedy these problems, but much more remains to be done. Encouraging examples are the closer surveillance of error rates, financial incentives to reduce these error rates, and child support collection programs.

Replacement or Reform?

Dissatisfaction with the categorical public assistance programs, especially AFDC, has become so intense that until recently major attention had shifted from piecemeal reforms to replacement of these programs with a guaranteed minimum income program. This suggestion and related programs are discussed in Chapter 16. SSI is a step in this direction.

Recently, however, many persons, including Martin Anderson, President Reagan's principal advisor on welfare matters, have expressed a strong preference for reforming the current welfare system, including AFDC. According to Dr. Anderson, the "dismal failure" of welfare is a myth.[13] True, the system is characterized by great inefficiencies, a high fraud level, terrible management, overlapping programs, many inequities, and a virtually nonexistent financial incentive to work. But, by two basic criteria—the completeness of coverage for those who really need help and the adequacy of the assistance it provides—Dr. Anderson maintains that the system is a brilliant success. In his opinion "virtually all people who are eligible qualify for government checks and government-provided services that automatically lift them out of the official ranks of poverty."[14] The number of poor people is very small and grows smaller every day. Furthermore, poverty statistics probably overstate the number of poor people.[15] They include many persons who do not reveal their true level of income, they count among the poor people with low annual incomes because they start work late in the year, and they omit income in kind such as food stamps, housing subsidies, and medical benefits.

Two philosophical approaches to welfare—the needy-only approach and the guaranteed income approach—dominate the thinking of welfare policymakers. Dr. Anderson asserts that most of the population favors the needy-only approach. Welfare payments should go only to needy people; people on welfare should be helped and encouraged to become self-sufficient. The guaranteed income approach, he believes, is favored by a highly visible minority. They believe that everyone is entitled to a guaranteed income without working. Some supporters of this approach argue that people like to work and even mild incentives will encourage them to leave the welfare rolls. Dr. Anderson disagrees. He cites the results of several research studies that suggest that "a reasonable level of a guaranteed income causes low-income workers to *reduce* the number of hours they work, and the larger the amount of the guarantee relative to their income, the more they tend to stop working."[16]

---

[13]Martin Anderson, "Welfare Reform," Chapter 6 in Peter Duignan and Alvin Rabushka (Eds.), *The United States in the 1980's* (Palo Alto, Calif.: Hoover Institution, Stanford University, 1980). Reprinted in Ref. 12, pp. 95–179.

See also Martin Anderson, *Welfare: The Political Economy of Welfare Reform in the United States* (Stanford: Hoover Institution Press, 1978).

[14]See Ref. 12, p. 46.

[15]See the comment on this issue in Chapter 14.

[16]See Ref. 13, p. 160.

In Dr. Anderson's view, therefore, reform of the present system, not a guaranteed income plan, is the answer. He advocates seven guiding points for such reforms[17]:

1 Reaffirm the needy—only philosophical approach to welfare and state this approach as explicit national policy.
2 Increase efforts to eliminate fraud.
3 Establish and enforce a fair, clear work requirement. Financial incentives do not work. A person should get welfare only if they are incapable of self-support.
4 Remove inappropriate beneficiaries such as strikers from the welfare rolls.
5 Strengthen child support enforcement provisions.
6 Improve the efficiency and effectiveness of welfare administration.
7 Shift more welfare responsibility from the federal government to state and local governments and private institutions. This point could lead to block grants to state and local governments, which would design their own programs.

The 1981 amendments moved in the direction advocated by Dr. Anderson. The Reagan Administration is expected to advocate more block grants.

National Commission on Social Security

Although the National Commission on Social Security devoted most of its attention to OASDHI, it also recommended the following changes in SSI:

1 Payments under this SSI program should be increased by 25% to raise benefits to about 90% of the poverty threshold. Recipients, however, should no longer be eligible for food stamps. For various reasons many eligible SSI recipients have not and are unlikely to participate in the food stamp program. States should be required to maintain their current level of supplementation.
2 The assets test for eligibility should be eliminated. The present test complicates program administration and denies SSI payments to some people with inadequate incomes.
3 The reduction of one-third in the basic payment when the recipient lives with others should be eliminated. The present provision discourages people from taking an eligible relative into their home.
4 The general income disregard should be increased from $20 to $40 and, in the future, should be indexed by the CPI.
5 The earned income disregard should be indexed to changes in the level of wages, beginning in 1981.

[17]See Ref. 13, pp. 170–177.

6 SSI payments should be indexed in the same manner as OASDI benefits, including a maximum limit in periods when wages rise less rapidly than prices.

The President's Commission on Pension Policy, whose report was summarized in Chapter 5, recommended that (1) SSI benefits be raised to the poverty level and (2) the assets test be eliminated.

GENERAL ASSISTANCE

General assistance, administered and financed by state and local governments, is the most basic and oldest assistance program in this country, but today it is essentially a residual program. Many persons who lack money to meet their basic needs are not eligible for assistance under the more liberal federal–state programs because of their inability to meet the age, disability, or other special requirements. For these persons general assistance is the only source of aid. Some persons receiving assistance under the federal–state program turn to general assistance for supplementary aid.

Operation of Program[18]

Eligibility

Not all of the needy who are ineligible for the federal–state programs qualify for general assistance. Almost one-third of the states limit their assistance primarily to unemployable persons or to families without an employable member. Half of the states that give assistance without regard to employability require that recipients accept assignment to a systematic work program or projects or public service jobs. Most of the others require only registration with the state employment service.

More than one-half require that applicants be state or local residents at the time they apply for benefits; another one-fifth have a durational residence requirement such as one year. Most of these states, however, make an exception either for emergency assistance or for short-time assistance to nonresidents, usually pending their return to their place of legal residence. Only a few states restrict aid to U.S. citizens.

In about three-fifths of the states specified relatives are expected to support the needy applicant. Most states disqualify applicants with property in excess of specified limits.

About two-thirds limit assistance to persons not eligible for SSI or AFDC.

[18]U.S. Department of Health, Education, and Welfare, Social Security Administration, Office of Family Assistance, *Characteristics of General Assistance in the United States,* 1978 ed. (Washington, D.C.: Government Printing Office, 1978).

Most of these states, however, would aid these recipients pending receipt of their SSI or AFDC benefits or in an emergency situation.

Benefits

About three-fifths of the states usually meet only emergency needs, give assistance only on a short-term basis, or meet continuing needs only in specified types of situations. For example, the most common uses of the California program are aid in emergency situations pending receipt of categorical assistance, short-time assistance to meet temporary need, foster care, transportation, and long-term care of chronically ill indigent persons who do not qualify for the federal–state programs.

About one-third of the states use the standard of assistance under their categorical assistance programs. Another one-third use standards that are less comprehensive in items covered in the budget or in the amounts allowed for the items. In the remaining one-third standards used by the local units are too varied to classify or there are no budget standards.

About half the states have the legal right to recover at least some assistance payments from the recipients or their estates.

Payments are limited to a specified dollar maximum in almost 30% of the states. A few of these states also limit the time when benefits can be paid. About 50% set no maximum except as it may result from the limited funds available. In the remaining states limitations on amount or duration vary among local units.

Unlike the categorical programs, general assistance often pays vendors of supplies or services instead of making cash payments to recipients. In about 20% of the states vendor payments are generally used. In another one-third both money payments and vendor payments are used, depending on the circumstances in the individual case.

Medical care benefits are provided in over two-thirds of the states. Vendor payments are most commonly used to provide this assistance.

Financing

State funds finance all the assistance and administrative costs in almost one-half of the states; local funds are used exclusively in another one-third. The remaining state plans are supported by both state and local funds.

Administration

General assistance is administered by a state agency through its local offices in about 40% of the states, and supervised by the state in almost 20%. In the remaining states local government agencies administer the program with little or no state supervision.

Operations

Table 15.1 shows that general assistance is the smallest program listed, both in regard to the number of recipients and the benefits paid. Average general assistance payments per recipient exceed average AFDC payments, but their duration is shorter. In October 1980 state averages ranged from $15 to $280.

Issues

The deficiencies of general assistance are apparent from the preceding discussion. Eligibility requirements, including residence requirements, exclude many poor persons and limit others to emergency assistance. Payment standards tend to be less than under the categorical programs and vary even more widely among states. The administration of the programs is more frequently criticized, and the state and local governments bear all of the financial burden. Nevertheless, general assistance helps many persons who have nowhere else to turn.

MEDICAID

All levels of government participate in programs that meet medical expenses. The most important of these programs is the federal–state Medicaid program established by the Social Security Amendments of 1965. Another source is general assistance, described above, which may include medical care allowances in cash payments or make direct payments to vendors of medical services such as doctors and nursing homes. Many states, cities, and counties operate general hospitals to serve the needy. The federal government also provides medical services for special groups such as needy Indians and Eskimos.

Historical Background

Medical assistance has been provided under federal–state public assistance programs since 1936. The Social Security Act of 1935 permitted states to consider medical care costs in determining *cash* payments under their federally supported public assistance program. A 1950 amendment provided federal financing of *direct payments to vendors* of medical services as well as cash payments to recipients covering their medical care costs. A separate matching formula for vendor payments, enacted in 1956, gave states a special incentive to make vendor payments under their categorical assistance plan.

In 1958 the separate matching formula was rescinded, but a change was made in the basic federal matching formula that enabled the states to secure more federal assistance in paying large medical bills. Under the earlier formula the matching was limited to some fraction of the total paid each month to each recipient up to some specified maximum. Under the new formula the matching was some fraction of the average amount paid per month per recipient. There was no limit on the amount paid any single recipient in cash or vendor payments. Poorer states also received relatively more federal aid for the first time.

As noted in Chapter 9, the first response by Congress to the movement in the late 1950s for a social medical expense insurance program for the aged was the Kerr–Mills Amendment of 1960. This amendment authorized additional federal financing of expenditures for vendor payments for medical care on behalf of OAA recipients. (A 1962 amendment extended this additional financing to vendor payments under combined OAA, AB, and APTD programs.) It also created a new program, Medical Assistance for the Aged (MAA), that helped aged persons whose income exceeded OAA standards but which was not sufficient to meet the costs of medical care. Under this program each state was required to state the income level that would determine whether a person was eligible for MAA. In most states persons with higher incomes were also eligible if they needed medical care, the cost of which was expected to exceed their resources. Only vendor payments were covered under the program. The plan had to provide both institutional and noninstitutional care. The federal government paid half the administration costs and 50–80% of the total expenditures, the exact percentage being computed under a formula based primarily on state per capita income. Shortly after 1960 all states had vendor payment programs for OAA recipients. Most, but not all, states had MAA plans.

Both Medicare and Medicaid were established by the Social Security Amendments of 1965. Medical Assistance (MA), the technically correct but less popular name for Medicaid, was designed to (1) replace by 1970 both MAA and vendor payments for medical care under the four categorical assistance programs, and (2) encourage the extension of vendor payment assistance to needy persons not eligible for the categorical programs. Currently all states except Arizona have MA programs. MAA had a short career, but many provisions of the Medicaid program were copied from MAA.

Federal Standards

To be eligible for federal financial support a state program must meet certain federal standards regarding eligibility requirements and services rendered.

Eligibility

With one exception, persons eligible for cash payments under SSI or AFDC must be made eligible for MA benefits. The exception is SSI recipients who qualify for SSI benefits only because the SSI payment standards are more liberal than those utilized by the state in January 1972 in its OAA, AB, or APTD programs. States *may* include such recipients, but they need not do so. However, if they elect to exclude these SSI recipients, they must deduct any medical expenses these recipients incur from their countable income in determining their eligibility for Medicaid. Until 1981 amendments children under 21 who would be eligible under the

AFDC program except for an age or school requirement had to be covered. States can now limit this coverage to children under 21, 20, 19, or 18 or any reasonable category of such children.

If a state does not include families with unemployed parents under its AFDC program, it may elect to extend Medicaid benefits to these families. Persons becoming ineligible for cash assistance because their earnings rise *must* be continued on Medicaid for four months after their eligibility would otherwise terminate. Persons who would be eligible for assistance under SSI or AFDC if their incomes were lower *may* also be included if they are medically needy. If a state does include all these medically needy, the defined economic level must be the same for all categories of needy people—the aged, the blind, the disabled, and members of an eligible family with dependent children. Under 1981 amendments, however, a state need not provide coverage for all medically needed categories.

A state *may* include *all* medically needy children under 21. Another *option* is the inclusion of children under age 21 in foster homes or private institutions for whom public agencies are providing some financial support but who are not covered under AFDC. These last two options are especially noteworthy because they extend Medicaid beyond the SSI and AFDC categories.

If the state elects to cover the medically needy as well as those receiving cash assistance, the maximum eligibility level permitted is $133\frac{1}{3}\%$ of the highest amount ordinarily paid in cash payments under its AFDC plan to a family of the same size without any countable income. This latter restriction was enacted in 1967, when a few states adopted eligibility incomes that Congress considered too high. New York, for example, had qualified a family of four with one wage earner if its annual income less income taxes and health insurance premiums was $6,000 or less. About one-third of the state's residents qualified under this standard.

Relatives can be held responsible for assisting the applicant only if the relative is a spouse or parent.

Services

Services that must be provided under the state program are the following:

1 In-patient hospital care.
2 Out-patient hospital care and rural health clinic services.
3 Other laboratory and x-ray services.
4 Skilled nursing facility and home health services for recipients age 21 or over.
5 Physicians' services at home, in the doctor's office, at a hospital or a skilled nursing facility, or elsewhere.
6 Early and periodic screening and diagnosis of recipients under age 21 and correction of defects and conditions discovered thereby.
7 Family planning services.

At its option the state may include other services such as private duty nursing services, clinic services, dental services, physical therapy, prescription drugs, eyeglasses, and treatment in mental hospitals for children under age 21. If the HHS Secretary approves, the state can cover *any* medical service recognized under state law.

The services provided the medically needy may be more limited in kind than the services provided cash assistance recipients. As a result of 1981 amendments the services need not be the same for all medically needed groups. The state is not required to offer a minimum number of services for any medically needy group, but if the state provides institutional services, it must also provide ambulatory services (physician, clinic, nurse practitioner, dental, and preventive services) to this group.

States can require prior authorization for certain services. They can also impose certain limitations (such as the number of days of in-patient hospital care) on both mandatory and optional services. However, for mandated services they cannot impose on the needy receiving cash assistance any deductible or other cost-sharing charge. In keeping with this principle, elderly and disabled needy persons receiving cash assistance who are eligible for the HI benefits described in Chapter 9 must receive assistance in meeting the deductibles and other cost-sharing charges under that program. At their option, states can require the *medically* indigent to pay nominal deductible or other co-payment amounts for any services, mandatory or optional.

States are not required to enroll aged or disabled recipients under SMI. If they fail to do so, however, the federal government does not finance any medical assistance costs that would have been covered under that program.

The Original Long-Term Goal

The 1965 law stated in Title XIX, Section 1903(e) that federal funds were not to be paid unless

> . . . the State makes a satisfactory showing that it is making efforts in the direction of broadening the scope of the coverage and services made available under the plan and in the direction of liberalizing the eligibility requirements for medical assistance with a view toward furnishing by July 1, 1975 comprehensive care and services to substantially all individuals who meet the plan's eligibility standards with respect to income and resources, including services to enable such individuals to attain or retain independence or self-care.

By 1975 this program was expected to provide comprehensive medical services for substantially all needy persons. In 1969, as concern over the cost of the program increased, the target date was postponed to 1977. The 1972 amendments repealed this section and Section 1902(d), which prohibited a state from reducing its aggregate expenditures for the state share of its Medicaid program from one year to the next.

Review Requirements, Standards, and Advisory Committees

Concern about rising Medicaid expenditures and the quality of long-term care caused Congress in 1967 to add two review requirements, to establish federal standards for skilled nursing facilities, and to create a Medical Assistance Advisory Council to advise the then Secretary of Health, Education, and Welfare on a continuing basis.

The first type of review required is a periodic medical review of the appropriateness of care furnished patients in long-term care institutions. The second is an ongoing review of the utilization, efficiency, economy, and quality of all care and services provided under the plan.

In 1972 the Medical Assistance Advisory Council was abolished, its function being assigned to the Health Insurance Benefits Advisory Council, which also advises the Secretary on Medicare. Medicaid now imposes essentially the same utilization review requirements as Medicare on its providers. The Professional Standards Review Organizations mentioned in Chapter 9 also review Medicaid operations. Federal matching payments for long-term stays in hospitals and nursing homes are reduced by one-third if the state fails to have an effective program of utilization control or independent professional audits of patients. A common certification process for skilled nursing facilities applies to Medicaid and Medicare. Finally, Medicaid is subject to many, but not all, of the Medicare cost controls and procedures. For example, until the 1981 amendments described below, unless a state obtained approval from the Secretary for an alternate method, it could pay only the reasonable cost of outpatient hospital services. For all other services the state did not have to use the Medicare method of payment, but the Medicaid reimbursement could not exceed the amount Medicare would pay. Vendors had to and still must accept the Medicaid payment as payment in full.

The 1981 amendments changed Medicaid administration in various ways. For example, state payments for inpatient hospital services must be reasonable and adequate to meet the costs that "must be incurred by efficiently and economically operated facilities" in order to meet applicable laws and safety standards. In the aggregate the amount paid cannot exceed the amount determined to be reasonable under Medicare. States must take into account, however, the atypical costs incurred by hospitals that serve a disproportionate number of low income patients. As will be indicated shortly, the federal grant formula encourages a qualified hospital review program. The act repealed the requirement that Medicaid payments for physicians and lab services could not exceed what Medicare would pay. However, instead of permitting recipients to choose where they purchase laboratory services and medical devices, states can elect to purchase these items through a competitive bidding process. Furthermore, states can require individuals who overutilize services to use particular providers. They can also limit the participation of providers who, following a hearing, are found to have abused the program.

To encourage the use of HMOs, HMOs need no longer within three years after they enter into a Medicaid contract have an enrollment of less than 50% Medicare and Medicaid beneficiaries. The percentage is now 75% and the Secretary can waive this requirement completely for public HMOs. States, however, are no longer limited to prepaid insurance arrangements with federally qualified HMOs. Other insurers can be used if they have made adequate provision against potential insolvency.

The HHS Secretary is authorized to waive certain requirements of the law to achieve certain program purposes provided he or she finds them to be cost effective, efficient, and not inconsistent with program intent. Under this authority the Secretary can restrict the provider from whom individuals can obtain primary care. Localities can act as brokers in selecting from among competing health plans. The Secretary can under certain conditions permit a state to cover personal care services and other services pursuant to an individual plan of home and community-based care to persons who would otherwise require institutional care. The total cost of all medical assistance for services under such plans cannot, however, exceed the cost of services to these persons if they were institutionalized.

These changes are consistent with the Reagan Administration emphasis on cost effectiveness and their belief that cost effectiveness is best achieved through flexibility in federal regulations and reliance on competition.

Financing

The federal government pays 75% of the costs of professional medical personnel, 100% of the costs of skilled nursing facility inspectors, 90% of the costs of state Medicaid fraud and abuse control units located organizationally outside the "single state agency", 90% of the cost of developing automated claims processing and management information systems, and 75% of the cost of operating such systems. The federal share of all other administrative costs is 50%. In addition, the federal government pays 90% of family planning services and 50–83% of all other medical care costs. The fraction is 50% for states with above average per capita income and varies between 50 and 83% for the other states. The exact formula was presented earlier in this chapter in the section on AFDC. Under the Omnibus Budget Reconciliation Act of 1981, however, the federal matching payments the state would otherwise receive under this formula will be reduced by 3% in fiscal 1982, 4% in fiscal year 1983, and 4.5% in fiscal year 1984. A state can lower this reduction by 1% for each of the following: (1) operating a qualified hospital cost review program, (2) sustaining an unemployment rate exceeding 150% of the national average, and (3) demonstrating recoveries from fraud and abuse (plus in 1982 third party recoveries) equal to 1% of federal amounts. A state can also receive an offset in its reductions if total federal Medicaid expenditures in a year fall below a specified target amount. For 1982 the target amount is 109% of the state's estimates for fiscal 1981. The targets for 1983 and 1984 will be the 1982 target adjusted for increases in the medical care expenditure component of the CPI. The Act also directed the General Accounting Office to study the feasibility and consequences of changing the federal medical assistance percentage.

States can require localities to finance part of the nonfederal share of Medicaid costs, but the state portion of the nonfederal share must be at least 40%.

Administration

Each state administers its own Medicaid program. The Health Care Financing Administration, a component of the U.S. Department of Health and Human Services, checks on whether the state programs are in compliance with the federal requirements.

One state agency must be designated as the "single state agency" responsible for overall administration of the program. As noted in Chapter 9, the Office of Program Integrity was created as part of the Health Care Financing Administration to strength fraud and abuse control in both Medicaid and Medicare. This office assesses state agencies' efforts to deter, detect, investigate, and prosecute Medicaid fraud cases and assists in these efforts.

State Plans

All states except Arizona have federally approved Medicaid programs.[19] Arizona has a large Indian population that is already covered under other federal programs.

Eligibility

In January 1978 15 states had elected not to cover all SSI recipients by using some aspect of their pre-SSI eligibility standard. About three-fifths of the states included medically needy persons under their MA program as well as those eligible for cash assistance benefits. The 1978 income level used to define the medically needy ranged from $1,296 for a single person in rural Louisiana to $3,600 in Hawaii, Massachusetts, and Rhode Island. The four-person income standard varied between $2,400, in Tennessee, and $6,600, in Hawaii. About two-fifths included *all* medically needy children under age 21. About two-thirds of the states provided medical assistance for some persons not eligible for the federal program such as persons age 21–65 who are not blind, disabled, or AFDC adults or people whose income exceeds the federal limitations.

---

[19]U.S. Department of Health, Education, and Welfare, Health Care Financing Administration, *Data on the Medicaid Program: Eligibility, Services, Expenditures* (Baltimore, Md.: Medicaid/Medicare Management Institute, 1979).

Services

In addition to the required services, commonly provided services were prosthetic devices (41 states), prescription drugs (48 states), clinic services (39 states), emergency hospital services (41 states), skilled nursing facilities for children under 21 (43 states), care for patients age 65 or over in institutions for mental care (41 states), dental care (31 states), eyeglasses (33 states), and chiropractors' services (28 states). Private duty nursing coverage is much less common (18 states).

Generally states provided the required services without any maximum limits or co-payment provisions. Many states, however, required prior authorization for all services or services beyond a specified limitation. About one-third of the jurisdictions limited care in a general hospital to a specified number of days, such as 21 or 60, per spell of illness or per fiscal year. About one-fifth limited the number of visits to a physician. About one-third required a small co-payment for prescription drugs. All states required Medicaid patients in long-term care institutions to contribute income in excess of the amount they required for personal needs to help pay the cost of their care.

All but a few states paid the Supplementary Medical Insurance premiums for recipients eligible for that program.

Almost all states covering medically needy persons provided this group with all the types of services available to cash needy persons.

Financing

About three-fourths of the states financed their share of the costs entirely out of state revenues. The others relied on both state and local funds.

Administration

In most states the single state agency responsible for the administration of the Medicaid program was either the state welfare agency or an umbrella resources agency. This agency, however, could contract with other agencies to carry out some of its functions. For example, in those states where the welfare agency was not the single state agency, it normally determined what AFDC and medically needy persons were eligible for these benefits.

About three-fifths of the states had contracted with the Social Security Administration to determine eligibility for SSI recipients or federally administered state supplements.

Over half the states have contracted with health insurers or fiscal agents to process claims for most or all services. Blue Cross–Blue Shield associations perform this function in most states. The second most common private claims processor is the Electronic Data System Federal Corporation. Almost one-third of the states process their own claims. A few have hired fiscal agents to process certain services such as dental services and drugs.

All states now have fraud control units to investigate and prosecute fraud in their Medicaid programs.

Operations

Table 15.4 shows the total medical vendor payments that have been made under public assistance programs in selected years since 1951. As noted earlier, the federal government first financed direct payments to vendors of medical care through 1950 amendments to the Social Security Act. Other important bench marks reflected in these data are the Kerr–Mills Amendments of 1960, which established MAA and the 1965 amendment that established Medicaid.

Total payments increased dramatically with the establishment of Medicaid. Medicaid covered needy persons not included under the programs it replaced and provided more comprehensive services.

By 1974 these payments exceeded the cash payments under all welfare programs combined. Although a small portion of the total, general assistance vendor programs have also increased significantly in the past decade.

About 22 million persons received Medicaid benefits in 1978, compared with 18 million in 1971. About 4 million were aged, 3 million disabled, 10 million children under age 21, and 5 million adults in families with dependent children. About 31% of the payments were for in-patient hospital care, 24% for intermediate care, 18% for nursing home care, 9% for physicians, 6% for prescribed drugs, 2% for dental care, and 11% for other services. Medicaid accounted for about 12% of total personal health care expenditures, 29% of the public portion of those expenditures. Annual payments per recipient rose from $353 in 1971 to $824 in

Table 15.4 Medical Vendor Payments Under Public Assistance Programs During Selected Years, 1951–1978 (In Millions of Dollars)

Year	Total	Federally Aided Programs			General Assistance[a]
		Medicaid	MAA	Other	
1951	103	—	—	57	47
1955	232	—	—	163	68
1960	522	—	5	415	102
1965	1,480	—	586	774	121
1966	2,008	1,194	293	436	84
1970	5,606	5,507	—	—	99
1975	14,555	14,177	—	—	378
1976	15,941	15,543	—	—	399
1977	17,739	17,140	—	—	600
1978[b]	19,700	18,800	—	—	900

Sources: Social Security Bulletins.

[a]Incomplete data.

[b]Estimated by author.

1978. Inflation, however, explained a large share of this increase. In constant 1971 dollars the 1978 expenditure per recipient was $512.

The federal medical assistance percentage is 50 for 14 states. The states with the highest percentages are Mississippi (78%), Alabama (71%), Arkansas (73%), and South Carolina (71%).

In 1978 10 states made two-thirds of the total payments[20]; 20 states made 82%.

About 60% of the poor population in the United States were Medicaid recipients. In two states, California and New York, Medicaid recipients exceeded the poor population; in eight states Medicaid recipients were less than 20% of their poverty population.

Total Medicaid expenditures per $1 million of *national* personal income were $10,734, the state and local share being $4,708. New York was the only state for which the total expenditures per $1 million of *state* personal income were over $20,000. Five states reported expenditures relative to $1 million of state personal income that were less than $5,000. These states were Alaska, Delaware, Florida, Nebraska, and Wyoming.

Issues

Because Medicaid is so closely related to the categorical cash public assistance programs, many of the criticisms directed at the eligibility conditions of those programs also apply here. However, many states cover needy persons not covered under the cash assistance programs.

Benefits vary among the states, but certain services must be provided in all plans and many states offer additional services.

The principal problems surrounding Medicaid have been its cost and the possibilities for fraud and abuse. Initially some states established income limits for the medically needy that Congress later judged to be unduly generous. The prices of medical service, fueled in part by both Medicare and Medicaid, rose much faster than expected. As a result, the accomplishment of the long-range goal of comprehensive coverage for all needy persons was deferred once and abandoned in 1972. Administration of the amounts paid doctors and hospitals has been tightened in various ways. Fraud and abuse continue to be serious problems, but control units established in recent years are beginning to reduce their level.

Some of the national medical expense insurance proposals analyzed in Chapter 9 would replace or change the role of Medicaid.

In addition to recommending changes in SSI, the National Commission on Social Security recommended the following changes in Medicaid:

1   All families whose income is 65% or less of the poverty standard should be
    eligible for Medicaid. This recommendation is designed to reduce some of the

---

[20]Ranked in order of their total expenditures, these states were New York, California, New Jersey, Wisconsin, Ohio, Texas, Massachusetts, Michigan, Illinois, and Pennsylvania. New York alone accounted for almost 19%, California for 14%.

disparity among the states and to cover some needy persons not currently covered.

2 The states' option to base Medicaid eligibility for SSI recipients on 1972 Medicaid standards, resulting in some SSI recipients not being eligible for Medicaid, should be eliminated.

3 Medicaid eligibility for disabled recipients of SSI should not terminate before the person becomes entitled to Medicare.

4 Reimbursement to physicians for Medicaid should be raised to the levels paid by Medicare. Because of current low reimbursement levels some physicians are reluctant to treat Medicaid patients. The fees under both programs will ultimately have to be reasonably equivalent to those paid for privately purchased services.

5 Neither Medicare nor Medicaid should be used as instruments to control health care costs. Competition, however, should be encouraged where it can help to restrain cost increases.

6 Coverage of abortions under Medicaid should be the same as that for any other covered medical procedure.

7 A separate program should be created to provide services other than acute care to needy persons requiring long-term care.

The Reagan Administration is expected to urge a reduction in the federal government's share of the cost of this program, greater flexibility as to how the states use the federal monies, and more emphasis on competition among medical providers.

SOCIAL SERVICES AND CHILD WELFARE SERVICES

In addition to the cash assistance payments provided under SSI and AFDC and the medical assistance under Medicaid, the Social Security Act provides social services and child welfare services for many low-income families.

Social Services

Originally social services were provided under the cash categorical public assistance programs (OAA, AB, APTD, and AFDC), but in 1974 Congress transferred the social service provisions of the Social Security Act to a separate Title XX. In 1981 Congress amended this title to establish a new block grant to states for social services of various sorts including, for example, many services formerly covered under the Community Services Act. The block grant reduced the total state allotment but gave the states more latitude in how the money can be spent. Under the new Title XX states receive an annual allotment for operating social service programs directed toward the following goals:

1 Achieving or maintaining economic self-support to prevent, reduce, or eliminate dependency.

2 Achieving or maintaining self-sufficiency, including reduction or prevention of dependency.

3 Preventing or remedying neglect, abuse, or exploitation of children and adults unable to protect their own interests, or preserving, rehabilitating, or reuniting families.

4 Preventing or reducing inappropriate institutional care by providing for community-based care, home-based care, or other forms of less intensive care.

5 Securing referral or admission for institutional care when other forms of care are not appropriate, or providing services in institutions.

Allotments based on state populations are limited to $2.4 billion in fiscal year 1982 rising gradually to $2.7 billion by fiscal year 1986.

Under the old Title XX, to qualify for these federally supported social services individuals and families had to be either SSI, AFDC, or Medicaid recipients or meet certain income requirements. No services other than protective services, family planning services, or information and referral services could be provided families with incomes above 115% of the state median income. In 1979 almost half of the social service recipients were AFDC, SSI, or Medicaid recipients, about 36% met the income requirements, and 15% did not. Child day care accounted for over 21% of the expenditures. Other services accounting for at least 10% of the expenditures were homemakers' services (14%), protective services and child foster care services (15%), and education, training, and employment (10%). Under the new Title XX there is no requirement that a certain percent of the funds be used for welfare recipients or that any services be limited to families with lower incomes. Furthermore, each state can, if it wishes, transfer up to 10% of its allotment for expenditures under separate health or energy assistance block grant programs.

Child Welfare Services

Under Title IV-B, not changed by the 1981 amendments, the federal government pays part of the costs incurred by state welfare agencies in establishing, extending, and strengthening child welfare programs. Each state receives $70,000 plus the remainder of the amount appropriated times a ratio that varies directly with the state population under age 21, and inversely with the state per capita income. Because the amounts appropriated have been much less than authorized, the federal share of the actual costs has been less than 7%. About 73% of the program expenditures are for foster care, including income maintenance for children not eligible for foster care under AFDC. The other major uses are day care (8%), protective services (8%), and adoption services (3%).

FOOD ASSISTANCE PROGRAMS

Food assistance programs fall into three major categories: all three programs are supposed to improve the diet of the poor, but they operate in quite different ways. They supplement cash assistance programs and serve some persons not eligible for those programs. Because these programs were originally minor appendages of farm price support policies, they are administered by the Department of Agriculture. Today they are more commonly regarded as part of the U.S. welfare program.

Under the food distribution program domestically produced commodities previously purchased by the federal government are distributed at the local government level to needy persons meeting certain eligibility requirements. Because this approach is much less important than the other two categories of food assistance programs and has been gradually declining in importance, only food stamp and child nutrition programs are discussed below.

Food Stamps

Under the food stamp program eligible families receive coupons that may be used to purchase any food except alcoholic beverages, tobacco, foods that would be eaten in the store, and ready-to-eat hot foods, like barbecued chicken. Food stamps can also be used to buy plants and seeds that will be used to grow food. Retailers desiring to accept coupons must be approved by the Department of Agriculture. Coupons accepted by retail food stores can be redeemed through approved wholesale food concerns or banks.

Program Characteristics

To receive food stamps the applicant must satisfy several requirements. First, recipients must usually be U.S. citizens or legally permanent aliens. Second, able-bodied recipients between 18 and 60 years of age must register for work, search for a job, and accept an offer of a suitable job. Students are subject to some special requirements. For example, they must work at least 20 hours a week, be enrolled in a WIN program or federally financed work–study program, or be responsible for at least half the support of a dependent person other than a spouse. Third, if the household includes elderly or disabled members, its *net* income during the next month from all sources, including OASDI and public assistance, must be less than a specified amount that increases with the size of the household. Each year this amount is adjusted to reflect changes in the cost of living. The objective is to qualify all such households whose net income (not gross income) is less than the poverty guideline established by the Office of Management and Budget (OMB) for each household size. During 1981 the maximum allowable monthly "net" income for a single person was $316, $418 for a 2-person household, $621 for a 4-person household, and $1,232 for a 10-person household. The net income is the gross income less the following items: (1) a standard deduction ($85 per household until July 1, 1983), (2) 18% (20% until 1981 amendments) of the gross earned income to cover work-related expenses and payroll taxes, and (3) in certain cases deductions for child care or care for disabled adults, excess shelter costs, and medical expenses. Prior to 1981 amendments this net income standard applied to all families but now families without elderly or disabled members must satisfy a tighter income requirement. Their gross (not net) income must not exceed 130% of the applicable federal poverty level.

In addition to the income requirements, single recipients must not have resources exceeding $1,500. This limit for households with two or more persons is $3,000 if at least one family member is age 60 or older; otherwise it is also $1,500. Not counted in applying these limits are certain resources such as the recipient's home and surrounding lot, household goods and personal belongings, life insurance policies, and, if their trade-in value is less than $4,500, the primary household vehicle plus one for each household member who is employed, training for a job, seeking employment, or temporarily unemployed.

The value of the coupon allotment varies according to the monthly *net* income and the number of persons in the household. Households without any income receive the estimated monthly cost of a nutritionally adequate diet for a family of their size. These amounts are adjusted each year to match increases in food prices. Households with income receive an allotment equal to the difference between the estimated cost of a nutritionally adequate diet and 30% of their monthly net income. The minimum benefit for any eligible family is $10. Some examples of the allotments during 1981 were as follows:

Monthly Net Income ($)	Family Members 1 ($)	2 ($)	4 ($)	10 ($)
0–1	70	128	233	525
99–101	40	98	203	495
199–201	10	68	173	465
299–301	10	33	138	430
399–401		10	113	405
499–501			83	375
599–601			53	345
699–701				315
.				.
.				.
.				.
1199–1201				165

The Food and Nutrition Service of the U.S. Department of Agriculture is the national administrator of this program. Local welfare offices, in compliance with federal directives, determine what households are eligible and their coupon allotment. SSI recipients may apply at the local Social Security Administration office. The federal government pays out of general revenues the full cost of the coupons and 50 or 60% of the administrative expenses. The federal share is 60% unless the state error rate exceeds 5%.

Under a separate Special Supplemental Food Program for Women, Infants, and Children (WIC) the federal government provides to certain families stamps that can be used only to purchase certain commodities, such as milk, that are considered desirable for children.

Historical Development

The Food Stamp Act of 1964 formally established this program. At first only 22 states participated, each setting its own eligibility standards and allotment schedule. Eligible households purchased food stamps that had a face value in excess of the amount they paid. This excess value was known as the "bonus" value of the coupons. The purchase price varied according to household income and size. Legislation passed in 1971, 1973, 1977, 1980, and 1981 changed the program significantly. The 1971 legislation liberalized the program. National eligibility standards were established, the allotments were to be set at a level sufficient to provide a nutritionally adequate diet, and these allotments were to be adjusted automatically for annual cost of living increases. The poorest recipients were given free food stamps, and able-bodied household members up to age 65 (except students and those needed at home to care for children) were required to register for work. As a result of 1973 amendments, the categories eligible to participate were increased and coupon allotments were adjusted semiannually instead of annually. The program's current basic characteristics were determined largely by 1977 legislation. The purchase requirement was eliminated. The benefit became what used to be the bonus value of the coupons. The deductions used to determine net income were revised from a more generous procedure to one close to that described above. The OMB poverty guidelines also replaced a more liberal eligibility standard. Work registration requirements were tightened for students and for caretakers, whose children now had to be under age 12. On the other hand, the maximum age was lowered from 65 to 60. Federal sharing of administrative costs was raised from 50 to 60% for those states with an error rate of 5% or less. Legislation in 1979 established a medical deduction for the aged and disabled persons and granted them an unlimited shelter deduction. Fraud provisions were also tightened. In 1980 Congress decided that it would be sufficient to adjust the cost of an adequate diet once a year instead of twice and further restricted the eligibility of students. The 1981 amendments tightened the income requirement for families without elderly or disabled members, reduced the earned income deduction used in the calculation of net income, increased the bases for disqualifying individuals for fraud and misrepresentation and the penalties assessed for such acts, and improved the government's ability to recover benefit overpayments.

Operations

Table 15.5 shows the number of persons who have participated in the food stamp program during selected years since it was initiated, the total bonus value of the coupons that have been allocated, and the average bonus per participant. The data reflect the important legislative changes noted above, the increase in the U.S. population, changes in the proportion of the population that is poor, and inflation. WIC benefits, not shown in this table, totaled about $350 million in 1978.

Table 15.2 indicates that only Medicaid has more recipients than the food stamp program. The dollar benefits are close to SSI payments, including state supplements.

Issues

Until the 1970s the food stamp program was severely criticized because of low participation rates. Many counties did not have food stamp programs, and in counties with programs many eligible persons chose not to participate. To participate families had to invest some of their limited cash in food stamps; the basic allotment was not sufficient to provide a nutritionally adequate diet; and no one was permitted to buy less than the basic allotment. Participation rates increased markedly in the early 1970s as eligibility and purchase requirements were relaxed, benefits increased, and more counties encouraged to establish such programs. More recently questions have arisen as to whether eligibility requirements were too low, benefits too generous, and administration too lax. The 1977, 1980, and 1981 amendments noted above were designed primarily to tighten the eligibility requirements, reduce the semiannual automatic adjustment in allotment levels to once a year, and tighten the administration, especially with respect to fraud.

Table 15.5   Food Stamp Program: Number of Participants, Bonus Value of Coupons, and Annual Average Monthly Bonus per Participant, Selected Fiscal Years, 1962–1979

Fiscal Year	Participants (In Thousands)	Bonus Value (In Millions of Dollars)	Annual Average Monthly Bonus per Participant ($)
1962	143	13	7.66
1965	424	32	6.39
1970	4,340	551	10.58
1975	17,063	4,386	21.42
1976	18,557	5,310	23.68
1977	17,058	5,058	24.71
1978	16,044	5,165	26.83
1979	17,710	6,485	30.51

Source: Social Security Bulletin, Annual Statistical Supplement, 1977–1979, Table 27, p. 79.

Child Nutrition Programs

Child nutrition programs currently or recently in effect include school lunch and breakfast programs, a child-care center food program, and a summer food program. The most important of these programs is the school lunch program, which currently costs the federal government about $2 billion per year.

Under the National School Lunch Act the federal government assists the states through grants-in-aid to establish, maintain, and expand school lunch programs. Most of the federal funds are used to purchase agricultural products and other foods for consumption by school children, but nonfood assistance that supports the school lunch program is also available.

Lunches served by participating public or nonprofit public schools must meet minimum nutritional requirements prescribed by the Secretary of Agriculture. Children who are members of poor households, as defined by poverty guidelines, must be served these lunches without cost or at a reduced price not exceeding 20 cents. In 1981 Congress required that households requesting such assistance document their incomes. The Secretary of Agriculture was also required to conduct a pilot study to verify the data provided on a sample of applications. Other children in participating schools pay higher, but still attractive, prices. Despite these low prices, student fees pay most of the costs not covered by the federal grants.

The federal government supports this program through (1) general assistance reimbursement rates and (2) special assistance reimbursement rates. In 1981 Congress set the general assistance rate at 10.5 cents per lunch for lunches served in school districts where less than 60% of the lunches are served free or at a reduced price and 2 cents more in the other districts. The special assistance rate is 98.75 cents for full meals and 58.75 cents for reduced-price meals. All these rates are to be adjusted each July 1. Each state is required to provide matching revenues to school districts equal to at least 30% of the federal general assistance reimbursements.

One of the criticisms of the program is that many schools in poor areas cannot afford to participate in the program because they lack cafeterias or matching funds.

Each school must include in its lunch program commodities designated by the Secretary as being in abundance either nationally or in the school area. This provision is designed to encourage the domestic consumption of agricultural commodities and other food—one of the stated objectives of the Act. The Secretary may also donate foods purchased under the farm price support program.

HOUSING ASSISTANCE PROGRAMS

The housing of poor families, like their diets, greatly affects their economic and psychological well-being. Consequently, a number of programs have been developed with the avowed objective of providing decent housing for all families. Like the food programs, these housing programs supplement public assistance benefits and have in some cases benefited the nonpoor at least as much as the poor. From the viewpoint of the poor the major federal housing programs are public housing, rental assistance, and interest supplements. All three are administered by the Assistant Secretary for Housing—Federal Housing Commissioner of the U.S. Department of Housing and Urban Development (HUD).

Public Housing

Public housing, initiated by the Housing Act of 1937, is designed to provide decent public housing to poor families at rentals they can afford. Although more funds are being allocated at present to rental assistance, public housing still helps many lower-income persons. Local public housing authorities develop and administer the housing units, financed in part by the federal government. The authorities may obtain this housing by constructing new units, rehabilitating existing units, purchasing units from private developers or builders (the Turnkey method), or leasing units from private owners. Families in public housing benefit because they pay subsidized rent and the number of dwelling units among which people at their income level can choose is increased.

Eligibility

Congress restricts eligibility for public housing to families whose income is no more than 80% of the median income in the area as adjusted for family size. To encourage the development of more housing for lower-income families, however, in 1981 Congress required that the proportion of units available under public housing and Section 8 (to be discussed shortly) for families whose income is between 50 and 80% of the median be sharply reduced. For example, on new or additional units becoming available after October 1, 1981, the proportion, to be applied on the average over all projects and programs, cannot exceed 5%.

The highest initial rent charged [which is usually 30% (20–25% until 1981 amendments) of the family income adjusted for family size] must be at least 20% less than the lowest rents for decent private housing. When its income rises above a ceiling set by local authorities, a family must leave the public housing.

Because the demand for public housing exceeds the available supply, other criteria have sometimes been used, such as "merit, demonstrated moral behavior, social need (such as the elderly and other displaced individuals), and veterans' preference."[21]

Benefits

The federal government provides financial and technical assistance. Annually the federal government covers the debt service on local authority bonds sold to pay

---

[21]*Background Papers, The President's Commission on Income Maintenance Programs* (Washington, D.C.: Government Printing Office, 1970), p. 339.

for the development or acquisition of public housing. It also provides operating subsidies to help the public housing agencies operate their projects, retain minimum operating reserves, and offset certain operating defects. Operating subsidies are based on what a well-managed agency would require to operate its units.

In some areas local authorities have been accused of using criteria other than income to discriminate against certain classes of applicants. They have also been accused of being inflexible and paternal. The design and construction of some of the housing have been severely criticized. The concept of public housing itself has been accused of segregating the poor and preserving ghetto life, though in a different setting. In fairness, however, it should be noted that some public housing has been efficiently administered and has clearly benefited its residents.

Rental Assistance

The major housing assistance program at the present time is authorized by Section 8 of the U.S. Housing Act of 1937 as amended by the Housing and Community Development Act of 1974. Section 8 and some related programs help low- and moderate-income families rent decent *private* housing. The income standard is that already stated for public housing. If the applicant's assets exceed $5,000 in value, 10% of their value is added to the applicant's income to determine eligibility. In addition to requiring that families with incomes below 50% of the area median income receive a larger share of the units available under public housing and Section 8 in 1981 Congress specifically directed newly constructed housing under this section to be "modest in design."

In addition to having low enough incomes, applicants must be one of the following: (1) handicapped; (2) disabled as defined under OASDI; (3) displaced as the result of a governmental action or federally declared disaster; or (4) elderly, which means that the head of the household or the spouse is at least 62 years of age. Furthermore, single persons are admitted to this program only under special conditions. (Singles can receive somewhat less generous assistance under other programs.)

Under Section 8, renters pay no more than the highest of (1) 30% of the family's monthly adjusted income, (2) 10% of the family's monthly income, or (3) that part of a family's welfare payments that is specifically designated to meet housing costs if the state adjusts this payment in accordance with the family's actual housing cost. HUD pays the remaining portion, which is determined by the "fair market rent" normally received for the unit.

Interest Supplements

Under the HUD Act of 1968 the Department of Housing and Urban Development subsidizes interest payments on home mortgages by families with incomes less than 95% of the area median income. The homeowner must make a down payment of at least 3% of the acquisition cost and pay on the mortgage at least

20% of his or her monthly income adjusted for family size. Interest costs can be reduced to as low as 4% under this program. In 1981 Congress prohibited the HUD Secretary from entering into new contracts for such interest supplements after September 30, 1983. After March 31, 1982 the Secretary can enter into new contracts only pursuant to earlier commitments.

EARNED INCOME TAX CREDIT

In 1975 Congress enacted an earned income tax credit (EITC) that helps families with low incomes.

Eligible families can subtract the credit from their federal income tax. If the credit exceeds the tax they would otherwise pay, these families receive a check for the difference as a tax refund.

The major purpose of this credit is to offset the effect on these families of the OASDI tax, which, unlike the income tax, is not a progressive tax. Because the net effect is cash assistance for such families, EITC is included in this chapter as a public assistance program. Because its major purpose is not public assistance, however, EITC possesses several, unique characteristics.

Only husbands and wives with a dependent child filing a joint return are eligible. Their adjusted gross income must be less than $10,000.

If the adjusted *gross* income is $6,000 or less, the earned income credit is determined by the earned income. Part of the table used to calculate the credit for 1980 returns is reproduced below:

Earned Income ($)		Earned income
Over	But Not Over	Tax credit ($)
0	50	3
⋮		⋮
100	150	13
⋮		⋮
1,000	1,050	103
⋮		⋮
2,000	2,050	203
⋮		⋮
3,000	3,050	303
⋮		⋮
4,000	4,050	403
⋮		⋮
5,000	6,000	500 (the maximum)
⋮		⋮
9,950	9,999	3

Note that the credit is $0 for families with either no earned income or one of $10,000 or higher. The maximum refund is $500.

If the adjusted *gross* income exceeds $6,000, the credit is the smaller of (1) the credit for the earned income as described above and (2) the credit in the same table for the amount corresponding to the total adjusted gross income.

If a family is eligible for a credit, it may request advance payments that will be included regularly in their pay. About 5 to 6 million families have filed returns each year, starting in 1976, claiming an EITC. The credits have exceeded $1 billion each year.

SUMMARY

Over 20 million persons currently receive aid from a complex welfare system that includes cash public assistance, Medicaid, social services and child welfare services, food assistance, housing assistance, and other programs. Some critics believe that the present system is so deficient that it should be replaced. Others favor extensive reforms.

Social insurance programs enable many families to escape poverty and reduce the degree of poverty among others. Social insurance, however, is designed primarily to provide wage-related benefits to victims of personnel risks. Minimum social insurance benefits are below poverty levels. They cannot be raised without distorting the present benefit structure nor raising benefits for all insured persons.

Public assistance programs provide cash benefits, medical care, food assistance, housing assistance, and other services for persons who can demonstrate their individual need.

Under the Supplemental Security Income (SSI) program aged, blind, and disabled persons are guaranteed a specified monthly income by the federal government. For persons living in their own households the 1981–1982 guarantee is $264.70. If both members of a couple are eligible, the guarantee is 150% of the amount guaranteed an individual. The actual payment is this guaranteed level less the person's "countable" income. Each July 1 the guarantee is increased to match increases in the Consumer Price Index. All states but one supplement the federal payment under certain conditions.

Aid to Families with Dependent Children (AFDC) assists children deprived of parental support because the father or mother has died, is disabled, or, as is most common, is continually absent from the home. Some state plans also help families with an unemployed parent. AFDC is a state and local government program financed in part by federal grants-in-aid. The federal grants and most state and local funding are derived from general revenues, not earmarked taxes.

To receive federal aid the state program must satisfy certain conditions. Although the states still have some flexibility in setting eligibility and benefit requirements, 1981 amendments greatly reduced this flexibility. The amount of assistance is determined by subtracting the applicant's income available for basic needs from his or her personal requirements as determined by the administering agency. The federal grant formula favors states with below average per capita income.

One major criticism of these two categorical cash assistance programs is that they exclude many poor persons. They cover only certain categories of the poor; many of these favored poor are excluded by low payment standards. The needs test used to determine eligibility and benefits is said to damage the recipient's self-respect and destroy any incentive to work and save. Some critics are more concerned about the number of fraudulent claims. Work requirements have been applauded by some, denounced by others. Eligibility requirements and benefits vary widely among states. A comparison of AFDC benefits with state budget standards reveals a substantial unmet need in many states. Some AFDC families, however, receive more than families headed by a full-time worker earning low wages. Financing these programs has become a major problem for poorer states and many large cities.

Those favoring the replacement of SSI and AFDC would turn to the guaranteed income approach discussed in Chapter 16. Many opponents of the guaranteed income approach agree that the welfare system, of which SSI and AFDC are part, is inefficient, poorly managed, inequitable, and deficient in its work incentives. Parts of the welfare system provide overlapping benefits and are characterized by a high fraud level. In their opinion, however, the guaranteed income approach would help many persons who are not needy and seriously reduce work incentives. These reformers would cover only the needy and establish a clear work requirement. They would transfer more responsibility from the federal government to the state and local governments.

General assistance, administered and financed by state and local governments, helps the poor who are not eligible for the federal–state programs or receive inadequate benefits under these programs. Eligibility requirements, however, tend to be restrictive, and the benefits low.

Medicaid, like AFDC, consists of approved state and local government programs financed in part by federal grants. The state programs must cover all persons covered under AFDC and most persons under SSI. They may, and in about three-fifths of the states do, cover medically needy persons who would be eligible for the cash assistance programs except for their income level. Finally, they may cover all medically needy children. The benefits are comprehensive, including hospital stays, physicians' services, and other medical care. The 1981 amendments reduced the federal share of the costs of this program and gave the states more flexibility in its administration.

Food assistance programs include surplus commodity distribution, food stamps, and free or reduced-price school lunch programs. Under the food stamp program eligible families receive coupons that can be used to purchase food. The objective is to qualify all households with elderly or disabled members with a *net* income below the poverty guideline. Currently a family of four in this category must have a monthly "net" income of $621 or less to participate. Other families must have a *gross* income below 130% of the poverty standard. The value of the coupon allotment varies according to the monthly net income and the number of persons in the household. For example, in 1981 the allotment for a family of four was $233 for a family with no income, $138 if the net income were $138. The U.S. Department of Agriculture administers this program.

The major housing assistance programs are public housing, rental assistance, and interest supplements. The principal beneficiaries are the poor close to the poverty threshold. These programs differ according to whether the housing units are owned and administered by public agencies or private persons, whether the subsidized persons live together or are scattered throughout the community, whether the program concentrates on new housing units or existing units, and whether a family must move out of the subsidized unit when their income rises. The 1981 amendments tightened the standards and phased out the interest supplements.

Because a family may qualify for cash, food, housing, and medical assistance, the combined effect of these benefits must be considered.

An Earned Income Tax Credit provides a tax credit or cash payment for husbands and wives with a dependent child and low income.

SUGGESTIONS FOR ADDITIONAL READING

Anderson, Martin. *Welfare: The Political Economy of Welfare Reform in the United States.* Stanford, Calif.: Hoover Institution Press, 1978.
A detailed analysis of the welfare system and thought-provoking reform proposals by an articulate supporter of the needy-only approach.

Brinker, Paul A. *Economic Insecurity and Social Security.* New York: Appleton-Century-Crofts, 1968.
Several chapters in this comprehensive text deal with public assistance and other ways of handling poverty problems.

Haveman, Robert H. (Ed.) *A Decade of Federal Antipoverty Programs.* New York: Academic Press, 1977.
A valuable collection of seven major papers, each with two commentaries by discussants, presented at a conference sponsored by the University of Wisconsin-Madison Institute for Research on Poverty to discuss the achievements, failures, and lessons to be learned from a decade of programs under the War on Poverty.

How to Think About Welfare Reform for the 1980's, Hearings before the Subcommittee on Public Assistance of the Committee on Finance, U.S. Senate, 96th Congress, 2nd Session, February 6 and 7, 1980. Washington, D.C.: U.S. Government Printing Office, 1980.
An excellent compilation of testimony on the present welfare system, its problems, and new directions for the 1980s.

Piven, Frances F., and Richard A. Cloward. *Regulating the Poor.* New York: Pantheon, 1971.
A highly critical commentary which asserts that public relief exists not to help the poor but to defuse political turmoil.

Programs of HUD. Washington, D.C.: U.S. Department of Housing and Urban Development, 1978.
A description of the various programs of the Department of Housing and Urban Development.

Rejda, George E. *Economic Security and Social Insurance.* Englewood Cliffs, N.J.: Prentice-Hall, 1976.
Chapters 17 and 18 of this comprehensive book cover the problems of poverty and the welfare system.

Stein, Bruno. *On Relief.* New York: Basic Books, 1971.
An economic analysis of the alternatives to the present system.

U.S. Department of Health, Education, and Welfare, Health Care Financing Administration, Medicaid/Medicare Management Institute. *Data on the Medicaid Program: Eligibility, Services, Expenditures,* 1979 ed. (revised). Baltimore, Md.: Health Care Financing Administration, 1979.
A detailed examination and analysis of state Medicaid programs and their operation.

U.S. Department of Health and Human Services, Social Security Administration, Office of Family Assistance, *Characteristics of State Plans for Aid to Families with Dependent Children,* 1980 ed. Washington, D.C.: U.S. Government Printing Office, 1980.
A detailed analysis of state AFDC plans and their operation.

U.S. Department of Health and Human Services, Social Security Administration, Office of Research and Statistics. *Social Security Bulletin, Annual Statistical Supplement, 1977–1979.* Washington, D.C.: U.S. Government Printing Office, 1980.
In addition to containing a wealth of statistical data on public assistance programs, this volume describes the present characteristics and historical development of SSI, AFDC, and food stamps.

Myers, Robert J. *Social Security,* 2nd ed. Homewood, Ill.: Richard D. Irwin, 1981.
Chapter 11 of this comprehensive book covers public assistance programs.

U.S. Senate, Committee on Finance, Subcommittee on Public Assistance, 96th Congress, 2nd Session. *Statistical Data Related to Public Assistance Programs,* Committee print. Washington, D.C.: U.S. Government Printing Office, 1980.
A highly useful summary and compilation of important statistical data on AFDC, SSI, food stamps, GA, Medicaid, social services, and child welfare services.

Wilcox, Clair. *Toward Social Welfare.* Homewood, Ill.: Richard D. Irwin, 1969.
Parts of this highly readable book deal with public assistance and other attacks on poverty.

Chapter Sixteen

Income Maintenance
and Other Plans

The focus of the discussion in Chapter 15 was on plans that sustain the poor, but only on the basis of demonstrated need and only as a residual source. Beginning in the 1960s, increasing attention was directed to an entirely different approach, one that utilized the idea of a "guaranteed annual income." Before looking at the details of guaranteed income proposals, it will be useful to compare the new approaches with the more conventional methods of providing for the poor.

Conventional methods such as the residual public assistances can be characterized in a number of ways. Need must be demonstrated, and assistance is provided only on an after-the-fact basis. Need must be demonstrated to some type of "social case worker" who, in effect, becomes a "supervisory counselor" to the person or family in need. Earnings of the needy are taxed. The former practice was to tax at the 100% level, but as indicated in Chapter 15, many changes have been made in recent years.

The features of such a system have led many to characterize it as degrading, uncertain, and providing little if any incentive to get off poor relief. And certainly, whatever the causes, this system has not had the effect of "eliminating" the problems of all the poor.

The newer income guarantee plans differ fundamentally from conventional poor relief. They are as dissimilar to the older plans as were the "new-look" employment guarantee approaches to conventional guarantee plans in the mid-1950s.

Under the new plans, income would be provided as a matter of right.[1] A minimal income level would be set, and those who fell below it would receive a payment from the government. (How and in what amount would depend on the program; details of various plans are presented below.)

Some form of incentive is built into most of the new plans. A dollar of earnings would not result in the loss of a dollar guaranteed income. Whether the present

---

[1]SSI, discussed in Chapter 15, was certainly a "new" plan. But here we focus on more "advanced" types.

social-work apparatus would be retained also varies by plan. Some plans would seek to substitute the income guarantee for the present role of the social worker; others would retain the social worker, but in a different capacity.

In addition to income guarantees, a variety of other approaches have appeared over the years. Some of these, such as family allowances, are not new. These varying approaches are discussed below.

INCOME MAINTENANCE PLANS

One of the earliest efforts to provide an income guarantee was the Speenhamland system, devised in England in 1795. Under this system a wage supplement was to be provided whenever earnings fell below a certain level (based on the cost of bread and on family size). It was believed that the costs would be only $\frac{1}{10}$ of those that would be incurred if the family were allowed to become completely destitute and then rehabilitation attempted.

It should be noted that this system addressed itself only to those gainfully employed. Hence, were a modern version of this plan to appear, it would not provide protection for the impoverished, many of whom, for a variety of reasons, are neither employed nor capable of being so. The Speenhamland system failed, however, in practice. Employers used it as a pretext to cut wages, and the state was put in the position of subsidizing labor costs.[2]

A variety of other income maintenance plans were proposed in subsequent periods. The first of the modern plans appears to have been put forth by Lady Rhys-Williams in Great Britain in 1943.[3] However, Winston Churchill had, as early as 1906, urged adoption of an income level below which society would not allow persons to live and labor.[4] The economist J. A. Schumpeter had made a similar proposal a year earlier than had Lady Rhys-Williams. Sir William Beveridge, in 1942, had in principle espoused the income guarantee approach. These plans envisaged an income guarantee combined with a series of broad measures designed to equalize income.

The modern thrust came in 1962 and 1963. In 1962 Professor Milton Friedman suggested a "negative income tax" to supplant other social welfare programs.

---

[2]For an insightful discussion on this issue—and on many topics in this and earlier chapters—see David Macarov, *Incentives To Work* (San Francisco, Calif. Jossey-Bass, 1970), pp. 10–12. Macarov's "References" on pp. 227–242 provide an invaluable listing of social welfare source materials as of 1970.

[3]In a lighthearted but not all discourteous tone the authors would note the kinds of checking required in any writing—whether it be a "conventional" text or an original, path-breaking research contribution. Is Rhys-Williams hyphenated or not? Secondary sources are most conflicting; original sources use the hyphen. Moreover, it appears clear that when one uses "Lady Rhys-Williams," one does not use the first names of Juliette (sometimes spelled Juliet) Henriette. The full card catalog library citation in the U.S. is: Rhys-Williams, Juliette Evangeline Glyn, Lady.

[4]See Maurice Bruce, *The Coming of the Welfare State*, 2nd ed. (London: B. T. Batsford, 1965).

In 1963 Robert Theobald recommended an income guarantee program.[5] These two proposals unleashed an avalanche of discussion and led to a variety of other plans, all of which embodied the income guarantee concept though differing in detail.

Certain elements are common to all of the modern income guarantee plans:

1   Minimum income budgets would be set for individuals and families, and those whose incomes fell below the budget line would receive a payment from the federal government.

2   The payment would be made as a matter of right; the "need" would have been demonstrated by the income deficiency itself.

3   In the majority of plans the transfer would be linked directly to the federal income tax mechanism. The filing of the tax form would, if the return showed an income deficiency, be prima facie evidence of that deficiency and would provide the basis for receiving the subsidy as a matter of right. An income deficiency would in effect show up on the tax form as "negative income"— an income below the poverty line. Hence the term "negative income tax."

4   The subsidy would vary in amount, depending on the specific plan. Under some plans 100% of the deficiency would be paid; in others only a fraction would be guaranteed, such as one-half or less. Obviously the "cost" of the plan would vary widely, contingent on the level of the guarantee.

5   An "incentive" condition would be built into the plan so that a dollar of earnings would not result in a dollar of income payment loss (until some maximum had been reached).

The various plans differ in several respects:

1   The methods utilized in making the income payment vary. Friedman, for example, would utilize a "negative income tax." Just as those whose incomes are above a certain level pay a tax, those with incomes below that level would be "reimbursed." Other plans use different approaches.

2   The amount of income to be "guaranteed" is variable under different plans. In general, most of the proposals do not envisage making up 100% of the income below the poverty line; instead, they would restore some percentage of that income. They also differ on the tax to be applied to additional income earned.

3   The role of the existing social welfare system would be changed under the new proposals. Friedman would have the new system supplant that currently existing. Other plans would retain some role for the social casework system.

[5]See Milton Friedman, *Capitalism and Freedom* (Chicago, Ill.: University of Chicago Press, 1962), pp. 190–92; Robert Theobald (Ed.), *The Guaranteed Income* (New York: Doubleday, 1967). The latter volume contains various other contributions besides those of Theobald himself as he had developed them four years earlier.

The Friedman Plan[6]

The Friedman plan is perhaps the simplest form of approaching a guaranteed income, via the use of the negative income tax. The plan is predicated on the basic assumption that if family units receiving over a certain level of income are liable for federal income taxes, those below that level should receive a payment from the government.

Hildebrand uses the following symbols to explain the plan:

E = the total amount of exemptions and deductions.

P = pretax gross income.

D = the deficit in net taxable income.

X = the fraction of income restoration (100%, 50%, and so on).

S = the amount of the subsidy.

Then $E - P = D$, and $D(X) = S$.

In the Friedman plan, $X = 0.50$, so $D(0.50) = S$. The subsidy from the Treasury to an eligible income tax reporting unit would be 50% of the amount by which all exemptions and deductions (E) exceed pretax gross income (P).

Let us shear away the changing "dollar dimensions" of the federal income tax structure and consider examples that are simple but not unrealistic for the time at which Friedman wrote (1962). P would include "all income"—wages, salaries, commissions, "profits," dividends, interest, rent, and capital gains—but would exclude "transfer" payments from Old-Age, Survivors', and Disability Insurance, unemployment compensation, and workers' compensation.

A "reporting household" would be entitled to a $600 "exemption" for each member, a "standard deduction" of $300 for the person filing the return, and another "standard deduction" of $100 for each additional household member. Thus a "low-income" family of four would be entitled to $2,400 in "exemptions" ($600 × 4) plus $600 in "deductions" ($300 + 3 × $100), for a total of $3,000. Hence $E = \$3,000$.

Assume $P = 0$. Then $D = \$3,000$, and with a 50% subsidy, $S = \$1,500$. Or assume $P = \$2,000$. Then $D = \$1,000$ and, again with a 50% subsidy, $S = \$500$.

But take the case of a man and wife, both under 65, with no children. Their exemptions total $1,200 ($600 × 2) and their deductions total $400 ($300 plus $100), for a total E of $1,600. Assume the husband earns $1,500. Here the subsidy would amount to only $50 (50% of D or $100). Now assume that both individuals

---

[6]In addition to a reliance on the original sources, the following discussion draws on the excellent monograph by George H. Hildebrand, *Poverty, Income Maintenance, and the Negative Income Tax* (Ithaca, N.Y.: New York State School of Industrial and Labor Relations, 1967); and the equally useful book by Christopher Green, *Negative Taxes and the Poverty Problem* (Washington, D.C.: Brookings Institution, 1967).

are over 65 and receive total OASI benefits of $1,500, which are not counted in
P. Because of the double exemption provisions for persons over 65, E becomes
$3,000. If the couple has no income other than the $1,500 from OASI, E is $3,000,
S would be $1,500, and the couple's spendable income would be $3,000.

Thus before age 65 a couple would receive $50; after, $1,500.

For the moment let us put to one side any evaluation of the Friedman plan
(or other plans) and look instead at its basic characteristics:

1   Those over a certain income level pay a tax *to* the government; those whose
    income falls below this level would receive a payment *from* the government
    —a subsidy, in effect.
2   The subsidy would be at the 50% level. Thus a family of four with a pretaxable
    income of $1,500 and deductions and exemptions of $3,000 would have a
    deficit of $1,500, and 50% of that deficit would be $750.
3   Implicit in the Friedman proposal is a 50% tax on "earnings." Thus again
    assume that the family of four has deductions and exemptions of $3,000 and
    no earnings. Their subsidy would be 50% , or $1,500. Now assume that the
    family has earnings of $2,000. At a 50% tax rate this would be reduced to
    $1,000, which, with the $1,500 subsidy, would total $2,500.

[The reader will find an interesting bit of arithmetic logic in the Friedman plan.
The final amount comes out the same whether one (1) taxes earnings at 50% and
then adds the full subsidy, e.g., $1,500 for a family of four, or (2) does not tax
earnings at all, but pays 50% of D.] The family is $1,000 "better off" than it was
before, but the $2,000 earnings have been taxed away, in effect, at a 50% rate.
Whether this is confiscatory is a moot question; certainly it is less confiscatory
than a welfare roll "earnings" tax of 100%, a common practice for a long period.

For comparative purposes Table 16.1 presents a payment schedule under the
Friedman plan for a family of four (see above for the designating symbols).

There is another issue in this and similar plans that merits attention. The
$3,000 total of exemptions and deductions used above was based on the federal
income tax structure in effect in 1966, the year used by Hildebrand for his
analysis. It is also, however, a close approximation to the figure of $3,000 used
as the "poverty line" for a family of four.

Is this a coincidence? Or is there a close relation between federal income tax

Table 16.1   Payments Under the Friedman Plan (In Dollars)

E	P	D	S (At 50%)	Total Income to Family
3,000	0	3,000	1,500	1,500
3,000	1,000	2,000	1,000	2,000
3,000	2,000	1,000	500	2,500
3,000	3,000	—	—	3,000

exemptions and deductions and minimum income budgets? What if exemptions and deductions greatly exceeded a minimum budget? What if the converse were true?

The authors have not been able to find any definitive linkage between the $3,000 of federal income tax exemptions and deductions and a minimum income budget of the same figure. Nor have they been able to find a specific relationship between subsequent increases in exemptions and/or deductions and the increase in minimum poverty level budgets. The rationale for such increases in exemptions and/or deductions appears to be related more (in, say, 1970–1980 and later) to anticipated beneficial fiscal impacts in shoring up a depressed economy than to poverty budgets as such.

It may be instructive, however, to speculate on these issues. Assume that a minimum income budget for a family of four is $3,000. Also assume in the first case that the federal income tax total exemptions and deductions for such a family is $1,500. The family has no taxable income, so $D = \$1,500$. At a 50% subsidy rate $S = \$750$. This is one-fourth of what is needed to approximate the minimum poverty income level. Assume, to the contrary, that federal income tax total exemptions and deductions add up to $6,000 for the same family. With zero income and a 50% subsidy rate, the family would receive a subsidy of $3,000, which would put it just at the mid-1960s poverty line.

If a negative income tax is to be used as a means of "getting families out of poverty," the tax structure needs to bear a close relationship to the poverty line. If it is out of line on the lower side, the subsidy will do little toward the eradication of poverty. If, however, it is out of line on the opposite side, the subsidy would provide, in effect a windfall gain.

The Tobin Plan[7]

The Tobin plan utilizes the negative income tax approach and a fractional guarantee principle; but it differs from the Friedman plan in its use of tax "credits" rather than "deductions" and, through its level of taxes on earnings, in its incentive effects.

Each person in a tax-reporting unit would be entitled to an initial tax credit or allowance of $400 per person. *All* income received by the unit—public assistance payments excluded—would be taxed at a rate of $33\frac{1}{3}\%$. (For large families the credit or allowance would fall to $150 for the seventh and eighth child and to zero thereafter.) OASDI beneficiaries would not be entitled to allowances, but minimum benefits of $400 per person would be stipulated for them.

Let us again use the family of four cited under the Friedman plan. Using the Tobin approach it would have a "credit" of $1,600 ($400 $\times$ 4) applicable against the income tax. If it had no other income, it would receive $1,600. Assume that

[7]See James Tobin, "The Case for an Income Guarantee," *The Public Interest,* No. 4 (1966), 33ff.; and "On Improving the Economic Status of the Negro," *Daedalus,* XCIV, No. 4 (Fall 1965), 878–898.

it had "other" income of $2,000. This would be taxed at $33\frac{1}{3}\%$ ($667) by deducting it from the credit of $1,600, thus leaving $933 "collectible" from the government. Total family income in this case would be $2,933 ($2,000 of earnings plus a $933 guarantee). Under the Friedman plan the minimum guarantee would be $1,500 (instead of $1,600 under the Tobin plan), and for $2,000 of other income the family of four would receive a total of $2,500 (Friedman) versus $2,933 (Tobin).

On a graduated income basis the Tobin plan would yield the results shown in Table 16.2 for a family of four.

The family of four would need to reach an income level of $4,800 from outside sources before its subsidy fell to zero. Above $4,800 of income no allowance is payable, but the credit of $1,600 can still be used as an offset against the $33\frac{1}{3}\%$ tax due on other income. In effect this plan provides for a two-stage income tax schedule, with one stage applicable to the lower-income structure and the other taking over at that point.

The rationale used by Tobin is that allowances should not negatively affect the incentive to work and save, nor should they penalize desertion; hence the low one-third tax on income. Moreover, the absence of a male household head would not make a family ineligible, whereas his presence would add another $400 credit. It is not fully clear if the plan would, as Hildebrand notes, check leakages to the nonpoor, but it does concentrate its benefits on the poor. In Tobin's view no one would be worse off, and many families would be in an improved situation.

The Lampman Plans[8]

While Professors Friedman and Tobin have advanced specific income guarantee plans, their areas of particular interest in economics tend to be elsewhere. One of Professor Lampman's major specialities is in income distribution, poverty, and similar matters. It is therefore no accident that this interest has produced a series of plans rather than a single proposal and led to many other contributions relating to the problems of poverty.

Table 16.2 Payments Under the Tobin Plan (In Dollars)

Total Credit	Other Income	Tax on Income $(33\frac{1}{3}\%)$	Available From Credit	Family Income to Family
1,600	0	0	1,600	1,600
1,600	1,000	333	1,267	2,267
1,600	2,000	666	933	2,933
1,600	3,000	1,000	600	3,600
1,600	4,000	1,333	267	4,267
1,600	4,800	1,600	0	4,800

[8]Robert J. Lampman, "Negative Rates Income Taxation" (Washington, D.C.: Office of Economic Opportunity, 1965).

Lampman's Plan I somewhat resembles that of Friedman. In place of a 50% subsidy of the deficit in net taxable income, Lampman would pay 14% of the "unused value" of E (exemptions and deductions). Again assume the family of four, with E (per person) of $750 for a total of $3,000. If the family has no income, 14% of $3,000, or $420, would be available as a transfer payment. The same procedure would pertain to varying income levels and exemptions and deductions. The limitations of this plan are apparent in closing the poverty gap. If one takes into account the "other" income of the poor, only 30% or so of the gap would be closed by this approach.

Lampman's Plan II has a number of variants. If one wished to completely close the poverty gap it would be feasible to transfer the difference between income received and the minimum poverty budget. Thus, with a minimum budget of $3,000, a family of four with no income would receive $3,000. With an income of $1,500, the subsidy would be $1,500. The tax on income in this case comes, of course, to 100%.

Other versions could be used. A flat 50% offset could be used: for each dollar of earnings, 50 cents would be deducted from the subsidy. Or the offset rate could be graduated downward: 75% for the first $1,000 of earned income, 50% for the second, and 25% for the third (in effect, an "increasing" incentive). In these two types the minimum guarantee would be fixed at $1,500, rather than $3,000, assuming no other income. Another version would pay a subsidy of $750, irrespective of other income between zero and $1,500, and a 50% offset for income between $1,500 and $3,000. A final alternative would set the minimum allowance (with no other income) at $2,000; up to $1,500 of such income the offset would be 75%, and between $1,500 and $3,000 it would be 33%. (The reader may wish to calculate how a family of four would come out under these various plans.)

There is one major difference between Lampman's approach and those of other economists, particularly Friedman's. Friedman would substitute the negative income plan for the comprehensive and varied social welfare system currently existing. Lampman would not; in place of a unitary system to aid the poor, he would utilize a pluralistic attack on poverty. This difference is more than a matter of "economic" philosophy and will be commented on shortly.

The Schwartz Plan[9]

Professor Schwartz in a sense echoed the words of Winston Churchill when he suggested, in 1964, that one's right to a livelihood needed to be recognized and guaranteed as a constitutional civil right.

His plan starts with a "family security benefit" in brackets of $3,000, $4,000, or $5,000 for a family of four; which of these brackets would be used would be contingent on social acceptance of the relevant bracket. In 1964 the $3,000 bracket was estimated at a cost to the economy of some $11 billion; the $5,000 bracket, at $38 billion.

[9]See Edward E. Schwartz, "A Way to End the Means Test," *Social Work,* IX, No. 3 (July 1964), 4ff.

The guaranteed payment would be offset at increasing percentage rates for incremental additions of other income. If the guarantee were $3,000 for a four-member family, $1,000 of other income would result in a net guarantee of $2,399. Thus the guarantee falls by $600, which is 60% of the incremental income of $1,000, or a 60% tax rate. At $2,000 of other income the guarantee falls to $1,699, a decline of $1,300. This $1,300 is deducted from the incremental income for a tax rate of 65 + %. With $3,000 of other income the effective tax becomes 70%. With "outside income" of $4,000 to $4,499, the guarantee is zero, but no tax is due, while above $4,500 the applicable tax schedule will come into play.

As Hildebrand points out, serious disincentive effects are to be found in this plan. The Friedman plan utilizes a uniform 50% tax; the Tobin plan, a uniform $33\frac{1}{3}\%$ tax. But the Schwartz plan involves significantly higher marginal rates. The first $1,000 of income is taxed at a 60% rate; the next $1,000 at 70%, and the third $1,000 at 80%.

The Schwartz plan appears insensitive to the notion of a rate of return for labor services or to the value of work versus leisure. Would those below the poverty line prefer to be subsidized or, if they could lift themselves out of poverty through employment opportunities offered to them, would they do so? This is not an easy question to answer. What if they are taxed at higher incremental rates for each $1,000 of income they are motivated to try to earn? Motivation might recede markedly. It is one thing to support progressively higher marginal tax rates as one moves from the $30,000 to the $40,000 annual income bracket. It is quite another matter at the lowest end of the income spectrum.

The Theobald Plan[10]

The Theobald and Schwartz plans suggest the ending of poverty through the guarantee of full maintenance for all. But the former differs from the latter in important basic and philosophical ways. A literal reading of Theobald would lead one to conclude that the economy is on the verge of unrivaled abundance and that, in place of more than plenty for all if only proper income distribution methods are followed, the real fear is large-scale and permanent unemployment.

The plans in the Theobald program are Basic Economic Security (BES) and Committed Spending (CS). The first would replace the present patchwork system of income maintenance; the second would maintain a steady stream of purchasing power, prevent hoarding, and preclude any possibility of an economic downturn through idle resources.

BES would start with a "due income," say, $1,000 for each adult and $600 for each child (for a family of four), thus totaling $3,200. No greater "due income" would be available for larger family units. "Other" income would be charged against the guarantee on a dollar-for-dollar basis, but a premium of 10% would be provided for earned income, apparently irrespective of amount.

[10]Robert Theobald, *Free Men and Free Markets* (New York: Clarkson N. Potter, 1963).

An arithmetic example may assist in explaining the Theobald plan. For a family of four the BES would be $3,200 ($1,000 plus $1,000 for the two adults, plus $600 plus $600 for the two children). Assume that the family unit has $2,000 of earned income, which would be deducted dollar-for-dollar from the BES, leaving $1,200 from BES, plus the $2,000 earned income for a total of $3,200. In addition, the family unit would receive the premium of 10% on the $2,000 (or $200) for total receipts of $3,400.

The "Notch" Problem

This problem arises from the dual features of negative income tax or other similar plans: (1) provision of a substantial income floor (to support a household) and (2) less than a 100% tax on earnings (to provide an incentive to work). (How much less than a 100% tax is "necessary" to provide work incentives is a matter of debate.)

An example will help in understanding the nature of this problem.

1 Suppose that the minimum income poverty line "guarantee" is $8,000 for a family of four with no earnings.

2 Further assume that the tax rate on earnings under the plan is 50% (for example, 50% of $2,000 in earnings, or $1,000, is retained; the other $1,000 is paid in taxes).

3 And, finally, a family with $8,000 or more of earnings is, by definition, excluded from coverage under the plan.

Our illustrative household has $2,000 in earnings. Of this, $1,000 is 50% and hence the $8,000 guarantee is reduced by $1,000, giving the family $7,000 plus the $2,000 for a total of $9,000. (Or, looking at it a different way, the family would receive $8,000 and keep $1,000 of the $2,000 earned.)

The "excluded" family, earning $8,000, could well seek to let its earnings fall below that cutoff figure (by working less) so as to qualify.

To solve this dilemma—the "notch" effect—most plans would provide decreasing graduated payments, to families above the poverty line, sufficient to exceed the income of families below the line. Such "phaseout" schedules have been developed, and, depending on the mechanics of the plan, tapering off to zero. A rule of thumb for the cutoff (zero) point is as follows: if the marginal tax on earnings is 50%, that is the same as taxing earnings one-half; if 25% ,it is one-fourth; and so on. As in our illustration, let the guarantee be $8,000. Then if the tax is 50% (one-half), multiply the $8,000 by the reciprocal of one-half, or two, which equals $16,000. If the tax is 25% (one-fourth), multiply by four, which equals $32,000, and so on for varying tax rates. Whether the "public" would find such payments palatable is open to question.

A Preliminary Summary of Income Maintenance Plans

Let us summarize these various plans, examining them from a variety of viewpoints:

1 Notwithstanding steady erosion of poverty during recent decades, there is no small amount of dissatisfaction, among economists and others, over the relatively large numbers of those still below the line of impoverishment. The American economy should do better than it has in the elimination of poverty. Although the "war on poverty" began well before the inner-city turmoils of the later 1960s, these problems accentuated interest in and efforts to resolve the status of those in the poverty zone.

2 There is no small amount of dissatisfaction among many segments of society toward the "Demonstrated need–assistance–social worker" approach to poverty. An "ideal" system to replace satisfactorily the present arrangements for handling the problems of the poor has not yet been found, but the present system clearly leaves a lot to be desired in its approach to the problems of poverty.[11]

3 The previously mentioned plans are indicative of the ingenuity and practicality that can be applied to the problem of poverty. It *can* be met, say many, with dynamic thinking and imaginative remedies. We leave it to the reader to ponder this.

THE PRESENT WELFARE SYSTEM[12]: A CRITIQUE

The various plans previously discussed can better be evaluated if we review again, but in a different light, the present welfare system. What are its shortcomings, and how would the various plans seek to meet these deficiencies and difficulties?

One set of problems relates to the "welfare poor." If one takes AFDC and general assistance, the core of the present systems, as the area of controversy, the following criticisms emerge[13]:

1 Inadequate benefits (in terms of the poverty gap—individually and collectively).

[11]One of the authors has held extensive discussions with social workers on this and related issues. Conflicting opinions were as numerous as the discussions. One conclusion seems clear, however; the present system is far from ideal. Opinions seem about equally divided between those who contend that the poor have no one to blame but themselves as against those who say that, given a chance, the poor could pull themselves out of poverty. The divergence of viewpoints generally is almost beyond belief. We are still as uncertain as we were 25 years ago.

[12]This and subsequent discussions have profited greatly from Theodore R. Marmor (Ed.), *Poverty Policy* (Chicago and New York: Aldine-Atherton, 1971).

[13]See Ref. 12, pp. 33–36.

2   Wide variations in payments among geographical regions and various categories of recipients.

3   Administrative arbitrariness and injustice, not only with respect to recipients but toward those who are eligible and deserving but are deterred from applying.

4   The costs of increasing benefits and the number of those eligible who might seek payments.

5   The deleterious effect of the present system on the family as a unit and on patterns of work behavior.

6   The inequity of a system that aids only certain categories of the poor and excludes others.

A second set of issues focuses on the problems of the nonwelfare poor: those who are poor but who, for some reason, cannot qualify under existing programs. A conspicuous example would include those who are employed but whose earnings are insufficient to get the individual or family above the poverty line. Aiding the working poor involves the basic issue of how to increase income without impairing incentives.

A final set of problems revolves around income distribution and its relation to poverty. Inequality in wealth and income is viewed as a contributory factor. There will always be a lowest 20% on the income distribution spectrum, but these individuals need not be below the poverty line. Historically, the income accruing to this lowest category has increased (in real terms) at rates that have permitted increasing numbers to escape from poverty. But it is also true that poverty can be viewed as relative deprivation, and this deprivation has been worsening. In 1959 the poverty line was 47% of median income, in 1968 it had fallen to 36%, and by 1980 it was still lower. However, solutions for this kind of problem are markedly different from those indicated above.

CRITERIA FOR EVALUATING INCOME AND MAINTENANCE PLANS

Let us now raise a variety of criteria and questions that seek to tie together poverty problem areas with various alternative solutions, including the plans discussed earlier.[14]

Adequacy of the Benefit Level

Two concepts of adequacy should be noted. The first is individual benefit adequacy; for the individual it can be measured by comparing the benefit (plus other

[14]These criteria and questions are based on Marmor, Ref. 12, pp. 36–54.

income accruing to the individual or family) with some standard such as the poverty budget. The closer the total income comes to the minimum budget, the more adequate the benefit. The second concept is aggregate program adequacy. For all individuals and families, how much of the poverty gap is closed by the program?

In late 1980 the Social Security Administration's poverty line budget was approximately $8,000 for an urban family of four. The poverty gap was well over $25 billion. Individual benefit adequacy would be measured by the degree to which benefits pull the recipient up to the minimum budget level, aggregate adequacy by how much of this gap is closed.

Stigma

While stigma is not as well understood as it might be, it is clear that critics of the present welfare system hold that the receipts of benefits on the basis of need and the use of a means test are, if not degrading, at least undesirable if one uses the "dignity of man" as a criterion. It is true that receipt of the benefits as a matter of right would tend to mitigate this problem. But as long as investigative checks are necessary in a program, the possibility of stigma exists. For example, what if the Internal Revenue Service concluded that it was necessary to check income tax returns (under a negative income tax plan) for those whose returns showed less than $3,000 (or some other figure) of income? The problems inherent in this procedure are clear.

Equitable Efficiency

The concept of equitable efficiency, developed by Burton A. Weisbrod, can be defined in terms of the degree to which actual redistribution of income approximates desired redistribution.

Two types of such efficiency can be identified: vertical and horizontal. Vertical efficiency measures the extent to which program benefits go only to the specific group for which they are designed. Visualize a program designed for benefit group A. Also visualize other benefit groups B, C, and so on, for whom this program is not intended. If the benefits, in fact, go only to the members of group A and no benefits spill over to other groups, then the vertical efficiency ratio of the program is unity. Assume half of the benefits do go to other groups. The efficiency ratio becomes 0.5.

Horizontal efficiency measures the extent to which benefits designed for a given group reach all of the group. A program is designed for group A. The benefits reach all members of the group; therefore the horizontal efficiency ratio is again unity. Conversely, if the benefits reach only half the group, the ratio is 0.5. The closer to unity the ratios, the higher the degree of equitable efficiency.

However, a number of qualifications need to be considered with both measures of efficiency. For example, it may be possible to achieve 100% vertical efficiency, but only at a very large increase in, say, administrative costs. Conversely, 100% vertical efficiency may single out a particular group to whom stigma then attaches. A low vertical efficiency ratio could mean windfall gains for groups for whom the program was not designed. Under the horizontal measure the possibility may exist for a trade-off between adequacy and efficiency. All members of a group might receive benefits, though at an inadequate level; or some members might receive adequate benefits, and others none at all or at inadequate levels.

Work Incentives

In terms of its emotional content this is probably the most highly charged of any of the criteria applicable to income maintenance programs. Any such program involves a transfer from those who have to those who do not. If it could be demonstrated that such programs would reduce work incentives to zero, thus creating a permanently subsidized class, the public and political acceptability of these schemes would also, in all probability, approach zero.

We know all too little about the impact of income maintenance programs on work incentives, although a number of experiments conducted in the last decade have shed some light on this problem.[15] The standard cliché appears to be that "most people would rather work, if given the opportunity, than live off welfare." But even if this is conjectured to be true, there are still important technical questions to be answered. What should be the level of the income guarantee? At what rate(s) should differential amounts of earnings be taxed? What should be the cutoff point of the guarantee?

As Marmor notes, given the absence of reliable information, most work-incentive judgments rest on a number of rule-of-thumb notions: (1) any income guarantee will reduce incentive if the marginal tax on earnings is above zero; or (2) the "work habit" is so ingrained that a marginal tax of, say, up to 50% will have little effect on incentives. But these are conjectures; the final evidence is not yet in.[16] We discuss this issue more fully later in this chapter.

Work-incentive impacts also fan out into many areas that affect the economy as a whole as much as they do the individual. Examples include the regional distribution of income, the allocation of productive resources, the mobility of labor, work performance, the extent and pace of automation, and the level and

---

[15] Four major experiments have been undertaken in the last decade in different geographical areas and among different "populations." The labor supply effects have been mixed, although the latest experiment shows adverse effects. The interested reader can refer to the following issues of the *Journal of Human Resources* for symposia and other summary articles: Spring 1974, Winter 1978, Fall 1979, Fall 1980. Also see I. Garfinkel and S. Masters, *Estimating the Labor Supply Effects of Income Maintenance Alternatives* (New York: Academic, 1978). *But,* see below for more detailed conclusions.

[16] For a generalized discussion on many of these issues see the interview with Sar A. Levitan, "Work and the Welfare State," *Challenge,* 20, No. 3 (July–August 1977), 29–33.

structure of wages. It is clear that the incentive question has important psychological and sociological overtones. But it also reaches into the area of technical micro- and macroeconomics and therein raises many varied and important questions of policy and performance.

Program Costs

The costs of an income maintenance program or transfer payment system are difficult to estimate or predict, for a variety of reasons:

1   The costs, of course, would vary with the type of income maintenance system introduced. A Schwartz or Theobald plan would "cost" considerably more than would a Lampman plan variation that sought, for example, to provide only 14% income restoration.
2   Were such programs to be federalized, there is involved a trade-off in costs between federal and state and local governments. On net balance, what would the new costs be? While no one could be expected to specify a given amount, the probability is high that costs would increase. Federal takeover is likely to pull up average payments.
3   What would the impacts of such a program be on work incentives? Again, the answer is beclouded, but the impacts on costs are clear.

Political Acceptability

This is a complicated issue, and can be viewed either as a constraint on various alternative proposals or as a variable. In early 1972 the posture of Congress seemed more a constraint than a variable, depending on how one viewed a possible vote in both chambers as contrasted with strong chairmen in each. The proposals of the Nixon Administration were viewed in the Senate, at least by some critical committees and chairmen, as disadvantaging the South. And the Carter Administration proposals in 1978 faced the same constraints.

An income maintenance program that does not have work incentives built into it is less likely to succeed than one that has. A program that lessens states' rights in welfare matters is also less likely to succeed. However, politics makes strange bedfellows, and final legislation may contrast interestingly with preceding speculation.

AN EVALUATION OF PROPOSED PLANS

Let us look at the various plans discussed above in terms of the criteria just specified. With respect to each criterion we shall use the figure 1 if the given plan completely accomplishes its designed purpose, and 0 if the opposite is true. In many cases only rough estimates can be made, as will be apparent from the discussion.[17] We do this as a useful exercise—an exercise in evaluating any income maintenance proposal (or for that matter, welfare "reform"), even though none of the above plans has any likelihood of enactment.

Adequacy of the Benefit Level

The Schwartz and Theobald plans would approximate 1 in terms of both individual adequacy and closing the poverty gap. Lampman's various plans would differ as to adequacy. His Plan I, with a maximum subsidy of $420 for a family of four, would (given a $3,000 poverty line) meet less than one-sixth of the needs; one of the variants of his Plan II, with a subsidy of $2,000, would meet two-thirds of the needs, with other plans falling in between. Hence the criterion would range from 0.14 to 0.66. Because of other incomes received by many of the poor, a greater part of the poverty gap would be closed. Plan I would close about 30%; the variations of Plan II would close over one-half of the gap.

The Friedman and Tobin plans would rate approximately 0.5 on individual adequacy for a family of four with no income (with Tobin's rating being slightly higher). Taking other incomes into account, both plans would close a little over half (about 58%) of the poverty gap.

Hence the Schwartz and Theobald plans would come closest to achieving the goal; Lampman's Plan I would do the least, with other plans scattered in between.

Stigma

Here one can only conjecture. Given the preponderance of current cultural and social attitudes toward poverty, it is our judgment that the Schwartz and Theobald plans would rate low: certainly not 0, but probably well below 0.5. All other plans would have less stigma attached, and any rating would depend on the nature and amount of auditing of tax returns undertaken by the Treasury. Again, given present attitudes, no plan could be free of stigma. Many of those who pay taxes would view critically those who receive a negative income tax return. But the degree of stigma would be less, we believe, than in the case of the nonnegative income tax plans.

Equitable Efficiency

With respect to both horizontal and vertical efficiency, the Schwartz and Theobald plans would approximate a rating of 1, though the vertical efficiency rating would have to be tempered by raising a question concerning the policing of the system, to see that those who dod not deserve benefits did not receive them.

[17]For a sophisticated application of these criteria to another series of proposals—the Uniform State Benefits and Federal Family Benefit Plans—see Ref. 16, p. 49.

Ratings for the other plans can only be conjectured. Vertical efficiency presumably would be high and might approximate 1, contingent on the kind of checks made by the Treasury on income tax returns. Horizontal efficiency also would appear to rate high—perhaps close to 1—but this would in no way be equated to benefit adequacy.

Work Incentives

On a *relative* basis the Schwartz and Theobald plans would, we believe, most adversely affect incentives. But how much "quantitatively," we are unable to estimate. The Tobin plan would least affect incentives because of its $33\frac{1}{3}\%$ marginal tax rate. But whether that tax rate can be translated into a criterion rating of $.33\frac{1}{3}$ is by no means clear.

Program Costs

For the mid-1960s the following costs appear. (For the early 1980s it would be necessary to adjust these amounts by taking into account the increase in poverty line budgets and the changes in the number of poor. Our own estimates are that costs would need to be revised upward—probably more than doubled.)

Schwartz suggested that his program would cost $11 billion, but revisions by Lampman and others suggest that approximately $29 billion is more realistic. The Theobald plan would net out at a still higher figure, since his basic guarantee for a family of four is $3,200, compared with $3,000 for Schwartz's.

Lampman's Plan I would cost only $2 billion. His other plans would vary in cost, with some $5 billion net for the variant with the highest benefit level. The costs of the Friedman plan would vary widely: from $1.5 billion to $11 billion in 1963, contingent on what savings might or might not be effected in other assistance programs and costs.

If one roughly averages the gross national product for the end of 1963 and the start of 1964, the figure is $600 billion (in 1963–1964 prices). Quadruple that figure for 1980 (in current dollars). The figure would be somewhat more than double in real terms. The Schwartz and Theobald plans would have "cost" about 5% of the gross national product; Lampman's Plan I, about one-third of 1%. Even though these percentages appear remarkably low, the problems of translating them into actual transfers are much more complex.

Political Acceptability

One might suggest that the Schwartz and Theobald plans would, in terms of underlying principle, have strong support in certain quarters. But their acceptance by whichever administration was in office, and by the Congress, would be very low indeed.

The basic idea of income maintenance and the use of the negative income tax approach is, however, a quite different matter. The Nixon "Family Assistance Plan" (discussed in the next section) was an income maintenance plan that utilized the negative income tax mechanism. Obviously its acceptability to that Administration was high, or the Administration would not have introduced it. Acceptability to the Congress was quite another matter. The Nixon Plan was stalled in Congress during more than two and one-half years of discussion. If a 50–50 chance implies an equal rating for passage or nonpassage, the political (Congressional) acceptability of the Nixon Plan was less than .5. And the Carter Administration proposals of 1978–79 did not have any better odds.

All of the plans discussed above would trend toward federalizing the welfare system. Political acceptability to the states, counties, and municipalities could well be mixed. In terms of fiscal relief the degree of acceptability would be high. The loss of local control is another issue and here the reactions could well be more mixed. This issue would be all the more cloudy, depending on what disposition was made of the "social worker apparatus" contingent on federal assumption of the burden.

In conclusion, it should come as no surprise that the lowest degree of acceptability would apply to those plans that would most fully meet the problem. This is said neither in praise nor in criticism of any of the various plans, but merely to note that the concept of a cultural lag is not to be disregarded when social issues are under consideration. Let us now turn to several more recent proposals.

THE "NEW" INCOME MAINTENANCE PLANS

The principal outlines of various of the "new" plans can be sketched in so that the reader will have the opportunity to visualize the differences between the proposals of the early and mid-1960s and those of later periods.[18]

The Nixon Welfare Reform: The Family Assistance Plan

We start with the Nixon Administration's initial Welfare Reform Plan (1969), which was basically a family assistance plan with income guarantees (but with qualifications).[19] The principal components in this plan were as follows:

1 The proposal centers on the family with children. For a family of four with an income of $720 or less the "guaranteed annual income" would be $1,600. Three points are relevant here: (a) a "family-oriented" income provision, (b) which, for a family of four, guaranteed a minimum of $1,600, and (c) for the

[18]We do not cover here the several plans proposed by the Nixon Urban Council in the first months of 1969. For a concise summary see Marmor, Ref. 12, pp. 48–54.

[19]"Welfare Reform: A Message from the President of the United States," House Document No. 94–146, *Congressional Record,* 115, No. 136.

family, a stipulation that the first $720 (or 12 months times $60 a month) would not be taxed. The plan is equivalent to a guaranteed annual income plan of $1,600 for such a family, with the proviso that the first $720 of annual earnings would be taxed at a zero rate.[20]

2   Income beyond $720 a year would be taxed at 50 percent. The resulting figures for a family of four would be those listed in Table 16.3. (Except for the exemption of $720 of annual earnings and a slight change in the base benefit, this plan resembles the Friedman plan.)

3   For a "typical" welfare family the above figures would hold, as they would for a family headed by an employed father or a working mother. But the picture would change markedly for the aged, the blind, and the disabled. For these the Nixon Plan would establish a minimum payment of $65 per month, with the federal government contributing the first $50 and sharing in benefits above that amount. (This would contrast to 1969 benefit schedules, which varied from $40 to $145 per month for such individuals.)

4   For the single adult who is not handicapped, or for a married couple without children, the proposal would not be applicable (although $300 in food stamps per person per year would still be available).

5   The bridge from welfare to work would be reinforced by training and child-care programs. The former would be implemented by a new and expanded manpower training proposal; the latter, by greatly augmented day-care centers, providing for 450,000 children.

Table 16.3   The Nixon Administration's 1969 Proposed Benefit Schedule: Family Guaranteed Income Plan, Excluding All State Benefits (In Dollars)

Earned Income	New Benefit	Total Income
0	1,600	1,600
500	1,600	2,100
1,000	1,460	2,460
1,500	1,210	2,710
2,000	960	2,960
2,500	710	3,210
3,000	460	3,460
3,500	210	3,710
4,000	0	4,000

[20]In early 1972 the guarantee had risen to $2,400, with liberal Congressmen pressing for a figure of $2,800. The marginal tax rates on earned income were less clear, as were the attitudes of selected Congressmen as to the entire plan. For example, Senator Russell B. Long proposed the following substitute in January 1972: (1) workers earning less than $3,968, the current officially designated poverty level, would have their OASDHI taxes refunded without loss of future benefits (and this could total $400 a year); and (2) employees earning less than $1.60 an hour would receive a federal payment for the difference. Two comments are relevant. First, Senator Long's proposal does not get at the poverty problems of the nonworking poor. Second, the wage subsidy is a direct descendant of the Speenhamland system.

6   The new system would greatly curtail welfare "red tape" and would significantly reduce administrative costs. Such savings would be brought about by the fact that the federal payment would be based on a "certification of income," with spot checks to prevent abuse. States would be given the option of having the federal government process the payment of state supplemental benefits, minimizing administrative burdens and providing for a single check.

7   While the proposed plan would require a sizable initial investment ($4 billion of federal funds), the yield of future returns to the nation would be great. The expectation was that the plan would significantly reverse the momentum of "work to welfare" and would turn the welfare system around.

Two important points are to be noted with respect to this proposal:

1   The plan is work oriented. Those who fail to seek or accept work would be disqualified; they must accept training opportunities and jobs when offered, or give up their rights to the proposed payments. In other words, no able-bodied person would have a "free ride" under a system that provides opportunities for training and work.

2   The plan is family oriented. It would end financial incentives to desertion, and would extend eligibility to *all* dependent families with children, without regard as to whether such a family were headed by a man or a woman. Thus a mother with three small children and no outside income would be assured an annual income of at least $1,600; a family with an employed father or working mother would receive the same benefits *and* the first $60 per month of earnings would be disregarded as respects benefits received.

It is interesting to note that the 92nd Congress adjourned in October 1972 without enacting minimum income legislation, although hectic debate took place in the closing days of the session. The House approved the measure; in the Senate it stalled. And, as history subsequently showed, the later days of this Administration were not propitious for further consideration of this or other later proposals. Nor did the Ford Administration make any basic changes.

In discussing these and other income guarantee trends Robert Lampman has noted that proponents of such plans are now lodged between a rock and a hard place; the "welfare system" currently provides as much or more in the way of benefits. This state of affairs affords much in the way of an answer to the frequently-raised question: "Why is welfare so hard to reform?"

The Carter Welfare Reform: The Program for Better Jobs and Income

No recent Administration—of necessity—is immune from meeting the welfare problem head on. Thus the Carter Administration plan: "The Administration's

Welfare Reform Proposal: An Analysis of the Program for Better Jobs and Income.[21]

The details of the Program were complex; we summarize the main features as follows:

1 The cornerstone of the proposal was the Program for Better Jobs and Income (PBJI). It was a work-oriented approach to welfare reform. It would have replaced AFDC, SSI, food stamp, and general assistance programs with a "universal cash assistance program." A four-person family with no member expected to work and no income would have received a maximum benefit of $4,200 (1978 dollars), irrespective of residence. (Families with a member expected to work and no income would have received a lower benefit.) States would have been encouraged to supplement these benefits with federal matching funds for a portion of the supplement.

2 In order to encourage recipients' work effort, a program of job search and subsidized public employment and training opportunities was included. The special public service employment (SPSE) and training program would have been available to principal family earners if they could not find private employment. Up to 1.4 million job and training slots would have been provided, designed to lead to opportunities in unsubsidized work.

3 An expanded earned income tax credit (EITC) would have provided a 10% benefit on earned income up to $4,000, plus a 5% benefit on additional earnings up to a maximum dependent on the number of tax exemptions claimed.

PBJI would increase federal but reduce state and local costs. In fiscal year 1982 the (estimated) gross total cost would be $50.9 billion: $42.3 federal, $8.6 billion state and local. For the same year a one-percentage point increase in the unemployment rate would call for between 170,000 and 214,000 additional public service jobs. A 1% increase in prices would increase federal expenditures by more than $500 million.

When the proposal was written (1978), the 1982 fiscal year estimate was that under the then existing policies some 7.1 million families (8.1% of all families) would have below-poverty threshold incomes. Were PBJI introduced and if benefits were to keep pace with inflation, the number of poor families would be reduced by 2.1 million, to 5.7% of all families.

There is a carrot and stick to the work incentive features of the plan. The carrot: a reduction in the rate at which benefits are decreased as a recipient

[21]The discussion herein is abstracted from the *Budget Issue Paper For Fiscal Year 1979* (with the same title as in the paragraph above). The *Paper* was prepared by the Congressional Budget Office, Congress of the United States (Washington, D.C.: U.S. Government Printing Office, April 1978). For a critical analysis of the Program, see *The Administration's 1979 Welfare Reform Proposal* (Washington, D.C.: American Enterprise Institute, 1979).

earnings increase. The stick: potential recipients expected to work would have benefits reduced for refusal to accept suitable work. The carrot again: if job search results in no private-sector work, the individual would, in turn, be eligible for SPSE jobs and training opportunities.

Several "limitations" to the plan are evident—and, to the credit of the analysts —they were duly noted. One specific example is that the maximum benefit of $4,200 would approximate 65% of 1978 poverty level budget for a family of four. How such a family would make up the other 35% is not clear except insofar as PBJI, SPSE, and EITC would be of help. The program would be at once simpler and yet more complex than the existing system. The complexities would arise from the state supplementation and grandfathering provisions and the national computer system designed to distribute benefits.

The proposal did not make its way through Congress. Other issues, foreign policy, oil and energy, industry deregulation, double-digit inflation, and other events intervened. As to costs, by mid-1980 the unemployment rate was up by two percentage points (not "optimal," but not a "disaster"); inflation, however, was in double-digit figures, not in percentages. Hence the $500 million increase previously noted should be increased by a factor of 10 at least.

The 1980 platforms of the Democrats and Republicans did not have welfare reform in the forefront, although shoring up the economy and providing jobs (a form of "income maintenance") was. Hence it is likely that we will continue along the same path with incremental, rather than sweeping, changes.

In light of the above the following is instructive.[22]

1   In the last 15 years government "transfers" have risen from $39 billion to $282 billion.

2   As a result "poverty" has been reduced by two-thirds. *But,* without the transfers, it is estimated that there would be just as many in poverty today as in 1965.

3   A major problem appears to reside in those "who could be working." One estimate is that 6 million people fall into this category.

4   Jobs tax credits appear to be an effective way of providing job-creating incentives to both employers and potential workers. This approach should be encouraged and increased. (Nothing is said, however, about the problems involved in creating jobs in a depressed economy such as in 1980.)

5   The negative income tax approach has desirable features but also work disincentives and is not likely to be a readily acceptable substitute.

6   And, as the reader is by now "well aware," there is no easy solution to reforming the income transfer system.

[22]See "Why Income Transfers Are So Hard to Cut," *Business Week,* September 29, 1980, 69–77.

A Brief Summary

It is difficult to predict what will eventuate by way of welfare reform, but three comments can be made:

1 There is considerable dissatisfaction with the present system: dissatisfaction by those who provide services and income and by those who receive them; dissatisfaction as to costs, differentiated benefits, stigma, and a host of other characteristics.

2 The philosophy of a guaranteed income (most likely through the negative income tax process) has gained increasing support and, indeed, was at the core of the Nixon and Carter Administrations' welfare reform proposals, but it may well not be in the future.

3 There is, however, enough difference of opinion in Congress about desirable alternatives so that the guaranteed income approach is by no means "guaranteed." And, as the following "suggests," the case for income guarantees may not be at all as strong as once supposed.

Two events have altered—or may well alter—the "optimistic" point of view on income guarantees. The first is the new Reagan Administration outlook and philosophy, commented on in Chapter 15 and noted below. The second flows out of the publication of the results and analysis of the Seattle and Denver Income Maintenance Experiments.[23] (These results appear to have influenced the Reagan philosophy.)

The results differ in varying and much less sanguine ways from the earlier three experiments. The Seattle–Denver sample sizes were larger than those of all previous experiments added together; hence there is more of an element of credence in this last study, even if it is admitted, as noted in the reports, that an "experiment differs from a permanent program."[24]

Several of the experiments' outcomes can be noted briefly; we use here the preliminary results as extrapolated to the national population.

1 "Fairly sizable" reductions in labor supply would take place in participating families, ranging from 6–11% for husbands, 23–32% for wives, and 0–15% for single female family heads. (Thus there does appear a disincentive effect.)

2 The least generous program tested would cost $4 billion less than the present welfare system, but 92% of welfare families would be worse off. A more

[23]See *The Journal of Human Resources,* XV, No. 4, Fall 1980. This issue is devoted entirely to these experiments, and it is essential reading for any serious student of the subject. Also see P. K. Robins, R. G. Spiegelman, S. Weiner, and J. G. Bell (Eds.), *A Guaranteed Annual Income: Evidence from a Social Experiment* (New York: Academic, 1980). This volume contains 17 detailed and informative articles.

[24]See Ref. 23, p. 473. See the cautionary comments on the relevance of this factor for future national planning and programming.

generous program would cost $30 billion more than the current one, but it would make one-fourth of all welfare families worse off.

3 Not extrapolated, but noted in the results, was the finding that these two experimental programs increased marital dissolution rates for blacks and whites, but not Chicanos. (Whether this was to be expected and whether it would be viewed as "undesirable" are complex issues. But, certainly from a cultural point of view, "breaking up the family" is hardly to be regarded as a laudable feature of income guarantee programs.)

Where does this all leave us in terms of the relatively hopeful optimistic views that many economists, social workers, and others (ourselves included) once had? The "results" as reported do not address this question. As we write this, the only conclusion we can reach is that these forms of negative income tax–income guarantee programs may well not be the wave of the future many of us had expected they would be. So, whither? We wish we were omniscient enough to know!

A "Post" Summary Comment: The Reagan Approach

We ended the last paragraph with a question. We raise another here: What will be the Reagan Administration's programmatic approach to the "welfare problem?" At the time of this writing we do not know.

But we make two conjectures:

1 Given the "philosophy" (discussed in Chapter 15) of Martin Anderson, the principal welfare advisor to the President, it does not appear that the "guaranteed income" approach will loom large in Administration proposals.
2 To us the results of the Seattle and Denver income maintenance experiments would seem to be more rather than less supportive of the Anderson views. Readers may wish to challenge this conclusion; we offer it as conjecture.

FAMILY ALLOWANCES

We conclude this chapter with a discussion of family allowances (also called children's allowances).[25] Such allowances are a halfway house on the path toward a guaranteed minimum income system. Conventional economic security programs in the United States—Old-Age, Survivors, and Disability Insurance, unemployment compensation, workmen's compensation—are labor-market oriented and protection is extended only to those who have a bona fide labor-force attach-

---

[25]Two useful volumes are (1) *Social Security Programs Throughout the World* (Washington, D.C.: U.S. Government Printing Office, 1980) for a comparative worldwide treatment; and James C. Vadakin, *Children, Poverty, and Family Allowances* (New York: Basic Books, 1968) for a more detailed analysis of the nature of such plans.

ment. A true guaranteed income program presumably would not require such an attachment.

Family allowances can be regarded as a first step toward an income guarantee. They do not, as presently constituted, provide such a guarantee, nor even approximate it. But neither do they necessarily require labor-force attachment, although this constraint exists in a large number of programs around the world.

Such allowances can be characterized in a number of ways. A family is granted, customarily on a monthly basis, a specified payment for each child below a certain age. The government thus provides a subsidy to the family, which helps in reaching a minimum income level. Under one type of family assistance plan, all families are eligible, irrespective of income, and "excess payments" are recaptured if the family income exceeds a certain level. Under the other type the allowance is predetermined on the basis of family size, family income, and/or some other set of requirements.

The first of such plans was enacted in New Zealand in 1926, followed by Belgium in 1930 and France in 1932. By 1980 over 65 countries maintained some form of family allowance. Two principal forms of this system are found. Some 15 countries—principally in Europe, but including Australia and New Zealand —have plans that do not require an employment relationship for protection to be provided. The remaining nations do require some such form of relationship, thus, of course, weakening the universality of coverage. The majority of countries provide benefits to all families with one or more children, though several countries require three, and several others four, before the family is eligible.

The existence of a child in the family is proof in and of itself that the family is eligible if other conditions are satisfied. Most commonly the allowance ceases when the child is 15 to 18 years of age, although in the U.S.S.R. the maximum age is 5 (or 12 if mother unmarried).

By any criterion family benefit allowances tend to be modest in most countries. In 1978 in Canada the federal minimum was $24 per month per child. Provincial supplements were also payable. In the same year the United Kingdom paid approximately $10 a month for the first child and $15 for each additional child; this provided an augmentation of less than 10% to the prototype family. Only in France do benefits rise perceptibly for a third child; in Paris in the late 1970s a family's third child augmented its income by 37%.

In these countries in which universal coverage exists the practice is to fund family allowance costs out of general revenues. In the remaining nations the revenue is raised from employer (not employee) contributions, and the government may provide supplementary revenues if employer payments do not meet costs.

Arguments For and Against Family Allowances

The main argument in favor of family allowances is that the welfare of the child should have priority over any other social objective. The child's need is the greatest, the child is least able to help himself or herself, and the child's development is critical for the future. Parental earnings are based on wages that do not take into account the number and need of the children in a family. Hence the ability to rear a family should not be limited by the earnings of the principal wage earner. Family allowances are one generalized approach to this problem.

Four principal arguments have been raised against family allowance plans:

1   They will lead to an increase in the birth rate. There is little doubt that such plans were introduced in a number of European countries after the decimating population impacts of World War I. Such predictions of population increase appear, however, to be ill-founded. Canada has a family allowance plan; the United States does not. Yet, their birth rate patterns are highly similar. France, with a program that is much more liberal than those of her neighbors, has had a lower birth rate.

2   They will lead to a misuse of the allowance: the parents would use the additional income for purposes other than that of the care of the children. With no exceptions that we could find, research on this issue suggests that this is not true: family allowances are used for the children.

3   They will weaken incentive. Except for France, the allowances are at such a minimal level that it is difficult to conceive of this possibility. In France some questions have been raised as to the impact on incentives, but there is little real documentation.

4   They are administratively inefficient. In the case of universal coverage systems there is more than a grain of truth to this assertion, since "recapture" then becomes necessary. But stigma is avoided. Also, if only the "needy" were to be served, an elaborate screening mechanism would be required.

Family Allowances in the United States

Family allowances have never reached a level of general acceptability—cultural, political, or social—in this country. Two principal factors appear to be relevant. The first relates to public attitudes toward religion and the birth rate. The second has been the reaction of organized labor, in terms of its views toward the traditional concept of a "living wage." While this latter attitude appears to have undergone a degree of modification since the mid-1950s, a major endorsement of the family allowance approach has never appeared.

In the United States family allowances have had at least 50 years of interest and support.[26] The most recent versions are those of Alvin L. Schorr and Harvey E. Brazer.[27] A 1969 statement by a group of economists and social workers

[26]See, for example, Paul H. Douglas, *Wages and the Family* (Chicago, Ill.: University of Chicago Press, 1927).

[27]See Alvin L. Schorr, *Poor Kids* (New York: Basic Books, 1966), and Harvey E. Brazer, "Tax Policy and Children's Allowances," in Eveline M. Burns (Ed.), *Children's Allowances and the Economic Welfare of Children* (New York: Citizen's Committee for Children of New York, 1968), pp. 140–149.

favored children's allowances and closely followed the general outlines of the Schorr–Brazer proposals.

The major dimensions of these proposals (for which we have found no updated figures) are as follows:

1 A benefit of $25 a month for each child under 6 years and $10 a month for each child between 6 and 18 (Schorr) versus $50 a month for each child under 18 years (Brazer). The gross cost (in 1965–1967 prices) would be $12.7 billion for the former, and some $42 billion for the latter. The difference in cost is a result of the significantly higher benefits under the Brazer plan.

2 The net cost for each plan would, however, be considerably reduced because of the way in which the proponents would alter the present income tax structure. Let us look at the Brazer plan with respect to this alteration. If the $50 per month allowance were universal and subject to income taxation, about $7 billion would have been recouped, bringing the net cost down to $35 billion.

Brazer (and Schorr) would *substitute* the family allowance for the exemption allowed ($600 per child) for dependent children. The net impact would be to introduce a significant element of the negative income tax at low income levels and increase the after-tax income of families with taxable incomes of less than $4,000, though reducing it for those with higher taxable incomes. Table 16.4 shows sample amounts for low income levels.

Brazer would go beyond this, however, in utilizing what he calls a "vanishing allowance"—a method designed to recoup the allowance from those it is not intended to benefit. (This would be an "after-the-fact" approach, would eliminate

Table 16.4 Effects of Children's Allowance Subject to Tax and Elimination of Exemptions for Dependent Children, for Married Taxpayer With Two Children (In Dollars)

Adjusted Gross Income	Present Law		With Children's Allowance		
	Tax	After-Tax Income	Tax	After-Tax Income	Increase in After-Tax Income
0	0	0	0	1,200	1,200
1,000	0	1,000	56	2,144	1,144
2,000	0	2,000	200	3,000	1,000
3,000	0	3,000	354	3,846	846
5,000	290	4,710	692	5,508	798
7,000	603	6,397	1,034	7,166	769

Source: Abstracted from Harvey E. Brazer, "Tax Policy and Children's Allowances," in Eveline M. Burns (Ed.), *Children's Allowances and the Economic Welfare of Children* (New York: Citizens' Committee for Children of New York, 1968).

the necessity of defining and identifying the poor "before the fact," and would thus obviate the need for a means test.)

The specific method proposed by Brazer would include the following: (1) children's allowances would be included in income; (2) exemptions for children eligible for the allowance would be disallowed; *and* (3) taxpayers would be required to add to their tax liabilities, as otherwise computed, an amount equal to a percentage of the children's allowances received. Using the bracket system, Brazer proposes that the net "value" of the allowance would range from the full $600 per year ($50 times 12 months) at low income levels to, for example, $60 ($5 times 12 months) for those with taxable incomes in excess of $12,000.

The total impact of these proposals would yield the results shown in Table 16.5.

Brazer holds that little can be said for financing a plan of this type by means other than the individual income tax. Financing through the social security payroll tax system would be inequitable since the tax base is limited and property income is excluded. Such an approach would be regressive and horizontally inequitable. Moreover, no "insurance principle" is involved.

A cursory evaluation of this plan suggests that it would rate high in terms of all the criteria developed above except political acceptability. Here the rating would seem to be low.

Children's allowances, particularly the more modern and sophisticated versions as developed by Brazer and Schorr, have a compelling economic and operational logic. But one may well ask whether the cultural, political, and social milieu in the United States will permit easy acceptance. Notwithstanding a wide-ranging group of proponents favoring such plans, it does not appear that the route to a guaranteed income will have as a first step a children's allowance plan. Events leading to the 1980s reaffirm this judgment.

Table 16.5 Net Change in Income After Tax, Owing to Substituting Children's Allowances for Exemptions, Taxing the Allowances, and Applying a Recoupment Rate (In Dollars)

Number of Dependent Children	Adjusted Gross Income						
	$ 0	$1,000	$3,000	$5,000	$7,000	$10,000	$15,000
1	600	600	339	209	124	27	13
2	1,200	1,144	618	355	218	39	−45
3	1,800	1,674	934	483	289	42	−81
4	2,344	2,008	1,186	590	315	36	−124
5	2,874	2,305	1,377	684	315	21	−129
6	3,112	2,562	1,572	832	304	−3	−226
7	3,280	2,700	1,710	910	322	−45	−305

Source: Same as for Table 16.4.

THE PATH TOWARD GUARANTEED INCOME

The materials in this chapter can be coordinated with those in the preceding two chapters and summarized in the following series of comments:

1 Poverty, in its economic sense, has both an absolute and a relative dimension. For any point in time a "poverty budget" can be constructed for single individuals, households without children, families in urban or rural settings, and so on. A "count" can then be made of those below the poverty line.

The relative dimension has two facets: (a) at any point in time it involves a comparison of the poor with the nonpoor; (b) more importantly, over a period of time it embraces the view that poverty is defined by more than a changing price level. For example, assume that a poverty budget had been constructed a half-century ago for a family of four. A similar budget for today would be higher, in dollar terms, than the original budget adjusted for price increases. Increases in productivity have sanctioned increases in the plane of living, which should also be shared with the "poor." If kerosene lamps were part of a poverty budget at some time in the past, one would expect that electricity has been substituted in more recent budgets.

2 With certain cyclical interruptions there has been a steady decrease in poverty in the United States, although the 1970s exhibited a plateau rather than a further decline. This reduction has been accomplished in part through the increase in numbers of those capable of self-support, and in part through economic security programs of one type or another. That is, even if there had been no such programs, increasing numbers would have lifted themselves out of poverty. For many of those living in poverty the after-the-fact help provided by social welfare programs has had the effect of mitigating their degree of poverty. How much farther poverty can be reduced before a hard-core group of those who cannot be made self-supporting is reached is a matter of conjecture. We seem to have a good way yet to go.

3 The increase over the decades in the number of those who have lifted themselves out of poverty and who have become self-supporting has not resulted in a corresponding reduction in welfare costs. One reason has been rising prices and hence the rising cost of welfare; another is less restrictive eligibility requirements.

There are, however, other reasons for increases in the number of those on welfare rolls. The development of new economic security programs is one example: persons and families formerly "excluded" now become "covered." The AFDC program is a case in point.

4 Growing dissatisfaction has developed with respect to the social welfare programs in which need must be demonstrated. The three causes for this dissatisfaction are the aforementioned increase in the number of those on welfare rolls,[28] the soaring costs of welfare, particularly in certain localities such as New York

---

[28]For example, "deserted families" on welfare have increased by 600% from 1965 to 1972. See Richard A. Snyder, "Welfare: Separating Myth and Fact," *The Wall Street Journal* (January 27, 1972), 10.

City, and the belief that the present system perpetuates welfare dependency and does not motivate people to get off welfare. Of the first two statements there can be little doubt; of the last there is still too little clarification between fact and myth.

It should be noted that the dissatisfaction is not all on one side. In recent years there have been demonstrations in many parts of the country by those *on* welfare. The protests have ranged over a variety of issues: eligibility requirements, low benefits, maladministration, and so on.

5   Two sets of forces have led to the present stage of thought and deliberation about welfare. One, as noted above, is the level of dissatisfaction with current programs. This has had the effect of "pushing" society, legislatures, politicians, and others into thinking much more acutely and seriously about welfare reform.

The other kind of force has "pulled" the same groups into generating ideas for welfare reform. Michael Harrington's *The Other America* and Milton Friedman's concept of the negative income tax are cases in point. In general, then, the past two decades have witnessed the beginnings of the "war on poverty" and a continued series of debates—some constructive, some more emotionally weighted— on problems and solutions.

6   It is not possible at this time to specify what the "new welfare" will be, but some conjectures can be made.

Whatever the precise nature of the new thrust (and new programming), we would have said previously that it would be increasingly federal in scope. We no longer hold this as firmly.

Similarly, we would have said that the thrust would be toward the provision of minimum income guarantees. Again this is by no means any longer a certainty.

In the short run at least, strong work-incentive features will characterize whatever program is developed (witness the Nixon and Carter proposals).

Irrespective of their merits, children's allowances as such are not likely to be at the core of the new programs. Assistance will be given to families with children, but not through children's allowances. "People's allowances" are more likely.

It is not clear what will happen to the conventional social-work structure if and as new welfare programming becomes a reality. Certain functions, such as appraising need and providing "supervision," could lessen in importance or even disappear, but other functions such as family counseling may continue or even increase.

The future of the vast miscellany of specific programs—food stamp plans and other subsidy programs, for example—is unsure. Presumably the many and varied "support programs" will diminish. Presumably, too, those programs relating to the development and maintenance of skills will be continued and increased, so as to enhance the labor marketability of individuals.

Economic growth is not without its problems, of which congestion, pollution, and urban decay are conspicuous current examples. But economic growth and high levels of economic activity are also the means through which millions have been able to lift themselves out of poverty. Hence any analysis that looks at the costs of growth must also consider the benefits it confers on the impoverished.

A rejoinder might, of course, be to place less emphasis on growth and more on equality in the distribution of income as a means of waging the war on poverty. But the battle is difficult enough and this suggestion adds a newer and more controversial dimension.

Many crosscurrents are at work in the domain of welfare reform. We have already noted Senator Russell B. Long's wage-subsidy proposal and its kinship to the Speenhamland system. An even more anomalous reaction was to be found in President Nixon's late 1971 veto of the Child Care Bill that had passed, by wide margins, in both the House and the Senate. The anomaly arises out of the fact that the Nixon Administration welfare reform proposals are closely tied to work-incentive constraints. It is difficult to visualize a mother in a "fatherless" family[29] being able to work if her children cannot be cared for while she is at her place of employment. The President may have felt he had good reason for his veto, notwithstanding bipartisan support of the bill. While the arguments put forth in the veto message seem less than fully convincing, what is more relevant is the example the veto provides of the shifting sands of welfare reform. The Carter Administration did not have to worry about vetoes; no controversial legislation was enacted.

Are societies and individuals the prisoners of their own past history? Based on experiences of recent decades, will the welfare problem worsen and spawn a culture of those who will remain on relief into perpetuity? In the long run this does not seem to be the case. Beginning—perhaps specifically—with workers' compensation statutes in the first two decades of this century, society has sought to ameliorate the lot of those who have been disadvantaged. The trend has not always been in the direction of improvement, but, notwithstanding lags, lapses, and lateness, it does seem clear that there is a distinct path toward improvement both in specific programs and in the attitude of one group of human beings toward another. Unless the past reverses itself, the future will see steady progress in the war on poverty, in welfare reform, and in the development of a useful and concerned citizenry.

SUGGESTIONS FOR ADDITIONAL READING

Those interested in the detail of the many plans/programs cited in this chapter should consult the appropriate items cited in the footnotes.

[29]For other past crosscurrent examples see the comment by Roger A. Freeman, former special assistant to President Nixon, when he recommended a "cash bonus for sterilization by welfare parents rather than for every additional baby." *The Wall Street Journal,* LII, No. 74 (January 28, 1972), 1. See also the views expressed in early 1972 by Senator Abraham Ribicoff, who was counted on as leading the Democratic members in the Senate in support of the Nixon Family Assistance Plan. The Senator, who admitted to "being away from social welfare planning too long," indicated that he could not do more at this time than support a "pilot test" of the Nixon plan. Hence the uncertainty grew —and it still grows.

"The Administration's Welfare Reform Proposals: An Analysis of the Program for Better Jobs and Income," in *Budget Issue Paper For Fiscal Year 1979*. Congressional Budget Office, Congress of the United States. Washington, D.C.: U.S. Government Printing Office, 1979.
The Carter Administration proposal. While detailed (of necessity), this paper is a model of clarity of expression and explanation. This could be well read in conjunction with the next-to-last citation below.

Danziger, Sheldon, Irwin Garfinkel, and Robert Haveman. "Poverty, Welfare, and Earnings: A New Approach." *Challenge*, 24, No. 2 (September–October 1979), 28–34.
In the words of the authors, "The present welfare system, based on income-tested transfers, is not effective in reducing poverty. It should be replaced with a simpler program that provides job opportunities and enforces child support by absent parents." Interesting reading.

Goodwin, Leonard. *Do the Poor Want to Work? A Social–Psychological Study of Work Orientations*. Washington, D.C.: Brookings Institution, 1972.
An interesting analysis of "motivation."

Green, Christopher. *Negative Taxes and the Poverty Problem*. Washington, D.C.: Brookings Institution, 1967.
A most useful descriptive and analytical survey.

Improving the Public Welfare System. New York: Committee for Economic Development, 1970.
A very useful summary ranging from a profile of poverty to proposals for change.

Lampman, Robert J. *Ends and Means of Reducing Income Poverty*. Chicago, Ill.: Markham Publishing, 1971.
Treats the origin and nature of the goal of reducing poverty and the range of available approaches.

Poverty Amid Plenty: The American Paradox. Report of the President's Commission on Income Maintenance Proposals. Washington, D.C.: Government Printing Office, 1969.
This is the *Report* of the Committee chaired by Ben W. Heineman, a railroad executive, who took on the difficult task of chairing a Presidential Committee charged with examining the welfare system. The *Report* was disowned by both Presidents Johnson and Nixon—thus illustrating the hazards of public service—but at the same time it is an invaluable, forthright, and perceptive document.

Rolph, Earl R. "The Case for a Negative Income Device," *Industrial Relations*, VI, No. 2 (February 1967), 155–165.
An interesting alternative approach to a negative income tax, utilizing the concept of a "credit income tax" concept.

Titmuss, Richard. *Essays on the Welfare State*. New York: Pantheon, 1963.
A far-ranging series of essays dealing with such varied topics as social administration teaching and research and issues of income redistribution in social policy.

Weil, Gordon, with Samuel I. Eskenazi. *The Welfare Debate of 1978*. White Plains, N.Y.: Institute for Socioeconomic Studies, 1978.
A useful summary of welfare reform proposals.

"Welfare Reform: A Message from the President of the United States," House Document No. 91–146, *Congressional Record*, 115, No. 136.
The welfare reform message of President Nixon as first enunciated in 1969. This "reform" proposal followed a tortuous and unresolved path and ultimately came to naught.

Williams, Walter. "The Continuous Struggle for a Negative Income Tax: A Review Article," *The Journal of Human Resources*, X, No. 2 (Fall 1975), 427–444.
An updated review and analysis of this approach; excellent bibliography.

Chapter Seventeen

The Problems and Treatment
of Substandard Conditions

The working and living conditions of American workers became a matter of widespread concern for the first time around the turn of the 20th century. Employment and living conditions were being generated that a changing public opinion would not long tolerate. Frederick Lewis Allen has written of this period that to read

> . . . reports of qualified observers of poverty at its worst in the big city slums and grim industrial towns at the beginning of the century is to hear variation after variation upon the theme of human misery, in which the same words occur monotonously again and again: wretchedness, overcrowding, filth, hunger, malnutrition, insecurity, want.[1]

What were employment conditions at the time? First, there was widespread employment of children, which increased steadily until 1910. Census records reveal that 16% of all children 10 to 15 years old were gainfully employed in 1880, and 18.4% were in 1910. These estimates are probably conservative, since child labor in home work and street trades could not be easily recorded. Much of this child labor was most heavily concentrated in agriculture and manufacturing, where accident rates among children were high. The average earnings of employed children, except during the war years, were reported at from $3 to $5 a week.[2]

Second, adult American workers of the period labored under similarly adverse conditions. Allen writes[3] that the average annual wage of the period for American workers was between $400 and $500, with unskilled workers averaging under $460 in the North and $300 in the South. A report[4] of male earnings in the

---

[1]Reprinted with permission from Frederick Lewis Allen, *The Big Change* (New York: Harper and Row, 1952), p. 57.

[2]S. Howard Patterson, *Social Aspects of Industry* (New York: McGraw-Hill, 1929), p. 200.

[3]Frederick Lewis Allen, *The Big Change* (New York: Harper and Row, 1952), p. 55.

[4]These data are taken from an interesting compilation of studies on working conditions for the period

"principal trades and industries" for the decade preceding World War I reveals that one-fourth of the heads of families earned less than $400 a year; and one-half of them earned less than $600. One-fourth of regularly employed women in the "principal manufacturing industries" earned less than $200 a year and two-thirds earned less than $400. Women and children were employed in greatest proportions in the low-pay industries, such as textiles and glass. For women, a workweek in excess of 55 to 60 hours was not uncommon.

This final chapter explores in more detail the problem of substandard conditions in employment, the development of protective legislation to deal with these problems, and current state and federal laws, especially the Fair Labor Standards Act.

THE NATURE OF THE PROBLEM

Oppressive working conditions, such as those briefly sketched above, pose a problem in economic security that cannot be resolved by approaches such as the social assistance and insurance measures considered in earlier chapters.

In earlier chapters major attention was directed to the problems of unemployment as they affect economic security. That these problems should be of great importance is not surprising, for in an industrial society the only means by which a worker can earn a livelihood is through the sale of personal services in a free labor market. Whether unemployment arises directly out of labor-market operation or is caused indirectly by other factors such as accidents, sickness, or old age, social insurance measures seek primarily to alleviate its undesirable consequences. Protection against substandard working conditions cannot be provided by these methods, however, for it is not the inability of workers to get a wage contract that is at issue here, but rather their inability to get a wage contract that meets the minimum standards under which a society will permit its members to be employed.

This distinction has significance beyond its use as a definition. Unlike unemployment-caused insecurity, control of substandard conditions requires, and has indeed involved, intervention into the wage contract and intervention directly into the labor market. And so two questions arise: should the government intervene in the freedom of individuals to enter contracts for employment? Can it intervene? The courts permitted qualifications of this freedom in the name of economic security only after extended resistance.

It bears repeating that substandard conditions are causal factors in generating poverty. Not all the impoverished are without jobs, but insofar as they work at substandard wages their incomes may well be insufficient. And substandard working conditions may lead to health problems and increased expenses.

---

from 1900 to World War I by W. Jett Lauck and Edgar Sydenstricker, *Conditions of Labor in American Industries* (New York: Funk and Wagnalls, 1917), Chap. 2.

CHANGING ATTITUDES TOWARD SUBSTANDARD CONDITIONS

Because of the vast improvement in the conditions of work over the past 100 years, most working conditions during this period would probably be termed "substandard" by today's standards. The terms of employment that free societies accept as reasonable have changed enormously over the years, as have educational, health, and living standards—and they are continuing to do so.

In the American colonies one of the chief benefits derived from manufacturers was considered to be the job opportunities created for children. As recently as 1910 it was estimated that about one-fifth of all boys between 10 and 15 years of age were employed. Today the Fair Labor Standards Act prohibits the employment in interstate commerce of children under 16 in most employments and under 18 in most hazardous work.

Similarly, the acceptable minimum standards for working conditions, working hours, and pay have changed with a changing social and economic environment. These changes have been achieved through legislation, the efforts of trade unions, the actions of employers and, in the case of improved hours and wages, by advances in productivity. Today our increased concern about poverty has come about not because there is anything strikingly new about the problems of the poor, but because we have become more sensitive to the painful contrast of poverty in the midst of affluence. As one writer pointed out, the more general the boon of prosperity, the more bitter the taste of poverty.[5]

THE DEVELOPMENT OF PROTECTIVE LEGISLATION

Before considering the provisions of the protective labor laws that are in effect in all U.S. jurisdictions today, it is useful to note several generalizations about their development.

Historically, movements for improving working standards have been directed more at a specific situation that has aroused public interest than at goals based on abstract principles. Definitions of minimum acceptable working conditions have been determined by contemporary economic, social, and political circumstances. Clyde Dankert notes that arguments for reduced hours at any particular time "usually bear a close relationship to the objective conditions prevailing at that time." The appearance early in the 20th century of a child labor movement in the South, for instance, was due less to a belief that children should be educated as well as protected from working conditions interfering with their adult development than it was to the realization of the inhumane effects of the widespread employment of children by the new Southern mills.

For these reasons arguments in support of government intervention into sub-

[5]Mollie Orshansky, "Counting the Poor: Another Look at the Poverty Profile," *Social Security Bulletin,* XXVIII, No. 1 (January 1965), 3.

standard conditions have changed with the times and the conditions. We may note that shorter hours were first advocated as necessary for leisure and for better citizenship. But later, with the coming of the factory system, this approach was abandoned for the argument that shorter hours were necessary to protect the worker's health. More recently adoption of a shorter workweek has been urged as a means of reducing unemployment and cushioning the effects of advancing technology.

Experience under the Fair Labor Standards Act has been similar. Both the original 1938 Act and its subsequent amendments were justified by arguments that are traditionally offered in support of minimum wage legislation—the need to provide minimum living standards, reduce poverty, increase purchasing power, and lessen employer exploitation of the worker. Important to the 1938 law, however, was the argument that the overtime penalty provisions would aid in spreading employment in that immediate post-Depression period. The 1955 amendment, which increased minimum wages during a period of high, full employment, found important justification in the argument that since the low wages paid in Southern states were acting as an inducement to Northern industry to migrate south, they were an unfair competitive advantage against Northern employers and a threat to trade union wage standards.

In short, demands that certain working conditions be declared substandard have varied at different times and have been based on many grounds, including those of civic improvement, safety, health, morals, and more recently, economic effects.[6] Although at all times these demands had the specific objective of improving the conditions of work, they did not necessarily focus on an abstract goal nor on a single set of principles.

Behind this condition of objective and value judgment criteria for improved working conditions there occasionally lurked the selfish motive of setting job standards for women that would reduce their competitive threat to men.

Support for protection has come from many and varying sources. Sometimes an aroused public opinion was the initiating factor, as in the case of the child labor movement in the South. Trade union support, which today is frequently at the head of campaigns to improve legislative standards, dates back to the interest of the Knights of Labor in child labor legislation and the eight-hour day, which this union gained for its members for a short time. Yet trade union support has by no means been uniform. In fact, trade unions never gave much support to men's hours movements and for a time actively opposed the enactment of minimum wage legislation for fear that minimum wages would become "maximum" wages and that the government's would enter into the wage-fixing arena.

Employers have improved working conditions on their own initiative, partially in response to the pressures of trade unions and of competition, and in part when

[6]H. A. Millis and R. E. Montgomery, *Labor's Risks and Social Insurance* (New York: McGraw-Hill, 1938), p. 249; Frank T. de Vyver, "Regulation of Wages and Hours Prior to 1938," *Law and Contemporary Problems*, VI, No. 3 (1939), 323–324.

the economies of such action were apparent. Finally, reform movements frequently had as their nucleus of support organizations like the Consumers' League and Women's Trade Union League (in the case of women's hours) and various public-spirited middle-class individuals and groups who carried the brunt of the fight for minimum wage legislation.

Cultural, economic, and social philosophy, in the broad sense, appear to have played a more minor role in the movements for legislative protection. Humanitarian considerations, it is true, were responsible for the recognition that, particularly with respect to children and women, conditions of work were cruel and inhuman by virtually any standard. From these premises came the regulation of child labor. Other arguments came to be more significant, and the movement eventually extended to hours regulation for women and men, and finally to wage regulation.

ORIGINS OF THE PROBLEM OF SUBSTANDARD CONDITIONS

Also, prior to analyzing the standards set by protective labor laws, several questions should be asked. Why do working conditions fall to "low" levels? Who or what is responsible? The answers to these questions have, of course, changed from the time of the master-slave relationship to the present-day wage system.[7] Since slaves were owned by a master who could buy and sell them, they were wholly at their master's disposal. The status of the serf in the period of feudalism was only slightly better. While a lord did not own his serfs, their freedom was narrowly limited by their legal obligations in a lord's service, and the government action was used to insure that economic force did not give the serf power to change these conditions.[8]

None of these legal ties binds today's workers, since the essence of the contemporary wage system is the worker's freedom of choice. Workers are legally free to choose their occupations and to change them to accept or reject working conditions that please or fail to please them, to change employers, to work in any part of the country that they choose, or indeed, to refuse to work altogether.

Given these legal labor-market freedoms and concomitantly those of the employer to hire and fire, it should follow that under competitive labor-market conditions employers would be the custodians or administrators of working conditions determined by the basic market forces of competition. It was one of Adam Smith's premises in his theory of equalizing differences (referred to in Chapter 7) that under a free wage system competing bids for labor would effectively regulate working conditions in different occupations. The regulating force

[7]Discussed by Maurice Dobb, *Wages* (London: Pitman Publishing, 1948), pp. 1–17.

[8]Thus the first real government regulation of working conditions was the oppressive 14th-century Statutes of Laborers, which set maximum wages—a policy followed in the later Elizabethan Statutes of Apprentices.

of competition lies in the threat to an employer posed by his employees' alternative opportunities.

Competition, however, appears to play a paradoxical role in its effects on working conditions. On the one hand, our competitive system leads all nations of the world in its ability to amass capital and to become increasingly productive. Furthermore, the gigantic increases in real national income due primarily to productiveness have, over the years, been distributed generously among American workers in the form of reduced hours of work and higher (real) wages. Working hours during the past century have been shortened from an approximate 69-hour week to the present 40-hour week, with lower hours in an increasing number of occupations. Average nonagricultural wages have increased from about 9 to 10 cents an hour to current levels above $7.

On the other hand, various social, political, and economic criteria have been used over the years to demonstrate that an unregulated wage system produces substandard conditions, and that at the beginning of the 20th century deplorable working conditions existed in this country.

These two apparently contradictory situations can be reconciled, however, when the distinction is made between labor-market competition on the one hand and product-market competition on the other. In part, the reasons that labor-market competition does not always bring about acceptable working conditions are similar to the reasons that it fails to bring about wage rates that fully reflect the accident hazard of occupations. The reasons are not wholly the same, however, and since they involve the effects of the product market, let us examine them more fully. There are three general reasons why competition may not adequately regulate working conditions, to which a fourth may be added. These are the following:

Barriers to Labor-Market Competition

Although workers enjoy full legal rights to choose among labor-market alternatives, they are not always willing nor able to fully exercise them. Hence the competitive regulating force of working conditions is seriously weakened by the labor-market imperfections referred to earlier: poor knowledge of alternatives, institutional (noneconomic) barriers to accepting alternatives, economic barriers to geographic mobility, and economic and social barriers to upward occupational mobility. To expect of free *legal* labor-market choice the full exercise of *economic* labor-market choice that will fully regulate working conditions is, in Dobb's words, to depend on so "one-sided a picture as to contrast in some respects grotesquely with reality."[9]

[9]See Ref. 7, p. 6. For an interesting picture of the relation of the worker to his labor market in 1923, see Paul H. Douglas, Curtice N. Hitchcock, and Willard E. Atkins (Eds.), *The Worker in Modern Economic Society* (Chicago, Ill. University of Chicago Press, 1923), pp. 226–228. For a more recent analysis see Herbert S. Parnes, "Research on Labor Mobility," *Bulletin 65* (New York: Social Science Research Council, 1954).

The Superior Bargaining Power of Employers

Partly because of these barriers to labor-market competition and partly because of the very nature of the employment relationship, employers enjoy bargaining advantages over their employees in setting conditions of work.[10] In the absence of trade unions, competition among workers for jobs tends to be greater than competition among employers for workers. Employers have better information about alternatives; moreover, they control revenues and payments.

Labor is much more difficult to move than is capital, and it is much more perishable. Since most workers with little savings cannot store their services, they have poor waiting power. These and other reasons explain in large part why our present-day public policy toward collective bargaining encourages the continuing development of trade unions as a means of gaining equality in bargaining power between employer and employee.

It must be stressed in considering the above two points that they are by no means applicable without exception. For instance, the employment of women was once opposed as a social evil on the grounds that women were being underpaid and exploited. Yet today women represent over 42% of the labor force. In the secretarial and other office jobs, in which demands for their skills are highest, women's working conditions tend to be excellent by almost any standard. Another illustration is that, despite possible labor-market imperfections, keen competition for the services of specialized professionals has forced employers to bid up their working conditions. This happens wherever demands for labor are strong. During periods of rising prosperity the overwhelming majority of workers enjoy working conditions far better than the statutory minimums. Yet even in these times there are many who do not.

Keen Product-Market Competition[11]

Despite the obvious virtues of competition among sellers of goods and services, it is historically true that where such competition is keen and combined with the labor-market imperfections referred to above, substandard conditions of employment tend to result. Employers have a strong incentive to maximize their employees' output during the immediate period of their employment. The Webbs observed that, as a result of the introduction of the factory system,

> . . . competition is always forcing him [the employer] to cut down the cost of production to the lowest point. Under this pressure, other considerations disappear in the passion to obtain the greatest possible 'output per machine.'[12]

[10]Discussed by K. W. Rothschild, *The Theory of Wages* (New York: Macmillan, 1954), Chap. 9.

[11]Based on K. W. Rothschild, *The Theory of Wages* (New York: Macmillan, 1954), pp. 51–52.

[12]Sidney and Beatrice Webb, *Industrial Democracy* (London: Longmans, Roberts and Green, 1897), p. 327.

The desire to increase productivity and reduce costs by greater employment of the fixed costs of the factory led to long hours of work and the employment of children. Children were worked without consideration for the subsequent effects on their adult health nor lack of education; adults were worked long hours and under serious hazards, with low pay. Over a period of years workers became less productive and had to be replaced. The result was not only inhumane; it was socially inefficient.

Although maximum short-run productivity may not produce maximum long-run productivity, price competition can force employers to maximize short-run output. And as long as there is an adequate labor supply employers have incentives to follow this policy. The private cost to an employer of doing so is less than the full social cost of depreciating workers. Where labor-market competition cannot be counted on to remedy this situation, government intervention is necessary. By intervening here to achieve improved working conditions, the government performs one of its most important economic functions, and as a result everyone benefits—employers gain greater long-run productivity, and workers enjoy better health and living standards.

Labor as a Human Commodity

Unequal bargaining power and the lack of competitive regulation, despite their effects on the terms of sale, might be tolerable except for one additional factor —the commodity involved is an unusual one. Like most other commodities in the economy, labor has a price and is bought and sold in a marketing process. But unlike any other commodity, labor is distinctive in that the service can never be isolated from the person who performs the service. In short, it is a human commodity. The attention currently commanded by the "human relations" aspects of employment is ample evidence of how widely this fact is appreciated today. The terms of the sale of labor involved human conditions that are not a part of any other market considerations.

STATE PROTECTIVE LABOR LAWS

The discussion now turns to the protective labor legislation that has been enacted by the states. This legislation deals with (1) working conditions, (2) child labor, and (3) hours and wages.

Working Conditions

Recognition of the need for regulating working conditions developed along similar lines in the United States and England, although at different times. In both countries the government intervened to protect those least able to protect themselves—those whose lack of bargaining strength prevented them from fully exercising their legal labor-market freedoms.

Dissatisfaction with substandard working conditions in England came in the late 18th century shortly after formalized adoption of laissez faire policies and was soon followed by legislative efforts to correct them. The first such enactment was the (1802) Factory Act, designed to protect pauper children who had been made apprentices. Only a few such laws were enacted for some time, but after 1850 the area of regulative control expanded, until by World War I all the leading industrial countries of Europe exercised extensive controls over working conditions, hours, and wages.

In this country almost all states, and many municipalities and other jurisdictions, have sought to regulate conditions of work to insure certain minimum standards. Since there is very little uniformity in this type of legislation, it is difficult to estimate the degree of quality of protection that it affords. Most of the laws apply primarily to women and children. For these two groups most states prohibit work in specified industries or occupations—those declared hazardous or a health menace—and require that seating, rest, and toilet facilities, stated meal periods, and sanitary drinking water be provided by the employer.

Where this protective legislation has been extended to include men, it sometimes requires "safe employment devices and safeguards" and, in a few states, provides for minimum pay for call-ins and split-shift work. Other regulations require approved ventilation standards (particularly in laundries), payments of wages at least twice monthly, time off for voting, and adequate lighting.

Because of enlightened personnel administration, trade union pressures, and the cost savings to an employer of a satisfied working force, many of the standards of these laws are not as high as the "going practice." Yet for some employees, particularly those in unorganized areas, these laws can be a genuine source of protection, when adequately enforced.

Child Labor

Of all labor legislation, the need for laws regulating the employment of children[13] was most generally accepted and received the most early widespread support. Nevertheless, the development of child labor legislation was piecemeal and slow. It was hampered by problems of law and enforcement as well as by powerful, though limited, opposition. In addition, the problem of child labor was extremely complex. Adequate protection required a minimum age and education before a child could work, a limit on the number of hours a child could work, and a prohibition against employment in hazardous occupations.

---

[13]For an excellent review of child labor legislation from its beginnings through the middle 1930s, see John R. Commons, *History of Labor in the United States,* Vol. III (New York: Macmillan, 1935), 403–456.

Action by the States

During the 19th century there was some support for the protection of children (some of which came from the Knights of Labor). By the turn of the century 28 state laws had been enacted. These early child labor laws embodied a variety of standards, but were, for the most part, limited to work in manufacturing. They set the minimum age limit at 12 years, and the workday at 10 hours. Only a few of the laws made some provision for required education.

Despite this apparent progress in regulating the employment of children, census data for the period indicated that the percentage of employed children 10 to 15 years old was increasing. This was partly due to poor enforcement and limited coverage of the laws and, in part, to the new industrial expansion of the South, an area in which labor laws were yet to be enacted (and in which they were to encounter their stiffest opposition).

A great deal of state child labor legislation was enacted after the turn of the century and until the period of the first federal action in 1916. By 1909 all but six states had minimum age requirements for factories. And during the period of greatest growth of labor and protective legislation (from 1911 to 1913) 31 states took action to improve child labor legislation.

These laws sought to do the following: (1) create administrative devices that would enable conclusive evidence of age that could not be circumvented by parents; (2) limit the maximum hours worked per week to a number that bore a rational relation to the amount of work that a child could (reasonably) do; and (3) make some educational provisions.

All states now have child labor laws. Like workers' compensation laws, they are constantly being revised, and certain elements are common to all of them, although their standards differ considerably.[14] State child labor laws seek to do the following:

1 Set a minimum age at which a child may legally accept work, qualified occasionally by school hours requirements.
2 Limit the maximum hours per day that a youth may be employed.
3 Limit employment during night hours.
4 Set age limits on certain dangerous occupations.
5 Require employment certificates.
6 Require school attendance.

[14]For the current status of state child labor, minimum wage, and other laws affecting working conditions, see "State Labor Laws", in *Labor Relations Reporter* (Washington, D.C.: Bureau of National Affairs, updated periodically). Each year the *Monthly Labor Review* summarizes recent changes in these laws.

Federal Approaches

Because of the diversity in child labor standards and the failure of some states to adequately enforce their laws, it became apparent that genuinely effective control could be achieved only by federal legislation. Even before 1900 pressure was building, and despite the fact that the states had enacted considerable legislation, by 1914 demands for federal action could not longer be ignored.

By 1916 support was so widespread that Congress, by a great majority, enacted the first federal child labor law. It was the first of four federal attempts at regulation that failed to survive legal hurdles.

An early federal control that did succeed, although briefly, set minimum age standards for the employment of children in the Codes of Fair Competition of the National Industrial Recovery Act (NIRA). The standards of the Codes varied, but typically they provided for a minimum age of 16, although some went as low as 14. The minimum age in hazardous employment was set at 18. The Codes succeeded in curtailing the employment of children, but the regulations fell in 1935 along with the rest of the NIRA when the U.S. Supreme Court held that in enacting the Codes, Congress had exceeded its power to regulate interstate commerce.[15]

Following the Schechter decision Congress acted to control child labor in an area that seemed safely within its powers, namely, contractors supplying the federal government. In 1936 the Walsh–Healey Public Contracts Act was passed, prohibiting contractors who supply the federal government with manufactures, products, or finished materials in values over $10,000 from employing children under 16 and women under 18. It does not apply to agriculture, retail trade, or the service occupations. This was the only successful enactment of federal child labor regulation before the passage of the Fair Labor Standards Act, which marked the end of a 22-year period of unsuccessful federal action in this field.

Hours

Although movements to control working hours for women and men are related both in time and in motivating forces, because of some differences in timing, theory, scope, and coverage, hours regulation for these two groups will be discussed separately here. Although hours regulation prior to the Fair Labor Standards Act was primarily a matter of state legislation, the federal government in its role as employer was actually the first to limit hours and undoubtedly influenced the actions of some employers and legislative groups. But federal regulation comparable to that of child labor has never been attempted in this field. The discussion below therefore concerns state regulations, with a brief added comment on federal action.

---

[15]*Schechter Poultry Corporation versus United States,* 295 U.S. 495 (1935).

Women's Hours

The successful regulation of women's working hours dates back almost as far as the first child labor laws. New Hampshire enacted a 10-hour law in 1847, and a few other New England states followed. By 1896, 13 such regulatory laws had been passed. These laws were, for the most part, limited to manufacturing, and by and large were not very effective, either because they were unenforceable or because they lacked realistic hours limits. Moreover, a court decision in 1895 declared an Illinois eight-hour law for women unconstitutional.[16] The court ruled that such laws interfered with the right of freedom of contract and liberty and that the necessary protection to health, safety, or morals that might make such interference justifiable was not present.

As a result, from 1909 to 1917 there was a great flood of state legislative activity in this field. The principle had been firmly established, had won legal acceptance, and most states enacted women's hours laws. After World War I, however, the movement never regained its prewar momentum, and the legislative revisions were limited to newer rules such as prohibitions against night work and required rest periods.

Until recently almost every jurisdiction had in some way regulated the hours of women, though the extent and quality of coverage varied widely among jurisdictions. However, the following generalizations can be made: (1) for reasons of health and safety most laws limited work in specified industries or occupations; (2) almost all the laws limited work to, say, eight hours a day and 48 hours a week; and (3) the effect of the maximum hours requirement was considerably weakened by the exemptions (most frequently domestics, agricultural workers, and waitresses) that appeared in virtually all the laws. Coverage in some of the laws was limited to certain industries or establishments.

Most of these women's "protective" laws have been repealed because they conflict with Title VII of the Federal Civil Rights Act of 1964, which bans employment discrimination on the basis of sex. Numerous Equal Employment Opportunity Commission and federal court decisions rejected such laws in several states as a basis for discriminatory practices.

All but a few states currently have their own fair employment practices laws. These state laws frequently cover more kinds of discrimination than does Title VII. Furthermore, whereas Title VII applies only to employers of 15 or more workers, some states cover employers of one or more. About two-thirds of the states have specific "equal-pay" provisions in separate statutes or in their fair employment practices laws.

About two-thirds of the states also now have laws patterned after the federal Fair Labor Standards Act, which require employers to pay higher wage rates for work beyond a certain number of hours per week. Seven of these laws apply only to women.

[16]*Ritchie versus People*, 155 Ill. 98 (1895).

Men's Hours

Regulation has never been as comprehensive in its scope nor coverage of men's working hours as it has of the hours of women and children. Until fairly recently laws were enacted almost exclusively in those employments where protection was very badly needed because of hazardous conditions or where they were fairly easy to enact because of advantageous political or administrative situations.

In 1840 a presidential order stipulated a 10-hour maximum workday in government Navy yards.[17] As early as 1968 Congress, with some success, limited the workday on contracts for government buildings and roads to 10 hours. An early case[18] upheld state and municipal employees' hours laws and those covering state workers under contract.

Regulation of hours in hazardous work was first approved by the Supreme Court in 1898,[19] when the court upheld a Utah law that regulated the hours of men working in mines. Later cases upheld the right to regulate hours of special groups such as railroad employees, mining workers, bus drivers, and others on the grounds of safety.

Although men's hours laws gained recognition and approval between 1911 and World War I, they did not play a part in that period of vigorous legislative activity. Public interest in men's hours laws was never great, and no particular movement to enact this legislation ever developed.

Attempts to achieve shorter hours have been an important part of trade union programs since the 1890s. Since unions have been successful in gaining this objective and because of the general feeling that men are better able than women to protect themselves in the labor market, this area of regulation has not been one of major legislative nor public interest in the overall movement to improve substandard conditions. After the passage of the Fair Labor Standards Act little was done until the passage of the overtime rate laws mentioned earlier, which usually apply to both men and women.

Federal Regulation

With the exception of work on railroads, Congress has never sought to enact legislation that would state maximum hours of work for men or for women. Its approach in the few areas in which it has attempted regulation has always been not to prohibit excessive hours of work, but rather to make excessive hours expensive through penalty "overtime" payments. The Codes of Fair Competition of the National Industrial Recovery Act provided for overtime payments, as did the 1916 Adamson Act and the Walsh–Healey Act. Each of these set the workday and provided for overtime payments. Apart from the instances in which the

---

[17]Discussed by Matthew A. Kelly, "Early Federal Regulation of Hours of Labor in the United States," *Industrial and Labor Relations Review,* III, No. 3 (April 1950), 362–374.

[18]*Atkin versus Kansas,* 191 U.S. 207 (1903).

[19]*Holden versus Hardy,* 169 U.S. 366 (1898).

federal government was acting as employer, these were the only federal regulations in this field prior to the Fair Labor Standards Act.

Wages

Wages were the last of the conditions of employment to be regulated by government intervention. Child labor and hours movements were well under way by the time Massachusetts enacted the pioneer minimum wage law in this country in 1912—one that set nonmandatory minimum wages for women and children. With but limited exception, early minimum wage laws applied exclusively to women and children and were justified as protecting these two groups from low wages resulting from competitive labor-market conditions.

State Attempts at Regulation

Although eight states quickly followed the lead of Massachusetts in enacting minimum wage laws (most of which called for enforcement), and despite apparent Supreme Court approval,[20] the movement never gathered much momentum. Only 15 states had enacted such laws when the movement encountered a serious legal setback. In 1923 the minimum wage law of Washington, D.C., was held[21] unconstitutional as an interference with the freedom of contract.

The effect of this decision was nearly ruinous. Laws in six other jurisdictions were declared unconstitutional; other states avoided court tests at the cost of full compliance. By 1933, wage laws existed in only nine jurisdictions, and some of these were not in effective operation.

Most early minimum wage laws were based on a concept of the minimum wage needed for living. In the Adkins case the court implied that a criterion more directly related to the value of the services performed by the employee might be a more appropriate basis for such legislation. Laws that embodied this concept and set minimum wages for "reasonable value of services" were enacted in some states. The New York law, however, was challenged and held unconstitutional despite its new basis.[22] It was not until 1937 that the U.S. Supreme Court gave full approval to state minimum wage laws by holding[23] the Washington law a valid exercise of state police power.

Some favorable legislative response followed this decision, and state legislatures enacted laws or broadened existing ones, in some cases even extending coverage to men. Yet for a number of years there was little legislative action on

[20]In *Stettler versus O'Hara,* 243 U.S. 629 (1917), the U.S. Supreme Court split evenly, Justice Brandeis abstaining, on the constitutionality of Oregon's minimum wage law, leaving intact its approval by the lower court.

[21]*Adkins versus Children's Hospital,* 261 U.S. 525 (1923).

[22]On the grounds of a violation of the due process clause of the Fourteenth Amendment. *Morehead versus New York ex rel. Tipaldo,* 298 U.S. 587 (1936).

[23]*West Coast Hotel Company versus Parrish,* 300 U.S. 379 (1937).

this front. Then, with the poverty program of the 1960s providing the incentive, there was a flurry of activity beginning in 1964, when Michigan enacted a minimum wage law, the first state to do so for five years. In 1965 three states (Delaware, Indiana, and Maryland) passed laws for the first time, two states amended their laws to bring men under coverage, and many states increased their statutory rates.[24]

The Current Status of State Minimum Wage Regulation

Minimum wage laws exist today in all but nine states.[25] Utah is the only state to limit coverage to women. Standards required by these state minimum wage laws vary greatly. In six states the standard is less than $2, the lowest being $1.25 in Georgia. In 18 states the standard exceeds $3, the highest being $3.85 in Alabama. Rates equal to or higher than $3.35 (the current federal level) are now provided under 11 laws.

For an estimated 17 million nonsupervisory workers who are outside the coverage of federal minimum wage regulation, state laws offer a wide variety of standards—in some cases better protection than under the federal law, and in others no protection at all. For the most part, however, state minimum wage protection falls far below federal standards.

Federal Approaches

Prior to the enactment of the Fair Labor Standards Act, attempts to intervene in the wage area were made almost wholly by the states, although from time to time there had been pressure for federal action—some as early as World War I.

Proponents of federal wage regulation argue that a uniform standard overcomes interstate cost differentials, which are always cited in opposition to increasing a state minimum wage level. A novel state approach to this problem was initiated in 1931 by Franklin D. Roosevelt. As Governor of New York, he succeeded in persuading seven states (Connecticut, Maine, Massachusetts, New Hampshire, New York, Pennsylvania, and Rhode Island) to sign an interstate wage compact. It provided for uniform wages and hours and was ratified by three of the states when passage of the Fair Labor Standards Act made its operation seem unnecessary. It later became ineffective.

Federal minimum wage action prior to 1938 was first limited to the Davis–Bacon Act (1931), which provided for the payment of prevailing wages on federal construction contracts over $2,000, then to the Walsh–Healey Act (1936), already mentioned, which required overtime and "prevailing wage" payments for suppliers of goods to the federal government, and finally to the NIRA Codes.

[24]*State Minimum Wage Legislation, A Major Weapon in the War on Poverty* (Washington, D.C.: U.S. Department of Labor, Women's Bureau, 1965).

[25]Alabama, Arizona, Florida, Iowa, Louisianna, Mississippi, Missouri, South Carolina, and Tennessee.

THE FAIR LABOR STANDARDS ACT

In 1938 government regulation of child labor, working hours, and wages was brought together under the Fair Labor Standards Act.[26] The inclusive provisions of the Act were unique in comparison with the scope and operation of the state protective labor laws that preceded it.[27]

Not only was the Fair Labor Standards Act comprehensive, but each of its several standards tended to be more rigorous and more inclusive. Its child labor requirements were higher than those of the provisions of many of the 1938 state laws; it fixed an absolute wage minimum, departing from the administrative arrangement of flexible minimum wage setting to which all state minimum wage laws had adhered; and while its hours provisions did not set absolute maximums, it was the opinion of students at the time that the law would probably give more impetus to a movement toward a shorter workweek than had been generated by the state hours laws. Furthermore, the new law extended wage and hour protection to men, discarding the widely held theory that, except for special cases where health or safety was involved, only women and children required government protection against the economic pressures of the labor market. Finally, it extended regulation of working conditions far beyond the narrow limits of earlier federal control, which, it will be recalled, was limited to situations in which the government was the employer, was being furnished goods by contractors, or was interested in safety.

Basic Provisions

The Fair Labor Standards Act (FLSA) establishes minimum wage, overtime pay, equal pay, child labor, and record keeping standards. Each of these standards is discussed below, plus who is covered and how the standards are enforced.

Coverage

Subject to certain exceptions, all employees of enterprises having workers engaged in interstate commerce, producing goods for interstate commerce, or handling, selling, or otherwise working on goods or materials that have been moved in or produced for such commerce by any person are covered. Excepted from all provisions of the Act, however, are workers in the following areas:

1 Retail or service establishments with annual gross sales or business volumes less than $325,000 ($362,500 beginning January 1, 1982).

[26]Statute 1060 (1938). The law is most widely referred to as the "Wage and Hour Law."

[27]Strictly speaking, this cannot be said when comparing the Act with earlier federal laws, since " . . . the Fair Labor Standards Act is a reenactment of subsection (3) of Section 7(a) of Title I of the National Industrial Recovery Act." Orme W. Phelps, *The Legislative Background of the Fair Labor Standards Act* (Chicago, Ill.: University of Chicago Press, 1939), p. 5.

2 Other enterprises (other than those engaged in laundering, cleaning, construction or reconstruction, operation of a hospital or medical care institution, or education) with an annual gross sales or business volume under $250,000.

3 Establishments that have as their only regular employees members of the owner's immediate family.

State and local government employees are covered unless they are engaged in "traditional" government activities, in which case they are subject only to the child labor and equal-pay provisions. The U.S. Supreme Court has defined "traditional" activities as those of schools, hospitals, fire protection, police protection, sanitation, public health, parks, and recreation.[28]

Employees not employed in a covered enterprise may still be entitled to protection under the FLSA standards if they are individually engaged in interstate commerce or in the production of goods for interstate commerce. Examples are communication and transportation workers, clerical or other workers who regularly use the mails, telephone, or telegraph for interstate communications or who keep records on interstate transactions, and employees who regularly cross state lines in the course of their work.

Domestic service workers such as maids, chauffeurs, cooks, or full-time baby sitters are covered, but only if they (1) receive at least $50 in a calendar quarter from their employer or (2) work a total of more than eight hours a week for one or more employers.

Protection is not available to almost 17 million nonsupervisory workers who are either not covered or are exempt. What are the reasons offered for these limits on coverage and exemptions?

As to coverage, Congress cannot legislate beyond its constitutional authority, which, in case of the commerce clause, is "to regulate commerce . . . among the several States. . . ." The FLSA is limited in application to employers "engaged in commerce or in the production of goods for commerce." Court interpretation has given broad scope to the coverage phrases of the Act to "extend it far beyond interstate commerce . . . to a whole complex of activities which precede commerce, broadly defined as production for commerce." Yet coverage of the Act is restricted by the fact that

> It does not . . . extend at all beyond commerce to the other complex of activities which follow commerce. . . . The effect on commerce of labor conditions in production of the article which subsequently moves, is recognized, though the effect on the same commerce of labor conditions in the distribution of the article which has moved, is not.[29]

---

[28]*National League of Cities versus Usery,* 426 U.S. 833 (1976).

[29]Hearings before the Senate Committee on Labor and Public Welfare, Subcommittee on Labor, 84th Congress, 1st Session, *Amending the Fair Labor Standards Act of 1938* (Washington, D.C.: Government Printing Office, 1955), p. 1779.

Note, however that since this statement was made the law has been extended to cover domestic workers.

As for exemptions, part of the answer can be found in the legislative history of the Act. Each volume of congressional hearings on this legislation is replete with pleas from trade associations and employer groups predicting financial ruin should their particular group of employees be covered. Frequently these requests for exemptions are transmitted by members of Congress.

The following are illustrative of the arguments advanced at one time for specific exemptions: farm workers and fishery employees (too hard to regulate hours and wages in an industry that is subject to natural and seasonal forces), handlers and processors of agricultural commodities (the costs of processing cannot be passed on to the consumers but must be borne by the farmers and, furthermore, these employees do not work under industrial conditions); small logging operations (need exemption to compete with large operators and also too difficult to enforce).

Minimum Wages

Section 6(a) of the FLSA states that every employer shall pay to each covered employee not less than $3.35 an hour, subject to a few exceptions. First, if an employee customarily and regularly receives more than $30 a month in tips, the minimum wage is reduced by this amount of the tips, but by no more than 50%. Second, the Secretary of Labor may prescribe rates less than $3.35 for employees in Puerto Rico, the Virgin Islands, and American Samoa. Third, employers in all areas may, under certain circumstances, pay less to learners, apprentices, and handicapped workers, and to full-time students in retail or service establishments, agriculture, or institutions of higher education.

In addition to the employees not covered under any of the FLSA provisions, some employees are specifically exempt from the minimum wage and overtime provisions. Examples are executive, administrative, and professional employees earning less than $155 weekly, outside sales persons, employees of certain seasonal amusement or recreational establishments, switchboard operators of small telephone companies, farm workers employed by anyone who used no more than 500 full-time equivalent workdays of farm labor in any calendar quarter of the preceding calendar, and casual babysitters.

Overtime Pay

Section 7 of the FLSA requires employers to pay employees compensation at a rate not less than one and one-half times the employee's regular rate for work during a workweek in excess of 40 hours. For example, if an employee paid $6 an hour works 45 hours in a workweek, he or she is entitled to $1\frac{1}{2}$ times $6, or $9, for each of the five hours in excess of 40. If a worker is paid a weekly salary, the regular rate is determined by dividing the salary by the number of hours per week under the employment agreement.

The Act specifies that time spent in preliminary or postliminary activities or in travel to the work site cannot be considered as "hours worked" unless payment for these activities is the custom of the industry or is expressly provided in a collective agreement.

In addition to those employees (1) exempted from all FLSA provisions and (2) those specifically exempted from only the minimum wage and overtime provisions, some employees are exempt from the overtime provisions only. Examples of these exempted employees are certain highly paid commission employees of retail or service establishments, employees of railroads and air carriers, taxi drivers, radio announcers, domestic service workers residing in the employers' residences, and farm workers.

Equal Pay

Section 6(d) of the FLSA prohibits wage differentials based in whole or in part on sex for persons employed in the same establishment on jobs that require equal skill, effort, and responsibility and which are performed under similar working conditions.

It is important to note that the Act uses the term "equal work" rather than "identical work." The difference between the two terms has taken on great significance in the enforcement of the Act. The concept of equal work includes equal skill, equal effort, equal responsibility, and similar working conditions, and not necessarily identical skill, identical effort, identical responsibility, and identical working conditions. This seems to have given greater interpretive flexibility to the Department of Labor and the courts in enforcing the Act.[30] Also, it has become incumbent on employers to review their pay practices in terms of the broader concept of "equal work." In a 1981 decision the Supreme Court, in a bitterly split decision, held that some women guards in Oregon had the right to sue for sex discrimination on the basis not of equal pay for equal work but on how much they were paid relative to male guards given the difference in their jobs.

Most employees subject to the FLSA, including executive, administrative, professional, and outside sales personnel, are covered. The provision applies to labor organizations as well as employers, and to public as well as private employers.

Child Labor

Section 12 of the FLSA prohibits "oppressive" child labor. The purposes of this prohibition are to (1) protect the educational opportunities of minors and (2)

---

[30]For details see Harry Snagerman, "A Look at the Equal Pay Act in Practice," *Labor Law Journal,* XXII, No. 5 (May 1971), 259–265. For two court decisions upholding this interpretation see *Schultz versus Wheaton Glass Company,* 421 F. 2nd 259 (C.A. 3, 1970), cert. denied, 398 U.S. 905, and *Corning Glass Works versus Brennan,* 417 U.S. 188 (1974). For a description of the most recent case, *County of Washington v. Gunther,* see "Women's Issue of the '80s," *Newsweek,* June 22, 1981, pp. 58–59.

prevent their employment in jobs and under conditions detrimental to their health or well-being.

In nonfarm work the permissible kinds and hours of work are as follows:

18 years or older—any job for unlimited hours.

16 or 17 years old—any nonhazardous job for unlimited hours.

14 and 15 years old—any nonmanufacturing, nonmining, nonhazardous job outside of school hours limited to no more than three hours on a school day, 18 hours in a school week, 8 hours on a nonschool day, or 40 hours in a nonschool week. Work may not begin before 7 AM nor end after 7 PM, except from June 1 through Labor Day, when work cannot end after 9 PM.

In addition, at any age children may work at certain jobs such as delivering newspapers, performing on radio or television, or working for parents in a solely owned business, except in manufacturing or hazardous jobs.

Permissible farm jobs are as follows:

16 years and older—any job for unlimited hours.

14 or 15 years old—any nonhazardous job outside of school hours.

12 or 13 years old—any nonhazardous job outside of school hours with the parents' written consent or on the same farm as the parents.

In addition, at any age children may be employed outside of school hours on farms owned or operated by their parents or, with the parents' written consent, in nonhazardous jobs on farms not covered by minimum wage requirements.

Record Keeping

Section 11(c) of the FLSA requires employers to keep records on wages, hours, and other conditions and practices of employment as the Secretary of Labor may prescribe. Records required for exempt employees differ from those for nonexempt employees. Special information is required on employees working under uncommon pay arrangements or who are furnished lodging or other facilities. The reasonable cost of such facilities is considered to be part of the employee's wages.

Administration

The myriad problems that arise in the administration of the FLSA can be grouped into problems of how to fix standards and how to enforce them.

Fixing Standards

Although the FLSA defines basic wage and hour standards, it leaves to the Administrator considerable areas of discretion in defining and delimiting the law's applicability. The Administrator is also called on to interpret the law for employees who are uncertain of their status. A great many questions must be decided. Who is an executive, an administrator, or an outside salesman within the meaning of the Act? What employments are "closely related" or "directly essential" to the production of goods for commerce? For that matter, who are "employees"? How is overtime to be computed? Who qualifies for the various exemptions? For seasonal industry exemption?

The Act gives the Administrator power to issue binding and authoritative regulations in connection with specific provisions of the Act. It also makes provision for employers or others affected by these regulations to appeal to the Administrator for their revision. These important regulations cover the many phases of the law that the Administrator must supervise.

The Administrator must set standards for employment of learners and revise these standards in the light of current economic conditions. He or she must issue certificates for the employment of apprentices, messengers, and handicapped workers. In addition, the Administrator must maintain wage standards in Puerto Rico and the Virgin Islands.

Shortly after passage of the Act in 1938, the Administrator was besieged by employers and unions seeking authoritative rulings as to the applicability of the Act in specific situations. In lieu of such rule-making power (which was not given to the Administrator in the Act) the Wage and Hour Division began in November, 1938, to issue interpretative bulletins—a practice it has followed ever since.

The first interpretative bulletin (October 12, 1938) made clear its nonofficial status by noting that

> . . . interpretations announced by the Administrator, except in certain specific instances where the statute directs the Administrator to make various regulations and definitions, serve only to indicate the construction of the law which will guide the Administrator in the performance of his administrative duties, unless he is directed otherwise by the authoritative rulings of the courts, or unless he shall subsequently decide that a prior interpretation is incorrect.

Today interpretative bulletins cover such areas as general enforcement policy, coverage, methods of wage payment, overtime compensation, and agricultural processing. While these bulletins do not have the status of substantive regulations, they do carry weight with the courts, which are faced with the question of interpreting the FLSA.

Enforcing Standards

Despite the many problems involved in fixing standards, the most difficult task of the Administrator is to enforce them. Although the law has always made private suits for back pay available to workers, experience indicates that enforcement cannot be left to the worker's own initiative. Rather, business establishments are inspected to insure compliance with required standards—through lawsuit if necessary.

With one exception, the Wage and Hour Division of the Employment Standards Administration of the U.S. Department of Labor administers and enforces the law with respect to private employment, state and local government employment, and certain federal employees. The Civil Service Commission enforces the law with respect to most federal employees. Effective July 1, 1979, the Equal Employment Opportunity Commission became responsible for enforcing the equal pay provisions.

Compliance officers located across the United States conduct investigations and gather data on wages, hours, and other employment conditions or practices. Where they find violations, they may recommend changes in employment practices.

Willful violations may be prosecuted criminally, and the violator fined up to $10,000. A second conviction may result in imprisonment. Violators of the child labor provisions are subject to a civil money penalty up to $1,000 for each violation.

The FLSA lists four ways in which a worker can recover unpaid minimum wages, overtime wages, or amounts owed in violation of the equal pay provisions:

1 The Wages and Hour Division may supervise such back payments.
2 The Secretary of Labor may bring suit for these back payments plus an equal amount as liquidated damages.
3 The worker may file a private suit for these back payments and an equal amount as liquidated damages, plus attorney's fees and court costs.
4 The Secretary may obtain an injunction to restrain any person from violating the law, including the unlawful withholding of proper minimum wage and overtime compensation.

A two-year statute of limitations applies to the recovery of back pay except when there is a willful violation, in which case the statute of limitations is three years.

Constitutionality[31]

The first challenge of the FLSA reached the Supreme Court in 1940, and in 1941 the Court reversed a lower District Court decision and held the new Act constitutional.[32] Darby Lumber, which had been charged with a violation of the wage and hour provisions, claimed that the FLSA, in violation of the rule in *Hammer versus Dagenhart,* used the power to regulate commerce to regulate essential interstate business. The Court repudiated this narrow view of what was a permissible regulation of commerce and overruled *Hammer versus Dagenhart.* The Court's

[31]In view of past decisions of the U.S. Supreme Court on state laws regulating conditions of work, there was a great deal of speculation about whether the Court would uphold the Fair Labor Act.
[32]*United States versus F. W. Darby Lumber Company,* 312 U.S. 100 (1941).

earlier decision in *West Coast Hotel versus Parrish* had already determined that wage regulation did not violate the Fourteenth Amendment. In the Darby case the court held that the Act did not violate the due process clause of the Fifth Amendment. Another decision[33] upheld the operation of the industry committees as a permissible delegation of powers, and they operated until they completed their work in 1944.

Trends[34]

When the FSLA became law in 1937, it set federal standards with respect to minimum wages, hours of work and overtime pay, and child labor. In 1963 equal-pay amendments prohibited sex-based pay differentials. In 1947 Congress enacted the Portal-to-Portal Act to curtail the basis for overtime claims based on time spent in preliminary or postliminary activities or in travel to work.

At the time the law became affective in 1938 only about one-third of the 33 million nonsupervisory employees were covered. Less than 3% of these covered employees were paid less than the 0.25 cent minimum wage. Not since that time have so few employees been affected when they were first covered or when their minimum wage was increased. On four occasions (1965, 1969, 1975, and 1977) at least 20% of the employee group affected earned less than their new minimum wage. The most significant groups of employees not covered under the original Act were farm workers, domestic workers, and retail and service workers.

The original provisions set the minimum wage at 25 cents the first year, 30 cents during the next six years, and thereafter the lesser of 40 cents or the rate (not less than 30 cents an hour) specified by the administrator. Actually all industries were required to pay the 40-cent minimum by July 17, 1944. Amendments in 1949 and 1955 increased the minimum wage to 75 cents and $1.00, respectively.

The 1961 amendments introduced a two-tier minimum wage. For workers covered prior to 1961 amendments the minimum wage became $1.15 until 1963, $1.25 thereafter. For newly covered persons the minimum wage was $1, rising to $1.15 in 1964 and $1.25 in 1965.

The 1966 amendments established three different minimum wage schedules: (1) one for workers already covered, (2) one for newly covered nonfarm workers, and (3) one for the newly covered farm workers. For workers covered prior to 1966 the minimum wage was raised to $1.40 in 1967 and $1.60 in 1968. For newly covered nonfarm workers the minimum was $1.00 in $967, rising to $1.15 in 1968, $1.30 in 1969, $1.45 in 1970, and $1.60 in 1971. For newly covered farm workers the minimum was $1.00 in 1967, $1.15 in 1968, and $1.30 in 1969.

[33]*Opp Cotton Mills versus Administrator,* 312 U.S. 126 (1941).

[34]This section is based largely on earlier editions of this text and on Peyton K. Elder and Heidi D. Miller, "The Fair Labor Standards Act: Changes of Four Decades," *Monthly Labor Review,* CII, No. 7 (July 1979), 10–16.

The 1974 amendments also divided the covered workers into three groups. For workers covered prior to 1966 the minimum was $2.00 in 1974, rising to $2.10 in 1975 and $2.30 in 1976. For nonfarm workers covered by 1966 or later amendments the minimum wage was $1.90 in 1974, rising to $2.00 in 1975, $2.20 in 1976, and $2.30 in 1977. For farm workers, who were first covered in 1966, the minimum became $1.60 in 1974, $1.80 in 1975, $2.00 in 1976, and $2.20 in 1977.

The 1977 amendments established *one* minimum wage for *all* covered workers —$2.65 during 1978, $2.90 during 1979, $3.10 during 1980, and $3.35 thereafter.

Table 17.1 summarizes this discussion and shows for each year the ratio of the highest minimum wage in effect that year to the gross average earnings of production workers in manufacturing. What Table 17.1 does not show is that before the passage of the 1949 amendments this ratio had reached an all-time low of 20%.

The 1961, 1966, and 1974 amendments expanded the Act to cover millions of additional workers. The 1961 amendments added 3.6 million workers, the 1966 amendments 10.4 million, and the 1974 amendments 6.7 million—roughly 20 million workers over 13 years. The 1961 amendments extended coverage primarily to employees of large retail and service establishments plus local transit, construction, and gasoline service station employees. The 1966 amendments covered farm workers for the first time. Coverage was limited, however, to farms employing seven or more workers. Many more retail and service establishment employees were covered because the dollar-volume test was substantially reduced. Exemptions were also narrowed or repeated for state and local government employees of hospitals, nursing homes, and schools and such groups as employees of hotels, restaurants, laundries, or agricultural processing firms. The 1974 amendments extended coverage to the remaining federal, state, and local employees,[35] certain workers in retail and service trades previously exempted, and to domestic workers.

The 1977 amendments raised gradually the annual dollar-value coverage test for retail or service establishments from the $250,000 level established under the 1966 amendments to $362,500 by 1982. The objective was to move enterprises of this sort into the covered category on the basis of the quantity of goods and services sold, and not because of inflation.

Operations[36]

In September 1979 over 60 million nonsupervisory employees were covered under the minimum wage provisions of the FLSA. Table 17.2 shows the number of

---

[35]In 1976, however, the U.S. Supreme Court held that "traditional" government employees are subject only to the child labor and equal pay provisions. See Ref. 28.

[36]This section is based on the *Minimum Wage and Maximum Hours Standards Under The Fair Labor Standards Act* (Washington, D.C.: U.S. Department of Labor Employment Standards Administration, 1980).

Table 17.1 History of Federal Minimum Wage Rates Under the Fair Labor Standards Act and Average Hourly Earnings and Average Weekly Hours of Production Workers in Manufacturing, 1938–1981

Effective Date	Minimum Hourly Wage (In Dollars) for Workers in Jobs First Covered by				Average Gross Hourly Earnings for Production Workers in Manufacturing[a]	
	1938 Act[c]	1961 Amendments[d]	1966 and Subsequent Amendments[b]		Amount ($)	Highest Minimum Hourly Wage as a Percentage of Gross Hourly Earnings
			Nonfarm	Farm		
Oct. 24, 1938	0.25	—	—	—	0.62	40
Oct. 24, 1939	0.30	—	—	—	0.63	48
Oct. 24, 1945	0.40	—	—	—	1.02	39
Jan. 25, 1950	0.75	—	—	—	1.44	52
Mar. 1, 1956	1.00	—	—	—	1.95	51
Sept. 3, 1961	1.15	1.00	—	—	2.32	50
Sept. 3, 1963	1.25	1.00	—	—	2.46	51
Sept. 3, 1964	1.25	1.15	—	—	2.53	49
Sept. 3, 1965	1.25	1.25	—	—	2.61	48
Feb. 1, 1967	1.40	1.40	1.00	1.00	2.83	49
Feb. 1, 1968	1.60	1.60	1.15	1.15	3.01	53
Feb. 1, 1969	1.60	1.60	1.30	1.30	3.19	50
Feb. 1, 1970	1.60	1.60	1.45	1.30	3.36	48
Feb. 1, 1971	1.60	1.60	1.60	1.30	3.57	45
May 1, 1974	2.00	2.00	1.90	1.60	4.42	45
Jan. 1, 1975	2.10	2.10	2.00	1.80	4.83	43
Jan. 1, 1976	2.30	2.30	2.20	2.00	5.22	44
Jan. 1, 1977	—	—	2.30	2.20	5.68	40
Jan. 1, 1978	2.65	2.65	2.65	2.65	6.17	43
Jan. 1, 1979	2.90	2.90	2.90	2.90	6.69[e]	43
Jan. 1, 1980	3.10	3.10	3.10	3.10	7.27	43
Jan. 1, 1981	3.35	3.35	3.35	3.35	n.a.	n.a.

Source: Social Security Bulletin, Annual Statistical Supplement, 1977–1979, Table 15, p. 65. Average gross hourly earnings for 1980 from Monthly Labor Review.

[a]For year in which minimum wage rate changes were effective.

[b]The 1966 amendments extended coverage to state and local government employees of hospitals, nursing homes, schools, and to employees of laundries, dry cleaners, large hotels and motels, restaurants, and farms. Subsequent amendments extended coverage to the remaining federal, state, and local employees not protected in 1966, to certain workers in retail and service trades previously exempted, and to certain domestic workers in private household employment.

[c]The 1938 Act was applicable generally to employees engaged in interstate commerce or in the production of goods for interstate commerce.

[d]The 1961 amendments extended coverage primarily to employees in large retail and service trades as well as to local transit, construction, and gasoline service station employees.

Table 17.2 Estimated Number of Employed Wage and Salary Workers in the Civilian Labor Force Classified by Their Status Under the *Minimum Wage* Provisions of the Fair Labor Standards Act, by Industry Division, United States, September 1979 (In Thousands)

	Number of Employed Wage and Salary Workers in the Civilian Labor Force				Number of Nonsupervisory Employees Subject to the Minimum Wage Provisions of the FLSA[a]				Number of Nonsupervisory Employees Not Subject to the Minimum Wage Provisions of the FLSA
		Activities Generally Exempt Under Section 13(a)(1) of FLSA[a]		Nonsupervisory Employees Excluding Outside Sales-workers					
	Total	Executive, Administrative, and Professional Personnel	Outside Sales Workers		Total	Subject Prior to the 1966 Amendments[b]	Subject as a Result of the 1966 Amendments[b]	Subject as a Result of the 1972, 1974, and 1977 Amendments	
All industries	94,158	17,320	2,362	74,476	60,129	42,880	13,327	3,922	16,709
Private sector	78,318	11,001	2,362	64,955	57,538	42,880	12,676	1,982	9,779
Agriculture[c]	1,551	79	—	1,472	540		515	25	932
Mining	980	114	—	866	861	861	—	—	5
Contract construction	4,984	502	4	4,478	4,461	3,645	816	—	21
Manufacturing	21,192	2,469	429	18,294	18,208	18,099	73	36	515
Transportation and public utilities[d]	5,242	596	7	4,639	4,611	4,513	98	—	35
Wholesale trade	5,206	740	882	3,584	3,559	3,328	231	—	907
Retail trade	15,054	1,494	136	13,424	10,938	5,020	5,464	454	2,622
Finance, insurance, and real estate	5,002	723	870	3,409	3,245	3,117	128	—	1,034
Service industries (except private households)[d,e]	17,339	4,284	34	13,021	9,958	4,297	5,351	310	3,097
Private households	1,768	—	—	1,768	1,157	—	—	1,157	611
Public sector	15,840	6,319	—	9,521	2,591	—	651	1,940	6,930
Federal government[e]	2,751	519	—	2,232	2,232	—	522	1,710	—
State and local government[e]	13,089	5,800	—	7,289	359[f]	—	129	230	6,930

Source: Minimum Wage and Maximum Hours Standards Under the Fair Labor Standards Act (Washington, D.C.: U.S. Department of Labor, Employment Standards Administration, 1980), Table 7.

[a]Section 13(a)(1) exempts from the minimum wage and overtime provisions of the Fair Labor Standards Act ". . . any employee employed in a bona fide executive, administrative, or professional capacity (including any employee in the capacity of academic administrative personnel, or teacher in elementary or secondary schools), or in the capacity of outside salesman. . . ." Included are all employees in the specified activities whether employed in covered or noncovered establishments.

[b]Relates to currently employed workers who would have been subject under criteria in effect prior to the 1974 Amendments. The services industry, however, includes employees of enterprises affected by phase out of the section 13(a)(2) exemption.

[c]Estimates for agriculture are based on average employment for the 10-month active season. For July 1979, a peak employment period, the estimate for total hired farm labor was 1,935,000, 1,841,000 for nonsupervisory employment and 686,000 for subject employment.

[d]Not strictly comparable to previous periods as a result of changes in estimating methodology.

[e]Estimates for educational services relate to October 1979.

[f]Estimated employment subject to the minimum wage relates to nonsupervisory employment in public transit, other public utilities, water transportation services, and state liquor stores.

persons covered by industry division and when they were first covered under the Act. About 81% of the nonsupervisory employees were covered—89% of such private-sector employees, 100% of such federal employees, and 5% of such state and local government employees. Of those covered, about 71% were subject to the law prior to 1966, 22% as a result of the 1966 amendments, and the remaining 7% as a result of the 1972, 1974, and 1977 amendments.

In 1980 the Employment Standards Administration estimated that when the minimum wage rose in 1981 to $3.35 an hour, almost 5.6 million nonsupervisory workers, 9.3% of the total, would be affected. The wage increase would be about $2.2 billion, a 0.3% increase in the annual wage bill.

During fiscal year 1979 the Wage and Hour Division conducted over 75,000 investigations under the monetary provisions of the Act. These investigations disclosed $54 million in minimum wage payments due 426,000 workers and $70 million in overtime underpayments due 287,000 employees.

In its enforcement of the equal-pay provisions the Division found that over $10 million was due over 14,000 employees.

Division investigations during 1979 also revealed that almost 3,000 establishments employed almost 13,000 minors in violation of the FLSA child labor provisions. The retail trade industry accounted for 69% of these illegally employed minors, the service industry for 14%. Almost one-third of these minors were employed in occupations deemed to be hazardous for the employment of children between the ages of 16 and 18. About 59% were employed in slaughtering, meatpacking or processing, or rendering; about 20% were motor vehicle drivers or outside helpers.

Proposals to Amend FLSA

Several bills have been introduced in Congress that would amend the FLSA in various ways. Most of these bills deal with the minimum wage and overtime pay provisions. Some economic issues associated with these provisions are discussed in the last section of this chapter.

One bill would increase the overtime rate to not less than two times the current regular rate of pay. This bill would also gradually reduce the 40-hour workweek standard to 35 hours. The bill would also establish procedures to eliminate or curtail involuntary overtime work. Another bill would extend minimum wage and overtime protection to covered and nonexempt employees of Congress, including clerical, blue-collar, and similar nonsupervisory employees. Still another proposal would adjust the minimum wage rate to match increases in average national earnings.

Other bills would have deferred the two most recent increases in the minimum wage. They would have established a lower minimum wage during the first six months of employment for workers below a specified age. Those supporting this change argue that it would increase the employment opportunities for young workers. Opponents prefer to expand these opportunities through training programs. The definition of employee would be amended to exclude illegal aliens.

The 1977 FLSA Amendments established a Minimum Wage Study Commission to conduct a study of the FLSA and the social, political, and economic ramifications of the minimum wage, overtime, and other provisions of the Act. The Commission was directed to study the following: (1) the beneficial effects of the minimum wage, including its effect in ameliorating poverty among working citizens; (2) the inflationary impact, if any, of increases in the minimum wage; (3) the indirect wage effect, if any, of the minimum wage; (4) the economic consequence, if any, of indexing the minimum wage; (5) the employment and unemployment effects, if any, of a wage differential for youth, the handicapped, and the aged; (6) the employment and unemployment effects, if any, of the full-time student certification program currently in the Act; (7) the employment and unemployment effects, if any, of the minimum wage; (8) the exemptions from the minimum wage and overtime requirements; (9) the relationship, if any, between the federal minimum wage rates and public assistance programs, including the extent to which minimum wage workers are also eligible for food stamps and other forms of public assistance; (10) the overall level of noncompliance with the requirements of the Act; and (11) the demographic profile of minimum wage workers.

The Commission included eight members, two appointed by each of the following secretaries: (1) Labor; (2) Commerce; (3) Agriculture; and (4) Health, Education, and Welfare. In its May 1981 report the Commission made the following recommendations:

1 The minimum wage should be adjusted regularly based on increases in all workers' average hourly earnings.
2 Congress should not adopt a lower minimum wage for younger workers. To do so, the Commission argued, would displace many adult workers without significantly increasing jobs for teenagers.
3 The overtime pay rules should apply to all executive, administrative, and professional employees earning less than twice the weekly wages of a minimum-wage worker. Currently this weekly pay level would be $268.

OTHER FEDERAL STANDARDS LAWS

Three additional federal measures regulate labor standards, and although their coverage is much smaller than that of the FLSA, they are nonetheless important in their particular fields. The Davis–Bacon Act of 1931 (amended in 1936), the Walsh–Healey Act of 1936, and the McNamara–O'Hara Act of 1965 regulate firms doing business with the government. These laws provide the means by which the government's purchasing policies can be used as leverage to protect labor standards.

The Davis–Bacon Act

The Davis–Bacon Act law applies to federal public works contracts—government construction projects (construction, alteration, and repair) that exceed $2,000. The law declares that it is government policy to pay to "mechanics and laborers employed directly on the site of the work" the prevailing minimum wage rates for such work. Since construction work is performed at specific sites, the relevant prevailing wage rates are typically those of the local building trades in individual towns, sites, or civil subdivisions that are affected. By setting a wage floor the law seeks to (1) protect labor standards and (2) prevent unfair competition for government business by contractors who obtain such business by paying low wages.

The law is enforceable by termination of contract, by blacklisting the violators from government business, or by withholding amounts due. Those who violate the controls may be denied the benefits of the Act or the opportunity to bid for and work under government-funded contracts.

For many years the Davis-Bacon Act and the others described in this section have been severely criticized by many business representatives. Their major objection has been that the rates paid on projects receiving federal funding do in fact exceed the prevailing rate in the area. The result is that public projects cost more and federal projects bid workers away from private projects, thus boosting private wages and limiting private projects. The most severe critics would repeal the law. Others would change how the prevailing wage is determined. For example, the Reagan Administration has indicated its intent to drop the 30% rule. Under this rule the Department of Labor can define the prevailing rate as that paid to 30% of the workers in a trade, all of whom may be higher-paid workers. Instead the administration would define the prevailing wage as either the average rate or the rate paid to at least a majority of the workers performing similar work in the area. The proposed rules would also prohibit the Department of Labor from using urban wage data to set pay rates in nearby rural areas. Finally, currently only one unskilled trainee—one for each three to five skilled workers, depending on local union contracts—may be used on the job. The proposal would permit one unskilled trainee for each skilled worker.

The Walsh–Healey Act

Labor standards protection of the Walsh–Healey Act covers employees of firms ("regular dealers" or "manufacturers") supplying the federal government with new or used materials in amounts exceeding $10,000. It applies to manufacturing, assembling, and handling.

Executives, administrators, professional workers, office, custodial, and maintenance workers, as well as agricultural workers and farm producers, are exempt from coverage. For covered firms the law stipulates standards in five areas: it prohibits child labor (males under 16 and females under 18 cannot be employed); it prohibits prison labor; it specifies certain safety and health standards; it sets minimum wages as specified by the Secretary of Labor; and it requires overtime at the rate of one-half times the basic rate for more than 8 hours a day or 40 hours per week.

The McNamara–O'Hara Act

Just as the Walsh–Healy Act provides labor standards protection for employees of firms providing *goods* to the federal government, the McNamara–O'Hara Act protects the employees of firms supplying *services* to the federal government.

THE AGE DISCRIMINATION IN EMPLOYMENT ACT

Background

Before the Age Discrimination in Employment Act (ADEA) was passed, many older job applicants were denied a job because of age. Others found that they were denied promotions or discharged because of age. Such discriminatory action deprived the economy of badly needed resources and also created financial, psychological, and physical hardship for the older workers. In order to remove job barriers for the older workers an attempt was made in Congress to include a provision, in the 1966 revision of the FLSA, prohibiting discrimination because of age. Although this provision was not included in the FLSA, a separate Act was passed by the Congress in 1967.

General Provisions

The ADEA was enacted to promote the employment of persons who are over 40 years of age and under 65 (increased to age 70 in 1978) and to prohibit discrimination in employment because of age in matters of hiring, job retention, compensation, and other terms, conditions, or privileges of employment.

This age discrimination ban applies to employers of 25 persons or more in industries affecting interstate commerce and to employment agencies that serve such employers. The law also applies to a labor organization if it is in an industry affecting interstate commerce—that is, if it has a hiring office procuring employees for an employer covered by this Act or if it has 25 members or more.

The term "employer" does not include federal, state, or local governments. Employers, employment agencies, and labor organizations under the Act's jurisdiction are not permitted to use printed or published notices or advertisements relating to employment that indicate any preference, limitations, specifications, or discrimination based on age.

Exceptions

The Act provides for the following exceptions:

1 Situations where age is a bona fide occupational qualification reasonably necessary to the normal operation of a particular business.
2 Situations where a differentiation is based on factors other than age.
3 Situations where the differentiation is caused by a bona fide seniority system or employee-benefit plan that is not a subterfuge to evade the purposes of the Act. No such system or plan, however, can force a worker to retire prior to age 70 solely because of age.

Enforcement

Enforcement procedures are essentially similar to those of the FLSA. The major difference is that the age discrimination law specifically requires that before any legal proceeding can be instituted, attempts must be made to eliminate discriminatory practices through informal methods of conference, conciliation, and persuasion. Only after such attempts have failed may the civil remedies and recovery procedures of the FLSA be used to enforce the provisions of the ADEA. Administration of the law is assigned to the Wage and Hour Division.

ECONOMIC ISSUES

The employment contract between an employer and employee can be visualized as embracing the common interest issues of wages, hours, and working conditions. Wages and hours are customarily made explicit, but this is not necessarily the case for working conditions except in specific risk-related situations. (As a personal example, the employment contract of the writer explicitly indicates salary and "hours"—in the sense of a nine-month academic year. Nothing is said, however, of the "hourly" work load within that nine-month period, nor are working conditions even mentioned.)

Government regulation of wages, as through minimum wage laws, involves a direct intervention in such employment contracts. Wages are the most "visible" part of these contracts: the wage is a price—the price of labor—and thus quantifiable. Hence it is no accident that economists have devoted most of their attention to the regulation of this wage component. Moreover, the "employment" consequences of minimum wages also relate closely to the interests of economists.

Hours are also obviously "visible" and can be quantified. But, except for periods such as after the passage of the FLSA of 1938, they tend to change slowly over time and have received less attention from economists.

Working conditions do not necessarily have either the comparable visibility or the specificity of relationship between the employee and his work environment. For example, how does one price out the specific "value" to an employee of a given set of working conditions? Hence this topic also has tended to receive less attention from economists.

In our discussion we shall invert the wages–hours–working conditions triad and take it up in inverse order, moving from the more "general" to the more "specific."

Working Conditions

As previously noted, it is difficult to quantify and hence price out the "value" *to an individual worker* of a given set of working conditions. There is no "market," in the customary usage of this concept, for such conditions. And, given the absence of a market, "competition" in improving such conditions has not been traditionally viewed as operative. (We focus here only on working conditions as they affect health and safety, and not on aesthetics. The latter may have an impact, but such analysis is beyond our scope.)

There has been considerable recognition, however, of this relationship between the work environment and the physical and mental well-being of employees as a group. Such recognition and concern eventually led to the 1970 enactment of the Occupational Safety and Health Act (OSHA), discussed earlier in this book. While other specialized protective statutes, such as the Federal Coal Mine Health and Safety Act, antedated OSHA, this law was the first comprehensive piece of federal work-place legislation.

Much of the "analysis" thus far of the impacts of OSHA has revolved around bureaucratic issues: the costs involved, the intricacies of specific regulations, inspection and enforcement, penalties, and so on. New approaches are, however, beginning to appear.

An excellent example of a new economic approach to the work place is to be found in a volume by Belton M. Fleisher and Thomas J. Kniesser.[37] They note that it is only recently that economists have used competitive equilibrium analysis to examine work-place safety. The approach of these authors is via the conventional use of equating the marginal benefits of safety improvements with their marginal costs. (In a sense, what is used is a benefit–cost approach; the optimal safety level is where marginal safety benefits are equal to marginal safety costs.) The analysis does not start with a "no-safety" level—which would be nonsensical; it proceeds from an existing situation.

The critic might say that this is a callous approach, since it puts a dollar value on human injury. But this is done all the time; merely look at workers' compensation benefit schedules. And employers, for a long time, have costed out safety improvements and workers' compensation premiums.

---

[37]See Fleisher and Kniesser's *Labor Economics,* 2nd ed. (Englewood Cliffs: Prentice-Hall, 1980), pp. 169–178. Useful references are also included in their discussion.

Fleisher and Kniesser themselves have not applied these techniques empirically. They do cite several studies whose results, however, are limited because of the influence of extraneous factors. One study, for example, indicates that the safety effects of OSHA have been minimal given the incentives not to comply and the fact that inspections have also been minimal (and the "fines" quite low in cases of violation). Nevertheless, this new analytical approach shows possibilities of providing useful results heretofore lacking.

Hours

Hours regulations tend to be of three types: (1) "maximum" hours of work for women, children, and others, designed to protect their well-being (their "safety"); (2) "maximum" hours for certain occupations such as airline pilots and bus drivers, where the safety of others is involved; and (3) "maximum" hours in situations in which more time can be put in but only at overtime rates. The first two involve "prohibition": more time cannot be worked legally. The third invokes a "penalty": extra hours can be worked, but only at penalty rates.

The first two types of regulations can be disposed of relatively easily. Here society has simply placed a higher value on the physical, mental, and emotional well-being of certain groups than it has on the freedom of members of these groups (and their employers) to work whatever (maximum) hours they might contract for. One could disagree with, for example, the specific hour ceilings, but less easily with the intent.

Overtime poses a different problem. One of the purposes of the FLSA of 1938 was to "spread the work" by presumably making it more costly to have a covered employee work more than 40 hours. This involves the "lump of labor" thesis; that is, there is only so much work to go around, and by penalizing an employer for working individuals over 40 hours, he would instead hire additional employees. In practice, it has not necessarily worked out in this fashion, since hiring additional employees (and possibly separating them later) is not cost free. Hence employment is by no means automatically increased. Moreover, overtime is customarily a sign that business is good and hence the employer can readily pay it. Insofar as overtime analytically interests economists today, it is usually in connection with work–leisure trade-offs. Overtime is visualized as a premium paid for giving up nonwork time that becomes more and more valuable the less one has of it. (Overtime, for example, will always call forth more work time than would a regular wage increase.)

Hours—and the length of the workday or workweek as these relate to *productivity*—have been the subject of much analysis, but primarily by psychologists and others. And legislatively mandated hour maximums have not been at the center of such analysis.

Wages

As noted earlier, the analytical preoccupation of economists has been greatest by far with the wages component of the wage–hour–working condition trilogy.

The accepted current "theory" of minimum wage regulation was developed by George Stigler in a 1946 article.[38] Stigler shows the following: (1) that if wages in a competitive labor market are raised by regulation above the equilibrium level, employment will fall; and (2) that in a monopsonistic labor market (employer controlled) a skillfully set minimum may raise both wages and employment. However, the degree of regulatory "skill" required in this latter case is exceedingly high, and if the wage is set above what would exist under competition, employment will fall. Stigler also notes that a minimum wage may "shock" employers into operating more efficiently, which would therefore sustain the higher wage. However, it is not likely that shocks could be effective indefinitely through time as the minimum was successively raised.

The empirical work on minimum wages has centered mainly on (1) the general employment impacts and (2) the effects on the employability of juveniles, particularly those in minority groups.

As to general employment effects, one body of studies, undertaken principally by the U.S. Department of Labor, can be summarized as follows: "employment in the areas affected by the extension of coverage of FLSA has increased, and there is no evidence of any restraining effect of the broader coverage of employment opportunity."[39] (Earlier U.S. Department of Labor studies conclude much the same with respect to initial imposition of minimums and successive increases.) The difficulty with these studies is that they do not take fully into account the contaminating influence of other factors such as economic growth, prosperity, or changing industry conditions.

An opposed group of analyses leads to different conclusions: that employment is adversely affected.[40] The consequences are consistent with what competitive theory would lead one to predict.

Hence what does one conclude in the absence of convincing results? Our own judgment is that minimum wage legislation may tidy up the ragged fringes of labor markets. There are enough imperfections in the operation of these markets that such tidying up is possible without significant adverse effects. But it is futile to believe that minimum wages can be set so as to lift all low-wage workers to a "comfortable income" level, however one would define that level. (It is interest-

---

[38]See Stigler's "The Economics of Minimum Wage Legislation," *American Economic Review,* 36, No. 3 (June 1946), 358–365.

[39]U.S. Department of Labor, Wage and Hour and Public Contracts Division, *Minimum Wage and Maximum Hour Standards under the Fair Labor Standards Act* (Washington, D.C.: U.S. Government Printing Office, 1969), pp. 3–4.

[40]A good summary is to be found in John M. Peterson and Charles T. Stewart, Jr., *Employment Effects of Minimum Wage Rates* (Washington, D.C.: American Enterprise Institute, 1969).

ing to note that unions, via collective bargaining, also set minimum wages and that the same constraints apply. This issue has also been the subject of much analysis.)

The evidence and conclusions with respect to minimum wages and juvenile employment are similarly not in full agreement, although the majority view would appear to support an adverse impact.[41] Where varying results appear, they seem to be based on the inclusion or exclusion of controls for the growth of teen-age population. If such controls are included, minimum wages have a major unemployment impact; if excluded, the reverse holds.

One of the most comprehensive studies on minimum wage effects was undertaken by Edward Gramlich.[42] He concludes, as to general impacts, that because of incomplete coverage, lack of compliance, part-time work, and so on, the minimum wage is less of a force for good or evil than people have believed. As to teen-agers, he suggests that the impacts are not so much as to result in unemployment but that, at the margin, such individuals are pushed into part-time work, with lower pay and poorer jobs.

The basic criticism of nondifferentiated minimum wages for juveniles is that their productivity does not warrant such pay, this for a variety of reasons: less education and training, lack of experience, poor work habits, and so on. Hence Gramlich and many others have suggested a lower minimum wage for younger workers. Needless to say, organized labor and others oppose such a proposal. The opposition rests on a belief that employers might substitute juvenile lower-wage help for higher-wage adults. To indicate the controversial nature of the differential the 1977 minimum wage bill was enacted only after an amendment to permit such a differential was defeated. And in the House of Representatives this amendment lost by one vote. As noted earlier, the Minimum Wage Study Commission opposed this differential in its 1981 report, but Congress is still considering this issue.

A Concluding Comment

1 We believe, with Gramlich, that minimum wages are less of a good or evil force than current attention warrants. Such minimums *are* useful in tidying up the market. But if the minimum goes much above, say, 50% of the median wage in manufacturing (as one yardstick), undesirable consequences could well result. (The 1980 ratio is about 0.45; it has not been above 0.50 since the 1960s.) Even the escalation of the minimum from $1.60 in 1964 to $3.35 in 1981 is not likely to increase the ratio.

[41]A useful summary of research and conclusions is contained in Robert S. Goldfarb, "The Policy Content of Quantitative Minimum Wage Research," *Proceedings of the Twenty-Seventh Annual Winter Meeting, 1974,* (Madison, Wisc.: Industrial Relations Research Association, 1975), pp. 261–268.

[42]See Edward M. Gramlich, "Impacts of Minimum Wages on Other Wages, Employment, and Family Incomes," *Brookings Papers on Economic Activity,* No. 2 (Washington, D.C.: Brookings Institution, 1976), pp. 409–451; see also the critical commentary on pp. 452–461.

2 We think that a good case can be made for a teen-age differential. We are less fearful (unwisely so?) that this would result in a wholesale substitution of juveniles for adults. Adults possess a variety of work performance characteristics not likely to be matched by the adolescent; hence displacement on any large scale is not likely.

3 One "different" use of the minimum wage not noted previously but that we leave with the reader is that wage minimums need to be revised upward regularly so as to keep pace with welfare benefit levels. If such revision is not undertaken and one is on welfare, why seek work? What are the consequences for incentives if one can do better by not seeking employment at the existing minimum? The reader may wish to pause and reflect on this issue and its implications.

SUMMARY

Government intervention into conditions of employment began as a movement to protect women and children. Today all states have child labor laws. All but a few states have fair employment practices acts that ban discrimination in employment based on sex. About two-thirds specifically require "equal pay" for men and women. About two-thirds require higher pay rates for work beyond a specified number of hours per week; a few still limit these laws to women workers. All but nine states have minimum wage laws. Only 11 of these laws set a standard equal to the federal minimum. Only one state limits its law to women.

In the past 40 years rising levels of income and a public policy favorable to collective bargaining have brought working conditions for many workers in intrastate commerce well above the minimum levels that state regulation has sought to achieve. But for significant numbers of workers, particularly in some areas of the South, and especially among agricultural workers, improved state legislative standards could achieve better conditions of work.

At the time the Fair Labor Standards Act was passed its comprehensive and far-reaching extension of government authority into working conditions was viewed with some apprehension. For although it was an extension of a century-old state movement for improved labor standards legislation, its child labor and wage and hour provisions set standards well above existing state standards.

The Fair Labor Standards Act establishes minimum wage, overtime-pay, equal-pay, child labor, and record-keeping standards affecting more than 60 million nonsupervisory workers. Subject to certain exceptions, all employees of enterprises having workers engaged in interstate commerce, producing goods for interstate commerce, or handling, selling, or otherwise working on goods or materials that have been moved in or produced for such commerce by any person are covered. Some workers are covered, but are exempt from certain provisions. For example, executives of covered enterprises are exempt from the minimum wage and overtime provisions.

The current minimum wage is $3.35 an hour. Employees who work more than

40 hours a week must be compensated at a rate not less than one and one-half times the employee's regular rate. Men and women must receive "equal pay" for "equal work." Children under 16 cannot be employed in most jobs; children under 18 cannot be employed in most hazardous jobs. Employers must keep such records on employment practices as the Secretary of Labor may prescribe.

The original Act included all of the present standards except the equal-pay standard, which was added in 1963. The Act covered only one-third of the nation's nonsupervisory employees. Only 3% of the covered workers earned less than the $0.25 an hour minimum wage. The Act has been amended many times, several of which raised the minimum wage. The 1961, 1966, and 1974 amendments added millions of new workers.

Other federal protective legislation includes the Davis–Bacon Act, the Walsh–Healey Act, the McNamara–O'Hara Act, and the Age Discrimination in Employment Act.

SUGGESTIONS FOR ADDITIONAL READING

Bureau of National Affairs. "Wages and Hours," *Labor Relations Reporter,* Washington, D.C., updated periodically.
Presents a summary of legislation, regulations, and court decisions, both state and federal, covering working conditions, wages, and hours.

Commons, John R. *History of Labor in the United States,* Vol. III. New York: Macmillan, 1935.
The entire third volume of this classic series is devoted to working conditions. It presents a detailed and comprehensive analysis of the development of legislation in this field.

Commons, John R., and John B. Andrews. *Principles of Labor Legislation,* 4th ed. New York: Harper and Row, 1936, Chaps. 2–4 and 6.
This book is still valuable for its expert insights into principles and administrative problems of labor legislation.

Report of the Minimum Wage Study Commission. Washington, D.C. 1981.
The final report of the Minimum Wage Study Commission established by the 1977 amendments to the Fair Labor Standards Act.

U.S. Department of Labor, Employment Standards Administration. *Survey of Working Conditions.* Washington, D.C.: Government Printing Office, 1971.
A detailed report of a nationwide survey conducted by the Survey Research Center, University of Michigan. The bulk of the report consists of statistical tables grouped into 13 major content areas. Preceding each set of tables is a brief commentary.

U.S. Department of Labor, Employment Standards Administration. *Minimum Wage and Maximum Hours Standards Under the Fair Labor Standards Act.* Washington, D.C.: Government Printing Office, 1980.
The latest annual report on how the Fair Labor Standards Act is operating. The Report includes an analysis of the wage bill impact of the 1977 amendments.

Epilogue

Whither Economic and Social Security?

After all the foregoing discussion it is legitimate to ask: Whither Economic and Social Security?

As authors, we do not know. But, that is not to our discredit, for we do not believe that anyone else knows either.

We are willing, however, to make a few conjectures as an epilogue.

1. In the last half century, giant strides have been made in the development of programs providing protection against economic insecurity—strides unparalleled in the preceding 300 years. To be sure, some would say that not enough has been done; others that we have gone too far too fast.

2. We do not believe any of the programs discussed herein will be "abolished," though they may be altered, consolidated, or replaced by other approaches.

3. But we contend that the decade of the 1980s will be a period of consolidation and consideration and will not see a breakthrough of any major new thrusts. The twin problems of inflation (and costs), and, incentives are likely to tamper significant changes. Incremental alterations are more likely to be the order of the day.

4. Yet we are optimistic that improvements will take place and that the end of the decade will see less economic and social insecurity than at present.

Index

599

Due Due